Sex between Body and Mind

Social History, Popular Culture, and Politics in Germany
Kathleen Canning, Series Editor

Recent Titles

Sex between Body and Mind: Psychoanalysis and Sexology in the German-speaking World, 1890s–1930s
Katie Sutton

Imperial Fictions: German Literature Before and Beyond the Nation-State
Todd Kontje

White Rebels in Black: German Appropriation of Black Popular Culture
Priscilla Layne

Not Straight from Germany: Sexual Publics and Sexual Citizenship since Magnus Hirschfeld
Michael Thomas Taylor, Annette F. Timm, and Rainer Herrn, Editors

Passing Illusions: Jewish Visibility in Weimar Germany
Kerry Wallach

Bodies and Ruins: Imagining the Bombing of Germany, 1945 to the Present
David Crew

The Jazz Republic: Music, Race, and American Culture in Weimar Germany
Jonathan Wipplinger

The War in Their Minds: German Soldiers and Their Violent Pasts in West Germany
Svenja Goltermann

Three-Way Street: Jews, Germans, and the Transnational
Jay Howard Geller and Leslie Morris, Editors

Beyond the Bauhaus: Cultural Modernity in Breslau, 1918–33
Deborah Ascher Barnstone

Stop Reading! Look! Modern Vision and the Weimar Photographic Book
Pepper Stetler

The Corrigible and the Incorrigible: Science, Medicine, and the Convict in Twentieth-Century Germany
Greg Eghigian

An Emotional State: The Politics of Emotion in Postwar West German Culture
Anna M. Parkinson

Germany's Wild East: Constructing Poland as Colonial Space
Kristin Kopp

Beyond Berlin: Twelve German Cities Confront the Nazi Past
Gavriel D. Rosenfeld and Paul B. Jaskot, Editors

Consumption and Violence: Radical Protest in Cold-War West Germany
Alexander Sedlmaier

Communism Day-to-Day: State Enterprises in East German Society
Sandrine Kott

Envisioning Socialism: Television and the Cold War in the German Democratic Republic
Heather L. Gumbert

The People's Own Landscape: Nature, Tourism, and Dictatorship in East Germany
Scott Moranda

For a complete list of titles, please see www.press.umich.edu

Sex between Body and Mind

Psychoanalysis and Sexology in the German-speaking World, 1890s–1930s

KATIE SUTTON

UNIVERSITY OF MICHIGAN PRESS
Ann Arbor

Published in the United States of America by
the University of Michigan Press
Printed and bound by CPI Group (UK) Ltd, Croydon, CR0 4YY

First published December 2019

A CIP catalog record for this book is available from the British Library.

ISBN 978-0-472-13160-0 (hardcover : alk. paper)
ISBN 978-0-472-12612-5 (ebook)

For Judy and Kevin

Contents

Digital materials related to this title can be found on the Fulcrum platform via the following citable URL: https://doi.org/10.3998/mpub.9861753

A Note on Translations and Editions

Unless otherwise noted, the translations from original German sources in this book are my own. In several instances, I have elected to cite prominent English translations of key works, as I explain below. A number of the texts examined in this book were published in multiple editions, and were sometimes revised substantially from one edition to another, or continued to be reissued and updated after the author's death. Where relevant, my analyses thematize these differences across editions (such as for Sigmund Freud's *Three Essays on the Theory of Sexuality*); my selection of particular editions was at times also constrained by available library and archival holdings, which are often fragmentary as a legacy of wars, histories of exile and professional upheaval, and sometimes also state censorship.

For Freud's works, my translations are based on the 2000 German-language *Studienausgabe* (Fischer, 2000), which contains additional editorial commentary and precise information on editions and revisions. For the *Three Essays* and Freud's famous case study "Little Hans," which I examine in chapters 1 and 2, I have chosen to cite from the renowned English translation by James Strachey in the *Standard Edition of the Complete Psychological Works of Sigmund Freud* (Hogarth Press, 1953–1974), which will be most familiar to English readers. Considered far more definitive than the A. A. Brill translation of the second edition in 1910, Strachey's translation of the *Three Essays* was based on the final, 1924 edition published in the *Gesammelte Schriften*, Freud's collected works. In each case the translated materials were checked against the *Studienausgabe* and the original, 1905 version of Freud's case, in order to appropriately historicize both Freud's own developments in thinking, and others' reactions to this text. For further discussion of these various editions I refer readers to the recent collection *Deconstructing Normativity? Re-reading Freud's 1905 "Three Essays,"* edited by Philippe Van Haute and Herman

Westerink (London: Routledge, 2017). In addition, my translations of the Minutes of the Vienna Psychoanalytic Society from the early years of the Freudian movement draw on, but do not strictly adhere to, Margarete Nunberg's English translation of 1967 (Herman Nunberg and Ernst Federn, eds., *Minutes of the Vienna Psychoanalytic Society*, trans. Margarete Nunberg, 4 vols. (New York: International Universities Press).

Many scholars have discussed the problems of translating Freud's use of concepts such as *Trieb* and *Instinkt*; here I have elected to follow much of the recent psychoanalytic historiography in translating Freud's use of *Trieb* as "drive" rather than "instinct" (except where I follow the Strachey translations). In contrast to psychoanalytic discussions of concepts such as the "death-drive" or "life-drive" as forces motivating individual behaviors and choices, in sexological contexts I have often opted for the broader term "instinct" when it comes to describing attempts to capture the essence of human sexual existence. This term was adopted by prominent British sexologist Havelock Ellis in his English-language writings, and is also used widely in the historiography of this field. For further discussion see Dagmar Herzog, *Cold War Freud* (Cambridge, UK: Cambridge University Press, 2017): 124; Adrian Johnston, *Time Driven: Metapsychology and the Splitting of the Drive* (Evanston, IL: Northwestern University Press, 2005): chapter 6; and Herman Westerink, "Freud's Discussion with Psychiatry on Sexuality, Drives and Objects in 'Three Essays,'" in *Deconstructing Normativity? Re-reading Freud's 1905 "Three Essays,"* edited by Van Haute and Westerink (London: Routledge, 2017): 30.

My thinking on the at-times untranslatable cultural specificities of historical sexological and psychoanalytic texts, particularly when it comes to terms that convey racialized thinking or gendered identity categories, has been influenced by recent critical investigations of this concept, including Heike Bauer, "'Not a Translation but a Mutilation': The Limits of Translation and the Discipline of Sexology," *Yale Journal of Criticism* 16, no. 2 (2003): 381–405; Heike Bauer, ed., *Sexology and Translation: Cultural and Scientific Encounters across the Modern World*, Sexuality Studies (Philadelphia: Temple University Press, 2015). Where I have chosen to follow widely available English translations, including for Albert Moll's *Das Sexualleben des Kindes* (1908, translated into English in 1913 by Eden Paul as *The Sexual Life of the Child*, New York: Macmillan; introduction by Edward L. Thorndike), or Wilhelm Stekel's *Die Geschlechtskälte der Frau (Eine psychopathologie des weiblichen Liebeslebens)*, first published in 1921 (translated into English by James S. Van Teslaar as *Frigidity in Woman, in Relation to Her Sex Life*, Disorders of the Instincts and the Emotions: The Parapathiac Disorders, New York: Livereight,

1943), I have carefully checked them against the German text, and included references to the original German terms where several interpretations are readily available; differences in emphases and italics are noted in footnotes.

Richard von Krafft-Ebing's influential 1886 study *Psychopathia sexualis: Mit besonderer Berücksichtigung der konträren Sexualempfindung. Eine medizinisch-gerichtliche Studie für Ärzte und Juristen* went through fourteen editions between 1886 and 1903, and continued to be revised and republished in the decades that followed, including under the oversight of Alfred Fuchs (in 1907, 1912, 1918) and Albert Moll (1924); for details of various editions see Harry Oosterhuis, *Stepchildren of Nature: Krafft-Ebing, Psychiatry, and the Making of Sexual Identity* (Chicago: University of Chicago Press, 2000: ix–x, 46–48, 152, 275–77). In the following I cite the 1918 German edition (Stuttgart: F. Enke), for which I provide my own translations, having cross-checked this material (to ensure its correct attribution to Krafft-Ebing himself rather than later editors) against the English translation of 1899, *Psychopathia sexualis with Especial Reference to Antipathic Sexual Instinct*, based on the 10th German edition.

Acknowledgments

This book has been a long time in the making, and I am very grateful to the many people who have helped along the way. First, I owe enormous thanks to the anonymous reviewers at the University of Michigan Press, who at several stages of manuscript production provided generous, detailed, provocative, and enriching clarifications and comments; this book is much improved as a result. My warm thanks also to Christopher Dreyer at the Press for supporting the project from its early stages into final production, and to Marcia LaBrenz and her copyediting team for paying such careful attention to the manuscript.

Research for this book, including travel to archives on several continents, was made possible by funding from the Australian Research Council, and the early stages of this project were greatly enhanced by being part of the Discovery Project team "Making the Case" at the University of Melbourne. In particular, I thank Birgit Lang, Alison Lewis, and Joy Damousi for their enthusiasm, mentoring, and good cheer, and Birgit for also granting permission to include in chapter 2 of this book a short revised section of an article we coauthored. This project has received institutional support from the University of Melbourne and, in recent years, the Australian National University, where my colleagues in SLLL, Gender Studies, and the "Gender and History" node of the Gender Institute have provided most helpful feedback. My thanks, in particular, to Catherine Travis and Kate Mitchell for providing support for travel to conferences and archives, and to the Research School of Humanities and the Arts for funding a half-year sabbatical that enabled me to finish drafting the manuscript.

I received much assistance from archivists and librarians both in advance of and during my visits, and particularly thank the staff at the Staatsbibliothek zu Berlin; members of the Magnus-Hirschfeld-Gesellschaft in Berlin (particularly Ralf Dose and Rainer Herrn); the Schwules Museum Berlin (particularly

Jens Dobler); the ETH library in Zürich; the Kinsey Institute Library and Archives in Bloomington, Indiana (especially Shawn Wilson and Liana Zhou); the Library of Congress in Washington, DC; the Harry Ransom Center in Austin, Texas; the Beinecke Library at Yale; the New York Academy of Medicine; the Abraham A. Brill Library at the New York Psychoanalytic Society and Institute (especially Nellie Thompson); the Oskar Diethelm library at the Weill Cornell Medical College (especially Marisa Shaari); the British Library special collections staff; and the Freud Museum and Wellcome Library in London.

Many people have read and commented on chapters and sections of the manuscript, and I am most grateful for their generous and thought-provoking engagement with the project. In particular, I extend warm thanks to Heike Bauer, Chiara Beccalossi, Katharina Bonzel, Manuel Clemens, Ivan Crozier, Laura Doan, Kate Fisher, Jana Funke, Birgit Lang, Kirsten Leng, Wesley Lim, Laurie Marhoefer, and Carolyn Strange. Commentators on conference papers while I was drafting and revising the manuscript also offered timely interventions and prodding; these included Peter Cryle, Jennifer Evans, Lesley Hall, Nicole Perry, Karin Sellberg, Elizabeth Stephens, Annette Timm, April Trask, Chris Waters, the "Rethinking Sexology" team at the University of Exeter, and attendees at the following panels, seminars, and symposia: "Sexual Pathologies since 1800" (German Studies Association conference in Kansas City, October 2014); the "Queer Objects" symposium at the ANU (October 2014); the "Democratic Subjectivities II" seminar (GSA in San Diego, October 2016); the "Anatomy of the Image" conference at Monash University (February 2017); the "Principles of Cultural Dynamics" workshop at the Freie Universität, Berlin (July 2017); the Medical Humanities seminar at the University of Exeter (October 2017); the History of Sexuality seminar series at the Institute of Historical Research in London (October 2017); the European Sexologies Network conference at the American University in Paris (October 2017); the "Visual Archives of Sexology" symposium at Birkbeck, University of London (December 2017); the "Sex, Knowledge and Expertise in Germany's Twentieth Century" panel at the European Social Science History Conference in Belfast (April 2018); the University of Auckland and Auckland Goethe Society (April 2018); and "Thinking Critically with the Normal" (Volterra, June 2018).

I can't imagine having completed this project without the steady encouragement, welcome distractions, and reminders from friends and family that there are other things in life. A few have been particularly involved in this project over the years, providing warm hospitality, welcome debriefs, and the odd single malt, including Isolde Lueckenhausen, Dominic Brash, Shae Parker McCashen, Ishita Palit, Les Thomas, Birgit Lang, Brangwen Stone, Laura Bergade, and Russell Thomas; since I moved to Canberra, Susy Macqueen, Rohan Chandran, Leslie Barnes, and Knox Peden have all made life that much sweeter. While in Berlin, we always relish the warm welcome from the Bonzels, Rossbergs, Schmillenkamps, and Tobers, as well as welcome breaks from the library with Suntje Schmidt, Tina Roth, Bjarne Utz, Gunda Herke, and the rest of the crew. My partner Katharina Bonzel has been on this journey through thick and thin, tagging along on incredible research trips, cooking dinners, fixing software disasters, helping out with broken limbs, and being an all-round rock, all while working on her own book—I can't thank her enough for sticking it out. Finally, this book is dedicated to my parents, Judy and Kevin, for modeling hard work, generosity, a love of books and adventures, and for their constant love and support.

Sections of this book originally appeared in different form in the following: "The Queer Cases of Psychoanalysis: Rethinking the Scientific Study of Homosexuality, 1890s–1920s," *German History* 34, no. 3 (2016): 419–44 (coauthored with Birgit Lang); "Sexual Pathologies and the Violence of War: Sexological and Psychoanalytic Responses to World War I," *Limbus: Australisches Jahrbuch für germanistische Literatur- und Kulturwissenschaft (Australian Yearbook of German Literary and Cultural Studies)*, ed. A. Lewis, F.-J. Deiters, A. Fliethmann, B. Lang, and C. Weller (Freiburg: Rombach, 2014): 197–218; "Sexological Cases and the Prehistory of Transgender Identity Politics in Interwar Germany," in *Case Studies and the Dissemination of Knowledge*, ed. K. Sutton, J. Damousi, and B. Lang (New York: Routledge, 2015): 85–103; "Trading Transvestite Cases in Sexology, Psychoanalysis, and Weimar Sexual Subcultures," in *Intercultural Encounters in German Studies*, ed. Alan Corkhill and Alison Lewis (St. Ingbert: Röhrig, 2014): 323–40.

Introduction: Sex between Body and Mind

> Things are moving! On the 27th the Berlin Psycho-Analytic Society will meet for the first time. For the time being, the following gentlemen (all of them physicians) will take part: Hirschfeld, Iwan Bloch, Juliusburger, and Koerber. . . . I believe others will soon join in. Dr Juliusburger in particular is very keen; he is *Oberarzt* [senior staff physician] in a private institution and is introducing psychoanalysis in spite of his superior's opposition.
> —Karl Abraham to Sigmund Freud, Berlin, 21 August 1908[1]

It was with considerable excitement, just a year after returning from a three-year residency at Zurich's Burghölzli psychiatric clinic, that thirty-one-year-old neurologist and psychiatrist Karl Abraham wrote to his Viennese mentor of his plans to form a society in the German capital dedicated to the study of the unconscious mind. Among the earliest adherents of the emerging psychoanalytic movement in Germany, Abraham was keen to spread the word among his medical peers, many like himself up-and-coming physicians from assimilated Jewish-German families keen to direct their expertise toward the pressing social problems of their day. For historians of sexuality, the lineup of names joining Abraham in this endeavor stands out as a roll call of some of the leading figures in fin de siècle German sex research: the politically active sexologist, sex reformer, and homosexual rights campaigner Magnus Hirschfeld, with his characteristic full moustache, little round glasses, and dashing bowties; the more reserved Iwan Bloch, a balding and bespectacled dermatologist and venereal disease specialist; the socialist sanatorium psychiatrist and *Sanitätsrat* (medical counselor) Otto Juliusburger; and the bearded, pipe-smoking psychotherapist Heinrich Koerber.[2] The study of human sexuality in an era of scientific and cultural modernity, as this lineup suggests, was one that crossed disciplinary lines, bringing together researchers from across and outside the biomedical sciences. This sense of common purpose also extended beyond the German-speaking world: a letter from Freud's leading British follower Ernest

Jones two years later addressed that nation's foremost "sex psychologist," H. Havelock Ellis, as his "fellow countryman, and fellow-worker in the sphere of sexology."[3] So what led Freud, in a letter to the young Swiss analyst Carl Gustav Jung in 1911, to dismiss Hirschfeld—who had just announced his departure from the Berlin Society—as "a flabby, unappetizing fellow, absolutely incapable of learning anything," and overly susceptible to "homosexual touchiness"?[4] And just how disparaging was Hirschfeld's own reflection, a good two decades later, that the line dividing physiological sex research and psychoanalysis had frequently been based "more on emotional than on rational" principles?[5] When, how, and why were lines drawn between adherents of the Freudian "talking cure" and those who saw themselves as contributing to a more broadly conceived and interdisciplinary "sexual science," or sexology (*Sexualwissenschaft*), in the first decades of the twentieth century?

Sex between Body and Mind charts, for the first time, the interwoven historical relationship between these two overlapping, competing, and as the twentieth century progressed, increasingly distinct medical-scientific knowledge cultures. It demonstrates the significance of German-speaking central Europe to the shaping of ideas about modern sexual subjectivity, as doctors, scientists, and a range of other social actors developed theories of sexuality and debated treatments for perceived sexual abnormalities. Long before the publication of Michel Foucault's influential *History of Sexuality, Vol. 1*, researchers working in the booming medical and scientific disciplines of the late-nineteenth-century German-speaking world were well aware of the significance of sex for modern identity.[6] "Among the most constant elements of self-consciousness in the individual," wrote Austrian-based German psychiatrist Richard von Krafft-Ebing in his bestselling 1886 textbook of sexual pathologies, *Psychopathia sexualis*—widely considered a foundational text for modern sexual science—"are the knowledge of representing a definite sexual personality and the consciousness of desire."[7] Sexuality in this era was broadly understood to encompass desires, behaviors, identities, and relationships; it was seen as both a biological and psychological phenomenon, a product of nature as well as nurture, and as being at the very heart of human subjectivity.[8] This book argues that encounters between sexologists and psychoanalysts throughout the first half of the twentieth century had a crucial impact not only on modern understandings of human sexuality, but on modern understandings of the self.

From an international perspective, German-speaking doctors, scientists, sex reformers, and other actors were central to early encounters between sexology and psychoanalysis. Jones acknowledged as much in his letter to Ellis, drawing his colleague's attention to the "various forward movements" relating to sex developing on the Continent, "particularly in Germany and Austria," although this was hardly news to Ellis, whose influential study *Sexual Inversion*, coauthored with John Addington Symonds, had first appeared in German in 1896 as *Das konträre Sexualgefühl* (Contrary Sexual Feeling).[9] Several decades later, following Hirschfeld's establishment of the world's first Institute for Sexual Science in Berlin in 1919, a correspondent wrote to the British Society for the Study of Sex Psychology (later the British Sexological Society) similarly emphasizing the pioneering international role of contemporary German researchers:

> The German Institute for Sexual Science (under the direction of Dr. Magnus Hirschfeld) carries great weight in intellectual and judicial circles in Germany, and its officials are often called upon to give expert opinions in the Courts. Not only in Germany, but in many other parts of Europe, the great sociological and educational value of the Institute is recognized by publicists: the British Society, at all cost, can render like solid service in this country.[10]

Sex between Body and Mind homes in on those predominantly German-speaking, central European contexts in which early practitioners corresponded, published, gathered at conferences and reading groups, set up research laboratories, and met with patients and informants, whose needs and concerns shaped their clinical practice in crucial ways. Although it draws links to late-nineteenth century developments, both political and scientific, the core focus is on the years between the fin de siècle, when conversations between these two fields began in earnest following the publication of Freud's *Drei Abhandlungen zur Sexualtheorie* (*Three Essays on the Theory of Sexuality*, hereafter *Three Essays*) in 1905, and the early 1930s, when the rise of German fascism forced many practitioners—including, but not limited to, those with Jewish heritage—into emigration and exile. This shift dramatically curtailed the scope and influence of what had become one of the richest international centers for the study of human sexuality.

Histories of this period highlight the complexity of notions of "Germanness" during these decades of political and social transition, as new ideas about sexual and gender identity were overlaid with questions of nationhood and citizenship. As thousands of people moved to the cities and into work in the factories of industrialized modernity, the upheaval of the failed revolution of 1848 and an all-consuming world war from 1914 dramatically transformed the Austro-Hungarian and Prussian Empires of the nineteenth century, with all their linguistic and ethnic diversity, into the democratic nation-states of the twentieth. Anxieties about a rapidly changing society shaped cultural and scientific commentary on shifting reproductive practices, the threat of venereal disease, and the politics of prostitution and marriage, while leading European experts warned of the dangers of racial "degeneration" and eugenic and moral decline.[11] Such fears were compounded by specifically gendered anxieties, including a perceived "crisis" of middle-class masculinity, a sense that "feminizing" nervous disorders were on the rise, a series of prominent homosexual scandals in the early 1900s, and the growing influence of the women's movement from the late nineteenth century.[12]

Discussions of gender and sexuality differed across the German-speaking world—Germany, Austria, and Switzerland, for example, had quite different laws around male and female homosexuality, and these in turn differed markedly from those of other countries, such as France. National histories of women's suffrage and university entry were distinct as well. But there were also important commonalities guiding these conversations—a sense of a larger collective "Germanness" reflected in a shared language and cultural heritage, and in shared scientific traditions. These conditions promoted intellectual exchange and mobility between the Vienna-based Freudians and their medical and scientific colleagues to the Prussian north, Swiss west, and among the German-speaking populations of Hungary, the later Czech Republic, Russia, Italy, and elsewhere, at a time when "ideas and individuals traveled frequently back and forth across relatively recently created territorial borders."[13] German-speaking intellectuals, writers, physicians, and jurists were fundamental in shaping modern understandings of sexual categories, identities, and politics that continue to influence our lives into the twenty-first-century present. In turn, they were shaped by their cultural and political context.[14] There were concerns, for example, that German-speaking central Europe was less highly industrialized (at least until the late nineteenth century) and oversaw fewer overseas colonial territories than some of its neighbors in Western Europe, even as Berlin and Vienna represented hotbeds of social and cultural modernity. Nationalist anxieties also arose regarding the birthrate and population vitality, especially in the wake of the defeat of the Central Powers in World War I. The following chapters focus particularly on how debates played out in the context of the German nation after unification in 1871, which underwent further significant political transformation following the fall of the monarchy and establishment of Germany's first democracy in 1918/19. At the same time, they show how larger, transnational experiences affected "German" sex researchers in a broader sense, from the psychoanalysts and sexologists serving in the field hospitals of World War I to the descent into dictatorship during the 1930s.

A quick survey of developments from the first decade of the new century highlights the speed and intensity of German sexual knowledge production during this period. Building on influential earlier studies of the "sexual psychopathologies" and "perversions" by nineteenth-century scholars such as Krafft-Ebing and Heinrich Kaan, a second generation of largely but not exclusively male researchers, many based in the progressive Prussian center of Berlin, were beginning in the years following the fin de siècle to explicitly label their work "sexual science," or *Sexualwissenschaft*.[15] The dermatologist turned sex researcher, Bloch, later claimed, if not completely accurately, to have forged this term in the first years of the new century:

> The expression "*sexual science*" [*Sexualwissenschaft*], coined by me in the year 1906 as the label for a new, independent field of research, quickly established itself as the umbrella concept [*übergeordneter Begriff*] for a number of closely linked facts and problems, and not just in the medical, but also in the anthropological, juridical, and theological literature, against all forms of resistance, because it played to the widespread conviction that the broad problem of sexuality had undergone immense expansion.[16]

While I return to questions of etymology below, Bloch was only one of a growing number of researchers in fin de siècle central Europe seeking to expand the study of sexuality beyond the perversions to encompass human sexual life in all its facets. The year 1908 saw the appearance of not one but two of the first dedicated sexological journals to appear anywhere in the world. The *Zeitschrift für Sexualwissenschaft* (Journal of Sexual Science) initially appeared for twelve months under the stewardship of Hirschfeld in Berlin and his medical colleagues Friedrich Krauss in Vienna and Hermann Rohleder in Leipzig. Although its first public outing was short-lived, the periodical enjoyed far greater success when it was reestablished by Bloch and neurologist and sex researcher Albert Eulenburg in 1914, riding out the tumultuous events of that year to manage a nearly two-decade run until 1932. Max Marcuse's *Sexual-Probleme* (Sexual Problems, 1908–1914), meanwhile, deliberately expanded the scope of its predecessor journal *Mutterschutz: Zeitschrift zur Reform der sexuellen Ethik* (Maternal Protection: Journal for the Reform of Sexual Ethics, 1905–1907). The latter had been established in 1905 as the organ of the League for the Protection of Mothers and Sexual Reform, following a scuffle with that journal's original editor, radical feminist and sex reformer Helene Stöcker.[17]

These new journals represented a concerted broadening of the themes of sexual science, even as they followed in the footsteps of earlier, more specialized publications. These included Hirschfeld's pioneering *Jahrbuch für sex-*

uelle Zwischenstufen (Yearbook of Sexual Intermediaries), which since its establishment in 1899 had worked to illuminate the medical, scientific, and cultural aspects of homosexuality and other "intermediary" sexual forms, which included everyone from intersex individuals to those whose gender identity did not align with their assigned birth sex. The *Jahrbuch* was also the organ of the political lobbying organization, the Wissenschaftlich-humanitäres Komitee (Scientific Humanitarian Committee, WhK), which since 1897 had worked to petition the Reichstag to decriminalize male homosexuality and to prevent the criminalization of female homosexuality when this was proposed in 1909.[18] Other predecessors to the new "sexual science" journals had focused on topics such as venereal disease and syphilis (*Zeitschrift für Bekämpfung der Geschlechtskrankheiten*, 1903–1914), gynecology (*Archiv für Frauenkunde und Eugenik*, later renamed *Archiv für Frauenkunde und Konstitutionsforschung*, 1914–1933), and eugenics (e.g., *Archiv für Rassen- und Gesellschafts-Biologie*, 1904–1943)—the last-mentioned also an important issue for left-wing sex reformers during this period.

Although he acknowledged the significance of these earlier publications, Bloch emphasized the need to address sexual science in broader terms: "*Sexual science* as an independent discipline is the science [or "knowledge," *Wissenschaft*] of the sexual, that is, of the manifestations and effects of sexuality in *physical* and *mental*, in *individual* and *social* relation."[19] Marcuse, too, construed this new field in a wide and interdisciplinary sense: "there is hardly a scientific discipline for which the sexual question does not belong to the scope of its research."[20] Moving beyond the narrower psychiatric framings of Krafft-Ebing and his contemporaries, the sexologist was beginning to emerge as a "new intellectual type," drawing on knowledge from "anthropology, biology, history, psychiatry and the medical sciences."[21]

In the same years that Bloch and his colleagues were loudly declaring sexual science to be a new, independent field, a few hundred miles to the German-speaking south neurologist Sigmund Freud published a short book that was quickly acknowledged as a game-changer. His *Three Essays* of 1905 raised eyebrows among the scientific community for its no-nonsense account of how sexual behaviors, desires, and sensations could be found in "normal" individuals well before puberty: in the infantile sucking of thumbs, in a child's feelings of desire and jealousy toward siblings and parents, or in the pleasures of excretory bowel movements.[22] Freud was already enjoying a growing reputation among Germany's educated middle classes thanks to his influential study of dreams as a channel to unconscious life, *Die Traumdeutung* (The Interpretation of Dreams, 1900), and his 1890s work with Josef Breuer treating the curious physical symptoms of "hysterical" patients, including the famous case of "Anna O."[23] Although his *Three Essays* was not the first study to consider children's erotic potential from a scientific perspective, it was widely viewed as putting the study of human sexual development on a new footing, not least due to Freud's forthright declaration that "polymorphous perversity" and "bisexuality" formed part of the shared human experience. These, too, were not exactly novel propositions—several years earlier Viennese philosophy student Otto Weininger had pointed to the "bisexual" combinations of masculine and feminine elements making up the sexual composition of any one individual in his 1903 study *Geschlecht und Charakter* (Sex and Character), while Freud's early correspondent Wilhelm Fliess had been working on ideas of universal bisexuality for some time. Bloch and a number of his sexological colleagues, including Hirschfeld and psychiatrist Albert Moll, were also intrigued by how physiological "bisexuality" early in life—and as early as the embryonic stage—might shape subsequent sexual development in ways that complicated dominant cultural assumptions of a binary sexual system.[24] Nor was Freud the first to delve into the sexual reaches of the human unconscious; psychiatrists such as Moll, August Forel in Zurich, and Munich-based psychiatrist and parapsychologist Albert von Schrenck-Notzing had long been using techniques of hypnosis, suggestion, and mesmerism to manipulate their patients' proclivities, whether sexual or otherwise.[25] Their work frequently drew—as did Freud's own—on the influential discoveries and methods of an earlier generation of French psychiatrists in the 1880s, including Jean-Martin Charcot and Hippolyte Bernheim.[26]

Freud's theory of human sexual development had many detractors in German fin de siècle medical and scientific circles—and internationally as well, after A. A. Brill's English translation of 1910[27]—but most reviews of the *Three Essays* grudgingly acknowledged his innovation in bringing together a coherent and seemingly universal theory of sexuality. The theory promised to explain all manner of "neuroses" and "perversions," framing these as developmental "inhibitions" or "aberrations" from the norm rather than as fundamentally pathological, hereditary, or degenerative deformities. Freud's new "psychoanalytic" school of thought was also beginning to attract an enthusiastic, if temperamental, circle of early adherents. Among the members of the "Wednesday Society" that met weekly in Freud's apartment were Viennese physicians Isidor Sadger and Wilhelm Stekel and Budapest-based doctor Sándor Ferenczi, each of whom devoted much attention in subsequent years to the meanings of sexual quirks, fantasies, and repressions for an individual's overall nervous disposition. They were soon joined in these investigations by Abraham's aforementioned Berlin Psycho-Analytic Society in 1908, while Jung and his director Paul Eugen Bleuler at the famed Burghölzli clinic began moving conversations about the human unconscious westward, toward the Swiss Alps. Although his intervention was intended in a rather less field-defining sense than Bloch's, it was also Freud whom historians have identified as actually coining the term "Sexualwissenschaft" some seven years earlier, in a 1898 publication on the etiology of the neuroses. In that paper, the father of psychoanalysis expressed his regret "that the science of sexuality is nowadays still considered fraudulent [*unehrlich*]."[28] From this phrasing, as German historian of sexuality Volkmar Sigusch observes, it is clear that Freud also saw himself as a practitioner of this new branch of knowledge.[29] Like the lineup at Abraham's first meeting in Berlin, this etymological anecdote points to the significant overlap between the actors and questions populating the fields of psychoanalysis and sexology in early-twentieth-century central Europe.

Sex between Body and Mind begins by exploring how Freud's slender volume, *Three Essays*, fundamentally challenged the explanatory modes of fin de siècle sexology, and how sexologists responded to this challenge. It then works to tease out precisely how, where, and why these two fields drifted apart during the first decades of the twentieth century, even as both sexologists and psychoanalysts continued to look keenly toward developments from across this emerging disciplinary divide. The first book to subject this relationship to systematic analysis, it interrogates the interpersonal, theoretical, and methodological negotiations between scholars who identified as "sexologists," "psychoanalysts," sometimes as neither, and sometimes as both at once. As one scholar has recently observed, "many of the people we today associate with the emergence of European sexology . . . did not self-identify as 'sexologists' even as they staked out a specialism in sexual matters."[30] The following chapters focus on moments of encounter: most immediately, between scientists, doctors, and other researchers who came to identify with the disciplinary labels of "sexology" or "psychoanalysis," but also between sex researchers and social actors situated beyond the clinics, consulting rooms, and laboratories of these two fields, from injured soldiers to feminists to early transgender rights activists.[31]

Neither a biographical nor an intellectual history, this book presents a comparative cultural history of early-twentieth-century German scientific sex research and psychoanalysis that is informed by impulses from queer and gender studies as well as the history of medicine, science, and historical epistemology. Its chapters explore how sexologists and psychoanalysts, working within broader frameworks of "sexual modernity" (explored below), each attempted to articulate definitive explanations of human sexual development in its "normal" and "pathological" variations, even as they at times questioned the binary logic of such oppositional concepts. At the same time, they were working hard to shore up the scientific and professional legitimacy of their own fledgling professional specializations. By focusing on neglected moments of cross-disciplinary encounter, *Sex between Body and Mind* sheds light on the richness and dynamism of sexual knowledge production in early-twentieth-century German-speaking Europe. This book argues that intellectual debates between these fields did not begin and end with clear distinctions between "nature" and "nurture," and that matters were always more complex than sexologists coming down on the side of biology and psychoanalysts focusing purely on the workings of the mind.

Nature versus Nurture: Sex Research in an Era of Scientific Modernity

Sexologists and psychoanalysts working in the decades after 1900 sought to justify their theories and methods to diverse professional and lay publics both by addressing pressing new challenges, such as the treatment of shell-shocked soldiers returning from the trenches of World War I, and by bringing new, scientific perspectives to bear on older "problems" such as homosexual behaviors. Drawing on nineteenth-century constructs of "scientific medicine" to offer new definitions and diagnoses of sexual conditions, sexologists and psychoanalysts spoke to the very heart of ideas about the modern subject.[32] Since the 1970s the phrase "sexual modernity" (or sometimes "sexual modernism") has come to encapsulate this late-nineteenth-century merging of ideas around sex and the self, as sexuality became increasingly dissociated from reproduction and more closely connected with pleasure, desire, and emotional intimacy. Scholars also began looking beyond the physiology of the body toward more psychologized understandings of sexuality, while developing ever-more-differentiated classifications of the "perversions," following in the vein of Krafft-Ebing. This was not just a shift among scientists; sexuality was increasingly construed within society more broadly as a constructive natural force central to both social life and individual identity, as "something like a semi-coherent entity—a complex of physiological and emotional impulses and sensations, acts and ideals—took shape and was designated as 'sexuality' in the collective imaginary."[33] Moving away from older religious and legal frameworks, and more than simply a politicized model of sexual liberation, ideas of sexual pleasure and development became central aspects of the "reflexive project of the self."[34]

Throughout much of the nineteenth century, psychiatrists and physicians interested in sexual questions had been torn between explaining the sexual instinct and its perversions as a product of heredity or environment, nature or nurture, although they generally believed that both played a role. Within psychiatry, an older, "anatomical" style of reasoning was swiftly giving way to explanations based on "impulses, tastes, aptitudes, satisfactions, and psychic traits."[35] At the time Freud's *Three Essays* hit the shelves, many medical sex researchers were placing particular emphasis on congenital factors, often searching patients' family histories for signs of hereditary abnormality or degeneration. Yet they, like the early Freudians, shared a fundamental assumption that complex combinations of biological and psychological factors lay behind the formulation of the *libido sexualis*, or sexual instinct. Berlin Institute for Sexual Science psychiatrist Arthur Kronfeld declared as much in 1921, when he argued that "both factors, the endogenous and the exogenous, are inextricably interwoven with one another."[36] Conversations across disciplinary lines also led both sexologists and psychoanalysts to expand their frames of reference in these decades. Sexologists, weighing the Freudian focus on patients' repressed experiences and fantasies as well as the clinical innovation of the "talking cure," began to more concertedly attend to environmental, experiential, and psychological factors. In turn, their own persistent emphasis on the workings of the body, including exciting new research into the "inner secretions" or hormones that gained speed from the 1910s, forced psychoanalysts to develop more complex accounts of the relationship between physiology and psychology.

Historians of sexuality have long acknowledged that conversations occurred across these two fields, but the specifics of this relationship are still little understood. Much of the scholarship on early-twentieth-century sex research has focused on actors celebrated as progressive pioneers of the sex reform movement, and in particular, on Hirschfeld and his world-leading Institute. Established in central Berlin at the dawning of Germany's Weimar Republic under the motto of "Justice through Science," the Institute was soon renowned both locally and internationally for clinical and outreach activities ranging from marriage counseling to experimental laboratory research on "intermediary" sexual forms.[37] Individuals such as Hirschfeld tend to fit the mold of the "public scientist," espousing the value of science for attaining a range of social and political goals, which in his case included better access to contraception, eugenically oriented marriage counseling, and homosexual rights.[38] Yet as a more critical strand of recent scholarship points out, while Hirschfeld's socialist-inspired advocacy of greater sexual freedoms for the working classes and "third sex" individuals has been "lionized" by contemporary German LGBTIQ activists (and not a few historians) seeking to reclaim his legacy "as the guiding light of a rational, scientifically driven human rights movement for sexual toleration," such celebratory modes of remembrance overshadow his involvement in more troubling practices, such as eugenic interventions or invasive treatments for homosexuality.[39]

Among Hirschfeld's contemporaries, actors such as Max Marcuse, Helene Stöcker, or Grete Meisel-Hess were also closely involved in reform movements promoting birth control, the protection of mothers, the prevention of venereal disease, and the abolition of state regulation of prostitution, especially with a view to assisting the working classes.[40] German researchers other than Hirschfeld also played a central role in establishing fledging international sexological associations. One such was the Ärztliche Gesellschaft für Sexualwissenschaft (Medical Society for Sexual Science), founded in January 1913 with Albert Eulenburg as inaugural chair and a broad sex-reform agenda. Its competitor organization, the Internationale Gesellschaft für Sexualforschung (International Society for Sex Research, INGESE), founded in November 1913 as the joint brainchild of Moll, Marcuse, and demographer Julian Wolf, emphasized "a strictly scientific approach to sexuality."[41] Yet whereas the reputations of fin de siècle sexologists such as Moll, Bloch, or Forel more or less equaled Hirschfeld's at the time, they have received far less attention in the sexual historiography of recent decades. This is probably because the links between their work and twenty-first-century sexual politics are less immediately apparent than with Hirschfeld, especially as they focused their careers more squarely on the spaces of the clinic and the pages of scientific journals than on political advocacy and social reform.

A handful of recent studies have gone some way toward redressing this, exploring, for example, Moll's pioneering early formulation of a two-part sexual instinct in his 1897 *Untersuchungen über die Libido sexualis* (Libido Sexualis), Bloch's unique contributions drawing on fields ranging from embryology to cultural anthropology, or Forel's influential work on hypnosis.[42] In Moll's case, the lack of attention from contemporary scholars, many working within the antinormative and politically progressive frameworks of queer theory, has undoubtedly been compounded by his own increasingly conservative political stance, which even saw him attempt to foil the career of his long-time competitor Hirschfeld by writing to the dean of the Paris medical faculty in 1934, where Hirschfeld was then in exile, and sending a copy of his comments to the German foreign secretary for the Nazi Party.[43] Other researchers have undertaken detailed critical biographies of pioneering figures such as Krafft-Ebing and Kaan,[44] or explored the links between German sex researchers and scholars working elsewhere in Europe from the nineteenth century onward, including Italian criminal anthropologist Cesare Lombroso and physician Paolo Mantegazza.[45] Extending earlier historical surveys, this recent scholarship foregrounds the centrality of continental European contributions to sexual science before the later era of Anglo-American dominance by Alfred Kinsey and others.[46] The role of German scholars in shaping the origins of modern sexual science and developing a new vocabulary of "Urnings," "inversion," and "homosexuality" has, moreover, been the focus of a series of new studies on early German-speaking "gay rights" activists such as Heinrich Hössli, Karl Heinrich Ulrichs, and Karl Maria Kertbeny from the 1830s onward.[47] In particular, historians point to the resonances between such early homosexual rights discourses—often grounded in congenital scientific arguments—and more recent brands of "born this way" activism or the hunt for a "gay gene" or "queer science" in the twenty-first century.[48]

Despite the success of these efforts in developing more nuanced histories of modern sexual science, the influence of Freudian thought has often remained a marginal concern. This ongoing neglect is particularly notable when one considers both the influence of psychoanalysis continuing into the post–World War II era, particularly in North America, and the central significance that the Freudians attributed to the sexual.[49] For critics such as Rita Felski, this is because the "Freudian revolution" in the early years of the new century erected "a seemingly impenetrable barrier between the modern view of sexuality as an enigmatic and often labile psychic field rooted in unconscious desires" on the one hand, and the physiological and congenital work of the nineteenth-century sexologists on the other. Felski points out that one of the key achievements of Foucault's *History* was to dissolve this barrier, revealing an essential continuity between Victorian and post-Freudian culture that centered on the shared conviction that sexuality holds the key to our identity—the hallmark, as already noted, of sexual modernity.[50] Yet even today, most histories of modern sex research persist in a rather one-sided approach, prioritizing either sexology or psychoanalysis, but rarely both, in their efforts to understand how individuals in the past conceived of their sexual identities.

Certainly, a number of scholars have examined aspects of this overlapping history, particularly by demonstrating Freud's indebtedness to, and his at times decidedly tetchy relationships with, contemporary sexologists such as Moll, Hirschfeld, and Ellis.[51] Several studies also explore how doctors treating dysfunctional heterosexual relationships and providing marital advice—subjects that remain, regrettably, somewhat on the margins of the present study—drew on both sexological and psychoanalytic approaches during these decades.[52] Meanwhile, Ulrich Clement reflects on the relationship between these fields in the postwar period, suggesting that sexology has always been more interested in psychoanalysis than *vice versa*. Yet he rather too quickly—as the following chapters show—asserts that psychoanalysis was "lost" to leading sexual scientists after Freud's dismissal of the seduction theory in the 1890s.[53] We still understand very little about the transfers and contestations between these two fields, and how these conversations shaped modern understandings of sex.

Cultural historians, too, have tended to prioritize either the sexological or the psychoanalytic in their studies of early twentieth-century fiction and film, while drawing much-needed attention to how sexological theories of inversion and homosexuality, in particular, infiltrated and were critically negotiated in literary works such as Aimee Duc's *Sind es Frauen?* (Are These Women?, 1903), Thomas Mann's *Der Tod in Venedig* (Death in Venice, 1911), and the 1919 silent film *Anders als die Andern* (Different from the Others, dir. Richard Oswald). This scholarship has also productively demonstrated the influence of literary works on sexual science, such as Krafft-Ebing's reliance on Leopold von Sacher-Masoch's 1870 novel *Venus im Pelz* (*Venus in Furs*) as illustrative material when it came to first articulating the categories of "sadism" and "masochism" as unique perversions. A further set of studies reveals the significance of psychoanalytic theories of repressed sexual fantasies and their effects in works of this era, such as Alfred Döblin's *Die beiden Freundinnen und ihr Giftmord* (Two Girlfriends Commit Murder, 1924) or G. W. Pabst's *Geheimnisse einer Seele* (Secrets of a Soul, 1926).[54]

Accounts of early homosexual reform movements, meanwhile, tend to place psychoanalysis at a considerable distance from political organizations such as the WhK, even as some scholars lament the "Freudian eclipse" that supposedly overshadowed not only the work of early activist-intellectuals such as Ulrichs and Kertbeny, but also later sexological thinkers such as Moll and Hirschfeld.[55] Yet the notion that the Freudian contribution to German gay history remained firmly entrenched in an ivory tower of theory while sexologists such as Hirschfeld were out on the barricades is complicated by the kinds of affiliation and collaboration illuminated in the following chapters, from Ferenczi's and Freud's involvement in the WhK to Sadger's decision to publish his first in-depth case of a homosexual patient in Hirschfeld's *Jahrbuch*. It is into this decidedly fragmented historiography that *Sex between Body and Mind* intervenes, demonstrating the importance of telling the history of early-twentieth-century sex research from a standpoint of dialogue and mutual influence rather than intractable divides.

Thinking With and Beyond Foucault

At a broad level, this book works to flesh out what remains in Foucault's work a rather general account of the *scientia sexualis* and its relationship to Freudian thought. More narrowly, it contributes to a critical vein in the scholarship emphasizing the more emancipatory and productive aspects of Foucault's account, which for many years was primarily taken up as a critique of the negative, prohibitive, and disciplinary effects of encounters between the doctors and patients of sexual science, psychiatry, and psychoanalysis. The historiography of sexuality in modernity remains deeply entangled with the arguments set forth in the first, and by far the most widely read, volume of Foucault's *History of Sexuality. Sex between Body and Mind* charts the historical relationship between German sexology and psychoanalysis in the early twentieth century in a way that is simultaneously indebted to the fundamental rethinking of sexual modernity undertaken by that work and to the wealth of critical scholarship it has inspired. In particular, scholars writing from the perspective of late-twentieth-century LGBTIQ rights movements have drawn on Foucault's work in undertaking important and powerful critiques of psychiatry's complicity in pathologizing and persecuting bodies deemed "other." Yet such readings have resulted in a rather one-sided picture of what were frequently mutually influential relationships between doctors, scientists, patients, and emerging sexual minority cultures.

Foucault singles out medicine and psychiatry as two of the key sources of a modern science of sexuality in the eighteenth and nineteenth centuries, alongside systems of education and criminal justice. This was particularly pronounced, he argues, after the psychiatric profession "annexed the whole of the sexual perversions as its own province," creating new labels and taxonomies of sexual disorder, from "Krafft-Ebing's zoophiles" to "Rohleder's automonosexualists."[56] Scholars since have charted a move from the narrowly psychiatric and forensic brand of late-nineteenth-century sex research that is Foucault's focus to a more broadly "scientific" and politicized mode in the early decades of the twentieth, questioning the weight of Foucault's emphasis on the medical and psychiatric.[57] During this period, a new generation of sexual scientists and their allies, including feminists and sex-reform activists, extended the reach of the *scientia sexualis* well beyond the walls of the physician's consulting room.

The significance of psychoanalysis in this larger narrative of the scientification and politicization of sexual knowledge in modernity has frequently been underplayed. Problematic translations of Foucault's text have contributed to this sidelining. "The strange position of psychiatry at the end of the nineteenth century would be hard to comprehend," argues Foucault in the English translation of his *History*,

> if one did not see the rupture it brought about in the great system of degenerescence: it resumed the project of a medical technology appropriate for dealing with the sexual instinct; but it sought to free it from its ties with heredity, and hence from eugenics and the various racisms. It is very well to look back from our vantage point and remark upon the normalizing impulse in Freud; one can go on to denounce the role played for many years by the psychoanalytic institution; but the fact remains that in the great family of technologies of sex . . . it was the one that, up to the decade of the forties, rigorously opposed the political and institutional effects of the perversion-heredity-degenerescence system.[58]

Although Foucault makes explicit reference to both "Freud" and the "psychoanalytic institution," his reference to the "strange position of psychiatry" is somewhat confusing in this context; a more accurate translation, as Arnold Davidson points out, would be the "singular position of psychoanalysis" (*la position singulière de la psychanalyse*), as "Foucault's whole point here is to distinguish psychoanalysis from psychiatry, and to claim that psychoanalysis effected a 'rupture' with respect to the 'great system of degeneracy.'"[59] Yet Foucault's attempt to clearly distinguish between psychiatry and psychoanalysis during this period is itself problematic, oversimplifying the complex overlaps between these fields and their practitioners, including on the question of degeneration. Historians have now shown that psychiatrists such as Krafft-Ebing and Moll had already begun distancing themselves from degeneration theory before the interventions of the Freudians, and highlighted significant parallels between Freud's and Krafft-Ebing's respective conceptual frameworks of "normal" and "perverse" sexuality and the nature of the sexual instinct.[60]

In the decades since Foucault's study, many scholars have persisted in reducing his argument around the emergence of a modern sexual science to one of prohibiting disciplinary effects. This ignores Foucault's own dynamic emphasis (albeit less pronounced than his focus on disciplinary power dynamics) on the ways that sexual knowledge production "lets itself be invaded by the pleasure it is pursuing."[61] Overly narrow readings have led scholars to claim that Foucault failed to recognize the "two-sided and contradictory nature" of doctor-patient encounters in favor of emphasizing their regulatory effects; some even characterize his account of sexologists pathologizing their subjects as "wholly dismissive."[62] In contrast, this book aligns itself with a strain of scholarship arguing that there is more to Foucault's original account than such "ossified and literal" readings suggest.[63]

To take a key example, Foucault famously posits a "reverse discourse" of homosexual identity that developed as a direct result of interactions with the early sexual scientists, enabling "homosexuality . . . to speak in its own behalf, to demand that its legitimacy or 'naturality' be acknowledged, often in the same vocabulary, using the same categories by which it was medically disqualified."[64] New scientific theories of homosexuality, Foucault argues, were not simply constraining, but could also be emancipatory in their effects, enabling individuals to categorize themselves according to new sexual identities, and hence to formulate new political subjectivities and demands. Although a wealth of research has foregrounded the significance of the "voices of perverts" for the history of sexual science,[65] some scholars persist in interpreting Foucault's assessment of sexual science in terms of "a deplorable medical colonization."[66] Others, however, emphasize the emancipatory potential also present in the *History*, pushing for "a more complex and contradictory picture of the historical production of sexuality, one involving sexual subjects and emancipation as well as 'top-down' disciplinary discourses."[67] A concern with the patients and subjects of modern sex research informs each of the chapters of this book, from homosexuals subjected to early conversion attempts to soldiers being treated for shell shock during World War I. These voices are foregrounded in the final chapter, which shows how new forms of "expert" sexological and psychoanalytic knowledge were being taken up by individuals who had begun to identify with the diagnosis of "transvestism." Borrowing a phrase from Ian Hacking, I show how the negotiations of trans-identifying individuals with new scientific categories "looped back" to shape the inquiries of the sex researchers in meaningful ways.

Discipline-Making, Scientific Encounters, and Trading Zones

Sexology and psychoanalysis as they developed in German-speaking Europe grew out of more established nineteenth-century medical specializations, including psychiatry, neurology, and physiology. Krafft-Ebing in Vienna, Moll in Berlin, and Forel in Zurich were all psychiatrists with experience treating patients in asylums and private clinics, and also advised on forensic and criminological matters. Bloch and Marcuse were both Berlin-based dermatologists specializing in sexual disease and dysfunction, while Hirschfeld, following a brief stint studying modern languages, established his early career in general medicine with an interest in natural therapies before moving more firmly into sexual medicine and political sex reform.[68] Freud trained first as a neurologist and neurophysiologist, during which time his visit to Charcot's clinic at the Salpêtrière in Paris in 1885 helped to shape his innovative early clinical work with Josef Breuer on the peculiar symptoms of "hysterics."[69] Yet whether their original specialization was in psychiatry, neurology, physiology, dermatology (which at this time always had a sexual-diseases component), or general medicine, most fin de siècle German sexologists and psychoanalysts shared a common ground in the expectations and training of scientific medicine. With Berlin widely acknowledged as a leading international hub of medical, psychiatric, and psychotherapeutic research, "medicine and biology became ever more authoritative determinants of what was sexually and socially 'natural.'"[70]

Scholars have long recognized that "sexology, from the beginning, has been a transnational, or at least a transatlantic phenomenon"; more recently, they have shown it to be an endeavor that stretched from Prague to Palestine and from New York to Calcutta.[71] Yet the precise ways in which this field developed in relation to the wider German medical and scientific professions, in dialogue with emerging sexual minority groups and activists agitating for political reform, differed considerably across the various national contexts of Germany, Britain, the USA, Russia, Australia, India, and elsewhere. More cultural historical and literary modes of sex research emerged in the English-speaking world during this period, for example, in works by Ellis, Edward Carpenter, and others, although they were also in regular dialogue with the German sex researchers around concepts such as "sexual inversion" and an "intermediate sex."[72] In contrast, German researchers drew more consistently on the academic authority and professional prestige that had accrued to medical research over the course of the nineteenth century, even as they approached their topic in an interdisciplinary mode.

From around the turn of the century onward, German physicians and scientists who were beginning to identify with the new labels of "sexual scientists" (*Sexualwissenschaftler/innen*) or "psychoanalysts" (*Psychoanalytiker/innen*) endeavored to establish these fields as distinct and independent specializations or disciplines. Disciplines are always social constructions as well as frameworks of knowledge production, and I use this term here to refer to "a scientific specialism with its own subject matter, journals, courses, credentials, and . . . a profession with its own organizations, criteria and role as expertise."[73] Both sexual science and psychoanalysis were still very much in the throes of discipline-making between the 1890s and 1920s. Of course, not every field of study necessarily becomes a discipline in the sense of a discrete professional entity; sometimes scholarly networks exhibiting a sense of collective purpose are best described in less formalized terms, as "communities," "institutions," or "schools."[74] I have elected to describe sexual science and psychoanalysis in these early decades of their emergence primarily as "fields," both to highlight the dynamic work of professionalization processes and to widen the net to consider how a broader spectrum of social actors produced sexual scientific and psychoanalytic knowledge. Here I follow Kirsten Leng, who draws on the work of Pierre Bourdieu and others to show how the language of fields "facilitates an understanding of early twentieth-century sexology as a socially embedded, interactional, and highly contested practice of knowledge production, one that was not limited to a select few (male) authors and canonical texts."[75]

As already observed, the new brand of German sex research that developed over the final decades of the nineteenth century and first decades of the twentieth confounds easy categorization due to its explicitly interdisciplinary scope. The very label *Sexualwissenschaft,* with its broad connotations of sexual "knowledge" or "scholarly inquiry," goes well beyond narrower English-language definitions of "science," frequently understood to refer primarily to "natural" sciences such as biology, chemistry, and physiology.[76] In an editorial for the new *Zeitschrift für Sexualwissenschaft* (Journal of Sexual Science) in 1908, Hirschfeld listed the diverse areas of scholarly inquiry he considered this field to encompass, including predictable specializations such as sexual anatomy, chemistry, physiology, psychology, and Darwinist-inspired research on evolution and comparative sexual biology. But he also included more politically, culturally, or socially oriented fields: sexual hygiene; sexual prophylaxis (a branch of sexual hygiene dealing with matters such as STD prevention or prostitution); sexual politics; and sexual legislation, ethics, and ethnology. To these he added the specific study of sexual varieties and pathologies.[77] The dermatologist Bloch's *Das Sexualleben unserer Zeit in seinen Beziehungen zur modernen Kultur* (The Sexual Life of Our Times in Its Relation to Modern Civilization), published a year earlier in 1907, further exemplifies this trend in its heavy focus on "anthropological-ethnological research."[78] German scientific sex research in the first decade of the new century was thus starting to be reconceptualized as a field that reached "beyond the medical," even as scholarly moves to attend to this broader scope have been hotly debated in recent years.[79]

The explicit interdisciplinarity of fin de siècle sexual science complicates any consideration of its relationship to psychoanalysis. As Jones's appeal to a shared "sexologist" identity suggests, the boundaries between these fields were frequently blurred, especially in the early days. Psychoanalysis was a telling omission from the long list of fields that Hirschfeld *did* consider part of the new *Sexualwissenschaft,* for example, but he did include it in discussions of sexual science elsewhere in this journal. Similarly, the inaugural volume of Marcuse's *Sexual-Probleme*, published in the same year as Hirschfeld's *Zeitschrift*—both of which, the editors clearly hoped, would set the agenda for the scientific study of sex—included not one, but two articles by Freud, on the topics of infantile sexuality and "cultural sexual morality and modern nervosity."[80]

The disciplinary boundaries of psychoanalysis were also far from clear during these years in relation to the more established branches of the "psy-sciences."[81] Psychology had emerged as a discrete field in late-nineteenth-century Germany under the leadership of figures such as Wilhelm Wundt, who in 1879 established one of the first psychological laboratories at the University of Leipzig.[82] Histories of that field, with its emphasis on experimental laboratory methods and topics such as sensory perception and memory, frequently bracket off the seemingly more esoteric and sexual concerns of the Freudians, with their focus on the mysterious workings of the unconscious and fantasy life, observing that "[p]sychologists hated the thought that sex, dreams, and neuroses were all psychology was about."[83] The historical relationship of psychoanalysis to psychiatry is hardly less ambiguous. Often, the Freudian school and its successors are dismissed as a brief "hiatus" or "transitionary phenomenon," which had its heyday in the early postwar decades in North America, before being overtaken by modern neurobiological approaches in psychiatry or approaches such as cognitive behavior therapy in psychology.[84] Psychoanalysis's postwar "halcyon days" and subsequent "transmogrification into a still culturally influential but professionally far more niche phenomenon" has been most recently charted by Dagmar Herzog in her work *Cold War Freud*.[85] Despite areas of overlap with these other "psy-sciences," psychoanalysis consistently distinguished itself through its concerted focus on the unconscious mind and its dedication to the clinical "talking cure," a therapeutic mode that emphasizes dialogue and the relationships of "transference" and "countertransference" between patient and analyst. The clinician's role in this context was to help uncover repressed, and often sexual, experiences and desires from the depths of their patients' memories, using these to explain and relieve their symptoms and neuroses.[86]

A sense of professional marginalization compounded the disciplinary insecurity of sexual scientists and psychoanalysts in these decades. First, there was the matter of their risqué subject matter—neurotics, masochists, fetishists, hysterics, and cross-dressers—which positioned their work on the borders of respectable medical research. Then there was the lack of academic recognition in the form of university chairs, at a time when the large European teaching and research universities had come to be considered the legitimate location for the production of "proper" scientific knowledge.[87] By the end of the nineteenth century, many German universities oversaw departments for newer specializations, including psychiatry, neurology, gynecology, and psychology, but it was not until after World War II that either sexual science or psychoanalysis really gained a foothold within the mainstream German academy; the first dedicated university chair in *Sexualwissenschaft* had to wait until the 1970s.[88] Certainly, Krafft-Ebing had been recognized by university chairs in Graz and Vienna, but this was as a professor of psychiatry rather than for his pioneering work on sexual pathology; Freud's professorship at the University of Vienna (in an application supported by Krafft-Ebing) was in neuropathology.[89] In contrast, although both Moll and Hirschfeld received a level of official recognition for their role as "medical counselors" (*Sanitätsräte*), neither enjoyed the legitimation of a state-sanctioned university professorship, instead conducting their work in private medical clinics or research institutes.[90]

Psychoanalysis also struggled to be recognized as a "system of legitimate knowledge" due to its its contested status as a "science."[91] This remained a sensitive point well into the new century, as evidenced by a famous tussle between Freud and Ellis, who declared his long-term Viennese correspondent an "artist who arose in science."[92] It was further complicated by Freud's nomination for the Nobel Prize for Literature in 1936 (alongside multiple nominations in the Physiology or Medicine category between 1915 and 1938).[93] The question of psychoanalysis's scientific status has continued to be debated with gusto in the decades since, and its interdisciplinary appeal is evident in the critical negotiation of Freudian ideas across fields ranging from feminist philosophy to film studies.[94] Freud himself encouraged this broad uptake through his increasing focus on cultural and historical themes in the later decades of his career in works such as *Civilization and Its Discontents* (*Das Unbehagen in der Kultur*, 1930). Indeed, cultural history and anthropology were never far from his purview; one need only consider his 1910 case study of Renaissance artist Leonardo da Vinci, or his 1913 essay compilation *Totem and Taboo: Resemblances between the Mental Lives of Savages and Neurotics* (*Totem und Tabu: Einige Übereinstimmungen im Seelenleben der Wilden und der Neurotiker*).[95]

The process of establishing psychoanalysis as an independent professional field, meanwhile, can be traced to the series of meetings that later became known as the "International Psychoanalytic Congresses," first held in Salzburg in 1908, followed by Nuremberg (1910), Weimar (1911), and Munich (1913). The first meetings outside of the German-speaking lands took place in

Budapest (1918) and the Hague (1920) in the immediate post–World War I period. Historian George Makari suggests the Nuremberg meeting of 1910 as a crucial date after which, in order to be considered a Freudian, a general interest in the new theoretical approaches would not suffice; "one had to accept psychosexual theory in its fullest elaboration."[96] Yet trained analysts also continued to take part in events such as the International Conference for Sexual Reform on a Sexual Scientific Basis, held in Berlin from 15 to 20 September, 1921, retrospectively considered the first meeting of the World League for Sexual Reform.[97]

The metaphor of "trading zones" usefully foregrounds the ways in which early-twentieth-century sexologists and psychoanalysts, through reciprocal dialogue, attempted to find areas of common ground from which to theorize human sexuality. Historians of science have shown that communication within and across scientific disciplines depends on finding a common ground, a boundary area or "trading zone" in which information is exchanged, which might require developing a common "creole" language. Even though each group might disagree as to the larger symbolic significance of that information, neither framework remains static as a result of such interactions.[98] Rather, "interpenetration" results in "a knowledge product to which neither discipline had access previously."[99] The production of new sexual knowledge, this book argues, was as much a result of dialogue between physicians and scientists working within related, but not identical, frameworks of reasoning as it was a process of disciplinary demarcation.[100] Such concepts enable us to understand how practitioners were able to move beyond defensive or "reductionist hierarchies" to negotiate new modes of knowledge production across disciplinary lines, without conceding the unique contributions of their own fledging specializations.[101]

The Limits of German Sexual Modernity

Sexologists and psychoanalysts thrashed out their ideas in the pages of scientific journals and monographs, but they also engaged with one another in more socially embedded ways: through conferences, reading groups, visits to one another's apartments, heated discussions following lectures, and personal correspondence. An awareness of the social and cultural contexts in which "embodied knowledge" is produced, often sharpened by individual egos and ambitions, pushes us to question how the social positioning of early sexological and psychoanalytic practitioners shaped their research, including intersections of race, religion, gender, class, and ability.[102] It is also important to consider whose contributions were marginalized by these new epistemic cultures. Such exclusions point to the limits of German sexual modernity.

Sexual science and psychoanalysis, with their risqué subject matter and "perverse" and "neurotic" patients, were each located on the margins of respectable German-speaking scientific medicine of the late nineteenth and early twentieth centuries. This positioning had racialized implications in the context of the still profoundly anti-Semitic German medical profession—many of the most prominent sexologists and psychoanalysts were of Jewish backgrounds—even as German sex research of this era was itself thoroughly implicated in the imperialist and Eurocentric frameworks of scientific racism and degeneration that had come to shape biological and anthropological research since the early nineteenth century.[103] During this era aspiring Jewish medical students could access only certain specializations, such as psychiatry, dermatology, and syphilology. All of these fields ranked low in the contemporary medical hierarchy, dealing with those society deemed mad, perverse, or criminal. Jewish doctors—regardless of whether they actively practiced their religion—also had far fewer opportunities than non-Jewish colleagues to attain academic appointments in the medical faculties of the German university system, or even to enter into private practice. Psychopathology and sexuality, as Sander Gilman has shown, were among the few areas "where Jews were permitted to function on the level of the academician." It was no coincidence that it was in these areas that Freud, Stekel, Hirschfeld, Bloch, and others of Jewish descent sought to make their mark on the profession.[104]

Despite frequently contending with discrimination in their own professional lives, the racialized assumptions of whiteness and European superiority underlying German science and medicine also shaped the priorities of many German-speaking sexologists and psychoanalysts. Anti-Semitic tendencies are also evident at times, particularly in the singling out of Jewish patients as more susceptible to mental illnesses such as "neurasthenia" (understood as an insufficient ability to cope with the stresses of urbanized and industrialized modern life) or in the depiction of Jewish men as feminized and liable to "deviance."[105] At a broader level, the very language available to the sexologists was deeply implicated, even for socially progressive and left-leaning researchers such as Hirschfeld, in assumptions about racial "purity" and fears of its "pollution."[106] This is particularly evident in pervasive eugenicist and Darwinist-inspired concerns with hereditary health and its links to national strength, to be achieved through careful sexual selection or "racial hygiene," and in discussions of the dangers of degeneration that might result from less-than-ideal sexual pairings or the perils of urban modernity. Eugenic ideas were not yet tied to the genocidal logics of National Socialism, but also enjoyed widespread popularity among socially progressive researchers and reformers during this period, including many in the early German feminist movement.[107]

Although themes of race and eugenics are not major foci of this book, which instead foregrounds explicit moments of cross-disciplinary encounter, the following chapters do consider how practitioners' own Jewish heritage may have influenced their perspective on issues such as degeneration, and also contributed to the major ruptures and forced emigration and exile that gutted each of these fields following the advent of National Socialism. And while the following chapters do not attend in detail to the racialized implications of debates between sexologists and psychoanalysts, I acknowledge that more detailed examination of theories of nonwhite sexualities, particularly in the interwar period, are urgently needed to give a fuller picture of early-twentieth-century sex research. Ideas about colonial and in particular black bodies have a complex place in the German history of sexuality, and one that can be traced across a much longer period than the state-enforced racial politics of the Nazis.[108] This is particularly true for the interwar period, when both sexological and psychoanalytic researchers increasingly turned their attention toward culture, religion, ethnicity, and sociopolitical context as factors shaping sexual subjectivity. Much remains to be said, in general, about the anthropological and sociological turn in the 1920s that saw the concerns of each of these fields expand well beyond the doctor's clinic. Ethnic and racial difference was used to undergird both more sinister and more socially progressive arguments in these decades. Sex researchers sometimes drew on anthropological and historical comparisons in ways that might be considered as prefiguring the horrors of National Socialist racial hygiene, but they also used such analogies to argue, along more emancipatory lines, for the universality of theories of a "third sex" or "sexual intermediaries," to expand discussions of alternative models of marriage and the family, or to deessentialize and historically contextualize gendered bodily styles. Hirschfeld's account of his "world tour" in the early 1930s, Bloch's invocations of cultural anthropology, or Freud's discussions of "totem" and "taboo" were most certainly tied up in the racist, colonialist, and nationalist assumptions of their day, but they also represented genuine attempts to expand the transnational scope of research into human sexuality and unconscious life, including through dialogue with non-European researchers.[109]

The history of sexual scientific research also needs to turn its attention more thoroughly to the ableist and heteronormative limitations and exclusions imposed by fin de siècle researchers. Sexologists' and psychoanalysts' assumptions of whiteness often aligned with middle-class, heterosexual male expectations of sexual behavior, gendered roles, employment, and family.[110] The "compulsory able-bodiedness," "compulsory heterosexuality" and "heteronormativity" thematized by disability and queer studies scholars in recent decades can often be found in the kinds of clinical and political interventions examined in the following chapters, such as the promotion of eugenic counseling for soon-to-be-married couples, or the search for a cure for same-sex behaviors.[111] Recent studies have highlighted the heteronormative sexual science at work in birth control reformer Marie Stopes's (hetero)sexual "rhythm charts," for example, or in the early genre of sexual and marital advice manuals; scholars have also shown how even early feminist critiques of the patriarchal double standard participated in essentializing heterosexuality, despite calling for more equitable and ethical gendered arrangements.[112] An assumed heterosexual reproductive ideal underpins many of the debates examined in this book, informing ideas about "normal" versus "aberrant" child sexuality, the effects of war-related trauma on heterosexual relationships, and discussions of female "frigidity" in the face of changing cultural gender norms.

The contributions of women sexologists and analysts have also been sorely neglected in the historiography of modern sex research. Although their work, like that of their male colleagues, was frequently complicit in promoting heteronormative, ableist, and racialized assumptions—as Leng emphasizes, the fact that many early German feminists were ardent promoters of racial hygiene and eugenic reforms created a sexual science that was "emancipating for some, inhibiting for others"—women such as Johanna Elberskirchen, Helene Stöcker, Anna Rüling, Hermine von Hug-Hellmuth, Karen Horney, and Helene Deutsch, to name only a few, authored important and often politically radical contributions to fin de siècle sexual scientific and analytic thought.[113] They frequently picked up on topics overlooked by their male colleagues: in-depth critiques of male heterosexuality, prostitution, marriage, nuanced studies of female same-sex desires, and women's sexual needs in times of war. They also opened up new avenues in the study of children's psychosexual process. They did so despite often poor access to formal medical or scientific training, and the "powerful current of outright misogyny" running through German sexual science of this era.[114] As the twentieth century progressed, women's voices in each of these fields became increasingly audible, with their works frequently reviewed and discussed in the early sexual scientific and psychoanalytic journals and societies.[115] Interventions by female analysts and sexologists can be found throughout this book, but come into focus in the context of interwar German sex research in chapter 5.

By offering a new reading of works by some of the best-known and a good smattering of lesser-known German contributors to these fields, *Sex between Body and Mind* aims to pave the way for a more nuanced and integrated history of sexual knowledge production in the early twentieth century, homing in on moments of encounter and debate rather than attempting to map the entire intellectual landscape. I am acutely aware that the following chapters focus primarily on sexological and psychoanalytic texts published by well-educated, white, middle-class men working within the racialized, ableist, and often heteronormative limitations of fin de siècle German medicine and science. My hope is that future studies will continue to deepen our understanding of the plurality of early-twentieth-century sex research, which a wealth of scholarship has already shown was enriched by a broad spectrum of social actors, from feminists, homosexual and trans rights activists, socialists, and birth control reformers to the more elite and conservative moral-purity associations or socially influential members of Germany's liberal intellectual middle classes.[116]

The following chapters use historical labels to refer to diagnoses as well as gendered and sexual identities that in some cases have changed considerably during the century or so since. While I explain now-obscure medical categorizations such as "psychosexual infantilism" as they occur, more careful explanation is required when addressing historical subjects. In general, I have attempted to strike a balance between using the labels that individuals applied to themselves, while maintaining legibility and relevance for a twenty-first-century audience. Until the late nineteenth century, concepts of "sexual inversion," "contrary sexual feeling," or "Urningism" had dominated medical thinking on both cross-gendered identifications and same-sex desires, and were also widely used in broader cultural contexts; in the final decades of the nineteenth century the label "homosexual" gained currency, but continued to circulate in parallel with these earlier terms.[117] Such labels were joined in the first decades of the twentieth century by "transvestism" (Hirschfeld's term) and "Eonism" (Ellis's coinage), which were used in distinction from homosexuality. The "transvestite" category was soon taken up by many gender-variant individuals themselves, as well as by those engaged in sexological and psychoanalytic discussions, and I use it as the most direct translation of the linguistically gendered German terms *Transvestit* (male-to-female transvestite) and *Transvestin* (female-to-male transvestite). In early-twentieth-century Germany these terms were used in a broad sense, to refer to a range of behaviors, desires and identities that we might today label "trans."[118] As such, I occasionally use "cross-dressing" and "trans-identified" to convey this wider sense of gender-variant practices, and the more recent terms "trans," "transgender," and "queer" to connect the analyses in this book to larger scholarly discussions.[119]

Whether considering the origins of infant sexuality, the treatment of homosexuality and shell shock, or the impact of hormone research, this book shows that in the early decades of the twentieth century, sex researchers were moving away from thinking about sex in relation to criminality, degeneration, or immorality, and were instead focusing more and more on ideals of "normal" and "healthy" sexual behavior and desires that aligned with a broader framework of sexual modernity. "The normal," as Hacking observes, had come by this period to stand not only for the "typical" or statistically frequent, but also "for what has been, good health, and for what shall be, our chosen destiny. That is why the benign and sterile-sounding word normal has become one of the most powerful ideological tools of the twentieth century."[120] By expanding their scholarly purview to the entirety of human sexual phenomena, including the "normal" and the "heterosexual," sexologists and psychoanalysts sought to claim a larger scope of influence for their emerging fields. Nonetheless, the debates examined in the following chapters demonstrate that ideas of the "abnormal," the "perverse," and the "pathological" continued to constitute pressing concerns during these decades.

The sexual life of the child, and by extension, the very origins and development of the human sexual instinct itself, constituted the first significant "trading zone" between sexology and psychoanalysis at the turn of the century. Chapter 1 demonstrates the intensity of calls for a turn to the "normal" during these years, and the ways in which this aligned with a focus on the child. Leading sexologists, including Moll and Hirschfeld, responded to provocative Freudian theories of infant sexual development, and their works in turn were taken up and debated, sometimes fiercely, in psychoanalytic contexts. This chapter argues that debates around when and how children become "sexual" reveal some shared paradigms between early sexological and psychoanalytic thought—including a clear acknowledgement that "sexual" life begins before puberty—but also some key areas of contestation, with many sexologists opposed to Freudian articulations of an "Oedipus complex." Discussions of child sexuality also showcase the transnational dimensions of early conversations between these two fields, as German-speaking researchers drew on the work of contemporaries such as Ellis and Jones in Britain or psychologists Sanford Bell and G. Stanley Hall in the United States.

Chapter 2 identifies debates around homosexuality (including concepts of "sexual inversion" and "contrary sexual feeling") as a second key moment of encounter between these two emerging fields. In doing so, it highlights the ongoing significance of the "abnormal" and "perverse" for the diagnostic and therapeutic work of sexologists and psychoanalysts in the years before World

War I. Same-sex desires had long been a concern of psychiatrists such as Krafft-Ebing, but etiological discussions were reinvigorated by the Freudians, who insisted on viewing inversion as an "aberration" of universal developmental processes rather than as a marker of a fundamentally different kind of person. They also suggested new possibilities for treatment by means of the talking cure—methods that were, at times, fundamentally at odds with the more congenital explanations of sexologists such as Hirschfeld. Theoretical and methodological tensions increasingly divided sexologists and psychoanalysts on this issue, even as shared concern for their patients drove moments of collaborative exchange; I argue that patient case histories represented a crucial "trading zone" for these transfers of knowledge across emerging disciplinary lines. At the same time, scientific debates were shaped by larger political and legal realities, including German and Austrian laws criminalizing same-sex activities, and a series of prominent homosexual scandals. Many early homosexual rights activists followed Hirschfeld in using scientific arguments of hereditary homosexuality to contest legalized discrimination. As a result, politics helped to drive a deepening wedge between these fields in the years before World War I.

Chapter 3 shows how the experience of World War I, in which many sexologists and analysts served as physicians in military hospitals, led to important developments in both of these fields. From 1914, the mass casualties, population displacements, and xenophobia of mass conflict pushed issues of violence-related sexual trauma, shell shock, and the suitability of homosexual and transgender soldiers to the forefront of sex research. Treating cases of "war neurosis" pushed psychoanalysts to revise older explanations of traumatic neurosis devised in peacetime, while the many cases of violence-related sexual dysfunction in soldiers returning from the front led sexologists to place greater emphasis on psychic factors in the development of sexual pathologies; they were also closely involved in discussions about conscription involving members of the "third sex." Toward the end of the war, sexologists turned increasingly to hormone treatments as a possible solution. Meanwhile, feminists and sex reformers pushed for greater attention to matters such as birth control and women's sexual health in times of war. Such dynamic developments belie assertions that the Great War represented a "setback" in the modern scientific study of sex.[121] Although sexologists and psychoanalysts prioritized different questions during these years, the war provided an opportunity to shore up their professional legitimacy within German society at large.

Chapter 4 argues that the study of the hormones signaled a shift toward a more thoroughly medicalized and physiological brand of modern sexology, while pushing psychoanalysts, including Freud, to turn their attention toward the body's inner chemistry. During the war years, research into the mysterious workings of the "inner secretions" had taken off in earnest, particularly under the leadership of endocrinology professor Eugen Steinach and his team in Vienna. Undertaking ovary and testicle transplant experiments on rats and guinea pigs in a quest to better understand human sexual development and pathology, hormone research promised exciting new directions for sexual science. This was particularly the case for those sexologists who remained committed to physiological explanations of the sexual instinct and its pathologies. Many embraced hormone-based arguments and treatments as a source of scientific authority, and continued to do so even as Steinach's experiments gradually fell into disrepute. While the Freudians remained committed to the talking cure, and the rift between these fields grew ever deeper, psychoanalytic considerations of "chemical" arguments show the ongoing interpenetrations feeding the production of sexual knowledge during these years.

Chapter 5 homes in on the contributions of interwar women analysts and sexologists, arguing that they changed disciplinary conversations within and between their respective fields, particularly around long-neglected questions of female sexuality. Focusing on diagnoses of female frigidity and homosexuality, this chapter situates scientific discussions against the context of rapidly changing gender roles and anxieties in the postwar German-speaking world. It argues that women analysts and sexologists—and in particular, psychoanalysts trained along Freudian lines, such as Karen Horney and Helene Deutsch—were frequently more attuned to such cultural factors than their male colleagues. More broadly, this chapter argues for women's increasing prominence in German-speaking sexology and psychoanalysis during these years, which represented something of a "golden age" for sex research characterized by the rapid growth of professional networks and publications and increasing efforts to disseminate expert knowledges to wider publics.

The final chapter rounds out this history of cross-field encounters by foregrounding the voices of patients and informants via the "case of the transvestite." It argues that sexological and psychoanalytic cases of trans-identified individuals offer important examples of how sexual knowledge was "traded" and critically negotiated between expert and wider publics, particularly during the liberalized era of Germany's Weimar Republic. Historians of sexuality have long recognized the need to draw on diverse and at times eclectic sources and methodologies—"marginal, idiosyncratic, and sometimes unexpected sites"—to do justice to nonnormative forms of identity and embodiment in the past.[122] Although early-twentieth-century German trans history has left only a fragmented documentary record, this chapter argues that Weimar-era publications produced by and for individuals we would today consider trans or queer—magazines that targeted "homosexuals," "transvestites," and a "third sex," to follow contemporary identity labels—functioned as a critical sounding board for the findings of sex researchers. Contributors carefully weighed the value of scientific theories and categories both for describing their own sense of self and as a basis for political activism.

An epilogue charts the fundamental rupture to German and Austrian sex research that began in the early 1930s and gained intensity in the following decade, as National Socialism forced many practitioners into emigration and exile. Although the thoroughgoing Nazification of German science and medicine did not completely halt either sexual scientific or analytic inquiry, it steered these fields in much more nationalist and sinister directions. Networks and conversations that had shaped the scientific study of sex until the early 1930s in German-speaking Europe were violently disrupted and partially relocated from the Old World to the New, with Anglo-American researchers coming to dominate international discussions in and between sexual science and psychoanalysis after World War II.

Sex between Body and Mind charts a process of growing divergence between sexual science and psychoanalysis across the first half of the twentieth century, while providing the first in-depth account of just how much interpenetration actually took place across these emerging professional boundaries. It argues that although psychoanalysis was sometimes considered within extended definitions of "sexual science," sexologists increasingly distanced themselves from concepts such as the castration and Oedipus complexes and the mysterious clinical methods of the "talking cure." Despite initial enthusiasm for Freudian lines of inquiry, sexologists found such developments hard to stomach in the longer run, turning instead to more pragmatic and often more interventionist therapies. In particular, this book shows that the growth of hormone research from the 1910s marked a key point of divergence, with the Freudians considering the "inner secretions" an interesting but only peripherally relevant factor—steering their research, instead, in ever more cultural and historical directions—whereas the sexologists seized on endocrine research as crucial to securing their own professional relevance. By the 1920s, these two fields had consolidated as distinct disciplinary entities, but only as a result of years of cross-fertilization, interpenetration, and boundary-drawing. Understanding these interactions is crucial to understanding the development of sexual categories and subjectivities that continue to shape our thinking today.

Whether considering the "sexualization" of children in the contemporary media, the ways in which ideas about "nature" versus "nurture" have shaped debates around gay marriage or homosexual conversion therapies, or the legal and medical recognition of trans identities, the sources examined in this book offer rich genealogies of current discussions, and point to the emergence of ideas central to our understanding of what it means to be human.

CHAPTER 1

Redefining "Normal": Childhood Sexuality in Fin de siècle Sexology and Psychoanalysis

One cool November evening in 1908, a group of twelve physicians and intellectuals gathered in Professor Sigmund Freud's Viennese apartment at the Berggasse 19 to discuss a new publication by Berlin psychiatrist and sexologist Albert Moll. Seven months earlier, these men (the first woman to join the group was Margarethe Hilferding in 1910; she was also the first woman to finish a medical degree in the Habsburg Empire) had voted to formalize their weekly Wednesday gatherings, when they met to discuss the study of the human unconscious, by changing their name to the Vienna Psychoanalytic Society (Wiener Psychoanalytische Vereinigung, hereafter WPV).[1] On this particular evening, the publication up for discussion was a weighty tome of over 300 pages, *Das Sexualleben des Kindes* (*The Sexual Life of the Child*), which had just appeared in a limited edition from Leipzig publisher F. C. W. Vogel, although from 1909 it enjoyed a larger run with a Berlin publishing house.[2] Aimed at a broad audience of educators, lawyers, judges, and physicians, and covering topics ranging from homosexuality to sex education, Moll's book was being touted in professional circles as the first thoroughgoing investigation of infantile sexuality; as one reviewer commented, "hitherto we did not have such a comprehensive and elaborate account of every aspect of the sexual life of the child."[3] The crucial factor for the gentlemen gathered in Freud's apartment, though, was that this book represented the first sexological reply to Freud's own psychoanalytic exploration of children's sexuality three years earlier in *Drei Abhandlungen zur Sexualtheorie* (1905), first translated into English as *Three Contributions to the Sexual Theory* in 1910 (based on the second, revised German edition), and again in 1949 as *Three Essays on the Theory of Sexuality* (hereafter *Three Essays*, based on the fourth and final edition of 1924).[4] Perhaps it was only to be expected that, at this gathering of dedicated Freudians, Moll's study received a lukewarm response: while some noted points of interest, others decried it as a stunning example of scientific ineptitude and even plagiarism. This reception was not entirely unprovoked. Moll enjoyed a sound reputation as a psychiatrist and sex researcher thanks to two significant 1890s publications on same-sex desire (*Die konträre Sexualempfindung* [Contrary Sexual Feeling, 1891]) and the sexual instinct (*Untersuchungen über die Libido sexualis* [*Libido Sexualis*, 1897]), but he was also known as a politically conservative and rather difficult colleague. Later that evening, Freud cited fellow Berlin sexologist Magnus Hirschfeld's assessment of Moll as "a petty, spiteful, parochial character."[5] In the opening chapter of *Sexual Life*, moreover, Moll had provocatively downplayed psychoanalytic contributions to the field, declaring "Freud has not systematically studied the individual manifestations of the sexual life of the child." Countering Freud's own—admittedly audacious—claim to have been the first to recognize the "regularity of a sexual drive in childhood," Moll characterized his own work as the first "comprehensive study of the subject."[6]

The meeting minutes, recorded by the Society's young secretary, Otto Rank, reveal that discussion of Moll's book raised the temperatures in the room. Physician Eduard Hitschmann dismissed it as "a semi-scientific work, unsystematic, a mere synthesis in which there is nothing original," even if it raised interesting questions about the childhood origins of pathology.[7] Alfred Bass declared that "Moll is not a match for psychoanalysis and has not grasped its essence," while hydrotherapist and neurologist Isidor Sadger, who had joined the group in 1906 and would soon become known for his own psychoanalytic studies of homosexuality and narcissism, criticized Moll's territorialism: "Moll . . . who was introduced to this literature by Krafft-Ebing and who was the first after Krafft-Ebing to occupy himself with these matters, considers it an invasion into his personal domain if another person also achieves something in this field. Such is also, for example, his relationship to Hirschfeld."[8] Freud was thus among friends when it came to his turn to speak, declaring Moll's book "inadequate, inferior, and above all . . . dishonest."[9] In an assessment infused with the psychoanalytic rhetoric of repression, Freud argued that Moll had written his book only after his own *Three Essays* led the Berlin sexologist to recognize the importance of child sexuality and that Moll's subsequent denial of Freud's influence could be explained by a latent awareness of this fact. Reiterating moderator Dr. Rie's opening words, Freud announced that "normal child sexuality had actually, as odd as it may sound, been discovered by him—Freud." Moll had also, Freud declared, failed to recognize the principal achievement of the *Three Essays* in bringing together an overarching theory of normal sexual life as well as the perversions and the neuroses, linking these to a universal "polymorphous-perverse" predisposition in infancy.[10] Thus, 1908 saw the beginning of an embittered race for intellectual precedence between these two researchers, who had once been on more respectful terms.[11] It also points to the beginnings of a much broader turf war in which Moll and Freud were two of the key players in these early years, alongside figures such as Hirschfeld, Sadger, Havelock Ellis, Iwan Bloch, and Wilhelm Stekel, who feature more prominently in later chapters of this book.

At a time when the disciplinary status of both sexology and psychoanalysis was anything but secure, this chapter argues that the first significant encounter between these two fields centered on competing conceptualizations of the sexual life of the child. Fin de siècle efforts to understand children's sexual development reveal emerging tensions between sexological and psychoanalytic thought, including around such central Freudian concepts as the "Oedipus complex" and children's "pregenital" and "polymorphous" sexuality. These debates also, I submit, tell a larger story about the history of early-twentieth-century sex research, demonstrating an increasing prioritization of ideas of "normal" sexuality in place of the dominant nineteenth-century focus on pathologies and "perverts." Taking a closer look at debates around child sexuality in the years after 1900 can help us ascertain exactly when and how "normal" human sexual subjectivity was seen to begin and end in this era of sexual modernity. In particular, this chapter charts how the Freudian insistence that normal sexual life begins from birth challenged sexologists to revisit their assumptions, which had previously focused on puberty. As a result of these encounters, a few practitioners (including Ellis, chiming in from across the English Channel) began to incorporate psychoanalytic ideas about infant development into their thinking. Others, including Moll, Hirschfeld, and August Forel in Zürich, took a more cautious line, one that also points to the professional threat that Freudian thought was beginning to pose to their own fledgling field. Yet critical backlash to Freudian ideas was also brewing from within the ranks of early psychoanalysis, with Carl Gustav Jung becoming one of the sharpest early critics of Freud's libido theory in the years before their break in 1913. The study of the child thus contributed to early fractures within the analytic movement as well as to increased boundary-drawing with other fields.

The early conflict between Moll and Freud about who had the authority to pronounce on the sexual life of the child came during a decade in which the disciplinary boundaries of psychoanalysis and sexology had so far been decidedly porous. Earlier in 1908, Moll had invited Berlin analyst Karl Abraham to collaborate on a new journal. Abraham agreed, and in the same year, as noted in the Introduction, founded the Berlin Psychoanalytic Society together with

Berlin-based sexologists Bloch, Hirschfeld, and Max Marcuse, among others.[12] This group not only extended the dedicated discussion of Freudian theory several hundred miles to the German-speaking north, but promoted professional exchanges among a first generation of self-declared psychoanalysts and physicians from other medical specializations. The same year saw the appearance, albeit short-lived, of the first dedicated sexological journal, the *Zeitschrift für Sexualwissenschaft* (Journal of Sexual Science) under Hirschfeld's editorship. As Hirschfeld explained, the *Zeitschrift* had grown out of the monthly reports of the Scientific Humanitarian Committee (Wissenschaftlich-humanitäres Komitee, WhK), but whereas that homosexual rights organization focused on the plight of "sexual intermediaries," the new periodical sought to address the entirety of sexual science—including, as Hirschfeld optimistically foresaw, the insights to be gained from "rational deep interrogation, *psychoanalytic exploration*."[13] Alongside programmatic editorials declaring the "birth" of this field, the *Zeitschrift* ran regular articles by members of the inner Freudian circle, including Freud himself.[14] Such interpenetrations point to the complexity of sexual knowledge production at the fin de siècle, even as the brewing conflict between Moll and Freud marks the start of growing efforts to distinguish psychoanalysis from sexology in the years that followed.

Demonstrating that sexological and psychoanalytic accounts in the years around 1900 cannot be separated along a clear body/mind split, this chapter also reveals the complex trading zone in which sexual knowledge of children's sexuality was produced. My concern in the following sections is less with explicating Freud's well-trodden theories of child sexuality than with examining how these were refracted through the lens of fin de siècle sexology: how, precisely, did sexologists respond to Freud's challenge to their own conceptions of the sexual instinct, drives, and behaviors, and their development from infancy through to adulthood? Although I focus particularly on Freud's *Three Essays* and Moll's *Sexual Life* as representative monographs from each of these fields produced within the space of five years, neither of these texts was produced in a vacuum; they are considered here in the context of broader discussions taking place within and beyond the German-speaking world. These include sexological studies by Hirschfeld, Ellis, and Forel, studies by early US-based psychologists such as Sanford Bell and G. Stanley Hall, and contributions by early Freudians, including Stekel and Jung. Of course, the child had already been an important figure in psychiatric, criminological, and physiological discussions for many decades, and also a focus of eighteenth-century intellectuals such as Samuel-Auguste Tissot and Jean-Jacques Rousseau. I thus begin by briefly charting this longer "science of the child," including some recent interventions by queer theorists.

A Brief History of Child Sexuality

The rise in medical discourses around children's sexuality from the late nineteenth century coincided with a broader shift from familial and religious to expert medical and scientific forms of sexual knowledge, famously charted in Foucault's *History of Sexuality*, Vol. 1. There he characterized the "pedagogization of children's sex" as one of four key "mechanisms of knowledge and power" centered around sex in the modern era, alongside the hystericization of women's bodies, the Malthusian reproductive couple, and the psychiatrization of perverse pleasures.[15] Over the course of that century, children's masturbation had increasingly come to be seen as a medical problem linked to conditions such as "infantile hysteria," "perversion," and other physical and mental illnesses.[16] This was a heavily gendered discourse: whereas concerns about boys' masturbation contributed to class-inflected ideas about male homosexuality, anxiety about girls was more closely linked to the emergence of gynecology and identities such as the hysteric.[17] Securing pedagogical expertise over masturbation helped to shore up the discursive authority of the medical profession, which in the late-nineteenth-century German-speaking world was rapidly gaining in class and status.[18] Moll's *Sexual Life* was both strategic and in tune with the *zeitgeist* in placing sexual and social hygiene front and center, including an entire chapter titled "Sexual Education." Freud, too, thematized children's sex education in several essays during this period.[19] Both authors thus addressed a topic that historians have identified as crucial to the late-nineteenth-century social hygiene and purity movements, and to broader eugenic concerns about national health, venereal disease, and degeneracy.[20]

Yet the understanding that one could have a "normal" or "pathological" childhood was not an invention of the fin de siècle. The sexual child had circulated in forensic, criminological and psychiatric discourses for several decades, forming part of a broader fascination with the "science of the child" marked by the 1877 publication of Charles Darwin's article "A Biographical Sketch of an Infant" in the world's first dedicated psychology journal, *Mind*.[21] Even earlier than this, though, the child had been central to Enlightenment-era studies by scholars such as Samuel-Auguste Tissot (*L'Onanisme*, 1760), Jean-Jacques Rousseau (*Emile, or On Education*, 1762), and Johann Gottfried Herder (*Treatise on the Origin of Language*, 1772), who had deliberated on topics ranging from the ill effects of masturbation to children's "ideal" education and training for citizenship. Whereas in the Middle Ages children were not frequently thought of as categorically different from adults, in the modern era the child came to occupy a position of intellectual, moral, and social distinctiveness.[22]

Within this longer history, the early twentieth-century "Freudian revolution" is often considered "a complete *volte face*" away from earlier pathologizing and moralizing attitudes, framing children's sexuality as natural, normal, and in need of open expression.[23] Yet by the twenty-first century, children's sexuality has again come to occupy a difficult cultural position, with growing concerns around children's sexualization in the media and consumer culture sitting in tension with a certain "erasure" of the sexual life of the child, which some scholars have attributed to a post–second wave feminism "climate of pedophilia panic."[24] Scholars working from the antinormative perspective of queer theory, meanwhile, have usefully challenged epistemological distinctions between "children" and "adults," taking up the question of age as a crucial vector of sexuality. Childhood itself, they suggest, may well be fundamentally "queer," in the sense that it gains meaning only in its discursive construction as the innocent, asexual "other" of adulthood. Illuminating how childhood eroticism is still frequently collapsed into euphemistic terms such as "exploration" or "capriciousness" and viewed as fundamentally different from, and prior to, "real" adult sexuality, queer theorists critique the regulatory effects of retrospectively assessing an individual's childhood sexual behaviors based on their subsequent sexual orientation or gender identity. Such interventions challenge dominant heteronormative assumptions that adult heterosexuality represents a fixed ideal for human sexual development.[25] In seeking to reclaim the diversity and ambiguities of children's sexual experiences and desires, this recent scholarship on the "queerness" of childhood returns repeatedly to early-twentieth-century analyses of infant sexuality, and particularly the interventions of psychoanalysis.

This chapter aims to deepen our understanding of the historical and intellectual context in which the Freudian interest in children's sexuality materialized in the opening decade of the twentieth century, and to show its close enmeshment with sexological research. Proponents of these two fields, I argue, developed mutually influential theoretical frameworks for discussing the figure of the child: Freud drew on the studies of his sexological contemporaries, and influenced their work in turn. There are, observes Arnold Davidson, two competing myths about Freud in the historiography: the first depicts him as a "lonely genius" and "triumphant revolutionary," while the second shows him "getting all of his ideas from someone else." These "someones" include Freud's early correspondent Wilhelm Fliess, with whom he discussed ideas of original universal bisexuality; his former teacher Jean-Martin Charcot; his longtime British correspondent Ellis; and his psychiatric colleague Moll, the figure most frequently credited with having "discovered infantile sexuality years before Freud."[26] One of the first to ascribe Freud's ideas to others was Frank Sulloway in his influential biography of the Viennese analyst, even as he engages in a certain degree of hero worship in declaring it a "reflection of Freud's subsequent greatness that his name has become associated with many important ideas about human sexuality that he did not originate."[27] Other scholars, too, have offered important readings of the links between Freud's ideas on children's sexuality and earlier sexual scientific thought, and to broader cultural and artistic discourses around the sexualized child in fin de siècle Viennese and Berlin modernity.[28]

My own analysis focuses less on the questions of intellectual precedence shaping these previous inquiries than on the ways in which the growing focus on child sexuality at the fin de siècle was symptomatic of a broader foregrounding and revisiting of "normal" sexuality. During this period sex researchers were seeking to lay claim to a universalizing field of expertise, working to move sex research out from the margins of medical-scientific inquiry. Nonetheless, as the following chapters of this book show, questions of pathology and perversion kept resurfacing in ways that problematized such universalizing claims.

Embracing the "Normal": The Shifting Priorities of Fin de siécle Sexual Science

It is a "very remarkable fact," observed Ellis in 1903, "that, although for many years past serious attempts have been made to elucidate the psychology of sexual perversions, little or no endeavor has been made to study the . . . normal sexual emotions." Although this research was still very much in its infancy it should, Ellis insisted, become the central focus of sexual science, for normal sexual phenomena "give the key to the abnormal."[29] Such comments by Britain's foremost sex researcher would not have gone unheeded by colleagues on the Continent, where Ellis was well known for his influential study of homosexuality, *Das konträre Geschlechtsgefühl* (*Sexual Inversion*), coauthored with cultural critic John Addington Symonds, which had first appeared in German translation in 1896 (the English original was only published several years later).[30] In the following years, Ellis's plea to his colleagues to reorient sexual science toward the study of "normal" human sexual development proved, if not causally responsible, at least symptomatic of a much larger shift among European and a few North American sex researchers. This aligned with the embrace of "sexual modernity" discussed in the Introduction, whereby sexuality from the late nineteenth century came to be viewed as a natural, positive phenomenon central to an individual's personality. This encompassed a growing focus on psychology rather than physiology, and a reduced emphasis on procreation in favor of valuing sexuality for its relational and pleasurable dimensions.[31]

As the new century dawned, the forensic emphasis of nineteenth-century German sex psychiatry, which had its beginnings in studies such as Heinrich Kaan's *Psychopathia sexualis* of 1844, and continued apace in the second half of the century with works by Richard von Krafft-Ebing, Moll, and others, became increasingly overshadowed by attempts to explain human sexuality in all its variety, and not just those pathologized "inverts," "fetishists," and "masochists" whom Krafft-Ebing had described as "nature's stepchildren."[32] Sexual scientists across Europe began churning out encyclopedic works seeking to pin down the very essence of the human sexual instinct in both its "normal" and "pathological" manifestations, often drawing on a range of natural and social scientific approaches. This reorientation toward the "normal" can be seen most clearly in a heightened push to investigate the desires and behaviors of the heterosexual majority.[33] German-speaking researchers were at the forefront of this research, with Moll's landmark 1897 study *Untersuchungen über die Libido sexualis* (*Libido Sexualis*), Bloch's *Das Sexualleben unserer Zeit in seinen Beziehungen zur modernen Kultur* (The Sexual Life of Our Time in Its Relations to Modern Civilization, 1907) and Forel's *Die sexuelle Frage* (The Sexual Question, 1905). Further afield, Ellis had also begun work on his multivolume magnum opus, *Studies in the Psychology of Sex* (1897–1928). These ambitious works reflect the growing pressure on sexual science to address the larger biopolitical concerns of early-twentieth-century modernity.

In his *Libido Sexualis*, for example—which developed the theoretical foundations for his subsequent discussion of child sexuality—Moll declared that, having previously dealt with pathological manifestations in his 1891 study of sexual inversion (*Die konträre Sexualempfindung* [Contrary Sexual Feeling]), he now planned to investigate the "normal sexual instinct/drive" ("*normalen Geschlechtstrieb*").[34] Bloch's *Sexualleben* marked a similar shift of gears away from the disease-oriented model of his 1902 *Beiträge zur Aetiologie der "Psychopathia sexualis"* (Contributions to an Aetiology of the "Psychopathia sexualis").[35] Across the Channel, Ellis saw the new edition of his *Studies* with Philadelphia firm F. A. Davis (1901–1928) as a chance to reorder the volumes in a way that emphasized the entirety of sexual life rather than its "abnormalities": he swapped the volume on sexual inversion, which he had penned first, with one dedicated to more obviously heterosexual phenomena, "The evolution of modesty, the phenomena of sexual periodicity, autoerotism."[36] Even Hirschfeld, who more than any other contemporary sex researcher had gained a reputation for his scholarship and activism on homosexuality as publisher of the *Jahrbuch für sexuelle Zwischenstufen* (Yearbook of Sexual Intermediaries, 1899–1923) and monographs such as *Das dritte Geschlecht* (The Third Sex, 1904), declared in 1908 that the "uncomplicated love between man and woman is the broad, fertile current, the main artery of life, and thus also for sexual science."[37]

The turn toward the "normal" in fin de siècle sexual science deserves recognition, I submit, as part of a broader critical historiography of ideas of the "norm" and the "normal" in modernity.[38] For sexologists in particular, this was also a strategic move, aimed at shoring up the broader relevance and credibility of their research. The urgency of such questions is apparent from ongoing assertions that "scholars . . . have at present only the vaguest sense of how and when a new regulatory force we now call 'normality' began to shape and influence how people thought about sexuality."[39] During the early to mid-twentieth century, older understandings of the norm as a statistical "average" were becoming conflated with ideas of the "healthy" and the "good."[40] From the final decades of the nineteenth century, sexology's reorientation toward "normal" sexual behaviors began to identify the child as a central focus of research. Sex researchers set about defining, revising, and contesting ideas about when and in what ways human sexuality manifested itself in childhood. Sexual scientific publications of the fin de siècle reveal a spike of interest in early developmental processes leading to "mature" and "healthy" adult sexuality, while presenting "precocious" (premature) child sexuality "as an epidemic menace that risked compromising not only the future health of adults but the future of the entire society and species."[41] Here sexual maturity was understood in largely genital, heterosexual, and reproductive terms, its beginning aligned with the onset of physical puberty. By redirecting their investigations toward the heterosexual "norm," and examining how this is forged from childhood—and aberrations from that norm, as well—sex researchers began rethinking what exactly "normal" sexuality entailed.

A key proponent of the "normal-from-puberty" argument was Krafft-Ebing, whose *Psychopathia Sexualis*—which by the time of his death in 1902 had expanded across twelve editions to encompass more than 300 case histories—characterized childhood as a period of "sexual neutrality." Preadolescent manifestations of the libido, including masturbation, argued Krafft-Ebing, were symptomatic of a "premature" (*vorzeitig*), generally congenital predisposition toward "severe degenerative neuroses or psychoses"—or at the very least, of a "neuropsychopathic constitutional condition." He labeled such cases of early sexual maturation "Paradoxia": manifestations of the sexual instinct occurring seemingly independently of physiological processes in girls younger than thirteen, and boys younger than fifteen (these being, he explained, the average European ages for the onset of menstruation in women and of beard growth, voice deepening, and "pollutions" in men). Pointing to criminal anthropologist Cesare Lombroso's discussions of children affected with such a "decided hereditary taint," he cited the case of one girl who "masturbated shamelessly and almost constantly at the age of three."[42] Krafft-Ebing also coined the term "erotic pedophilia" (*paedophilia erotica*) to describe the sexual desire for, and abuse of, children.[43] For Krafft-Ebing, signs of sexuality before puberty were a clear sign of pathology, and children themselves were out of bounds as the object of adult sexual attentions.

The assumption that "spontaneous sexual impulses" in early childhood were a product of neuropathic degeneration was one shared by many late-nineteenth-century sexologists, even though Krafft-Ebing himself moved away from degeneration frameworks later in his career.[44] Researchers today tend to define "precocious puberty" as beginning between the ages of six and nine;[45] similarly, "normal" sexuality for most physicians of Krafft-Ebing's era was that which developed from adolescence onward.[46] Yet this assumption was problematized by a number of studies published in the decades before Freud's and Moll's major works on this topic. In 1879 Budapest physician Sámuel Lindner published a paper on the erotic nature of children's "voluptuous" thumb-sucking (subsequently cited by both Moll and Freud); Viennese physician Stekel published a paper "On Coitus in Childhood" (1895) seven years before first meeting Freud; German psychologist and philosopher Max Dessoir formulated influential theories of the human sex drive that proved particularly important for Moll's work on this topic, and Ellis coined the term "auto-erotism" to describe children's sexual pleasures.[47]

Moll's two studies from the 1890s laid the foundations for his analysis of child sexuality in the years after 1900. In particular, his 1899 *Libido Sexualis* garnered praise—from no less than Ellis—as "the most thorough attempt yet undertaken to investigate the fundamental problems of the sexual impulse."[48] (Moll later returned the favor, describing Ellis as "in my opinion, the leader of all those at present engaged in the study of sexual psychology and pathology."[49]) Particularly significant for his later work on children's sexual development was Moll's theoretical separation of the sexual instinct into two parts. The "detumescence" impulse described the physiological urges directed at physical release, such as ejaculation, while the "contrectation" impulse described more emotional and psychological aspects of the sexual instinct, characterized—at least for "normal" development—as intellectual and physical attraction to the opposite sex. Moll emphasized—some years before Freud—that both of these impulses could be found even among quite young children, with infants as young as one or two capable of experiencing pleasurable genital sensations, "a kind of pleasurable sensation, a kind of tickling," and even erection and masturbation. To illustrate these claims, he cited recollections of childhood love sentiments by famous figures such as Dante and Byron from as early as five to ten years of age, as well as several case studies from his earlier, 1891 study of "contrary sexual feeling" that suggested masturbation in infants as young as two days old.[50] In *Libido Sexualis* Moll also put forth a number of other influential ideas and distinctions: he separated the instinct to procreate from the sexual drive envisaged in terms of pleasure; he questioned existing distinctions between the "normal" and the "pathological," as well as the complex relation between inborn ("nature") and environmental ("nurture") factors; and he emphasized the psychological components of sexuality. He thus offered, as historians have shown, a distinctly modern formulation of the sexual instinct, and one that demonstrates important lines of continuity with Freud's later contributions.[51]

As Moll's first major contribution to scientific research on the sexual instinct, *Libido Sexualis* did not escape Freud's attention, even if he privately dismissed the German sexologist's detumescence-contrectation distinction as "Spanish walls, which prevent insight into the real state of affairs," rejecting the notion of "detumescence" as entirely inapplicable to children, and "contrectation" as "an utterly impossible and artificial concept."[52] (Sadger foreshadowed this scathing assessment at the aforementioned WPV meeting, rejecting Moll's concepts as mere "empty phrases: new labels to cover up for deficient knowledge."[53]) Such criticisms notwithstanding, the heavy annotations in Freud's personal copy of Moll's most famous work suggest that he took the latter's interventions quite seriously; in a letter to Fliess, Freud even recorded his "delight" at finding in Moll's book ideas about the "erogenous zones" of infantile eroticism that closely aligned with his own.[54] Recent revisionist historiography has cast new light on Moll's pioneering theoretical contributions to the history of sexuality, working to counter the long neglect of an actor who was, at the turn of the twentieth century, one of the leading lights of German sex research, despite his reputation for being rather stuffy and conservative.[55] By foregrounding Moll's work here, my analysis also draws attention to his prominence within fin de siècle German sex research as one of the key players in early debates between the sexual scientists and the newer Freudian school.

Across the Atlantic, a number of North American psychologists also made influential contributions to these European discussions. In *Adolescence* (1904),

G. Stanley Hall focused on the period of puberty and youth; he worked from the recently established Clark University in Massachusetts, site of Freud's only visit to the United States some seven years later. Two years earlier, Sanford Bell had been among the first to attempt a large quantitative study of child sexuality, analyzing data from more than 2,500 "healthy" schoolchildren and adolescents in coeducational schools.[56] Bell's finding that the "emotion of sex-love" may manifest in children as young as three broke new ground, and was subsequently cited by Freud, Moll, and Ellis (as well as, many years later, Alfred C. Kinsey).[57] In 1905 Lewis M. Terman, too, described "the indubitable fact that even in normal, healthy children the sexual instincts are often aroused very early," although, acknowledging the slipperiness of ideas of the norm, he noted that there was still "no agreement" on how exactly to define the standard underlying diagnoses of "precocity."[58]

Like Krafft-Ebing and most of his contemporaries, in the 1880s and 1890s Freud, too, had been reluctant to acknowledge an innate sexual drive as part of normal preadolescent experience. This was an eventful period in the young Viennese doctor's life—in 1886 alone, having recently returned from studies in France, Freud had turned thirty, married the Hamburg-born Martha Bernays, and quit his neuropathology lectureship at the University of Vienna to enter private practice.[59] Freud's resistance to notions of infant sexual desire at this point in his career contrasted sharply with his later insistence on their universal significance. In a much-cited 1896 essay on the origins of hysteria, he even used examples of hysteria in prepubertal children to argue *against* the sexual etiology of this condition, insisting that sexual behavior in children resulted from abuse or seduction by an adult or older child.[60] By this stage, Martha and Sigmund Freud themselves had no fewer than six children, with their youngest, Anna, joining the family in 1895.

Freud's trauma-oriented "seduction theory" created waves among the psychiatric profession of the 1890s. At an 1896 meeting of the Society for Psychiatry and Forensic Psychology (Verein für Psychiatrie und forensische Psychologie, later the Verein für Psychiatrie und Neurologie), of which Freud was a member from 1895 to 1901, then-president Krafft-Ebing dismissed it as a "scientific fairy tale," even though he was otherwise supportive of his younger colleague's career.[61] Shortly afterward, in a now-famous moment for the history of psychoanalysis, Freud radically revised his seduction theory following his own self-analysis, finding that child sexual abuse was so common that it could not itself be considered decisive for the formation of adult neuroses. Instead, he came to prioritize the role of sexual fantasies and their repression over actual traumatic childhood experiences.[62] As Jung later noted, many unknowing critics nonetheless continued "senselessly to attack this theory, not realizing that it is more than fifteen years since it was abandoned."[63]

This revision was also central to Freud's broader thinking about the etiology of the neuroses. By the time he published *Three Essays* in 1905, followed in 1909 by his famous case study of Little Hans, finding a young boy's phobia of horses to have decidedly sexual undertones, the founder of psychoanalysis had not only revised his views on seduction, but had come to view sexual expressions as a normal and necessary aspect of childhood. The following section reads Freud's 1905 essays against both Moll's 1908 monograph on child sexuality and other responses from contemporary sexologists, arguing that mutual interpenetrations of knowledge shaped these theorizations of the sexual life of the child, and contributed to a broader reassessment of the standards of "normal" sexuality.

Contesting Infant Sexuality at the Fin de siècle

Moll's *Sexual Life* and Freud's *Three Essays* appeared on the German market within the space of three years. *Three Essays* enjoyed almost immediate attention within and beyond the German-speaking world, with one early American reviewer describing the 1910 translation by A. A. Brill as "the very best thing that has been written on the theory of sex in English."[64] Even some twenty years later, Hirschfeld declared it "Freud's most important book for sexology," and the work that had assured him an "everlasting reputation" in the history of sex research.[65] Moll's *Sexual Life* was also widely read and reviewed by physicians, pedagogues, lawyers, and psychologists, and first appeared in English translation in 1913.[66] Unlike Freud's study, however, Moll's faded into obscurity in subsequent decades, and has received far less attention from historians of sexuality, which scholars variously attribute to his troubled professional relationships, his lack of a university position, his at times impenetrable writing style, the growing intellectual appeal of Freud's approach, and his political conservatism and lack of the kind of activist profile that makes Hirschfeld such an attractive figure to today's progressive historians.[67] None of this was helped by Freud's decision, when revising his *Three Essays* in 1910, to refrain from any detailed treatment of his German colleague's recently published study; instead, he merely added a couple of footnotes noting that *Sexual Life* provided "no occasion" for altering his original literature review.[68]

These two works—the two most significant sexological and psychoanalytic accounts of child sexuality in the decades following 1900—cannot be differentiated straightforwardly on the basis of "nature" versus "nurture," or "congenital" versus "acquired" conditions. Although Moll's intellectual roots in nineteenth-century somatic psychiatry led him to insist that conditions such as homosexuality are frequently linked to congenital weakness, his work also considers nonphysiological phenomena such as hypnosis—an area in which his work had already been most influential—as well as, tentatively, the decidedly psychoanalytic realms of imagination, fantasy, and dreams, to which Freud had laid claim with his own widely read *Die Traumdeutung* (The Interpretation of Dreams, 1900).[69] Freud, too, carefully considered both "congenital" and "acquired" explanations, particularly in the first of his *Three Essays* on the "sexual aberrations." Although he placed more emphasis than most contemporary sexologists on interpersonal influences and infantile fantasies, Freud's strongly dualistic emphasis on physiological as well as psychological factors famously led one biographer to cast him as a "biologist of the mind."[70] These fin de siècle sexologists and psychoanalysts, in short, shared a distinctly modern view of the human sexual instinct as a rich combination of the physiological and the psychological, experience and affect.[71] So what *did* distinguish their theories of infant sexual development, and what might these distinctions tell us about shifting ideas of sexual subjectivity at the turn of the twentieth century?

Freud's *Three Essays* addressed three separate but linked themes that together form a broad account of human sexuality and its development over the lifespan. The first essay, "The Sexual Aberrations," discusses the etiology of deviations from the norm such as inversion, fetishism, or masochism (I return to this essay in chapter 2). The second, "Infantile Sexuality," provides an account of "normal" sexual development from birth to puberty, and is my primary focus here. The third, "The Transformations of Puberty," accounts for the subsequent transition between the "auto-erotic" phase of infancy and adult sexual maturity, including reorientation toward an external sexual object and the subordination of the "erogenous" zones of infantile eroticism to the genitals as the core site of sexual pleasure. The overriding achievement of *Three Essays* lay in formulating a universal (although implicitly male) theory of infant sexual development, outlining a series of "pregenital," unconscious infantile processes that Freud considered crucial to both normal maturation and the emergence of "neuroses" and "perversions."[72]

Moll had also provided a wide-ranging account of human sexual maturation with his articulation of the contrectation and detumescence drives in his earlier *Libido Sexualis*, described by one prominent historian as "the most comprehensive and sophisticated general theory on sexuality" before Freud's

Three Essays and Ellis's *Studies*.[73] At the same time, Moll's work fell short of Freud's not only in its exhaustiveness, but in establishing a dedicated movement of followers. Whereas Moll had oriented his theoretical reflections toward the emergence of adult-like sexual expressions in much older children, Freud pushed his contemporaries to consider much earlier stages of development as coming within the realm of the "normal"—and indeed, as crucial to maintaining society's norms of adult heterosexuality. His work also offered a larger framework within which to situate earlier research on the child, such as Lindner's work on thumb-sucking or Bell's cases of "sex-love." Although many now regard it as an achievement of synthesis as much as innovation, it was certainly ambitious in its universalizing reach.[74] Freud's loudly proclaimed "discovery" of infantile sexuality was also received by many contemporaries as a radical intervention, and its theoretical layers, which built up over the course of several editions, require careful unpacking. As the editors of a recent scholarly collection devoted to the 1905 edition of this work insist, the *Three Essays* were "anything but inevitable," and as well as merely synthesizing earlier clinical insights and theories, provoked "their fundamental revision in the light of a new conceptual framework."[75]

For fin de siècle sexology, Freud's study had a mixed impact. On the one hand, it proved a productive impetus for sexual scientists to delve more deeply into the roots of normal and perverse sexuality, revisiting older distinctions between acquired and congenital conditions. Yet the new psychoanalytic framework also threatened the classificatory authority that sexologists such as Moll were seeking to claim. From the outset of his slim volume, Freud explicitly "spares" himself the trouble of a detailed literature review, instead subsuming under an initial footnote all relevant sexological discussions to date, noting merely the significance of—unspecified—works by "Krafft-Ebing, Moll, Moebius, Havelock Ellis, v. Schrenck-Notzing, Löwenfeld, Eulenburg, I. Bloch, M. Hirschfeld" as well as articles published in Hirschfeld's *Jahrbuch für sexuelle Zwischenstufen* (Yearbook for Sexual Intermediaries).[76] This rhetorical move, described by one historian as both a "sensation" (*Paukenschlag*) and a thoroughly dismissive gesture, freed Freud to draw on existing sexological findings as he chose.[77] This is not to say that he did away with scientific citations altogether: later pages mention works by Hirschfeld, Moll, Lindner, and Krafft-Ebing, among others. Clearly, though, Freud considered it inadvisable to clutter with too many references a study for which he was claiming pioneering status.[78]

But just how pioneering *was* Freud's claim that "normal" sexual life began in earliest infancy? In *Sexual Life*, Moll also argued for the existence of "normal" sexual manifestations in children who had not yet reached puberty: "we have been forced to admit the fact that in the child sexual processes are much more extensive than has commonly been believed."[79] Here he could draw not only on the work of scholars such as Bell, but on his own previous research into the links between childhood masturbation and adult perversions. In his 1891 study of contrary sexual feeling, for example, Moll reported on an "epidemic" of mutual masturbation at a Berlin boarding school, but found that none of the boys later became homosexual. This acknowledgement of child sexual activity as normal even prior to adolescence represented an important shift from studies such as Krafft-Ebing's. At the same time, Moll's 1908 study was typical of sexological thought more broadly in conceding this "normal" status only for sexual activity occurring during the later, "second period" of childhood, between the ages of eight and fourteen.[80]

Consequently, Moll rejected Freud's significantly enlarged definition of infant sexuality, which encompassed a series of "auto-erotic" (a coinage Freud attributed to Ellis) and, most provocatively, "pregenital" phases of sexual development, including the so-called "oral" and "anal" stages.[81] Moll also dismissed Freud's sexual theory of the neuroses, viewing conditions such as hysteria, neurasthenia, and anxiety as far removed from any "true relationship to the sexual life of the child." He was critical of the claim that "infantile amnesia" prevented the memories of earliest childhood from being available to conscious recall, and only recoverable through the new analytic method, and he warned "against the exaggerations of those who interpret everything in sexual terms."[82] Many early critics of psychoanalysis shared his skepticism; as Jung observed in 1912, "the very idea that children might be sexual, and that sexual thoughts might play any part in their lives, aroused great indignation."[83]

While Moll was prepared to accept Freud's finding that the infant body displayed a range of nongenital "erogenous zones"—described by Freud as "a part of the skin or mucous membrane in which stimuli of a certain sort evoke a feeling of pleasure"—he remained committed to a genitally oriented definition of sexuality. As a result, Moll classified as "sexual" only those behaviors seen to be of the same kind as adult sexuality, and insisted that only in extremely rare cases do children experience a "voluptuous acme" or orgasm comparable to adult ejaculation.[84] As Freud remarked to those gathered in his apartment in 1908, "Moll actually understands sexuality as consisting of 'genitality.'"[85] Despite being accused of theoretical naivety by Jung ("with his long experience he really should have more understanding of your work," the Zürich psychiatrist had complained to his Viennese mentor[86]), Moll's position was not necessarily less theoretically sophisticated *per se*, but rather stemmed from a differing definition of "sexuality" that relied on proximity to adult forms of sexual expression. The response it generated from the early Freudians, though, was remarkable in the extent to which the attack became personalized. In a letter to Jung, Freud responded to Moll's criticisms (including of the psychoanalytic method of relying on a small number of patient histories) by suggesting that he possessed "the intellectual and moral constitution of a pettifogging lawyer."[87] A few months later, Moll visited Freud's Viennese apartment, presumably to discuss their respective views on child sexuality; he later recounted in his memoirs Freud's "great sensitivity" at that meeting, as Freud "produced my book about the *Sexual Life of the Child* and pointed with agitation to a particular section."[88] Freud, meanwhile, described in a letter to Jung how he

> let him [Moll] have it; I attacked the passage in his notorious book where he says that we compose our case histories to support our theories rather than the other way round, and had the pleasure of listening to his oily excuses. . . . Then he complained that I was too sensitive, that I must learn to accept justified criticism; when I asked him if he had read "Little Hans," he wound himself up into several spirals, became more and more venomous, and finally, to my great joy, jumped up and prepared to take flight. . . . He had stunk up the room like the devil himself, and partly for lack of practice and partly because he was my guest I hadn't lambasted him enough.[89]

In his later biography of Freud, Ernest Jones reported, with a certain British understatement, that Moll had been "a less welcome visitor . . . Freud thought very poorly of him and he said he gave Moll a bad time."[90] Described by one scholar as "certainly one of the less edifying episodes in the history of the psychoanalytic movement," I suggest that it is productive to read this scene of obvious antagonism as more than simply a clash of personalities—which it most certainly was, with Freud later declaring to Stekel that "Moll is a spitfire (*Giftkröte*), who is not deserving of anything more than a dry review."[91] Rather, the ferocity of Freud's response reflects a desire to stake out and protect the intellectual turf of the new psychoanalytic movement, and thus marks an important moment in the emerging intellectual struggle between these two fields.

The distinction between adult (genital) and infant (pregenital) definitions of sexuality proved particularly contentious when it came to assessing Freud's formulation of the "oral" and "anal" stages. According to Freud, the infant's first sexual activities involve an oral autoerotic stage characterized by rhythmic practices such as thumb-sucking.[92] Moll contested this, declaring "that there is here no intimate connexion between the act of sucking and the sexual life," and that "with just as much reason, every movement might be regarded as sexual—as, for instance, the clenching by a child of its little fists." Moll's genital definition of sexuality also led him to critique Lindner's 1879 account of children's "pleasure sucking," including finger sucking, ear rubbing, and genital stimulation: "there is no proof whatever for the view . . . that this 'voluptuous sucking' (*Wonnesaugen*) is a truly sexual process." Instead, he argued that infant self-stimulation merely indicates "a specific genital sensation to which the child responds"—and thus even erections or masturbation could be nonsexual, resulting from physical causes such as distension of the bladder.[93] He introduced a slight contradiction into his argument, however, by then citing sexologist Hermann Rohleder's finding (*Die Masturbation* [Masturbation, 1899]) that where "such sucking movements" occur with especial frequency, they might be linked to masturbation and read as evidence of a "congenital morbid predisposition."[94] This move reaffirmed the possibility of infant sexuality, even while declaring it pathological.

A number of Moll's contemporaries concurred. Nerve doctor and general practitioner Leopold Loewenfeld, occasional editor of a neurological pamphlet series and a "loyal opponent" of Freud since the 1890s, drew criticism from early WPV member Sadger for questioning the sexual nature of children's thumb-sucking.[95] Meanwhile, Zurich psychiatrist, neuroanatomist, and entomologist Forel, who had directed the famous Burghölzli psychiatric clinic from 1879 to 1898, pointed to several neurodevelopmental factors that, he argued, made the Freudian eroticization of infancy "scientifically inadmissible." First, there was the fact that thumb-sucking begins almost immediately after birth, when the cerebrum is still underdeveloped. Secondly, infants' sexual organs are still in an embryonic state, and thus biologically incapable of emitting sexual feelings into the spinal cord. Although Forel considers it "without doubt" that somewhat older children—say, from the age of three or four—occasionally experience "vague sexual feelings," this is a long way, he insists, from declaring infant sexuality "the rule, as Freud's school claims."[96] Like Moll, Forel in his widely read *Die sexuelle Frage* (The Sexual Question, 1905), also refuted the sexual etiology of the neuroses, insisting that the causes "cannot always be found in the second or third year of life, as Freud suggests."[97] Such criticisms notwithstanding, Forel's decision to engage with psychoanalysis at all at this late stage in his career was seen by at least one reviewer as evidence of the "significant activity and plasticity" of his approach.[98]

The formulation of the anal stage, meanwhile, described children's capacity to use bowel movements as both a source of pleasure and a means of expressing compliance or disobedience. Like the oral phase, Freud argued, this stage was observable by the third or fourth year of life. A few years after *Three Essays*, he vividly illustrated such infantile pleasures and protests in his case study "Little Hans." Based on his friend Max Graf's observations of his young son, the child's own voice is here at several removes from Freud's readers, mediated by both his own father and by the analyst who interpreted his friend's notes. Fixations on anal processes play an important role in this analysis: "Quite unexpectedly, and certainly without any prompting by his father, Hans now began to be occupied with the 'lumf' complex, and to show disgust at things that reminded him of evacuating his bowels." Freud then traced the boy's sudden fear of horses to incestuous desires for his mother, a desire to see her "widdler," and subsequent fears that his own "widdler" might be forcibly removed by his father in an early example of the castration complex; Freud's observations of this case led him to pay more attention to Oedipal motivations in subsequent revisions of the *Three Essays*.[99] A year later, Jung offered a similar account of a girl he dubbed "Anna," whose "neurosis" he linked to the birth of her younger brother, noting that it contains elements that "confirm how much is typical about 'little Hans.'"[100] Anna, too, was fascinated by bodily orifices, coming to associate the act of birth with excretion. This led her to conduct a series of "investigations" and declare a desire to "kill" her (still-hypothetical) younger sibling, before she finally experienced improvements in her neurotic state as she gradually discovered the facts of life from her parents.[101] Despite their powerful illustrative qualities, such cases provided grist to the mill for contemporaries keen to critique the new psychoanalytic approach, not least because they used "neurotic" infants as a basis for theorizing about "normal" sexual development.

Freud's articulation of the anal phase drew a more varied response from sexological colleagues. Moll was again skeptical; while prepared to accept that, in a few children, the activity of the erogenous zones might include "gentle scratching of the anal region and buttocks" or even flagellation, he flatly rejected any more universalizing formulations of this stage, and in particular, the Freudian postulation that sexual pleasure might be gained from "voluntary retention of the faeces" ("I have not yet been able to satisfy myself that these processes always, or even usually, have any connexion with the sexual life").[102] Yet not everyone agreed. Ellis, always well-informed about Continental developments—he corresponded regularly with German colleagues, including Hirschfeld and Bloch, and maintained a lively correspondence with Freud from the 1890s until their respective deaths in 1939[103]—vocally supported Freud's linking of scatophilia and infant sexual life. Although he declared

Moll's *Sexual Life* "the most able and judicious book yet written on this subject" and agreed with the Berlin sexologist that the age of "seven or eight" marked the point after which childhood sexual activities may be considered "as coming within the normal sphere," Ellis also developed a more nuanced response to the psychoanalytic framework of infant sexuality than many of his German peers.[104] Writing in his *Studies* that "there appears to be no limit to the age at which spontaneous masturbation may occur," Ellis had, in fact, highlighted the pleasurable sensations of urination, defecation, and breast-feeding even before the appearance of *Three Essays*, leading some scholars to claim that he anticipated "much of the Freudian doctrine."[105] With regard to the anal stage, Ellis asserted in a 1913 essay, "Sexual Problems," his agreement with Freud that sexual impulses in children are "very frequently, perhaps normally, scatalogic," while also seizing the opportunity to explore the urinary excretory functions, one of his abiding personal and intellectual interests. Emphasizing the "intimate connection, physical and psychic" between the channels of urination, defecation, and the sexual centers, Ellis celebrated these as "a rudimentary form of the artistic impulse, at the same time a manifestation of power." He thus not only agreed with, but expanded on, Freud's deliberations, arguing that pleasurable sensations apply equally to the bladder and the bowel, and may also (biographical accounts suggest that here, he was perhaps drawing on personal experience) retain this erotic function beyond infancy: "it is certain that even in later life the contents of the bladder are sometimes retained for the same reason."[106]

Such discussions surrounding the sexual potential of the excretory functions spurred further inquiries. Working within psychoanalytic frameworks, Otto Rank and Isidor Sadger both considered urethral eroticism between 1910 and 1912;[107] continuing this dialogue, Ellis penned a 1913 article, "The Relation of Erotic Dreams to Vesical Dreams," where he engaged at length with psychoanalytic ideas about dreams and the unconscious, while challenging Rank's prioritization of the sexual over the vesical (urinary) impulse.[108] In 1913 Jones even issued an invitation to Ellis to join a new Psycho-Analytic Society to be founded in London.[109] In their correspondence they, too, discussed the specifics of urinary eroticism, with Jones explaining that "the conflict of priority between sexual versus vesical is for us [psychoanalysts] no problem," but rather "is solved by recognizing that the pleasurable sensations" relating to the urinary functions "belong to the 'Lust' group that we call sexual in the broader sense."[110] As Ellis's nuanced response to Freud's ideas shows, *Three Essays* did not merely challenge sexological definitions of "normal" sexuality, but provided a productive impetus to further inquiry, creating fruitful moments of exchange across the solidifying boundaries of these medico-scientific specializations.

As well as articulating a series of "pregenital" phases of infant sexual life, Freud challenged sexological understandings of human development with his formulations of the infant's "polymorphous perversity," the "Oedipus complex," and the "latency phase." Least conceptually problematic was the first of these concepts: the understanding that children are fundamentally open to all kinds of sexual influences and irregularities at a stage of life during which mental barriers of shame and morality are not yet fully constructed. As Freud explained—in rather misogynistic terms—infants "are thus like an uncultivated woman whose sexuality may remain normal, but who can find all sorts of perversions to her taste under the influence of a clever seducer."[111] To an extent, though, the "polymorphous" label was simply a new take on a concept that had been current in medical circles for some time. In *Sexual Life*, Moll had described the significance of an "undifferentiated sexual impulse" in childhood, building on the work of German psychologist and philosopher Max Dessoir, who in 1894 had argued that the earliest, "neutral" stage of childhood, which is free of psychosexual attraction, is followed by an "undifferentiated stage." During this stage, as Moll explains, "the direction of the impulse is not yet completely differentiated," but "oscillates to and fro, and depends on the external objects which happen to be in the vicinity." This may result in "quite normal children" demonstrating signs of homosexual as well as heterosexual excitement—or, sometimes, an attraction to animals or other "perverse" sentiments. On reaching maturity, this undifferentiated stage is generally replaced by "differentiation," as the libido narrows its focus to heterosexual relationships. Some individuals, however, continue to show signs of perverse inclinations, remaining in what Dessoir termed an "embryonic" state.[112] Dessoir's findings, in turn, closely align with Freud's later discussion in *Three Essays* of the developmental inhibitions leading to aberrations from the sexual norm.

Moll, for his part, made some adjustments to Dessoir's categorizations, particularly the assertion that the "undifferentiated" phase occurred in girls between twelve and fourteen and in boys between thirteen and fifteen. Drawing on his own theory of the duality of the sexual instinct, as well as Bell's observations of schoolchildren, Moll argued that by as early as the age of eight "the phenomena of the contrectation impulse become so frequent . . . that at this time of life these phenomena must be regarded, not merely as not pathological, but further, as not even abnormal." He presented a number of case histories illustrating this "undifferentiated" stage, in which patients recall childhood "crushes" on tutors or friends' older siblings, or intimate relationships with fellow students of the same sex. Moll used these cases, in particular, to argue that same-sex desires were both common and often temporary. His "Case 2," a thirty-year-old male with "no morbid condition," for example, describes how an early "immeasurable, passionate love" for a fellow male pupil was superseded by romantic feelings for a girl in his dancing class, although it was not until he reached the age of twenty that his homosexual inclinations disappeared completely: "I am now, I believe, in every respect a healthy male."[113] For Ellis, too, "there is normally in all boys and girls a trace of homosexual feeling," even if sexual impulses in children generally take on a diffused form; like Dessoir and Moll, Ellis resisted assuming that "the first delicate growths of what will later become a mighty instinct . . . are perverse."[114] This insistence that temporary homosexual behaviors could later turn into a heterosexual orientation was critical to subsequent debates about the etiology and treatment of the "perversions," examined in the next chapter.

Far more contentious than the notion of polymorphous perversity was Freud's formulation of the "Oedipus complex." Drawing on Greek mythology, he argued that the child must overcome and ultimately repudiate original incestuous and jealous impulses toward their parents, who form the primary sexual objects, to achieve a state of mature adult heterosexuality. Freud had first articulated the Oedipus complex in his 1899 study of dreams (the publication of which was forward-dated to 1900), and continued to explore its workings in a number of essays during the 1900s and 1910s, although he only discussed it directly in *Three Essays* in revisions to the 1920 edition. There he described the Oedipus complex as a universal challenge that everyone must individually master if they are not to fall victim to neurosis or perversion; at the same time, he noted its already controversial status as "the shibboleth that distinguishes the adherents of psycho-analysis from its opponents."[115] Scholars have characterized Freud's growing focus on Oedipal arguments in later editions of the *Three Essays* in terms of a "normalizing" turn, particularly when compared with the radical potentiality of his earlier thinking on the polymorphous perversity of childhood; he had even provocatively postulated that kissing represents a "perverse" act, not being strictly driven by the sexual apparatus.[116] They also highlight contradictions introduced across the various editions of Freud's text between the less object-oriented stages of pregenital infancy and the object-driven explanations of the Oedipal phase, while noting that incestuous fantasies were never entirely absent from Freud's original account, and that even so-called "autoerotic" stages such as thumb-sucking were often linked to an original object relation, in this case with the mother's breast.[117] Nonetheless, Freud's Oedipal framework represented an important reappraisal of the normal/pathological distinction by arguing that the same Oedipal explanations lay behind the "perversions" and "normal" human development.

Sexological skeptics of Freud's Oedipal arguments included Moll and, somewhat later, Hirschfeld, whose initial enthusiasm for Freudian thought hit a limit on this point. Moll's insistence on a genital definition of sexuality and the unknowability of children's sexual feelings led him to dismiss as fruitless any attempt to "distinguish a boy's love for his mother from his nonsexual friendship for a little girl" ("*in the mind of the child the various feelings comprised under the idea of 'sympathy' [friendship, affection for parents, love of children, sexual love] cannot always be marked off each from the other after the manner of provinces on a map*").[118] Although Moll could refer only to the 1905 edition of Freud's text, in which the Oedipus complex had not yet been described in explicit terms, we nonetheless see here a rejection of Freud's focus on the incestuous feelings shaping infant development.

Hirschfeld did not clearly articulate his position on the Oedipal concept until the interwar period, by which time Freud had also more fully elaborated his ideas. Hirscheld had also become decidedly less enthusiastic about psychoanalysis in the interim, although he was never an outright opponent. As noted in the Introduction, Hirschfeld had been one of the original members of Abraham's Berlin Psychoanalytic Society in 1908, and he also collaborated closely with Abraham during these early years, both in developing a "psychobiological questionnaire" for collecting patient case histories, and in the joint preparation of expert court statements.[119] As Abraham wrote to Freud in 1909, Hirschfeld "altogether takes the kindest interest in me."[120] Following a visit from Hirschfeld in 1908, Freud had similarly observed (to Jung) that the Berlin sexologist "is moving close to us and from now on will take our ideas into account as much as possible."[121] The honeymoon was short-lived, however. In 1911 Hirschfeld withdrew from the Berlin group. In his later biography of Freud, Jones noted Hirschfeld's resignation, but gives no reasons for it, instead remarking that Freud had invited his Berlin colleague "to lunch at his home on at least two occasions."[122] Abraham, however, came close to the core of the problem when he lamented to his Viennese mentor that Hirschfeld "displayed an ignorance about Ψα [psychoanalysis] that was outright shocking. [. . .] It was most probably only the emphasis on sexuality that made analysis attractive to him, especially at a time when his own sex research met with hostility." Such concerns about Hirschfeld's lack of comprehension or adoption of Freudian ideas were certainly part of the problem, but his decision to formally leave the analytic fold was compounded by personal attacks on his character by Jung, in particular. In correspondence with Freud, Jung had harshly described Hirschfeld and Abraham's psychoanalytical questionnaire as "a perfectly idiotic concoction that does Hirschfeld no credit" and a "desecration" of the word "psychoanalysis." Jung had also made his criticisms more publicly known at the 1911 International Psychoanalytic Congress in Weimar, which Hirschfeld attended, and although the precise wording of his attack has gone unrecorded—an attack which clearly formed the breaking point for Hirschfeld's formal involvement with the Freudians—homophobic insults may well have played a role.[123]

In the years that followed, Hirschfeld gradually arrived at a compromise: he acknowledged that Freudian theory had introduced some important concepts to sexology, such as the concept of repression (*Verdrängung*), but saw the Oedipus complex as an unnecessary and abstract "detour" that served only to refract attention away from sexuality's fundamental seat in the body.[124] In 1917, he also declared Freud's emphasis on universal incestuous tendencies "a completely erroneous auto- and altero-suggestion [*sic*]." He did, however, accept that a child's love for parents or siblings may contain a "lightly erotic undercurrent that does not fully penetrate the consciousness," and that even conscious incestuous feelings "may well be more frequent than is generally assumed"; Hirschfeld noted that this view was shared by fellow Berlin sexologist Max Marcuse, editor of the journal *Sexual-Probleme* (Sexual Problems).[125] In contrast, Ellis again took a more nuanced approach to the incest question that at least partly anticipated Freud's own. Emphasizing the erotic relationship between the breast-feeding mother and her child, in 1900 Ellis had characterized the maternal transfer of fluids as "the one true physiological analogy to the relationship of a man and a woman at the climax of the sexual act," an argument Freud subsequently cited in *Three Essays*.[126]

Sexologists, as these sources show, were beginning to critically engage with, and also take sides on, Freudian formulations of the Oedipus complex and the stages of infant sexuality. Picking up on some arguments while rejecting others, their responses to Freud's ideas demonstrate the depth to which these had penetrated sexual scientific discourse by the first decade of the new century, but also that sexologists were prepared to push back against the aspects—such as the attribution of incestuous feelings to newborn infants—that they perceived as taking things a little too far.

Freud's ideas were not only controversial with sexological contemporaries, but sowed seeds of dissent among fellow psychoanalysts. In 1912, still committed to Freudian methods as chair of the International Psychoanalytic Association (IPA), which had been founded in Nuremberg in 1910, the Zurich-based Jung used a lecture series to articulate various criticisms of Freud's account. In many ways, this critique went deeper than that of the sexologists, challenging not only Freud's understandings of the polymorphous perversity of infancy, but more fundamentally, his formulation of the nature and workings of the libido itself. Jung joined skeptics such as Moll and Forel in disputing Freud's characterization of gestures such as sucking as sexual pleasures, arguing that the first period of life is focused only on the functions of nutrition and growth, "so that to speak of manifest sexuality in infancy would be a contradiction in terms."[127] (Taking a different tack, Abraham had argued that nutrition and sexuality remained linked at this stage.[128])

Jung instead sought to develop a conception of the libido that was not exclusively sexual ("*Obtaining pleasure is by no means identical with sexuality*") and thus adjusted Freud's triphasal model of infant development. He argued that there is, first, a "presexual" stage, until the ages of around three to five, characterized by the functions of nutrition and growth, and that only during a second, "prepubertal" phase does the germination of sexuality take place, as the libido gradually transfers from the oral zone to other areas of the body, "where it may provide occasion for the first attempts at masturbation."[129] Echoing Moll and Dessoir, Jung stressed that in both boys and girls before puberty, the libido is of "a sexually undifferentiated character, which could also be termed bisexual," and that only quite late in puberty does it reach "its final differentiation, corresponding to the sex of the individual." While Jung broadly followed Freud's articulation of the Oedipus complex, agreeing that the first love for both sexes belongs to the mother, he offered a more specific—albeit brief—account of female development in the form of the "Electra complex." Daughters, he argues, develop an attraction toward the father and a jealous attitude toward the mother, in a reference to the mythological Electra's revenge on her mother Clytemnestra, who had murdered Electra's father.[130] (Like Jung, Moll was also more attentive to female sexuality during this period than Freud, soberly describing phenomena such as female ejaculation, although with the disclaimer "that the sexual life of the girl is still much more obscure to us than that of the boy."[131]) Jung's postulation of an alternative complex was quite possibly an attempt to widen the distance between himself and Freud, who later responded by explicitly rejecting Jung's terminology.[132]

Even today, some commentators criticize Freud's inclusion of pregenital motives and fantasies in psychoanalytic understandings of the sexual instinct as a "watering down" or excessive symbolization of the concept of sexuality.[133] Certainly, the Freudians focused much more on the latent and repressed desires and fantasies of their patients than on the kinds of manifest expressions of sexuality that had garnered the attention of earlier sex psychiatrists such as Krafft-Ebing—fetishes, cross-dressing, and other "perverse" sexual practices.

Jung's assertion of an alternative norm for the beginning of sexual life placed him somewhere between Freud's insistence on the pregenital sexuality of infants and the sexologists' emphasis on later childhood. His distance from Freud's positions widened further when he echoed sexological colleagues such as Forel and Ellis in rejecting Freud's characterization of polymorphous infant sexuality as "perverse," noting that this label had been fuel to the fire for psychoanalysis's critics. Instead, he argued that the perversions must be understood as "disturbed products of a developed sexuality," and thus of a different order than the initial, "rudimentary and provisional" stages of "normal" sexuality.[134] Jung also disagreed with Freud's argument that there was a sudden sexual quieting during a "latency" phase between early childhood and puberty. Attributing this term to his early correspondent Fliess, Freud had argued that during this latency phase the production of sexual excitation does not cease, but is redirected or "sublimated" into energy for other purposes, allowing the infant to erect barriers or "inhibitions" based in disgust and shame. These esthetic and moral values would later steer the sexual instinct, he argued, in culturally acceptable directions.[135] Jung, however, countered that it would be biologically unique—and thus highly unlikely—for a process such as the onset of sexuality to *begin* to flourish, only to be retracted and reappear later in a similar form, such as masturbation. Instead, he concluded that "what he [Freud] calls a disappearance is nothing other than the *real beginning of sexuality*, everything preceding it being but a preliminary stage to which no real sexual character can be attributed."[136]

Jung's interventions ultimately proved symptomatic of an irreconcilable difference that contributed to the famous split between these two pioneering analysts in 1913, with Jung resigning as president of the IPA in 1914.[137] They particularly threatened the early Freudian movement, as Lutz Sauerteig observes, because Jung's desexualized libido theory promised to be less objectionable to the broader professions of psychology and psychotherapy.[138] Jung deemed the Freudian emphasis on sexuality too narrow to support a wider theory of human psychology; as a result, he—along with Alfred Adler, who also broke from Freud in these years around questions of sexuality to found his own school of "individual psychology"—is only a marginal player in the remaining chapters of this book. For both the inner Freudian circle and contemporary sexologists, on the other hand, sexuality continued to represent the very core of human existence, and the key to understanding the modern subject.

Discussions surrounding children's sexuality in the years that followed continued to respond to innovations from within and beyond sexology and psychoanalysis. In the emerging field of developmental psychology in the 1920s and 1930s, Viennese children's psychologist Charlotte Bühler worked to expand understandings of infant sexuality as a phenomenon clearly distinct from that of adults. For Bühler, while there was convincing evidence of masturbatory and other pleasure-oriented activities in even very young children, it was not until puberty that this early *Wollust* (pleasure)—embedded in a "completely different total structure" than adult sexuality—begins to assume a mature form, oriented toward climax and a sexual partner. Other contemporary psychologists shared this view, such as Breslau (now Wrocław) psychologist William Stern.[139] Following the Austrian *Anschluss* in 1938, Bühler continued her work in children's and youth psychology at universities and hospitals in Norway, Minneapolis, and Los Angeles; a children's clinic in Vienna now bears her name.[140]

While the figure of the child faded somewhat from sexological attention after the fin de siècle, children's sexuality and subjectivity has continued to be of central concern to psychoanalysts throughout the twentieth century, thanks particularly to the contributions of women analysts. Hermine Hug-Hellmuth is often heralded as the first child psychoanalyst, although from as early as the 1910s Russian analyst Sabine Spielrein, who had undergone analysis with Jung, joined her in this endeavor; tragically, Hug-Hellmuth was murdered in 1924 by her nephew and former patient Rolf.[141] Later, Sigmund and Martha Freud's daughter Anna not only established child analysis as a discrete field, but brought it to an international audience, along with colleagues such as Melanie Klein.[142] When the National Socialist seizures of power in Germany and then Austria forced many of these researchers to leave German-speaking central Europe, analysts such as Klein in the United States and Anna Freud and Donald Winnicott in London continued to develop this field as a semi-independent specialization, despite tensions between the "Freudians," the "Kleinians," and the "British middle group."[143]

In the 1910s and 1920s, meanwhile, new research into the endocrinal glands and hormones forced a revisiting of these early debates about the nature of the sexual instinct and its "normal" development. Spearheaded by the sex organ experiments of Eugen Steinach and his team in Vienna, research into the inner secretions added complexity to questions of children's physiological and psychological development. It also (as I show in chapter 4) led Freud to revise a section of his *Three Essays* on "Chemical Theory," although he did not fundamentally transform his theoretical framework. Moll had even vaguely foreshadowed this shift in *Sexual Life* when he observed that the "chemical" theory of the glands had recently gained ground over the older "nervous" theory, even if the precise functioning of these glands was still unclear.[144] Inner-secretions research was starting to compel observers of child sexuality, as Arthur Kronfeld of the Berlin Institute for Sexual Science noted several years later, to acknowledge a "normal" hormonal and physiological basis for human sexual development from earliest infancy, beginning well before the immature organism is capable of reproduction.[145] Whereas Freud's *Three Essays* had forced sexologists to sit up and take notice, chemical research into the glands promised to return some of the scientific authority that figures such as Moll and Hirschfeld had been forced to concede to psychoanalysis in these crucial questions of etiology. This tale of how the pendulum began to swing back—from an increasingly psychologized framework of sexual modernity at the turn of the century to a renewed focus on the body's organic functions by the 1920s—represents a crucial moment in the relationship between these two fields in the early twentieth century, and in the larger narrative of this book.

Fin de siècle discussions of child sexuality demonstrate the extent to which sexologists had already begun to critically engage with newer Freudian modes of thought by the first decade of the new century. They also show the degree to which psychoanalysts, including Freud, were enmeshed in existing sexological and psychological discussions, from earlier theorizations of the "undifferentiated" sexual impulses of childhood by scholars such as Dessoir and Moll, to Ellis's more contemporary writings on the eroticism of urination and breast-feeding. Such interpenetrations of knowledge were the source of tensions, particularly around the Oedipal complex, that point not just to theoretical differences, but to the perceived professional threat posed by the Freudian school to sexological explanatory modes. But within psychoanalysis as well, Freud's theory of infantile sexual development was starting to ruffle feathers, with Jung developing an alternative formulation of the libido that soon proved irreconcilable with Freud's own.

These debates around the child evidence a shifting conceptualization of infantile sexual life in the first decades of the twentieth century. They also laid the crucial groundwork for discussions of children's sexual subjectivities, vulnerabilities, and agency during the century that followed, and can still be detected into the present in the approach of queer theorists and other scholars to questions such as sexual abuse and the development of nonheteronormative sex-gender identities. They highlight, furthermore, some key theoretical and methodological distinctions between sexology and psychoanalysis that continued to be negotiated in the years to follow. With their intellectual roots primarily in psychiatry, medicine, and the biological and natural sciences, sexual scientists' skepticism about what they considered to be psychoanalysts' less empirically demonstrable theories and methods is already evident in the debates examined here. This was particularly the case when it came to illustrating radical new concepts such as the Oedipus complex using a handful of neurotic cases such as that of "Little Hans," rather than, as in larger psychological studies such as Bell's, a broader cross-section of the "healthy" population. Psychoanalysts, meanwhile, were more concerned with identifying the core developmental processes of infancy, and with using this foundation to show how ideas of the "normal," the "neurotic" and the "perverse" belonged to a single developmental spectrum.

The history of sexuality has much to gain from a more concerted historicizing of the "normal" as a category shaping sexual knowledge in the early twentieth century. Fin de siècle debates about children's sexual development offer valuable insights into the precise ways the normal was being defined when it came to understanding the beginnings and scope of sexual subjectivity. As scholars such as Moll and Freud raced to establish their authority on matters of child sexuality, they were also staking claims to the capacity of their respective fields to establish the limits of "normal" human sexuality. The next chapter explores the implications of these diverging approaches for ideas about homosexuality. This, as we shall see, became a central locus for discussions of "normality" and "perversion" and the extent to which these were shaped by congenital or acquired influences.

Chapter 2

Treating the "Perversions": The Prewar Homosexuality Debate

> Because many homosexuals possess the desire, certainly justified, to experience heterosexual feelings, we must be grateful to every doctor who presents new treatment possibilities. For some time now, since it emerged that hypnotic treatment was not fulfilling expectations, Prof. Freud in Vienna and his pupils . . . have attempted to use psychoanalysis to find a new way of advancing therapeutically. Naturally, it is still not possible to arrive at a conclusive judgment concerning the new technique [*Verfahren*], however we do not want to refrain from pointing both doctors and homosexuals toward Freud's analytic method, which in any case tackles the question of sexual status in a fundamentally deeper and more exhaustive manner than hypnosis.[1]

This cautiously enthusiastic statement about the possibilities of the Freudian method for the treatment of homosexual patients was penned by one of early-twentieth-century Germany's leading scientific researchers of homosexuality, Magnus Hirschfeld of Berlin. Hirschfeld was also one of the most vocal advocates for the repeal of Paragraph 175 of the Criminal Code, which criminalized "intercourse-like" (*beischlafähnliche*) sexual acts between men, and he frequently appeared in court cases speaking as a medical expert for the defense. Celebrated today as a giant of the early German gay rights scene, he even has a Berlin street named after him. Films, novels, biographies, and plays celebrate his life, and his Institute appeared in a recent series of the acclaimed television drama *Transparent* (Jill Sulloway, 2014–). "Hirschfeld . . . has once again been made the face of homosexual emancipation, as he was for most of his adult life."[2] His prominence in German homosexual history and historiography lends particular significance to his comments on the new psychoanalytic method, which appeared in the world's first journal dedicated to the scientific investigation of homosexuality, the *Jahr-*

buch für sexuelle Zwischenstufen (Yearbook of Sexual Intermediaries, hereafter *Jahrbuch*). As noted in the Introduction, that journal had been founded in 1899 under the auspices of the Scientific Humanitarian Committee (Wissenschaftlich-humanitäres Komitee, WhK), an anti–Paragraph 175 lobby group first established in 1897. WhK activists contested the enshrining of Prussia's punitive Paragraph 143 in the criminal code as Paragraph 175 following Germany's unification in 1871, while to the south, both female and male homosexuality were outlawed under Austria's Paragraphs 129b and 130 of 1852.[3] As editor, Hirschfeld made the bold decision in 1908 to publish a lengthy case study of a "feminine male urning" by Viennese analyst Isidor Sadger, an early member of Freud's Wednesday Society and an analyst particularly attuned to sexological developments; Hirschfeld's above note was attached to that article.[4] The case of "S.M.," which Sadger recorded in shorthand during their many sessions, presented the first in-depth psychoanalytic account of an openly homosexual patient by any of the early Freudians. (Same-sex desires had featured in Freud's famous cases of "Dora" and "Anna O.," but these took the form of repressed bisexual fantasies rather than conscious same-sex identification.) Sadger used the case to publicize his ambitious claim that he had found a "cure" for even avowed homosexuality through the artful application of psychoanalytic techniques. By allowing his male patients to access hidden heterosexual desires, Sadger later explained, he "gave [the patient] back not only potency with women, but also, and this is decisive, changed his sexual ideal itself."[5]

Hirschfeld's publication of Sadger's case highlights the willingness of sexual scientists at the fin de siècle to engage with the newest branch of the "psy-sciences," and to exploit the possibilities of the new Freudian methods for the good of homosexual patients. Yet Sadger's claim to have found a cure did not sit easily with the early homosexual emancipation movement; for the WhK, the main problem was not same-sex desire per se, but rather the social persecution of homosexuals. The organization's advocacy for homosexual rights was buoyed by the Hirschfeldian argument of "Justice through science," and the conviction that same-sex desire represented a naturally occurring, inborn form of "sexual intermediacy." Its strategy of basing civic rights claims on the naturalness of homosexual desire had a long history, having already been articulated in the writings of German lawyer Karl Heinrich Ulrichs and others from the late 1860s; recent studies have extended this timeline even further back to early-nineteenth-century thinkers such as Swiss writer Heinrich Hössli.[6] Framing homosexuality as an anthropological variant that was not itself pathological, many fin de siècle activists argued that it should be neither legally persecuted nor necessarily medically altered. At the same time, leading figures in this movement, Hirschfeld among them, were supportive of patients who sought to alleviate their situations by changing themselves, and looked with interest to the latest research, even across solidifying professional lines.[7] How, then, did debates about homosexuality shape the race for scientific legitimation between sexologists and psychoanalysts? Their investigations of childhood, as I argued in the previous chapter, formed part of a broader shift toward examining "normal" sexuality, generally defined as heterosexual and reproductive. The "normal" was also beginning to dominate psychological research on other topics, from the workplace to parenting to consumer culture.[8] This trend resonated with a growing and diverse sex-reform movement, which drew attention to questions of heterosexual marital happiness, birth control, and eugenics alongside concerns with the rights of sexual minorities.[9] Yet even as sex researchers turned their attention toward the normal, the study of sexual "perversions" and "pathologies" remained crucial to their clinical and theoretical work.

This chapter argues that medical debates around homosexuality enabled new interpenetrations of knowledge between pre–World War I sexology and psychoanalysis. I situate shifting theoretical and therapeutic approaches to same-sex behaviors against changing understandings of sexual norms and their relation to the perversions, arguing that, in an era of sexual modernity, practitioners in each of these fields were moving toward less dialectical understandings of what was normal and healthy, and what was not. My focus on both theory and therapy reflects Freud's own distinction between the "scientific structure" of psychoanalytic theory and its applications as both a method of inquiry and a mode of treatment.[10] The first section of the chapter situates early-twentieth-century debates between analysts and sexual scientists against a longer history of medical understandings of same-sex desire, which had revolved particularly around the question of whether homosexuality always had an inborn element, or could be acquired at some point after birth. As this analysis shows, the nature-versus-nurture question did not follow clear disciplinary lines either before or after 1900; psychiatrists, sexologists, and psychoanalysts all engaged in intricate maneuvering between biological and environmental arguments.

I then show how Freud and his followers—Sadger in particular—prompted sexologists to take a new look at older theoretical ideas surrounding sex-gender "inversion" (which had aligned same-sex desires with cross-gendered traits), whether by emphasizing the significance of the sexual "object" of attraction over cross-gendered behaviors, or by offering more nuanced explanations of how early childhood influences might evolve into adult homosexual desire. Freudians also, as Sadger's early case shows, began exploring the therapeutic possibilities of the "talking cure." One of the most significant rifts in these fin de siècle discussions of homosexuality, I argue, was actually not along the solidifying disciplinary lines of sexology and psychoanalysis. Rather, it was between researchers committed to acquired explanations and conversion therapy on the one hand, and those advocating biologically determinist positions on the other, which groups such as the WhK used to support the political case for decriminalization. Sometimes, these two positions converged in conflicted ways (in Hirschfeld's writings, in particular). Linking these two camps, however, was a broader attempt by both sexologists and psychoanalysts to formulate new models of sex-gender variations and their relationship to the "normal." In this, they built on the work of late-nineteenth-century scholars such as Richard von Krafft-Ebing and Albert Moll, who had helped to establish a scientifically rational discourse of sexual modernity distanced from older legal and moralistic framings, and had begun to develop less oppositional models of normality and pathology.[11] Psychoanalytic interventions, I argue, pushed these sexological deliberations further, as the Freudians sidelined congenital versus acquired distinctions to focus instead on the stages of infancy as the key to sexual disorders.

In recent decades the history of homosexuality has become one of the most well explored aspects of modern sexual historiography. The late nineteenth century, if we follow Foucault's widely cited and at times contested argument, saw the invention of the very concept of the homosexual as a "species" and "morphology," and not just an individual who practiced certain behaviors.[12] Amidst a flourishing of scientific interest in same-sex desire, German-speaking scholars played a leading role. Historians have carefully traced shifts in the language and conceptualization of same-sex identification in these decades, charting the emergence of competing terminologies of the "urning," the "invert," and the "homosexual," and investigating the role of medical and psychiatric discourses in shaping wider cultural ideas about homosexuality.[13] They have also paid much-needed attention to the role of patients and other informants in shaping these medical discourses.[14] The German-speaking world was so important in these developments that several recent studies even attest to the German "invention" or "discovery" of modern ideas of (homo)sexuality, from the coining of this term in 1868 by Viennese-born Hungarian journalist Karl Maria Kertbeny to psychiatrist Carl Friedrich Otto Westphal's role as author of the first psychiatric study of "contrary sexual feeling" in 1869, and Ulrichs's early legal defenses of the rights of "Uranians."[15] As noted above, German-speaking activists also pioneered the establishment of organized homosexual rights movements such as the WhK.[16] Debates in the late-nineteenth- and early-twentieth-century German-speaking world, historians have shown, laid the foundations for the sexual politics of the post-Stonewall era.[17]

Sexual scientific debates about homosexuality in the 1900s and 1910s centered squarely on the experiences of male-born individuals. Although some sexologists included cases of female inversion in their major works on sexual pathology—usually as a parallel but reverse phenomenon to male "inversion"—they acknowledged that much remained unknown.[18] Even the prewar sex-reform and feminist movements largely ignored the question.[19] Not until Freud's 1920 "Psychogenesis of a Case of Homosexuality in a Woman" did the Viennese school begin to examine female inversion in any detail; I examine interwar theorizations of female homosexuality, including by female analysts such as Karen Horney and Helene Deutsch, in chapter 5.[20] In the period between the fin de siècle and the First World War, academic interest in questions of (male) same-sex desire was buoyed by a series of scandals that rocked Kaiser Wilhelm II's inner circle. The suicide of industrialist Friedrich Alfred Krupp and the so-called "Harden trials" featuring prominent military men turned homosexuality into a pressing legal, social, and scientific question for intellectuals across the political spectrum; scholars such as Hirschfeld were called to give evidence at trial (which he did, although not without damage to his reputation).[21] In this tense social environment, questions of nature versus nurture and body versus mind took on a new urgency. Following the publication of Freud's *Three Essays* in 1905, the suggestion by some Freudians that homosexuality might even be eliminated entirely via the "talking cure" was a provocation for many sexologists, and as this chapter argues, prompted a second key phase of encounter between these two emerging fields in the years before World War I.

Searching for Causes in Late-Nineteenth-Century Sexual Science

Modern sexual science was born out of the study of sexual pathologies, evidenced by the identical title of two pivotal nineteenth-century studies by Heinrich Kaan (1844) and Richard von Krafft-Ebing (1886): *Psychopathia sexualis*.[22] In the 1880s French psychiatrists such as Valentin Magnan, Jean-Martin Charcot, and Alfred Binet helped to shape sexual pathology into a discrete research field, joined by the likes of Italian criminal anthropologist Cesare Lombroso and sexologist Paolo Mantegazza. By the 1890s, German and Austrian experts—Krafft-Ebing foremost among them—took the lead in shaping the new specialization of "sex psychiatry."[23] The end of that century famously saw an "explosion" of discourses surrounding sexual deviance; a rich historiography now traces how the pathologizing implications of this shift were countered by the rise of more emancipatory discourses of sexual modernity, human rights, and sexual identity politics. A move away from older discourses of degeneration, criminality, and pathology was symptomatic of the wider intellectual current of sexual modernity that since the late nineteenth century had started to replace older imperatives of bourgeois Christian morality with an Enlightenment-inspired scientific and political liberalism.[24]

Most late-nineteenth-century sex researchers conceptually merged same-sex attraction with gender-atypical characteristics; it was not until the early twentieth century that researchers such as Hirschfeld and Havelock Ellis in Britain explicitly separated "homosexual" phenomena from ideas about "transvestism" or "Eonism" (although earlier scholars such as Moll and Krafft-Ebing had made preliminary moves in this direction).[25] The final decade before 1900 witnessed a spike in attempts by German-speaking physicians to uncover the roots of same-sex desire, building on several decades of scholarship on the phenomenon variously known as "uranism," "inversion," or "contrary sexual feeling," including the aforementioned political and legal writings of Kertbeny and Ulrichs and psychiatric studies by Westphal and Wilhelm Griesinger.[26] In the 1890s works by Moll (*Die conträre Sexualempfindung* [Contrary Sexual Instinct, 1891]), Hirschfeld (*Sappho und Sokrates* [Sappho and Socrates, 1896]), and psychiatrist Albert von Schrenck-Notzing (*Die Suggestionstherapie bei den krankhaften Erscheinungen des Geschlechtssinnes, mit besonderer Berücksichtigung der conträren Sexualempfindung*, 1892, translated into English in 1895 as *Therapeutic Suggestion in Psychopathia Sexualis (Pathological Manifestations of the Sexual Sense): With Especial Reference to Contrary Sexual Instinct*) were joined by the first volume of Hirschfeld's *Jahrbuch* (1899). In the first years of the new century, this literature expanded to encompass Hirschfeld's cultural-anthropological tour of Germany's metropolitan homosexual milieu in *Berlins drittes Geschlecht* (Berlin's Third Sex, 1904) and a growing number of literary and autobiographical accounts.[27] Works associated with the growing "masculinist" branch of fin de siècle homosexual activism that took shape around activists such as Adolf Brand and Benedict Friedlaender were also an important part of this wider German homoerotic and sexual-scientific literature; I briefly discuss some of these below. In addition, scholars from across Europe contributed in fields ranging from medicine to literature and philosophy, including Ellis and John Addington Symonds (*Sexual Inver-*

sion, 1897) and Edward Carpenter (*The Intermediate Sex,* 1908) in Britain, French scholars Julien Chevalier and Marc André Raffalovich, and Russian syphilologist Benjamin Tarnowsky.[28] By the first decade of the new century, studies of the "perversions" may no longer have constituted the entire tree of sexological inquiry, but they remained one of its biggest branches. Indeed, just as the previous chapter charted an increasing focus on "normal" (hetero)sexuality in the years around 1900, we might view the renewed attention to questions of homosexuality and perversion during this period as part and parcel of this phenomenon, with the "normal" always in dynamic tension with the possibility for deviation.

A central question in these fin de siècle discussions was whether inversion was inborn or acquired. And although many sexologists and psychiatrists in the final decades of the nineteenth century considered congenital explanations for sex-gender inversion, sometimes linking these to ideas about hereditary degeneration, the notion that homosexuality could be acquired via external influences was far from a Freudian innovation. Psychiatric researchers had long inquired into the immoral or negative influence of environments such as prisons and boarding schools, and by the turn of the century, a number of prominent scholars—Krafft-Ebing, Ellis, and Moll among them—were starting to preempt the psychoanalytic position that homosexuality might only be fully explained with reference to nurture as well as nature. This aligned with the increasingly psychologized priorities of an era of sexual modernity, with mental disorders increasingly viewed as the cause, rather than the result, of "unnatural" acts, and sexual behaviors viewed as complex entanglements of body and mind.[29] Well before Freud's *Three Essays*, scholars working in the asylums and clinics of the late nineteenth century had begun to question older distinctions between the normal and the abnormal, the healthy and the perverse.[30]

In the final decades of the nineteenth century, degeneration had also emerged as a conveniently flexible framework of explanation, for both congenital and acquired disorders.[31] If reproductive heterosexuality was the end result of evolutionary progress, sexual disorders provided examples of natural processes moving "backward," as Krafft-Ebing explained: "every anomaly of the psychosexual constitution may be clinically viewed as a sign of functional degeneration."[32] Describing a form of hereditary morbidity that passed from one generation to the next, this theory was articulated most thoroughly by French physician Bénédict-Augustin Morel. Far from being shrouded in an aura of intellectual regression, degeneration was embraced by many late-nineteenth-century scientists as a cutting-edge response to the latest Darwinist thought.[33] As we have seen, however, in the years surrounding the fin de siècle many scholars began to distance themselves from degeneration-based explanations, including Krafft-Ebing, who came by the end of his career to view homosexuality as a variation rather than a product of degeneration; shortly before his death he even signed a WhK petition seeking to abolish Paragraph 175, and supplied a handwritten letter of support that Hirschfeld published in his *Jahrbuch* in 1902.[34] Ideas of hereditary degeneration continued to haunt sexual scientific discourses for many years beyond that point, however, with researchers frequently looking to their patients' family histories for signs of "hereditary strain" such as alcoholism, mental illness, or high suicide rates. Freud, too, distinguished between "congenital" and "degenerate" forms of inversion, noting that while degeneration arguments had become "fashionable," they should only be assumed where there is considerable impairment or a severe deviation from the norm. Like most fin de siècle sexologists, including Hirschfeld, Freud accepted degeneration as a possible factor under the conditions of "civilized" modernity, but rejected its applicability to the majority of inverts. Speaking against degeneration theories, he noted, was the fact that some of the most prominent men in history were homosexuals, a point Hirschfeld was also fond of making.[35]

Krafft-Ebing's influential account of "contrary sexual feeling" considered both acquired and inborn contrary sexual feeling in men and women, and identified a series of subcategories for each. He distinguished between those for whom "perversion" was a permanent constitutional disorder, and the temporary immoral behaviors or "perversity" of "normal" individuals. Noting the scarcity of scientific literature on female inversion (which he attributed partly to German laws—which criminalized only male homosexuality—while noting that his country of work, Austria, did criminalize "intercourse-like" acts between women[36]), over successive editions of *Psychopathia Sexualis* Krafft-Ebing fine-tuned his classifications to posit inversion as one of the four main perversions alongside sadism, masochism, and fetishism. He divided "inborn" contrary sexual feeling into "psychosexual hermaphrodisia" (broadly corresponding to a bisexual object-choice), "homosexuality" (an exclusive desire for one's own sex), "effeminatio" and "viraginity" (categories closely aligned with what would today be termed trans identifications), and finally "androgyny" (in women) and "gynandry" (in men), in which the individual's physical form begins to correspond to their "abnormal" sexual feeling; he also devised subcategories for "acquired" inversion.[37] Several years later, Ellis simplified Krafft-Ebing's schema, identifying only two main categories of inversion in men and women: he aligned "true," "active" or "congenital" inversion with cross-gendered characteristics—"masculine" women and "feminine" men—

and distinguished these from a more passive variety of inversion that was "only slightly marked."[38]

The increasing entanglement of congenital and acquired arguments is evident from Moll's 1891 study of *Die konträre Sexualempfindung* (Contrary Sexual Feeling). In this work, with its rich historical and anthropological examples that set a precedent for later studies by Hirschfeld and others, Moll argues that even in "acquired" cases one finds examples of perverse ideas traceable back into childhood, while even among "pronounced urnings" one frequently finds evidence of at least temporary attraction to the opposite sex. "Degeneration" arguments are featured—Moll argues that all cases of contrary sexual instinct have in common a "neuro- and psychopathic strain"—but are also put into perspective, as he notes that there is no medical agreement on the precise content of this "strain."[39] Significantly, for Moll, contrary sexual feeling was separated from the normal not by any "unbridgeable chasm," but rather by "numerous *intermediary forms*"—a position that foreshadowed both Hirschfeld's later work on "sexual intermediaries" and Freud's emphasis on the "polymorphous perversity" of infancy.[40] Moll continued to develop his theory of inversion in his 1897 *Libido Sexualis*, where he clarified that, as with hereditary conditions such as muscular atrophy, it is the *predisposition* (*Anlage*) to inversion that is inborn, but that illness does not manifest until well after birth. Consequently, environmental influences were crucial in explaining why a perversion manifests at a particular point in time, and suitably timed prevention strategies might nip it in the bud altogether, including protecting the individual from dubious reading materials that might endanger the blossoming of "normal" sexuality.[41]

Others placed an even stronger emphasis on acquired factors. Russian physician Benjamin Tarnowsky described how school pupils can acquire homosexuality under the influence of older students whom they wish to impress: "The acquired active pederast becomes completely impotent with respect to women."[42] Berlin dermatologist and sexologist Iwan Bloch, meanwhile, whose works were starting to enjoy a wide readership among the general public as well as medical colleagues, attributed most cases of same-sex love to "external, occasional factors" such as a disagreeable marriage or fear of venereal disease; he also went further than Moll and Krafft-Ebing in insisting that "an originary predisposition . . . is very improbable, or in any case most rare."[43] Bloch was particularly concerned about masturbation, arguing in his major study *Das Sexualleben unserer Zeit in seinen Beziehungen zur modernen Kultur* (1907, *Sexual Life of Our Time*) that onanism blunts normal sensibility such that increasingly strong sexual stimulation is required—leaving an individual vulnerable to homosexual advances.[44] He did not dismiss congenital arguments outright, though, agreeing with Krafft-Ebing, Ellis, and others that effeminate male homosexuals might also display physical symptoms such as greater fat storage or a weaker musculature.[45] Even more than Moll, Bloch engaged with a rich range of anthropological and cultural sources, from the ancient Greeks to Oscar Wilde—an aspect of his work that recent scholarship has begun to explore for the way it expands our understanding of early sexual science.[46] Bloch linked his ideas on acquired homosexuality to "scientifically dignified" research on universal (physical) bisexuality by physician Wilhelm Fliess and philosopher Otto Weininger, to Hirschfeld's research on sexual intermediacy, and to the "undifferentiated" stages of puberty emphasized by Moll and Dessoir.[47] He concluded that, while same-sex behaviors remained a "riddle" (*Rätsel*) in a cultural and evolutionary sense, they could not be simply designated pathological or degenerate, and over time he came to agree with the WhK that same-sex activity should be free of legal censure (largely, argues one historian, due to Hirschfeld's influence).[48] Although hardly a vocal advocate of Germany's "third sex," we might speculate that this Jewish dermatologist-sexologist's culturally relativist, antihereditary (and thus antidegeneration) arguments were also a response to the kinds of biological determinist discourses within German psychiatry and criminology that persistently linked sexual perversion, pathology, degeneracy, and crime to ideas of Jewish difference. As Sander Gilman convincingly argues, such factors were critical in shaping Freud's account of human sexuality, and undoubtedly played a role in the work of other Jewish sex researchers of this period as well.[49]

Two further notable interlocutors in these fin de siècle discussions were Hirschfeld, who followed up on his earlier works with a mammoth 1,000-page-plus study *Die Homosexualität des Mannes und des Weibes* (The Homosexuality of Men and Women) in 1914, which surveyed wide-ranging medical, anthropological, and sociological themes, and German psychiatrist and criminologist Paul Näcke, who died in 1913. Both were strong proponents of congenital arguments.[50] Fin de siècle sexologists were thus deeply divided on the question of how best to explain homosexuality well before the Freudians entered the scene, although most were convinced that both nature and environment had a role to play. Consequently, they also took diverse approaches to treatment and prevention.

Hypnosis, Castration, and Hormones: Clinical Approaches to Homosexuality before Freud

For those convinced that homosexuality was, at least sometimes, a product of environmental influences, hypnotic suggestion was a popular treatment option in the late nineteenth century. In acquired cases, Krafft-Ebing deemed psychotherapy most useful in combating harmful influences, removing sexual neuroses, and promoting heterosexual feelings. He advocated inducing in the patient a deep hypnosis and making targeted suggestions to them during this state, a method popularized by Charcot in his treatment of hysterics.[51] This proto-psychotherapeutic method was particularly promoted in the German-speaking world by physician and parapsychologist Schrenck-Notzing from the 1880s, who considered it particularly well suited to treating homosexual patients, and reported on a number of allegedly successful treatments. Such methods formed, in turn, an important foundation for Freud and Josef Breuer's 1890s studies of hysteria, and point to the popularity of hypnosis as a treatment mode in the years before 1900.[52] Sexologists including Moll, Bloch, and Forel each showed enthusiasm for this method's potential to counteract, as Forel put it, the "evil" (*Übel*) of homosexuality. Bloch even considered hypnotic suggestion to be a possible solution in congenital cases, where he compared the suppression of homosexual tendencies to the broader social requirement that individuals control their urges: "human society must demand control of the instinct, just as it demands control of the sexual instinct in relation to the opposite sex."[53]

Leading German scholars of homosexuality were, however, becoming increasingly skeptical of hypnotic suggestion by the late 1890s. Moll advised caution where same-sex desire appeared to be inborn, arguing that only a deep hypnosis conducted at the right time, before the sexual instinct is too deeply rooted, might achieve real results; he feared that many supposed "cures" simply resulted in a form of "artificial coitus" reliant on homosexual fantasy.[54] Hirschfeld's assessment was even blunter:

> I remember one youth who was of such a feminine nature that apart from the actual genital apparatus there was not the least thing about him that was masculine. He allowed himself to be hypnotized for over a year by a South German colleague, without success. I personally know of only one homosexual who informed me that he felt himself freed of his same-sex urges by a course of suggestive treatment by the colleague [neurologist Alfred] Fuchs in Vienna.

As a firm advocate of congenital explanations, Hirschfeld added that "if external influences were capable of changing the direction of the drive, then the same-sex drive would have been extinguished long ago."[55] In his 1914 study, he stepped back even further from hypnotic therapies, concluding based on observations of posttherapy patients "*that supposedly cured homosexuals either had not been cured or were not homosexual.*"[56] Näcke agreed, considering the prognosis in cases of inborn homosexuality to be poor indeed: "*any therapy is certainly without prospect and I am yet to see a relevant case that stands up to stringent scientific critique.*" Despite pointing to the heteronormative assumptions underlying such treatments ("Would it not sound absurd were one to try in the same fashion to transform a hetero- into a homosexual?"), Näcke preempts later psychoanalytic approaches in expressing hope that, at least in bisexuals, a remaining heterosexual component might be strengthened by psychotherapeutic means.[57] Such arguments also underlay the emphasis on childhood prevention in many sexological and psychiatric works of this era, which advocated discouraging gender-atypical "affectations," masturbation, and access to sexually explicit literature, combined with improved nutrition, physical exercise, and appropriate sex education, to reduce the likelihood of same-sex behaviors becoming dominant.[58]

The question of homosexual therapy raised important questions concerning sexologists' ethical and medical duty toward their patients. When was intervention desirable, and when might it have harmful effects? What if the "urnings" in question were happily in love, or suffering from nervous conditions, or did not consider themselves ill? Should doctors encourage marriage and reproduction, and if so, how did this align with their duty to society? Most agreed that the duty to the patient was foremost: physicians were required by oath to respond to a distressed patient's wish for treatment, even if they saw the primary cause of their distress as social or familial rejection.[59] But they also had a duty to avoid causing their patients further distress: "Actually, first of all we must ask ourselves whether one should intervene therapeutically against contrary sexual feeling in the first place, and whether its elimination does not in fact do more harm to the individual or society."[60] Under the influence of Darwinian arguments, sexologists were also starting to consider their eugenic responsibilities to society at large, arguing that it was their duty to prevent seemingly "cured" urnings from passing on their nervous disposition to the next generation. Moll floated the possibility that homosexuality was a form of natural evolutionary "self-correction"; Hirschfeld argued along similar lines in explaining why homosexuals should not marry; Forel echoed Ulrichs's much earlier suggestion that urnings might be best served by being permitted to marry one another, a "socially harmless" practice that would give them some peace.[61]

In the face of such uncertainties, more clinically minded sexologists offered pragmatic advice. Hirschfeld, in particular, emphasized practical coping strategies as part of his "adaptation" or "assimilation therapy," arguing that doctors have a duty to reassure their patients that homosexuality is neither a vice nor a sin ("not a misfortune in itself, but rather made so by . . . unjust prejudice"), and to offer tips on how to steer clear of blackmailers and the law.[62] Although earlier researchers had at times encouraged intercourse with prostitutes, this was now a less popular option. "To seriously believe that a homosexual can transform into a heterosexual through forced sexual intercourse with a female person betrays a certain naivete," argued Moll. Hirschfeld agreed (a rare occurrence in their tense professional relationship) that this was just as distasteful as suggesting that a "normal-feeling man" have sex with a man.[63] In light of the legal situation, where same-sex behaviors could land men in jail, as well as the dangers of venereal disease, some sexologists also discussed the pros and cons of abstinence, suggesting that this could also be supported by medical means, including bromine or water treatments. They acknowledged, though, the high physical and mental cost to the patient, and Hirschfeld, who had collected the largest amount of quantitative data on homosexual practices, declared lifelong abstinence among the gay male population to be highly unusual, practiced by as few as 2 percent of individuals.[64]

Such protestations notwithstanding, Hirschfeld was also willing to contemplate more interventionist measures, such as surgical castration. He wavered on this issue, not least due to his conviction that the seat of the sexual instinct lay in the brain rather than the genitals ("if you want surgically to eliminate the offending organ, you will have to remove the brain")—and he was understandably wary of those who advocated excising homosexuality via lobotomy, noting that several attempts had already occurred. The psychical center of homosexuality should be discovered only, he insisted, when "through the correct analysis of homosexuals people have been convinced about the superfluous nature of such operations."[65] On the other hand, he favored castration for adult men who sexually assaulted children, and agreed with Näcke that castration could lessen the intensity of the sexual instinct, even if it could not magically change an individual's orientation.[66] His conflicted position on whether homosexuality represented a curable condition was evident in his encouragement of Sadger's psychoanalytic therapies, and also characterized his later support for new hormone therapies, discussed in chapter 4. Indeed, as early as 1912 Hirschfeld was enthusiastically foreshadowing the kinds of cross-gendered organ-transplant experiment that Viennese endocrinologist Eugen Steinach and his team would soon bring to international attention, and pondering the applications of such experiments for homosexual patients. For homosexual men, he envisaged, this might involve transplanting "normalsexual" testicular substances; equally, "it seems reasonable that supplying normal-female sexual hormones in the form of ovarian substance to the body of a homosexual woman could stimulate in her a metabolic change . . . and thereby influence her sexual inclinations."[67] In general, Hirschfeld advocated that doctors be guided by their homosexual patients' own assessment of how their distress might best be alleviated; at times, however, this pragmatism produced contradictions between his theoretical positions, clinical methods, and political activism.

Others were similarly enthusiastic about new hormone-based methods. A 1914 editorial in Hirschfeld's *Jahrbuch* articulated the hope that these might soon solve the "age-old mystery" of this condition; Bloch even speculated that they might deliver a "new theory" of homosexuality, the sexual chemistry of which was "still completely opaque." Accordingly, the *Jahrbuch* editors called on "*all homosexual men and women*" to contact the WhK to undergo "painless and safe" blood testing in the name of science.[68] On the other hand, blood transfusions, a topic discussed many years earlier by Ulrichs (who in the 1860s had fielded an unusual request from an American medical student for a transfusion in order, he hoped, to be temporarily transformed into an urning for research purposes), had gone out of fashion.[69] These examples point to the rapidly shifting scientific foundations of pre–World War I research on homosexuality, while pointing to the ways in which the choices of individual patients and their doctors were framed by social and legal concerns, from a fear of isolation to the threat of a jail term.

Beyond the immediate circles of medicalized sex research, questions of hereditary versus acquired inversion, and the relationship between same-sex desire and a "masculine" or "feminine" gender identity, were also being debated by authors, cultural critics, members of the popular Wilhelmine-era "life reform" movements, and in particular, representatives of the culturally oriented "masculinist" groups of German fin de siècle homosexual activism.[70] Robert Tobin characterizes two prominent strands of German research on homosexuality in this era: first, a "Greek" or "Hellenic" model—universalizing, masculinist, oriented toward classical Greek culture and intertwined with conservative and at times openly anti-Semitic thought—and second, a "Jewish model": minoritizing, medicalized, invested in notions of gender inversion, and linked to progressive, emancipatory politics.[71] In this book my focus is primarily on the latter, foregrounding discussions between mostly medically trained sexologists and psychoanalysts, many of them themselves Jewish, and the ways in which these played out via medical journals, monographs, and professional societies. It is important to emphasize, however, that these discussions took place within a broader cultural context in which ideas about the origins and treatment of homosexuality, its connection to the latest hormone research, and indeed, the broader findings of the new Freudian school, were also being taken up in very different ways.

Adolf Brand and Benedict Friedlaender, cofounders of the homoerotic association *Gemeinschaft der Eigenen* (Community of the Autonomous/Self-Owned), which seceded from the WhK following heated debates during its first decade, were two of the key proponents of the "Greek" school of masculinist homosexual activism and cultural production. Through its magazine *Der Eigene* (The Autonomous/The Self-Owned), the first homosexual emancipation periodical (it was founded in 1896, a year before the establishment of the WhK), this group promoted a more "virile," gender-normative alternative ideal to the inversion-oriented theories of Hirschfeld or, before him, Ulrichs, who had famously described "Uranians" as possessing a "female soul in a male body."[72] Although Bloch dismissed the magazine as "purely popular and belletristic," it was more nuanced than this; starting life "as a literary publication with a vaguely anarchist slant," as one historian describes it, it soon became one of the most prominent German vehicles of what it termed "the love of friends" or "manly culture."[73] The *Gemeinschaft der Eigenen* was also an organization, however, from which "shrill anti-Semitic tones" emanated. This was particularly the case during the 1920s, when *Der Eigene* published a vicious caricature of Hirschfeld, and when Ernst Röhm, who in the early 1930s became Commander of the SA, the Nazi Party's paramilitary wing, before becoming embroiled in scandal, was not far from its inner circle.[74] Interested in the newest hormone research only to the extent that it might help to explain more "virile" brands of male homosexuality, representatives of the masculinist movement such as the zoologist Friedlaender pulled no punches in describing how Hirschfeld's theory turned homosexuals into "psychological freaks of nature" and "pitiable half-women." Arguing that inversion-based arguments were conducive to gaining neither legal equality nor social respect, Friedlaender was nonetheless a card-carrying member of the WhK, and published in Hirschfeld's *Jahrbuch* on several occasions. Another member of these circles, Hans Blüher, best known for his work on the *Wandervogel* youth movement and for popularizing Friedlaender's theory of "physiological friendship" between men, similarly rejected Hirschfeld's category of the "inverted effeminate," although he echoed the Berlin sexologist's emphasis on congenital arguments, arguing that the homosexual disposition was inborn.[75]

The masculinists objected to what they saw as a persistent medicalization of homosexuality as a pathological and effeminate aberration, and were more interested in explaining homosexuality in cultural and historical terms. In typically nationalist and gendered rhetoric, Blüher insisted that, while he had observed many "doubtless healthy cases of inversion" while studying the German youth movement, these were distinct from the racially inferior and "inbred" decadents of ancient Rome, who clearly belonged to the "pathological" category of the feminine male homosexual. Instead, he and others in this movement idolized the upstanding, muscular esthetic of the ancient Greeks. Unwilling to condone Blüher's anti-inversion stance, Hirschfeld edited out the last two pages of his essay "Three Fundamental Forms of Homosexuality" before publishing it in his *Jahrbuch* in 1913.[76] Meanwhile, the then twenty-three-year-old Blüher had drawn Freud's attention by submitting an article to the new psychoanalytic journal *Imago* in 1912/13. In particular, the masculinists appreciated Freud's writings on sublimation, which they used to support a specific cultural role for homosexuals in society. In private correspondence, Freud generously commented to Blüher that "what I have read in your work is much cleverer (*gescheiter*) than most of the homosexual literature and more correct than most of the medical literature"—a not-so-subtle critique of Hirschfeld and the WhK. He later made this criticism explicit, noting that "the problem of homosexuality may not yet be settled . . . but your work represents a major advance beyond that of the W. H. Komité"; nonetheless, Freud had also made regular donations to the Austrian WhK subgroup following its foundation in late 1906.[77] Despite Freud's own Jewishness and medicalizing stance, his appreciative response to Blüher makes sense when one considers that Blüher saw in Freud's theories of universal bisexuality and the sexual object the key to same-sex desire, as well as to the specific appeal of masculine homoeroticism.

The Freudian Intervention

While there were thus important divisions within Wilhelmine-era sex research and homosexual activism that belie any generalizing statements, Freud's *Three Essays* and the interventions of analysts within his inner circle prompted many sexologists to revisit their existing theories of homosexuality, and by extension, their clinical and therapeutic practices. Freud placed the question of inversion front and center in his 1905 work, particularly in his first essay on the sexual aberrations. Even in his earlier writings on hysteria he had started to frame homosexuality as a symptom of developmental inhibition rather than hereditary or degenerative pathology ("When, therefore, any one has *become* a gross and manifest pervert, it would be more correct to say that he has *remained* one, for he exhibits a certain stage of *inhibited development*"[78]), but he did not disregard congenital factors altogether.

Rather, he argued—as sexologists such as Krafft-Ebing and Moll had been doing for some time—that the "choice between 'innate' and 'acquired' is not an exclusive one."[79] Crucially, he also moved discussions of homosexuality toward ideas of the "sexual object" (*Sexualobjekt*), the *individual* from whom the sexual attraction proceeds, as opposed to the "sexual aim" (*Sexualziel*), the *activities* toward which the sexual instinct is directed. Focusing on the object of attraction led Freud to bracket inversion off from other perversions of the "normal" sexual aim (fetishism, scopophilia, sadism, masochism), which all remained conceptually linked to heterosexuality.[80] In this emphasis, his position was more in line with the masculinist wing of the homosexual rights movement, for it led Freud to distance his theory of same-sex desire from earlier studies of "inversion" that had emphasized gender-atypical characteristics. Freud did, however, retain the "inversion" label for discussing same-sex behaviors, and he also roughly followed the classifications of earlier sex researchers by dividing this into, first, individuals who are "absolutely" or exclusively inverted.[81] A second category he termed "amphigenously inverted" or, following Krafft-Ebing, "psychosexually hermaphroditic," where the object of attraction might belong to either sex. A third group of individuals were only "occasionally" inverted, often due to extenuating circumstances such as imprisonment or war.[82]

A back and forth between congenital and acquired arguments continues throughout *Three Essays*. As Hirschfeld later noted with approval, Freud's object-oriented explanation did not entirely expunge ideas of congenital inversion.[83] Although Freud restricted innate homosexuality to "the first, most extreme class of inverts," he refused to consider this group completely distinct from the other categories. Instead, he argued that across all groups, one could frequently identify an early childhood experience that left a determining sexual impression, even if this had been subsequently repressed. It was more productive, he suggested, to ask why many people subjected to such influences did *not* become inverted (a position not far from Dessoir and Moll's earlier discussions of the "undifferentiated" stage of childhood, which he cites).[84] Acquired explanations are foregrounded when Freud cites research suggesting that inversion might be reversed by hypnotic suggestion, or when, in his third essay on the transformations of puberty, he describes same-sex education, the presence of manservants, or the early loss of a parent as compounding factors. Elsewhere, though, he gestures toward hereditary causes, noting the frequency of venereal disease in the extended families of neurotic individuals, and concluding that an "abnormal" sexual constitution may often be a "last echo" of the patient's "syphilitic heritage."[85] In short, for Freud the sexual constitution was not decisive in determining an individual's sexual desires; rather, the same constitution could lead to quite different results depending on environmental factors—a position that aligned quite closely with that of many of his sexological predecessors. But he also argued that efforts to determine precise combinations of congenital and acquired factors missed the point—the true nature of inversion must proceed from an understanding of the psychic mechanisms developed in early childhood.[86]

Freud developed this aspect of his theory of homosexuality, and of the perversions more broadly, over the course of subsequent editions of *Three Essays*. Early Oedipal arguments make an appearance in additions to the second edition in 1910, which he expanded in 1915 and again in 1920 via a lengthy footnote. Here Freud noted that factors working against the development of same-sex desires could include, in male patients, fond recollections of maternal affection and a competitive relation with the father, or in female patients, a hostile relation to their own sex.[87] Despite a disclaimer that psychoanalysis is still a long way from establishing a complete homosexual etiology, Freud explained how an inadequately resolved Oedipal conflict in the male invert, involving a period of intense early fixation on and (over)identification with the mother, can result in narcissistically seeking out sexual objects who resemble himself. While not immune to sexual stimulation by women, inverts develop psychic patterns whereby the resulting excitation is transposed onto a masculine object. Freud continued to add to this brief explanation over the next two decades, drawing on his 1909 case of "Little Hans" and 1910 study of the artist da Vinci to expand his discussion of castration anxiety (stimulated by the sight of female genitals); a corresponding shift in sexual object from the mother to a "woman with a phallus"; a "negative" Oedipus complex, in which the child identifies with the opposite-sex parent; the transformation of anger toward same-sex siblings into love by way of reaction formation; and a prolonged fixation on the anal zone.[88] Although he mentions girls' development in passing, it was not, as already noted, until his 1920 "Psychogenesis of a Case of Homosexuality in a Woman" that Freud first attempted a detailed explanation of female inversion.[89]

Throughout his career, Freud's views on homosexuality remained complex. Ultimately, he concluded that it was neither a "vice" nor an "illness," but merely "a variation of the sexual function produced by a certain arrest of sexual development."[90] Writing to Ernest Jones in 1921, Freud also affirmed the right of homosexuals to themselves become psychoanalysts.[91] His insistence that homosexuality represented a variant of universal Oedipal processes diverged from the congenital theories popularized by Hirschfeld and the WhK, and from the emphasis on hereditary degeneration in many earlier psychiatric and sexological studies. Sexological theories, Freud added, were inevitably skewed toward the pathological by the clinical contexts in which most cases were observed (although as we will see below, sexologists leveled similar criticisms against the Freudians due to their focus on "neurotic" cases).[92] Arguing for a less stringent divide between the normal and the pathological, Freud insisted that inversion was part of a spectrum of human sexual variation: "Psycho-analytic research is most decidedly opposed to any attempt at separating off homosexuals from the rest of mankind as a group of a special character."[93]

This spectrum model of normality and pathology, which viewed aberrations as inhibitions of normal development rather than fundamentally distinct conditions fixed to particular bodies, aligned with Freud's insistence on the original bisexuality and "polymorphous perversity" of infancy. As such, it could be used to explain not only homosexuality, but a wide range of other so-called perversions and neuroses. And although earlier researchers such as Bloch had also emphasized original bisexuality in discussing inversion, Freud went further than most in suggesting that the mechanisms of heterosexuality are equally in need of explanation:

> [F]rom the point of view of psycho-analysis the exclusive sexual interest felt by men for women is also a problem that needs elucidating and is not a self-evident fact based upon an attraction that is ultimately of a chemical nature. A person's final sexual attitude is not decided until after puberty and is the result of a number of factors, not all of which are yet known; some are of a constitutional nature but others are accidental.[94]

Psychoanalysis, according to Freud, demonstrates that all human beings are capable of making a homosexual object choice, and in fact have already done so in their unconscious.[95] In support of this spectrum model, Freud pointed to his Swiss colleague C. G. Jung's observation that "neurotic" and "normal" individuals contend with the same problems: "We no longer ask whether the patient has a father or mother complex, or unconscious incest fantasies which tie him to his parents, for we know today that everybody has them."[96] Normal and neurotic patients, Freud agreed, were not sharply distinguishable; the main difference was that "the healthy have learned how to deal with these complexes."[97] By moving away from congenital and degeneration models and focusing instead on universal psychological processes, psychoanalysts emphasized the potential for any individual, regardless of biological disposition, to diverge from the expectations of "normal" heterosexual development.

While Freud thus questioned heterosexual norms with a directness unusual in the contemporary literature, his spectrum model was not actually radically different from that of other writers working within the context of fin de siècle sexual modernity. As we have seen, Krafft-Ebing, Moll, Bloch, and Hirschfeld also strongly emphasized psychological explanations of homosexuality, and had similarly refocused their explanations of the sexual instinct away from reproduction and toward ideas of pleasure (the older Forel, in contrast, took a more conservative line, rejecting as "extreme" the Freudian premise that the perversions emerge from a universally shared predisposition, and insisting that the "normal" must always be oriented toward the reproduction of the species[98]). Focusing on connections between Krafft-Ebing and Freud, historians Elizabeth Stephens and Peter Cryle have shown that both scholars deployed a decidedly relational understanding of "normal" and "perverse" sexuality, viewing abnormality as a question of degree rather than kind: "Scxual abnormalities, according to Krafft-Ebing, were not opposed to but rather intensifications of normal forms of sexuality."[99] Harry Oosterhuis extends the comparison to Moll,[100] who had argued that "perverse" sentiments may well make an appearance in the early lives of individuals whose subsequent sexual development is "normal."[101] Ellis agreed that, rather than being fundamentally pathological, the perversions were best understood as mere "exaggerations of instincts and emotions that are germinal in normal human beings."[102] Scholars remain divided on the extent to which Freud's thinking on these issues represented a continuity or break with that of his predecessors; what is clear is that moves to relativize ideas of the normal and pathological were also at work in the psychiatric profession more broadly, with historians showing that sharp distinctions between the "insane" and the "normal" gave way to a far less diametrical framework during these decades.[103]

Freud's framing of homosexuality as a symptom of developmental inhibitions thus built on, as much as it broke with, earlier sexological deliberations regarding "normal" and "abnormal" sexuality, and congenital and acquired behaviors. It did so, however, in a way that underlined psychoanalysis's universalizing claims to be a mode of inquiry that potentially applied to all human beings: "[Normal sexuality] had become a focus for psychoanalytic research not because there were so many normal people hitherto overlooked by medical research, but because there were so few."[104] As Gilman points out in a sophisticated reading of psychoanalysis's self-positioning, Freud's universalizing approach to mental illness can also be considered a response to anti-Semitic ostracization. "His desire was to move the argument about the madness of the Jews away from the question of race and to universalize it," which he did by emphasizing the "ubiquitous presence of human sexuality—in all of its manifestations."[105] Freud's investigation of sexual aberrations in *Three Essays* concludes in a somewhat ambiguous fashion, with the "unsatisfactory" finding that "far too little remains known of the biological processes constituting the essence of sexuality to be able to construct a theory adequate to the understanding alike of normal and of pathological conditions."[106] This uncertainty foreshadowed the increasing grappling by sexologists in the 1910s and 1920s with the biological influence of hormones. It was not, however, until his 1920 revisions to *Three Essays* that Freud addressed this question in any detail; I take up these revisions in chapter 4. Such uncertainties notwithstanding, Freud affirmed the contribution that psychoanalysis could make to understanding homosexuality, and forcibly emphasized the independence of this field from biological research.[107]

Psychoanalyzing Homosexuality after Freud[108]

Freud's arguments laid the groundwork for further analytic studies in subsequent years, for if homosexuality was now understood as a developmental inhibition rather than fundamentally pathological, it could also be potentially reversed through the "talking cure." As the Budapest representative for the WhK and a member of the Wednesday group and later the Vienna Psychoanalytic Society, Sándor Ferenczi had keenly followed Freud's early interest in the relationship between homosexuality and paranoia, and in 1914 he articulated two of his own distinct pathological symptom complexes. "Subject homoeroticism" (*Subject-Homoërotik*) described a feminine, passive brand of invert whose "developmental anomaly" was probably congenital (and for whom psychoanalysis was thus unlikely to offer a cure), while "object homoeroticism" (*Objekt-Homoërotik*) described a more common form of masculine, active homosexual attracted to younger or more feminine men. Men in the latter category, Ferenczi suggested, may sometimes be amenable to a version of psychoanalytic therapy aimed at replacing homosexual attraction with bisexuality.[109] At around the time of his break with Freud, Viennese analyst Wilhelm Stekel also drew on ideas of universal bisexuality to describe the "masked" forms that repressed homosexuality might take, such as an attraction to androgynous-looking members of the opposite sex: "all human beings who depart from a specifically male or female line can in this sense have an erotic appeal."[110] Unusually within psychoanalytic circles at this period, he also applied his arguments to women, suggesting that frustrated homosexual desires could explain the sexually precocious behaviors of female prostitutes and nymphomaniacs. In other respects, however, Stekel was more conservative than his analytic peers, harking back to older theories of inversion that conflated cross-gendered behaviors with same-sex desires, and describing "transvestism" as merely an expression of repressed homosexuality (an argument to which I return in chapter 6).[111]

The most tenacious attempts to pursue a psychoanalytic "cure" for homosexuality, understood as a lasting return to heterosexuality, were undertaken in these years by Sadger. Sadger's relationship to Freud was ambivalent, but not overly antagonistic.[112] His ideas about homosexual etiology and treatment are among his most significant contributions to early psychoanalytic theory, and he first presented them at the inaugural International Psychoanalytic Congress in April 1908, in spite of Freud's protestations. They centered on the assumption that even the most masculine male invert has, at some point, experienced a period of heterosexual attraction that therapy might uncover: "behind the most masculine sexual ideals of any urning one can, without exception, find proof of female *Ur*-lovers."[113] Identifying narcissism as a crucial factor, Sadger argued that in heterosexuals and homosexuals alike, a prepubertal narcissistic episode marks an interim stage in the transition from infantile autoeroticism to an external sexual object; during this stage, an individual seeks out sexual objects that align with his own image.[114] This stage of "secondary autoeroticism" occurs when the primacy of the genitals has already been established, but not yet to the exclusion of the earlier erogenous zones such as the mouth and anus. Sadger arrived at this extension of Freud's account of child sexual development while analyzing a thirty-two-year-old Danish count, whose "multiple perversions" included "completely flagrant" anal eroticism, fantasies of self-coitus and self-flagellation, and a penchant for testicle-stroking and voyeurism.[115] Like Freud, he did not deny the relevance of congenital factors in some cases, and gestured toward degeneration arguments by using terms such as "strain" (*Belastung*) or "pathological brain composition." In his enthusiasm, though, Sadger claimed that even hereditary considerations did not necessarily preclude a successful therapeutic outcome, as long as the patient honestly desired it.[116]

Through normalizing attempts to recover patients' underlying heterosexual desires, Sadger described how, for example, he "cured" his patient "S.M." (the subject introduced at the beginning of this chapter) during four months of treatment, which brought the hidden feminine types behind the patient's masculine sexual ideals to consciousness, with the latter gradually losing their appeal until the patient was exclusively attracted to women.[117] Yet longer-term success remained elusive; Sadger was repeatedly frustrated by patients who "prematurely" broke off their analysis, and we can only speculate on his patients' own assessments of their encounters with this enthusiastic member of the new psychoanalytic profession.[118] In general, he approached his homosexual patients in a somewhat conflicted fashion, which may possibly have been for more personal reasons than the available sources reveal. Publicly, he supported the legal recognition of "sexual intermediaries" (even though this seemingly contradicted his push to convert patients to heterosexuality), but he was also sharply critical of the homosexual rights movement for using the "guise" of science in ways that might undermine therapeutic success. If individuals believed their condition was congenital—as the WhK was wont to argue—they were much more likely, in Sadger's view, to retrospectively adjust their memories to fit this theory, and he saw this as dealing a fatal blow to analytic intervention.[119] Other analysts raised similar concerns. "The theories of the Scientific-Humanitarian Committee are naturally tendentious deliria," lamented Freud in a letter to Ferenczi.[120] Ferenczi, too, criticized the widespread adoption of Hirschfeld's theory of sexual intermediacy by individuals happy to have found a scientific crutch for their politics.[121] Although sympathetic to efforts to decriminalize homosexuality, and well aware of the social and legal pressures that might cause patients to keep their sexual histories hidden, these early Freudians remained skeptical of the "scientific" basis on which groups such as the WhK were basing their claims.

Competing Methods: The Struggle for Clinical Authority

Whereas sexological investigations of same-sex desires prioritized etiological questions, psychoanalysts were more attuned to questions of therapy, and while practitioners in each of these fields were, as noted above, developing a less pathologizing approach to the sexual perversions than had characterized the work of many nineteenth-century scholars, divisions soon emerged around questions of treatment and method. Some sexologists, particularly in the first decade of the new century, were keen to explore the potential of analytic approaches in cases of inversion. Sadger reflected on Hirschfeld's "obvious amicability" in publishing his 1908 case in the *Jahrbuch*; Forel was similarly intrigued by psychoanalytic methods that could seemingly return patients to "normal" by bringing forth memories of influential childhood experiences.[122] Such researchers proceeded on the relatively nonjudgmental understanding, also characteristic of Krafft-Ebing's foundational work, that whatever might help patients was worthy of exploration. Others, however, developed a more defensive and even condemnatory approach.

Hirschfeld, for his part, again occupied a conflicted stance. On the one hand, as one of the most forceful proponents of the view that homosexuality, like other sexually "intermediary" forms, often had a congenital basis, he questioned the necessity of therapeutic intervention ("no medical, operative, diet, psychological or other methods are capable of destroying a condition and a drive which indissolubly attaches to one's individuality for the duration of one's life"), and linked this conviction of its immutability to arguments for extending homosexuals' legal rights.[123] This was exactly the kind of stance the psychoanalysts saw as sounding a death knell for clinical intercession. On the other hand, Hirschfeld lamented that his medical colleagues all too often failed to help homosexual patients rather than enlightening them about their condition. The suffering of such patients, he insisted, was largely social in its causes, and it was to this end that he had developed his pragmatic "adaptation" therapy. It was thus with obvious satisfaction that he cited a statement by Freud, published in a Viennese newspaper in 1905, that the homosexual does not belong in court, and should not be treated as a patient.[124] In particular, Hirschfeld lambasted analytic colleagues who were in the habit of publicly undermining the statements of homosexual patients; Sadger, for one, had written a series of articles on this theme.[125] Yet such defenses of homosexual rights and the immutability of this condition must be read against Hirschfeld's openness to exploring psychoanalytic attempts at a "cure," as well as his own later dabbling in hormonal and surgical interventions. These activities suggest a stance driven more by the distress of individual patients than a clear overriding scientific and political position.

Concern for patient well-being was also of central importance to colleagues such as Bloch, who even changed his political position on this basis. Whereas in 1902 he had argued that revoking Paragraph 175 would amount to an official sanctioning of homosexuality and promote the corruption of youth, by 1907 such arguments were overshadowed by humanitarian concerns for patients' mental health and a more nuanced account of their psychological trauma in the face of social discrimination, which he diagnosed as a peculiar type of "homosexual neurasthenia." Bloch also echoed the WhK's protests against the plague of blackmail and suicides resulting from Germany's criminal law, arguing that homosexuality should be acknowledged as a "typically biological phenomenon."[126]

Moll, on the other hand, joined the Freudians in disparaging "agitators" who "falsify the data of science" in pursuing congenital arguments (criticisms that clearly implicated Hirschfeld and the WhK), and he warned that parents, schoolmasters and physicians might be led astray for the sake of repealing Paragraph 175: "In the interest of truth, in the interest of the children endangered by these perversions, and in the interest of civilization, these misstatements must be contradicted."[127] Moll stopped short of agreeing with Freudian explanations of homosexuality ("The general etiology which [Freud] assumes to exist can from no point of view be regarded as sound"[128]). He also warned the reader to be "on his guard against numerous exaggerations" by members of that school.[129] But he did agree with them on several key points. Firstly, Moll echoed Freud's description of neurotic disease as a "summation" of factors, insisting that any given illness may have "a dozen causes or more."[130] He also aligned himself with both the psychoanalytic search for a cure and earlier psychiatric experiments with hypnotic suggestion when in 1908 he wrote that the (homo)sexual instinct might be "educated" into desirable channels. He advocated a psychotherapeutic approach he termed "associational therapy," aimed at "checking" perverse manifestations before they could flourish. His support for less congenitally driven explanations was, in turn, noted approvingly in psychoanalytic circles, including by Freud's early English translator Brill.[131]

At the level of theorizing homosexuality, then, a split was emerging less along disciplinary lines than between researchers committed to biologically determinist arguments, who viewed homosexuality as a naturally occurring sexual variation, and those convinced that same-sex behavior identifications could be acquired after birth, and could thus either be prevented or treated through appropriate medical intervention. Questions of congenital and acquired etiology thus continued to shape debates about homosexuality well into the new century, even as practical considerations and the needs of patients at times led practitioners to blur the lines between these positions.

In contrast, a much clearer divide between these two fields can be seen when it comes to assessing questions of method. Sexologists criticized psychoanalytic methods on two main grounds. First, they feared that analytic patients were overly vulnerable to suggestion and overinterpretation, which put into question psychoanalysts' claims to have truly "cured" homosexual patients. Second, they argued that psychoanalysts relied too heavily on just a few case studies of "neurotic" individuals in formulating universal theories of human sexuality. Concerns about the potential for analytic misinterpretation and suggestion were deemed especially problematic by the more empirically minded sexologists. Moll criticized Freudian patient histories as "illusions of memory," with their retrospective focus likely to lead some patients to mistakenly believe that they had only ever experienced same-sex inclinations. He also attacked psychoanalytic modes of interpretation for "arbitrarily" designating objects from patients' accounts as "symbolic representatives of the genital organs," or reading dreams "symbolically at will" (a practice that Moll presumably saw as quite removed from his own discussion of patients' dreams in several of his case studies).[132] Others agreed with him, arguing that while there may be some truth to Freudian interpretations of the symbolic, far too much is "exaggerated beyond measure and overestimated . . . in connection with the sexual," while "the subtle and slender clues which Freud frequently follows in interpreting dreams cannot fail sometimes to arouse doubt in his readers' minds."[133] Looking back on these discussions almost two decades later, Hirschfeld offered a somewhat more generous assessment:

> We can go along a good distance with Freud and his school on the subject of symbolisms, but not everywhere and not through thick and thin. . . . Because symbols are products of fantasy, this also gives unlimited room to the fantasy of the interpreter, and many analysts make of this the widest possible use.[134]

As this statement reveals, though, he continued to view Freudian interpretation as leaving rather too much space for the analyst's whims and fantasies.

The influence of the analyst also led sexologists to question the permanence of any alleged analytic "cures." For Moll, "the patient's confidence in his physician, and the fact that the treatment requires much time and patience, are two such powerful factors of suggestion, that provisionally it is necessary to regard it as possible that suggestion explains the whole matter."[135] Although Moll himself flirted briefly with analytic techniques, he later turned this experience into the basis of a damning critique: "*The importance of the factor of sexual experiences in the causation of disease has been greatly over-estimated by Freud.*"[136] For Hirschfeld, too, Sadger's "cure" of S.M. was, at best, a short-term product of suggestion, and at worst, of outright clinical intimidation (evident in the analyst's "vain attempt to convince the patient that at age four he had homosexual feelings for his father"[137]), while Forel singled out Stekel's accounts of "masked homosexuality" as exemplary of the kinds of "suggestive fashionable complaints" that do not stand up to rigorous scientific critique.[138] At times, the Swiss psychiatrist's critiques of analytic methods also took on decidedly anti-Semitic overtones, as Forel described a Freudian tendency

> to translate the products of great phantasies into reckless [*gewagte*] hypotheses, to dogmatize these hypotheses and then, through a labored, almost Talmudic exegesis, to support these through the construction of all sorts of sophistries [*Spitzfindigkeiten*] that reach into the extreme [. . .] so that one is gingerly led out of the territory of science and into that of sectarian theology.[139]

Such arguments point to solidifying methodological boundaries between these fields, and resonated with criticisms from the wider medical profession (which at times were similarly tinged with anti-Semitic skepticism). As one psychologist declared, "It can hardly astonish that most psychiatrists, neurologists and psychologists steer clear of [Freud's theory of dream interpretation] so long as he and his pupils produce interpretative stunts whose relation to true scientificity is as for a photograph in relation to the painting of a master."[140] For sexologists, meanwhile, such criticisms of the Freudian method had the benefit of implicitly lending weight to their own, more empirical methods as a more "scientific" and "objective" approach.

Sexologists' second major concern was that psychoanalysts relied too heavily on a handful of cases of "neurotic" individuals. Psychoanalytic theory might have the capacity to explain its own clinical histories, argued Moll, but those histories could not in turn substantiate the kinds of universalizing claims that the Freudians were trying to make.[141] Näcke protested that Sadger, in particular, had gone too far in claiming to have found the "philosopher's stone": "I would like to know *how many* urnings he, Stekel, Freud and others have seen outside of the consultation hours at all! It won't be many."[142] In contrast, sexologists saw their own emphasis on case studies of "healthy" individuals as better able to illuminate normal sexual development. Näcke cited *Jahrbuch* bibliographer Numa Praetorious—a gentlemen with extensive connections in the contemporary "third sex" community—who reported that he had not witnessed a single successful cure among any of his many hundreds of homosexual acquaintances.[143] Hirschfeld, meanwhile, boasted that he had gathered evidence of no less than 10,000 nonclinical cases of homosexuality. His research, which had examined same-sex behaviors among diverse occupational groups and social classes, from butchers to university students, had found that approximately 1.5 percent of the population was homosexual and a further 3–4 percent bisexual, and was cited approvingly by Freud in *Three Essays*.[144] In a piece penned with physician Ernst Burchard, Hirschfeld warned that because psychiatrists overwhelmingly see pathological cases, they are too willing to consider homosexuality in terms of disease, and to thus overlook the many "psychologically healthy homosexuals" leading "normal occupational and professional lives." These authors also critiqued the unconscious heterosexual bias of psychiatric researchers who seek to explain homosexuality without being able to "definitively ascertain *hetero*sexuality"—although in doing so, they unwittingly echoed Freud's own insistence that heterosexual development is equally in need of explanation.[145] In turn, Freud occasionally conceded the need for large-scale studies of "healthy" individuals to complement theoretical findings developed on the basis of cases such as "Little Hans" or "Dora." Nonetheless, he continued to justify the analysis of neurotic patients as an "irreplaceable investigative method" that offered unique insights into the links between symptoms, fantasies, and behaviors.[146]

Despite such methodological concerns, a number of sexologists saw value in adopting at least certain aspects of the Freudian technique when dealing with homosexual patients. "The cathartic process of yielding up and bringing to the surface suppressed elements of consciousness," wrote Ellis, "may not suffice to render the sexual impulse normal, [but] it certainly renders it less injurious, and at the same time restores the whole psychic life to some degree of harmonious equilibrium."[147] Hirschfeld's enthusiasm, already seen in his promotion of Sadger's work, was also evident from his aforementioned collaboration with Karl Abraham on the development of a "psychobiological (or sometimes 'psychoanalytic') questionnaire," which sought to inquire systematically and in-depth into a subject's personal particulars, family life, childhood, and current physical and psychological condition. Hirschfeld hoped that this format would make the insights and methods of the Freudian school more accessible to sexual science, being less vulnerable to "subjective untruths and objective falsehoods," and thus constitute "a usable foundation for the methodology of sexual-analytic interrogation."[148] Although this adjectival coinage suggests an impending merging of disciplinary perspectives, it largely failed to eventuate in the following years (as foreshadowed by Jung's criticisms of the questionnaire, discussed in chapter 1). Instead, even Hirschfeld, one of the more analytically aware sexologists of his generation, became ever more skeptical of Freudian innovations such as the Oedipus complex; in turn, Hirschfeld's early dabbles with Freudian theory came under fire. As with Moll's fin de siècle work on the child, this attack went beyond intellectual differences to assume a decidedly personalized form.

In the year that war broke out across Europe, Hirschfeld published the aforementioned study of homosexuality that is widely regarded as his magnum opus; in it, he declared that "the cases reported by Sadger in the *Jahrb. f. sex. Zwischst.* and in the *Zeitschrift f. Sexualwissenschaft* do not give the convincing impression of true and lasting cures."[149] He drew support from Stekel, now estranged from the Freudians; Stekel, having himself praised Hirschfeld's study as "indispensable for every sex researcher," observed that he had "never seen a complete cure of homosexuality through psychoanalysis."[150] A few months later, Sadger reviewed Hirschfeld's study in the *Internationale Zeitschrift für Psychoanalyse* (International Journal of Psychoanalysis) in the unkindest terms. Complaining that Hirschfeld had blatantly misrepresented Sadger's own psychoanalytic work with homosexual patients, Sadger suggests that the German sexologist had only feigned a genuine engagement with this new field, omitting "all that was unfavorable" from his book. Throwing himself into "every medical fashion that suits," where psychoanalytic findings become too "uncomfortable," argues Sadger, Hirschfeld

> attempts to understate or entirely suppress these, for example the fixation on the mother or the heterosexual archetypes of the homosexual lovers, and most particularly, our therapeutic successes, or when we revealed that even the "absolute" invert was originally attracted to the opposite sex, and that it is thus impossible that the same-sex orientation of the drive was "inborn."

Within six years, Hirschfeld's initial generosity in publishing Sadger's case—"yes, the same H., who otherwise literally oozes goodwill"—had been thoroughly negated, with any hint of a psychoanalytic cure "struck out, the successes concealed and pushed away," in the interests of buttressing Hirschfeld's own conviction that homosexuality is inborn.[151] Psychoanalytic achievements in the treatment of same-sex desire, Sadger perceptively concludes, "cannot suit H.," as the "whole house of cards of 'innateness' [*Angeborenheit*] . . . collapses into nothing."[152]

The ferocity of Sadger's review points, as had the earlier conflict between Freud and Moll, to a second significant moment of disciplinary boundary-drawing in the years between Freud's *Three Essays* and World War I; a heated splitting off from former collaborators and what had been genuine attempts at finding points of convergence, such as the psychobiological questionnaire. Underlying this growing split, alongside more theoretical and methodological concerns, was an underlying push for scientific legitimation: by downplaying sexological expertise, while claiming that psychoanalysis offered the only method that could reverse homosexual desire, Sadger attempted to use the homosexual question to draw clearer boundaries around his own solidifying field of expertise. For sexologists such as Hirschfeld, meanwhile, an acknowledgement that there may be some merit to Freudian techniques sat in tension with the way psychoanalytic ideas undermined ideas about the congenital immutability of homosexuality. Rather than engaging more deeply with psychoanalytic explanations in the years that followed, many sexologists found it preferable to turn their attention toward sketchy initial research into the "inner secretions," which they hoped—with some justification—might buttress their own scientific contributions.

The claim that homosexuality could be cured once and for all by a series of sessions on the couch remained for fin de siècle sexual scientists a speculative one, plagued by shaky interpretive techniques. Yet this reading of prewar homosexuality debates shows that the boundary between psychoanalysis and sexology in these years, although not without its tensions, remained a mutually porous one. First, although the Freudians sidelined congenital factors, they never attempted to banish biology altogether from the theoretical toolbox. For Freud, as for many sexologists seeking to uncover the originating causes of the "sexual aberrations," it was just as false to look solely to constitutional factors as it would be to consider only environmental influences. Secondly, this analysis reveals the depth of sexologists' engagement with Freudian explanations of same-sex desire, even if these generally fell short of a full-scale embrace, and involved rejecting certain analytic methods as scientifically flawed.

As sexologists and psychoanalysts moved away from the older psychiatric view of homosexuality as a degenerative condition, and questioned whether it was even necessarily a lifelong affliction, new political and clinical questions emerged. Was homosexuality a pathological condition fundamentally distinct from "normal" heterosexuality, or was it a temporary aberration that might befall anyone under certain circumstances? Was it desirable to seek to return a patient to a "normal" state of sexual behavior and desire through therapeutic intervention? For Sadger, the psychoanalyst who pursued these questions most thoroughly in the prewar period, the answer to this last question was clearly "yes," even if others—including Freud—had their doubts. For activist-scholars such as Hirschfeld, on the other hand, the psychoanalytic emphasis on environmental and interpersonal factors was fatally incompatible with the conviction that a congenital theory of homosexuality provided the soundest basis for a new brand of identity politics.

Historians of sexuality are increasingly insisting that we examine the very different registers at work in historical descriptions of the "normal"—a term that has sometimes been used to designate that which is healthy, at other times that which is legal, moral, or statistically dominant.[153] The pre–World War I debates around homosexuality examined here mark an important moment of encounter and divergence in the development of modern sex research, as practitioners across a solidifying disciplinary divide began to subscribe to new understandings of the "norm" defined according to a register of physical and mental health rather than morality or criminal predisposition. "Normal" sexuality and its "perversions" or "aberrations" were increasingly being envisaged in relational rather than oppositional terms. Psychoanalysts emphasized the potential for any individual to diverge from the social expectations of "normal" heterosexual development, and at least some were convinced that such aberrations from the norm might be successfully treated using the talking cure. For more biologically minded sexologists such as Hirschfeld, on the other hand, surgical interventions such as castration remained a distinct possibility. Yet running alongside such seemingly oppositional techniques, and reflecting the complex entanglements of ideas about body and mind that occupied sex researchers across the board during this period, were a wide spectrum of clinical approaches and theoretical positions that often combined approaches with a view to helping distressed patients. Older psychotherapeutic methods of suggestive hypnosis sat alongside preventive measures aimed at removing morally dubious influences and pragmatic "adaptation" therapies aimed at assisting homosexual patients deal with the challenges of everyday life under the shadow of German and Austrian criminal law.

During the 1910s and 1920s, research into the "inner secretions" increasingly complicated these distinctions between normal and pathological, body and mind, promising new physiological and chemical possibilities for intervening in an individual's most intimate sexual desires and behaviors. More immediately, however, World War I descended over Europe, and debates about the nature and treatment of the perversions took a distant second place to the care of the war wounded. This increasingly occupied the working hours of medically trained sexologists and psychoanalysts, just as it did for their colleagues in other medical specializations, as many were called to serve at hospitals near the front lines. The experience of violent conflict produced pressing new questions for each of these fields, which are explored in the next chapter.

Chapter 3

How World War I Changed Sex Research: War Neurotics, Shell Shock, and Sex in an Era of Industrialized Violence

> Th[e] tremor had been removed by pure suggestive methods, but one morning it returned, as the patient expressed it "by itself." On closer questioning, he remembered that the shaking had re-appeared in conjunction with a terrifying dream during the previous night; the actual content of the dream he had forgotten. During hypnosis the patient immediately became conscious again of the dream, and by means of it of those events that still compelled him to shake his arm. During the night he had dreamed of a Russian with a black beard who sprang on to his bed in order to strangle him. He awoke in anxiety and terror with his arm shaking. The patient had seen [in his dream] the face of this Russian appear over the parapet during a furious hand grenade fight just when he [the patient] was on the point of fixing a grenade fuse and was suddenly blown over. He lost consciousness with his rage undischarged and an incipient movement that served as a mimic abreaction of this anger.[1]

This patient, who presented at a field hospital with a severe tremor of the right arm that involved oddly circular movements, was one of the many thousands treated for shell shock in the military hospitals of the Central Powers during the long years of trench warfare and machinated violence from 1914–1918. His doctor, Berlin physician Ernst Simmel, had been stationed during the war at a field clinic in the eastern Prussian outpost of Posen. He was at the forefront of those experimenting with psychoanalytic techniques to combat the nervous disorders associated with the violence of the front. Several sessions with Simmel, using an adapted form of the psychoanalytic "talking cure" with a strong focus on dream analysis, revealed in the patient an unconscious memory of twisting the top off a hand grenade just before he lost consciousness in an explosion, as the above account, mediated by his analyst, reveals. Subsequently, the patient's physical symptoms disappeared—or at least, he was deemed recovered enough for his doctor to cease clinical treatment. During the war Simmel chalked up considerable success in relieving the symptoms of traumatic war neurosis, or shell shock, in just two to three therapeutic sessions, through a combination of hypnotic, suggestive, and psychoanalytic methods. Although an outsider to psychoanalysis's inner circle before 1918, Freud responded enthusiastically to Simmel's publication of a book on war neurosis during that final year of the war, and in September he was invited to speak at the Fifth International Psychoanalytic Congress in Budapest.[2]

Although international in both name and outlook, the realities of the war meant that the Congress was attended primarily by German-speaking participants from the Central Powers, particularly from the German and Austro-Hungarian Empires. While the hostilities had temporarily curtailed professional mobility and international networks—especially with respect to researchers located in Allied nations such as Britain and in North America—they drew to the Budapest Congress official military representatives keen to set up psychoanalytic centers in army hospitals. Specifically, they sought ways to both investigate and humanely and efficiently treat the mysterious nervous illnesses associated with the battlefield. It was to this audience that Simmel described his treatment of multiple cases of war neurosis, explaining the condition as a protective psychological mechanism aimed at preventing the development of a more damaging war psychosis. In his introduction to the published conference proceedings, *Zur Psychoanalyse der Kriegsneurosen* (1919)—the English translation appeared two years later as *Psycho-Analysis and the War Neuroses* (1921)—Freud reflected on the impact of the preceding years of violent conflict in raising the profile of his fledgling discipline. Although certainly not wishing a return to the war, he somewhat ruefully observed that its end marked a lost opportunity for further detailed study of war neuroses, the symptoms of which had, in many cases, seemingly disappeared when the conflict ended.[3] Psychoanalysis, its status still tentative within the wider medical profession, appeared set to gain both respectability and prestige if practitioners could prove themselves useful in treating soldiers suffering from uncontrollable shaking, hysterical tics, and other neurotic outbursts—soldiers who might today be diagnosed as suffering symptoms of posttraumatic stress disorder.[4]

The unprecedented scale of industrialized, machine-driven violence also forced a rethinking of medical understandings of sexual dysfunction beyond the realm of Freudian theory. As Berlin physician Ernst Burchard sagely foresaw in 1915, writing in the recently reestablished *Zeitschrift für Sexualwissenschaft* (Journal of Sexual Science), "new questions for the field of sexual science doubtless lie hidden behind the uproar of this war."[5] The conflict pushed medically trained psychoanalysts and sexologists out of their civilian practices, clinics, and consulting rooms and into military and field hospitals, where they treated thousands of traumatized soldiers as well as civilians. The unique challenges and symptoms they confronted forced practitioners to reevaluate their previous assumptions and form new opinions about numerous conditions, from the causes and treatment of trauma-related impotence and shell shock to the military suitability of soldiers who identified as homosexual or whom we would today consider "trans."

The experience of the Great War constitutes a pivotal, yet largely unexplored chapter in the relationship between psychoanalysis and sexology in the early decades of the new century. Certainly, historians have acknowledged—as Freud himself did in 1918—the significance for psychoanalysis of the experience of treating war neurotics, thereby bringing this field to wider professional and public attention.[6] As the interest of military officials suggests, psychoanalysis's patient base was no longer restricted to the mostly bourgeois urban clients who had visited the private consulting rooms of Freud and his early followers in the late 1890s and 1900s, inspired by his and Josef Breuer's path-breaking work with hysterics and his fascinating insights into the interpretation of dreams. The war's impact on sexology, in contrast, has rarely been examined, and little has been done to counter one historian's claim of more than two decades ago that "World War I proved to be a major setback to the German sexological movement."[7] This chapter challenges such assessments, arguing that, far from representing a simple "setback" in the history of twentieth-century sex research, World War I was in fact a highly productive moment in these early decades of sexological and psychoanalytic professionalization, inspiring important new areas of research inquiry, but also intensifying budding tensions between these two fields. Debates about the treatment of shell-shocked soldiers or the military aptitude of conscripts who might today be classified as homosexual, queer, or trans demonstrate an openness to new approaches and a nuanced responsiveness to current events that reached across consolidating disciplinary boundaries. The war pushed sexologists into deeper levels of engagement with the newer theories of psychoanalysis, which many were prepared to accept as part of an enlarged diagnostic and clinical tool kit, but it also forced psychoanalysts to revisit some of their theoretical assumptions surrounding sexuality and the neuroses. Meanwhile, the field of hormone research offered promising new directions for researchers seeking to comprehend the nature and treatment of sexual "pathologies," and for the more physiologically oriented field of sexology, offered an important means for practitioners to start to more firmly distinguish their expertise from that of the Freudian school.

The first section of this chapter takes up the question of shell shock or war neurosis, offering a close reading of psychoanalytic responses to a condition that challenged Freudian theories of traumatic neurosis developed in peacetime, particularly in response to railway accidents, that had generally assumed a sexual etiology. Faced with the apparently nonsexual symptoms of traumatized soldiers, psychoanalysts were pushed to revisit existing explanations in ways that might take into account the physical violence of war. I then show how sexologists, who had frequently favored biological and congenital explanations of sexual pathology, responded to their own experiences of treating war victims by revising aspects of their theories of human sexual behavior, particularly in relation to more obviously "sexual" disorders such as impotence. Sexologists also considered the impact of high male mortality on marriage and birth statistics, increased abortion rates, and war-related prostitution and venereal disease; a number of female sexologists were particularly vocal in stressing the war's gendered impact on women's as well as men's sexual lives. As the war progressed, sexual scientists intensified their study of the "internal secretions," or sex hormones, knowledge of which was progressing by leaps and bounds following physiologist and endocrinologist Eugen Steinach's return to Vienna in 1912. Meanwhile, leading sexologist Magnus Hirschfeld initiated new discussions around the military aptitude of homosexual- and cross-gender-identifying soldiers in his pioneering journal of homosexuality and "intermediary" sexual categories, the *Jahrbuch für sexuelle Zwischenstufen* (Yearbook of Sexual Intermediaries), one of the most important scientific sources for the history of homosexuality in early twentieth-century Germany.

Psychoanalysis and the "War Tremblers": Revisiting the Sexual Etiology of the Neuroses

Psychoanalysts during World War I were fascinated by the problem generally referred to in contemporary German medical literature as "war neurosis" or "war hysteria" (*Kriegsneurose* or *Kriegshysterie*). Although better known in the English-speaking world as "shell shock," British psychoanalyst Ernest Jones was among those to reject that term for its focus on only one of multiple possible causal factors, preferring the German-derived "war shock" (*Kriegsschock*).[8] The distinctive type and extent of trench warfare that developed in World War I, with machine guns and long-range weaponry working to immobilize combat and push soldiers into a certain passivity, created a particularly modern brand of nervous condition.[9] By the end of the war, doctors were diagnosing an epidemic of "hysterical men"; over 600,000 German soldiers were treated for mental disorders in military hospitals.[10] The most common physical symptom of the war neurotic was an uncontrollable shaking of the legs or entire body, leading to the coinages "war trembler," or *Kriegszitterer*, and "trembling neurosis" (*Zitterneurose*). Other physical symptoms of traumatic neurosis resembled those familiar from peacetime diagnoses of hysteria: muscle tics, blindness, convulsive attacks, mutism, and partial paralysis.[11]

Historians emphasize that shell shock should not be understood simply as a mental illness triggered by violent trauma, but as intricately bound up with culturally and temporally specific influences on subjectivity, including ideas of masculinity, normalcy, and the policing of such categories.[12] It has sometimes been theorized as a "social disease," constructed by doctors and working in ways that underscored existing social prejudices; shell-shocked soldiers joined the ranks of other "outsiders," such as Jews, criminals, homosexuals, and the insane.[13] Shell shock was also understood in inherently gendered ways, placing its victims outside of the masculine "ideal" and yet offering one of the only forms of escape from an uncontrollable reality: "If it was the essence of manliness not to complain, then shell shock was the body language of masculine complaint, a disguised male protest, not only against the war, but against the concept of manliness itself."[14] In the immediate postwar era, shell shock also became closely bound up with understandings of sexual abnormality and aggression, as sexual disorders, brutalization, and violence were among the most widespread traumatic symptoms displayed by men who had returned from the front.[15] For psychoanalysts, it represented precisely the kind of condition that their theories and methods might help to unpack where previous clinical approaches had stalled: using one-on-one therapy to reveal and work through the layers of trauma that had led to the "neurotic" symptoms in the first place.

Shell shock had not been foreseen as a particular problem in the early days of the war, which many German leaders and intellectuals had welcomed as an antidote to the nation's perceived nervous "crisis" in the face of the industrialization and urbanization of the modern era. In 1914, Emperor Wilhelm II predicted the onset of a "war of nerves" that might counter what commentators such as Oswald Spengler had lamented as the "decline of the West," and start reversing the perceived "soft aestheticism" of middle- and upper-class German men.[16] Some sexologists during these years also adopted this rhetoric. In a lecture held at the Medical Society for Sexual Science in December 1914, Burchard declared that many sex-related illness appeared to be "favorably influenced by the powerful sublimation of war," which Berlin neurologist, psychiatrist, and sex researcher Albert Eulenburg had described as a "steel bath of nerves."[17] Commentators across the political spectrum echoed this positive early assessment. Left-wing female emancipist and sex reformer Henriette Fürth declared in 1915 that, although eleven months of conflict had created new social problems relating to women's marriage prospects and single motherhood, it had also begun to strengthen and heal the population, with many finding new powers in themselves: "The physically weak were strengthened by the unaccustomed exertions of military service and endured these with aplomb. Imagined neuroses disappeared in the trenches. The mentally weak found within themselves unknown sources of strength."[18] Optimism about the "steeling" effects of the war for national strength and potency, however, soon began to appear misplaced. In his 1920 memoir *In Stahlgewittern* (Storm of Steel), Ernst Jünger vividly described his experience of shock following a shell hit, where after managing an initial retreat he collapsed into "convulsive sobbing" followed by "extreme indifference"—not unlike the soldier with the hand grenade tremor above.[19] Far from steeling the nation for modernity, industrialized warfare and rationalized slaughter soon proved more conducive to producing nervous breakdown on an industrial scale, as historian Andreas Killen observes.[20] It quickly became apparent that dealing with this crisis of nervous illness would require innovative approaches to diagnosis and treatment.

In particular, psychoanalysis appealed to the military powers and hospital staff as a potentially more humane and efficient method of treating patients' symptoms and returning them swiftly to the front line, compared to older treatments such as the controversial "Kaufmann method" (named after Austrian Jewish neurologist Fritz Kaufmann). This "surprise attack" approach combined painful electrical currents or mock surgeries with verbal suggestion to form a much more physically invasive therapy than the hypnotic suggestion frequently deployed by nineteenth-century psychiatrists. Although widely employed in military psychiatric units during World War I, the Kaufmann method drew criticism for being overly brutal, and was seen as contributing to a breakdown of morale and high rates of relapse. It relied on the shock of therapy to increase the patient's will to recover and make a return to the front seem the more attractive option. This attention to the patient's will reflected, in turn, a shift in medical understandings of traumatic neurosis: what had previously been viewed as a somatic illness involving physical changes in the nervous centers—a view associated with prominent Berlin neurologist Hermann

Oppenheim—was increasingly explained in psychological terms. This shift was enshrined at the 1916 War Conference of German psychiatrists in Munich, which adopted a more fully psychological definition of neurosis.[21]

For sufferers, this development was not without problems: a number of doctors and politicians began to argue that war neurotics were not affected by any genuine disability, but were simply "malingerers," mostly from the lower social classes, who suffered from "pension neurosis" and were merely seeking "refuge" in their illness to receive a disability pension—accusations that shifted the blame away from the trauma of war and onto individuals.[22] The ethics of "helping" patients by rendering them fit to return to the battlefield also remained highly questionable.[23] These developments paved the way, however, for a much more serious consideration of psychoanalytic explanations by doctors stationed in military hospitals, keen to embrace a less invasive treatment mode. Paying greater scientific attention to the individual subjectivity of soldier patients, the new methods were without doubt more humane than the use of electrical currents.[24]

In the German military, Simmel was at the forefront of those experimenting with psychoanalytic techniques. Following his appearance in Budapest, in 1920 he became a founding member of the Berlin Psychoanalytic Institute polyclinic, together with Karl Abraham and Russian analyst Max Eitingon. The clinic provided treatment free of charge to patients on low incomes. Simmel developed close links to other socialist doctors and intellectuals, including writer and physician Alfred Döblin.[25] He saw the war neuroses as proving the correctness of Freudian views on hysteria, whereby physical symptoms were considered to be conversions of psychological conflicts. The unconscious played an important role, repressing events and feelings hostile to the ego.[26] Describing another soldier who presented with a paralyzed arm but no obvious physical injury, Simmel explains how analysis revealed that at the moment of a violent grenade explosion, the patient had believed his arm to be ripped off completely. Simmel used hypnosis to correct this unconscious belief, "reattaching" the arm in the patient's consciousness. While this treatment drew on somewhat dated Freudian approaches—Freud himself had moved on from hypnosis by this stage—Simmel also experimented with more recent psychoanalytic methods such as dream analysis. This becomes apparent in the aforementioned example of the patient traumatized by the incident of the hand grenade and a Russian opponent.[27]

No longer dealing with upper-middle-class Viennese society ladies and gentlemen, but confronted instead with the grim realities of the trenches, analysts thus began to adapt Freudian methods to suit their nontraditional psychoanalytic patient base: mostly uneducated soldiers from the working classes and peasantry. Simmel was aware that the limitations on time and resources in military hospitals meant that he could focus only on alleviating specific symptoms rather than a complete course of treatment: "An analytical cure of the entire personality . . . will have to be reserved for the psychological clinic of the future."[28] While other pioneers of psychotherapy, including Fritz Stern, Willibald Sauer, and Fritz Mohr, had adapted Freud and Breuer's cathartic method for treating hysteria for cases of war-induced "male hysteria,"[29] Simmel's methods provided an important reference point for members of Freud's inner circle, who took their investigations in more Oedipal directions. These included Sándor Ferenczi and Abraham, both of whom had been serving as military doctors during the conflict, Ferenczi as director of clinical neurology at the Maria Valerie barracks hospital in Budapest and Abraham as head of a psychiatric ward in the eastern Prussian outpost of Allenstein (now Olsztyn in Poland). Their roles were prominently noted on the title page of the Budapest proceedings, presumably in an effort to harness the prestige of national service to the still-controversial methods of the Freudian school. In his introduction to those proceedings, Freud expanded on Simmel's explanation of the war neuroses, describing a conflict between the individual soldier's prior, "peacetime" ego and a new, "warrior" ego.[30] Ferenczi and Abraham, meanwhile, were more interested in exploring whether theories developed in peacetime concerning the specifically sexual etiology of the neuroses could also be applied to neurotic soldiers.

The emphasis on sexuality was by far the most contentious aspect of psychoanalytic approaches to the war neuroses, as several speakers at the Congress observed. Analysts presenting on this topic were careful to emphasize that war shock, like other forms of traumatic neurosis, must be understood not as belonging to the area of explicitly genital sexuality, but to an earlier, narcissistic stage of development. This approach reflected Freudian psychoanalysis's broad understanding of sexuality as "Eros," as well as its emphasis on the sexual phases of infancy. Simmel himself remained ambiguous on the extent to which this inner conflict was necessarily a sexual one, causing skepticism toward his work in certain analytical quarters.[31] Freud, meanwhile, insisted that it had become possible to extend the libido theory to the "narcissistic" neuroses, and put forth the concept of a "narcissistic libido":

> Only by advancing and making use of the idea of a "narcissistic sexual hunger (libido)," that is to say, a mass of sexual energy that attaches itself

> to the ego and satisfies itself with this as otherwise it only does with an object, has it been possible to extend the sexual hunger (libido) theory to the narcissistic neuroses, and this entirely legitimate development of the concept of sexuality bids fair to do for these severer neuroses and for the psychoses all that one can expect from an empirically and tentatively progressing theory. The traumatic neurosis of peace time will also fit into this group when researches into the correlation undoubtedly subsisting between shock, anxiety, and narcissistic sexual hunger (libido) have reached success.[32]

Ferenczi and Abraham each used their papers at the Congress to take up this understanding of the libido, examining it in conjunction with the stages of childhood sexual development outlined by Freud in his 1905 *Three Essays on the Theory of Sexuality*. Both researchers argued along remarkably similar lines (causing Abraham to point out that they had not in fact collaborated), each seeking to develop a causal explanation of traumatic war neurosis framed in terms of infantile regression. Asking why the violent trauma endured by almost all soldiers at the front results in neurosis only in some cases—why, as Abraham puts it, one soldier might be repeatedly injured and return to the front without any signs of neurosis, while another can fall without injury but subsequently develop the severest symptoms—both analysts concluded that it was due to a combination of individual predisposition and childhood experience.[33]

Abraham argued that even before going to war, many war neurotics already suffered from inhibitions of the libido, such as impotence, with their development more or less locked in the narcissistic stage. The extreme circumstances of wartime, however, demand constant self-sacrifice and the renunciation of narcissistic tendencies. Although this is something with which healthy and psychologically mature individuals can cope, it can destabilize those with a neurotic predisposition. A further factor contributing to neurosis development was the all-male military environment, which Abraham saw as threatening the already shaky heterosexuality of the narcissistic individual.[34] Analysts including Freud and his Viennese follower Isidor Sadger had for some years seen homosexuality and narcissism as closely linked (see chapter 2), with Sadger declaring that "*the path to homosexuality always leads via narcissism, that is, the love for one's own self/ego.*"[35] Revealing a degree of patriotism not unusual among central European sex researchers during this period, Abraham argues that war requires the sacrifice of one's ego and the suppression of such narcissistic tendencies for the sake of the community and nation. This was more difficult for latent homosexuals, for whom war represented a particularly volatile experience.[36] Finally, war threatened the individual's sense of immortality, with narcissistic security giving way to a sense of powerlessness. The individual regresses in his behavior until, as Ferenczi writes, the patients seek "to be pampered, cared for, and pitied like children. One can therefore speak of a reversion into the childish stage of self-love." Both analysts also consider the politicized question of "pension neurosis" (*Rentengier*) in these infantilizing terms; their brusque analytic assessments are hardly likely to have aligned with their patients' own sense of their condition. According to Ferenczi, it is not so much a case of individuals producing illnesses to achieve actual monetary or personal gain, such as compensation or escape from the front; these, he insists, are only secondary benefits of illness (*Krankheitsgewinne*). Rather, "the primary motive for the illness is the pleasure itself of remaining in the secure retreat of the childish situation once so unwillingly left behind."[37]

These key representatives of early-twentieth-century psychoanalysis thus reaffirmed sexuality as a central factor even in neuroses triggered by what appeared to be obviously nonsexual, violent experiences, such as grenade explosions or burial under debris. Viewed in this way, even an absent or weak sex drive could be taken as proof of sexual etiology, albeit repressed rather than manifest. Nor was anyone fully immune to this condition, because as Ferenczi emphasized, the narcissistic stage represents an important phase in the libido development of every human being, not just neurotics.[38] By attempting a causal explanation rather than simply addressing symptoms, as earlier psychiatric methods of electric shock therapy had done, psychoanalysts situated theirs as the only theory with the potential to truly explain and cure war neurosis—as Sadger had previously done for homosexuality. While cautioning that these theories were still in development, Abraham nonetheless boldly proclaimed their therapeutic potential: "Psycho-analysis, which enables us to penetrate deeper than any other method into the structure of the war neuroses, will perhaps take therapeutic precedence."[39] In this vein, Viennese lay analyst and one of the early women in Freudian inner circles, Hermine von Hug-Hellmuth, wrote in the nonspecialist sex-reform journal *Geschlecht und Gesellschaft* (Sex and Society) in 1914 that

> there is no war neurosis in the sense of the war being its maker (*Erzeuger*); its deepest roots, its germinal seeds lie in that place where we must seek all neuroses and psychoses, and where we also find them: in a particular constitution, in current hurts (*Schädlichkeiten*) of the sex life and in sexual dreams, thoughts and fantasies from early childhood days.[40]

In taking this early stance on the roots of war neurosis, Hug-Hellmuth anticipated some of the discussions at the Budapest Congress by several years, in addition to exploring, as male analytic colleagues were not yet doing, specifically gendered questions arising from the conflict (she attributed an increase in women demonstrating neurotic symptoms, for example, to an overidentification with the early casualties being shipped back from the front).[41] These early shows of confidence in the new methods also resonated with Freudians across the globe; Melbourne physician Paul G. Dane in 1925 deemed psychoanalytic treatment in such cases "altogether more satisfactory to patient and doctor than any other method," producing relief that can be "so dramatic and profound that this is in itself a highly valuable effect."[42]

The experience of treating war neurotics forced analysts to rework and extend their existing theories of traumatic neurosis. They applied older notions of arrested sexual development to new situations of violent combat to explain why some but not all exposed individuals developed the symptoms of shell shock. This explanatory model was not without its drawbacks, potentially stigmatizing patients by locating their pathologies in constitutional deficiencies and sexual inadequacy rather than war trauma.[43] More productively, though, the experience of treating traumatized soldiers encouraged analysts to develop new methods that could accelerate the lengthy "talking cure" established by Freud, which conventionally involved several days per week of treatment over a period of months or even years. Psychoanalysts' responses to World War I also set the stage for a number of important new theoretical developments within that field during the interwar period, including the concept of the ego (*Ich*), which receives an early mention in Freud's introduction and several other papers presented at Budapest. Freud subsequently developed this concept in his 1923 publication *The Ego and the Id*, while German analyst Carl Müller-Braunschweig explicitly referenced the military experience in his discussion of the links between war trauma and a "warrior" versus a "peacetime" ego in a 1923 article on *Angst* or fear and the libido.[44] The clinical study of war neurosis, as Veronika Fuechtner points out, provided the crucial "theoretical stepping-stone" for the maturation of this concept.[45] The war experience also pushed Freud to continue developing his broader theory of trauma, and to introduce new categories such as the repetition compulsion, whereby patients repeatedly return in nightmares to the scene of a traumatic event. Finally, it facilitated his innovation in *Beyond the Pleasure Principle* (1920) of the "death instinct" ("Thanatos") as a force equally important to the "life instinct" ("Eros") in the human psyche.[46]

Sexology and Male Impotence: Combining Theories of Body and Mind

While the violence that war inflicted on the soldier's body and psyche led psychoanalysts to revisit their theories of the sexual etiology of the neuroses, sexologists approached the sexual problems associated with the conflict in broader terms. A survey of one of the earliest and most significant German sexological periodicals, the *Zeitschrift für Sexualwissenschaft* (Journal of Sexual Science), reveals wide-ranging contributions on topics including prostitution and venereal disease, laws on sadistic crime, the impact of mass casualties and forced abstinence on population health, the military aptitude of homosexual and "transvestite" soldiers (a label I return to below), and in a more self-reflexive vein, the responsibilities of sexual science in times of conflict. These contributions highlighted the urgent questions raised by the war, but also enabled sexual scientists to champion the relevance of their own fledgling branch of medical-scientific inquiry. Whereas psychoanalysts focused on traumatic neurosis and shell shock, sexologists prioritized the question of "traumatic impotence": sexual dysfunction among male soldiers that was believed to be directly caused by war violence. (A couple of analysts, including Ferenczi, had investigated impotence from a Freudian perspective, but these investigations remained on the periphery of psychoanalytic research in these years.[47]) From a cultural-history perspective, this preoccupation with male virility was not new, but it took on a new sense of urgency as unprecedented numbers of soldier patients returned from the front complaining of (hetero)sexual disorders.[48]

The concept of trauma was central to sexual scientific assessments of the war's impact on soldiers. Internist Friedel Pick of the German University in Prague and editor of the journal *Archiv für Dermatologie und Syphilis* (Archive for Dermatology and Syphilis) undertook a major quantitative study of this phenomenon, finding widespread evidence of impotence, weakened sex drive, and premature ejaculation among soldiers under his treatment. He attributed these disorders to exertion, poor nutrition, and physical shock to the nervous system from exploding grenades. Pick's findings appeared in prestigious German and Austrian medical journals such as the *Deutsche Medizinische Wochenschrift* (German Medical Weekly) and *Wiener klinische Wochenschrift* (Viennese Clinical Weekly), and resonated widely with his contemporaries.[49] Psychoanalysts criticized his disregard of psychological factors, but welcomed his empirical charting of the frequency of sexual disorders among soldiers:

> Dr. Pick's experimental results provide a valuable affirmation of the psychoanalytic claim regarding the primary role of libidinal disturbances in

> the neuroses, and particularly in the traumatic neuroses. By questioning those under his care in his ward . . . Pick found that of 100 patients 13 complained of profound disturbances of the sexual function—more or less complete impotence, or premature ejaculation. In most of these patients there was evidence of a grenade concussion or burial under a landslide [. . .], five cases displayed severe neurasthenia without trauma, and one case showed high-level anemia with *colitis ulcerosa*. The coincidence of sexual disturbance and neuroses is highly instructional for the analyst.[50]

Analysts thus interpreted Pick's findings as confirmation that sexual disturbances play a central role in the traumatic neuroses. Sexologists, on the other hand, took Pick's evidence of the effects of violent conflict as an impetus to more precisely categorize the physical as well as psychological causes of traumatic impotence.

One of the key sexological considerations of trauma-based impotence was a 1918/19 article in the *Zeitschrift für Sexualwissenschaft* by then-editor Bloch, who lamented the overwhelming neglect of sexual dysfunction in research on wartime neurosis. Citing his own observations of seventy to eighty cases over the previous three years, both inside and outside of military hospitals, he insists that the physiological and the psychological are often closely interlinked in such cases ("the old categorization of impotence into the two major clinical forms of the so-called 'organic' and the so-called 'nervous' or 'psychic' impotence no longer holds").[51] One must carefully distinguish among the diverse physical causes of traumatic impotence, he argued, including injuries to the genitals, brain, spinal cord, and other parts of the body, those caused by sensations of pain or sudden cold (*Schmerzlähmung*), and those caused by grazes, direct blows, or concussion. Complicating this picture is the recognition that physical injuries are often accompanied by psychological shocks (*seelische Erschütterungen*); Bloch further divides psychic traumas into conscious and unconscious variants.[52] In addition, he cited the workings of the still little understood "internal secretions," observing that greater awareness of hormonal function was already forcing a reevaluation of older mind-body distinctions in the study of sex.[53]

Bloch's article appeared in the second incarnation of the *Zeitschrift*, which enjoyed a relatively long run from 1914 to 1932, and succeeded an earlier, short-lived publication of the same name, which Hirschfeld had edited for twelve issues (a single volume) in 1908. That journal was subsumed into dermatologist and sexologist Max Marcuse's *Sexual-Probleme*, and both of these early periodicals demonstrate the strong crossovers between sexological and psychoanalytic publishing during these years. As noted in the Introduction, Freud published several early essays in *Sexual-Probleme*; he also authored a piece, "Hysterical Fantasy and Its Relation to Bisexuality," for the 1908 *Zeitschrift*, although this had originally been intended for inclusion in Hirschfeld's *Jahrbuch*.[54] In a letter to his Jewish colleague penned on Christmas day, Freud congratulated Marcuse on the merger of his publication with Hirschfeld's, "from which I expect a very especial elevation of the new organ."[55] Overseeing the new *Zeitschrift* from 1914 was the Berlin-based Medical Society for Sexual Science (Ärztliche Gesellschaft für Sexualwissenschaft), founded in 1913 under Albert Eulenburg's leadership. Eulenburg edited the journal together with Bloch, and Hirschfeld was one of its frequent contributors. From April 1917 until early 1919, Bloch was sole editor, and in April 1919 Max Marcuse took over the editorial helm, where he remained until March 1932, when the journal dissolved, presumably a victim of the late-Weimar economic crisis.[56] Freud himself declined an offer to join the Society in 1913, probably because Wilhelm Fliess was also a member; the two were no longer on speaking terms. He also distanced himself from the new *Zeitschrift*. Ernest Jones later commented that its "allusions to psycho-analysis were not encouraging enough for Freud to be willing to have any more to do with the undertaking"; Freud himself noted to Abraham his "intention to go on maintaining reserve" regarding the journal, describing its attitude toward psychoanalysis as "not very alluring."[57] Nonetheless, during the four wartime years following its establishment the *Zeitschrift* not only published reviews of works by Freud, Sadger, and others, but also articles by scholars with a close relationship to Freudian theory, including Abraham, Karen Horney, Carl Müller-Braunschweig, Theodor Reik, Bruno Saaler, Lou-Andreas Salomé, and Wilhelm Stekel. Such cross-disciplinary publishing activities once again demonstrate the willingness of the early Freudians not only to engage in sexological forums, but to see themselves as working within a larger remit of "sexual science."

Writing his article on traumatic impotence in the midst of these cross-field collaborations and growing territorialism, Bloch takes a middle line. Certainly, he takes psychoanalytic theory seriously in emphasizing the unconscious as well as conscious variants of psychic trauma. Sudden and acute mental shocks, he notes, are likely to result in more severe cases of impotence; he cites the case of a young male patient who lost sexual function after watching his mother die suddenly of a heart attack. Although hesitant about the Freudian emphasis on "the *incest motif* . . . as a source of psychic trauma and an allegedly frequent cause of impotence later in life," Bloch nonetheless expresses confidence that psychoanalysis has much to reveal "about the possible revelation of unconscious psychic traumas." He even gives examples: if a child's witnessing a gruesome scene such as the slaughter of a chicken or the beating of another child coincides with sexual arousal, this can fixate "abnormal" sadistic or masochistic associations, leading to the development of impotence later in life.[58] Yet Bloch also diverges from psychoanalytic tenets in several ways, particularly in his insistence that even "psychic" forms of traumatic impotence are probably affected by hormonal factors:

> For after intense psychic agitations it has been shown without question that there is, for example, a strong increase of the adrenal secretions, of adrenalin, in the blood. And so everything points to the fact that the nature of impotence following from psychic trauma is to be sought in a disturbance of the endocrinal system—one which, however, is still unknown to us.[59]

His colleague Felix A. Theilhaber agreed: "Neurology has not yet come so far that it can completely detach the insults delivered by the war (fright, overexertion etc.) from the effects of pathological internal secretions."[60] This insistence that the inner secretions could influence not only clearly physical ailments such as menstrual disturbances, but also seemingly psychological disorders and trauma, was thoroughly in keeping with the latest findings in sexual science.

Sexologists were thus increasingly laying their hopes on the potential of endocrinal research to thoroughly transform not only the understanding of war-related sexual disorders, but sexual pathologies in general. As editor of the *Zeitschrift*, Bloch went to considerable lengths to underscore this exciting new frontier of sexual scientific research. Although his inaugural editorial of 1914 had pointed to the importance of Freudian psychoanalysis in uncovering the "significance of early sexual infant and youth experiences," it also emphasized the "enormous significance" of the inner secretions, identifying as the next major project for sexology the establishment of the "meaning of the individual glands of internal secretion for the sexuality of both sexes in terms of physiology and pathology."[61] Six years earlier, Bloch's *Das Sexualleben unserer Zeit* (The Sexual Life of Our Time) had already suggested a possible connection between homosexuality and "embryonic disturbances of the sexual chemistry," a few months before Berlin-based colleague Albert Moll cautiously noted, in *The Sexual Life of the Child*, the growing influence of the "chemical" theory of the glands.[62] Moving now beyond the vagueness of these prewar formulations, and extending the conceptual boundaries of experimental human biology to the invisible workings of the glands, Bloch's positioning of the hormones at the forefront of sexual scientific research signaled the beginnings of a new brand of sexology defined by the technological advances of the twentieth century; I return to the role of hormones in chapter 4.

The overwhelming focus of male sexologists on male sexual needs in wartime did not go uncriticized. The aforementioned Henriette Fürth was one of a number of female sex reformers and sexologists whose contributions have tended to hover at the margins of the historiography, but whose views appeared alongside those of male colleagues in the *Zeitschrift*, suggesting they reached a similarly broad readership. Fürth articulated a scathing assessment of the lack of attention to women's wartime needs:

> The general assumption goes something along the line that women possess a lesser sexual need than men. This assumption, like all of our guiding life principles and laws, is dependent on men for its creation, form and applicability, and it is their will that sustains it.[63]

Echoing these views was radical feminist Helene Stöcker, who in a 1916 piece on wartime sexual abstinence insisted on the masculine bias of sexual scientific research: "a portion of the current grievances—this can really not be disputed—can be traced back to the fact that it has only ever been the needs and pronouncements of *one* sex that have been considered."[64] Such concerns for the war's impact on women's sexual lives remained in the minority in the *Zeitschrift* during these years, although a few male commentators also considered topics such as women's reduced opportunities to have sex and have children, the increase in menstrual and pregnancy disturbances, and the use of military hospitals for gynecological procedures.[65] They foreshadow a growing emphasis on female sexuality in the postwar period, however, during which—as I show in chapter 5—women sexologists and analysts began to play a much more prominent role.

Suitable for Service?: The "Sexual Intermediaries" in Wartime

The violence of war raised new questions for the study of sexual pathology, as the dysfunctions presented by soldiers exposed the limits of older explanatory models. These challenges increased practitioners' receptiveness to ideas that crossed conventional medical specializations. Psychoanalysts gained the increasing respect of the broader medical profession, while sexologists looked to several sources in developing creative solutions to clinical problems, accepting that psychogenic factors could better explain traumatic neurosis while also turning their attention toward the exciting new possibilities of endocrinal research. Although this produced a potentially contradictory web of etiological explanations, it reflects the complexity and porosity of sexual scientific knowledge production during these decades. Increasingly, though, sexologists such as Bloch were leaning toward inner-secretions research, not least as a means of undergirding their own scientific authority. With new specialist journals and societies, sexology and psychoanalysis had each gone some way toward becoming distinct professional disciplines by the second decade of the new century, and this was helped rather than hindered by the war experience. Nonetheless, neither field had yet attained the level of scientific legitimacy or independence enjoyed by more established disciplines such as psychiatry, neurology, and gynecology, and other signs of disciplinary maturity, such as dedicated professorial posts and specialist training institutes, remained either nonexistent or at an embryonic stage. Addressing new challenges was an important means for practitioners in these fields to justify their new theories and methods to a wider audience. A further problem that suddenly gained significance during the war years was whether sexually "intermediary" individuals—those who were attracted to individuals of the same sex, or cross-dressed, or in some other way failed to conform to dominant norms of masculine heterosexuality—should be deemed fit for military service. Although this debate concerned only a small segment of the population, it shot to the heart of questions of German military strength and nationalism, and produced some unexpected responses from members of the medical profession.

Sexologists, in particular, concerned themselves with this question, although in doing so they at times drew—not uncritically—on arguments inspired by psychoanalysis. The scholar-activist Hirschfeld and his medical colleague Ernst Burchard, both active in WhK (Scientific Humanitarian Committee) homosexual rights circles, and future colleagues at Hirschfeld's Institute such as Otto Juliusburger (also active in the WhK), wrote during the war years on the patriotism and military suitability of homosexual and gender-atypical individuals. They took quite different positions on these issues, however: while Hirschfeld and Burchard often affirmed the capacity of homosexuals for military service (particularly in the case of "virile" homosexual men and some female-born soldiers passing as men), Juliusburger argued against conscription based on such individuals' pathological status. In addition, sexologists argued that wartime service might sometimes be best undertaken in more gender-suitable roles, such as ambulance driving. This applied particularly to individuals who would today be considered "trans" or "transgender," and included occasional cross-dressers, individuals assigned male at birth who lived more permanently as women, and the broad spectrum of experiences and identifications summarized by Hirschfeld in a major study of 1910 under the label "transvestites."This category, as noted in the introduction, was seen by contemporaries to encompass (including by Hirschfeld himself) a broad range of cross-gendered behaviors and desires.[66]

The mass casualties of the first months and years of war produced concerns among German political commentators, physicians, and psychiatrists not only about the impact of war on returning soldiers, but about the consequences for national strength of conscripting "less than first-class material" into the military, on the one hand, and the dangers of sacrificing "the healthy and vigorous part of Germany's male population" on the other.[67] These eugenic and nationalist anxieties combined with food shortages and a falling birthrate to create a sense of crisis around the general health of the population, particularly during times of war.[68] Deciding who was fit enough to be sent to—or back to—the front line was an important aspect of these larger discussions, and psychiatrists were granted greater jurisdiction in this matter by the military authorities in Germany than in other European countries at this period. They also had the power to decide whether deserters should be held psychologically responsible for their actions—in many other places, deserters faced immediate court-martial.[69] For individuals who fell under the broad "third sex" category—those who might today be considered queer or trans, and who may have variously identified with categories such as "homosexuals," "inverts," "urnings," or "transvestites"—there was much at stake in debates around military aptitude, just as scholars have shown that the stakes were especially high for Jewish German citizens.[70] Debates about military suitability had the potential to further pathologize "third sex" individuals as second-class outsiders. Alternatively, they could offer reconciliation with a mainstream society that had criminalized male homosexual practices under Paragraph 175, and marginalized transgender practices under "public nuisance" and "gross mischief" laws. By serving their country, such individuals could prove their worth via patriotic ideals of citizenship and duty.[71]

Otto Juliusburger, writing from the Lankwitz sanatorium in Berlin's Steglitz district in 1915, took a difficult stance on this matter, at least from a twenty-first-century queer or trans rights perspective. Although his tone is sympathetic, he used "scientific" arguments to fundamentally question whether homosexuals and transvestites were even capable of true patriotic feeling, leading him argue that most were unsuitable for military service. While this position would have brought relief to some individuals understandably wary of conscription, it also relied on a pathologizing of the "third sex" that put people placed in this category—whether voluntarily or by the medical profession—at odds with nationalist and patriotic discourses. Drawing on psychoanalytic theory, Juliusburger argued that the same infantilizing developmental disturbance that led to the urge to dress in women's clothing—he used the term "psychosexually indifferentiated" to describe these transgender cases—also prevented the development of the masculine aggression and virility required on the battlefield.[72]

Juliusburger's writings and career in many ways straddled the fields of early-twentieth-century sexology and psychiatry: born in the then-German city of Breslau (now Wrocław in Poland) in 1867, he trained in psychiatry and worked at a private hospital before the war. Along with Hirschfeld and Bloch, he had joined Abraham's Berlin Psychoanalytic Society in 1908. He also became a founding member of the Berlin branch of the International Psychoanalytic Association following its foundation in 1910, and soon became an advocate of psychoanalytic approaches in his immediate clinical contexts.[73] A few years later in 1919, in his role as *Sanitätsrat* (medical counselor), Juliusburger collaborated closely with Hirschfeld at the Institute for Sexual Science in Berlin, and both doctors were well-known experts in court cases on sex-related crimes. An active member of the interwar World League for Sexual Reform, and known for his left-leaning law-reform advocacy (and, like his Swiss counterpart August Forel, for his antialcohol campaigning), Juliusburger's interest in "third sex" matters was confirmed by his membership and later chairmanship of the WhK.[74]

Juliusburger wrote on the issue of "third sex" suitability for service in 1915 as part of an ostensibly broad treatment of the war neuroses in the leading psychiatric journal *Monatsschrift für Psychiatrie und Neurologie* (Psychiatric and Neurological Monthly), edited by Karl Bonhoeffer. Bonhoeffer was head of the psychiatric department at Berlin's prestigious Charité teaching hospital, and during the war years he oversaw the publication of numerous pieces on war-related mental illness, from epilepsy to pathological tremors. Like Freud, he viewed the war as a unique opportunity to raise the standing of his own specialization, "an experiment of near-gigantic dimensions for psychiatry."[75] Among these contributions, Juliusburger's stands out in two ways: first, for its integration of psychoanalytic themes, and second, for its consideration of "war neurotics" exhibiting same-sex or transgendered desires.

In turning to psychoanalytic explanations, Juliusburger echoed analysts such as Ferenczi in arguing that the war should generally be viewed as the trigger rather than the ultimate cause of a patient's pathology, setting off "pre-existing, pathologically predisposed energies." In making this argument, he introduces four patient cases. The first (Patient 1) involved an unmarried thirty-five-year-old male who had entered psychiatric treatment in a state of "heightened restlessness," and who feared immanent disaster if called up for service, such as accidentally shooting a comrade and undergoing a trial by martial law. Using medical therapies to still his unrest, Juliusburger ascertained a clear streak of "infantilism" in the patient's rapid mood swings, and diagnosed "irrational logic" on questions such as vegetarianism and in his reactions to seemingly minor incidents, such as receiving an unappetizing meal: "the patient behaved like a stubborn, petulant child."[76] Reporting this patient's history very much in the style of the early narrative cases of psychoanalysis, such as Freud's "Dora" or "Little Hans," Juliusburger pays great attention to his fantasies and dreams, and although Patient 1 makes no mention of same-sex desires or cross-gendered identifications, Juliusburger categorizes his "entire habitus" as obviously exhibiting a typically infantile "feminine element." With a certain degree of heteronormative condescension, Juliusburger then explains his patient's pacifism and lack of patriotism as consequences of this inhibited development: "It wasn't possible for him to form and comprehend the thought of the necessity of the nation state."[77]

Juliusburger sees this same absence of patriotic feeling in his next case: "Lonnie" (Patient 2), a former interior decorator, singer, waiter, and entertainer who had reportedly had a series of long-term relationships with men, and had survived only the briefest period of military service before landing in a field hospital. Lonnie expresses a strong cross-gendered identification to his/her doctor: "*He is unhappy whenever he can't go as a woman*"—an identification Juliusburger recognizes as akin to the cases in Hirschfeld's 1910 study.[78] Describing his patient as thoroughly feminine in voice, hair, eyes, and behavior, Juliusburger considers one of his dreams so obvious that it barely requires analysis: "it is transparent in its naïve, childlike composition and eloquently attests to the strong infantile factor in the patient's psyche." For such an individual, Juliusburger sympathetically observes that peacetime presents a torturous enough process of having to go to work in despised male clothing; the challenge of military service is simply a step too far, with the enforced masculine aggression of the battlefield leading to a clear state of "psychosexual instability or dissociation."[79] It is thus a combination of the patient's femininity and an underlying infantile disturbance that Juliusburger sees as hindering the psychic processes required to develop the will and energy necessary to cope with military service, and to commit to "higher" ideals of sacrifice for a larger cause:

> The concept of the state, the consciousness of integration into the bigger picture, the intensive feeling of duty, of also sacrificing oneself . . . can only come about through comprehensive psychic processes of fusion and higher synthesis. They are impossible when that process characterized as sublimation or the transformation of lower into higher quality psychic energies cannot come into operation.

Describing individuals such as this patient as "markedly defective human beings" (*ausgesprochene Defektmenschen*), Juliusburger takes a Darwinian line with strong undertones of hereditary degeneration, describing the inhibitions leading to such conditions as a kind of atavism or evolutionary throwback, while noting that previous eras of human history knew no such thing as loyalty to a political ideal or state.[80] Such degeneration ideas, despite being rejected by researchers such as Krafft-Ebing in the years around the fin de siècle, remained current in scientific circles well into the 1920s, including among sexual "progressives" such as Hirschfeld, before being manipulated in the service of National Socialist ideologies in the 1930s.[81] In Juliusburger's analysis, the overlaying of nationalist and eugenic discourses provides a historically and culturally specific framework for the pathologization of queer and trans subjectivities.

Juliusburger diagnoses similar tendencies in a final case study, a male tailor of women's clothing whose feminine movements he considers "organically so deeply rooted" that they can surely not have been acquired, as the patient insists they were, through "conscious or unconscious adaptation" to the habits of female clients at the clothing store. While this self-diagnosis by the patient points to the wider circulation of psychoanalytic ideas among nonmedical readers by the second decade of the new century, for Juliusburger the case is another example of severe "psychosexual dissociation," and he considers mental breakdown inevitable under military conditions, given the patient's lack of masculine aggressiveness.[82]

By highlighting "infantile" tendencies in his neurotic patients, Juliusburger's work aligns with, and indeed partially anticipates, the discussions of Ferenczi, Abraham, and others at the 1918 Budapest Congress about the Oedipal roots of the war neuroses. He carefully distinguishes these cases from the psychiatrist Oppenheim's earlier discussions of traumatic neurosis on the grounds of gender: whereas Oppenheim's patients exhibited no comparable developmental disturbance, the feminine traits of Juliusburger's patients are offered as evidence of their psychosexual immaturity. He also sees this at work, albeit in an inverse fashion, in his one female case, a twenty-seven-year-old widow who had attempted suicide following her husband's violent death in battle. This patient presents with a masculine build—including "complete absence" of breast development—and cross-gendered identifications: "she freely offered up the information that she feels herself more as a boy," as was apparently underscored by her fondness for beer, wine, sorbet, and cigarettes. Paradoxically, while this patient's masculine longings lead her to express a wish to cut off her hair and join the army, Juliusburger declares her intellectually and emotionally incapable of patriotic feeling: "by no means did she want to do this in order to defend the fatherland, but rather to foster her old fondness for sport." On the basis of these cases, Juliusburger condones military service only for the "virile," heteronormative male population, and declares that the quickest resolution of symptoms for psychiatric patients in this category can be achieved by declaring them unfit for service.[83]

While some of Juliusburger's patients might have found relief in this psychiatric assessment, it entailed accepting a diagnosis of permanent pathology and second-class citizenship at a time of heightened national need. Other sex researchers, including Burchard and Hirschfeld, took a quite different approach to the military suitability of "third sex" individuals, challenging dominant cultural associations between heteronormativity and patriotism. They did so in nuanced and at times contradictory ways that tended to affirm the capacity of homosexuals, but not trans individuals, for soldierly roles. In a piece for the *Zeitschrift*, Burchard argued that, as with cases of nervous illness, aptitude for service must be decided on an individual basis, and must distinguish between the respective situations of intersex (he uses the then-current term "hermaphrodite"), homosexual, and transvestite individuals. "Hermaphrodites," he argued, should be excluded from military service not because of deficient national feeling, but because their physical difference would produce shame and difficulty in communal contexts. Transvestites should be considered in an analogous fashion to physical hermaphrodites, in light of recent endocrinological research suggesting that the foundation of their condition similarly had physiological roots to be found in the sex glands. For many transvestites, argues Burchard, reluctance to be engaged in active service "is not at all a fear of danger or exertions, but rather the feeling of utter unsuitability for continuous life as a man." He notes that some male-to-female transvestites had even appeared in female clothing in response to military summons, asking not to be excused but rather to work in gender-appropriate roles in nursing or the army canteen; others, Burchard suggests, are well-suited to ambulance service. In addition, Burchard acknowledges a contingent of female-to-male transvestites who, like Juliusburger's fourth case, actively seek out combat roles, although unlike his colleague, Burchard refrains from undermining such desires as infantile.[84]

Hirschfeld was also vocal on the question of homosexual and transvestite aptitude for service. Familiar to those in the know as an expert witness for issuing "transvestite certificates," which permitted the wearers to cross-dress without hindrance by the police, Hirschfeld also devoted an entire section to the question of military suitability in his late-wartime series of volumes, *Sexualpathologie* (Sexual Pathology).[85] He notes that the WhK had issued a "special warning" to transvestites to avoid cross-dressing in wartime for fear of being considered spies, but like Burchard, he reports that a number of people had appeared at military draft calls in women's clothing, including famous female imitator Willy Pape, known as "Voo Doo." Others brought along photographs of themselves in female dress, and several had requested official reports from Hirschfeld asking that they be excused from recruitment due to their "feminine character" (*weiblichen Einschlag*). In a simultaneously pathologizing and protective gesture, Hirschfeld echoes Juliusburger's finding that a good proportion of transvestites are unsuitable for military service due to "nervous ailments of a more severe nature." If called up, he suggests, they will often fall victim to hysterical symptoms and need to be released anyway.[86] Hirschfeld was thus—perhaps surprisingly, given his advocacy for transvestite individuals—against their compulsory military service. Although this may have had something to do with his own increasingly pacifist stance as the war progressed—which was made explicit in his widely received 1916 work *Kriegspsychologisches* (The Psychology of War)—it conflicted with what Heike Bauer has recently described as his "jingoistic defense of queer soldiers" in the early years of the conflict.[87]

Hirschfeld was, moreover, not alone in viewing male homosexuals as far more suitable military conscripts than transvestites. Perceiving little if any reluctance to volunteer for active service among male homosexuals, Burchard observed that they had "an enthusiasm for war that arguably exceeds the average"—a far cry from Juliusburger's diagnoses of "psychosexual infantilism," and a view that also ran counter to the assumption of analysts such as Abraham that homosexuals were more liable to succumb to war neuroses.[88] For Burchard, (male) homosexuals' "lust for war" can be traced, not as one might expect to a wish to "rehabilitate" themselves in a society that has marginalized them; neither is it entirely attributable to the undeniably attractive prospect of living for a time in an exclusively male milieu. Rather, the homosexual enjoys a naturally *greater* ability than his heterosexual counterparts to dedicate himself to the higher causes of national community because he is not tied down by immediate familial or reproductive concerns. Pointing to high numbers of war medals among homosexual servicemen, he concludes that "homosexuality in and of itself thus must by no means determine suitability for military and war service."[89] Burchard's position was echoed by psychiatrist Kurt Mendel, who argued that homosexuality per se did not make a man unsuitable for duty, except where this combined with transvestitism and "severe nervous disturbances on a psychopathic basis"—where, however, it might have a damaging and even "infecting" influence on their environment.[90]

The loudest protests against the notion that homosexuals, transvestites, and other "intermediary" sexual subjects were in any way inferior soldiers or patriots can be found in the Quarterly Reports (*Vierteljahresberichte*) of the WhK, which during the war years replaced the expensively produced *Jahrbuch für sexuelle Zwischenstufen*. The Quarterly Reports ran regular columns with titles such as "From Times of War," which provided a pacifist critique of the latest "murderous" and "insane" events while emphasizing the unique contributions of homosexual combatants, in the explicit hope that these might further the homosexual rights cause: "That this fight for the freedom of nations and people also benefits the homosexuals who have so diligently dedicated themselves to the cause is our hope and confidence." This column brought together a wide array of what might today be considered "queer" perspectives, from travelogue-like descriptions of landscapes and people and tales of war injuries written from the beds of field hospitals—where it is primarily the author's own identification and choice of publication venue that "queers" the narrative—to more explicitly homoerotic or non-gender-normative themes: poems mourning how the war had torn away male lovers, or joyful tales of newfound intimate relationships.[91] A further regular column, "Women as Soldiers in the World War," gathered clippings from a wide range of German-language newspapers to report on females engaged in military roles from Turkey to the United States, often passing as men in order to do so. Two typical young females serving as men in the Polish legion were described as "nowhere . . . second to their comrades, and their superiors speak of them with the greatest approval"; here, too, the tone is one of great courage and admiration, in stark contrast to some of the more pathologizing medical accounts.[92]

Such defenses of the wartime contributions of "sexual intermediaries" or members of a "third sex" reverberated into the interwar era. Hirschfeld compiled many of the examples previously published in the Quarterly Reports into his *Sittengeschichte des Weltkrieges* (*Sexual History of the World War*, 1930), alongside discussions of prostitution, morality, and heterosexual eroticism in and out of the trenches.[93] Stories of homosexual and transgender bravery also flourished in many of the new subcultural publications to emerge in Weimar-era Berlin aimed explicitly at homosexual and transvestite readers, often with links to sexual rights organizations such as the League of Human Rights (Bund für Menschenrechte) or the German Friendship Association (Deutscher Freundschafts-Verband). From the mid-1920s to early 1930s, long-running female homosexual magazines *Die Freundin* (Girlfriend) and *Frauenliebe* (Womanly Love) set forth the wartime tradition of the Quarterly Reports with articles on brave female-to-male cross-dressing soldiers, bearing titles such as "Heroic Deeds of a Hungarian Woman in the World War."[94] In 1932 the regular column "Transvestites' World" in *Die Freundin* even published an eight-part series by male-to-female transvestite Emi Wolters on "Transvestites in the World War." Wolters, a former senior lieutenant in the German military who had been taken captive by the Russians, drew on more than 100 letters sent in by like-minded *Artgenossen* (literally members of the same "species"), as well as newspaper reports and Hirschfeld's *Sittengeschichte*, to highlight the patriotic deeds and courage under fire of both male-to-female and female-to-male transvestites. Defying popular clichés of cross-dressing spies and conscription dodgers, Wolters investigated the diverse roles of trans and cross-dressing individuals during the war, including as entertainers and female imitators in the prisoner-of-war camps, where comedic or theatrical cross-dressing was also a regular activity of nontransvestite and heterosexual soldiers in their downtime. Such activities were tolerated by the military authorities, as one historian observes, "as a temporary act of relief from the stress of war"; in this they might be compared to the similarly "non-transgressive" cross-dressing balls that other scholars have examined in contexts such as gold rush–era San Francisco.[95] Yet spaces also developed for individuals for whom cross-dressing was more than a temporary "relief." As Wolters reports, the efforts of transvestite performers were sometimes so appreciated by the other men that they even received special privileges: "Yes, one went so far as to allow these mock women (*Scheindamen*) to dress as women even off the stage."[96] Such sources provide an important insight into perspectives that move beyond the mediated patient biographies published by clinical sex researchers and analysts, highlighting the unique contributions of trans and queer subjects both on and behind the front line.

Defending the patriotism of homosexual and transvestite soldiers in World War I by drawing attention to brave homosexual troops, undercover female soldiers, and morale-boosting performers, "third sex" writers challenged psychoanalytic-inspired accounts such as Juliusburger's that undermined the possibility of third sex patriotism based on assumptions of developmental defects. Juliusburger's colleagues, meanwhile, took a more mixed line, defending the military capacity of homosexual soldiers—particularly those exhibiting more masculine characteristics—while arguing that trans individuals were constitutionally unsuited for battle, and should be protected from such roles (although "protection" was undoubtedly mixed, in some cases, with a fear of "infecting" other troops). The sympathetic application of medical expertise to these relatively uncharted waters undoubtedly helped to protect some individuals from nervous breakdown or steer them toward more suitable service roles, even as the pathologizing implications of the sexological accounts examined contrast with the increasingly vocal protests of an emerging homosexual and trans subculture.

With the end of the war in 1918 and the birth of Germany's Weimar Republic in the following year, sadistic violence and sexual disorders increasingly overtook the tremors of the shell-shocked soldier as the primary symptoms of war trauma. These legacies of the war's violence also shaped the cultural realm in significant ways, with sex murderers and rapists spiking in prominence in the artistic and literary representations of interwar Germany. Scholars have discussed at length the undertones of male war violence and misogynistic resentment against those who remained safe at the home front in paintings by Otto Dix, George Grosz, and others, whose male perpetrators glower over dismembered female corpses, and in Franz Biberkopf's violent sprees against women in Alfred Döblin's modernist classic *Berlin Alexanderplatz*.[97] Nor was linking the violence of the trenches to displaced sadism on the home front a novel suggestion for contemporaries—in 1915, Burchard had already predicted a connection between war and a rise in sex crimes, although he noted that "viable" evidence could only reasonably be expected once peace had been reestablished.[98]

By the late Weimar period, such displaced violence was widely acknowledged as part of the long-term fallout of war. When Hirschfeld published his *Sittengeschichte* in 1930, he argued that the normalized violence of war had extended well beyond the soldier veterans themselves to shape the entire psychology of postwar German society, unleashing sadistic instincts and sexual restraints: "the World War can and must be characterized not only as a historical catastrophe, but from the perspective of the history of morality, also as *the greatest sexual catastrophe* that has ever befallen civilized humankind."[99] For commentators such as Hirschfeld and criminologist Erich Wulffen, war neuroses were only the beginning of the sexual-sadistic psychological problems resulting from the global conflict. Consequently, it was not so much psychoanalytic work on the war neuroses as Freud's identification of the "death instinct" that Hirschfeld later considered to be the most significant analytic finding to arise from the violence of war.[100]

The Great War represents a crucial chapter in the larger story of these two mutually entangled fields, as conversations that had begun in earnest in 1905 with Freud's *Three Essays* were given new momentum in the face of the mass violence experienced by soldiers in the trenches of World War I. Psychoanalysts and sexologists in the crisis years of 1914–1918 showed an ability to respond in a prompt and nuanced fashion to the new challenges raised by the war, which many had experienced firsthand from the field hospitals near the front, whether by revising theories of traumatic neuroses and sexual dysfunction originally developed in peacetime, or by offering sympathetic, if not unproblematic, assessments of the capacity of "sexual intermediaries" to represent their nation in times of need. The latter discussions continue to haunt us today, with long and torturous debates around gays and trans people in the military persisting—to take the case of the United States—in only recently repealed "don't ask, don't tell" policies on homosexuals in the services, as well as frightening new bans on trans soldiers put forth by President Donald Trump.[101]

The competing sexological and psychoanalytic approaches examined in this chapter represent only a fraction of the massive scope of medical and psychiatric treatment required by soldiers returning from the front lines—even in Germany, where psychiatry enjoyed particularly strong recognition by military authorities.[102] Yet from a history-of-sexuality perspective, this period is of great significance, for a number of reasons. It shows an ongoing acknowledgement by sexologists that psychoanalysis might have useful contributions to make to their own, more orthodox field; it demonstrates that psychoanalysts were prepared to revisit their own theories of the neuroses in light of current events; and it shows the rise of a critical "third sex" discourse and publications that would become increasingly influential into the Weimar years. Most importantly for the narrative of this book, it shows how endocrinal research was driving an ever-larger wedge between sexological and psychoanalytic approaches by the second decade of the new century as the global conflict coincided with the popularization of the sex-hormone research pioneered by Eugen Steinach and his team in Vienna. The impact of this research on these two fields continued to be felt well into the 1920s, and the following chapter examines how this new brand of chemically oriented argument raised important new questions about the relationship between sexuality, subjectivity, body, and mind.

CHAPTER 4

Discovering the Sex Hormones: Rethinking Sexual Pathologies and Therapies after World War I

"For a long time," researchers of the body's inner chemistry on the one hand and of psychoanalysis on the other "passed each other by without regard, one might even say with 'pride,'" reflected prominent German sexologist Magnus Hirschfeld in 1926. This mutual scientific disregard was something he had, moreover, experienced in person. Many years previously, in the winter before the war, Hirschfeld had made a trip from Berlin to Vienna. He recorded the details of this trip in the first volume of his five-volume textbook series *Geschlechtskunde* (Sexual Science, 1926–1930), in which he recalls that, in the course of one day, he had visited two gentlemen now recognized as "leading personalities of these respective fields."[1] As subsequent paragraphs reveal, these two figures were none other than Eugen Steinach, professor of physiology and pioneer of modern endocrinal and organ transplant research at Vienna's Academy of Sciences (Akademie der Wissenschaften), and that most famous resident of the Berggasse no. 19, Sigmund Freud.

In the morning of that sojourn through the world of cutting-edge Viennese medicine, Hirschfeld reports how he enjoyed a stimulating few hours observing the gonad transplant experiments on rats and guinea pigs being undertaken by Professor Steinach and his team at the Vivarium, a former aquarium and later also zoo in Vienna's Prater amusement park, built for the Vienna World Exposition of 1873. Since 1903, it had housed the city's privately funded Institute of Experimental Biology (Biologische Versuchsanstalt).[2] Hirschfeld then recounts the reaction to his tales of the morning's activities later that afternoon, during an audience with the father of psychoanalysis:

> Still completely under the impression of the artificially feminized and masculinized laboratory animals, I told of the astonishing experiments

> that I had just observed and openly expressed my admiration for this scientific *tour de force* that was enabling such new and deep insights into the finer mechanisms of the body-soul (*Körperseele*), only to be greeted with the same hostile, distancing words that I had heard only a few hours earlier when speaking of psychoanalysis: "These things do not interest me."[3]

It was, he observes, less a case of outright antagonism than "complete indifference," although the famous sexologist and homosexual rights activist acknowledges that the years since his visit had brought a degree of mutual respect between practitioners of these diverse fields. Indeed, by the 1920s Freud had not only begun to cite Steinach's research in his own writings, but had decided to put himself under the knife: in 1924, he underwent the popular "Steinach" vasoligature procedure, a form of vasectomy pioneered by the research team at the Vivarium, which was aimed at rejuvenating male energy and sexual potency.[4] Yet writing in 1926, Hirschfeld was aware that, for at least some scholars, the idea of conjoining body and soul in sex research retained an "illegitimate" character: "Biology over here, psychology over there—the body over here, the mind over there—matter over here, strength over there—Steinach over here, Freud over there!"[5]

As this anecdote suggests, research into the mysterious workings of the endocrinal glands in the first decades of the twentieth century—and in particular, the rather juicily named "internal secretions" of these glands, which after the war became more widely known as "hormones"—marked an important shift in the study of human sexuality. The findings of Steinach and his team quickly reverberated across various branches of medical and scientific research, but their impact on the two academic fields most invested in theorizing sexuality and treating its purported aberrations, sexology and psychoanalysis, has only recently started to attract the serious attention of historians. Within this scholarship, psychoanalysis barely makes it out of the footnotes, with scholars paying far more attention to how figures such as Hirschfeld drew on Steinach's findings to buoy his homosexual rights activism.[6] This focus is not unjustified: Hirschfeld was not only one of Germany's foremost sexological voices during these decades, but his response to Steinach's research was also more detailed than that of many of his peers. His political motivations, moreover, mean that his response is relevant to the history of modern homosexual rights movements as well as the history of science.

Considering the works of Hirschfeld alongside lesser-known actors, the following analysis expands the history of twentieth-century sex research by offering the first detailed account of the impact of internal-secretions research on wartime and interwar psychoanalysis, and on that field's relationship with sexual science. I argue that the popularization of "hormone" research in the 1920s—a term coined by London-based physiologist Ernest Starling in 1905[7]—raised new questions for both fields, but also marked a pivotal moment in processes of professionalization and disciplinary establishment, at times seeming to support and at other times threatening to undermine the truth claims of sex researchers. In particular, I show that it offered sexologists a powerful new basis from which to shore up their field's authority by refocusing attention on the significance of physiological processes, in the form of the invisible workings of the body's inner chemistry.

The boom in hormone research in the 1910s and 1920s forced sexologists and psychoanalysts to reevaluate their understandings of the sexual instinct and its role in shaping the human constitution. Growing awareness of the influence of the internal secretions drove scholars to revisit distinctions between body and mind, and to reconsider the respective significance of congenital and acquired factors in the development of the perversions. Was homosexuality, to take a key example, henceforth to be considered a condition rooted in physiology, as sexologists such as Hirschfeld had long insisted? And could it, by extension, be treated via hormonal intervention? Did the new hormone research negate the Freudian assumption that same-sex desires could be traced back to inhibited psychosexual development? Previous chapters have shown how sexologists from German-speaking central Europe, including Hirschfeld, Albert Moll, August Forel, and Iwan Bloch, faced a major challenge to their explanations of human sexuality with the publication of Sigmund Freud's *Three Essays on the Theory of Sexuality* in 1905—a particular test for more congenitally and physiologically oriented researchers such as Hirschfeld. Freud, as we have seen, had insisted on the universal significance of infant psychosexual development, including the "pregenital" stages of oral and anal eroticism and the negotiation of the Oedipus complex.[8] Proposing a more thoroughly psychologized theory of human sexual development that went beyond existing psychiatric accounts in claiming to explain the universal development of the neuroses, Freud's ideas subsequently infiltrated sexological explanations of conditions ranging from sex-gender "inversion" or homosexuality to trauma-related impotence.

In this context of scientific interpenetration, the research fronted by Steinach and his Viennese team raised new questions for both fields, but lent particular ammunition to sexology, promising to help secure the independence and relevance of a field that had only recently begun to explicitly distance itself through journals and conferences from more established disciplines such as biology, psychiatry, and criminal anthropology. After decades of weighing acquired versus congenital explanations for the "perversions," hormone research seemed to provide definitive proof that an individual's innermost sexual constitution was determined above all by the workings of the glands. Excitement centered especially on the potential to use hormone-based therapies to treat patients suffering from seemingly debilitating disorders, as lab-based technologies now vied for authority with the older scientific genre of the patient case history.[9] In turn, sexology's reorientation toward physiological and hormonal explanations prompted responses from psychoanalysts, whose own professional standing had risen significantly thanks to their involvement in treating war neuroses.

This chapter begins with a brief survey of late-nineteenth- and early-twentieth-century hormone research, before undertaking a comparative reading of wartime and interwar writings around two discrete diagnoses. The first, psychosexual infantilism, was an early-twentieth-century sexological label for delayed sexual development, and encompassed physical as well as psychological symptoms; its analysis represents something of a lacuna in the history of sexuality. The second, homosexuality, has already featured prominently in chapter 2 as the center of debates about congenital versus acquired sexual perversions, and as the focus of normative scientific attempts to find a "cure" for this condition. The perceived urgency of this research was underpinned by the social and political vilification of homosexuals in the German-speaking world, with male same-sex acts criminalized under Germany's notorious Paragraph 175, while in Austria both female and male homosexual acts were punishable under Paragraphs 129b and 130.[10] Some of the texts I examine are well known: I place *Three Essays* under the microscope, for example, to determine the precise impact of Steinach's research on foundational psychoanalytic assumptions. I contrast this with less-familiar works, including a key study on psychosexual infantilism by psychiatrist Arthur Kronfeld, a prominent figure in interwar German sex research as a founding member of Hirschfeld's Institute for Sexual Science in Berlin in 1919 and a frequent speaker at the Berlin-based Medical Society for Sexual Science (Ärztliche Gesellschaft für Sexualwissenschaft) since its establishment in 1913. Known for his innovations in psychotherapy, contemporary psychoanalysts recognized Kronfeld as one of the sexologists working most clearly "under the banner of Freud" due to his acceptance of the libido theory and ideas about infantile sexual development.[11] Yet he has also been characterized as "one of the most important early critics of psychoanalysis," based particularly on a widely cited article from 1911, in which he complained of Freud's lack of evidence for his theories of the unconscious.[12] Kronfeld's work has tended to float at the margins of the history of sexuality, possibly because he wrote largely for medical specialists, but it was taken seriously by psychoanalytic and sexological contemporaries—particularly, we might speculate, because his understanding of Freudian ideas ran deeper than that of many of his sexological colleagues.[13] In the following, I read such writings by interwar sexologists and psychoanalysts in the context of diagnoses of psychosexual infantilism and homosexuality to show how hormone research shifted the relationship between these fields, providing a boost to sexology at a crucial moment in its disciplinary history. This chapter also brings questions of therapy into the foreground, arguing that the needs of patients were an important factor shaping the clinical priorities of both sexologists and psychoanalysts—not all of which could be adequately addressed by the new hormone therapies.

The Exciting World of the Hormones: Steinach and the "Internal Secretions"

Internal-secretions research offered scientists in the early twentieth century exciting new insights into "normal" as well as "abnormal" human development. Eugen Steinach achieved widespread scientific fame, including six nominations for the Nobel Prize, in the later years of World War I for his experiments with the endocrinal glands, before his work fell into disrepute by the 1940s.[14] He died in exile in Switzerland in 1944, where he continued to work after his career as a Jewish scientist in National Socialist Vienna became untenable—and even though his work on human "rejuvenation" achieved through testicular graftings, vasectomies, and other methods had become clouded by associations with quackery, commercial self-interest, and lack of verifiability.[15] This contrasted markedly with the tone of upbeat optimism surrounding his team at the Vivarium—famous among biologists as the "Sorcerers' Institute"[16]—in the years after 1912, when he returned to Vienna after two decades at the German University in Prague. Experimenting with sexual development in rats and guinea pigs by castrating young animals before puberty, the team found that the animals failed to reach sexual maturity. They then showed that testicle and organ transplants on castrated animals—including autotransplants where gonads were removed from and then reinserted into the same animal—could restore inhibited secondary sex characteristics, such as mammary development or sex-specific hair growth. These experiments, which worked by deliberately distorting biological processes, quickly became more daring, as the team began grafting ovaries onto castrated male animals and testicles onto neutered female animals.[17] On this basis, Steinach and his team decided that the sex glands were not only responsible for reproduction, but excrete "inner" or "internal secretions" necessary for sexual maturation. They understood these internal secretions to be a product of the "interstitial" or "Leydig" cells, which Steinach somewhat inaccurately dubbed the "puberty gland" (*Pubertätsdrüse*), and found that they were not only sex-specific, but could also be manipulated.[18] As a result, castrated animals could be "feminized" or "masculinized" in ways that seemingly contradicted their biological sex, affecting not only physiological development, but behavioral patterns such as mating or suckling. Steinach characterized these behavioral and psychological effects as an "erotization [*Erotisierung*] of the central nervous system."[19] Further experiments involving simultaneous transplants of ovaries and testicles into castrated male animals produced—in the few cases where these grafts "took"—so-called "experimental hermaphrodites." These animals exhibited a male build but feminized mammary tissue and lactation, and sexual behavior cycled between masculine and feminine at two- or three-monthly intervals: males that had once been attacked by other males now became sexually interesting to them.[20] All of this seemed to prove that, even if sex was predetermined by genetics, as Steinach believed it was (the term "gene" had been coined in 1909, although its content continued to be debated), it could also be modified via the glands.[21]

It did not take long before the team at the Vivarium began thinking beyond lab rats and guinea pigs to consider applications in human beings—a level of experimentation encouraged by the scale of injuries being presented by soldiers returning from the front. The Biologische Versuchanstalt attracted substantial state subsidies even in the later years of the conflict—despite the Austrian government's strapped financial circumstances—based on the possibility that it might produce new and effective treatments for the demasculinizing symptoms of injury-related castration as well as the pervasive threat of homosexual "effeminacy."[22] While the initial surgeries (described below) focused on restoring masculinity to soldiers suffering castration symptoms, along with the potential that the new hormone treatments might be a means of achieving youthful "rejuvenation," particularly in the frail or elderly, it was the implications for "effeminacy" that grabbed the wider public's attention. Could a person suffering from weakness, lack of energy, or impotence, Steinach wondered, be reinvigorated and remasculinized by stimulating the internal secretions? Could a homosexual man be "cured" by transplanting a testicle from a "normal," heterosexual male? In 1918, he declared that they could, in an assertion of the normalizing potential of the new endocrinal therapies. Although his bold claim echoed similar assertions made during the preceding decade by psychoanalysts such as Isidor Sadger, also based in the Austrian capital, for Steinach the cure for homosexuality was to be found not on the couch, but in the chemical manipulation of the body.[23] Fueling debates among biologists, sexologists, doctors, and psychoanalysts, his research also added new impetus to political activism, particularly among those who sought to defend homosexuality as a congenital anomaly. One of the foremost proponents of this view was, of course, Hirschfeld, famous not only as one of Germany's leading sexual scientists, but as a prominent homosexual rights activist and cofounder of the Scientific Humanitarian Committee (WhK).[24]

Although Steinach's experiments raised internal-secretions research to new levels of scientific and public awareness, he was not the first to experiment with the mysterious workings of the glands. For several decades, albeit with less success, scientists had been investigating both the seemingly age-defying potential of the hormones and their impact on sexual behavior and development. In the 1880s, French-American-Mauritian endocrinal physiologist Charles-Edouard Brown-Séquard had shown experimentally that the removal of the adrenal glands led to loss of life. He later risked his scientific reputation when he reported to a Paris audience on how he had successfully "rejuvenated" himself using injections of a liquid testicular extract taken from dogs and guinea-pigs. While Brown-Séquard's findings met with skepticism in the popular and medical press, his early attempt at organotherapy marked the start of something big, as the medical marketplace was "flooded with extracts and various preparations of virtually every organ . . . which were prescribed for virtually every conceivable disorder that did not respond to orthodox treatment."[25] Across Europe, North America, and beyond, enthusiasm for organ-based therapies grew apace, despite the fact that, for many orthodox physicians, they represented little more that outlandish and unproven quackery, concerns reinforced by the poor quality of many of the "extracts" on the market.[26] By the end of World War I, however, the boom in gland therapies helped to stimulate a wave of more scientifically respectable, laboratory-based research, such as that taken up by Steinach and his team, with the cooperation of major pharmaceutical companies such as Schering. This resulted in a new wave of clinical applications, as high-quality, potent hormone extracts were made available, often drawn from the thyroid and adrenal glands.[27] In the early 1930s even Hirschfeld had jumped on the bandwagon, collaborating with Institute physician Bernhard Schapiro in the development of the pharmaceutical product "Testifortan." This impotence treatment, based on freeze-dried testicular tissue from bulls, became an important source of income for the Berlin Institute in its final years before the Nazi seizure of power, particularly when it began to be marketed under the brand name "Titus Pearls" (*Titus-Perlen*).[28] Just as nineteenth-century scientific medicine had turned to the "objective" experimental approaches and instruments of physiology, in the interwar period the laboratory-based study of hormonal functions was embraced as a key site of medical innovation, one that promised to be of particular import and legitimation for the scientific study of sexuality.[29]

Other treatments for men included the aforementioned, highly fashionable—although subsequently discredited—"Steinach" vasoligature procedure. By 1936, Viennese urologist Viktor Blum observed that there were now more than 1,000 research papers dealing with this minor surgical intervention, while Steinach himself noted "countless" reports from as far afield as Delhi, New York, Cuba, and Leningrad.[30] In their 1940 retrospective *Sex and Life*, Steinach and Josef Loebel explained the methods that had led to developing this operation. Observing how early experimental vasectomies on rats had caused lethargic, senile animals to gain weight, develop glossy fur, and exhibit an increased sex drive, they also describe the first human experiments, performed in the late 1910s by Steinach's Viennese colleague, urologist and surgeon Robert Lichtenstern. These experiments took place without the patients' knowledge (to avoid the distortions of suggestion) in the course of surgeries ostensibly treating conditions such as testicular abscess. The logic underlying this operation was that vasoligature would destroy the germinal, sperm-producing cells of the testicle, stimulating the remaining hormone-secreting interstitial cells to rejuvenating effect. The researchers were delighted with the results. Their first subject, a forty-three-year-old coachman named Anton W., had originally presented as a "perfect example of pre-senile exhaustion," including greatly reduced work capacity, loss of appetite, and poor physical condition. Three months later, he could boast increased appetite and weight, fresh hair growth, and muscle development, and by the time eighteen months had passed, "this man with his smooth, unwrinkled face, his smart and upright bearing, gives the impression of a youthful man at the height of his vitality."[31]

Such wartime surgeries were a boon to the Steinach team's research and to sexual science more broadly. In 1918 new *Psychopathia sexualis* editor Alfred Fuchs even incorporated a brief discussion of the "Steinach-Lichtenstern" experiments into the latest edition of Krafft-Ebing's still-bestselling forensic study, noting their theoretical significance and attractiveness for homosexual individuals facing social stigma (even as he warned that in most cases, psychological therapy remained the only suitable option).[32] The Steinach vasoligature operation, meanwhile, was being widely touted as a scientific vehicle of national regeneration and increased productivity, and became enormously popular following the war; American-German journalist George Viereck and American novelist Gertrude Atherton were among those to argue that Germany could make use of this procedure to help recover from its post-war economic woes.[33] With surgeons around the world rushing to specialize in this popular technique, it is not surprising that Freud was among those who agreed to be "Steinached" in 1924, hoping to hinder the progress of his oral cancer.[34] Nor was he alone in pursuing a return to a more youthful, healthier self: when Irish poet William Butler Yeats underwent the procedure, he reported that it revived not only his "creative power" but also his "sexual desire."[35] Freud's response was less enthusiastic: several months after his surgery he wrote that "up to now I have felt nothing reassuring from the effects of the Steinach operation."[36] Yet this did not prevent one observer from reporting back to Steinach that Freud "was very satisfied with the result," feeling "that the malignant growth of his jaw had been favorably influenced."[37]

More experimental methods were also trialed: French-Russian physician Serge Voronoff achieved notoriety in the 1920s after implanting "monkey-glands"—testicular tissue from apes—into ageing men as a treatment for senility. Like Steinach, Voronoff also experimented with treating homosexuality, although his claims of success remained undocumented;[38] his work was recorded with some excitement by London-based Jewish Australian sexologist and gynecologist Norman Haire—an enthusiastic, if often socially awkward intermediary between Continental, Anglophone, and later also North American sexological developments.[39] For women, meanwhile, the nineteenth-century gynecological boom in oophorectomy, or ovary removal procedures, once used to treat illnesses ranging from nervous disorders to breast cancer, had fallen from favor due to poor postoperative results and an increasing awareness of unfortunate side effects. There was no direct equivalent of the Steinach operation to "rejuvenate" the female body; instead, practitioners looked to supplementary treatments such as ovarian extracts, including a new "Progynon" preparation that Steinach developed together with pharmaceutical company Schering-Kahlbaum. Other therapies included X-ray irradiation of the ovaries or more complicated procedures such as tubal ligations and even ovarian transplants; Steinach was optimistic about the potential of such transplants, but left their trialing to others. This may also have been due to the difficulty experienced by earlier researchers, such as Viennese gynecologist Josef Halban, in getting the grafts to "take," in an era in which the immunological science of transplant rejection was little understood.[40] Haire was among those who nonetheless experimented with female as well as male surgical and hormone treatments during these years to treat women suffering from conditions such as amenorrhea or excessive facial hair. As he wrote to his distinguished senior colleague Havelock Ellis in 1927, "My Steinach cases continue to be satisfactory with a few disappointing exceptions. I have done quite a number latterly and have three female cases under treatment at present." Haire and many others continued to pursue these methods even as the Steinach methods were starting to fall from grace in the larger medical profession.[41]

Later transsexual research pioneer Dr. Harry Benjamin was another of Steinach's many admirers at this period, and recorded in his diaries of the 1920s and 1930s his regular visits to the Vivarium. Benjamin was fascinated not just by the vasoligature procedure (which he soberly assessed as having "a definite value in balancing endocrine disturbances, relieving symptoms of age and prolonging efficiency—no more and no less"), but by the possibilities of radiation for female rejuvenation.[42] Born in Berlin in 1885 and trained in medicine in the German city of Tübingen, Benjamin had emigrated to the United States in 1913 and become an enthusiastic proponent of Steinach's research in the 1920s; he later reported that he "studied with [Steinach] in Vienna nearly every summer until the late 1930s."[43] One of Benjamin's patients played a particularly important role in increasing public knowledge of the new endocrine science. The aforementioned novelist Gertrude Atherton had sought treatment from Benjamin for "mental sterility" or writer's block. In such cases, radiation treatment was often combined with diathermy, using electrodes to warm the reproductive organs with the aim of stimulating ovarian function; Atherton later raved about how this therapy resulted in "a black cloud lifting from my brain."[44] Irradiation continues to be used today for the purpose of tissue repair, but despite Atherton's enthusiasm, its effectiveness in "rejuvenating" women ultimately proved limited, and seems to have relied not a little on the powers of positive suggestion. This also applied to many of the early organotherapy methods based in hormone extracts, although some of them did contain active ingredients that have since been verified as effective and continue to be found in over-the-counter and prescription medicines. The development of synthetic hormones, too, used today particularly in trans medicine and hormone replacement therapies, had its direct roots in this early endocrinological research.[45]

A documentary film explaining Steinach's experiments for a popular cinema audience, *Der Steinach-Film* (The Steinach Film), did much to publicly disseminate the latest internal-secretions research. It hit the cinemas in January 1923, with images of rats undergoing castration operations, microscope tissue slides, and "masculine" women shaving off moustaches and beards. At a time when newspapers and magazines from Berlin to New York were enthralled by tales of gender crossings and bodily rejuvenations, this film publicized sex-organ transplants among mainstream audiences as a potential mode of treatment not only for men castrated by disease or accident, but for those individuals that Hirschfeld had dubbed "sexual intermediaries," including male-to-female "transvestites" and females who lived as men.[46] I have argued elsewhere that the increasing use of lens-based technologies of photography and film points to something of a visual turn in the production and dissemination of sexological knowledge in the first decades of the twentieth century. Distancing themselves from the feared distortions of the subjective, text-based case study, sex researchers were beginning to embrace seemingly more objective types of evidence, including photographic and moving images, which had the added benefit of being able to communicate expert knowledge about human sexuality in an entertaining and educational fashion.[47] The *Steinach-Film* was no exception, attracting attention even well beyond the German-speaking world, as is evident from an exchange of letters in early 1923 between Haire and Ellis. Haire was quickly becoming one of interwar Britain's most prominent sexological voices, and gaining a reputation as one of the leading practitioners of the Steinach procedure in that country. With great pleasure he reported to Ellis that he was now performing vasectomies under local rather than general anesthetic ("yesterday [I saw] a patient whom I vasectomied a year ago to the day—he is a transformed man"), and even offered to drive Ellis from the latter's home in Brixton to see the *Steinach-Film*. The aging Ellis responded that he was regrettably unable to attend, but drew on his Continental connections to put his younger colleague in touch with Hirschfeld in Berlin, who was planning a visit to the third International Sex Congress in London—a simple gesture, but one that again points to the significance of German scholars in transnational sex research networks during this era.[48]

Glandular therapy was thus threatening—or promising, depending on one's point of view—to displace all manner of existing therapeutic methods, even those directed, like psychoanalysis, toward the workings of the mind. "How much closer to the true and wholesome are we led by these facts," declared American gynecologist Samuel Bandler of the new hormone research, "than by the aberrations of the theories of Freud"; others similarly declared endocrinal investigation set to "control the future of human nature" in a way that may well "render a good many of the Freudian dicta obsolete"—or at least force these into a "synthesis" with the newer theories of the glands.[49] Not surprisingly, Steinach's complex and at times contradictory contributions to the scientific understanding of sexual difference received mixed responses from researchers working within sexological and psychoanalytic frameworks. For two conditions in particular, psychosexual infantilism and homosexuality, hormone-based therapies seemed to offer particularly promising outcomes.

Revisiting Sexual Development: Kronfeld's "Psychosexual infantilism" (1921) and Freud's Revisions to *Three Essays*

In 1921, two years after its foundation in a stately building in Berlin's central Tiergarten district at In den Zelten 9a–10, Hirschfeld's Institute for Sexual Science oversaw publication of the slender volume "On Psychosexual Infantilism, a Constitutional Anomaly." It was the first of a new monograph series entitled *Sexus*, edited by Hirschfeld and aimed at disseminating the Institute's research findings. The author was Institute staff member Arthur Kronfeld, originally from Heidelberg, who between 1919 and 1926 worked at Hirschfeld's Institute as leader of the "Department for Psychological Sexual Complaints" (*Abteilung für seelische Sexualleiden*) treating disturbances such as impotence and various nervous conditions. Active in Weimar-era homosexual rights circles, he later founded his own neurological practice in Berlin, but emigrated and died during the period of National Socialism.[50] In this pamphlet, Kronfeld defines psychosexual infantilism as a diverse grouping of developmental abnormalities linked by physiological or psychological immaturity, which he situates within a constitutional biology framework. Constitutional biology, as one historian has recently summarized, was a "central organizing paradigm in cutting-edge research in neurology, physiology, anatomy and endocrinology" during these decades. For Kronfeld, psychosexual infantilism represented one of a series of little-understood, "partial" constitutions, caused by a combination of morphological, functional, and evolutionary factors.[51] Symptoms could range from the physical, such as thyroid-related growth anomalies, to the psychological, including exhibitionism, narcissism, fetishism, and pedophilia—and in a distinct class of cases, homosexuality.[52] Kronfeld attributed the coinage of "psychosexual infantilism" to Hirschfeld and his WhK colleague Ernst Burchard, who in 1913 had discussed "sexual infantilism" in terms of pathological inhibitions such as aplasia of the testicles or fetishistic desires.[53]

Defining infantilism as the abnormal persistence of developmental stages that would "normally" be quickly passed through, Kronfeld's study at first seems to closely follow Freud's model of inhibited development as the source of the neuroses and perversions. Yet he soon diverges from psychoanalytic accounts by insisting that, while developmental inhibitions (*Entwicklungshemmungen*) may be externally triggered, they require an underlying constitutional basis. Crucially, Kronfeld linked this constitutional basis to the internal secretions, insisting on the influence of the gonads from early infancy onward in ways that helped to crystallize earlier sexological speculations in this direction. In his prewar study *The Sexual Life of the Child* (1908), for example, Moll had tentatively associated the secondary sexual developments of *later* childhood and adolescence with the body's chemical functions. Kronfeld takes this further, making a case for the impact of the sexual glands even in very young infants, before the organism is capable of producing mature reproductive cells.[54] He also linked the maturation of the gonads to the development of behavioral inhibitions—a process theorized in Freud's *Three Essays* in clearly psychologized terms as a product of the latency phase.[55]

Kronfeld has been described as the "theoretical head" of Hirschfeld's Institute; the interdisciplinary sophistication of his account can be seen not only in his discussion of the latest endocrinal research, but in his integration of psychoanalytic thought.[56] Although disagreeing on various details, Kronfeld defends Freud's theory of infantile sexuality as an "everlasting achievement" for science, from Freud's emphasis on object choice and environmental factors to his recognition that the "perversions" in fact display distinct constitutional similarities in the form of developmental delay, or "infantilism."[57] Kronfeld's admiration for Freud's insights is tempered, however, by his questioning of their methodological soundness and some of Freud's more daring theoretical assumptions: he criticizes the Oedipus complex as overly "schematic," for example. He also considers formulations of the libido comparing emotional and instinctive processes in children with adult sexuality "unfortunate," and he attacks psychoanalytic case studies (as Moll had similarly done) for their lack of representativeness, their suggestibility, and the ethical problems involved in extracting sexual information from children. Freud's findings, he concludes, add value but must not be utilized in isolation. Instead, they must be placed within broader legitimizing frameworks of constitutional biology research.[58]

Nor could psychoanalysts simply ignore the implications of endocrine research for their own explanations of human sexual development. A note of caution can already be detected in a 1919 letter from Freud to Sándor Ferenczi applauding a scientific paper his Hungarian friend had written, which mentioned the latest results from the Vivarium: "But do you have permission to disclose anything of Steinach's secret discoveries?"[59] A year later, Freud found himself compelled to address this new research in his fourth, 1920 edition of *Three Essays*—although his response to the "discovery" of the sex hormones, as the editors of his collected works observe, is remarkable for how little he needed to modify his own hypotheses.[60] Freud's revisions cite Steinach's sex-organ experiments as an extension rather than a reversal of his previous discussion of the causes of sexual excitation; he also creatively deploys them to underwrite his ideas about universal bisexuality. In his first two essays, Freud's annotations are confined largely to the footnotes. Here he observes that the Steinach experiments shed "a bright light" not only on the organic determinants of homoeroticism, but on sexual characteristics in general, showing that glandular transformations can be psychosexual as well as somatic. He cites an experiment reported by Alexander Lipschütz in which a "passive homosexual" male, who had lost his testicles to tubercular illness, subsequently exhibited a range of "female" secondary characteristics, including hair growth and fatty deposits. Following a testicle transplant, the patient "began to act as a man" and direct his libido "in a normal fashion toward women."[61] Despite this impressive new experimental evidence, however, Freud sticks to his guns in insisting that these new findings fail to "put the [i.e., Freud's own] theory of inversion on a new basis," and maintaining his primary commitment to relational and environmental explanations of homosexual development (even as he acknowledged that the hormones might help to establish a basis for such development). Even more damningly, he contends that these new findings do not offer a "cure" for homosexuality—a conservative but self-serving position at odds with Steinach's own, rather more gung-ho experimental attempts to treat homosexual men via testicle transplant.[62] As we will see, however, Freud was reluctant to put forward an alternative psychoanalytic "cure" for this condition (as some of his followers had attempted to do), because he did not deem same-sex desires to be inherently pathological. As such, his updated writings on this topic represent a less normative stance than that of many of his medical contemporaries.

Revising his third essay, "The Transformations of Puberty," Freud included his most substantial discussion of Steinach's research. Rewriting and expanding an extended passage on chemical theory, he first explains Steinach's experiments to his readers, before tentatively linking the "hermaphroditic" chemical and anatomical functions of the puberty gland to existing psychoanalytic understandings of universal bisexuality and latency:

> It has become experimentally possible (E. Steinach) to transform a male into a female, and conversely a female into a male. In this process the psychosexual behaviour of the animal alters in accordance with the somatic sexual characters and simultaneously with them. It seems, however, that this sex-determining influence is not an attribute of that part of the sex-glands which gives rise to the specific sex-cells (spermatozoa and ovum) but of their interstitial tissue, upon which special emphasis is laid by being described in the literature as the "puberty-gland." It is quite pos-

> sible that further investigation will show that this puberty-gland has normally a hermaphrodite disposition. If this were so, the theory of the bisexuality of the higher animals would be given anatomical foundation. It is already probable that the puberty-gland is not the only organ concerned with the production of sexual excitation and sexual characters. In any case, what we already know of the part played by the thyroid gland in sexuality fits in with this new biological discovery. It seems probable, then, that special chemical substances are produced in the interstitial portion of the sex-glands; these are then taken up in the blood stream and cause particular parts of the central nervous system to be charged with sexual tension.[63]

Not only did the discovery of the sex hormones leave Freud's overarching theory of sexual development intact, but a number of his earlier writings suggest that he had anticipated such findings from as early as 1895, including in an exchange with Fliess ("it is probable that further research of a similar kind will produce a direct confirmation of this presumption of bisexuality") and in a 1906 essay emphasizing the "chemical factor" in the development of the neuroses.[64] Freud was prepared to acknowledge the influence of the glands, but not to see them as decisive in shaping an individual's sexual subjectivity.

In different ways, sexologists and psychoanalysts each responded to the latest hormone research by attempting to underpin existing theories of human sexual development and its "inhibitions" with a more sophisticated understanding of the body's endocrinal processes. At the same time, Kronfeld's study reveals an increasingly matter-of-fact acceptance by interwar German sexologists of certain aspects of Freudian theory, despite ongoing reservations about clinical methods; in this, his approach to psychoanalysis continued in the vein established by prewar sexologists, even as he lends more weight to endocrinal factors. Freud's revisions to his *Three Essays*, meanwhile, suggest an attempt to harness the scientific legitimacy of hormone research to psychoanalytic ideas, including universal bisexuality and the latency period. It was no coincidence that Freud's revisions return to the question of sexual inversion, moreover, for the homosexual subject was central to these interwar debates about the clinical and therapeutic significance of the hormones. This was most evident in the work of Germany's leading scientist-activist in the field of homosexuality, Magnus Hirschfeld.

Hirschfeld, Homosexuality and Hormones: The Internal Secretions as "Cure"?

The possibility that hormone manipulation might offer a permanent "cure" for homosexuality—understood as a successful diversion of the homosexual's desires from same-sex to "normal" (heterosexual) object choices—caused great excitement in interwar sexual science. The pressing needs of patients in the here and now sharpened the need to distinguish between clinical realities and the exciting future possibilities of hormone-based therapies, and further altered the terms of the conversation between sexology and psychoanalysis. Intrigued by Steinach's claim that he could cure a man of his homosexuality by replacing his testicles with those from a heterosexual male, even Hirschfeld was known to have quietly sent off a number of his patients to undergo castration operations with surgeon Richard Mühsam.[65] He did so despite being Germany's most vocal proponent of the view that homosexuality was a naturally occurring, immutable, and thus defensible "intermediary" sexual variant. The normalizing push to intervene in the lives of homosexual-identified subjects—even if in the name of creating for them what queer scholars describe in terms of a more "livable" life—thus came into direct conflict with the larger tenor of Hirschfeld's sexual politics.[66]

Within the growing body of Hirschfeld scholarship, several recent biographers have considered the rather glaring contradiction between his conviction, on the one hand, that homosexuality might not only be explained but possibly treated along invasive biological lines, and on the other his political campaigning for equal rights and recognition for the "third sex." While some rightly emphasize the severity of homosexual stigmatization within the legal constraints of Wilhelmine Germany, and point to the constant risk of reputation damage or even patient suicide that came with such constraints, others note that this only partially explains why Hirschfeld opted for castration surgeries in some cases (and indeed, why he had earlier expressed an open-minded approach toward the "conversion" attempts of psychoanalysts such as Sadger). Most likely, his overriding concern for his patients meant that he simply failed to see either the contradictions in his own approach or the damage that the surgeries themselves might do to patients.[67] Concern for patients was, after all, the guiding motivation for his development of the "adaption therapy" discussed in chapter 2, whereby Hirschfeld advised physicians to work with patients not to "heal" their condition, but rather to strengthen their self-esteem and develop strategies for living with their sexuality without coming into conflict with the law.[68] Although narcissistic factors such as status and fame undoubtedly helped to propel his public outreach activities, Hirschfeld's lifelong work to reduce the sufferings caused by living in a society intolerant of sexual diversity is evident in his ongoing advocacy for homosexual patients and politics, in the establishment of marital and transvestite counseling clinics at his Institute, and in his touring interwar Germany lecturing on topics such as birth control.[69]

Hirschfeld's publications on homosexuality from the late wartime and interwar years demonstrate a number of trends that, together with Kronfeld's pamphlet, offer vivid examples of how European sexologists at this period were attempting to juggle and integrate new hormonal and psychoanalytic explanations into their responses to the pressing needs of patients. First, they highlight a growing conviction that the glands held the key to the mysteries of human sexual development. Second, they offer evidence of sexologists selectively adopting psychoanalytic concepts, even as they worked to shore up the boundaries of their own medico-scientific specialization. Hirschfeld's monolithic 1914 study *The Homosexuality of Men and Women*, for example, showed an early interest in connecting theories of homosexuality to the latest endocrine research, which he observes "indeed holds a seductive fascination" (*etwas Bestechendes*), and offered "the most promising means of arriving at clarity concerning the remaining causes of homosexuality." Although Hirschfeld saw Steinach and his team as leading the way, he also mentions the promising "Abderhalden" method of blood investigations, while his 1912 work *Naturgesetze der Liebe* (Natural Laws of Love) trumpets his own coinage of the terms "Andrin" and "Gynäcin" (never widely adopted) to describe the sex-specific "juices" necessary for sexual maturation.[70]

Pointing to the wider enthusiasm among sexologists for these new methods, Max Marcuse's journal *Sexual-Probleme* (Sexual Problems) also published a number of pieces on castration experiments in these years, including in animals, and regularly highlighted the latest research on the glands in its "Rundschau" column.[71] For his part, Hirschfeld was sympathetic to the desire of homosexual patients to seek out the latest treatments, but initially hesitant about the prospects of organotherapy, questioning whether available testicle-based hormone preparations could really have "practical results" when the workings of the internal secretions "are still so dark and complicated."[72] He did, however, look to the "chemical" theory of sexuality as a powerful discursive means of separating homosexuality from older associations of degeneracy and vice, and emphasized developments in embryological and evolutionary research suggesting that humans developed from an original bisexual or hermaphroditic origin, which supported in turn his own theory of human sexuality as a continuum of naturally occurring but immutable intermediary forms. Hirschfeld thus combined a Darwinian antidegeneration position with the belief that homosexuality was an immutable and inborn condition. This stance placed him in line with the Freudians on the former point, and at odds with them on the latter.[73]

The war experience opened up spaces for a more accelerated and experimental brand of sex research, as sexual scientists drew on the authority they had gained during their mobilization in field hospitals treating German soldiers.[74] During these years Hirschfeld continued to explore the implications of Steinach's sex-gland experiments for theories of homosexuality (as well as developments in embryological research, such as Iwan Bloch's 1908 suggestion that inversion may be attributable to chemical changes in the fetus),[75] and carefully translated these findings for general audiences via his public lectures and even a silver-screen appearance in the 1919 silent film *Anders als die Andern* (*Different from the Others*, dir. R. Oswald). He even claimed some of the credit for Steinach's decision to investigate "hermaphroditized" animals in the first place, arguing that this merely confirmed "the standpoint on homosexuality and related phenomena that I have put forth in the *Jahrbüchern für sexuelle Zwischenstufen* and other writings for the past twenty years."[76] This view is also shared by some historians: "It seems probable that Steinach's animal experiments would not have led so quickly to human experiments without the Zwischenstufentheorie [Hirschfeld's theory of sexual intermediacy] as the missing link."[77] By the early 1920s, Germany's most outspoken sexologist found himself in a position to look back on an exciting quarter-century of "extraordinary progress," during which his field had extended beyond its initial status as "an appendage of the psychiatric clinic . . . lacking its own autonomy" to connect with a rich body of experimental physiological research.[78] Moving beyond the test tubes and lab coats of the Vivarium, hormones had swiftly become a crucial legitimizing foundation of a modern sexual science.

This was particularly important for sexologists as they confronted the growing influence of psychoanalytic accounts in explaining the workings of the sexual body and mind. Hirschfeld's own relationship with psychoanalysis, as earlier chapters of this book have demonstrated, was a rocky one. After signing up as an enthusiastic founding member of the Berlin Psychoanalytic Society in 1908, by 1911 Hirschfeld had abandoned that pioneering group following attacks by Jung and complaints of his analytic ignorance by others such as Abraham.[79] Such personal slights compounded considerable theoretical differences of opinion on matters such as the Oedipus complex. Yet Hirschfeld, like many of his sexological colleagues, actually remained closely attuned to psychoanalytic developments in the years that followed. By the time he penned his major, multivolume works of sexual science and sexual pathology of the late 1910s and 1920s (including his three-volume *Sexualpathologie* [*Sexual Pathology*, 1917–1920], and his last major textbook series *Geschlechtskunde* [Sexual Science, 1926–1930]), he had quietly adopted a number of Freudian concepts. (His final monographs on the war and his 1933 travelogue *Weltreise eines Sexualforschers* [The World Journey of a Sex Researcher] took a more cultural-historical and ethnological turn.) He was prepared to accept, for example, the central psychoanalytic idea of repression (*Verdrängung*), and even to acknowledge a lightly erotic "undercurrent" in parental and sibling love. His ongoing engagement with psychoanalytic writings is evident from the numerous references he makes in these volumes to early Freudians such as Sadger, Otto Rank, and Wilhelm Stekel.[80] In other respects, though, Hirschfeld's later works represent a concerted attack on the Freudians, chalking up their reluctance to acknowledge constitutional and hormonal factors to an irrational opposition to biological research. Cheekily turning the Freudian rhetoric of "resistance" against its own practitioners ("*The sex life has its roots in the life of the glands*, in the constitutional and not the accidental. Will psychoanalysis gradually arrive at this goal, against which it currently puts up so much resistance . . . ?"[81]), he argued that psychoanalysis lacks the scientific approach necessary to account for the physiological underpinnings of the sexual instinct: "An external inducement (*Anlaß*) is only ever a stimulus, never a decisive internal cause."[82] In such ways, and more forcefully than even Kronfeld had done, Hirschfeld used the legitimizing potential of hormone research as a means to bolster sexual science against the growing currency of psychoanalytic accounts.

Although many of the details of exactly what the hormones did remained fuzzy, sexual scientists had thus begun to adopt and articulate a theory of the sexual instinct as chemically determined. This turn toward the body's inner chemistry formed part of the broader transformations characterized by historians of this period as typical of "sexual modernity," and sat—at times uneasily—alongside a growing emphasis on psychologized understandings of the sexual instinct, exemplified by the rise of psychoanalysis. A move toward ideas of scientific modernity is also evident in the shifting evidentiary modes being used to describe sexual subjectivity, away from the autobiographical idiosyncrasies of the patient case history and toward explaining the sexual instinct using experimental, laboratory-based methods. This was no mere revival of nineteenth-century frameworks of degenerative constitutional inheritance, from which sexologists and psychiatrists had been distancing themselves for some time—especially, if we follow Michel Foucault, under the influence of the Freudians.[83] Not the outdated concept of degeneracy, but rather the cutting-edge field of hormone research was at the core of this paradigm shift, seen by some, at least, to hold the potential to completely rewrite theories of the sexual body and its behaviors.

Sexologists' new prioritization of the internal secretions also had implications for therapeutic encounters with patients. While many sexual scientists were happy to embrace chemically based hormone therapies as part of their arsenal of treatment options, the final section of this chapter shows that these at times proved inadequate to addressing patient concerns, some of which were better suited to the more relational methods of psychoanalysis. Psychoanalysts, meanwhile—without outright refuting the biological findings of Steinach and others—continued to prefer the "talking cure" from the couch.

After Steinach: Psychoanalysis, Hormones, and Therapeutic Pragmatism

Psychoanalysts did not share the conviction of sexologists such as Hirschfeld, Bloch, or Kronfeld that the new hormone therapies would revolutionize the understanding and treatment of sexual conditions. At a time when Steinach's findings were enchanting not only the scientific world, but much wider publics thanks to enthusiastic media coverage, sell-out screenings of *Der Steinach-Film,* and advertisements for commercial hormone preparations, Freud had made only minor modifications to his theory of human sexual development. As detailed above, he saw these experiments as confirming rather than undermining his ideas of a universal bisexual disposition and the infant's polymorphously perverse desires. By this stage, too, a number of Freud's followers had been busy for some years peddling the psychoanalytic method as the first truly promising treatment of the causes rather than just the symptoms of conditions such as homosexuality. As early as 1908, as examined in chapter 2, Sadger in particular had used publications in major sexological journals to argue that psychoanalysis offered unprecedented insights into the unconscious origins of developmental inhibitions, including same-sex desires, and was uniquely positioned to present "a real possibility of a cure."[84] Freud, however, was not convinced that homosexuality could be either completely "cured" or even fully explained by psychoanalysis.

In the same year as he undertook his final revisions to *Three Essays*, Freud published "The Psychogenesis of a Case of Homosexuality in a Woman" (1920). This account of his treatment of an eighteen-year-old woman provided an opportunity to further consider the possibilities and limits of hormone research. Because the parents of his young patient had pushed her into analysis involuntarily with the express hope of shifting her sexual orientation, Freud argued that the conventional analytic goal of solving a neurotic conflict did not apply, because the patient was neither sick nor suffering. Rather, he writes that in such instances, psychoanalysis could hope at best to open up "access to the opposite sex" and thus restore a patient's "full bisexual functions. After that it lay with him [*sic*] to choose whether he wished to abandon the path that is banned by society."[85] Despite having previously framed same-sex desire in terms of inhibited psychosexual and, specifically, narcissistic development, Freud now cautioned that psychoanalysis should not attempt to fully explain this condition, but rather content itself with revealing the psychological mechanisms that lead to a particular object choice: "There its work ends, and it leaves the rest to biological research." He acknowledges that other factors necessarily play a role in determining the patient's lasting orientation, including factors that are "probably of an internal nature."[86] It is with respect to the latter that Freud sees Steinach's experiments as offering new insights, and he even speculates that surgical therapies for inversion may ultimately prove more effective than analytic methods. For the time being, though, as early Freudian Eduard Hitschmann remarked in 1928, psychoanalysis would work to "cure without consideration of the hormones," continuing to present a strong alternative at a time when "honest researchers admit that there is still no effective masculine or feminine hormone preparation."[87]

Broadly speaking, then, sexologists and psychoanalysts had come to agree that any explanation of homosexuality—or, for that matter, any number of developmental "inhibitions" or "perversions"—must acknowledge highly complex combinations of physiological and psychological factors, recognizing the workings of the internal secretions as well as those of the psyche. Yet Freud also issues a note of warning in his 1920 case, observing that Steinach's alleged "successes" in treating homosexuals via testicle transplants had so far been restricted to a narrow group of male individuals exhibiting a clearly marked somatic "hermaphroditism": "it would be premature, or a harmful exaggeration, if at this stage we were to indulge in hopes of a 'therapy' of inversion that could be generally applied." It was, moreover, impossible to tell whether such therapies might be analogously applied to female homosexuality, for example via ovarian transplants. (These had been suggested by Berlin-based sex researcher Hermann Rohleder as an ideal treatment for female patients, but even he noted that, given the difficult nature of this operation, a more practical approach might be libido reduction achieved by X-ray treatment of the ovaries.[88]) Paying more attention to his patients' subjective identifications and desires, Freud argued that replacing a female patient's "probably hermaphroditic ovaries" with ones that are "hoped to be of a single sex" offered little hope of practical application, because a "woman who has felt herself to be a man, and has loved in masculine fashion" will seldom agree to be forced into a feminine role.[89] Freud thus paid lip service to Steinach's research, only to dismiss it as irrelevant to the actual treatment of female homosexuality.

In later years, Freud not only remained reticent about psychoanalysis's capacity to cure homosexuality, but also reluctant to endorse even the desirability of such a cure. In a frequently cited "Letter to an American mother" from 1935, he wrote that, although homosexuality is a result of developmental inhibition, the problems faced by the homosexual are primarily those of social intolerance. Speaking now in consciously lay terms rather than the expert language of analysis, Freud used the intimate space of a personal letter from a kindly physician to a mother concerned for her child's well-being to make a larger case for the role of psychoanalysis in modern society. It is by confronting the larger challenges and prejudices of daily life, he suggests, rather than simply the neuroses of the individual, that psychoanalysis might best offer its patients a guiding light:

> The answer is . . . we cannot promise to achieve it [a cure]. . . . What analysis can do for your son runs in a different line. If he is unhappy, neurotic, torn by conflicts, inhibited in his social life, analysis may bring him harmony, peace of mind, full efficiency whether he remains a homosexual or gets changed.[90]

Well into the 1930s, then, it was far from clear whether Freud's revolutionary methods would, or more importantly should, ever be able to truly convert homosexuality along heteronormative lines. After all, earlier claims to have achieved a cure, whether by physiological or psychological intervention, remained fragile or unsupported. Steinach's failure to achieve lasting success led him to cease authorizing castration operations on male homosexuals. As Ellis wrote to the enthusiastic Steinachian Haire in 1921, "I have not at present come across a full report of a case of reversal of homosexual feeling by transplantation."[91] Many testicle implants in homosexuals not only failed, but had to be removed, resulting in lateral or complete castrations with significant physical and mental consequences. As a result, Steinach stopped his involvement in these surgeries in 1923, with historians deeming the method "conclusively discredited" by 1924.[92] Sadger, too, we might recall, had been unable to prove that his reorientations of homosexual patients toward heterosexual desires resulted in any more than a temporary "cure," most likely the product of short-term suggestion rather than long-term psychosexual transformation. In this context, it is significant that Freud used his letter to a concerned mother not to defend the approach of Sadger and other followers of this method, but rather to question whether psychoanalysts should even strive toward this end.

Yet as his letter also makes clear, even analysts who may not have seen their method as a potential cure did view it as a means of achieving partial or short-term symptom relief from the psychic turmoil suffered by many homosexual patients under existing social and legal constraints. They found agreement on this point within sexological circles, with physicians such as Kronfeld and Moll joining Hirschfeld in developing a range of therapeutic techniques to treat patients with psychosexual conditions, some of which drew closely on psychoanalysis's talking cure. It was becoming clear that there were practical benefits to be had from applying a combination of methods, which might include conventional psychiatric treatments, chemically based hormone preparations, and the couch-based therapies of the Freudians. One commentator even suggested that Steinach's testicular transplants would be most successful when followed by a course of analytic treatment: "The surgeon, cooperating with the psycho-analyst, restores endocrine and psychic harmony—a task that would be too difficult for either without the aid of the other."[93]

Such therapeutic pragmatism is also evident in Kronfeld's recommendations for the treatment of psychosexual infantilism, where the urgent needs of patients and entanglement of "endogenous" and "exogenous" factors necessitated a multifaceted approach. Despite viewing psychoanalytic theory as flawed and partial, Kronfeld suggests that analytic *methods* may well prove useful in such cases, particularly in separating the libido from its current fixation. Although he does not go so far as to allow that these methods might enable full development of the sexual instinct in constitutionally inhibited patients—standing in the way of success were the patient's suggestibility, curiosity, and lack of loyalty to the truth—he suggests that they might encourage maturation, especially when deployed together with established psychiatric methods such as deep-sleep hypnosis and suggestion.[94] This advocacy of a therapeutic middle road integrating older psychiatric techniques aligned with the treatment for homosexuality developed by Kronfeld's Berlin-based colleague Moll; shying away from the more extreme biological and psychological options of surgical castration and psychoanalysis, Moll argued in favor of "psychohygiene" and psychotherapy.[95]

Hormone therapies were particularly attractive for doctors treating patients with somatic rather than strictly behavioral symptoms. For obviously physical manifestations such as stunted growth, Kronfeld enthusiastically promotes the use of organ extracts and injections, or X-ray reduction of the thymus, a lymphoid organ in the chest. Although he cautions that many of the more experimental organotherapies were still at the "pie in the sky" stage (*Zukunftsmusik*), Kronfeld also cites the benefits of the popular Steinach procedure.[96] Yet just as a lack of permanent success had already caused Steinach to stop authorizing castration as a treatment for homosexuality, his less-invasive vasoligature procedure also faded from glory toward the end of the interwar period, going out with a fizzle rather than a bang. Sullied by criticisms that it relied largely on the powers of suggestion, and unable to realize its own grand claims of restoring youthful vigor—leading Steinach himself to suggest the less-dramatic language of "reactivation" and "restitution"—fears of adverse further consequences, including the suggestion that it might shorten rather than prolong life, undermined the operation's popularity. As a result, by the late 1930s "rejuvenation was ridiculed and Steinach's pioneering early research marginalized," and very few people sought this procedure for rejuvenation purposes during the Nazi era.[97] Perhaps it was an early inkling that such gland manipulations remained far from perfect that led Kronfeld in 1921 to concede that, for the time being, psychotherapeutic methods offered the most practicable approach toward alleviating the symptoms of psychosexual infantilism. In making this utilitarian argument, Kronfeld cites the urgency of intervening in cases of infantilism that manifested as pedophilia: there was a need to prevent these individuals from socially or legally endangering themselves or others. For these (male) patients, he recommends "very energetic" hypnotic therapy, aimed at diverting erotic attention away from their wayward or infantile sexual objects and toward the "normal sexual act with an adult woman."[98] Such patients did not have time to wait for science to catch up.

Freud, too, remained open to potential syntheses of psychoanalytic and hormone-based treatments, as can be inferred not only from his personal medical choices, but from his later interwar publications. Having in *Three Essays* and in the 1920 case of a homosexual woman subtly extended his theories of human sexual development and homosexuality in the immediate postwar years to incorporate the findings of Steinach, Lipschütz, and others, Freud returned to the question of the internal secretions in 1926. He did so in the somewhat unlikely context of an essay discussing the suitability of training lay analysts (as opposed to medically trained physicians) in psychoanalytic methods. In this essay, Freud declares that the knowledge of the body's inner workings and chemistry that one acquires through medical education should remain an important prerequisite for analytic instruction, particularly in the absence of dedicated psychoanalytic training institutes. At the same time, he warns that individuals who have undergone such education must "not mistake their preliminary education for a complete training," and must

> resist the temptation to flirt with endocrinology and the autonomic nervous system, when what is needed is an apprehension of psychological facts with the help of a framework of psychological concepts. . . . [A]ll those problems which relate to the connection between psychical phenomena and their organic, anatomical and chemical foundations can be approached only by those who have studied both, that is, by medical analysts.[99]

Among those taking a similar line were Berlin socialist analyst and physician Heinrich Meng, a strong advocate of addressing social and public health issues via psychoanalysis and coauthor of a *Popular Psychoanalytic Handbook* (1926) with Viennese analyst Paul Federn. Meng explained that new endocrinological research, while significant, "gives us only a partial view on that which is truly decisive in real life," and insisted that environmental factors must form part of any attempts to prevent the development of perversions and neuroses.[100] Several years later, in 1933, Freud reiterated his views on the matter in a series of introductory lectures on psychoanalysis, describing his optimism that a greater knowledge of hormonal effects might one day provide "the means of successfully combating the quantitative factors" of neurotic illness. He cautions, though, that "we are far from that to-day." In the meantime, there was still a clear need for the talking cure.[101]

The expansion of hormone research in the 1910s and 1920s actively reshaped the relationship between sexology and psychoanalysis in ways that had already been foreshadowed in fin de siècle discussions of child sexuality and homosexuality and pursued with greater conviction by sexologists during the war, forcing practitioners of each field to reconsider their theories of human sexual development. Sexology took a fairly decisive turn during these interwar years toward understanding the sexual instinct and its pathologies via the glands of internal secretion, and used this to counter the psychologically oriented reasoning of the Freudian school in a much more self-assured fashion than had been possible in earlier debates. This new sexological confidence created a situation where practitioners were able to selectively incorporate psychoanalytic findings and methods without fear of damaging sexology's newfound status as a discrete medical field. Leading sexual scientists, including representatives from Hirschfeld's pioneering Berlin Institute, acknowledged Freud's achievement in bringing together an overarching theory of sexual disorders within a framework of universal sexual development, and endorsed a cautious adoption of specific Freudian techniques. But they continued to contest Freudian understandings of the libido, the Oedipus complex, and even definitions of "sex" itself, and sharply criticized clinical methods they deemed to stray too far from the established techniques of empirical science.

For psychoanalysis the boom in endocrine research did not cause any fundamental theoretical reassessments—certainly none of the magnitude of psychoanalysis's own challenge to sexology a decade or so beforehand. Yet Steinach's research did prompt analysts toward a more detailed consideration of how sexual identity might be shaped not just by environmental and interpersonal influences, but by chemical factors intrinsic to the self. Whereas the modernization of sex research in the late nineteenth century had encompassed a stronger focus on psychological components of human sexuality, the advent of internal secretions research in the first decades of the twentieth century saw an increasing acknowledgement of invisible biological processes as factors shaping sexual behaviors and desires. As they responded to these new research trends, sexologists and psychoanalysts were also compelled by their patients' need to find treatment options that would provide relief in the here and now. While rarely offering a full-blown "cure"—and sometimes, as with the Steinach operations, ending rather in full-blown failure—they began to innovatively combine methods ranging from vasoligature to hypnosis, and from hormone therapies to sessions on the couch.

Interwar negotiations around cutting-edge hormone research illustrate an increasing confidence among sexologists and psychoanalysts alike that their fields had come to constitute independent and respectable medico-scientific disciplines, equipped to cope with challenges to their theories and methods. For psychoanalysis, this process of professionalization had been propelled by the experience of World War I, as practitioners trained in analysis found themselves responsible for treating soldiers traumatized by shell shock, and were able to offer their superiors less invasive, seemingly more humane therapeutic methods than conventional psychiatry. For sexology, it was not so much the war itself as the wartime expansion of endocrinal research—which found early applications in treating injured soldiers, as the Steinach-Lichternstern operations showed—that offered an important new foundation on which to cement its independent status. While the majority of conversations between these two fields in the first decades of the twentieth century had focused, either implicitly or explicitly, on men and male sexuality as the core subject of sexual scientific research, this chapter has also shown that women's sexual experiences and desires were beginning to be taken more seriously by researchers, whether in the context of new hormone interventions directed at the ovaries, or in Freud's case of a female homosexual patient. The next chapter homes in on these themes of female sexuality, arguing that these formed one of the most exciting foci of interwar German scientific sex research, not least due to the forceful interventions of a growing number of women sexologists and psychoanalysts. These women changed the male-dominated conversations both within and between their respective fields. They point to the inherently gendered and historically contingent ways in which sexuality shaped a person's very sense of self and possibility in the context of early-twentieth-century modernity.

CHAPTER 5

Changing the Conversation: Theorizing Female Sexuality in Interwar Sex Research

In the early autumn of 1930 the Austrian capital of Vienna hosted the third official conference of the World League for Sexual Reform (WLSR), a transnational—although predominantly European—network of researchers and political activists that had been meeting for several years to discuss issues ranging from birth-control politics to the latest hormone research. At that meeting, German socialist feminist and high-profile sex reformer Helene Stöcker offered a biting critique of the masculine blind spots of many male Freudian psychoanalysts writing on female sexuality. Although some members of this movement had made "brave progress" in their investigations of the female libido, she cautioned that even in those writings

> we find unconscious allegiances and delusions [*Bindungen und Verbledungen* (*sic*)] in their *masculine* approach, for example when they demand that everyone must assume his "sex role" (masculine or feminine)—whereby it is silently assumed that the woman must continue to quietly take on the role of the dominated sex. But why should one's sex determine "the sex role," that is, one's role in life more broadly? . . . Why shouldn't rather the *entirety* of our *being* help both sexes to *grow out of* the "limits of sex," as Romantic philosophy put it so aptly?[1]

Stöcker was one of quite a few women sex researchers working in the decades surrounding World War I at the intellectual and political intersection of sexual science, feminism, and sex reform. These researchers drew on the respectability of German medicine and science to undergird often decidedly radical arguments for gender equality and social and welfare reform. Stöcker's critique of the assigned passivity of the female sex role, and her challenge to the very assignation of roles by sex, was shared by other women sexologists of this era, as scholars have now shown in some detail.[2] Pinpointing her statement as a product of interwar sexology are, first, her focus on social and cultural factors, and second, her engagement with now widely known psychoanalytic theories of sexual development.

Views such as these had been rapidly gaining an audience in the years since World War I. Two years earlier, during his presidential adddress at the 1928 WLSR meeting in Copenhagen, famous German sexologist Magnus Hirschfeld singled out for acclaim the association for maternal protection and sex reform of which Stöcker was head, the Bund für Mutterschutz (League for Maternal Protection, the BfM), established in 1905. The BfM encompassed a wide spectrum of Germany's left-wing sex reformers, including prominent social democrats, welfare campaigners, sociologists, and physicians; approximately a third of its members were men, including sexologists Albert Moll, Iwan Bloch, Albert Eulenburg, and (until an early falling out with Stöcker in 1907), Max Marcuse. Among its female ranks were many of the leading women sexologists and feminists of this era, including Henriette Fürth, Grete Meisel-Hess, Adele Schreiber, and Mathilde Vaerting.[3] Together with his own Institute for Sexual Science, Hirschfeld declared the BfM to be one of the glorious achievements of an increasingly "unified sexual science" in the first quarter of the new century.[4]

In this context, Stöcker's critique of the prevailing sex-gender system and contemporary male researchers performatively enacted a sense of feminist solidarity. While declaring a debt of thanks on behalf of "we as women" to researchers such as Havelock Ellis and Alfred Adler (a former Freudian who in 1909/10 broke with the Wednesday Psychological Society to found his own school of "individual psychology"[5]) for starting to look beyond assumptions of men's "absolute superiority," she insisted that continuing societal disregard of women forced commentators such as herself to protest against the "female role."[6] In drawing connections to women's broader sociopolitical positioning in contemporary German society, Stöcker's comments have important parallels with the writings of German-speaking women psychoanalysts of the interwar period, including increasingly influential Freudians such as Helene Deutsch in Vienna and Karen Horney in Berlin.

In 1925 Horney reviewed the first book-length psychoanalytic study of female sexuality, Deutsch's *Zur Psychoanalyse der weiblichen Sexualfunktionen* (*Psychoanalysis of the Sexual Functions of Women*).[7] Deutsch had herself undergone analysis with Freud in 1918/19 and joined the Vienna Psychoanalytic Society in 1918, and she penned this work while serving as the founding president of the Society's Training Institute (Sigmund Freud's youngest daughter Anna Freud was secretary)—roles that point to the particular prominence of women in the early analytic movement, especially compared with most other medical and scientific fields of this era.[8] Deutsch was responsible for assessing all new potential trainees, and by 1925 "was on the way to becoming one of the most famous teachers in the history of Freud's movement."[9] Reflecting on Deutsch's study of female sexuality, one detects more than a hint of relief in Horney's declaration that

> First of all, it is of the greatest value that such an undertaking to submit the entirety of the female sexual functions to a psychoanalytic consideration has been ventured in the first place. And we approach this study with double the interest . . . because here again we have not just any old subtopic of normal psychology being brought into the domain of psychoanalytic research, but nothing less than woman's entire sexual life.[10]

Both Horney and Deutsch assumed, like many of their fellow analysts, a fairly reverent stance toward Freud's work. Rather than radically questioning the attribution of gendered and sexed identities, as Stöcker and others were doing, they took up the "woman question" within a binary gendered framework, but added rich nuance to Oedipal accounts of sexual development. Their interventions into existing psychoanalytic explanations were especially significant when it came to questions of female sexuality and child analysis (on the latter, see chapter 1).

This chapter shows how women analysts and sexologists in the interwar period reoriented contemporary sex research—I focus on the questions of frigidity and homosexuality—by offering socially embedded critiques of sexual "dysfunctions" and sex-gender relations that went far beyond the scope of many of their male colleagues. Why, these scholars asked, did some women fail to respond in an acceptably heteronormative fashion to male sexual overtures, or develop a sexual orientation toward other women, and what might this have to do with the state of gender relations since the war? Although female sexologists and psychoanalysts made crucial intellectual contributions to their respective fields during these years, their contributions represent a still frequently overlooked chapter in the history of modern sex research. Women's writings across these two fields were frequently complicit in problematic dominant discourses that replicated heterosexist models of reproductive sexuality, ableist and racialized investments in ideas of health and eugenic improvement, and imperialist assumptions about civilized Europeans and primitive others. Kirsten Leng's recent work draws particular attention to these more ambivalent aspects of female-authored sexology, even as she highlights how they challenged "male-authored knowledge, particularly about women."[11] The following analysis joins a growing body of critical gender historiography in showcasing some of the limits of male-authored sexual science, building on existing accounts by looking across disciplinary divides to bring female analysts working in the Freudian tradition into the center of analysis.[12] As such, this chapter offers the first truly comparative reading of interwar sexological and psychoanalytic writings by and about women.

While I focus here particularly on interventions by Freudian analysts such as Horney and Deutsch, I read their works in the context of wider interwar conversations around gender and sexuality. I begin by briefly charting the larger landscape of German sexual science in the context of Weimar-era liberalized democracy (and to the German-speaking south, the similarly left-leaning "Red Vienna" of the 1920s). Women researchers played an active and prominent role in the increasingly internationalized sex-research and sex-reform movements of these years, including many nonanalytic sex researchers such as Stöcker, Vaerting, and the today little-known Olga Knopf (an Adlerian analyst) and physician Julie Bender. I show how these commentators linked their critiques to broader cultural discourses surrounding the "New Woman" and changing gender and sexual expectations in post–World War I Germany, while undertaking a closer examination of the writings of female analysts on frigidity and homosexuality. These gender-based critiques, I argue, not only firmly situated their research questions within the time and place of interwar central Europe, but also offered a distinctly—if not flawlessly—feminist framework for understanding the sexual constraints on modern women.

Feminizing, Popularizing, and Internationalizing Interwar Sex Research

Women and female sexuality had become significant topics of medical and scientific interest in the years before World War I, with the growth of gynecology as a discrete specialization marked by new journals such as the *Archiv für Frauenkunde und Eugenik* (Journal of Women's Studies and Eugenics) in 1914. These topics took on a new urgency in the years following the war in the face of wider biopolitical concerns about population decline and regeneration, and visible changes in women's participation in the workforce and public life. On the one hand, this was an era of great optimism and opportunity: Austrian women finally achieved suffrage in 1918, and German women a year later with the signing of the Weimar Constitution. During these years, "a new political imaginary" of citizenship helped lay the groundwork for a more woman-centered approach to sexual questions.[13] On the other hand, it was an era fueled by a pervasive sense of gender "crisis," as conservative critics spread rumors that women were among the groups (Jews were another) contributing to a "stab in the back" of German troops during the war, and a widely discussed "surplus" of women of marriageable age, who were seen to be competing for jobs with the men who had returned, often injured and broken, from the front lines. Even as historians have shown that gender relations were already widely perceived as being in a state of upheaval well before the war's beginning, the conflict had done much to stoke nationalistic and conservative fears of social and moral degeneration and decay.[14] The interwar media landscape was rife with half-playful, half loudly condemnatory reports on the changing rules of heterosexual relationships and the "masculinization" of German women, with the sexually, socially, and financially independent "New Woman"—deemed by scholars to have been both a media construct *and* a new social reality—serving as ready code for those concerned about the state of German gender relations. With her monocle, tuxedo, and short-cropped hair, the "masculinized" modern woman also stood as an increasingly legible signifier of female same-sex desire.[15]

Against this backdrop of intersecting gender "crisis" and nationalist concerns that repeatedly forced sexual questions—reproduction, prostitution, venereal disease, abortion—into the foreground of public debates, the interwar years proved a particularly productive period for the expansion of sexual scientific and psychoanalytic research networks, and for women's increasing role within those spheres. The foundation of Germany's Weimar Republic and the fall of the Austro-Hungarian monarchy to the south ushered in something of a golden age for German-speaking sex research marked by a liberalized and democratized public sphere, which in turn enabled the dissemination of expert sexual knowledges among wider lay publics and emerging sexual minority groups. Political and economic stabilization following the inflation of 1923 combined with relaxed censorship laws to lay the groundwork for exciting new centers (including Hirschfeld's Institute), collaborations, and networks for the study of human sexuality, and for the reinvigoration of sexual scientific journals that had been established in more precarious times.[16] These included the *Zeitschrift für Sexualwissenschaft*, *Geschlecht und Gesellschaft*, and Hirschfeld's *Jahrbuch,* each of which had been either discontinued or drastically pared down during the war years (although the *Jahrbuch* soon fell victim to the inflation crisis of 1923). New monograph series were established (e.g., "Sexus," 1921–1926; "Monographs on Sexual Science," ed. Rohleder, 1921–

1924), and prominent German-speaking sexologists such as Hirschfeld, Moll, Marcuse, and August Forel continued to be regarded as international leaders in their field, publishing major reference works such as Marcuse's *Handwörterbuch der Sexualwissenschaft* (Concise Dictionary of Sexual Science, 1923), a new edition of Moll's *Handbuch der Sexualwissenschaften* (Sexual Science Handbook, 1921, first published 1912), a popular edition of Forel's *Die sexuelle Frage* (The Sexual Question, 1924), and Hirschfeld's multivolume *Geschlechtskunde* (Sexual Knowledge, 1926–1930).

This liberalized public sphere provided new spaces for negotiating questions of gender and sexuality, from sex work to birth control, eugenics to abortion, homosexual rights to those of single and working mothers. Networks between clinical sex researchers and politicized sex reformers expanded, with the birth control and eugenics movements particularly successful in gaining traction both at home and abroad, thanks not least to the work of pioneers such as Stöcker in Germany, Marie Stopes and Stella Browne in Britain, and Margaret Sanger in the United States.[17] Sex research was also finding its way into popular culture: the documentary *Steinach-Film* (1923), released in a popular as well as scientific version and featuring tantalizing images of female imitators, bearded women, and mating animals, was only one of a raft of "social hygiene" and "sex education" films produced in these years, often under the banner of major studios such as Ufa and in collaboration with high-profile researchers such as Hirschfeld, Eugen Steinach, or Karl Abraham. These included films on venereal disease, prostitution, abortion, homosexual blackmail and suicide, while G. W. Pabst's psychoanalytic thriller *Geheimnisse einer Seele* (*Secrets of a Soul*, 1926) took audiences on a spectacular journey into the unconscious roots of murderous desires.[18] At a more grassroots level, socialist psychoanalysts also engaged in public outreach programs, establishing "psychoanalytic polyclinics" in Berlin and Vienna to promote analytic education and therapies, often offered free of charge.[19]

The establishment of the WLSR under the leadership of honorary presidents Hirschfeld, Forel, and Ellis, with an administrative base in Hirschfeld's Institute, was an important symptom of the popularization and internationalization of sex research during these years, what scholars have dubbed the "new internationalism" or "global turn" of interwar sexual science.[20] German-speaking researchers dominated this organization, the first official meeting of which was retrospectively declared to have been the International Society for Sex Research conference in Berlin in 1921.[21] Seven years later, approximately thirty sex researchers and activists from across Europe gathered in Copenhagen with the goal of "pursuing science not for its own sake, but in service to humanity," exchanging papers on experimental endocrinology, birth control, and companionate marriage. A number of speakers also addressed the place of psychoanalysis within the wider project of sex reform. The proceedings, published in German, French, English, and Esperanto, point to an optimistic international outlook after the years of global conflict.[22]

Like other sex-reform organizations such as the BfM in Germany and the British Sexological Society in the UK, the WLSR included many women and political activists among its members.[23] The 1929 meeting took place in London, overseen by gynecologist and sexologist Norman Haire and English socialist feminist Dora Russell, who noted that among the delegates from some twenty-five nations were a "remarkable . . . number of courageous and intelligent professional women from Germany."[24] Significantly for the larger narrative of this book, the WLSR proceedings signal the ongoing preparedness of leading proponents of *Sexualwissenschaft* to consider psychoanalysis as part of the project of sexual scientific research, even if they did not agree with all aspects of Freudian thought. In London, Hirschfeld explicitly included "psycho-analysis" in his opening speech as one of the fields lending sexology "the dignity of an independent science"; the conference also featured papers by Heinrich Meng on Freud's early neurological research and Jungian Barbara Low on children's sex education.[25] (Freud cordially sent along a letter, read aloud by Haire, expressing his regret at being unable to take part.[26]) By the time of the fourth meeting in Vienna in 1930, the WLSR had expanded almost tenfold to attract more than 2,000 members and visitors; Hirschfeld boasted that, through its affiliated associations, the League could claim an "extended" membership of as many as 130,000. Local organizing committee president, socialist educator, and Austrian League for Sexual Reform leader Josef K. Friedjung made much of the host city's scientific traditions, reminding listeners that "our unassuming little Austria" was the home of no less than Krafft-Ebing and Freud,[27] while Hirschfeld brushed over growing disciplinary divides by warmly congratulating Freud for recently winning the Goethe Prize from the city of Frankfurt.[28] Although the now-seventy-five-year-old Freud did not attend in person—it is unclear whether due to poor health or lack of interest—the organizers agreed that "the senior master of Psychoanalysis" should receive a telegram. In return, Freud sent a greeting wishing the participants every success, as did Steinach, who invited participants to visit his labs and witness his experiments with sex hormones.[29] Hosted with the support of the socialist city government and engaging with questions such as public hygiene and housing reform, the Vienna meeting points to a broader shift within early-twentieth-century German-speaking sex reform from a more strictly scientific endeavor to a movement with an increasingly social, cultural, anthropological, and political orientation.[30]

The WLSR is exemplary of the kind of cross-disciplinary interpenetrations that also continued to characterize leading sexual scientific journals during the interwar years. The *Zeitschrift für Sexualwissenschaft* still regularly incorporated discussion of psychoanalytic themes, and despite Freud's own rather tepid enthusiasm for the sex-reform movement, a number of those at the periphery of the psychoanalytic movement made efforts to reach out to colleagues across disciplinary as well as geographic and linguistic lines. Wilhelm Stekel, for example, following his acrimonious split with Freud in late 1912, collaborated with New York–based literary psychotherapist Samuel A. Tannenbaum to found the new analytic periodical *Psyche and Eros* (1920). When this journal folded in 1922, he established a second publication, *Fortschritte der Sexualwissenschaft und Psychanalyse* (Proceedings in Sexual Science and Psychanalysis), which appeared sporadically from 1924 to 1931. Tannenbaum, meanwhile, joined with New York physician and editor William J. Robinson to initiate the explicitly interdisciplinary *Journal of Sexology and Psychanalysis*, featuring many translated articles by German-speaking researchers.[31]

It was into this internationalized, politicized, and popularized sex–research landscape that German women analysts and sexologists intervened in increasingly vocal ways, building on the prewar efforts of German and Austrian feminists such as Stöcker, Johanna Elberskirchen, Anna Rüling, and Meisel-Hess. German women still had relatively poor access to formal medical and scientific training; while a wealthy few had been able to travel to Switzerland for university study since the 1870s, women were only permitted to register for formal study at German tertiary institutions "under severely restrictive conditions" between 1900 and 1909.[32] As a result, they were "largely absent from the membership rosters . . . and from the editorial boards of the first explicitly sexological societies."[33] A key exception was the BfM, in which women maintained prominent leadership roles throughout the life of the organization.[34]

While women had been at the margins of the analytic profession during much of the 1900s and 1910s (an exception was child analyst Hermine Hug-Hellmuth), during the 1920s female analysts began to constitute a much stronger presence, as Deutsch, Horney, Ruth Mack-Brunswick, Melanie Klein, and Freud's youngest daughter Anna, together with Joan Riviere in England and Jeanne Lampl-de Groot in Amsterdam, "left their stamp on the psychoanalytic profession."[35] In particular, they drew overdue attention to questions of female sexuality, a topic that psychoanalysis had blatantly neglected in its early years.

Freud acknowledged as much when, in 1925, he reflected that in earlier works on the sexual life of the child,

> we regularly took the male child, the little boy, as the object. With the little girl, we thought, it must be a similar process, although also in some way different. At what point of the developmental process this difference was to be found was not obviously apparent.[36]

That this had begun to change by the early 1920s is also evident in Freud's own writings. Following large gaps between his early case study, "Dora" (1900), and a 1915 case of female paranoia, and after rejecting Jung's challenge that the Oedipal account should be refigured as a specifically female "Electra complex" when describing girls' development,[37] in 1920 Freud published his first extended consideration of female homosexuality, followed by a 1925 essay on anatomical difference and a 1931 piece on female sexuality. Together, these constitute the bulk of his publications on a topic he famously described in 1926 as still "a *dark continent* for psychology."[38] The next sections of this chapter turn to the ways in which women analysts and a few sexologists in these years challenged Freud's models and developed new ideas about female frigidity and homosexuality in particular. Their negotiation of female sexuality, I argue, was firmly embedded in the gender politics of their day, and although analysts' interventions were often less radical than those of their sexological contemporaries, they permanently transformed psychoanalytic research around the "woman question" in more feminist directions.

Rethinking Frigidity through Feminist Cultural Critique

Interwar discussions of female frigidity tread a difficult line from the perspective of today's feminists. As historians of sexuality emphasize, they are best judged not according to twenty-first-century feminist and queer standards, but rather with a view to the specific cultural context in which they emerged, when flappers, career girls, and New Women were competing with nationalist, heteronormative expectations of a return to traditional gender roles and reproduction in the wake of World War I.[39] In this section, I examine how a number of female intellectuals turned their attention to questions of women's sexuality in ways that led to more sophisticated understanding of sexual dysfunction and its possible treatments. Although their theorizations remained constrained by essentializing gender expectations, including ideals of "passive," vaginal sexuality, and of motherhood as a woman's ultimate goal, they also show how these issues were being reconceived in light of women's increasing involvement in German political and cultural life.

Male impotence had been a long-standing concern of German sexual science, particularly during World War I, when traumatic frontline violence and hundreds of thousands of male war deaths exacerbated nationalist concerns about population health. Less audible in historical accounts of this period, as noted in chapter 3, are the concerns voiced by feminist scholars about women's sexual needs and hardships during times of war. These frequently encompassed criticism of the gendered double standards that allowed prostitution and venereal disease to flourish. Such critiques aligned with a feminist push since the 1890s to acknowledge as "natural" a woman's right to sexual fulfilment, but also with an ongoing stigmatization of women deemed sexually "frigid."[40] With women traditionally viewed as naturally "colder" than men, it was not until the late nineteenth century that female sexual dysfunction became defined as a problematic gynecological symptom, and female potency was established as the "normal" state of being.[41]

In the decades around 1900 German psychiatrists such as Richard von Krafft-Ebing, Albert von Schrenck-Notzing, Albert Moll, and Berlin physician Otto Adler (later secretary of the Medical Society for Sexual Science, Ärztliche Gesellschaft für Sexualwissenschaft) brought ideas about female frigidity to the attention of the wider medical profession. What had once been viewed as a rare condition was increasingly considered in "epidemic" terms, and as an important target for clinical treatment.[42] Krafft-Ebing aligned his discussion of "sexual anesthesia" with late-nineteenth-century degeneration arguments (viewing frigidity as an effect of brain rather than genital degeneration), while Schrenk-Notzing opposed such degenerationist explanations, but also focused on psychologized treatments such as hypnotic suggestion ("In the majority of cases, endoscopial examination of the urethra reveals nothing").[43] Others situated this condition in more culturally relativist terms. Havelock Ellis in England viewed the rise of frigidity as a product of modern "artificial civilization"—a perspective that resonated, as we shall see, with interwar commentators such as Horney and Deutsch. Otto Adler's *Die mangelhafte Geschlechtsempfindung des Weibes* (Deficient Sexual Sensation in Women, 1904), meanwhile, provided the first dedicated sexological treatment of this topic.[44] Subsequent editions addressed, not without sympathy, the concerns of the militant feminist movement, advocated for women doctors, and looked to psychoanalysis rather than medical or surgical intervention as the most appropriate treatment for vaginismus (vaginal cramps and spasms preventing coitus), arguing that the

Freudian school seemed particularly "equipped to bring together the theoretical and practical possibilities for a cure."[45] Adler's work was nonetheless critically reviewed in psychoanalytic journals, with one commentator in 1926 describing the latest edition as "already outdated on publication, for it completely ignores the fundamental works published since its first release by Abraham, Horney, and others and contents itself with Stekel as its sole psychoanalytic source."[46]

Wilhelm Stekel's two-volume study of female frigidity in 1920 was the first dedicated psychoanalytic study of female frigidity to hit the shelves, almost two decades after Adler first published his study.[47] This is notable given the centrality of sexual "inhibitions" and "repressions" to Freudian theory; it also underlines the analytic neglect of female sexuality in the 1900s and 1910s. Stekel insisted on the psychological causes of female sexual dysfunction—an "inner refusal" hidden from the patient's consciousness—while arguing that these were frequently masked by organic symptoms. He considered "unconscious homosexuality" to be a contributing cause in many cases, arguing that in a typical female patient, frigidity "had a fourfold root" combining same-sex desire, moral inhibitions, hatred for the father, and an infantile fixation on the mother.[48] Stekel was convinced the condition was curable, and that physical symptoms point to a reversible repression of libidinal drives ("The anaesthetic woman is merely a woman who has not discovered the form of sexual gratification which alone can be adequate in her case").[49] He also linked the rising incidence of frigidity to feminism and the "masculinization" of modern women: "it is distinctly a social manifestation."[50] Not fundamentally averse to feminist goals (Stekel was critical of the sexual double standard, which "punishes not the transgressions but the transgressor [. . .] if the transgressor be a woman,"[51] and advocated equal rights), but he declared that, under improved legal and social circumstances, it would nonetheless be necessary for women to return to "the calling of motherhood" for the problem of frigidity to be truly resolved.[52] He thus affirmed a heteronormative and culturally conservative vision of social relations.

Stekel's study paved the way for a number of illuminating studies of this condition by female analysts in subsequent years. These reached something of a high point in the radical 1930s writings of French intellectual Marie Bonaparte, who had herself undergone analysis with Freud; she was so concerned with her own perceived frigidity that she underwent a harrowing series of genital surgeries in an attempt to align her clitoral sexual sensitivity more closely with the vagina.[53] As Peter Cryle and Alison Moore show, surgery for Bonaparte formed a compromise between female clitoral "virility" and pleasure, symbolic of a strong modern womanhood, while still affirming the heteronormative social requirement of penetrative coitus.[54] Her view that the duality of female genital organs (clitoris and vagina) was a problem for modern women's heterosexual pleasure resonates with the writings of 1920s female intellectuals such as Viennese individual psychologist Sofie Lazarsfeld and sexologist Mathilde Vaerting. While not focusing on frigidity *per se,* these scholars similarly used their work, as recent research has shown, to negotiate tensions between feminist demands for gender equality and the biopolitical concerns of heterosexual reproduction.[55] Cryle and Moore, meanwhile, move swiftly from Stekel to Bonaparte with the justification that analysts such as Deutsch and Horney, writing in the 1920s, largely adhered to the Freudian argument that a shift from clitoral to vaginal sexuality was required for mature womanhood to be achieved. In the following, I turn our attention back to these 1920s studies, arguing that they demonstrate some of the ways in which women researchers had already begun challenging psychoanalytic theories of female sexuality during the first decade after the war.

The work of the Berlin-based Horney is of particular interest here because she published in leading psychoanalytic journals as well as more interdisciplinary sexual science publications. A 1926 essay, "Inhibited Femininity," published in the *Zeitschrift für Sexualwissenschaft* took frigidity as its central theme. Horney used this essay to explain psychoanalytic concepts to a broad readership, in a nod to the journal's interdisciplinary forum (Horney also had strong connections to Berlin-based sexologists such as Iwan Bloch, Otto Juliusburger, and Heinrich Koerber[56]). But she also moved beyond the close examination of intrapsychic dynamics by situating female sexual dysfunction in the context of post–World War I gender relations. Although less engaged in socialist politics than fellow Berlin analysts such as Ernst Simmel, Horney was already known in analytic circles for her incisively feminist studies of the female castration complex, penis envy, and the "flight from femininity." A talented analyst overseeing trainees with the Berlin Psychoanalytic Institute, she was often frustrated by the gender politics and perceived dogmatism of that Institute's older analysts.[57] Growing up in Hamburg in the early 1900s, she had been well aware of the radical feminist movement led by Lida Gustav Heymann to abolish prositution in that city, although her sympathies lay more closely with the BfM. Although not a BfM member herself, Horney and Stöcker shared a number of biographical similarities. Both women rebelled against their religious families and subsequently attended university at a time when this was hardly the expected female norm. Horney was in broad agreement with the BfM's advocacy of a "New Ethic," encompassing "free" (non-state-sanctioned) marriage, access to contraception and abortion, recognition of illegimate children and their mothers, sex education, and women's sexual empowerment. It is also highly likely that Horney and Stöcker knew one another personally, as Stöcker joined the Berlin Psychoanalytic Institute when Horney was one of only a handful of female members.[58]

For Horney, there were two key positions on frigidity within the contemporary medical profession: one that saw it as equivalent in severity and urgency to male impotence, and another that considered it so common as to barely qualify as pathological, merely describing the "normal sexual behavior of the culturally civilized woman."[59] Psychoanalysis, Horney observes, focuses on the individual, asking whether the sexual dysfunction is merely an isolated symptom or a sign of a deeper, underlying problem preventing a woman from forming satisfying heterosexual connections. Generally, she argues, frigidity is the product of an underlying "masculinity complex" that combines feelings of female inferiority, penis envy, inhibited familial relationships, and an unconscious rejection of the female genitalia, the pathology of which is unconsciously reaffirmed with every menstrual period. Horney acknowledges that such analytic interpretations are often met with disbelief—including, no doubt, by some readers of the *Zeitschrift*—but emphasizes that they are supported by a wealth of case materials.[60] Horney's critique is both theoretical and sociopolitical. Broaching the question of why this condition is so common among modern women, Horney shifts her gaze beyond Oedipal relations to consider "supra-individual, cultural factors"—revealing early signs of what one historian has recently described as the "incipient culturalist" Horney would later become.[61] Horney concludes that the problem is often not so much a rejection of sexual intimacy, but rather an unconscious rejection of the female role in a society that consistently undervalues the achievements and perspectives of women ("It is, after all, well known that our culture is a masculine culture").[62] In a Eurocentric vein, Horney contrasts penis envy among "civilized" women with the sexually naïve but healthier phallic cults of "primitive" peoples. Compounding this situation, she argues, is the gendered double standard that permits men to split their erotic attention, as Freud had shown, into a "sensual" (*sinnlich*) and a "spiritual" or "psychological" (*seelisch*) current. Women, Horney observes, are condemned by social norms to direct their desire strictly toward their marital partner, and this triangulation of desires can easily lead to frigidity.[63] She thus develops a Freudian-inspired analysis of frigidity that, in its political embeddedness, echoed earlier attacks on the gendered double standard by feminist sexologists such as Stöcker and Meisel-Hess.[64] In other writings from this period, Horney also challenged fellow analysts with her concept of "womb envy," suggesting that this might be a far greater problem for men than envy of the penis for women.[65]

Horney's Viennese colleague Helene Deutsch, meanwhile, included an entire chapter on the topic of frigidity in her 1925 monograph, and continued to investigate this condition in the years that followed. Born in 1884 in Przemyśl, Galicia (now Poland), Deutsch received her PhD from the University of Vienna in 1912; when she entered that institution's medical school in 1907 only seven women had done so before her. Strongly influenced by Freud's *Interpretation of Dreams* and theories of infant sexuality, she was also fascinated by socialist politics, attending a congress featuring Rosa Luxemburg while still in medical school. (As the *New York Times* reported in 1978, even in her eighties Deutsch participated in anti-Vietnam war demonstrations in the United States, where she had fled from the Nazis with husband Felix.[66]) During her studies she also worked at the university's psychiatric clinic, leaving in 1916 to work with Freud, with whom she underwent a year-long analysis. In 1924 she became the first woman to lead the Vienna Psychoanalytic Training Institute.[67]

Like Horney, Deutsch observed that female frigidity was much more frequent than its male counterpart, and she agreed that it demanded a distinctly gendered form of psychoanalytic inquiry.[68] Deutsch's explanation differs from Horney's, though, in her emphasis on the Oedipal requirement—first outlined by Freud in *Three Essays*—that an early, prepubertal phase of clitoral, "phallic" sexuality must be repressed during puberty for mature, vaginal sexuality to take its place. In later works, Freud elaborated on the dual transition that girls must undergo in changing the leading sexual organ from the clitoris to the vagina, and the sexual object from the mother to the father.[69] These findings opened up a theoretical space for further inquiries into a "pre-Oedipal" phase of female sexuality.[70] In particular, Horney and Deutsch were drawn to Freud's commitment to the idea of original bisexuality, on which basis he proposed both an active ("masculine") and passive ("feminine") aspect to each individual's negotiation of the Oedipal compex.

The analytic insistence on differently gendered psychosexual processes conflicted, of course, with calls by contemporary female sexologists such as Stöcker for an abandonment of sex assignation processes altogether. Vaerting, too, who began publishing in sexological journals in 1914, was arguing by the early 1920s that "sex differentiation is merely the outcome of the position of dominance or subjection and is not a product of inborn biological characteristics."[71] Nor was Freud unaware that he was taking a potentially antifeminist stance. Even as he praised the "estimable and rich" writings of Horney, Deutsch, and others on the castration and masculinity complexes, Freud argued that girls experience a "narcissistic wound" and "feelings of inferiority" from the realization of their lack of a penis.[72] Confronting the castration complex—which they blame on the mother—leads to a loosening of the maternal connection, paving the way for the Oedipal wish for a child by the father. If the libidinal paternal connection is disrupted, however, overidentification with the father can ensue, so that the girl returns to the earlier "masculinity complex" and becomes fixated in that state.[73] In this way, Freud drew attention back to pre-Oedipal development, suggesting that girls come to reject the Oedipus complex in a far more gradual manner than boys. Provocatively, he used this finding to argue that women had a more ambiguous stance on moral and legal questions, and to counter the "opposition of the feminists, who want to impose on us a complete equalization [. . .] of the sexes." Yet Freud also tempers his antifeminist language when he observes that most men, too, "remain far behind the masculine ideal," and that in any case, "pure masculinity and femininity remain theoretical constructions with uncertain contents."[74]

Drawing on this rather ambivalent framework, Deutsch explains that in cases of frigidity, the transition from the "phallic" clitoris to mature motherhood remains incomplete due to a refusal to fully give in to "feminine-passive-vaginal-reception." Like Horney, she argues that the sufferer is reminded of this disruptive element with every menstrual period, and again, traumatically, with the act of defloration, experienced as not only sexually disappointing, but as a form of narcissistic injury.[75] While Deutsch's emphasis on vaginal sexuality was not unusual in psychoanalytic thinking of this period, she also shared with Horney and other female analysts a concern with the historical constraints framing discourses of female sexuality—British analyst Joan Riviere, for example, had described the performative "masks" of femininity, such as coquettish flirtation, that women were forced to wear in public to disguise more "masculine" careers or intellectual pursuits.[76] Linking modern women's heightened propensity for libidinal dysfunction to "our cultural conditions," Deutsch argued that cultural constraints on girls mean that they have far fewer opportunities to sublimate their sexual instincts into intellectual and social works, and were instead expected to focus on producing children.[77]

Deutsch expanded on this cultural-historical aspect of her frigidity analysis in a lecture held at the 11th International Psychoanalytic Congress in 1929.[78] Here her concerns were more theoretical, as she argued that penis envy only gradually replaces the pleasures of early clitoral satisfaction, and that the "masculinity complex" can never fully be overcome.[79] More radically, Deutsch challenged Freud's earlier writings on anatomical gender differentiation by postulating that between the clitoral and the vaginal stages one finds a "post-phallic" phase, during which the girl is anatomically condemned to a form of regressive masochism, frequently expressing a desire to be castrated at the hands of the father.[80] Deutsch thus contested the directness of Freud's account, while agreeing that female maturation remained dependent on the transition from clitoris to vagina. It was on the latter point that her work proved vulnerable to challenges by later feminist thinkers, starting with Bonaparte in the 1930s and extending through to "second-wave" intellectuals such as Kate Millett in the US—who rejected not only the Freudian designation "phallic" to describe clitoral autoeroticism, but also discussions of female genital inferiority by Deutsch, Bonaparte, and others.[81] Also deeply skeptical of such findings were later French psychoanalytic feminists; in a typical critique, Luce Irigaray inisted that the allegedly "frigid woman" had merely been forced to adhere to male models of "sexual 'techniques' which do not correspond to her sexuality."[82]

Despite these limitations from the perspective of late-twentieth-century feminism, Deutsch succeeded in tracing a more nuanced trajectory of the libido in the early years of a girl's life than Freud had done, showing exactly where and how this might go awry to result in female sexual dysfunction. Attending closely to early object relations, Deutsch postulates a "phallic" connection to the mother similar to that experienced by boys:

> In the period of "penis envy" we still see the small girl turning to the mother with her libidinal demands, so that the primary connection to the mother, just as in the boy, takes on an active "phallic" current. Before the competition with the mother for the love of the father results in a negative relationship to her, we often see this tender connection destroyed by a frequently very aggressive rage against the original love object (the mother).[83]

The roots of frigidity, argues Deutsch, lie in the repressions that can occur during this infantile-masochistic phase, which she links to Horney's "flight from femininity." But the causes, she suggests, are also anatomical, as "a kind of organ memory" turns the phallically oriented clitoris into a major hindrance to the transferral of arousal to the vagina.[84] Motherhood, Deutsch concludes, has provided the historical means by which women could resolve their masochistic tendencies and lack of opportunities for sexual satisfaction ("no analytic observer can deny that in the mother-child-relationship . . . [there are] libidinal powers in play that are closely related to the man-woman relationship"), protecting generations of women from adverse neurotic consequences.[85] Frigidity was now on the rise, however, due to the decline in a certain type of woman capable of such indirect, masochistic "joyous-tender feeling[s] of giving pleasure." Declaring that "this female type is dying out," Deutsch connected women's rising rates of frigidity to broader interwar discourses concerning the financially, sexually, and socially independent and "masculine" modern woman.[86]

At first glance, Deutsch's linking of modern female neurosis to women's emancipation echoed the much more conservative commentary of some male contemporaries. Prominent Weimar-era gynecologist Hugo Sellheim, for example, used articles for the popular illustrated media to argue that pregnancy was the best form of exercise for women, and that women's competitive sport—another symptom of women's excessive "masculinization"—represents "a complete and utter failure in respect to thc thc woman's original feminine capacity."[87] *Zeitschrift* author Professor Ratner of Copenhagen, meanwhile, referenced the latest endocrinological research merely to confirm age-old misogynist stereotypes, as he suggests that the inner secretions "flood the entire female body and take full possession of it practically until menopause." So strongly is the female psyche under this sexual influence, argues Ratner, that utilizing women of reproductive age for other goals such as intellectual work "is against nature and finds the most terrible revenge" in the form of diseases of the reproductive anatomy and a declining birth rate.[88] Such sensationalist and only barely medicalized rhetoric was not unusual in a period during which the masculinization of Germany's womanhood was being denounced as the source of all manner of social ills.[89]

In this context, it is important to draw out the nuances of Deutsch's account. Her work treads not only a more cautious, but also, I submit, a much more feminist line than Freud's, particularly when she argues that the analyst's role in such cases is not to ensure reproductive capacity, but rather to resolve patients' inner conflicts such that they might achieve erotic pleasure. Although her arguments remain embedded in ideas of maternal satisfaction and heteronormative reproduction, they are also grounded in a sense of female agency and self-determination, as she insists that

> Women would never have permitted the social order across multiple historical epochs to keep them separate from the possibilities of sublimation on the one hand, and sexual satisfaction on the other, if she had not found in the reproductive function a magnificent satisfaction for both![90]

Deutsch's account of frigidity, in sum, is a somewhat ambivalent one, juggling an affirmation of women's increased role in German society with a confirmation of traditional norms of motherhood and family. As one critic observes, while her work "has clearly given feminists cause for dismissing her views," when taken together with her life and clinical practice it becomes much more complex: "Tensions and contradictions in her work have gone largely unnoticed because her most dogmatic and biological thinking is in easily accessible short papers, while her revisionist observations are embedded in lengthy and sometimes tedious case histories."[91] Certainly, in the historical context in which Deutsch was working, hers was not an antifeminist stance. Even if it fell short of the radical gender critiques of some of her sexological contemporaries, her investment in a maternal model of female sexual maturity aligned with the vocal maternal feminist branches of the contemporary women's movement, including Stöcker herself, who had written in 1905 that "the great significance of woman for humanity lies in motherhood."[92]

An alternative perspective on the etiology of frigidity was offered by analysts working within the Adlerian school of "individual psychology," who used concepts such as "inferiority complex" and "overcompensation" to describe factors shaping personality in the context of dominant social hierarchies. Alfred Adler had split with Freud in the early days of the analytic movement based on what he considered the latter's overemphasis on sexual factors; in 1914 he founded the *Internationale Zeitschrift für Individualpsychologie* (International Journal of Individual Psychology) with Viennese colleague Carl Furtmüller, and his thought enjoyed particular popularity among Austrian Social Democrats.[93] Women were unusually prominent in this movement, making up around half of the Viennese Association of Individual Psychology in the 1920s; recent scholarship has focused particularly on Sofie Lazarsfeld's writings on gender and sexuality, which echoed those of contemporary women sexologists in combining demands for gender fluidity with more essentialized heteronormative expectations.[94] In 1930 Adler's journal also published a specific investigation of frigidity by Viennese physician Olga Knopf. As might be expected from her intellectual positioning, Knopf does not respond directly to Freudian discussions by Horney, Deutsch, and others, but she does echo their socially and culturally contextualized interpretations, citing the remarkably high—if empirically untested—statistics observed by fellow scholars that the proportion of "frigid" women in the wider population ranged between 40 percent and 80 percent.[95]

With a typically Adlerian emphasis on individual responsibility, Knopf stresses that it is within the power of "a woman herself to free herself of this evil," although she observes that it is often difficult to even verbalize frigidity in a time when it has only recently become respectable for women to speak more openly on sexual matters.[96] Citing Adler's 1907 study "On the Inferiority of Organs" and her own previous work applying individual psychology to gynecology, Knopf explains that vaginism results from "reflexes that have become autonomous" and that can gradually appear independently of, or even against, the patient's will, as an "*expression of defense.*" As a result, the woman remains passive in a moment during which her partner is experiencing the "highest affirmation of life."[97] The reason is that girls are brought up to learn that woman is a "second grade creature," while boys are brought up conscious of their "manly rights." Education aimed at protecting girls' virginal virtue, moeover, tends to depict sexuality as "something ugly, dirty, demeaning to the woman."[98] The "virile woman," she observes, is most likely to get "stuck" in this process—Knopf cites the American "flapper type" and the European "demi-vierge." The goal of individual psychology in such cases is not to ascertain at which point a woman gets "stuck," but rather *why* she does; attaining a more positive attitude toward men and the female sexual role, they might acknowledge "that there is more joy in giving than in taking."[99] Knopf thus at once celebrates society's greater openness in discussing female sexuality, while ultimately affirming a passive, "feminine" role for women.

Such negotiations of frigidity by women analysts working within the Freudian and Adlerian modes are problematic for the way they continue to emphasize heternormative gender role expectations, whether by adhering (as in Deutsch's case) to a maternal model of sexual maturity or (as with Knopf) by advocating that women accept a passive sexual role and be primarily givers rather than receivers. Yet they also engaged with the gender politics of their historical moment with more nuance than their male colleagues; in particular, their emphasis on the "virile" or "masculine" woman highlights the importance of situating these analyses within a cultural context where the "New Woman" was a daily feature of German media coverage, and discussions of changing gender roles spoke to deep national and cultural anxieties. The intellectuals examined in this section developed detailed analyses of female frigidity, and offered new perspectives on treatment. In the process, they pushed the blame away from individual women and insisted on viewing female sexual "dysfunction" as a product of wider social and cultural change—and the fault of men as well as women.

Challenging the "Dark Continent" of Female Homosexuality

Just as discussions of female frigidity only came to serious sexological and later psychoanalytic attention in the years following the fin de siècle, it was not until the 1920s that female homosexuality became a more central concern, particularly for Freudian researchers. In this section I show how women analysts and a few nonanalytic researchers expanded understandings of female same-sex desire, contesting Freudian narratives of female Oedipal development and making a case for the particular role of women physicians and analysts in treating women for sexual complaints. During the 1920s, Horney and Deutsch in particular offered some of the most theoretically innovative explorations of female same-sex desire to date, examining their female patients' fantasies and desires along specifically gendered lines. Working from positions of "situated knowledge" as women treating other women, they challenged not only Freud's own writings, but also the tendency of earlier male sexologists to view this phenomenon as analogous to male same-sex desire.[100] In particular, they shied away from congenital explanations, while not denying these as a possible factor (a wise position, given the uncertain state of endocrinological research). Instead, they correctly observed that it was only into the psychological roots of same-sex desire that psychoanalysis might offer insights.

In the decade before World War I, as discussed in chapter 2, male sexologists and analysts had debated theories of congenital and acquired homosexuality and appropriate modes of treatment, at times examining female inversion in parallel with male homosexuality, but rarely as a central theme. Several feminist intellectuals, such as Anna Rüling, Johanna Elberskirchen, and Rosa Mayreder, also offered radical new theories of female same-sex desire during these years, "envision[ing] a female subject unmoored from the expectations of reproductive heterosexual womanhood" and articulating a "rational" vision of emancipated female masculinity.[101] In subsequent years, research on the hormones opened up new possibilities for conceptualizing same-sex desire, although attempts to intervene clinically via hormone treatments, as we have seen, met with little success. At a theoretical level, though, discussions of homosexuality had stagnated by the early Weimar years. Even Freud's first extended case of a female homosexual patient, published in 1920, did not so much explore new theoretical ground as turn its attention to the broader environmental and social factors contributing to homosexual identification.[102] In a case discussed in the previous chapter in the context of hormone research, Freud examined an eighteen-year-old who had fallen in love with an aristocratic older woman and been dragged into analysis by her disapproving parents, who tasked Freud with "bringing their daughter back to the norm" following a suicide attempt.[103] Defying this demand, while Freud agreed to treatment he emphasized that he would not attempt to convert her to a heterosexual life course ("the successes of psychoanalytic therapy in treating . . . homosexuality are far from numerous"), but instead viewed homosexuality as a complex phenomenon that was not easily abandoned, nor was it necessarily pathological. Under the most forgiving conditions, he suggested, psychoanalytic treatment might direct patients to embrace their bisexual function, and thus "open up the path to the other sex."[104]

The general lack of scholarly attention to female homosexuality was not lost on women physicians and sex reformers. In a review of Freud's case in the *Zeitschrift*, Käthe Hoffmann picked up on Freud's own observation that "female homosexuality has been overlooked by criminal law and neglected by psychoanalysis."[105] In the same journal a year earlier, left-wing physician Julie Bender responded to an article by male colleague Eric Stern that had argued for the existence of a specific female inverted "type." Stern had used three case studies to illustrate a condition he connected closely to severe mental disturbances ("All three are *psychologically severely altered individuals, in whom inverted sexuality is only a symptom of the psychological disturbance*").[106] Bender—whose framing of her piece suggests that she identified as heterosexual—takes a less pathologizing line, drawing on her own experiences as a doctor to argue for the existence of "genuine" homosexuality, contending that male colleagues tended to downplay both the prevalence and constitutional foundations of this condition. Bender gives the example of a female lab worker alongside whom she had worked in a dermatological clinic, whom she declares "not a normal woman" despite a "gracious, feminine build," because of her masculine mannerisms with her colleagues and the way she "assumed the role of the dominating man" in a sexual relationship with one particular female coworker.[107] Bender thus aligns herself with older, gender-inverted explanations of female homosexuality, while refusing to link this condition to severe mental illness in the way that some medical colleagues were continuing to do.

Female homosexuality had not been a focal point of the German sex reform and feminist movements of the early twentieth century. In the prewar years, as one historian observes, "the BfM generally acted, effectively, as if lesbianism were a nonissue," only publishing a few pieces on this topic in its journal *Die Neue Generation* (The New Generation) in 1908, when a series of scandals shook the contemporary homosexual rights movement.[108] Stöcker's own writings on this topic were somewhat ambiguous; although she was a vocal opponent of Paragraph 175—including during debates about whether this should be extended to women in 1911—she also hoped that psychoanalysis might help return homosexuals "in many cases to a normal mode of feeling."[109] BfM member Johanna Elberskirchen was much more outspoken on the matter. Openly homosexual herself, and one of only four female chairpersons of the WhK (a role she took on in 1914), Elberskirchen had studied science and then law in Switzerland, and was later heavily involved in left-wing and women's suffrage campaigns.[110] Declaring that her own position as a woman made her a more "objective" scientific observer, Elberskirchen—celebrated by German LGBTIQ activists today—presented a resounding challenge to "male-authored knowledge" (Leng's term), as she insisted on viewing female homosexuality not as inversion, but rather in terms of same-sex love. As such, she described female couples as those in which "both love in the other the same sex—the feminine, not the masculine," positioning this as both a thoroughly feminine and more spiritual form of sexual subjectivity.[111] Other prewar activists, such as journalist Anna Rüling and intellectual Rosa Mayreder, also put forth theories of female homosexuality in the first decades of the twentieth century. Rüling advocated a special social role for the masculine homosexual woman ("I am convinced . . . that the homosexual Woman is particularly capable of playing a leading role in the international women's movement for equality"), while Mayreder presented a vision of a "synthetic human" free of the constraints of binary sexuality (although with a clear affinity, as Leng observes, for the masculine end of the spectrum).[112]

Despite being less politically active than homosexual rights advocates such as Elberskirchen or Hirschfeld, women analysts such as Horney and Deutsch offered far more complex discussions of the gendered specificity of female same-sex identifications than their psychoanalytic predecessors had done. They also shared some views in common with women doctors and scholars working outside of Freudian frameworks, particularly regarding the importance of having female clinicians to treat female patients—including those who presented on account of same-sex desires, albeit not restricted to such patients. Focusing on sexual complaints was not without problems for female doctors themselves, however, who risked damage to their reputations. Max Marcuse, while encouraging more unmarried female doctors to work in this area, acknowledged the risk that they might themselves be suspected of sexual licentiousness. Bender also critiqued the judgmental behavior of many male medical colleagues; presumably having been burnt herself, as someone who published regularly on women's health and sexuality.[113] Bender notes that the problem for women doctors' reputations lay less with chatty patients than with male colleagues: "a large percentage considers themselves justified in linking any interest by an unmarried female colleague in sexual questions to their active participation in sexual life."[114] Women may now have had access to medical training, but their agency was still sharply policed by antifeminist prejudice within the profession.

Women analysts working in the Freudian tradition justified the need for well-trained female practitioners on more specifically psychoanalytic grounds. As Freud himself acknowledged in his 1931 essay "On Female Sexuality,"

> it really seems that female analysts like Jeanne Lampl-de Groot and Helene Deutsch could perceive these facts [regarding girls' psychosexual development] more easily and clearly in that with their informants the transference was aided by a suitable mother replacement.[115]

In a 1927 essay on the Oedipus complex in women, Dutch analyst Lampl-de Groot had observed that the early stage of negative Oedipal attitude in women can only be reached through a lengthy and advanced analysis, ideally at the hands of a female analyst. "Perhaps with a male analyst it may be very hard to bring this period to light at all," she suggests, "for it is difficult for a female patient to enter into rivalry with the father-analyst, so that possibly treatment under these conditions cannot get past the analysis of the positive Œdipus attitude."[116] To a degree, Freud's 1920 case had affirmed this difficulty, as he observed that while a relationship of transference is unavoidable, his eighteen-year-old patient had "transferred to me [Freud] her fundamental rejection of men, which had dominated her since her disappointment by her father." Realizing this, Freud broke off the treatment and advised her to continue her sessions with a woman doctor.[117] He thus acknowledged the advantages that women analysts could bring to the treatment of female patients, even as he remained defensive regarding his own theoretical insights, noting significant differences between himself and "the feminists among the men, but also our female analysts" when it came to judging the effects of penis envy and the "masculinity complex."[118]

In a 1932 essay, "On Female Homosexuality" (the title of which explicitly referenced Freud's earlier piece, and which was based on a paper initially intended for the cancelled 1931 International Psychoanalytic Congress), Deutsch addresses this question of women analysts in more detail.[119] Again focusing on the psychoanalytic transference, where patients were encouraged to project their fantasies and desires onto their analyst as an essential part of the therapeutic process, Deutsch observes that women clinicians could offer their female patients a very different projection surface than their male colleagues:

"The transference onto me [from her female patient] was very strong. . . . The patient felt herself so happy to have finally found a good, understanding mother from whom she could receive everything that her own mother had not provided."[120] In an interesting twist on the pervasive cultural discourses of female masculinization noted above, Deutsch also describes the significance for female homosexual patients of being able to project fantasies of a *masculinized* or cross-gendered persona onto their female therapists: she recounts one patient's dreams of herself and colleague Anna Freud—between whom the patient was trying to choose a therapist—in which the latter featured smoking cigars and "*wearing men's clothing*."[121] By emphasizing the contributions of a specifically female perspective on analytic work, Deutsch and Lampl-de Groot offer examples of how women analysts, like women sexologists of this era, "mobilized their gender as a unique epistemic location from which to produce sexual knowledge."[122]

Deutsch based her observations on the homosexual question on expansive case material—eleven patients observed over twelve years—the timing of which suggests that she had already started collecting her findings when Freud published his 1920 case. Her analysis focuses on uncovering and reinterpreting complex layers of pre-Oedipal and Oedipal factors, and diverged from Freud's earlier case in two key ways. First, while Freud had still felt compelled to consider whether homosexuality was a congenital condition or one acquired through environmental influences—leading him to update his *Three Essays* in 1920 to respond to the latest hormone research, as we have seen—twelve years later, Deutsch barely deems it necessary to touch on this topic. Freud had concluded that his female patient demonstrated a form of inborn homosexuality, but one only fixed as such after puberty; he thus deems the very question of congenital versus acquired homosexuality as misleading and its value as "only very minimal."[123] Psychoanalysis, he declared, must "satisfy itself with revealing the psychological mechanisms that lead to the decision of object choice."[124] In Deutsch's piece, however, while physiological concerns resonate in her decision to examine her patients for signs of physical as well as psychic inversion, she concludes that most of her patients did not display any indications whatsoever of masculine traits, and clearly prioritizes analytic interpretative modes. She concludes that, while the "phallic-masculine" form of female homosexuality remains the most obvious, it has tended to be overemphasized in ways that disguise underlying, pregenital tendencies.[125]

The second difference concerned when and why homosexual tendencies congeal into a permanent state. Freud had diagnosed the shift to homosexuality as occurring in his teenaged patient following the birth of her third brother when she was sixteen. Stressing the significance of overidentification with a masculine father figure, Freud argues that after her youngest sibling's birth, the patient shifted her interest from young children to mothers and eventually older women. Her "infantile fixation" combined with a strong "masculinity complex" (demonstrated by a strong sense of competition with her older brother and "powerful penis envy"[126]) to result in a choice of an older female lover who embodied both maternal and fraternal elements, thus "combining the satisfaction of homosexual and heterosexual desires."[127] In contrast, Deutsch used sessions with her female homosexual patients over the course of many months to dig back through what she considered to be more superficial layers of penis envy and masculine identification to instead locate the roots of homosexual feeling in an earlier, "pre-phallic," oral stage of the mother-child relationship. This was, however, subsequently overlaid by the Oedipal influence of the father, in what Deutsch describes as "not a simple fixation on the mother as the first object of love, but rather a complicated process of return."[128] For Deutsch, this long detour is crucial to understanding the true development of female homosexuality as beginning in infancy and finding confirmation during puberty. An underlying aggression toward the mother is transformed through the later homosexual relationship into love, allowing the patient to seek satisfaction in a symbolic flight back to a maternal figure.[129]

Although Deutsch adopts a respectful stance toward Freud's arguments—"she remained a Freudian loyalist," observes one historian—her findings substantially expanded on his 1920 elaboration of female homosexual identification.[130] She also built on Freud's much more recent essay on female sexuality, in which he had emphasized two substantial findings: the "strongly underestimated" duration of a girl's original connection to the mother, and the intensity of that connection, which he argues is proportionately mirrored in the later transference to the father. Although varying between individuals, he finds that this original maternal connection

> in numerous cases reached well into the fourth, in one case into the fifth year, thus involving by far the longest portion of the early sexual blossoming [*Frühblüte*]. Yes, one had to allow the possibility that a number of female beings remain stuck in the original connection to the mother [*Mutterbindung*] and never manage a proper transition toward men.
>
> The pre-Oedipal phase in women thus achieves a level of significance that we had not previously attributed to it.[131]

While Freud acknowledged Deutsch's work as demonstrating "the phallic activity of the girl and the intensity of her maternal connection,"[132] Deutsch's own essay goes further in insisting on both the significance of this pre-Oedipal phase and its complex overlaying by the later Oedipal relationship. In short, she questioned Freud's assumption that female homosexuality results from masculine identification combined with a fairly straightforward fixation on the mother.[133]

In terms of therapeutic outcomes, though, there are important alignments between Freud's 1920 case and Deutsch's later study. Freud, as we have seen, agreed to analyze his young patient only after making clear that his goal was to help her recover from her depression, not remove her same-sex desires. Deutsch agrees that it is not so much a "cure" as a relief of neurotic symptoms that psychoanalysis could provide. Certainly, an element of heteronormative expectation haunts her observation—more than in Freud's case—that analysis could *not* generally achieve "a further and more favorable dissolution of the connection to the mother, allowing her to give up homosexuality and turn toward men." Nonetheless, Deutsch sympathetically testifies to the relief of patient suffering that psychoanalytic therapy might provide, and happily reports meeting one of her patients a year after the analysis had ended to find a "flourishing, radiant human being" whose depression and suicidal tendencies had completely disappeared.[134] On the basis of such careful, if not unproblematic, negotiations of female same-sex desire, I disagree with Dagmar Herzog's recent finding that Deutsch was one of the interwar female analysts who "participated in elaborating antihomosexual sentiment." Herzog does, however, aptly capture the tensions in Deutsch's work when she writes that "there was a stark vacillation between, on the one hand, a genuine, at times intrusive-voyeuristic and at other times almost envious, concern with investigating the sexual practices of lesbians; and on the other, the eager attempt to develop further Freud's reflections on lesbian object-choice."[135] In these final years of intellectual flourishing before the National Socialist seizure of power, female analysts expanded the scope and depth of analytic theories of female homosexuality. Their work formed part of a broader affirmation of the place of women intellectuals—and the specific contributions they could make *as* women, from positions of "situated knowledge"—within medicalized sex research.

The occasionally ambivalent gender politics of these pioneering women researchers working across the sexological-psychoanalytic divide was, I have argued here, at least partly the product of strategic choices responding to a particular historical moment, in which the figure of the emancipated, masculinized "New Woman" was symbolically butting heads with cultural conservatives fearful that changing gender expectations would lead to a fall in the birthrate, moral decay, and general national decline. Women sex researchers, themselves contending with precarious positions within the German medical and scientific professions, successfully advanced a number of more nuanced models of female sexuality and gendered agency, but they sought to do so in ways that would be heard by their male colleagues. And their voices were, indeed, being heard—or more often, read—in ways that contributed to larger conversations. Most of the pieces examined in this chapter were published in the leading German sexological, Freudian (and in Knopf's case, Adlerian) journals of the day, indicating that they had not only undergone strict peer review processes, but were likely to be on the radar of a broad cross-section of relevant professional colleagues. The uptake of female-authored sexological and psychoanalytic knowledge can be seen in Freud's own references to a number of women analysts in his interwar writings, a rare, if not uncomplicated citation in the context of his larger oeuvre (Freud rarely cited others in the main text of his essays, and as one influential biography observes, his atitudes toward women in particular "were part of larger cultural loyalties, his Victorian style").[136] As feminist theorist Sara Ahmed argues, citation practices are a "successful reproductive technology, a way of reproducing the world around certain bodies."[137] Read from this perspective, Freud's references to Horney, Deutsch, Lampl-de Groot and others point to the power of overt recognition in shoring up women's influence within a school of thought still very much under the sway of its Viennese founder.

Investigations of frigidity and female homosexuality by Freudian women analysts changed wider analytic conversations around the "woman question"—on which, as Freud himself acknowledged, too little research had been done. Both Horney and Deutsch remained committed Freudians during the period discussed here, although Horney developed a more critical relation to Oedipal frameworks following her move to the United States in 1932. After that point, she joined a "neo-Freudian" camp, placing greater emphasis on interpersonal, social, and cultural factors.[138] We can see the beginnings of this shift in her interwar writings: together with Deutsch and others, Horney brought a uniquely female analytic perspective to bear on questions of female sexuality in the context of Weimar-era sexual politics. Having themselves overcome structural hurdles to women's higher education and professional acknowledgment, these analysts situated their clinical inquiries in the context of feminist arguments around female agency, gender equality, and women's "right" to sexual pleasure. In addition, their embodied presence as women physicians brought a new dynamic to doctor-patient interactions, enabling patients to project different kinds of desire and fantasy onto the bodies of their analysts.

Although they discussed female dysfunction and same-sex desire from quite different perspectives than the Freudians, female intellectuals and practitioners such as Stöcker, Elberskirchen, Bender, and Knopf also offered important contributions to discussions of frigidity and homosexuality during this period, while echoing the analysts' emphasis on the need for more women doctors with whom female patients might broach sexually intimate questions. Women intellectuals working in this "golden" era of German sex research drew on the respectability and prestige of scientific arguments to pursue more elaborate discussions of female sexuality, but they also changed the conversations in their fields by orienting their discussions toward contemporary gender politics and a critique of unjust double standards. This also helped to pave the way for more concerted interventions into scientific discussions of sexuality by members of new sexual minority groups, including homosexuals and individuals who did not identify with their assigned birth sex. The final chapter of this book explores these interactions between sexologists, psychoanalysts, and emerging sexual publics by focusing on the "case of the transvestite," showing how individuals critically adapted and rearticulated medical knowledge about their innermost sex-gender identities.

CHAPTER 6

The Case of the Transvestite: Expert Knowledges, Subjects, and Trans Identity Politics

> Case 1, 1910. Thirty-year-old merchant "Mr A." assigned male at birth (AMAB),[1] tells Berlin sexologist Magnus Hirschfeld about their desire since earliest childhood to dress in feminine clothing: "*I wanted so sincerely to be a girl and often dreamed of this with eyes wide open*, making plans for the future etc." Hirschfeld notes—with a nod to degeneration discourses—that his patient comes from healthy parental stock and exhibits a masculine physicality that is countered by a high voice and theatrical disposition. He includes A.'s story in a new study of "transvestism."[2]
>
> Case 2, 1921. A twenty-eight-year-old artist, who identifies as masculine but was assigned female at birth (AFAB), visits Viennese psychoanalyst Wilhelm Stekel seeking to be cured of their vaginal "anesthesia." He diagnoses an unfulfilled childhood fixation on the mother that has transformed into an obsession with the father—"Her desire to be a man is a consequence of her strong identification with the father"—resulting in a case of "pronounced" but potentially curable transvestism.[3]
>
> Case 3, 1924. Self-identified transvestite Toni Fricke (AMAB) writes a letter to the Berlin-based magazine column "Welt der Transvestiten" (Tranvestites' World) welcoming the establishment of this new forum: "A general need has been met now that we finally have the opportunity to have our say." Criticizing a lack of medical understanding, and describing her own troubled history of cross-identifying desires and the stress of having to hide her condition from the world, Fricke advocates for social tolerance of transvestites.[4]

Each of these cases represents an attempt to explain a condition that in the early twentieth century was just beginning to be conceptualized by sex researchers as a distinct sex-gender phenomenon: the desire to dress or live completely as a member of the "opposite" sex. Individual life narratives, or cases, are at the center of these theorizations of transgendered behaviors and desires. Two of the above excerpts were published in scientific monographs—one a major sexological study, the other an examination of female frigidity from a psychoanalytic perspective—while the third appeared in a new magazine aimed at a "third sex" audience, distributed primarily via newsstands and subscriptions. They demonstrate the different ways in which the experiences of individuals whose gender identity did not correspond to their physical anatomy were being taken up by medical experts and emerging sexual subcultures in interwar Germany. This chapter shows how the question of gender identity constituted one of the last significant sites of encounter between sexologists and psychoanalysts in the years following World War I, one that marks an increasingly irreconcilable theoretical and therapeutic divergence between these fields. Yet it also looks beyond this race for scientific authority, examining the critical perspectives of the individuals and patients whose stories were at the heart of medicalized discussions, to argue that new medical categories for gender-variant identities were being taken up beyond the discussions of sexological and psychoanalytic "experts" in ways that reflect the political priorities and identifications of the world's first organized transgender movement.

Sexologists and psychoanalysts of the 1910s and 1920s used what they described as "transvestite" or "Eonist" patient histories to establish new diagnostic categories and treatments. These diagnoses were particularly exciting because sex researchers had only recently begun to divorce them from older sex-gender categories of "inversion," which merged same-sex desire with cross-gender identifications. For sexologists, it was an area in which they could hope to make truly new advances to the older classificatory schema of pioneers such as Krafft-Ebing. For psychoanalysts, it opened up new therapeutic challenges that subtly differed from the older search for a homosexual "cure," at a time when patients were increasingly viewing psychoanalysis as an attractive and practical form of sexual therapy, including for marital problems.[5] Narratives of transvestism were also, as Fricke's letter shows, beginning to be taken up by emerging subcultural publics. The following analysis argues that contributors to new Weimar-era subcultural "transvestite" publications adapted and rearticulated the medical knowledge produced by sexologists and psychoanalysts to suit the interests of a new branch of minority identity politics. In adopting this focus, my analysis follows recent trends toward studying smaller archives in the history of sexuality.[6] Homing in on the interactions between differently invested groups that emerged around the diagnosis of transvestism, I foreground the ways in which expert sexological and psychoanalytic knowledges were taken up by the subjects at their center, creating what scholars have theorized in terms of "circuits of knowledge exchange and transformation." These doctor-patient relationships involved not simply strict hierarchies or repressive pathologizations, but also mutually fascinating and enjoyable "*spirals of power and pleasure*."[7] Specifically, I argue that expert diagnostic labels "looped back," to use Ian Hacking's phrase, to not only shape the self-understanding of people who were beginning to associate their own subjectivities with a "transvestite" label, but also to use that label to organize and demand political rights.[8] This involved participating in medical research and adopting some of its definitions and concepts, but also at times pushing back against "expert" definitions when these were seen to undermine the identifications and priorities of trans-identified individuals.

This chapter focuses on "transvestite" cases for three reasons. First, this phenomenon is of particular relevance for both the history of sexuality more broadly, and the more specific histories of sexual science and psychoanalysis, because it was a uniquely twentieth-century categorization, the product of decades of debate and discontent with older categories such as "inversion" and "contrary sexual feeling." From these genealogical roots, it emerged as the conceptual counterpart, despite a lag of several decades, to the late-nineteenth-century diagnosis of "homosexuality." As a result, it is particularly well suited to examining competing theorizations of sexual subjectivity in twentieth-century cultural and scientific modernity.

Second, this diagnosis raised new questions for sexologists and psychoanalysts, intensifying earlier struggles between these fields surrounding child sexual development, the nature of the perversions, and the role of the internal secretions or hormones. Only a handful of scholars took up the challenge in depth, including Hirschfeld and his British colleague Havelock Ellis in the sexological camp, and Stekel and his assistant Emil Gutheil representing the analytic tradition—with the psychoanalysts taking a more pathologizing and skeptical approach toward their trans-identifying patients. While I focus here on specific considerations of the "transvestite" diagnosis by sexological and psychoanalytic researchers, questions of gender identity were also gaining broader currency in these years both within and beyond each of these fields: we might think, for example, of the connections drawn between cross-gendered desires and paranoia in Freud's famous Daniel Paul Schreber case.[9]

Third—and most importantly, from the perspective of trans history, which has often been neglected in the historiography of modern Germany—the Weimar Republic was a particularly important time and place in the history of transgender identity politics. Following the war and revolution of 1918/19, which ushered in a liberalized public sphere and reduced censorship, new publications aimed not only at "homosexual" publics—which have now been widely studied—but at specific "transvestite" audiences blossomed during the Weimar Republic, often with a base in Berlin. Although the Weimar transvestite media were quite middle-class and "respectable" in orientation, which resulted in the marginalization of certain subjectivities, within these limitations they represented, as I argue in the final section of this chapter, an important sounding board in which transpeople could engage in the critical negotiation of expert knowledges.

Transvestite Cases in Early-Twentieth-Century Sexology

Building on the early taxonomizing efforts of psychiatrists Richard von Krafft-Ebing and Carl Friedrich Otto Westphal, and of lawyers and writers including Karl Maria Kertbeny and Karl Heinrich Ulrichs, in the early twentieth century European sexologists began to move away from older theories of "inversion" and "Urningism," which viewed same-sex attraction and cross-gendered characteristics as intimately intertwined, and to consider "transvestism" and "homosexuality" as distinct sex-gender phenomena. Although terms such as "contrary sexual inversion" continued to be used into the early twentieth century, in discussions of same-sex desires and behaviors they were gradually overshadowed by Kertbeny's coinage of "homosexuality," which came to be defined primarily in terms of sexual object choice.[10] This terminological shift better accounted for homosexual men and women whose gender presentation was considered too "virile" (in male homosexuals) or too typically "feminine" (in women) to constitute genuine inversion—the hunky Greek-god-like figures who regularly appeared in Adolf Brand's homoerotic magazine *Der Eigene* (The Autonomous/Self-Owned), for example, or homosexual women who did not conform to stereotypes of the smoking, drinking, cane-swinging bluestocking. However, it failed to account for cases where cross-gendered characteristics constituted the primary symptom.[11]

In 1910 Hirschfeld, already well known for his writings on Germany's "third sex" and "sexual intermediaries," coined the terms *Transvestitismus* ("transvestism"/"transvestitism") and *Transvestit/in* ("transvestite" [male-to-female/female-to-male]), publishing *Die Transvestiten: Eine Untersuchung über den erotischen Verkleidungstrieb* (The Transvestites: The Erotic Drive to Cross-Dress). Most of the seventeen case studies in that voluminous work involved cross-dressing individuals AMAB who identified as heterosexual, and a few who lived permanently as women. These cases had the benefit of clearly distinguishing between the formerly merged categories of homosexual and transvestite, but this clarity came at the expense of diversity: only one of his case studies had been AFAB, as Hirschfeld assumed that most female-to-male transvestites were homosexuals (i.e., sought relationships with women).[12] Nonetheless, Hirschfeld did acknowledge at least the theoretical possibility that male-to-female transvestite tendencies could also coincide with homosexual desires, as in a 1923 article he defined the five chief varieties of transvestism as heterosexual, bisexual, homosexual, narcissistic, and asexual, and also introduced the term "psychological transsexualism" (*seelischer Transsexualismus*), paving the way for later, more surgically oriented discourses.[13]

Other sex researchers also developed theories of cross-gendered identification in this period. Foremost among them was Ellis, who in two 1913 articles suggested the term "Sexo-Aesthetic Inversion" before publishing his study *Eonism and Other Supplementary Studies* as volume 7 of his *Studies in the Psychology of Sex* in 1928.[14] In that work he named this phenomenon after an eighteenth-century cross-dressing French diplomat and spy; as he explained in a letter to Norman Haire, "I call it Eonism, after the Chevalier d'Eon, as I do not regard the cross-dressing as always the most essential feature."[15] Like Hirschfeld, Ellis noted that homosexuality and Eonism could sometimes be found together, but insisted that "Eonism, where it appears in homosexual persons, is perhaps merely a secondary result of the sexually inverted psychic state." He divided his category into a more-common variant confined mainly to cross-dressing, and a less-common but more "complete" variant in which "the subject so identifies himself with those of his physical and psychic traits which recall the opposite sex that he feels really to belong to that sex."[16] For Ellis, the fact that Eonism is "wide-spread over the world among peoples of all stages of culture" showed that this was a deeply rooted instinct, the possibilities of which are always latent.[17] Further contributors to this pan-European conversation included German zoologist and anthropologist Ferdinand Karsch-Haack, who suggested the terms "transsensibel" and "Transmutist" as less focused on clothing than Hirschfeld's category; sexologist Max Marcuse, who in 1916 wrote an article on the *Geschlechtsumwandlungstrieb* (drive for sex transformation); psychiatrist Paul Näcke, who preferred Hirschfeld's subtitle focus on the "drive to cross-dress" (*Verkleidungstrieb*) to the less transparently German "Transvestismus"; and Freudian dissident turned "individual psychologist" Alfred Adler, who preferred the term "psychic hermaphroditism" (*psychischer Hermaphroditismus*).[18]

Ultimately, though, it was Hirschfeld's term that was taken up most prominently by doctors and cross-identifying individuals in early-twentieth-century

Germany. Notwithstanding debates about its etymological shortcomings (Latin: *trans*, to cross, and *vestis*, dress), "transvestism" was generally understood (as Hirschfeld himself insisted, and as discussed in the introduction to this book) to encompass a diversity of gender-variant practices and identities. Its broad uptake can be attributed both to Hirschfeld's professional prominence and his reputation for outspoken political advocacy in defense of the "third sex": as well as appearing frequently in court cases involving male homosexuality and blackmail, Hirschfeld was well known within certain circles as a doctor who would provide medical certificates to transvestites applying for police permits to wear clothing of the "opposite" sex.[19] His Berlin Institute housed a dedicated transvestite counseling center, and among his closer acquaintances at least, he was known for his own cross-dressing practices.[20] One colleague described how in late 1911, he and several other physicians were invited to Hirschfeld's apartment, where they were introduced to "approximately ½ dozen transvestites, of whom two appeared in elegant ladies' evening attire."[21] Such factors undoubtedly facilitated Hirschfeld's access to wider communities of trans-identified individuals for his research.

These communities and their significance for German trans history have only recently received serious attention from historians of sexuality. In previous research, I and other scholars have shown that self-identified "transvestites" were an increasingly vocal presence in German cultural life, beginning in the pre–World War I period, when the Berlin police department was among those issuing the aforementioned "transvestite certificates" or "passports." The Weimar era saw a blossoming of transvestite media both in conjunction with and sometimes at odds with the political and social organizations of female and male homosexuals. Although these groups shared some issues—gender variance was an important category for esthetic, erotic, and personal identity for many same-sex-desiring individuals in the 1920s, as older associations with the concept of "inversion" suggest—they did not share certain other goals. Not all groups, for example, sought the legal capacity to change one's name or the right to "cross-dress" in public without being subject to arrest.[22] The need to fight for such "rights"—for this period was also an important chapter in terms of conceptualizing LGBTIQ politics in terms of broader "human rights" discourses, which historians have traced in the German context back to at least the 1830s[23]—was a dominant feature of 1920s trans activism. As one commentator observed, drawing also on discourses of Empire and colonialism, "without a fight, we will never achieve the place in the sun that is our right."[24] Recent scholarship on German trans history, drawing on a wide range of legal, photographic, and subcultural sources, emphasizes that it is important not to reduce this history to medical and scientific frameworks, and to acknowledge that many gender-variant experiences will never be captured by the fragmentary historical documents that have survived. As I argue here, however, sexological and, to a lesser extent, psychoanalytic studies were an important aspect of trans "world-making" during this period, with many trans-identified individuals reporting fairly positive experiences with medical professionals, and using medical cases as a basis from which to start formulating their own narratives, as I examine in the final section of this chapter.

Anthropological and historical examples were an important feature of both Hirschfeld's and Ellis's groundbreaking studies—from famous stage performers, to gender-variant tribal practices in non-Western cultures, to individuals AFAB who had passed as men and served their countries as soldiers—but their core evidence consisted of case histories gathered from patients and informants. Both sexologists used their case studies to underline ideas about congenital transvestite causality, although they also acknowledged that psychological factors played a marginal role. This foregrounding of the body of the transvestite patient reflects a continued sexological investment in ideas about the physiological causes of sex-gender aberrations, while references to the general health of extended family members as well as the patients themselves point to lingering ideas about hereditary degeneration. Ellis notes that his patient "J.G.," for example, had a "highly strung" and "quick tempered" father and a "phlegmatic" mother, although three siblings "seem to have been normal."[25] In other cases, it is an absence rather than presence of degenerative symptoms that is noted. Introducing his fifth case, "Mr E.," Hirschfeld writes that his patient is "ca. 40 years old, comes from healthy parents. Divergent features or signs of degeneration cannot be established among his relatives."[26] Similarly, in the case of twenty-seven-year-old female-to-male transvestite "Helen N.," Hirschfeld notes that her father had "died of appendicitis" but her mother was "alive and healthy."[27] In contrast, some other sexologists of this era found scant evidence to link transvestism and degeneration: "based on external appearance, the people I saw certainly did not given a degenerate impression."[28]

Sexologists also foregrounded their patients' bodies by referencing the latest advances in "inner secretions" research, which had been popularized following Eugen Steinach's groundbreaking experiments in wartime Vienna. In extreme cases, they argued, transvestites might even develop visible physical characteristics associated with the "opposite" sex. Ellis maintained, for example, that while transvestites were physically far less marked by their condition than "hermaphrodites" (as sexologists of this era described intersex conditions[29]), their condition could nonetheless be traced to an inborn and possibly hereditary endocrinal basis. This had consequences for therapeutic intervention: "the path lies open for its modification by suitable gland implantation. It falls short of disease; it is . . . simply a variety, though, one may add, an abnormal, in the strict sense a pathological, variety."[30] Developments in this field led Hirschfeld to add a note to the second edition of *Die Transvestiten* in 1925:

> The studies of the inner secretions in particular remove all doubt that we are dealing here not with a purely psychological matter, not with deeply rooted habits or even, as some continue to insist, with a disguised form of homosexuality, but rather that the transvestite represents a special sexual type, a psychobiological (physical-mental) [*körperseelische*] variant of the human species.[31]

The conviction that transvestism could often be explained on physiological grounds also influenced how sexologists presented their patient histories.

Most of the sexological cases published by Ellis and Hirschfeld are told in the first person, separated by quotation marks and font from the surrounding text. While such stylistic considerations reinforce a sense of authenticity, these texts were shaped in crucial ways by editorial decisions. For one thing, the selection of cases for publication depended on how well they illustrated sexological theories. And while many read as fairly spontaneous autobiographical accounts, structural similarities between Ellis's cases suggest that informants were probably responding to a set questionnaire. Detailed descriptions of the subject's early childhood development and cross-dressing ("The wish to wear the clothes of the other sex is my earliest definite recollection"[32]) serve, as Ivan Crozier observes, to reinforce Ellis's theory that any sexual behavior must have a congenital component.[33] Hirschfeld's patients similarly recount childhood experiences of cross-dressing and non-gender-normative play: "Mr A." describes how as a child he liked to play with dolls and learned to crochet, and as a youth always desired to wear girls' clothes: "often I got up during the night and tried to take clothing from the wardrobe of the landlord's daughter."[34]

The typical sexological transvestite case history proceeds from such descriptions of cross-gendered childhoods to describe experiences of puberty, including a growing awareness of difference and the first emergence of explicitly sexual behavior, such as masturbation. Many of these observations aligned with Hirschfeld's titular description of this condition as an "erotic drive," which he foregrounded in his case presentations through parenthetical observations labeled "*vita sexualis*." In this vein, Hirschfeld discusses the frequent masturbatory practices and sexual preferences of his sixth patient, "Mr F.":

> While wearing women's clothing he finds it easy to masturbate to orgasm [*usque ad orgasmum*], *without* needing to *think* of female or male persons; yes, he has even experienced ejaculation without touching his member. . . . *He twice entered into a marriage of love, from which two children were produced.*[35]

F. (Hirschfeld assigned his patients sequential letters) also notes that as a child of ten he had dreamed of walking the streets with real, pierced earrings, and that such dreams produced "an erotic feeling of well-being."[36] Yet others insisted that the urge to wear female clothing was not of an erotic nature, but simply an expression of their true selves. In doing so, they resisted expert narratives from within the very framework of the sexological case. As one patient observed, "*the appeal of women's clothing has nothing erotic about it.* It is as though the feminine aspect of my character periodically bursts forth in a particularly strong manner; then I love the masquerade, because it corresponds to my psychological condition."[37] Ellis, too, concluded that a condition that he had once "been inclined to regard . . . as representing a combination of feminism with fetichism [*sic*]" often in fact had little to do with sexual arousal: "not only is there usually no primary inversion in these cases, but there is no true fetichism, the garment possessing no marked dynamic erotic power in itself, or when worn by another person, but only when worn by the subject himself." As he explained, rather than an "impulse of disguise" (Ellis's translation of Hirschfeld's term *Verkleidungstrieb*), by adopting the dress of the "opposite" sex the Eonist "feels on the contrary that he has thereby become emancipated from the disguise and is at last really himself"—a conclusion that, as we shall see, resonated with the self-description of many trans-identifying individuals of this era.[38]

Many of the case studies also describe the patient's experiences of cross-dressing as an adult, including the desire to convincingly "pass" in public. As Hirschfeld's "Mr. N" observed,

> I would be overjoyed . . . if I could go out strolling in broad daylight, if only for short distances, dressed as a lady together *with actual ladies* [*mit wirklichen Damen*]. Previously I sometimes allowed myself this passion, occasionally in the evenings and on solitary walks; I gave it up, though, as it seemed to me too dangerous.[39]

Typically, patients conclude their narratives with reflections on how their cross-dressing has affected their adult sexual relationships, in ways that tend to reaffirm the heterosexuality of the narratives selected for publication (a heterosexuality defined, however, based on anatomical sex rather than gender identity). Hirschfeld's "Mr. B.," for example, reassures readers that: "*I have never felt a particular inclination toward men*, only when dressed as a lady have I *enjoyed* flirting and *playing with them*"; similarly, "Mr. N." declared that "*I am not homosexual,* on the contrary, I can say that I was a real Don Juan."[40] In a few cases, though, "homosexuality" is mentioned as a possibility, with "Mr. D" offering that, while he had not yet engaged in same-sex relations, "It seems to me that there are no sexual acts with a man that would disgust me."[41] Such statements sat in tension with Hirschfeld's finding that most transvestites were heterosexual; as one scholar observes, "even when his informants were clear about an issue, he discounted crucial aspects of their stories."[42] For a number of patients, the primary focus of the narrative is clearly the desire to live full-time as a woman or man, and sometimes also to undergo surgical bodily transformation. "Metalworker O" (Case 16 in Hirschfeld's casuistry) declares that "life will lose all its appeal for me if I am not able to wear skirts."[43] "Mr. C" even described the desire to be pregnant, explaining that "My longing is not restricted to a women's outfit [*Frauenkostüm*], but extends to a complete life as a woman."[44] Twenty-five-year-old C.T. in Ellis's collection, meanwhile, described their gender identity in a way that resonates more closely with late-twentieth-century understandings of transsexual identity, explaining how they had "often thought seriously of castration. . . . I know that I should be immensely happier if my sexual organs were removed."[45]

These case studies of "transvestism" and "Eonism" reflect sexologists' focus on biological and hereditary factors as the primary, albeit not exclusive, cause of trans identifications. The cases overwhelmingly present transvestism as an inborn, untreatable condition, even as they gesture toward the possibility of new hormone-based interventions. Ellis and Hirschfeld presented their cases in ways that claimed interpretive authority over their patients' narratives: "relying upon cases . . . was inconceivable without the predominant authority of the doctor."[46] Yet these narratives also had a life beyond an immediate sexological readership, entering a wider trading zone of knowledge exchange. In particular, the figure of the transvestite was taken up within psychoanalytic discussions of the early 1920s in ways that point to a growing divide between these two cultures of modern sex research.

Psychoanalytic Approaches to the Transvestite Case

Picking up on fin de siècle debates about the sexual life of the child, the nature of the perversions, and more recent research into the inner secretions, in the years after World War I the recently minted category of transvestism became a further, if somewhat peripheral, focus of the professional rivalry between sexologists and psychoanalysts. Since Freud's *Three Essays* in 1905, as previous chapters have shown, a particular point of contention between these two fields was the psychoanalytic emphasis on developmental inhibition as the key to the perversions, a theory that threatened to undermine the often more physiological models of the sexologists. Seeking to better understand the internal psychic dynamics of cross-gendered identifications, psychoanalysts followed sexologists by delving into questions of transvestite diagnosis and therapy. For them, too, patient histories constituted a crucial medium of evidence. Indeed, the case history had retained even more currency for psychoanalysts than it did for sexologists of this period, who were increasingly turning to methods such as questionnaires, experimental laboratory research, and even photography.[47] From a psychoanalytic perspective, the interpretation of individual cases had been the cornerstone of diagnosis and therapy ever since Freud and Josef Breuer's 1890s examination of the quirks and sufferings of hysterics. It can be traced through the chapters of this study from Freud's analysis of the infantile sexual phenomena exhibited by "Little Hans," to Sadger's case of a Danish count suffering "multiple perversions," and the cases of "war neurotics" used by Simmel, Ferenczi, and Abraham to explain "hysterical" episodes triggered by battlefield violence. Admittedly, the emphasis on individual cases had begun to fade somewhat by the 1920s, as Freud's own theoretical works such as *The Ego and the Id* or *Civilization and Its Discontents* took a more abstract and cultural historical turn.[48] Nonetheless, the case study remained the key analytical genre of evidence, and thus the obvious entry point for approaching the category of transvestism.[49]

Although there were strong similarities between the kinds of narrative provided by trans-identified patients to sexologists and psychoanalysts, practitioners working on each side of this growing disciplinary divide diverged considerably in their framing and interpretation of such cases, particularly when it came to causation and treatment. Whereas diagnosis dominated the sexologists' mission, psychoanalysts were more interested in trying to "cure" transvestite patients, and sought to explain transvestite causality along Oedipal lines.[50] One of the most detailed psychoanalytic discussions of transvestism from this period was Stekel's "Fragment der Analyse einer Transvestitin" (Fragmentary Analysis of a Transvestite), published in 1921 as part of his two-volume work on female frigidity.[51] Labeled 'fragmentary' because the patient broke off treatment before Stekel deemed it complete, this case details the analysis of an educated young individual AFAB complaining of lack of responsiveness during sexual intercourse with men. Stekel, an early member of the Vienna psychoanalytic school before his expulsion in 1912, was, as Ellis remarked, the analyst "who has most often discussed the nature of cross-dressing"; he presented further cases in his works *Onanie und Homosexualität* (Onanism and Homosexuality) and *Der Fetischismus* (Fetishism).[52] Perhaps it was precisely Stekel's intellectual isolation outside of the hallowed inner Freudian circle by the 1920s that led him to pursue a topic given only glancing attention in earlier psychoanalytic studies. At the same time, his interest in the sex-gender identification of this female-born patient resonates with the larger analytic reorientation toward female sexuality in the interwar years (see chapter 5).[53]

The first section of Stekel's text consists of the anonymous patient's own account. Unlike the first-person narratives published by Hirschfeld and Ellis, she (I follow the patient's own choice of female pronouns) writes in a distanced, third-person voice. Assuming that Stekel republished the patient's account directly, as he claims, this stylistic choice can be interpreted as a conscious alignment with the expectations of the medical or psychoanalytic case. As the patient herself reports, "*Until her sixth year patient regarded herself as a boy for some unknown reason dressed in girl's clothes, in spite of the reassurances of her environment.*"[54] For many years, the patients of sex researchers had seen the benefits of framing their autobiographical accounts in distinctly medical ways; some of Krafft-Ebing's patients even added diagnostic observations in the margins of their written accounts to more closely resemble a physician's case notes.[55] By writing in the third person, Stekel's patient loses some of the sense of individual authenticity conveyed in the sexological cases of Hirschfeld and Ellis, distancing herself from her own narrative—possibly as a protective mechanism, whether to express a certain resistance to her own non-normative desires, or to overcome a sense of underlying shame or discomfort in order to tell her story.[56] Yet this also has the discursive benefit of placing herself on a level with her analyst, as she offers up her story as evidence for Stekel's diagnostic explanations.

Despite this shift in register, the content of Stekel's patient's case echoes sexological case histories of transvestism in several respects. Like Hirschfeld's and Ellis's informants, she lists her history of physical ailments, describes her childhood preference for boys' games, her teenage experiences of humiliation when forced to wear feminine clothing, and her preference for "masculine" sexual roles, in which she does the active courtship.[57] Unlike the patients in many sexological cases of transvestism, she expresses satisfaction with her occasional homosexual practices, which she adamantly wishes to maintain. Rather than seeking a conversion to "normal" sexuality, she hopes only that psychoanalysis might help her to (also) achieve "proper" sexual responses with men.[58] Clearly familiar with the generic expectations of the medical case, her account also reveals fluency in the language of psychoanalysis, as she describes her inner psychic processes: "One self dissects everything into the clear field of consciousness, is sceptical [*sic*], cool. The other self in her is saddened by the feelings of the first, yearns for the unconscious, yearns to be 'like the others.'"[59] The patient speculates on possible Oedipal causes for her pathology, including an emotional fixation on the mother and a possible erotic fixation on the father, and self-diagnoses a personality split as well as sadomasochistic and compulsive thoughts. She also explains her decision to seek treatment with reference to psychoanalytic concepts, suspecting that her ill health was due to what Karl Abraham had termed a "flight to illness" (*Flucht in die Krankheit)*.[60]

Picking up on this self-diagnosis, Stekel offers several explanations for his patient's "frigidity," including a fear of childbirth and sexual penetration.[61] He echoes her attribution of her transvestism to a succession of childhood fixations, first on her mother, and when this love was not returned, on her father ("In her neurotic endeavor to combine all these clashing trends in herself she became man and woman. She grew up a transvestite. She identified herself more and more with her supreme love objective—her father!").[62] According to Stekel, treatment depended on whether she could wean herself from these overinvested familial ties, ideally via an older man who could act as a father figure. As he rather condescendingly informs his patient, "In your innermost self you are a woman of housewifely instincts,—with a 'craving for respectability,'" imposing his own assumptions about his patient's "true" gender identity.[63] He dismisses as mere "poses" her tendencies toward "Bohemianism," sexual anarchism, and atheism, and questions her desire to be "exceptional" and to paint, which is a traditionally masculine-coded area of cultural production. As he reflects at the conclusion of the analysis, "Does artistry really mean more to her than peace and happiness, quiet and satisfaction?"[64] It is, perhaps, no accident that this openly masculine, well-educated patient starts arriving late or not at all to therapy sessions at about the time Stekel begins to argue along such antifeminist—and indeed, transphobic and homophobic—lines.

While Stekel used this case to support an Oedipal theory of transvestite causality, with other patients exhibiting cross-gendered behaviors he tended to diagnose latent homosexuality. This interpretation was in line with other analysts such as Abraham, Isidor Sadger, and Stekel's assistant Emil Gutheil, who viewed transvestism as caused by the castration complex, repressed homosexuality, or both. Abraham, for example, interpreted the desire of a "hysterical" male patient to be a woman as "pointing us toward the homosexual components of the patient's drives." These included a strong identification with the mother, whose severe menstrual headaches the patient reportedly "shared."[65] (In contrast, Ellis assessed the facts of Abraham's case as "primarily an example of Eonism," sharply observing that analysts' insistence on describing their patients' condition "exclusively on psycho-genetic grounds" sometimes directly contradicted their patients' own self-perceptions.)[66] Such apparent lack of understanding also angered at least some self-identified transvestites, who reported frustration at psychoanalysts who interpreted denials of homosexuality as an admission of the same.[67]

We can only imagine that such frustration must have informed the reaction of thirty-four-year-old public servant "Elsa B." to a series of analytic sessions conducted by Stekel's assistant, Gutheil, and published in Stekel's study on fetishism in 1923. As Gutheil observes in an introductory note, "The patient entered the analysis under one condition: *that we do not destroy the arrangement of her sexual drive* [*sexuelle Triebeinstellung*]. She purely sought a medical certificate in order to apply for a police permit to wear male clothing."[68] Yet far from simply being issued with the required documentation—which she hoped, as she expressed in a letter to Stekel, would allow her "a human existence"—Elsa B. subsequently sat through (seemingly more or less willingly) more than thirty analytic sessions.[69] These delved deeply into her childhood (when she had been neglected), her early same-sex experiences, her traumatic encounter with an exhibitionist, and her current relationship with her landlady Justine, whom she referred to as "mother." In Gutheil's detailed case notes, Elsa B. describes dressing in male clothing, an urge that she had experienced since childhood, as being like the "tense expectation of a pleasure, which then expresses itself as relaxation, calming and contentedness."[70]

As with Stekel's patient, Elsa B.'s understanding of her "condition" (again, I follow the patient's own use of female pronouns) differed significantly from Gutheil's assessment of her case. In a language that references sexological-congenital explanations of transvestism, she reports, "I describe my condition as inborn and no doubt [*wohl*] abnormal, however not at all pathological. I am also unaware of any nervous complaints."[71] Gutheil's interpretation, in contrast—completed in consultation with Stekel—drew heavily on his interpretation of the patient's dreams and familial relationships, leading him to diagnose a heady combination of the castration and Electra complexes, including a fixation on her mother, identification with her brother Eduard and long-deceased father, a religious "Madonna" complex in which Elsa B. featured as the suckling Christ child, and narcissism. Identification with a sexual object of the opposite sex served, Gutheil argued, as the basis for the patient's homosexuality.[72] He was also keen to determine whether Elsa B.'s transvestism fit the theoretical category of fetishism (the label under which this case was published), noting that Hirschfeld had rejected this connection on the basis that the fetishist initially takes his object of choice in connection with a second person, but not primarily as a part of himself, as is the case with transvestism. Although declaring that this approach "only brushes over the surface of the problem," Gutheil and Stekel conclude that, despite certain internal similarities, transvestism is not an example of "genuine" fetishism, but rather "constitutes a special form of compulsive neurosis, in which the desire for the genitals of the opposite sex is displaced onto the clothing." Fetishism, moreover, has a retrospective tendency (referring to an object encountered in the past), whereas transvestism is prospective in outlook, envisaging a future "miracle" of sexual metamorphosis.[73]

In the early 1920s Hirschfeld's Institute coworker Arthur Kronfeld also attempted to interpret along analytic lines a phenomenon whose essence, he declared, still lies "completely in the dark."[74] Although emphasizing that individual variation makes it difficult to place transvestites into any kind of unitary category, Kronfeld relied heavily on theories of narcissism, together with "a peculiar form of reciprocal identification with the mother" and hints of the castration and Oedipus complexes.[75] Although Kronfeld agreed with Hirschfeld that many male-to-female transvestites were heterosexual, he focused far less than his Berlin colleague on physical symptoms, instead suggesting—in a manner no doubt highly offensive to his patients—that their "physical build often contradicts these [cross-gendered] tendencies in almost grotesque fashion." He also agreed with Ellis that this was not an overwhelmingly erotic phenomenon, and emphasized environmental factors: "no special hereditary biological 'gene' [*erbbiologischen 'Gene'*] is required," he insists, to explain the transvestite condition.[76] In the trading zone of scientific encounter that such cases opened up, sexologists and psychoanalysts viewed each others' interpretations with a critical eye, as the next section of this chapter shows.

Competing Cases

Sexologists were keen to maintain their disciplinary authority over a diagnosis that had, after all, been a sexological rather than analytic innovation. Ellis conceded the value of psychoanalysis in developing a fuller perspective on trans identities, but rejected the tendency among Freudians to "overthrow[ ] the constitutional view altogether."[77] The danger of psychoanalytic approaches, he argued, is that they overlook all-important biological factors, including the internal secretions, focusing instead on psychological findings that might, in the absence of a vulnerable constitutional foundation, "be of no importance at all."[78] On the other hand, both Gutheil and Stekel firmly rejected Hirschfeld's "biological theory of transvestitism."[79] While Gutheil expressed gratitude for Hirschfeld's achievement in providing the first detailed case histories of this condition, he critiqued the latter's alleged neglect of his patients' latent homosexuality, attributing it to a broader failure to deploy analytic techniques: "In point of fact the reason why the most significant researcher could overlook such an important characteristic of transvestism lies purely in the circumstance that *Hirschfeld*, in his extensive and content-rich study, eschewed the techniques of psychological depth research [*Tiefenforschung*]."[80]As a result, argues Gutheil, Hirschfeld completely ignores the "incest problem," despite the fact that "some of his patients articulate this in very clear terms" [*eine ziemlich deutliche Sprache darüber führen*].[81] A good decade earlier in a 1911 review for the *Zentralblatt*, Stekel had criticized the superficiality of Hirschfeld's theory along very similar lines, arguing that "it appears to me that he has not exhausted the depths of the problem and places too much weight on the statements of his transvestites," who tend to deny homosexual desires, while failing to investigate their "unconscious stirrings" (*unbewussten Regungen*).[82] Such arguments resonated with psychoanalytic critiques of the early 1910s concerning the alleged inauthenticity of homosexual patient statements.[83]

A few within homosexual rights circles also disagreed with Hirschfeld's separation of homosexuality and transvestism, including leftist intellectual Kurt Hiller, who in the Weimar period became a leading figure in the WhK, and who drew on psychoanalytic arguments to contest Hirschfeld's new categorization.[84] Although an ally of Hirschfeld's in the early Weimar years—like Hirschfeld, Hiller privately had relationships with men without publicizing his homosexuality—they disagreed on political tactics: whereas Hirschfeld sought to change public opinion through science, Hiller thought "inverts" should form their own political party in the Reichstag; he also advocated a strategy of "mass self-denunciation" (or publicly "coming out," as we might say today), controversial in homosexual rights circles at this time.[85] The two were at opposite sides of a major rift within the WhK in the late 1920s over, among other things, a proposed reform to Paragraph 175 that would have come at the expense of the rights of male prostitutes (Hirschfeld wanted the reform; for Hiller the cost was too high). While Laurie Marhoefer has recently shown that this struggle was key to Hirschfeld's resignation in 1929 from the group that he had himself cofounded, the animosity between them was certainly compounded, not only by their very different approaches to political activism, but by Hiller's criticisms of "effeminate" homosexuals and transvestites—which put him more in line with the masculinists in the movement—in contrast to Hirschfeld's vocal support for these groups.[86]

Hirschfeld responded to Stekel's criticisms in the second volume of his 1920s series *Sexualpathologie* (Sexual Pathology), arguing that the focus on repressed homosexual urges was not so much completely false as clinically unhelpful: "for *clinical* consideration it comes down not so much to that which is latent as that which is manifest, and there can be no doubt that for many transvestites homosexuality is every bit as disagreeable [*unsympathisch*] as for the majority of heterosexuals."[87] Ellis, meanwhile, took issue with the fact that Stekel accepted Hirschfeld's clinical case histories while completely opposing the latter's biological conception of causality. Pointing to Hirschfeld's unparalleled knowledge of homosexuality among contemporary sexual scientists, Ellis remarks, "It is hardly likely that he would overlook the anomaly of which he is the chief expert in a class of cases which he was the first to study with care on a large scale." For Stekel, Ellis observes, even patients exhibiting apparently "normal" (heterosexual) desires were in fact "really masked sexual inverts." Ellis—who had a history of disagreeing with Stekel's case interpretations—conceded that everyone possesses latent possibilities, but declared it unprofitable to classify the population according to a condition that most patients never reach.[88] Ellis also responded in unusually firm fashion to Gutheil's case: "Certainly it would hardly be possible to pile up a greater number of complexes and perverse fantasies on to Elsa B.'s devoted head. They seem to be plentiful enough to account for anything." He points to a series of "very definite" facts seemingly ignored by Gutheil, but "in which he might well have found a grave significance if he had not felt bound to reject altogether the possibility of any constitutional element in the case." These included the age disparity between the patient's parents at conception, "a known cause of deviations in the offspring"; her premature birth; and a parental neglect that "furnished exactly the favoring conditions demanded by any perverse innate germs"—thus emphasizing the significance of hereditary and degeneration arguments over psychosexual development. As a result—and while careful to observe that Gutheil und Stekel do not speak for all analysts—Ellis scathingly concludes that "one can well understand the sceptic [*sic*] feeling that the psycho-analyst is a kind of spider who spins his pathological web-complex so widely and so elaborately only in the hope that somewhere, at all events, the fly must become entangled."[89]

Despite this critical stance toward the case studies of Stekel and Gutheil, Ellis's openness to psychoanalytic approaches shines through in his discussion of his own cases, such as that of a thirty-seven-year-old heterosexual married Welshwoman whose "anomaly" manifested only in her erotic dreams, when she imagined herself as a young man of twenty-three making love to a young woman,[90] or forty-eight-year-old "R.L.," of whom Ellis suggests that "if we were to investigate him psycho-analytically, we might possibly find the influence of an infantile attachment to his mother."[91] He thus offers hesitant approval of the insights offered by psychoanalysis, despite being highly critical of analysts' neglect of biological or hereditary factors. Ellis's attempt to reconcile theories of body and mind, as well as the divergent methods of physiological and psychoanalytic inquiry when it came to such cases, bears citing at length:

> Those investigators who concentrate on the constitutional foundations of psycho-sexual anomalies, and those investigators who explore the mechanisms revealed by psycho-analysis are alike performing necessary tasks. Nothing is now more certain than the influence of the varying balance of the internal secretions in building up the psychosexual constitution. Nothing also is more illuminating than the mechanisms which the masters of psycho-analysis have revealed in unraveling the varied experiences of the individual. Both are essential to a complete interpretation of the varied cases that arise. Evil only ensues when, in one party or the other party, there is a failure to realize the immense services which the opposite party is rendering.[92]

This insistence on lending even weight to biology and psychology was shared, Ellis notes, by leading British analyst Ernest Jones, who "clearly assumes the existence of both sets of factors in all psycho-analytic investigations."[93] This integrative stance was, as we have seen in previous chapters, typical of Ellis's overall attitude toward the findings of the Freudians.

Others similarly sought to reconcile organic and acquired explanations of trans identifications during this period. In 1924/25, New York–based physician Lothar Goldmann published an article series "Über das Wesen des Umkleidungstriebes" (On the Nature of the Drive to Cross-Dress) in the German periodical *Geschlecht und Gesellschaft* (Sex and Society), in which he addresses a wide range of possible causes, although in keeping with broader shifts in medical attitudes, and in contrast to Ellis, he clearly rejects degeneration arguments. Based on observations that, as Ellis later noted, "seem to have been made chiefly in Berlin," Goldmann concludes that while hormonal influence is significant ("without doubt, it exercises an influence on every cell of the body"), some cases may well be primarily psychological in nature. On this basis, he distinguished between actively and passively acquired transvestism.[94] Pointing to the wider dissemination of such expert medical discourses, Goldmann's article series was also published in pamphlet form and advertised in 1920s German homosexual periodicals such as *Die Freundin* (Girlfriend) and *Das 3. Geschlecht* (The 3rd Sex).

For their part, psychoanalysts were far less prepared to take a middle line. Not until 1929 did analyst Otto Fenichel start to accept the possible separation of transvestism and homosexuality that sex researchers such as Ellis and Hirschfeld had been proposing for almost two decades, but that Stekel and Gutheil had largely rejected.[95] In a paper delivered to the 11th International Psychoanalytic Congress in Oxford that July, in which he presented a detailed case of a forty-year-old husband and father who expressed fantasies of being a woman, Fenichel cited Hirschfeld's articulation of transvestism as a "specific form of perversion." He affirmed the emphasis of earlier psychoanalytic studies on the castration complex and identification with a phallic mother figure (for male-to-female transvestism), while suggesting that a simpler form of penis envy could explain female-to-male transvestism.[96] Such late-1920s analytic engagements with transvestite topics were, in turn, barely acknowledged within sexological discussions in the German-speaking world until the 1950s and 1960s.[97]

Contestations over transvestite cases demonstrate their function as a cross-disciplinary "trading zone" in the sense described by Peter Galison. Although they retained their basic structure as (auto)biographical patient narratives with a number of shared features, they also underwent stylistic adaptation and reinterpretation as they moved across the theoretical frameworks of interwar sexology and psychoanalysis. But what about the self-identified "transvestites" at the heart of these cases? In the following I show that people who were beginning to shape their sense of self around new medical categories rearticulated sexological and psychoanalytic models of the transvestite case, reimagining this genre in less normalizing and more emancipatory ways.

From Patients to Activists: Subcultural Negotiations of the Medical Case

Scholars have done much to shed light on how sexological—and to a lesser extent, psychoanalytic—theories were taken up within interwar literature and popular culture in and beyond the German-speaking world.[98] Yet the "looping" between medical and broader publics was far from a one-way street. Sexological and psychoanalytic accounts of the perversions are unthinkable without the first-person accounts supplied by patients and other informants, which in turn shaped the priorities of individual researchers. Homosexual activist and writer Kertbeny, and later Hirschfeld, both pointed in their writings to the suicides of friends, acquaintances, and patients as affective prompts for their own scholarly inquiries.[99] In a more positive vein, Hirschfeld noted that "higher than expected interest" from readers of his *Transvestites* study led him to publish an illustrated companion volume, working together with Berlin artist Max Tilke. This rich collection of fifty-four plates consisted predominantly of images volunteered by readers of his earlier study, dressed according to their gender identity.[100] A brochure announcing the foundation of the Weimar transvestite organization Vereinigung D'Eon (D'Eon Association) further highlights the wider "loopings" of Hirschfeld's study at this period. Since the publication of *Die Transvestiten*, the authors report, "thousands of people have notified the Magnus Hirschfeld Institute for Sex Research [*sic*], professing that they are transvestites and requesting his assistance in their psychological distress."[101] Meanwhile, psychoanalytic explanations had also begun to infiltrate publics beyond the largely bourgeois patient base of the early Freudians. Although they still tended to be read in more elite and avant-garde circles, interwar innovations such as the Berlin psychoanalytic polyclinic, overseen by the Institute, established in 1920 by Karl Abraham, Max Eitingon, and Georg Simmel to treat primarily lower-income patients at no fee, brought analytic methods to a much larger cohort of patients along socialist-inspired principles, as did a similar clinic in Vienna.[102] The remainder of this chapter shows how individuals who recognized themselves in the "transvestite" cases of sexology and psychoanalysis began appropriating and reimagining this medical category for political and community-building purposes, at times leading them to directly contest "expert" medical definitions.

The Weimar Republic's reduced censorship restrictions and rapidly expanding urban environments opened up rich new spaces for the expression of nonnormative gendered and sexual subjectivities.[103] In addition to a blossoming of homosexual political organizations, bars, literature, and magazines, the 1920s and early 1930s saw the emergence of a number of transvestite-specific organizations and media, mostly based in Berlin. Bearing titles such as the aforementioned "Transvestites' World" or "The Transvestite," these identity-oriented social groups and magazine columns were very much products of the dialogue between scientific knowledge cultures and the broader sociopolitical contexts in which these had emerged. The magazine columns constitute some of the first examples of print media worldwide to specifically address issues that would today be classified under the broad banners of "trans" or "transgender." With the exception of a short-lived magazine dedicated entirely to transvestite concerns, *Das 3. Geschlecht* (The 3rd Sex, 1930–1932), these columns mostly appeared in periodicals aimed at female homosexual readers. Here they received a warmer welcome than in the often overtly masculinist male homosexual periodicals, while reflecting a degree of overlap in transvestite and female homosexual organizations and social events during these years. The columns included many confessional autobiographical pieces, but also short stories and poems, advice columns on questions such as fashion and makeup, and opinion pieces on medical or legal questions such as "Transvestites and the Police."[104]

Contributors to the Weimar transvestite media frequently drew on sexological and psychoanalytic assessments of "transvestites," "sexual inversion," and "intermediary" sexual forms to articulate a discourse of cross-gendered identity. Friedel Werner insisted that, far from being an acquired "aberration" (*Verirrung*), science had shown transvestism to be an "inborn predisposition"; Fred Ursula agreed that "Transvestism . . . is a predisposition, just like homosexuality, although these are not identical."[105] In a programmatic opening article for *Das 3. Geschlecht*, Anne von den Eken carefully reminded readers of the original female sex organs present in all embryos and the "countless intermediary forms between one sex and the other"; this magazine also advertised works by Hirschfeld, Ellis, and Bloch, and published "popular scientific" articles that reformulated in lay terms theories of gender by prominent scholars such as Karsch-Haack or Austrian philosopher Otto Weininger.[106] Other commentators carefully teased out the distinctions between transvestism and fetishism, masochism and sadism, all commonly framed by sexologists in gendered terms.[107]

In such ways, the columns translated and adapted scientific discussions to suit the needs of a trans-identified readership. They also offered occasional "from below" accounts of encounters with medical practitioners.[108] In 1931, columnist Em(m)i Wolters described how, over forty years earlier, "my case study" had been one of the first to become known to the sex researchers; she later revealed that the sexologist she had seen was Hirschfeld himself.[109] Others pointed to the new scientific approaches toward non-gender-normative bodies and behaviors inspired by the latest endocrine research: Toni Fricke described undergoing blood tests with the famous researcher Professor Abderhalden in Halle to prove "that I am, so to say, internally a hermaphrodite."[110] Sexologist Goldmann had also discussed Abderhalden's tests on the blood serum of a transvestite—possibly Fricke herself—observing that these tests verified theories of the original hermaphroditic constitution of the gonads.[111]) Such positive tales of personal encounters with medical researchers support the findings of other historians that sexological encounters could be comforting and self-affirming, as well as having pathologizing effects.[112] They also sound notes of warning, however, with Eken advising that transvestites only turn to doctors who have "engaged extensively with research on sexual intermediaries," and who understand that their goal is not to alter the "physical or sexual predisposition" of their patients, but rather to protect them, through education and advice.[113]

A particularly clear example of the "loopings" between sex researchers and an increasingly organized and politicized transvestite subculture can be found in discussions of medical and surgical options for trans-identified individuals. Many contributors—and by extension, readers—of the Weimar transvestite magazines were familiar with at least the theoretical possibility of gender confirmation procedures, including the research being carried out by Hirschfeld's Institute for Sexual Science. The most famous case of this period was that of Danish artist Lili Elbe in the early 1930s, whose posthumously published memoirs—the subject of a recent film—followed a series of surgeries in Dresden.[114] Yet Elbe was not alone in seeking the "highest possible forms of physical transformation possible today." In 1931 Institute-affiliated doctor Felix Abraham wrote an illustrated report of surgeries performed at the Institute on "two homosexual transvestites," domestic worker Dora (Rudolph) R. and artist Toni (Anton) E. In his report, Abraham sympathetically observes that their journey "essentially reflects that which is generally longed for by transvestites."[115] Such surgeries, which involved castration (removal of the testicles) and penile amputation followed by vaginal construction, were not widely accessible to trans-identified individuals in the Weimar years, and carried with them a significant risk of complications (for Dora R. and Toni E., the risk of surgery was deemed less than that posed by the potentially "life-threatening complications" of highly probable "self-mutilation").[116] Nonetheless, they played an important role in the developing transvestite imaginary mediated by the Weimar-era magazines. A short story titled "Girl-boy," for example, describes how a female-born child named Selma grows up to become a male bridge engineer following the intervention of a sympathetic outsider, who had seen through external appearances to the teenaged Selma's "true" identity. Following a stay in a sanatorium, Selma describes to the former stranger how she "became a 'case'" for the scientific authorities, and how (an ellipsis smooths over the details of this fictionalized medical encounter) "in a nutshell, it just required a simple operation—and I became a real man."[117] Not all accounts of gender realignment surgery were quite so positive; one anonymous contributor—possibly a member of the editorial team on a pedagogical mission—described a friend whose urge to cross-dress was (so the author claimed) purely erotic, and not that of a "genuine" transvestite. The friend subsequently underwent castration surgery and was deeply unhappy, which the author uses to warn others against such methods: "I will content myself with that which can be achieved by natural means."[118]

As well as making a theme of direct encounters with the medical professions, transvestite authors adapted the generic structures of the sexological and psychoanalytic case history in autobiographical narratives published in these magazines. These life writings frequently adopted a confessional trope of "*sich bekennen*" (approximately "to confess" or "to openly acknowledge" something), and thus bore strong links to both older traditions of religious confession, described by Foucault as "the general standard governing the production of the true discourse on sex," as well as much later discourses of "coming out" as gay, lesbian, or trans.[119] They function as an emancipatory project of strategic and creative self-transformation, and like the cases of the sex researchers, typically begin with the author's first-person recollections of cross-gendered inclinations in childhood, such as dressing up in a sister's clothes or envying boys their trousers, haircuts, or rifles: "My female soul showed itself from an early age," writes Ursula.[120] By focusing on a life stage when, as "Mimi" insisted, the subjects were too young for "perversity" to play a role ("this tendency must decisively be a hereditary one"), these accounts of trans identifications in childhood underwrote sexological ideas about transvestism as a natural, inborn condition.[121]

Such childhood recollections are followed, as in the medical cases, by the author recounting realizations of difference during puberty: from the pain of being forced to keep one's gender identity a secret to the satisfaction accompanying a first purchase of gender-variant clothing. Ursula describes this moment: "I was utterly satisfied, even though only half of my wishes had so far been fulfilled"; similarly, E.K. explains how "all at once things got better with this drive to cross-dress [*Umkleidungstrieb*]. It was like a big letting out of breath."[122] Again echoing the sexological cases—for the case study is a genre that "organizes singularities into exemplary, intelligible patterns"[123]—a further critical moment for many was the first public outing during which they successfully "passed," described by Lily from Hamburg as "the most beautiful, happy, pure moment of my life to date."[124] The narratives typically end by lamenting the difficulties the author has faced as an adult in finding an understanding sexual partner, and the practical, legal, and social problems involved in attempting to live a transgendered life. A few, though, describe a more positive experience of "coming out" to family, friends, and colleagues, such as E.B., who expressed delight at finding a girlfriend "who understands me, and with whom I can be exactly who I am."[125] By emphasizing certain aspects of their life stories and brushing over others, these narratives collectively assume the contours of a recognizable genre of transvestite life writing, and resonate with several longer memoirs and novels published in Germany since the fin de siècle.[126] In spite of obvious parallels between these autobiographical chronicles and the case histories published by sexologists and psychoanalysts, subcultural authors were not simply bowing down to the interpretive power of medical authority, but rather negotiating scientific models in critical and selective ways.

There were good strategic reasons for such critical appropriations, from the promotion of transvestite rights and political advancement to the mediated creation of a sense of shared gender-variant identity. Whereas, for example, the anonymizing use of initials and pseudonyms in the medical case studies ostensibly worked to protect the subject's privacy, in transvestite contexts this practice took on new meanings. More than a pseudonym, assuming an identifiably male or female name—or a gender-ambiguous one such as "Toni" or "Gert"—worked as a powerful performative act to affirm the author's gender identity. In a similar vein, male-to-female columnists referred to one another as "fellow sisters," and to themselves as "women" or "ladies"; as contributor Maria declared, "I want to be judged and recognized as a woman."[127] These examples of what more recent queer theorists have described in terms of "world-making" or the articulation of "livable" spaces functioned to delineate a politics of belonging for an increasingly articulate transvestite minority.[128] Distinct subcultural priorities are also evident in the selective uptake of scientific ideas. In particular, while many commentators drew strength from sexological theories of transvestism as inborn, some criticized what they considered an excessive emphasis on clothing and pathology. This critical attitude is evident in the following statement by Lina Es, who demonstrates her familiarity with scientific discourses by citing the work of Hirschfeld, one Dr. Thomalla (presumably Curt Thomalla, head of the UFA film studio's Medical Film Archive), and Steinach: "The transvestite is [. . .] not to be blamed for his hermaphroditism and is also not to be blamed for having been born. [. . .] It is also fundamentally incorrect to speak of [clothing in terms of] *disguise* [*Ver*kleidung]. It is not a disguise, but a *change* of clothing [*Um*kleidung] and name that is sought."[129] Wolters offered a similarly sharp assessment of the latest medical "knowledge": while praising Hirschfeld's research in general terms, she criticized his assessment of transgender phenomena as a "pathological" drive to cross-dress (*"krankhafter" Verkleidungstrieb*), and distanced herself from the "not-quite-suitable word transvestism."[130] Publisher and gay rights spokesperson Friedrich Radszuweit also took a critical stance toward medical assessments of transvestism, using his editorial weight to draw attention to unsympathetic pieces in competitor journals, and even republishing a piece by one Hans Scheimann in which transvestism was declared both a "pathological empirical symptom" and a repressive and compensatory mechanism "analogous to kleptomania." Transvestite readers, Radszuweit declared, should come to their own conclusions on such pieces: "The transvestites have the floor."[131]

In a more emancipatory vein, medical research was also redeployed as a basis from which to demand legal and social recognition, including freedom from police harassment. This strategy was familiar from the homosexual rights movement; the WhK had long based its fight against Paragraph 175, as seen in previous chapters, on "scientific" understandings of homosexuality as an inborn and unchangeable condition.[132] Such arguments echo in the words of Dolly S., who argues that "Not just in our own circles, [. . .] but also generally it must be made known that we are dealing not just with a childish folly, but with a most primitive internal drive, with our entire psychological sensibility, and thus not with the unnatural, but with the natural."[133] In the two decades since Hirschfeld's *Transvestites* study, then, this sexological label had come, at least for some readers, to acquire the status of an essential identity, and also formed a basis for new kinds of political organization. Examples include the establishment of a (short-lived) "Special Transvestite Group" in 1929 by the homosexual rights organization Bund für Menschenrechte (League of Human Rights), while in 1930 the competing Deutscher Freundschafts-Verband (German Friendship Association) oversaw the foundation of the aforementioned Vereinigung D'Eon (D'Eon Association).[134] Such politicized identity movements could also boast a number of successes by the end of the Weimar period, as the number of official applications for gender-neutral names and for transvestite certificates significantly increased compared to the Wilhelmine era.[135] In a further example of subcultural "loopings," applicants often drew explicitly on medicalized arguments in making their cases to the authorities; describing the process of applying for these legal documents, one commentator observed that a medical examination had revealed "masculine inner matter (testicles)," despite a feminine "external structure."[136]

For other members of this consolidating subculture, though, psychoanalytic theories better reflected the sense of self. In an article with the telling title "Can transvestism be acquired?," Irene D. describes how as a child she had been forced to cross-dress because her guardian aunt could not afford gender-appropriate clothing, and how she subsequently developed a transvestite sensibility: "Since then I have been a transvestite, beforehand I was just a boy dressed in a girlish way. . . . Who is to blame for my transvestism? According to my own view, only the fact that I was raised as a girl."[137] Others similarly emphasized environmental and relational factors: "I was . . . at the time not a transvestite due to an inner drive, but due to external inducements and upbringing."[138] Views such as this remained in the minority in the transvestite periodicals, not least because they undermined the politically strategic hypothesis that transvestism was an innate identity. Consequently, the editors of "Transvestites' World" observed that they had only published Irene D.'s contribution "in order to convince her of her completely incorrect view": "We do not agree with the thoughts outlined here, on the contrary, we cannot, on the basis of our years of experience, identify with them at all."[139] A similar example of community self-policing can be found in responses to "Fräulein Gerda," who described how she, too, had been forced as a child to wear girl's clothing, and subsequently resisted cross-dressing for an extended period before returning to it later in life. "If you have managed to remain without disguise [*Verkleidung*] for fifteen years," declared another reader, "then it is out of the question that you are a genuine transvestite, in my opinion you are a bisexual [*ein Bisexueller*]."[140] Such disciplining of transvestite narratives aligned with the magazines' generally cautious attitude toward Freudian theories. In one "popular scientific" contribution to *Das 3. Geschlecht*, the author observed that while Freud's research had shown that an individual's sexual character probably underlies many spheres of their psychological life, "he goes too far in the development of his theory, which thus becomes one-sided."[141] Such subcultural tensions surrounding transvestite causality point to both the new political possibilities created by the looping of medical theories, and the ways in which these were utilized to delimit understandings of "genuine" transvestism.

The dominant voices in the transvestite media clearly viewed the congenital clarity of sexological definitions as more conducive to their political claims, and were prepared to sacrifice recognition of some transvestite subjectivities for the sake of these goals. Within the terms of Weimar transvestite politics, recognition was about more than legal rights; it was also about establishing a community for "fellow sufferers" (*Leidensgefährten*) that might reduce feelings of individual isolation damaging to mental health.[142] Anna Maria H. declared that she was sharing her story to "show that it is also possible for us transvestites to structure our lives and achieve happiness in a way that is in line with our nature," while Fricke described the "persistent, nerve-murdering psychological pressure" constantly threatening to undermine transvestite health.[143] Other contributors told of how reading others' life stories had opened their eyes to their own transvestite "tendencies" (*Neigung*) or "predisposition" (*Veranlagung*), about which they had not previously dared to speak for fear of ridicule.[144] Such solidarity could represent a crucial psychological crutch in the face of ongoing social ostracism. As Mimi lamented, "if people knew what we transvestites suffer, they would certainly be milder in their judgments"; Loni Rex reported with even greater emotion that "it is not going too far when I say that the enlightenment [*Aufklärung*] you have given me [through your magazine] saved my life."[145] Adapting what had started as a medical diagnosis to link their individual situations to those of others like themselves, contributors encouraged fellow readers to become politically active in the defense of a shared identity.

Yet just as appeals to congenital arguments marginalized individuals who understood their condition along less biologically determinist lines, the transvestite solidarity promoted by the transvestite magazines was one characterized by exclusions. The mostly middle-class contributors to the Weimar transvestite media imposed their own standards of bourgeois respectability, citizenship, and decency on their fellow readers as they formulated claims to full recognition by the German state. As Vereinigung D'Eon leader Marie Weis announced in 1930, only when the conditions of transvestite respectability had been achieved would it be possible to publicly identify with this label and fight for rights on that basis.[146] Respectability in this context meant conforming to bourgeois standards of appearance, behavior, and morality, with an emphasis on "passing" in public, wearing subtle and unflashy clothing, and not engaging in activities such as prostitution or crime. This meant, however, that individuals who did not conform, including sex workers and criminals, but often also people who were working-class, homosexual, or female-to-male transvestites, were excluded from the terms of Weimar transvestite belonging, at times even brutally dismissed as "the scum of humanity" or "morally inferior," or linguistically marginalized as "also-transvestites."[147]

Such exclusions were also typical of Weimar sexual politics more broadly, a process of pragmatic compromise that Marhoefer has recently described as the "Weimar settlement on sexual politics."[148] It is crucial, then, to consider the limits of the sources examined here. As valuable as they are in documenting the world's first explicitly transvestite political and community movement, they do not reflect the subjectivities of those trans-identified individuals who may have conceived of their gendered and sexual identity in ways quite removed from either the respectability-driven understanding of the magazines' middle-class identity politics, or the medicalized discourses of sexology and psychoanalysis. Attending to the nuances of historical subjectivities and political formations demands that we think critically about such exclusions, but also beyond the categories of today's LGBTIQ identity politics to acknowledge the otherness and, at times, the "topsy-turvydom" of gendered and sexual identities in the past.[149] Allowing voices such as Irene D.'s and Fräulein Gerda's to complicate narratives of a Weimar transvestite identity based primarily on sexological-congenital understandings does not lessen the significance of this early movement for trans history. Rather, it illustrates how a range of expert discourses—including psychoanalytic as well as sexological understandings of nonnormative gender identifications—contributed to the "loopings" that shaped transvestite self-understanding during these years.

The three different approaches to the transvestite case examined in this chapter represent three different ways of "telling a life" through the lens of modern sexual categorizations, and of making that life both "public" and "scientific."[150] By examining mutual interpenetrations of medical and subcultural discourses, I have shown that this looping was a dynamic process of critical negotiation, as individuals previously "sorted" by sexologists and psychoanalysts (to again borrow a phrase from Hacking) used their own publications to rebel against scientific classifications and rearrange the terms of their self-identification. The new genre of transvestite life-writing established in Weimar-era periodicals, I have argued here, exhibited strong links to, but also significant differences from, the medicalized frameworks of the sexological and psychoanalytic case history from which it had emerged. By intervening in the looping process, authors developed a discursive basis from which to expound the political goals of an increasingly tangible transvestite public, laying the foundation of late twentieth-century trans rights movements. In the process, though, they reinforced those narratives that aligned with normative ideas of transvestite respectability and congenital causality, while policing alternative understandings of trans subjectivity for the sake of political coherence.

This analysis of competing models of transvestism from the 1910s to 1930s also reveals the significance of the case study genre itself as a trading zone of knowledge exchange; a disciplinary and cultural hybrid that could transfer new knowledge about transvestite subjects between different readerships, while remaining open to multiple appropriations. Divergent interpretations by sexologists and psychoanalysts of their patients' narratives of gender-atypical experience highlight the ongoing conflict between congenital and acquired models of sexual pathology. Indeed, they show how the struggle between "body and mind" had gained a renewed intensity in the interwar period following the rapid expansion in hormone research. More firmly than ever, sexologists were coming down on the side of biology, while psychoanalysts focused their attention on the workings of the subconscious (attributing transvestism to "latent" homosexuality or an unresolved castration complex) while paying even less heed to physiological arguments than in earlier discussions of child sexuality, homosexuality, or the war neuroses.

The promising advances in both medicalized research on trans bodies and a new brand of "transvestite" political activism examined in this chapter came to an abrupt halt with the National Socialist takeover. German transvestite and homosexual publications were soon culled under the harsh new censorship regime after January 30, 1933, although scholars have traced historical fragments of trans experience into the Nazi era.[151] It was not for another two decades that a new current of research into the medical and surgical options for, and inner psychic dynamics of, trans-identified individuals properly took root, now across the Atlantic, spearheaded by German émigré doctor and former Steinach student Harry Benjamin.[152] Similarly, it was also not until after World War II that the next significant wave of trans activism emerged in the United States, initially evidencing a similar politics of normative respectability and the exclusion of unruly others that had shaped the Weimar movement.[153] These developments mark a decisive break with the trading zone of sexological, psychoanalytic, and subcultural knowledge that had begun to circulate in German-speaking Europe in the Weimar years, even as individual actors formed important threads of continuity between the interwar and postwar periods. This break, and the transnational relocation of sexological and psychoanalytic knowledge that ensued, is the subject of this book's epilogue.

Epilogue

"Emphasize in the most friendly manner that although I have become a victim of the Hitler regime, like so many German intellectuals, my power to work is not yet broken, and that from Nice, the place to which I have withdrawn, I am occupied with the preservation of my scientific investigations in the interest of a better future."[1] In March 1935, one month before his death in the French coastal city of Nice, almost two years after the ransacking of his Institute for Sexual Science by Nazi students in Berlin, and a good five years after leaving Berlin for a world tour from which he never returned, the exiled Magnus Hirschfeld sent this letter to his Australian-British colleague Norman Haire, with whom he had for some years been in regular contact as organizers of the transnational World League for Sexual Reform. Hirschfeld's request poignantly demonstrates his ongoing commitment to the sexological cause, despite his financially and geographically difficult situation and poor health. Haire also wrote to his British mentor Havelock Ellis concerning Hirschfeld's plans to organize, from exile, a translation into English of his major 1914 study of homosexuality. "The American publisher ought to insist," Haire notes, with a reference to both Germany's new political regime and its impact on the once-thriving Weimar-era homosexual subculture, "on Hirschfeld bringing [his work] up to date by revising, where necessary, those parts concerning the laws both in Germany and in other countries. . . . It would be of interest for him to add an appendix concerning the change under Hitlerism. I am told that the Lokale [homosexual pubs] are mostly closed, except for a few where entrance is reserved for Nazis and their trusted sympathizers."[2] That the international sex research community was well aware of the looming threat to their German-speaking colleagues is also evident in a letter from Ellis to Haire in January 1932—a full year before the National Socialist seizure of power—in which Ellis expressed his approval of Hirschfeld's politically timely world tour: "I suspect he is wise to follow the psycho-analysts in going to America."[3]

As Hirschfeld was in Paris watching the destruction of his Institute via newsreels, transnational networks of medical and lay analysts were busying themselves with the bureaucratic technicalities of paving a path into exile for German-speaking colleagues, many of whom were, like Hirschfeld, especially vulnerable to Nazi persecution on the basis of their Jewish backgrounds. "We have incorporated a Psychoanalytic Institute of Los Angeles," wrote physician David Brunswick to his New York colleague Dr. Monroe A. Meyer in September 1933, "and Dr. [Ernst] Simmel of Berlin has agreed to come in January as Educational Director to take up general educational work for us and for the community. We must now enable him to procure a permanent immigration visa, preferably a professorial one." This would involve sending to Simmel, who as we have seen had first made his mark on the German-speaking analytic community with the expedited treatment of shell-shock victims in World War I,

> a letter addressed to the consul, showing that he has been for many years a teacher at the Berlin [Psychoanalytic] Institute, that he is coming to teach and be Educational Director at our institute, and guaranteeing (1) that we are inviting him to fill a position that no American is both qualified and willing to fill, and (2) that he will not become a public charge. . . . The first guarantee seems to be the crux of the matter . . . and could be backed up, I suppose, only by a letter signed by Dr. Brill in his capacity as President of the American Psychoanalytic Association.[4]

Five years later, just two months after the Nazi annexation of Austria in March 1938, one Dr. Caprio made similar inquiries on behalf of Wilhelm Stekel at the New York Psychiatric Institute and Hospital, "asking about any possible university appointments for Dr. Steckel [*sic*]." As a hospital administrator wrote to the Institute for Psychoanalysis in New York, "I discouraged him in this respect, stating that university appointments were very difficult to obtain for refugees" and suggesting that "undoubtedly Dr. Steckel [*sic*] would be happier in the practice of psychoanalysis in one of the smaller cities in this country," where there was less competition and psychotherapy was "badly needed."[5]

The advent of the National Socialist dictatorship, as these fragments of correspondence suggest, had the gravest consequences for the many Jewish physicians working in the still medically and scientifically marginalized fields of sexology and psychoanalysis in 1930s Germany and Austria. Although versions of sexual science and analytic therapy each continued to leave their marks on Nazi-era science, the looming threat of fascism forced the majority of these practitioners, including most of the more liberal and reformist members of their respective fields, either to abandon their groundbreaking research altogether, or to attempt to transport it into exile. In the cultural memory of this period, the destruction of Hirschfeld's Institute in the first months of Nazi rule has come to symbolize the brutally anti-Semitic, homophobic, and antiliberal violence that put an abrupt end to the early history of socially progressive sex research in the German-speaking world.[6] Other self-proclaimed *Sexualwissenschaftler* with Jewish backgrounds suffered similar ruptures in their careers and lives: former *Sexual-Probleme* (Sexual Problems) editor Max Marcuse emigrated to Palestine shortly after the 1933 book burnings; Hirschfeld's Institute colleague Arthur Kronfeld left for Switzerland and later the Soviet Union in 1935; Iwan Bloch had already died in Berlin in 1922, having missed out on a professorial habilitation because he refused to convert to Christianity. The increasingly politically conservative and nationalist Albert Moll, meanwhile, who had converted from Judaism in 1895, was among those who remained in Berlin. Despite expressing approval for the political developments, he, too, lost his medical registration under the new regime, and in a poignant coincidence, died on the same day as his long-time intellectual combatant Freud in 1939.[7]

Freudian-style psychoanalysis was another early intellectual victim of the end of Weimar democracy, denounced by the Nazis as a "Jewish science."[8] Although psychoanalytic and other psychotherapeutic schools continued to be influential into the Nazi era, and were even considered crucial to the war effort between 1939 and 1945, advising on matters ranging from military leadership training to war neurosis and homosexuality, a growing backlash against practitioners of the "talking cure" was already in the air before 1933. In 1931 the nationalist Munich-based cultural magazine *Süddeutsche Monatshefte* (South German Monthly) dedicated a special issue to the topic "Against psychoanalysis," the contents of which constitute a veritable manifesto against the Freudians by prominent German psychiatrists such as Siegfried Placzek, Gustav Aschaffenburg, and Alfred E. Hoche.[9] From 1933, the Berlin Psychoanalytic Institute began its process "of largely self-imposed alignment with national socialist policy (*Gleichschaltung*)," soon leading to the exclusion of Jewish psychoanalysts from the profession by their own former colleagues.[10] The pioneering Institute was subsumed under the umbrella of the so-called Göring Institute, known officially as the German Institute for Psychological Research and Psychotherapy and led by National Socialist individual psychologist Mathias Göring, in what constituted a clear rejection of the more sexually oriented and "Jewish" theories of the Freudian school (individual psychology founder Alfred Adler had himself been born Jewish but converted to Protestantism in 1904; he died in exile while on a lecture tour in Scotland in 1937, having moved to the United States in 1934). A number of prominent Weimar-era analysts continued to pursue their careers under this new structure, including Carl Müller-Braunschweig. After the war Müller-Braunschweig was also instrumental in forming the German Psychoanalytic Association (DPV, not to be confused with the rival German Psychoanalytic Society, DPG), which from 1950 was recognized by the International Psychoanalytic Association, pointing to the continuities as well as breaks with Weimar-era psychoanalysis into the National Socialist era. Others became active critics of the regime, and in some cases members of the resistance movement.[11] Of the prominent Vienna-based analysts examined in this book, Sigmund Freud and his analyst daughter Anna landed in the northern suburbs of London in 1938, where he died in 1939; others sought new careers and lives across the Atlantic. Isidor Sadger was one of many to be killed in the Nazi death camps, dying in Theresienstadt in 1942.[12] As a result of these brutal and rapid developments, the conversations that had shaped both early Freudian thought and the modern science of sex more broadly began to shift their center of gravity away from German-speaking Europe and toward the English-speaking world.

US-based analysts and their professional societies went to considerable lengths to aid colleagues fleeing Nazi-occupied Europe, with the American Psychoanalytic Association establishing an Emergency Committee on Relief and Immigration in 1938.[13] Although some were excluded from this mission on political grounds, including Marxist psychoanalyst Wilhelm Reich,[14] many of these émigré analysts soon significantly influenced locally born practitioners and training institutes, including in long-running debates about whether to allow lay analysts into the profession. "When these up-rooted analysts took refuge in New York, they sought to remake their lost world," observes George Makari, leading to frequent tussles with home-grown analysts, "who shared the same name but differed intensely over their identities."[15] The trauma faced by Central European émigrés shaped their research and theoretical priorities as they integrated themselves professionally, culturally, and linguistically into the rich existing North American analytic landscape that, like North American sexology, had developed its own traditions, research foci, and leaders in the decades since the fin de siècle. The new journal *The Psychoanalytic Study of the Child*, founded in 1945, has been characterized by historians as "a creative response to the traumas and losses" endured by many émigré analysts; an "effort to recreate a sense of continuity with an irretrievably lost European psychoanalytic community" that fixed on the child as a point of future-oriented optimism.[16] Shortly before his death, meanwhile, Freud wrote to the British Psychoanalytic Society declaring that he now considered London to be the "main site and center of the psychoanalytic movement"—although as Makari points out, this gesture "was not devoid of pathos; over the years Freud had expressed similar feelings to leaders in Zurich, then Budapest, then Berlin, only to watch each of those hubs either desert him or collapse."[17] It was, however, a clear sign of the relocation of psychoanalytic thought away from the German-speaking world, and the beginning of an era in which émigrés and Anglo-American analysts were to dominate the global conversation. Caught between a precarious life and an almost certain death, hundreds of exiled analysts found themselves compelled to adapt their clinical practice and ideas to suit a very different linguistic, cultural, and professional climate.

As well as transforming international psychoanalytic networks, the political upheaval all but ended the careers of many who for years had combined their sex research with left-wing political activism, from involvement in homosexual rights movements to birth-control politics and eugenic reform—the latter undergoing a drastic shift from a source of optimistic rallying for early marriage reformers, feminist activists, and others, to be horrifically manipulated under the guise of Nazi racial science.[18] In 1937 honorary British Sexological Society member and long-time pacifist and feminist sex reformer Helene Stöcker wrote to that sympathetic international organization from exile in Switzerland. There she was attempting to write a history of the European sex reform movement in the almost complete absence of her personal library, "collected over the course of 40 years, [which] is unfortunately located in Germany, and there is no possibility of getting it out."[19] In 1939 Haire described to an elderly Ellis the growing despair of the international academic community in the face of such blows to German-speaking Jewish and non-Jewish colleagues, shortly before Ellis's own death later that year:

> Stekel is now practicing in London and came down to my cottage last Sunday, and poor old Helene Stöcker, who is now a refugee in London, came down too. I have been very busy with medical refugees. It is very depressing to see all our old friends and acquaintances, who took part in international congresses, in distress, and to hear every week that some more of them have committed suicide—and as the years go by, those of us who have been at all willing to shoulder the burden of supporting, or partly supporting, any of them, find that the possibilities of discovering sources of help for further refugees are becoming smaller and smaller. The refugee problem seems to have no solution.

Haire went on to list some of the many scholars who had reportedly committed suicide, including "Karl Giese, who was Hirschfeld's secretary, and Dr. Felix

Abraham, who was one of Hirschfeld's assistants at the institute in Berlin," as well as "Bondy (the leader of the Czechoslovakian sex reform movement) . . . and I have read dozens of letters from other people who took part in our congresses begging for help to get out of the Axis countries."[20] Even *Der Eigene* editor and homosexual rights campaigner Adolf Brand, who, as we have seen, could count many anti-Semites and *völkisch* nationalists among his masculinist circles—including, for a time, SA leader Ernst Röhm—wrote to the British Sexological Society lamenting "the utter hopelessness of continuing my life's work in the new National Socialist Germany."[21] Brand's despair is especially notable given the ongoing enthusiasm among Nazi-era sex researchers for investigating both inborn and acquired forms of homosexuality. This research drew, at times contradictorily, on a combination of biomedical and psychological approaches while participating in a system that brutally persecuted many homosexual and transgender individuals.[22]

In the years after World War II it was above all the English-speaking world that took over as the center of international sex research, and from the late 1940s onward eyes were increasingly on the United States. With an impact some likened to that of the atomic bomb, the large-scale sex surveys conducted by Alfred C. Kinsey and his team in Indiana, *Sexual Behavior in the Human Male* (1948) and *Sexual Behavior in the Human Female* (1953), initiated a new phase in sexology's history that focused on examining the practices of "average" Americans, including the invention of the famous homosexual-heterosexual "Kinsey scale."[23] In subsequent years, American sexology shifted ever further toward laboratory-oriented studies of physiological sexual response, driven by researchers such as Virginia Johnson and William Masters in Missouri, and an increasingly dominant sex therapy movement. By midcentury, too, sex advice columns in popular periodicals such as *Sexology* were beginning to play a key role in disseminating "scientific" knowledge about sex to broader readerships across North America, echoing the role played by interwar German media and cinema.[24]

Although practitioners at times looked back to the history of pre–World War II German-speaking sexual science, this new brand of American sexology was a largely homegrown affair, with US roots stretching back for several decades. In 1938 a commentator in the *Sexology* journal remarked on the degree of the break with Europe:

> Since Hitler began his purge of "non-Aryans," we seem to have imported many of Germany's greatest research teachers and doctors who have brought knowledge and science to the enrichment of American medicine.

> Yet—strange, isn't it?—we have assimilated so much of the science of Germany but have slighted that for which Germany was most famous—the sciency [*sic*] of *Sexology*.

Describing Hirschfeld's Institute, the author laments that "there has been nothing adequate built to replace this Institution designed to aid scientists in their researches in sex."[25] It was thus often with a nostalgic backward glance across a period of traumatic rupture rather than a strong sense of continuity with older European traditions that North American sexology gained a foothold in the postwar era, even as scholars have traced important lines of connection between Kinsey and prewar German-speaking researchers, including Hirschfeld.[26] An important exception was in the area of trans medicine, with former frequent visitor to the Steinach labs Harry Benjamin responsible for introducing the concept of "transsexualism" to American sexual science and medicine from the 1950s. He was also one of the key figures in developing surgical gender confirmation procedures in the middle decades of the century—his work in particular stands as an important thread of continuity with German and Austrian research of the interwar era.[27]

Much more influential than the émigré sexologists on North American medicine and the academy were the exiled analysts, many of whom became key figures in the growing postwar networks of US psychoanalytic institutes and training centers, such as Karen Horney in Chicago and Sándor Rádo at Columbia. Psychoanalytic thought enjoyed a series of renaissances in the US in the decades after World War II, dubbed by one scholar a "golden age" of popularization, coming to dominate the field of psychiatry by the 1950s.[28] The groundwork had, of course, been laid in the first decades of the twentieth century with Freud and Jung's 1909 visit to Clark University in Massachusetts, after which mainstream American psychiatry had "warmed" to psychoanalysis, "fashioning it into a peculiarly American dynamic psychiatry organized around the operation of mental forces identified by Freud."[29] "Psychoanalysis, in all its unruly complexity," as another recent account declares, "became an integral part of twentieth-century social and intellectual history," reaching its intellectual and popular zenith from the 1940s to the 1980s.[30] And although its hegemony over American psychiatry and psychology proved temporary, fading over the decades in the face of psychiatric drug-based therapies and cognitive-based therapeutic approaches, psychoanalysis was also taken up in the postwar era as a pivotal lens of inquiry in other fields, including the humanities, not least thanks to the influence of Jacques Lacan and the French feminist psychoanalysts, where it has served as a key platform for critical, feminist, and queer theory.[31]

This book has shown that it is historically incorrect to simply locate psychoanalysis within an extended ambit of German-speaking "sexual science" or *Sexualwissenschaft* by the 1910s and 1920s. More productively, we might view the relationship between these two fields in terms of a Venn diagram, with clear areas of intersecting interest and interpenetrations of knowledge—not least via the evidentiary medium of the case study—but also areas of concern and method that were clearly separate and unique to each of these fields as they developed into stand-alone specializations between the 1890s and the early 1930s. An initial enthusiasm for cross-disciplinary exchanges, I have argued, gave way to a modern science and medicine of sexuality defined along increasingly segmented lines, even as "scientific" knowledge about sexual subjects became ever more implicated in the needs and concerns of broader sexual publics. The final volume of the *Zeitschrift für Sexualwissenschaft*, which appeared during the economic and political crisis years of 1931/32 (a note inserted by the publishers notes that the journal's cessation was due to the "the unfavorable economic situation in Germany"[32]) provides a telling illustration of this deepening rift; across the eight issues in this volume, psychoanalytic approaches are either barely acknowledged or quickly dismissed. A piece called "Education and the Sex Drive" contains no mention of the numerous writings on either topic by members of the Freudian school, while the author of "Sexual Symbolism of Language" clearly considered it necessary to preface an otherwise sympathetic account of Freudian dream interpretations with a long list of recent antianalytic accounts, declaring that "there have been many sins in the interpretation of dream life and of artistic production by Freud's pupils, who often deport themselves more pontifically than the Pope."[33] A prominent half-page advertisement for the aforementioned anti-Freudian issue of the *Süddeutsche Monatshefte* can have left little doubt in readers' minds that the latest sexual science no longer had much in common with the writings of the Freudian school.

The Introduction to this book outlined some of the ways in which historians of sexual science in recent years have worked to expand the boundaries of that field, whether by examining contributions from fields "beyond the medical" or by paying overdue attention to the contributions of women and researchers working outside of the cultural contexts of Europe and North America. Whereas these studies push for an expanded understanding of "sexual science" as it emerged in the context of late-nineteenth- and early-twentieth-century modernity, the central concern of *Sex between Body and Mind* has been somewhat different. By examining scholarly debates, clinical practices, the establishment of professional networks, and interactions between sex researchers and wider sexual publics, I hope to have shown just how much is overlooked when historians examine the history of twentieth-century sex research in ways that prioritize either sexological or psychoanalytic frameworks. In the early years of the century, I have argued, it is difficult to even clearly distinguish between "sexologists" and "psychoanalysts" in light of the strong enthusiasm for collaboration, whether in groups such as the Berlin Psychoanalytic Society, interdisciplinary journals such as the *Zeitschrift für Sexualwissenschaft*, or trialing new methods such as Abraham and Hirschfeld's psychobiological questionnaire. As the decades progressed, though, the chapters of this book have traced a growing divide that accompanied an increasing sense of disciplinary self-consciousness and legitimacy between and across these two fields.

By showing how the theoretical categories surrounding modern sexual subjects underwent challenge after challenge at the nexus of sexology and psychoanalysis, *Sex between Body and Mind* has demonstrated how these encounters contributed to the molding of new disciplinary frameworks in twentieth-century science and medicine, as well as a rethinking of ideas about sexual "norms" and their relationship to conditions deemed "pathological." The embattled emergence of modern sexual ideas cannot be extricated from the story of how new professional and disciplinary fields emerge, through multilayered processes of dissemination, boundary drawing, and interpenetration. These disciplinary struggles between early sexology and psychoanalysis took place not just at the level of theory, but also around questions of methodology and treatment, as can be seen in the quite different trajectory of the case study as a genre of evidence across these two fields. Both during and after the period examined in this book, psychoanalysts continued to focus their attention on the close analysis of "neurotic" individuals, who had usually entered analysis voluntarily and who could generally afford both the time and expense of a lengthy one-on-one treatment, although periods of stress saw concessions to the need to treat patients more quickly and cheaply, such as in the field hospitals of World War I or the new psychoanalytic polyclinics established in interwar Berlin and Vienna. In contrast, sexologists from the turn of the century onward, while continuing to compile ever-growing case collections to illustrate their diagnostic categories, also began to prioritize seemingly more objective, empirical methods, from experimental laboratory research to interventionist hormonal and surgical treatments. In particular, they hoped that larger data sets of "healthy" individuals might distinguish their research both from the perversion-driven "sex psychiatry" of the late nineteenth century, and from their more immediate psychoanalytic competitors.

It was the expansion of hormone research from the 1910s, however, that was most decisive in drawing a boundary between these two fields. Sexologists seized on the inner secretions as a source of disciplinary legitimacy, enthusiastically emphasizing the physiology of the sexual body via the role of the hormones—even after Steinach's own experimental methods had started to fall into disrepute. Psychoanalysts, meanwhile, although still very much committed to the talking cure, increasingly steered their inquiries in broader cultural historical directions through works such as Freud's *Civilization and Its Discontents* (1930). Volkmar Sigusch describes this as a split between the increasingly "'objective-exact' science" of the sexologists and a push toward "something intuitive-speculative, as in cultural studies and philosophy" by psychoanalysis.[34] By the interwar period, even as individual practitioners maintained a mutual interest in developments across disciplinary lines, these two fields were becoming increasingly distinct, self-assured, and influential professional entities.

Some of the developments of this period have proven longer-lasting than others. Today only a relatively small number of researchers and scholars internationally apply the specific labels of "sexologist" or "clinical sexologist" to their own work, even if clinically oriented sex therapists and sexual counselors abound in the era of the "psy-sciences." Despite the media sensations surrounding the Kinsey and later Masters and Johnson reports, and even the odd university chair—including, as noted in the introduction, Sigusch's own at the University of Frankfurt in the 1970s—postwar sexology never truly solidified into a modern academic discipline to the extent of other fields in the human and social sciences whose genealogy can similarly be traced to the late nineteenth century, such as psychiatry, criminology, or sociology. That said, the postwar history of sexological research, and the extent to which this did or did not overlap with the numerous postwar "renaissances" of psychoanalytic thought, is a topic still much in need of scholarly attention. Sigusch, Ulrich Clement, and others have charted some of this ground for West Germany. We know far less about the place of scientific sex research in the German Democratic Republic or other Eastern European states during the era of the Iron Curtain—although Katerina Lišková's new study, *Sexual Liberation, Socialist Style*, examining sexology in communist Czechoslovakia, stands as an exciting sign of things to come. Neither do we know very much about the extent of postwar breaks and continuities in Austrian and Swiss sexology.[35] New research into other national contexts suggests that much might be gained by comparing developments between the German-speaking research hub of the early twentieth century and parallel or intersecting developments elsewhere, such as medical-scientific developments in Latin America and the Romance cultures of southern Europe, or the growth of less medicalized and more culturally oriented traditions of sex research in places such as Britain.[36]

Psychoanalysis, as outlined above, fared somewhat better than sexology in terms of maintaining a sense of disciplinary continuity. Yet for some decades, as Dagmar Herzog has recently argued in *Cold War Freud*, it was a more conservative, desexualized and Christianized strand of the analytic tradition that survived and thrived in the postwar United States, pandering to both homegrown religious conservatism and wider Cold War anxieties that combined questions of morality and pervasive homophobia with anticommunist sentiment. As a result, normative, conversion-oriented approaches became the rule in dealing with homosexual or trans-identified patients. This growth of "psychoanalytic homophobia," combined with "loosening sexual mores and the ascent of competing sexological research" were key factors, Herzog convincingly argues, in the subsequent abrupt decline of psychoanalysis's prestige from the later 1960s and 1970s.[37] Beyond North America, though, the disciplinary profile of psychoanalysis received significant boosts in the postwar era from post-Freudian schools of thought such as the Jungians and the Lacanians, whose interventions decisively shaped the twentieth- and twenty-first-century analytic profession in places ranging from Australia to Argentina.[38]

Notwithstanding the dramatic transformations in sex research between the first and second halves of the twentieth century, the debates examined in *Sex between Body and Mind* continue to influence and haunt our thinking about sex today. In many cases, they form the very foundation of contemporary ideas about gender, sexuality, and sexual citizenship, from still-fraught discussions and moral panics about the "sexualization" of children to discussions of gay marriage or transgender rights. The labels coined and diagnoses thrashed out across disciplinary lines in German-speaking research in the early twentieth century continue to shape our understandings of questions of "nature" versus "nurture," for example, even as conversations about the physiological locations of sexual identity and behavior have increasingly shifted from the hormones to the genes. The insistence of fin de siècle German sexologists and psychoanalysts on the complexity of human sexuality, their willingness to consider both body *and* mind when it came to explaining and treating perceived deviations from the sexual norm, and their problematization of the very idea of a diametrical opposition between "normal" and "pathological" sexual phenomena offers a valuable cautionary tale in the face of ongoing research to uncover, for example, a "gay gene." They point to a more complex and interdisciplinary history of modern sex research than scholars have previously acknowledged. Finally, these historical debates offer a critical context for understanding twenty-first-century sexual and gender-identity politics, and for moving beyond one-sided intellectual frameworks in the present as well as the past.

Notes

INTRODUCTION

1. Letter 46A, Abraham to Freud, Berlin, 21 August 1908, in *The Complete Correspondence of Sigmund Freud and Karl Abraham, 1907–1925*, ed. Ernst Falzeder (London: Karnac, 2002), 56.

2. For biographical information see Volkmar Sigusch and Günter Grau, eds., *Personenlexikon der Sexualforschung* (Frankfurt am Main: Campus, 2009).

3. Letter, Jones to Ellis, 12 June 1910, in Add70539 Havelock Ellis Papers 1039A. Correspondence, 10/11. British Library Manuscripts and Archives (hereafter Havelock Ellis Papers).

4. Letter 278F, Freud to Jung, 2 November 1911, in William McGuire, ed., *The Freud/Jung Letters: The Correspondence between Sigmund Freud and C. G. Jung*, trans. Ralph Mannheim and R. F. C. Hull, Bollingen Series (Princeton, NJ: Princeton University Press, 1974), 453–54.

5. Magnus Hirschfeld, *Geschlechtskunde (auf Grund dreißigjähriger Forschung und Erfahrung)*, vol. 1. Die körperseelischen Grundlagen (Stuttgart: Julius Püttmann, 1926), 206.

6. Michel Foucault, *The History of Sexuality* (3 vols.), vol. 1: *The Will to Knowledge* (London: Penguin, 1998).

7. R. von Krafft-Ebing, *Psychopathia sexualis: Mit besonderer Berücksichtigung der konträren Sexualempfindung: Eine medizinisch-gerichtliche Studie für Ärzte und Juristen*, 15th ed. (Stuttgart: F. Enke, 1918), 186.

8. See, for example, Anna Clark, *Desire: A History of European Sexuality* (New York: Routledge, 2008), 3; Arnold I. Davidson, *The Emergence of Sexuality: Historical Epistemology and the Formation of Concepts* (Cambridge, MA: Harvard University Press, 2001); Anthony Giddens, *Modernity and Self-Identity: Self and Society in the Late Modern Age* (Cambridge, UK: Polity Press, 1991); Harry Oosterhuis, "Sexual Modernity in the Works of Richard von Krafft-Ebing and Albert Moll," *Medical History* 56, no. 2 (2012): 133–55.

9. Letter, Jones to Ellis, 12 June 1910, in Add70539 Havelock Ellis Papers 1039A. Correspondence, 10/11. See also Henry Havelock Ellis and John Addington Symonds, *Das konträre Sexualgefühl* (Leipzig: Wigand, 1896).

10. Letter to the editor, unsigned, n.d. (ca. 1928, as written fifteen years after foundation of the BSSSP): British Sexological Society collection, Harry Ransom Center (hereafter B.S.S. collection), 1.1, Letters Unidentified/Assorted "A." On this society see Lesley

A. Hall, "'Disinterested Enthusiasm for Sexual Misconduct': The British Society for the Study of Sex Psychology, 1913–1947," *Journal of Contemporary History* 30 (1995): 665–86; Laura Doan, "Sexology's Afterlives: On the Queer Circuitries of Expert Knowledge in Modern Britain, 1913–1930," *Gender & History* 31, no. 2 (2019): 304–18 .

11. Two of the most significant works on these themes in German were Max Nordau, *Degeneration* [Entartung, 1892] (New York: Howard Fertig, 1968); Oswald Spengler, *Der Untergang des Abendlandes: Umrisse einer Morphologie der Weltgeschichte*, 2 vols. (Vienna [1918]; Munich [1919]): Braumüller; Beck, 1918). German scholars writing on degeneration frequently engaged with broader European discussions, including by Italian criminal anthropologist Cesare Lombroso (*Criminal Man*, 1876, and *Criminal Woman*, 1893), and Bénédict Augustin Morel (*Physical, Intellectual, and Moral Traits of Degeneration in the Human Species*, 1857). On the intersections between sexology and degeneration discourses see Daniel Pick, *Faces of Degeneration: A European Disorder, c. 1848–1918* (Cambridge, UK: Cambridge University Press, 1989); Paul Weindling, *Health, Race, and German Politics between National Unification and Nazism, 1870–1945* (Cambridge, UK: Cambridge University Press, 1989), 102–9.

12. See Kathleen Canning, "Claiming Citizenship: Suffrage and Subjectivity in Germany after the First World War," in *Gender History in Practice: Historical Perspectives on Bodies, Class & Citizenship* (Ithaca, NY: Cornell University Press, 2006), 212–37; Norman Domeier, *Der Eulenburg-Skandal: Eine politische Kulturgeschichte des Kaiserreichs* (Frankfurt am Main: Campus, 2010); Andreas Killen, *Berlin Electropolis. Shock, Nerves, and German Modernity* (Berkeley: University of California Press, 2005); Marti M. Lybeck, *Desiring Emancipation: New Women and Homosexuality in Germany, 1890–1933* (Albany: State University of New York Press, 2014); George L. Mosse, *Nationalism and Sexuality: Respectability and Abnormal Sexuality in Modern Europe* (New York: H. Fertig, 1985); James Steakley, *The Homosexual Emancipation Movement in Germany* (New York: Arno Press, 1975).

13. Kirsten Leng, *Sexual Politics and Feminist Science: Women Sexologists in Germany, 1900–1933* (Ithaca, NY: Cornell University Press, 2017), 5. Leng points to the ways in which not only a sense of transnational Germanness, but also "*European* interconnectedness" shaped the experience of elites invested in sexual knowledge production before 1914; see also Ute Frevert, "Europeanizing Germany's Twentieth Century," *History and Memory* 17 (2005): 87–116.

14. See, in particular, Robert Beachy, *Gay Berlin: Birthplace of a Modern Identity* (New York: Knopf, 2014); Edward Ross Dickinson, *Sex, Freedom and Power in Imperial Germany, 1880–1914* (Cambridge, UK: Cambridge University Press, 2014); Laurie Marhoefer, *Sex and the Weimar Republic: German Homosexual Emancipation and the Rise of the Nazis* (Toronto: University of Toronto Press, 2015); Scott Spector, Helmut Puff, and Dagmar Herzog, eds., *After "The History of Sexuality"? German Genealogies with and beyond Foucault* (New York: Berghahn Books, 2012); Scott Spector, *Violent Sensations: Sex, Crime & Utopia in Vienna and Berlin, 1860–1914* (Chicago: University of Chicago Press, 2016); Robert Deam Tobin, *Peripheral Desires: The German Discovery of Sex* (Philadelphia: University of Pennsylvania Press, 2015).

15. I have attempted to keep the use of scare quotes to a minimum, even when ref-

erencing historically shifting and contested terms such as "perversion," "pathology," "aberration," "deviance," "normal," "homosexuality," and "inversion." As my focus is on interrogating the changing ways in which such terms were understood and deployed by early-twentieth-century sex researchers and their subjects, my use of these terms, following Oosterhuis, is intended as "merely denotative" rather than implying any value judgment. See Harry Oosterhuis, *Stepchildren of Nature: Krafft-Ebing, Psychiatry, and the Making of Sexual Identity* (Chicago: University of Chicago Press, 2000), 7n2. On the etymology of "perversion," first recorded in English medical use in 1842, see Arnold I. Davidson, "Styles of Reasoning, Conceptual History, and the Emergence of Psychiatry," in *The Disunity of Science: Boundaries, Contexts, and Power* (Stanford: Stanford University Press, 1996), 89–91.

16. Iwan Bloch, "Aufgaben und Ziele der Sexualwissenschaft," *Zeitschrift für Sexualwissenschaft* 1, no. 1 (April 1914): 2.

17. On the gendered implications of this falling-out see Leng, *Sexual Politics*, 58–61. For an overview of early European sexological periodicals (1890s–1930s), starting with the short-lived *Vita sexualis* (1895/1896), see Volkmar Sigusch, *Geschichte der Sexualwissenschaft* (Frankfurt am Main: Campus Verlag, 2008), 103–17.

18. On the 1909 *Proposal for a German Criminal Code*, which sought to increase penalties for male same-sex acts and expand criminalization to women, see Tracie Matysik, "In the Name of the Law: The 'Female Homosexual' and the Criminal Code in Fin de Siècle Germany," *Journal of the History of Sexuality* 13, no. 1 (2004): 26–48.

19. Bloch, "Aufgaben und Ziele," 3–4. Several years earlier, Bloch had offered a detailed survey of early sexual scientific publications, including the "fairly insignificant" 1890s periodical *Vita sexualis,* Hirschfeld's "highly dignified" *Jahrbuch*, Adolf Brand's homosexual monthly *Der Eigene* (The Autonomous/Self-Owned); Friedrich S. Krauss's annual *Anthropophyteia*, which focused on folkloric and ethnological themes; several journals specializing in dermatology and venereal disease, and several nonmedical journals, including Hans Groß's criminological *Archiv für Kriminal-Anthropologie und Kriminalistik*; Stöcker's *Mutterschutz*; life reformer Karl Vanselow's *Geschlecht und Gesellschaft* (Sex and Society), and several eugenics periodicals (*Politisch-Anthropologischen Revue*, ed. Ludwig Woltmann; *Archiv für Rassen- und Gesellschafts-Biologie,* ed. Alfred Ploetz). Iwan Bloch, *Das Sexualleben unserer Zeit in seinen Beziehungen zur modernen Kultur* (Berlin: Marcus, 1907), 823–24.

20. Max Marcuse, "'Sexual-Probleme.' Ein Wort zur Einführung," *Sexual-Probleme* 1, no. 1 (1908): 2.

21. Chris Waters, "Sexology," in *Palgrave Advances in the Modern History of Sexuality*, eds. H. G. Cocks and Matt Houlbrook (Houndmills, Basingstoke, UK: Palgrave Macmillan, 2006), 42.

22. Sigmund Freud, *Drei Abhandlungen zur Sexualtheorie* (Leipzig: F. Deuticke, 1905). For discussion of different editions and translations, see chapter 1.

23. Sigmund Freud, "Fragment of an Analysis of a Case of Hysteria (1905 [1901])," in *The Standard Edition of the Complete Psychological Works of Sigmund Freud (24 vols.)*, vol. 7 (1901–1905): *A Case of Hysteria, Three Essays on Sexuality and Other Works* (London, 1953), 1–122; Sigmund Freud, *The Interpretation of Dreams* (London: G. Allen & Unwin, 1954).

24. "Bisexuality" during this period was generally understood as the coexistence of male and female characteristics rather than erotic desire for both sexes. See George Makari, *Revolution in Mind: The Creation of Psychoanalysis* (New York: Harper, 2008), 86ff., 151ff.; Chandak Sengoopta, *Otto Weininger: Sex, Science, and Self in Imperial Vienna* (Chicago: University of Chicago Press, 2000); Frank Sulloway, *Freud, Biologist of the Mind: Beyond the Psychoanalytic Legend* (New York: Basic Books, 1979). See also Otto Weininger, *Geschlecht und Charakter. Eine prinzipielle Untersuchung* (München: Matthes & Seitz, 1997); Bloch, *Sexualleben*, 595–97. For a nuanced reappraisal of Weininger's notoriously misogynistic and anti-Semitic arguments, which are not a focus of the following chapters, see Spector, *Violent Sensations*, 195–201.

25. See Mirjam Bugmann, *Hypnosepolitik. Der Psychiater August Forel, das Gehirn und die Gesellschaft* (Köln: Böhlau, 2015); Andreas-Holge Maehle, "The Powers of Suggestion: Albert Moll and the Debate on Hypnosis," *History of Psychiatry* 25, no. 1 (2014): 3–19; Volkmar Sigusch, "The Sexologist Albert Moll—between Sigmund Freud and Magnus Hirschfeld," *Medical History* 56, no. 2 (2012): 184–200; Andreas Sommer, "Policing Epistemic Deviance: Albert von Schrenck-Notzing and Albert Moll," *Medical History* 56, no. 2 (2012): 255–76.

26. See Makari, *Revolution*, 14–18, 27–34, 46–48; Eli Zaretsky, *Secrets of the Soul: A Social and Cultural History of Psychoanalysis* (New York: Vintage, 2004), 24–26.

27. Sigmund Freud, *Three Contributions to the Sexual Theory*. Authorized translation by A. A. Brill, with an Introduction by James J. Putnam. (New York: Journal of Nervous and Mental Disease Pub. Co., 1910).

28. Sigmund Freud, "Die Sexualität in der Ätiologie der Neurosen (1898)," in *Gesammelte Werke*, vol. 1 (London: Imago, 1952), 498.

29. Sigusch draws attention to Freud's more incidental earlier use of the term "Sexualwissenschaft" (first published in the *Wiener klinischen Rundschau*, and discovered by historian Rainer Herrn), while arguing that it was already gaining currency before Bloch claimed it as his invention—for which Bloch himself gave various dates, but always between 1904 and 1906. Sigusch, *Geschichte der Sexualwissenschaft*, 50–51, 68, 262, 296. Others attribute the term to life reform activist Karl Vanselow, founder of *Geschlecht und Gesellschaft* [Sex and Society]; see Lutz Sauerteig, *Krankheit, Sexualität, Gesellschaft. Geschlechtskrankheiten und Gesundheitspolitik in Deutschland im 19. und frühen 20. Jahrhundert*, MedGG-Beihefte (Stuttgart: Franz Steiner Verlag, 1999), 55. The English term "sexology" is of American origin, coined by Elizabeth Osgood Goodrich Willard in the 1860s; see Leng, *Sexual Politics*, 17n26.

30. Bauer in Ivan Crozier and Heike Bauer, "Sexology, Historiography, Citation, Embodiment: A Review and (Frank) Exchange," *History of the Human Sciences* 30 (2017), http://www.histhum.com/?p=367.

31. On the notion of "sexual publics" see Lauren Berlant and Michael Warner, "Sex in Public," *Critical Inquiry* 24, no. 2 (1998): 547–66.

32. Michael Hagner, "Scientific Medicine," in *From Natural Philosophy to the Sciences: Writing the History of Nineteenth-Century Science*, ed. David Cahan (Chicago: University of Chicago Press, 2003), 49–87.

33. Dagmar Herzog, *Sexuality in Europe: A Twentieth-Century History* (Cambridge, UK: Cambridge University Press, 2011), 3.

34. Giddens, *Modernity and Self-Identity*, 164. See also Dickinson, *Sex, Freedom*, 3–7, 304–16; Anthony Giddens, *The Transformation of Intimacy: Sexuality, Love and Eroticism in Modern Societies* (Cambridge, UK: Polity Press, 1992); Oosterhuis, "Sexual Modernity," 140–41; Jennifer Terry, *An American Obsession: Science, Medicine, and Homosexuality in Modern Society* (Chicago: University of Chicago Press, 1999), 12; Charles Taylor, *Sources of the Self: The Making of the Modern Identity* (Cambridge, MA: Harvard University Press, 1989). Robinson's 1976 study was important in establishing this "predominant paradigm of sexuality in our culture," but was also, as Dean points out, limited in its focus on pleasure and liberation. See Carolyn J. Dean, *Sexuality and Modern Western Culture* (New York: Twayne, 1996), xiv–xv; Paul Robinson, *The Modernization of Sex: Havelock Ellis, Alfred Kinsey, William Masters and Virginia Johnson* (New York: Harper & Row, 1976).

35. Davidson charts a shift away from older "functional" explanations of the perversions, which attempted to locate these in relation to specific organs and bodily structures. Davidson, "Styles of Reasoning," 98. See also Davidson, *Emergence*.

36. Arthur Kronfeld, *Über psychosexuellen Infantilismus, eine Konstitutionsanomalie*, ed. Magnus Hirschfeld, Sexus: Monographien aus dem Institut für Sexualwissenschaft in Berlin (Leipzig: Ernst Bircher, 1921), 20.

37. On Hirschfeld's Institute and politics see Heike Bauer, *The Hirschfeld Archives: Violence, Death, and Modern Queer Culture* (Philadelphia: Temple University Press, 2017), 78–101; Ralf Dose, *Magnus Hirschfeld: The Origins of the Gay Liberation Movement*, trans. Edward H. Willis (New York: Monthly Review Press, 2014), 51–57; Atina Grossmann, "Magnus Hirschfeld, Sexualreform und die Neue Frau: Das Institut für Sexualwissenschaft und das Weimarer Berlin," in *Magnus Hirschfeld: Ein Leben im Spannungsfeld von Wissenschaft, Politik und Gesellschaft*, eds. Elke-Vera Kotowski and Julius H. Schoeps (Berlin-Brandenburg: be.bra wissenschaft, 2004), 201–16; Rainer Herrn, "Vom Traum zum Trauma. Das Institut für Sexualwissenschaft," in *Magnus Hirschfeld*, 173–200; Manfred Herzer, *Magnus Hirschfeld und seine Zeit* (Berlin: de Gruyter, 2017), 287-93; Manfred Herzer, *Magnus Hirschfeld: Leben und Werk eines jüdischen, schwulen und sozialistischen Sexologen*, 2., überarbeitete Aufl. (Hamburg: MännerschwarmSkript Verlag, 2001); Elena Mancini, *Magnus Hirschfeld and the Quest for Sexual Freedom* (New York: Palgrave Macmillan, 2010); Marhoefer, *Sex and the Weimar Republic*, 3-15; Andreas Pretzel, "Disziplinierungsbestrebungen. Magnus Hirschfeld und die Ärztliche Gesellschaft für Sexualwissenschaft," in *Magnus Hirschfeld*, 137–56; Sigusch, *Geschichte der Sexualwissenschaft*, 345–64.

38. Frank M. Turner, "Public Science in Britain, 1880–1919," *Isis* 71, no. 4 (1980): 590.

39. Jennifer Evans, "Introduction: Why Queer German History?," *German History* 34, no. 3 (2016): 378. See also Bauer, *Hirschfeld Archives*; Kirsten Leng, "Magnus Hirschfeld's Meanings: Analysing Biography and the Politics of Representation," *German History* 35, no. 1 (2017): 96–116; Andreas Seeck, ed., *Durch Wissenschaft zur Gerechtigkeit?: Textsammlung zur kritischen Rezeption des Schaffens von Magnus Hirschfeld* (Berlin: LIT Verlag, 2003). For a typically celebratory version of Hirschfeld's life and work, see Mancini, *Magnus Hirschfeld*.

40. See Dickinson, *Sex, Freedom,* 190–214; Atina Grossmann, *Reforming Sex: The German Movement for Birth Control and Abortion Reform, 1920–1950* (New York: Oxford University Press, 1995); Leng, *Sexual Politics;* Cornelie Usborne, *The Politics of the Body in Weimar Germany: Women's Reproductive Rights and Duties* (Basingstoke, UK: Macmillan, 1992).

41. Ivan Crozier, "'All the World's a Stage': Dora Russell, Norman Haire, and the 1929 London World League for Sexual Reform Congress," *Journal of the History of Sexuality* 12, no. 1 (2003): 20–21. See also Herzer, *Magnus Hirschfeld und seine Zeit,* 224-27.

42. No full biographical study of Moll or Bloch yet exists, but in 2012 the journal *Medical History* dedicated a special issue (vol. 56, no. 2) to reclaiming Moll's scientific contributions to sexology, psychiatry, forensics, and medical ethics; see chapter 1. A recent study of Forel that focuses particularly on his work with hypnosis is Bugmann, *Hypnosepolitik*. For recent discussions of Bloch's interdisciplinary brand of sexual science see chapter 2.

43. Sigusch, "The Sexologist Albert Moll," 184ff. (this incident is recounted at p. 197); Sigusch, *Geschichte der Sexualwissenschaft*, 264ff.; Lutz D. H. Sauerteig, "Loss of Innocence: Albert Moll, Sigmund Freud and the Invention of Childhood Sexuality Around 1900," *Medical History* 56, no. 2 (2012): 181–82.

44. Oosterhuis, *Stepchildren*; Benjamin Kahan, ed., *Heinrich Kaan's "Psychopathia Sexualis" (1844)*, trans. Melissa Haynes (Ithaca, NY: Cornell University Press, 2016); Volkmar Sigusch, "Heinrich Kaan: der Verfasser der ersten 'Psychopathia sexualis': Eine biographische Skizze," *Zeitschrift für Sexualforschung* 16 (2003): 116–42.

45. Chiara Beccalossi, "Madness and Sexual Psychopathies as the Magnifying Glass of the Normal: Italian Psychiatry and Sexuality c. 1880–1910," *Social History of Medicine* 27, no. 2 (2014): 303–25; Sigusch, *Geschichte der Sexualwissenschaft*, 52–53, 121–43.

46. Important survey works include Vern L. Bullough, *Science in the Bedroom: A History of Sex Research* (New York: Basic Books, 1994); Lawrence Birken, *Consuming Desire: Sexual Science and the Emergence of a Culture of Abundance, 1871–1914* (Ithaca, NY: Cornell University Press, 1988); Edward M. Brecher, *The Sex Researchers* (Boston: Little, Brown, 1969); Robinson, *The Modernization of Sex.*

47. See, for example, Ralph M. Leck, *Vita Sexualis: Karl Ulrichs and the Origins of Sexual Science* (Urbana: University of Illinois Press, 2016), 105–12; Spector, *Violent Sensations*, 73–165; Tobin, *Peripheral Desires*, 27–50; this scholarship is discussed further in chapter 2.

48. See Marhoefer, *Sex and the Weimar Republic*, 209–14; Tobin, *Peripheral Desires*, 230–43. A prominent proponent of the "gay gene" thesis is Simon LeVay, *Queer Science: The Use and Abuse of Research into Homosexuality* (Cambridge, MA: MIT Press, 1996).

49. Dagmar Herzog, *Cold War Freud: Psychoanalysis in an Age of Catastrophes* (Cambridge, UK: Cambridge University Press, 2017); Franz X. Eder, *Kultur der Begierde: Eine Geschichte der Sexualität* (Munich: Beck, 2002), 11.

50. Rita Felski, "Introduction," in *Sexology in Culture: Labelling Bodies and Desires, eds.* Lucy Bland and Laura Doan (Cambridge, UK: Polity Press, 1998), 1.

51. On Freud's encounters with Moll and Ellis, see Volkmar Sigusch, "Fantasie oder Verhalten: Sigmund Freud und das Verhältnis von Psychoanalyse und Sexualwissenschaft," in *Geschichte der Sexualwissenschaft* (Frankfurt am Main: Campus, 2008), 261–84; Sulloway, *Freud, Biologist*; Sander L. Gilman, "Sigmund Freud and the Sexologists: A Second Reading," in *Sexual Knowledge, Sexual Science: The History of Attitudes to Sexuality*, eds. Roy Porter and Mikuláš Teich (Cambridge, UK: Cambridge University Press, 1994), 323–49. On Hirschfeld's relationships with the Freudians see Rainer Herrn, "Der Anfang vom Ende—Die Don Juan-Figur in Sexualwissenschaft und Psychoanalyse," *Mitteilungen der Magnus-Hirschfeld-Gesellschaft*, no. 22 (1996): 27–37; Mancini, *Magnus Hirschfeld*, 71–78; Herzer, *Magnus Hirschfeld*, 2001, 153–97. The following histories of psychoanalysis also include substantial references to sexological thinkers and traditions: Veronika Fuechtner, *Berlin Psychoanalytic: Psychoanalysis and Culture in Weimar Republic Germany and Beyond* (Berkeley: University of California Press, 2011); Makari, *Revolution*; Zaretsky, *Secrets of the Soul*.

52. See especially Christa Putz, *Verordnete Lust: Sexualmedizin, Psychoanalyse und die "Krise der Ehe," 1870–1930* (Bielefeld, Ger.: Transcript, 2011); Peter Cryle and Elizabeth Stephens, *Normality: A Critical Genealogy* (Chicago: University of Chicago Press, 2017), 279–91.

53. Ulrich Clement, "Zum Verhältnis von Sexualwissenschaft und Psychoanalyse," *Zeitschrift für psychosomatische Medizin* 39 (1993): 63–74, at 63.

54. In the German context see Claudia Breger, "Feminine Masculinities: Scientific and Literary Representations of 'Female Inversion' at the Turn of the Twentieth Century," *Journal of the History of Sexuality* 14, nos. 1/2 (January 2005): 76–106; Elisabeth Bronfen, "Geheimnisse einer Seele. Gedanken zu Pabsts psychoanalytischem Film," in *Psychoanalyse in der modernen Literatur: Kooperation und Konkurrenz*, eds. Thomas Anz and Christine Kanz (Würzburg: Königshausen & Neumann, 1999), 61–82; Fuechtner, *Berlin Psychoanalytic*; Birgit Lang, Joy Damousi, and Alison Lewis, *A History of the Case Study: Sexology, Psychoanalysis, Literature* (Manchester, UK: Manchester University Press, 2017); Anna Katharina Schaffner, *Modernism and Perversion: Sexual Deviance in Sexology and Literature, 1850–1930* (Houndmills, Basingstoke, UK: Palgrave Macmillan, 2011); Tobin, *Peripheral Desires*. Much work has also been done on the British context, see for example Heike Bauer, *English Literary Sexology: Translations of Inversion, 1860–1930* (Basingstoke, UK: Palgrave Macmillan, 2009); Bland and Doan, *Sexology in Culture*.

55. Leck, *Vita Sexualis*, 2, see also 28–29.

56. Foucault, *History of Sexuality*, vol. 1, 30, 43. On Rohleder's work on female frigidity, masturbation, and the connections between abstinence and neurasthenia, see Dickinson, *Sex, Freedom*, 261–63; Sigusch and Grau, *Personenlexikon*, 595–601.

57. On the move from the psychiatric to the scientific see Howard Chiang, "Historicizing the Emergence of Sexual Freedom: The Medical Knowledge of Psychiatry and the Scientific Power of Sexology, 1880–1920," *Gender Forum: An Internet Journal for Gender Studies* 24 (2009): 1–6. For discussions of Foucault's overemphasis on the medical and psychiatric see Edward R. Dickinson and Richard F. Wetzell, "The Historiography of Sexuality in Modern Germany," *German History* 23, no. 3 (2005): 298–302; Philippe Weber, *Der Trieb zum Erzählen: Sexualpathologie und Homosexualität, 1852–1914* (Bielefeld, Ger.: Transcript, 2008), 42.

58. Foucault, *History of Sexuality*, vol. 1, 119.

59. Davidson, *Emergence*, xi.

60. See Cryle and Stephens, *Normality*, 262–79; Oosterhuis, "Sexual Modernity"; Oosterhuis, *Stepchildren*, 88–89, 100ff.

61. Foucault, *History of Sexuality*, vol. 1, 45.

62. See, for example, Birken, *Consuming Desire*, 14; Leck, *Vita Sexualis*, 3.

63. Spector, *Violent Sensations*, 85.

64. Foucault, *History of Sexuality*, vol. 1, 101.

65. This term is from Oosterhuis, *Stepchildren*, 9–10. See also Ivan Crozier, "Pillow Talk: Credibility, Trust and the Sexological Case History," *History of Science* 46 (2008): 375–404; Geertje Mak, *Doubting Sex: Inscriptions, Bodies and Selves in Nineteenth-Century Hermaphrodite Case Histories* (Manchester, UK: Manchester University Press, 2012); Klaus Müller, *Aber in meinem Herzen sprach eine Stimme so laut: Homosexuelle Autobiographien und medizinische Pathographien im neunzehnten Jahrhundert* (Berlin: Rosa Winkel, 1991); Spector, *Violent Sensations*; Weber, *Trieb*.

66. Leck, *Vita Sexualis*, 6.

67. Scott Spector, "Introduction. After *The History of Sexuality*? Periodicities, Subjectivities, Ethics," in *After "The History of Sexuality"? German Genealogies with and beyond Foucault*, eds. Scott Spector, Helmut Puff, and Dagmar Herzog (New York: Berghahn Books, 2012), 6. See also the other essays in that volume, and Dickinson and Wetzell, "Historiography," 298–302; Eder, *Kultur der Begierde*, 17; Spector, *Violent Sensations, 15, 85-89;* Terry, *An American Obsession*, 17; Tobin, *Peripheral Desires*, xiii.

68. For biographical details see Sigusch and Grau, *Personenlexikon*.

69. See Peter Amacher, *Freud's Neurological Education and Its Influence on Psychoanalytic Theory* (New York: International Universities Press, 1965); Sander L. Gilman, "The Struggle of Psychiatry with Psychoanalysis: Who Won?," *Critical Inquiry* 13, no. 2 (1987): 294; Makari, *Revolution*, 27–29.

70. Faramerz Dabhoiwala, *The Origins of Sex: A History of the First Sexual Revolution* (Oxford, UK: Oxford University Press, 2012), 358. On the social prestige of nineteenth-century German science and medicine, see Hagner, "Scientific Medicine"; Charles E. McClelland, *State, Society and University in Germany* (Cambridge, UK: Cambridge University Press, 1980); Lutz Raphael, "Die Verwissenschaftlichung des Sozialen als methodische und konzeptionelle Herausforderung für eine Sozialgeschichte des 20. Jahrhunderts," *Geschichte und Gesellschaft* 22, no. 2 (1996): 165–93; Paul Weindling, "Bourgeois Values, Doctors and the State: The Professionalization of Medicine in Germany 1848–1933," in *The German Bourgeoisie*, eds. David Blackbourn and Richard J. Evans (London: Routledge, 1991), 198–223.

71. Birken, *Consuming Desire*, 16. More recently, see Heike Bauer, ed., *Sexology and Translation: Cultural and Scientific Encounters across the Modern World*, Sexuality Studies (Philadelphia: Temple UP, 2015); Veronika Fuechtner, Douglas E. Haynes, and Ryan M. Jones, eds., *Towards a Global History of Sexual Science, 1880–1950* (Oakland: University of California Press, 2017).

72. Havelock Ellis and John Addington Symonds, *Sexual Inversion: A Critical Edition*, ed. Ivan Crozier (Basingstoke, UK: Palgrave Macmillan, 2007); Edward Carpen-

ter, *The Intermediate Sex: A Study of Some Transitional Types of Men and Women* (London: Allen & Unwin, 1908). See, for example, the discussion of interdisciplinarity in Kate Fisher and Jana Funke, "British Sexual Science beyond the Medical: Cross-Disciplinary, Cross-Historical, and Cross-Cultural Translations," in *Sexology and Translation: Cultural and Scientific Encounters Across the Modern World* (Philadelphia: Temple University Press, 2015), 95–114.

73. Nikolas Rose, "Assembling the Modern Self," in *Rewriting the Self: Histories from the Renaissance to the Present*, ed. Roy Porter (London: Routledge, 1996), 226. On the history of disciplinarization and the ways in which power relations shape disciplinary knowledge, see Jan Goldstein, "Foucault among the Sociologists: The 'Disciplines' and the History of the Professions," *History and Theory* 23 (1984): 175–76; Jan Golinski, *Making Natural Knowledge: Constructivism and the History of Science* (Cambridge, UK: Cambridge University Press, 1998), 70–72; Donald R. Kelley, ed., *History and the Disciplines: The Reclassification of Knowledge in Early Modern Europe* (Rochester, NY: University of Rochester Press, 1997); M. C. Lemon, *The Discipline of History and the History of Thought* (London: Routledge, 1995); Fernando Vidal, *The Sciences of the Soul: The Early Modern Origins of Psychology*, trans. Saskia Brown (Chicago: University of Chicago Press, 2011), 3–4, 6–7.

74. As Vidal observes, to speak of "a" discipline is frequently "a convenient abstraction." Vidal, *Sciences of the Soul*, 5–6. See also David Cahan, "Institutions and Communities," in *From Natural Philosophy to the Sciences: Writing the History of Nineteenth-Century Science*, ed. David Cahan (Chicago: Chicago University Press, 2003), 291–328; Timothy Lenoir, *Instituting Science: The Cultural Production of Scientific Disciplines* (Stanford, CA: Stanford University Press, 1997).

75. Leng, *Sexual Politics*, 33–34. See also Pierre Bourdieu, "The Specificity of the Scientific Field and the Social Conditions of the Progress of Reason," *Social Science Information* 14 (December 1975): 19–47.

76. Even today, *Wissenschaft* is used in German to designate knowledge production across the humanities and social and natural sciences, although distinctions are drawn between the *Geistes-*, *Sozial-* and *Naturwissenschaften*. In English, too, "science" and "scientist" have historically defied narrow definition, with the "scientist" label coined by philosopher and historian William Whewell in the 1830s to unite astronomers, chemists, botanists, and others. Since then, the unifying feature of "science" has overwhelmingly been understood in terms of a distinct method. See Richard R. Yeo, "Scientific Method and the Rhetoric of Science in Britain, 1830–1917," in *The Politics and Rhetoric of Scientific Method* (Dordrecht, Neth.: D. Reidel, 1986), 259, 261, 273–74; Turner, "Public Science," 591.

77. Magnus Hirschfeld, "Einteilung der Sexualwissenschaft," *Zeitschrift für Sexualwissenschaft* 1, no. 10 (1908): 569–88. This publication ceased after the first volume of twelve issues in 1908, and was distinct from the more successful periodical of the same name published from 1914 under the editorship of Albert Eulenburg and Iwan Bloch.

78. Bloch, *Sexualleben*, 506.

79. Jana Funke and Kate Fisher, "Sexual Science beyond the Medical," *Lancet* 387 (2016): 840–41. For an example of competing perspectives on the proper disciplinary

focus of history of sexology research see Crozier and Bauer, "Sexology, Historiography, Citation."

80. Sigmund Freud, "Über infantile Sexualtheorien," *Sexual-Probleme* 1, no. 12 (December 1908): 763–79; Sigmund Freud, "Die kulturelle Sexualmoral und die moderne Nervosität," *Sexual-Probleme* 1, no. 3 (March 1908): 107–29.

81. This term is from Rose, "Assembling the Modern Self," 232.

82. On the "birth" of psychology as a scientific discipline see Kurt Danziger, *Constructing the Subject: Historical Origins of Psychological Research* (Cambridge, UK: Cambridge University Press, 1990); Vidal, *Sciences of the Soul*, 3; David Hothersall, *History of Psychology* (Philadelphia: Temple University Press, 1984), xiv–xv, 52, 80ff. Further afield, psychology's disciplinary debut was marked by the appearance of new journals such as *Mind* in 1876 and the *American Journal of Psychology* in 1887.

83. Duane P. Schultz and Sydney Ellen Schultz, *A History of Modern Psychology*, 9th ed. (Belmont, CA: Thomson and Wadsworth, 2008), 437–39.

84. These terms are from Shorter's study, which exemplifies a tradition of more hostile approaches toward psychoanalysis within the history of psychiatry: Edward Shorter, *A History of Psychiatry: From the Era of the Asylum to the Age of Prozac* (New York: Wiley, 1997). For more nuanced accounts of this relationship see Elizabeth Lunbeck, "Psychiatry," in *From Natural Philosophy to the Sciences: Writing the History of Nineteenth-Century Science*, ed. David Cahan (Chicago: University of Chicago Press, 2003), 663–77; Mark S. Micale, "Preface," in *Beyond the Unconscious: Essays of Henri F. Ellenberger in the History of Psychiatry*, ed. Mark S. Micale, trans. Francoise Dubois and Mark S. Micale (Princeton, NJ: Princeton University Press, 1993), viii; Ulrike Hoffmann-Richter, "Die Wiener akademische Psychiatrie und die Geburt der Psychoanalyse," in *Gründe der Seele: Die Wiener Psychiatrie im 20. Jahrhundert*, eds. Brigitta Keintzel and Eberhard Gabriel (Vienna: Picus, 1999), 69–70.

85. Herzog, *Cold War Freud*, 56.

86. Sigmund Freud, *Introductory Lectures on Psychoanalysis (Parts I and II)*, vol. 15, *The Complete Psychological Works* (London: Hogarth, 1963); Freud, *Introductory Lectures on Psychoanalysis (Part III)*, vol. 16 (1917–1917), *The Complete Psychological Works* (London: Hogarth, 1963).

87. This marked a shift away from centralized national societies such as the Royal Society in England. See Golinski, *Making Natural Knowledge*, 66–78; Roger Hahn, *The Anatomy of a Scientific Institution. The Paris Academy of Sciences 1666–1803* (Berkeley: University of California Press, 1971), 175–76; Thomas S. Kuhn, *The Essential Tension: Selected Studies in Scientific Tradition and Change* (Chicago: University of Chicago Press, 1977), 146–47, 226–27; Thomas S. Kuhn, *The Structure of Scientific Revolutions*, 3rd ed. (Chicago: University of Chicago Press, 1996), 3–6; Reba N. Soffer, *Discipline and Power: The University, History, and the Making of an English Elite, 1870–1930* (Stanford, CA: Stanford University Press, 1994).

88. Sigusch notes that this was his own professorial appointment at the University of Frankfurt. Sigusch, *Geschichte der Sexualwissenschaft*, 463.

89. Oosterhuis, *Stepchildren*, 88–89.

90. Dose, *Magnus Hirschfeld*; Sigusch, "The Sexologist Albert Moll."

91. On the production of "legitimate knowledge" see Foucault, *History of Sexuality*, vol. 1, 72; Danziger, *Constructing the Subject*, 118–19.

92. This exchange, including Freud's rather scathing responses—he declared Ellis's assessment a "highly sublimated form of resistance," as Jones later reported (see Letter Freud to Ellis, 8 November 1925, Havelock Ellis papers, Yale University, Box 1, Folder 22)—has been widely discussed by historians of psychoanalysis and biographers. See Ernest Jones, *Sigmund Freud, Life and Work: The Last Phase, 1919–1939*, vol. 3 (London: Hogarth, 1957), 21; Phyllis Grosskurth, *Havelock Ellis: A Biography* (New York: Knopf, 1980), 292, 387; Meg Harris Williams, "Psychoanalysis as an Art Form," *British Journal of Psychotherapy* 25, no. 3 (2009): 381–92; Ivan Crozier, "Taking Prisoners: Havelock Ellis, Sigmund Freud, and the Construction of Homosexuality, 1897–1951," *Society for the Social History of Medicine* 13, no. 3 (2000): 447–66; Sulloway, *Freud, Biologist*, 305–15.

93. Freud's nominations can be viewed via the Nobel Prize Nomination Database: https://www.nobelprize.org/nomination/redirector/?redir=archive/show_people.php&id=3209. See also Carl-Magnus Stolt, "Why Did Freud Never Receive the Nobel Prize?," *International Forum of Psychoanalysis* 10, nos. 3–4 (2001).

94. On debates around psychoanalysis as a "science," and the process of differentiating this field from psychiatry, see Gilman, "Struggle of Psychiatry," 293–95; Davidson, "Styles of Reasoning," 75–100; Adolf Grünbaum, *The Foundations of Psychoanalysis: A Philosophical Critique* (Berkeley: University of California Press, 1984); Hoffmann-Richter, "Die Wiener akademische Psychiatrie."

95. Sigmund Freud, *Civilization and Its Discontents*, ed. and trans. James Strachey (New York: Norton, 1962); Sigmund Freud, "Eine Kindheitserinnerung des Leonardo da Vinci (1910)," in *Sigmund Freud Studienausgabe Band X: Bildende Kunst und Literatur* (10 vols.), eds. Alexander Mitscherlich, Angela Richards, and James Strachey, vol. 10 (Frankfurt am Main: Fischer, 2000), 87–159; Sigmund Freud, *Totem and Taboo: Some Points of Agreement between the Mental Lives of Savages and Neurotics*, trans. James Strachey (London: Routledge and Paul, 1950).

96. George Makari, "Mitteleuropa on the Hudson: On the Struggle for American Psychoanalysis after the Anschluß," in *After Freud Left: A Century of Psychoanalysis in America*, ed. Burnham, John C. (Chicago: University of Chicago Press, 2012), 112. See also Makari, *Revolution.*

97. Ralf Dose, "The World League for Sexual Reform: Some Possible Approaches," *Journal of the History of Sexuality* 12, no. 1 (2003): 1–15.

98. Peter Galison, "Introduction: The Context of Disunity," in *The Disunity of Science: Boundaries, Contexts, and Power, eds. Peter Galison and David J. Stump* (Stanford, CA: Stanford University Press, 1996), 14–15; Peter Galison, "Computer Simulations and the Trading Zone," in Galison and Stump, *The Disunity of Science,* 118–57. While recent investigations into the cultural, linguistic, and transnational dimensions of early sexual science have seized on the concept of "translation," my focus is less on linguistic and cultural-historical differences than interactions across consolidating disciplinary lines. Cf. Bauer, *Sexology and Translation.*

99. Steve Fuller, "Talking Metaphysical Turkey about Epistemological Chicken and the Poop on Pidgins," in Galison and Stump, *The Disunity of Science*, 184.

100. On the importance of commensurable "styles of reasoning" in establishing scientific credibility, see Davidson, "Styles of Reasoning," 75–100; Ian Hacking, *Representing and Intervening: Introductory Topics in the Philosophy of Natural Science*

(Cambridge, UK: Cambridge University Press, 1983), 71; Karin Knorr Cetina, *Epistemic Cultures: How the Sciences Make Knowledge* (Cambridge, MA: Harvard University Press, 1999).

101. This phrase is drawn from feminist critiques of scientific knowledge production. See Donna Haraway, "Situated Knowledges: The Science Question in Feminism and the Privilege of Partial Perspective," *Feminist Studies* 14, no. 3 (1988): 580.

102. This phrase is from Hagner, "Scientific Medicine," 79. See also Danziger, *Constructing the Subject*, 3–5; Karin D. Knorr-Cetina and Michael Mulkay, eds., *Science Observed: Perspectives on the Social Study of Science* (London: Sage, 1983), 1–17.

103. Sander L. Gilman, "Sexology, Psychoanalysis, and Degeneration: From a Theory of Race to a Race of Theory," in *Degeneration: The Dark Side of Progress*, eds. J. Edward Chamberlin and Sander L. Gilman (New York: Columbia University Press, 1985), 72–96.

104. Gilman, "Struggle of Psychiatry," 295, 298–300, 305, 308. On the status of sexual doctors and venereologists see also Weindling, *Health, Race*, 102. On the influence of Hirschfeld's Jewishness on his career, see Bauer, *Hirschfeld Archives*, 26, 92–96; Dose, *Magnus Hirschfeld*, 32–37; Herzer, *Magnus Hirschfeld*, 2001.

105. See Daniel Boyarin, *Unheroic Conduct: The Rise of Heterosexuality and the Invention of the Jewish Man* (Berkeley: University of California Press, 1997); Christina von Braun, "'Der Jude' und 'Das Weib.' Zwei Stereotypen des 'Anderen' in der Moderne," in *Deutsch-jüdische Geschichte im 19. und 20. Jahrhundert*, eds. Ludger Heid and Joachim Knoll (Stuttgart: Burg, 1992), 289–322; Sander Gilman, "Jews and Mental Illness: Medical Metaphors, Anti-Semitism, and the Jewish Response," *Journal of the History of the Behavioral Sciences* 20 (April 1984): 150–59; Gilman, "Sigmund Freud," 329; Nancy A. Harrowitz and Barbara Hyams, eds., *Jews & Gender: Responses to Otto Weininger* (Philadelphia: Temple University Press, 1995).

106. See Heike Bauer, "'Race,' Normativity and the History of Sexuality: The Case of Magnus Hirschfeld's Racism and Early Twentieth-Century Sexology," *Psychology and Sexuality* 1, no. 3 (2010): 239–49; Christina von Braun, "Die 'Blutschande.' Wandlungen eines Begriffs: Vom Inzesttabu zu den Rassengesetzen," in *Die schamlose Schönheit des Vergangenen. Zum Verhältnis von Geschlecht und Geschichte*, ed. Christina von Braun (Frankfurt am Main: Neue Kritik, 1989), 81–111; Veronika Fuechtner, "Indians, Jews, and Sex: Magnus Hirschfeld and Indian Sexology," in *Imagining Germany, Imagining Asia* (Rochester, NY: Camden House, 2013), 111–30.

107. Ann Taylor Allen, "German Radical Feminism and Eugenics, 1900–1908," *German Studies Review* 11, no. 1 (1988): 31–56; Ann Taylor Allen, "Feminism and Eugenics in Germany and Britain, 1900–1940: A Comparative Perspective," *German Studies Review* 23, no. 3 (2000): 477–505; Loren R. Graham, "Science and Values: The Eugenics Movement in Germany and Russia in the 1920s," *American Historical Review* 82, no. 5 (1977): 1133–64; Leng, *Sexual Politics*, 184–220. On eugenicist politics in Germany more broadly see Richard Weikart, *From Darwin to Hitler: Evolutionary Ethics, Eugenics, and Racism in Germany* (New York: Palgrave Macmillan, 2004); Weindling, *Health, Race*.

108. On colonial-era sexualities see Sara Lennox, "Race, Gender, and Sexuality in German Southwest Africa: Hans Grimm's 'Südafrikanische Novellen,'" in *Germany's*

Colonial Pasts, eds. Eric Ames, Marcia Klotz, and Lora Wildenthal (Lincoln: University of Nebraska Press, 2005), 63–75; Tobin, *Peripheral Desires*, 134–61; Lora Wildenthal, *German Women for Empire, 1884–1945* (Durham, NC: Duke University Press, 2001). On the Weimar period, when attention turned particularly to black French troops in the Rhine occupation, see Julia Roos, "Women's Rights, Nationalist Anxiety, and the 'Moral' Agenda in the Weimar Republic: Revisiting the 'Black Horror' Campaign against France's African Occupation Troops," *Central European History* 42, no. 3 (2009): 473–508; Iris Wigger, "'Black Shame'—the Campaign against 'Racial Degeneration' and Female Degradation in Interwar Europe," *Race & Class* 51, no. 3 (2010): 33–46. On the Third Reich, see Tina Campt, *Other Germans: Black Germans and the Politics of Race, Gender, and Memory in the Third Reich* (Ann Arbor: University of Michigan Press, 2004). On the post–World War II period see, for example, Franz X. Eder, "National and Racial Images of the Sexual 'Other' in the German-Speaking Countries (1950s–1970s)," *Sexuality & Culture* 21, no. 2 (2017): 362–81; Christopher Ewing, "'Color Him Black': Erotic Representations and the Politics of Race in West German Homosexual Magazines, 1949–1974," *Sexuality & Culture* 21, no. 2 (2017): 382–403; Priscilla Layne, "'Schwarz ist in': Racial Fetishism, Sexuality, and Black Masculinity in Lothar Lambert's *1 Berlin-Harlem*," *German Studies Review* 39, no. 2 (2016): 335–52.

109. For nuanced discussions of early sexology's positioning between Eurocentric frameworks and transcultural exchange see Bauer, *Hirschfeld Archives*, 13–36; Bauer, *Sexology and Translation*; Fuechtner, Haynes, and Jones, *Towards a Global History*. See also Magnus Hirschfeld, *Die Weltreise eines Sexualforschers* (Brugg, Switz.: Bözberg, 1933).

110. For an American perspective on how sex-advice literature often worked in ways that erased categories of heterosexuality and whiteness, see Julian Carter, *The Heart of Whiteness: Normal Sexuality and Race in America, 1880–1940* (Durham, NC: Duke University Press, 2007).

111. See, for example, Robert McRuer, "Compulsory Able-Bodiedness and Queer/Disabled Existence," in *The Disability Studies Reader*, 4th ed., ed. Lennard J. Davis (London: Taylor & Francis, 2013), 369–80; Adrienne Rich, "Compulsory Heterosexuality and Lesbian Existence," *Signs: Journal of Women in Culture and Society* 5 (1980): 631–60; Michael Warner, "Introduction: Fear of a Queer Planet," *Social Text* 9, no. 4 (1991): 3–17.

112. See Cryle and Stephens, *Normality*, 179–291; Edward Ross Dickinson, "'A Dark, Impenetrable Wall of Complete Incomprehension': The Impossibility of Heterosexual Love in Imperial Germany," *Central European History* 40 (2007): 467–97; Laura Doan, "Marie Stopes's Wonderful Rhythm Charts: Normalizing the Natural," *Journal of the History of Ideas* 78, no. 4 (2017): 595–620; Leng, *Sexual Politics*, 152–83; Putz, *Verordnete Lust*. On making heterosexuality the object of analysis see Jonathan Ned Katz, *The Invention of Heterosexuality* (New York: Dutton, 1995).

113. Leng, *Sexual Politics*, 14. See also Allen, "German Radical Feminism"; Atina Grossmann, "German Women Doctors from Berlin to New York: Maternity and Modernity in Weimar and Exile," *Feminist Studies* 19, no. 1 (1993): 65–88; Grossmann, *Reforming Sex*; Kirsten Leng, "Permutations of the Third Sex: Sexology, Subjectivity, and

Antimaternalist Feminism at the Turn of the Twentieth Century," *Signs: Journal of Women in Culture and Society* 40, no. 1 (2014): 227–54.

114. Dickinson, *Sex, Freedom*, 267.

115. In addition to Leng's research on women sexologists, see Mary Jo Buhle, *Feminism and Its Discontents: A Century of Struggle with Psychoanalysis* (Cambridge, MA: Harvard University Press, 1998); Christiane Ludwig-Körner, *Wiederentdeckt—Psychoanalytikerinnen in Berlin* (Gießen, Ger.: Psychosozial-Verlag, 1999); Makari, *Revolution*, 420–44; Nellie Thompson, "Early Women Psychoanalysts," *International Review of Psychoanalysis* 14 (1987): 391–408; Zaretsky, *Secrets of the Soul*, 193–216.

116. See Dickinson, *Sex, Freedom*; Grossmann, *Reforming Sex*; Elke-Vera Kotowski and Julius H. Schoeps, eds., *Magnus Hirschfeld. Ein Leben im Spannungsfeld von Wissenschaft, Politik und Gesellschaft* (Berlin: be.bra wissenschaft, 2004); Leng, *Sexual Politics*; Marhoefer, *Sex and the Weimar Republic*; Britta McEwen, *Sexual Knowledge: Feeling, Fact and Social Reform in Vienna, 1900–1934* (New York: Berghahn Books, 2012); Andreas Pretzel, "Sexualreform im Spannungsfeld weltanschaulicher Voraussetzungen und sozialpolitischer Auseinandersetzungen," in *Verqueere Wissenschaft? Zum Verhältnis von Sexualwissenschaft und Sexualreformbewegung in Geschichte und Gegenwart*, eds. Ursula Ferdinand, Andreas Pretzel, and Andreas Seeck (Münster: LIT, 1998), 229–42; Kristine von Soden, *Die Sexualberatungsstellen der Weimarer Republik, 1919–1933* (Berlin: Hentrich, 1988).

117. For a recent account of these linguistic shifts and parallels see Tobin, *Peripheral Desires*. In referring to same-sex desires, I have elected to use "homosexual" as a term that spanned German medical discourses as well as legal, cultural, and subcultural contexts, as opposed to the more informal "gay" or "lesbian," for although terms such as *Lesbierin* were in use in early twentieth-century Germany, these often referred to only a particular subset of same-sex identifications. In this I follow Leng, *Sexual Politics*, 115n1. I note, however, the protests of other scholars that "homosexual" has also acquired more negative associations than terms such as "gay" and "lesbian" in the century since, even as it is acknowledged "as a term of positive self-definition" in the early twentieth century. See Marhoefer, *Sex and the Weimar Republic*, 220n13; Clayton J. Whisnant, *Queer Identities and Politics in Germany: A History, 1880–1945* (New York: Harrington Park, 2016), 11.

118. Susan Stryker, *Transgender History* (Berkeley, CA: Seal Press, 2008), 17. As Marhoefer observes, "'Transvestite' meant different things to different people." Marhoefer, *Sex and the Weimar Republic*, 63, also 59–61. This term is rejected by many trans activists today due to its narrow associations with cross-dressing and fetish communities rather than a broader range of trans experience. For a survey of these changing terminologies see Stryker, *Transgender History*, 1–29.

119. See discussion of "cross-dressing" in Clare Sears, *Arresting Dress: Cross-Dressing, Law, and Fascination in Nineteenth-Century San Francisco* (Durham, NC: Duke University Press, 2015), 20–21. On the "limits of naming and self-naming" in historical contexts see Laura Doan, *Disturbing Practices: History, Sexuality, and Women's Experience of Modern War* (Chicago: University of Chicago Press, 2013), 141.

120. Ian Hacking, *The Taming of Chance* (Cambridge, UK: Cambridge University Press, 1990), 169.

121. Bullough, *Science*, 71.

122. See Ann Cvetkovich, *An Archive of Feelings: Trauma, Sexuality, and Lesbian Public Cultures*, Series Q. (Durham, NC: Duke University Press, 2003), 7.

CHAPTER 1

1. On the founding of the Wednesday Psychological Society in 1902 and its name change in 1908, see George Makari, *Revolution in Mind: The Creation of Psychoanalysis* (New York: Harper, 2008), 129–30, 135, 153, 177–78. On Hilferding see Eveline List, *Psychoanalyse. Geschichte, Theorien, Anwendungen* (Vienna: Facultas, 2009), 33.

2. Albert Moll, *Das Sexuelleben des Kindes* (Berlin: Walther, 1909). Subsequent references in this chapter cite the following translation: Albert Moll, *The Sexual Life of the Child, with an Introduction by Edward L. Thorndike*, trans. Eden Paul (New York: Macmillan, 1913).

3. (Emil) Meirowsky, *Zeitschrift für Bekämpfung der Geschlechtskrankheiten* 10 (1909/1910), 255. For a summary of reviews of Moll's text see Lutz D. H. Sauerteig, "Loss of Innocence: Albert Moll, Sigmund Freud and the Invention of Childhood Sexuality Around 1900," *Medical History* 56, no. 2 (2012): 175–76, 175n128.

4. Sigmund Freud, *Drei Abhandlungen zur Sexualtheorie* (Leipzig: F. Deuticke, 1905); Sigmund Freud, *Three Contributions to the Sexual Theory*. Authorized translation by A. A. Brill, with Introduction by James J. Putnam (New York: The Journal of Nervous and Mental Disease Pub. Co., 1910); Sigmund Freud, *Three Essays on the Theory of Sexuality.* Authorized Translation by James Strachey (London: Imago, 1949). In the following I cite from the 1962 edition of this text: Sigmund Freud, *Three Essays on the Theory of Sexuality. Translation by James Strachey* (London: Hogarth, 1962). For a close examination of the multiple editions of Freud's work see the essays in Philippe Van Haute and Herman Westerink, eds., *Deconstructing Normativity? Re-Reading Freud's 1905 "Three Essays"* (London: Routledge, 2017).

5. Freud in Herman Nunberg and Ernst Federn, eds., "Diskussion über Molls Buch Das Sexualleben des Kindes, 58. Protokoll, Vortragsabend: am 11. November 1908, anwesend Prof. Freud, Bass, Federn, Graf, Hitschmann, Joachim, Rank, Rie, Reitler, Steiner, Sadger, Wittels," in *Protokolle der Wiener Psychoanalytischen Vereinigung*, vol. 2 (Giessen, Ger.: Psychosozial-Verlag, 2008), 43–45. On Moll's politics, which became increasingly conservative over time, see Harry Oosterhuis, "Sexual Modernity in the Works of Richard von Krafft-Ebing and Albert Moll," *Medical History* 56, no. 2 (2012): 137–38; Volkmar Sigusch, "The Sexologist Albert Moll—between Sigmund Freud and Magnus Hirschfeld," *Medical History* 56, no. 2 (2012): 184–200.

6. Moll, *Sexual Life*, 14, xii; Sigmund Freud, "Drei Abhandlungen zur Sexualtheorie (1905)," in *Sigmund Freud Studienausgabe Band V: Sexualleben*, vol. 5, 81.

7. Nunberg and Federn, "Diskussion über Molls Buch," 40–41. On Hitschmann's and Rank's involvement in the Society see Makari, *Revolution*, 135, 153, 164–65.

8. Nunberg and Federn, "Diskussion über Molls Buch," 39–41. On the rivalry between Moll and Hirschfeld see Volkmar Sigusch, "Albert Moll und Magnus Hirschfeld. Über ein problematisches Verhältnis vor dem Hintergrund unveröffentli-

chter Briefe Molls aus dem Jahr 1934," *Zeitschrift für Sexualforschung* 8 (1995): 122–59.

9. Nunberg and Federn, "Diskussion über Molls Buch," 43.

10. Freud in Nunberg and Federn, 43–45.

11. On this rivalry see Volkmar Sigusch, *Geschichte der Sexualwissenschaft* (Frankfurt am Main: Campus Verlag, 2008), 264–68; Sigusch, "The Sexologist Albert Moll," 184–92; Sauerteig, "Loss of Innocence," 180–82.

12. While Makari includes Moll in the list of early members of Abraham's association, I have not been able to verify this information: Makari, *Revolution*, 237. On the establishment of this group see also Veronika Fuechtner, *Berlin Psychoanalytic: Psychoanalysis and Culture in Weimar Republic Germany and Beyond* (Berkeley: University of California Press, 2011), 8, 12. On the journal collaboration between Moll and Abraham see Isabel Sanfeliu, *Karl Abraham: The Birth of Object Relations Theory*, trans. Kate Walters (London: Karnac, 2014), 45.

13. Magnus Hirschfeld, "Zur Methodik der Sexualwissenschaft," *Zeitschrift für Sexualwissenschaft* 1, no. 12 (1908): 683, 702.

14. See, for example, Sigmund Freud, "Hysterische Phantasie und ihre Beziehung zur Bisexualität," *Zeitschrift für Sexualwissenschaft* 1, no. 1 (1908): 27–34; S. [*sic*] Sadger, "Ist die konträre Sexualempfindung heilbar," *Zeitschrift für Sexualwissenschaft* 1, no. 12 (1908): 712–20; Wilhelm Stekel, "Die sexuelle Wurzel der Kleptomanie," *Zeitschrift für Sexualwissenschaft* 1, no. 10 (1908): 588–600.

15. Michel Foucault, *The History of Sexuality: The Will to Knowledge*, vol. 1 (London: Penguin, 1998), 103–4, see also 27–30, 41–49.

16. On the medicalization of child sexuality and masturbation, see Arnold I. Davidson, *The Emergence of Sexuality: Historical Epistemology and the Formation of Concepts* (Cambridge, MA: Harvard UP, 2001), 54, 117–18; Sterling Fishman, "The History of Childhood Sexuality," *Journal of Contemporary History* 17, no. 2 (1982): 269–83; James Kincaid, *Child-Loving: The Erotic Child and Victorian Culture* (New York: Routledge, 1992); Thomas Laqueur, *Solitary Sex: A Cultural History of Masturbation* (New York: Zone, 2003); Patrick Singy, "The History of Masturbation: An Essay Review," *Journal for the History of Medicine and Allied Sciences* 59, no. 1 (2004): 112–21.

17. Eve Kosofsky Sedgwick, "Jane Austen and the Masturbating Girl," in *Questions of Evidence: Proof, Practice, and Persuasion across the Disciplines*, eds. James Chandler, Arnold I. Davidson, and Harry Harrotunian (Chicago: University of Chicago Press, 1994), 112.

18. R. Danielle Egan and Gail Hawkes, *Theorizing the Sexual Child in Modernity* (Basingstoke, UK: Palgrave Macmillan, 2010), 24, 76; Paul Weindling, "Bourgeois Values, Doctors and the State: The Professionalization of Medicine in Germany 1848–1933," in *The German Bourgeoisie*, eds. David Blackbourn and Richard J. Evans (London: Routledge, 1991), 198–223.

19. Sigmund Freud, "Zur sexuellen Aufklärung der Kinder (1907)," in *Sigmund Freud Studienausgabe Band V: Sexualleben*, vol. 5, 159ff.; Sigmund Freud, "Über infantile Sexualtheorien (1908)," in *Sigmund Freud Studienausgabe Band V: Sexualleben*, vol. 5,169ff. Freud had pressured Max Marcuse to publish this second essay quickly in

his journal *Sexual-Probleme* in order to beat Moll to the post: Letter, Freud to Marcuse, 14 August 1908 (Berchtesgarden), Sigmund Freud Archives, Library of Congress: Box 37, Folder 13, Marcuse, Max, 1908–1910.

20. Egan and Hawkes, *Theorizing the Sexual Child*, 4, 6, 52–54; Foucault, *History of Sexuality*, vol. 1, 144, 152; Paul Weindling, *Health, Race, and German Politics between National Unification and Nazism, 1870–1945* (Cambridge, UK: Cambridge University Press, 1989); Frank Mort, *Dangerous Sexualities: Medico-Moral Politics in England since 1830*, 2nd ed. (London: Routledge, 2000).

21. Charles Darwin, "A Biographical Sketch of an Infant," *Mind*, June 1877, 285–94.

22. Sally Shuttleworth, *The Mind of the Child: Child Development in Literature, Science, and Medicine, 1840–1900* (Oxford, UK: Oxford University Press, 2010), 221–32 at 221; Philippe Ariès, *Centuries of Childhood; A Social History of Family Life*, trans. Robert Baldick (New York: Knopf, 1962); Hugh Cunningham, "Histories of Childhood," *American Historical Review* 103, no. 4 (1998): 1195–1208.

23. Fishman, "The History of Childhood Sexuality," 270.

24. Egan and Hawkes, *Theorizing the Sexual Child*, 1–9; Steven Angelides, "Feminism, Child Sexual Abuse, and the Erasure of Child Sexuality," *GLQ: A Journal of Lesbian and Gay Studies* 10, no. 2 (2004): 142–47.

25. Angelides, "Feminism, Child Sexual Abuse," 161–167 (cited here at 167); Kathryn Bond Stockton, *The Queer Child, or Growing Sideways in the Twentieth Century*, Series Q (Durham, NC: Duke University Press, 2009), 1–17, 27.

26. Arnold Davidson, "How to Do the History of Psychoanalysis: A Reading of Freud's 'Three Essays on the Theory of Sexuality,'" *Critical Inquiry* 13, no. 2 (1987): 256–57.

27. Frank Sulloway, *Freud, Biologist*, 277–319 at 277.

28. Sigusch foregrounds Moll's influence, insisting that "[a]ll of the ingredients" for Freud's innovations "were already there" in the works of contemporary sexual scientists; Kern's earlier essay aligns with this assessment. Oosterhuis emphasizes similarities between Freud's findings and earlier works by both Moll and Krafft-Ebing; and Sauerteig offers an important contextualization of medical debates around child sexuality against larger cultural and aesthetic influences: Sigusch, *Geschichte der Sexualwissenschaft*, 261–84, esp. 264, 277n1; Sigusch, "The Sexologist Albert Moll"; Stephen Kern, "Freud and the Discovery of Child Sexuality," *History of Childhood Quarterly* 1 (1973): 117–41; Oosterhuis, "Sexual Modernity"; Sauerteig, "Loss of Innocence."

29. Havelock Ellis, *Analysis of the Sexual Impulse, Love and Pain, The Sexual Impulse in Women* (6 vols.), vol. 3, *Studies in the Psychology of Sex* (Philadelphia: F. A. Davis, 1903), Appendix B.

30. On the book's fraught publication history in the context of English censorship laws, see the introduction to Havelock Ellis and John Addington Symonds, *Sexual Inversion: A Critical Edition*, ed. Ivan Crozier (Basingstoke, UK: Palgrave Macmillan, 2007).

31. See Oosterhuis, "Sexual Modernity"; Harry Oosterhuis, *Stepchildren of Nature: Krafft-Ebing, Psychiatry, and the Making of Sexual Identity* (Chicago: University of Chicago Press, 2000), 58–59; Davidson, *Emergence*, 30–65; Foucault, *History of Sexuality*.

32. Oosterhuis, *Stepchildren*, 1–2, 95–96.

33. On sexological investigations of marriage and heterosexuality see Christa Putz, *Verordnete Lust: Sexualmedizin, Psychoanalyse und die "Krise der Ehe," 1870–1930* (Bielefeld, Ger.: Transcript, 2011).

34. Albert Moll, *Untersuchungen über die Libido sexualis* [1897] (Berlin: Fischer's Medicin. Buchhandlung, 1898); Albert Moll, *Die konträre Sexualempfindung* [1891], 3rd rev. Ed. (Berlin: Fischer's Medicin. Buchhandlung, 1899).

35. Iwan Bloch, *Beiträge zur Aetiologie der Psychopathia sexualis. Mit einer Vorrede von Albert Eulenburg* (Dresden: Dohrn, 1902).

36. Havelock Ellis, *The Evolution of Modesty, the Phenomena of Sexual Periodicity, Auto-Erotism* [1910], 3rd ed. (7 vols.), vol. 1, *Studies in the Psychology of Sex* (Philadelphia: F. A. Davis, 1925).

37. Magnus Hirschfeld, "Einteilung der Sexualwissenschaft," *Zeitschrift für Sexualwissenschaft* 1, no. 10 (1908): 585; see also Magnus Hirschfeld, *Berlins Drittes Geschlecht* [1904], ed. Manfred Herzer (Berlin: Rosa Winkel, 1991).

38. Only a few studies to date have explicitly foregrounded the "normal" as a factor shaping the priorities of modern sexual science. These include a chapter, "Sexology and the New Normality," by Egan and Hawkes; "Normal Soap and Elastic Hymens" by Doan; and "Sexology, Psychoanalysis, and Sexual Hygiene Literature" by Cryle and Stephens. See Egan and Hawkes, *Theorizing the Sexual Child*, 75–96; Laura Doan, *Disturbing Practices: History, Sexuality, and Women's Experience of Modern War* (Chicago: Chicago University Press, 2013), 164–94; Peter Cryle and Elizabeth Stephens, *Normality: A Critical Genealogy* (Chicago: University of Chicago Press, 2017), 261–93. Terry's study of medicalized discourses of homosexuality in the United States locates this turn to the normal—"the health and well-being of the modern heterosexual procreative family"—in the 1920s, almost two decades later than I do here; see Jennifer Terry, *An American Obsession: Science, Medicine, and Homosexuality in Modern Society* (Chicago: University of Chicago Press, 1999), 120–58.

39. Doan, *Disturbing Practices*, 168. The historical specificity of ideas of "norms" and the "normal" also remains an underexplored problem for queer theory, as Wiegman and Wilson point out. Robyn Wiegman and Elizabeth A. Wilson, "Introduction: Antinormativity's Queer Conventions," *Differences* 26, no. 1 (2015): 2, 6.

40. Cryle and Stephens, *Normality*; Doan, *Disturbing Practices*, 164–73; Waltraud Ernst, "The Normal and the Abnormal: Reflections on Norms and Normativity," in *Histories of the Normal and the Abnormal: Social and Cultural Histories of Norms and Normativity* (Abingdon, UK: Routledge, 2006), 1–25. These scholars build on older critical discussions of the restrictive as well as productive capacity of norms, including Foucault, *History of Sexuality*, vol. 1, 135ff.; François Ewald, "Norms, Discipline, and the Law," *Representations* 30 (1990): 138–61; Georges Canguilhem, *On the Normal and the Pathological*, ed. Robert Cohen, trans. Carolyn Fawcett, with an introduction by Michel Foucault (Dordrecht, Neth.: D. Reidel, 1978).

41. Foucault, *History of Sexuality*, vol. 1, 146.

42. R. von Krafft-Ebing, *Psychopathia sexualis: Mit besonderer Berücksichtigung der konträren Sexualempfindung: Eine medizinisch-gerichtliche Studie für Ärzte und Juristen*, 15th ed. (Stuttgart: F. Enke, 1918), 36–37, 182. On Krafft-Ebing's linking of

childhood masturbation and perversion see also Oosterhuis, *Stepchildren*, 57, 62, 131–33.

43. See R. von Krafft-Ebing, *Psychopathia Sexualis with Especial Reference to Antipathic Sexual Instinct: A Medico-Forensic Study*, English translation of 10th German ed. (London: Rebman, 1899), 521ff.; Oosterhuis, *Stepchildren*, 44f., 117, 278. For recent studies of sexological approaches to child abuse and cross-generational sex see Heike Bauer, *The Hirschfeld Archives: Violence, Death, and Modern Queer Culture* (Philadelphia: Temple University Press, 2017), 57–77; Jana Funke, "'We Cannot Be Greek Now': Age Difference, Corruption of Youth and the Making of 'Sexual Inversion,'" *English Studies* 94, no. 2 (2013): 139–53; and for a nuanced argument for taking age as a vector of analysis in the construction of the modern sexological category of male homosexuality, and as a deliberate point of distinction from new discourses of pedophilia, see Kate Fisher and Jana Funke, "The Age of Attraction: Age, Gender and the History of Modern Male Homosexuality," *Gender & History* 31, no. 2 (2019): 266–83.

44. On this shift in Krafft-Ebing's thought see Sulloway, *Freud, Biologist*, 289ff.; Oosterhuis, *Stepchildren*, 100ff.

45. This categorization is still contested; see Celia Roberts, *Puberty in Crisis: The Sociology of Early Sexual Development* (Cambridge, UK: Cambridge University Press, 2015); A. S. Parent et al., "The Timing of Normal Puberty and the Age Limits of Sexual Precocity: Variations Around the World, Secular Trends, and Changes after Migration," *Endocrine Review* 24, no. 5 (2003): 668–93.

46. For surveys of German and English-language medical studies of child sexuality, masturbation and hysteria from the 1860s onwards, see K. Codell Carter, "Infantile Hysteria and Infantile Sexuality in Late Nineteenth-Century German-Language Medical Literature," *Medical History* 27, no. 2 (1983): 190ff.; Sauerteig, "Loss of Innocence," 167–68.

47. Sámuel Lindner, "Das Saugen an den Fingern, Lippen, etc. bei den Kindern (Ludeln)," *Jahrbuch für Kinderheilkunde und physische Erziehung*, Neue Folge, 14 (1879): 68–89; Wilhelm Stekel, "Ueber Coitus im Kindesalter," *Wiener medizinische Blätter* 16 (April 18, 1895): 247–49; Max Dessoir, "Zur Psychologie der Vita sexualis," *Zeitschrift für Psychiatrie* 50 (1895): 941–75; H. Havelock Ellis, "Auto-Erotism: A Psychological Study," *Alienist and Neurologist* 19 (1898): 260–99. Ellis's study cited evidence of "spontaneous masturbation" even in very young infants, and was reprinted in volume 1 of *Studies in the Psychology of Sex*; see Sulloway, *Freud, Biologist*, 308.

48. Ellis, *Analysis of the Sexual Impulse*, 1903, vol. 3, 247–48.

49. Moll, *Sexual Life*, 15.

50. Moll, *Untersuchungen*, 94, 8–11, 44–46; Moll, *Die konträre Sexualempfindung*.

51. See, in particular, Oosterhuis, "Sexual Modernity."

52. Letter, Freud to Blüher, 10 July 1912, in Box 18, Folder 6, Blüher, Hans. 1912 and Folder 7, 1912–13, Sigmund Freud Archives, Library of Congress: General Correspondence 1871–1996.

53. Isidor Sadger in Nunberg and Federn, "Diskussion über Molls Buch," 39–41.

54. Sulloway, *Freud, Biologist*, 301; Sauerteig, "Loss of Innocence," 167–68.

55. See, in particular, a 2012 issue of *Medical History* devoted to readdressing the

historiographical neglect of Moll's work, including Sigusch, "The Sexologist Albert Moll"; Oosterhuis, "Sexual Modernity"; Sauerteig, "Loss of Innocence." See also Sigusch, "Albert Moll und Magnus Hirschfeld"; Andreas-Holge Maehle, "The Powers of Suggestion: Albert Moll and the Debate on Hypnosis," *History of Psychiatry* 25, no. 1 (2014): 3–19. An analysis of citation statistics in Ellis's influential *Studies* further points to Moll's contemporary influence, with Moll cited 120 times in contrast to 96 for Bloch, 77 for Krafft-Ebing, 75 for Freud, and 71 for Hirschfeld: Sulloway, *Freud, Biologist*, 299, 306.

56. G. Stanley Hall, *Adolescence: Its Psychology and Its Relations to Physiology, Anthropology, Sociology, Sex, Crime, Religion and Education* (2 vols.) (New York: Appleton, 1904); Sanford Bell, "A Preliminary Study of the Emotion of Love between the Sexes," *American Journal of Psychology* 13, no. 3 (1902): 325-54. On Freud's visit see Nathan G. Hale Jr., *Freud and the Americans: The Beginnings of Psychoanalysis in the United States, 1876–1917* (New York: Oxford University Press, 1971).

57. Freud highlights Bell's assessment of the lack of research on child sexuality: Freud, "Drei Abhandlungen," 2000, 81n2. Sulloway, however, plays down the influence of both Bell and Hall on Freud: Sulloway, *Freud, Biologist*, 198n18. Moll cites Bell repeatedly: Moll, *Sexual Life*, xii, 15, 69, 73f., 78f., 148, 151, 188f., 208. Ellis cites Bell's study as evidence of the frequency of "the emotions of normal love" prior to puberty: Havelock Ellis, "Sexual Problems: Their Nervous and Mental Relations," in *Modern Treatment of Nervous and Mental Diseases*, eds. William Anson White and Smith Ely Jelliffe (Philadelphia: Lea & Febiger, 1913), 104. See also Alfred C. Kinsey et al., *Sexual Behavior in the Human Female* (Philadelphia: W. B. Saunders, 1953), 103n2.

58. Lewis M. Terman, "A Study in Precocity and Prematuration," *American Journal of Psychology*" 16, no. 2 (April 1905): 174, 145. Terman was particularly known for his work on intelligence and children of genius; for an insightful reading of his works through a history-of-sexuality lens, see Peter Hegarty, *Gentlemen's Disagreement: Alfred Kinsey, Lewis Terman, and the Sexual Politics of Smart Men* (Chicago: University of Chicago Press, 2013).

59. Makari, *Revolution*, 21–29; Katja Behling, *Martha Freud: A Biography* (Cambridge, UK: Polity, 2005).

60. Sigmund Freud, "Zur Ätiologie der Hysterie (1896)," in *Sigmund Freud Studienausgabe Band VI: Hysterie und Angst*, vol. 6, 51–81.

61. Oosterhuis, *Stepchildren*, 88–89; Peter Gay, *Freud: A Life for Our Time* (New York: Norton, 1988), 136–40.

62. Freud summarizes his revision in "Meine Ansichten über die Rolle der Sexualität in der Ätiologie der Neurosen, in Löwenfeld, *Sexualleben und Nervenleiden*, 4th ed. (Wiesbaden: Bergmann, 1906 [1905 MS]), 242–51 (reprinted in the *Studienausgabe Band V*, 148–57); "Das Erleiden sexueller Traumen usw.," *Zentralblatt für Nervenheilkunde* (Nov. 15, 1907), 190. See also Angelides, "Feminism, Child Sexual Abuse," 155; Sauerteig, "Loss of Innocence," 163, 169.

63. C. G. Jung, "The Theory of Psychoanalysis," in *The Collected Works of C. G. Jung: Freud and Psychoanalysis*, eds. Herbert Read, Michael Fordham, and Gerard Adler, vol. 4, Bollingen Series (New York: Pantheon Books, 1961), 107.

64. W. White, "'Three Contributions to the Sexual Theory' by Prof. Sigm. Freud [Review]," *Journal of Nervous and Mental Disease* 38 (1911): 126–28.

65. Magnus Hirschfeld, *Geschlechtskunde (auf Grund dreißigjähriger Forschung und Erfahrung)*, vol. 1. Die körperseelischen Grundlagen (Stuttgart: Julius Püttmann, 1926), 226.

66. Moll, *Sexual Life*.

67. Harry Oosterhuis, "The Pre-Freudian Modernization of Sexuality: Richard von Krafft-Ebing and Albert Moll," in *Deconstructing Normativity? Re-Reading Freud's 1905 "Three Essays,"* eds. Philippe Van Haute and Herman Westerink (London: Routledge, 2017), 45–46; Sauerteig, "Loss of Innocence," 181–82; Sigusch, "The Sexologist Albert Moll," 184ff.; Sigusch, *Geschichte der Sexualwissenschaft*, 264ff.

68. Freud, "Drei Abhandlungen," 2000, 82. Other analysts echoed this judgment, including Isidor Sadger in "Sexualität und Erotik im Kindesalter. Eine psychoanalytische Studie," *Moderne Medizin* 6 (1915), 11–17, 21–27, cited in Sauerteig, "Loss of Innocence," 180.

69. See, for example, Moll, *Sexual Life*, 88, 95f., 276; Sigmund Freud, *Interpretation of Dreams*.

70. Sulloway, *Freud, Biologist*, 3.

71. See, in particular, Oosterhuis, "Sexual Modernity," 150–51.

72. Freud, "Drei Abhandlungen," 2000.

73. Oosterhuis, "Sexual Modernity," 136.

74. See, for example, Sulloway, *Freud, Biologist*, 310; Oosterhuis, "Sexual Modernity," 136–37; Volkmar Sigusch, "Fantasie oder Verhalten: Sigmund Freud und das Verhältnis von Psychoanalyse und Sexualwissenschaft," in *Geschichte der Sexualwissenschaft* (Frankfurt am Main: Campus, 2008), 261–84.

75. Van Haute and Westerink, "Introduction: Excavating a Theory of Sexuality," in *Deconstructing Normativity?*, 1.

76. Freud, "Drei Abhandlungen," 2000, 47n1.

77. As Sigusch points out, Freud even misspelled several of the authors' names: Sigusch, *Geschichte der Sexualwissenschaft*, 263, 274.

78. In the 1910 edition Freud extended this first footnote to acknowledge Sadger's influence, but also to underline his "own experience": Freud, "Drei Abhandlungen," 2000, 47n1.

79. Moll, *Sexual Life*, 109.

80. Moll, 1–2. For surveys of Moll's theories on child sexuality, see Egan and Hawkes, *Theorizing the Sexual Child*, 89–94; Sauerteig, "Loss of Innocence," 164, 167, 177.

81. Freud, "Drei Abhandlungen," 2000, 88.

82. Moll, *Sexual Life*, 14, 109. On infantile amnesia in Freud's work, see Egan and Hawkes, *Theorizing the Sexual Child*, 102–5, 108.

83. Jung, "The Theory of Psychoanalysis," 94.

84. Freud, *Three Essays*, 1962, 34f.; Moll, *Sexual Life*, 91, 58f..

85. Freud in Nunberg and Federn, "Diskussion über Molls Buch," 45.

86. Jung and Freud had been corresponding about the idea of publishing a number of short articles in Moll's new journal, the *Zeitschrift für Psychotherapie und med-*

izinische Psychologie [Journal of Psychotherapy and Medical Psychology]. Letters from Freud to Jung, Vienna, 19 May 1908, and from Jung to Freud, Burghölzli-Zürich, 1 June 1908, McGuire, *The Freud/Jung Letters*, 152–55.

87. Letter 114F, Freud to Jung, 12 November 1908: McGuire, 179.

88. See Albert Moll, *Ein Leben als Arzt der Seele. Erinnerungen* (Dresden: Reissner, 1936), 54–55; Sigusch, *Geschichte der Sexualwissenschaft*, 266.

89. Letter 141F, Freud to Jung, 16 May 1909: McGuire, *The Freud/Jung Letters*, 223. Freud echoed these comments in letters to Ferenczi, where he reports how he "scolded him [Moll] and almost threw him out. He is a disgusting, vicious, maliciously pettifogging individual"; and to Abraham, where he declared—although without providing evidence—that "several passages in the *Sexual Life of the Child* would actually have merited a charge of libel." Letter 52, Freud to Ferenczi, 25 April 1909, *The Correspondence of Sigmund Freud and Sándor Ferenczi*, eds. Eva Brabant, Ernst Falzeder, and Patrizia Giampieri-Deutsch, trans. Ingeborg Meyer-Palmedo, Peter T. Hoffer, and Peter T. Hoffer, vol. 1: 1908–1914 (Cambridge: Belknap, 1996), 54–55; Letter 65F, Freud to Abraham, 18 February 1909, *The Complete Correspondence of Sigmund Freud and Karl Abraham, 1907–1925*, ed. Ernst Falzeder (London: Karnac, 2002), 65.

90. Jones, *Sigmund Freud, Life and Work* vol. 2, 51.

91. Freud's letter to Stekel, a few months before they had their falling out, concerned a piece the latter was writing on Moll for the latest issue of the *Zentralblatt*. Letter, Freud to Stekel, 11 March 1912. Sigmund Freud Archives, Library of Congress: General Correspondence 1871–1996, Box 42, Folder 13. See also Oosterhuis, "The Pre-Freudian Modernization," 45.

92. Freud, "Drei Abhandlungen," 2000, 87–89.

93. Moll, *Sexual Life*, 171–73.

94. Moll, 173. See also Jonathan Gillis, "Bad Habits and Pernicious Results: Thumb Sucking and the Discipline of Late-Nineteenth-Century Paediatrics," *Medical History* 40 (1996): 55–73; Edward Ross Dickinson, *Sex, Freedom and Power in Imperial Germany, 1880–1914* (Cambridge, UK: Cambridge University Press, 2014), 262–63.

95. Isidor Sadger, "L. Loewenfeld, 'Über die Sexualität im Kindesalter,' Sexual-Probleme (Juli/August 1911) [Review]," *Zentralblatt für Psychoanalyse* 2, no. 3 (1912): 142–43.

96. August Forel, *Der Hypnotismus oder die Suggestion und die Psychotherapie: Ihre psychologische, psychophysiologische und medizinische Bedeutung*, 6th ed. (Stuttgart: Ferdinand Enke, 1911), 196–97.

97. Forel, *Die sexuelle Frage* (gekürzte Volksausgabe) (Munich: Ernst Reinhardt, 1924), 156.

98. A. Maeder, "A. Forel, Der Hypnotismus oder die Suggestion und die Psychotherapie [Review]," *Zentralblatt für Psychoanalyse* 1, no. 12 (1911): 598–99.

99. Freud, *Three Essays*, 1962, 51ff.; Sigmund Freud, "Analyse der Phobie eines fünfjährigen Knaben ['Der kleine Hans'] (1909)," in *Sigmund Freud Studienausgabe Band VIII: Zwei Kinderneurosen*, vol. 8, 9–123. This translation is from Sigmund Freud, *Two Case Histories ("Little Hans" and the "Rat Man")*, ed. and trans. James Strachey, vol. 10, *The Complete Psychological Works*, 126. See also Herman Westerink,

"Freud's Discussion with Psychiatry on Sexuality, Drives and Objects in 'Three Essays,'" in *Deconstructing Normativity?*, 36, 41.

100. C. G. Jung, "Über Konflikte der kindlichen Seele," *Jahrbuch für psychoanalytische und psychopathologische Forschungen* 2 (1910): 33–58.

101. Jung, 35, 39, 43, 48.

102. Moll, *Sexual Life*, 91, 143. Cf. Freud, "Drei Abhandlungen," 2000, 84.

103. British Library Manuscripts collection: Havelock Ellis Papers Add70524–70589. Additional correspondence with Freud is held in the Havelock Ellis collection at Yale University, MS195, and in the Sigmund Freud Archives at the Library of Congress: Box 25, Folder 1.

104. Ellis, "Sexual Problems," 105.

105. Ellis, *Evolution of Modesty*, vol. 1, 238; Sulloway, *Freud, Biologist*, 308. Sulloway singles out the essay Havelock Ellis, "Analysis of the Sexual Impulse," *The Alienist and Neurologist* 21 (1900): 247–62. Ellis also highlighted the work of other scholars on this topic, including Hirschfeld's research on infants' finger and toe-sucking: Ellis, *Evolution of Modesty*, 1:181.

106. Ellis, "Sexual Problems," 129. On his personal interest in this topic, see Havelock Ellis, *My Life* (London: Spearman, 1967), 69–70; Phyllis Grosskurth, *Havelock Ellis: A Biography* (New York: Knopf, 1980), 227–28.

107. J. [*sic*] Sadger, "Über Urethralerotik," *Jahrbuch für psychoanalytische und psychopathologische Forschungen* 2 (1910): 409–50; Otto Rank, "Die Symbolschichtung im Wecktraum und ihre Wiederkehr im mythischen Denken," *Jahrbuch für psychoanalytische und psychopathologische Forschungen* 4 (1912): 51–115.

108. Havelock Ellis, "The Relation of Erotic Dreams to Vesical Dreams," *Journal of Abnormal Psychology*, September 1913, 163–64. Ellis's interest in urinary eroticism occupied him throughout his career; see also Havelock Ellis, "The Bladder as a Dynamometer," *American Journal of Dermatology*, May 1902; Ellis, *Evolution of Modesty*, vol. 1, 195.

109. Letter, Jones to Ellis, 10 September 1913. British Library Manuscripts, Havelock Ellis Papers 1039A, Add70539; Correspondence: Folio 18/19.

110. Letter, Jones to Ellis, 20 November 1913. British Library Manuscripts, Havelock Ellis Papers 1039A, Add70539; Correspondence: Folio 20.

111. Freud, *Three Essays*, 1962, 57.

112. Dessoir, "Zur Psychologie"; Moll, *Sexual Life*, 60–61.

113. Moll, *Sexual Life*, 64–70 (cited at 66-67, 69-70), see also 82–86. Moll had already begun this work of extending Dessoir's undifferentiated phase back to childhood in *Libido sexualis;* Sauerteig, "Loss of Innocence," 164.

114. Ellis, "Sexual Problems," 105–6.

115. Freud, *Three Essays*, 1962, 91–94. See also Freud, *Interpretation of Dreams*, 462.

116. See, for example, Egan and Hawkes, *Theorizing the Sexual Child*, 99, 165n34; Van Haute and Westerink, "Excavating," 2–3; Westerink, "Freud's Discussion," 32–33.

117. See, in particular, Rachael Blass, "Understanding Freud's Conflicted View of the Object-Relatedness of Sexuality and Its Implications for Contemporary Psychoanalysis," in *Deconstructing Normativity*, 6–27.

118. Moll, *Sexual Life*, 175–77 (emphasis in original).

119. Archival versions of this questionnaire are held in the Norman Haire Collection at the University of Sydney Manuscripts Collection (HAIRE 3.20 [1] Correspondence. Magnus Hirschfeld), and (in English translation, with handwritten answers) in the Magnus Hirschfeld Papers at the Kinsey Institute ("The Hirschfeld Scrapbook").

120. Letter 60A, Abraham to Freud, Berlin 13 January 1909, in Falzeder, *Correspondence of Sigmund Freud and Karl Abraham*, 75.

121. Letter 82F, Freud to Jung, Vienna 14 April 1908, in McGuire, *The Freud/Jung Letters*, 138.

122. Jones, *Sigmund Freud*, vol. 2, 81.

123. Letter 116A, Abraham to Freud, Berlin, 29 October 1911, in Falzeder, *Correspondence of Sigmund Freud and Karl Abraham*, 140, 1; Letter, Jung to Freud (140J), 12 May 1909, in McGuire, ed., *The Freud/Jung Letters*, 221; for more details on Jung's attack and this "homophobic" interpretation, based on a close reading of correspondence between Freud, Jung, and Abraham surrounding the Congress, see Manfred Herzer, *Magnus Hirschfeld und seine Zeit* (Berlin: de Gruyter, 2017), 151-53 (on Jung's anti-Semitic and homophobic comments in relation to others associated with the movement, see also 148-49).

124. Hirschfeld, *Geschlechtskunde*, vol. 1. Die körperseelischen Grundlagen, 202–3, 242.

125. Magnus Hirschfeld, *Geschlechtliche Entwicklungsstörungen mit besonderer Berücksichtigung der Onanie*, vol. 1, *Sexualpathologie. Ein Lehrbuch für Ärzte und Studierende* (Bonn: A. Marcus & E. Webers, 1917), 80. On Marcuse and his journal's positioning within the Wilhelmine sex reform movement see Dickinson, *Sex, Freedom*, 245; Kirsten Leng, "The Limits of Transnationalism: The Case of Max Marcuse," in *A Global History of Sexual Science, 1880–1960*, eds. Veronika Fuechtner, Douglas E. Haynes, and Ryan M. Jones (Berkeley: University of California Press, 2018), 424–26.

126. Ellis later included this essay, "The Analysis of the Sexual Impulse" (1900), in volume 3 of his *Studies*: Ellis, *Analysis of the Sexual Impulse*, 1903, 15. He also discussed the erotic relationship between the "suckling mother" and her child in Ellis, "Sexual Problems," 105. Much later, he clarified that the term "incest" should only be used with adults: Havelock Ellis, *Eonism and Other Supplementary Studies*, vol. 7, *Studies in the Psychology of Sex* (Philadelphia: F. A. Davis, 1928), 26.

127. Jung, "The Theory of Psychoanalysis," 105–6.

128. Karl Abraham, "Untersuchungen über die früheste prägenitale Entwicklungsstufe der Libido," *Internationale Zeitschrift für ärztliche Psychoanalyse* 4, no. 2 (1916): 81.

129. Jung, "The Theory of Psychoanalysis," 107 (emphasis in original); C. G. Jung, "The Concept of Libido," in *The Collected Works of C. G. Jung*, vol. 4, eds. Herbert Read, Michael Fordham, and Gerard Adler, Bollingen Series (New York: Pantheon Books, 1961), 117, 127–28.

130. C. G. Jung, *The Collected Works of C. G. Jung*, vol. 4, 151, 153–54.

131. Moll, *Sexual Life*, 59.

132. Sigmund Freud, "Über die weibliche Sexualität (1931)," in *Sigmund Freud Stu-*

dienausgabe Band V: Sexualleben, vol. 5, 178–79. See also Jill Scott, *Electra after Freud: Myth and Culture* (Ithaca, NY: Cornell University Press, 2005), 8.

133. Ulrich Clement, "Zum Verhältnis von Sexualwissenschaft und Psychoanalyse," *Zeitschrift für psychosomatische Medizin* 39 (1993): 64.

134. Jung, "The Concept of Libido," 128. In a later essay in the same volume, Jung reiterated this view: "The earlier, infantile state represents a normal application of libido, whereas the reversion of libido to infantile ways is something abnormal": 163.

135. Freud, "Drei Abhandlungen," 2000, 85, 85n1.

136. Jung, *Collected Works*, vol. 4, 165 (emphasis in original).

137. Makari, *Revolution*, 277ff.

138. Sauerteig, "Loss of Innocence," 178.

139. Charlotte Bühler, "Zum Problem der sexuellen Entwicklung," *Zeitschrift für Kinderheilkunde* 51, nos. 4–5 (1931): 612–42; William Stern, "Die Anwendung der Psychoanalyse auf Kindheit und Jugend. Ein Protest. Mit einem Anhang: Kritik einer Freudschen Kindes-Psychoanalyse, von Clara und William Stern," *Zeitschrift für angewandte Psychologie und psychologische Sammelforschung* 8 (1913/1914): 71–101; see also Sauerteig, "Loss of Innocence," 159, 178–80.

140. Charlotte Buehler Institute: http://www.charlotte-buehler-institut.at/charlotte-buehler-info/.

141. See, for example, S. Spielrein, "Die Äußerungen des Ödipuskomplexes im Kindesalter," *Internationale Zeitschrift für ärztliche Psychoanalyse* 4, no. 1 (1916): 44–48; Hermine Hug-Hellmuth, "Zur Technik der Kinderanalyse," *Internationale Zeitschrift für ärztliche Psychoanalyse* 4, no. 1 (1921): 179–97. See also Angela Graf-Nold, *Der Fall Hermine von Hug-Hellmuth: Eine Geschichte der frühen Kinderanalyse* (München: Verl. Internat. Psychoanalyse, 1988); Michael Plastow, "Hermine Hug-Hellmuth, the First Child Psychoanalyst: Legacy and Dilemmas," *Australian Psychiatry* 19, no. 3 (2011): 206–10.

142. Anna Freud, *Einführung in die Technik der Kinderanalyse: vier Vorträge am Lehrinstitut der Wiener Psychoanalytischen Vereinigung* (Vienna: Internationaler Psychoanalytischer Verlag, 1927); Melanie Klein, "Die Rolle der Schule in der libidinösen Entwicklung des Kindes," *Internationale Zeitschrift für ärztliche Psychoanalyse* 9 (1923): 323–44; Melanie Klein, "Frühstadien des Ödipuskonfliktes," *Internationale Zeitschrift für Psychoanalyse* 14 (1928): 65–77.

143. See Nellie L. Thompson and Helen Keable, "The Psychoanalytic Study of the Child: A Narrative of Postwar Psychoanalysis," *American Imago* 73, no. 3 (2016): 343–82; Claudine Geissmann and Pierre Geissmann, *A History of Child Psychoanalysis* (London: Routledge, 1998); Beatriz Markman Reubins, *Pioneers of Child Psychoanalysis: Influential Theories and Practices in Healthy Child Development* (London: Karnac, 2014).

144. Moll, *Sexual Life*, 107–9.

145. Arthur Kronfeld, *Über psychosexuellen Infantilismus, eine Konstitutionsanomalie*, ed. Magnus Hirschfeld, Sexus: Monographien aus dem Institut für Sexualwissenschaft in Berlin (Leipzig: Ernst Bircher, 1921).

CHAPTER 2

1. Magnus Hirschfeld, editorial footnote, in Isidor Sadger, "Fragment der Psychoanalyse eines Homosexuellen," *Jahrbuch für sexuelle Zwischenstufen* 9 (1908): 424.

2. Laurie Marhoefer, *Sex and the Weimar Republic: German Homosexual Emancipation and the Rise of the Nazis* (Toronto: University of Toronto Press, 2015), 214. On Hirschfeld's complicated historical legacy for contemporary LGBTIQ politics, see Heike Bauer, *The Hirschfeld Archives: Violence, Death, and Modern Queer Culture* (Philadelphia: Temple University Press, 2017); Jennifer Evans, "Introduction: Why Queer German History?," *German History* 34, no. 3 (2016): 371–84; Kirsten Leng, "Magnus Hirschfeld's Meanings: Analysing Biography and the Politics of Representation," *German History* 35, no. 1 (2017): 96–116.

3. On the removal of female homosexuality from the Prussian legal code in the mid-nineteenth century see Claudia Schoppmann, *Nationalsozialistische Sexualpolitik und weibliche Homosexualität*, 2nd ed. (Pfaffenweiler, Ger.: Centaurus, 1997), 79–81; Tracie Matysik, "In the Name of the Law: The 'Female Homosexual' and the Criminal Code in Fin de Siècle Germany," *Journal of the History of Sexuality* 13, no. 1 (2004): 26–48.

4. Sadger, "Fragment der Psychoanalyse," 321–424; Ulrike May-Tolzman, "Zu den Anfängen des Narzißmus: Ellis-Näcke-Sadger-Freud," *Luzifer-Amor: Zeitschrift zur Geschichte der Psychoanalyse* 4, no. 8 (1991): 53. On the "urning" terminology see Florian Mildenberger, "Kraepelin and the 'Urnings': Male Homosexuality in Psychiatric Discourse," *History of Psychiatry* 71, no. 3 (2007): 321–35.

5. S. [*sic*] Sadger, "Ist die konträre Sexualempfindung heilbar," *Zeitschrift für Sexualwissenschaft* 1, no. 12 (1908): 714. On this and Sadger's other early homosexual cases, as well as Freud's early treatment of homosexuality, see Birgit Lang and Katie Sutton, "The Queer Cases of Psychoanalysis: Rethinking the Scientific Study of Homosexuality, 1890s–1920s," *German History* 34, no. 3 (2016): 419–44.

6. On Hössli and Ulrichs see Ralph M. Leck, *Vita Sexualis: Karl Ulrichs and the Origins of Sexual Science* (Urbana: University of Illinois Press, 2016); Robert Deam Tobin, *Peripheral Desires: The German Discovery of Sex* (Philadelphia: University of Pennsylvania Press, 2015); Clayton J. Whisnant, *Queer Identities and Politics in Germany: A History, 1880–1945* (New York: Harrington Park, 2016), 19–20.

7. For a succinct summary of Hirschfeld's views see Ralf Dose, *Magnus Hirschfeld: The Origins of the Gay Liberation Movement*, trans. Edward H. Willis (New York: Monthly Review Press, 2014), 68–74. Hirschfeld detailed his early views on homosexual causality and sexual intermediacy in Magnus Hirschfeld, "Ursachen und Wesen des Uranismus," *Jahrbuch für sexuelle Zwischenstufen* 5, no. 1 (1903): 1–193.

8. Nikolas Rose, "Assembling the Modern Self," in *Rewriting the Self: Histories from the Renaissance to the Present*, ed. Roy Porter (London: Routledge, 1996), 231.

9. In particular, see Atina Grossmann, *Reforming Sex: The German Movement for Birth Control and Abortion Reform, 1920–1950* (New York: Oxford University Press, 1995).

10. On this distinction see Sander L. Gilman, "The Struggle of Psychiatry with Psychoanalysis: Who Won?," *Critical Inquiry* 13, no. 2 (1987): 293.

11. See, in particular, Harry Oosterhuis, "Sexual Modernity in the Works of Richard von Krafft-Ebing and Albert Moll," *Medical History* 56, no. 2 (2012): 133–55.

12. Michel Foucault, *The History of Sexuality*, vol. 1 (London: Penguin, 1998), 42–44. For critical discussion of this claim in the German context see Scott Spector, Helmut Puff, and Dagmar Herzog, eds., *After "The History of Sexuality"? German Genealogies with and beyond Foucault* (New York: Berghahn Books, 2012).

13. George Chauncey Jr., "From Sexual Inversion to Homosexuality: The Changing Medical Conceptualization of Female 'Deviance,'" in *Passion and Power: Sexuality in History*, eds. Kathy Peiss, Christina Simmons, and Robert A. Padgug (Philadelphia: Temple University Press, 1989), 87–117; Lucy Bland and Laura Doan, *Sexology in Culture: Labelling Bodies and Desires* (Cambridge, UK: Polity Press, 1998); Arnold I. Davidson, *The Emergence of Sexuality: Historical Epistemology and the Formation of Concepts* (Cambridge, MA: Harvard UP, 2001); David M. Halperin, *One Hundred Years of Homosexuality: And Other Essays on Greek Love* (New York: Routledge, 1990); Gert Hekma, "'A Female Soul in a Male Body': Sexual Inversion as Gender Inversion in Nineteenth-Century Sexology," in *Third Sex, Third Gender: Beyond Sexual Dimorphism in Culture and History*, ed. Gilbert Herdt (New York: Zone Books, 1994), 213–39; Roy Porter and Mikuláš Teich, *Sexual Knowledge, Sexual Science: The History of Attitudes to Sexuality* (Cambridge, UK: Cambridge University Press, 1994); Vernon A. Rosario, *Science and Homosexualities* (New York: Routledge, 1997).

14. See, in particular, Harry Oosterhuis, *Stepchildren of Nature: Krafft-Ebing, Psychiatry, and the Making of Sexual Identity* (Chicago: University of Chicago Press, 2000); Scott Spector, *Violent Sensations: Sex, Crime & Utopia in Vienna and Berlin, 1860–1914* (Chicago: University of Chicago Press, 2016), 116ff.

15. Kertbeny (born Karl-Maria Benkert and later known by his Hungarian name as Károly Mária Kertbeny) coined the term "homosexual" in a private letter to Ulrichs on May 6, 1868. Carl Friedrich Otto Westphal published "Die conträre Sexualempfindung: Symptom eines neuropathischen (psychopathischen) Zustandes" in the *Archiv für Psychiatrie und Nervenkrankheiten* 2, no. 1 (1869/1870): 73–108. Ulrichs's core arguments can be found in Karl Heinrich Ulrichs [pseud. Numa Numantius], *Forschungen über das Räthsel der mann-männlichen Liebe (1864–1879)*, Reprint, 12 vols. (Berlin: Rosa Winkel, 1994). See Robert Beachy, "The German Invention of Homosexuality," *The Journal of Modern History* 82, no. 4 (2010): 801–38; Leck, *Vita Sexualis*; Spector, *Violent Sensations*, 73–77, 87–100; Robert D. Tobin, "Kertbeny's 'Homosexuality' and the Language of Nationalism," in *Genealogies of Identity: Interdisciplinary Readings on Sex and Sexuality*, eds. Margaret Breen Sönser and Fiona Peters (New York: Rodopi, 2005), 3–18; Tobin, *Peripheral Desires*, 1–25, 122ff.

16. A substantial literature on German homosexual identity politics in the Wilhelmine and also Weimar periods now exists in English and German; for a good recent survey see Whisnant, *Queer Identities*. In addition to the sources cited above see, in particular, Manfred Baumgardt, "Die Homosexuellen-Bewegung bis zum Ende des Ersten Weltkrieges," in *Eldorado: Homosexuelle Frauen und Männer in Berlin 1850–*

1950. Geschichte, Alltag und Kultur, ed. Michael Bollé (Berlin: Rosa Winkel, 1984), 17–27; Robert Beachy, *Gay Berlin: Birthplace of a Modern Identity* (New York: Knopf, 2014); Edward Ross Dickinson, *Sex, Freedom, and Power in Imperial Germany, 1880–1914* (Cambridge, UK: Cambridge University Press, 2014), 152–76; Marti M. Lybeck, *Desiring Emancipation: New Women and Homosexuality in Germany, 1890–1933* (Albany: State University of New York Press, 2014); Günter Schmidt, "Allies and Persecutors: Science and Medicine in the Homosexuality Issue," *Journal of Homosexuality* 10, no. 3–4 (1985): 127–40; James Steakley, *The Homosexual Emancipation Movement in Germany* (New York: Arno Press, 1975); Andreas Sternweiler and Hans Gerhard Hannesen, eds., *Goodbye to Berlin? 100 Jahre Schwulenbewegung* (Berlin: Rosa Winkel, 1997).

17. On these historical connections to contemporary LGBTIQ identity politics and "human rights" discourse see Leng, "Magnus Hirschfeld's Meanings"; Marhoefer, *Sex and the Weimar Republic*, 209–14; Leila J. Rupp, "The Persistence of Transnational Organizing: The Case of the Homophile Movement," *American Historical Review* 116, no. 4 (2011): 1014–39; Tobin, *Peripheral Desires*, 230–43.

18. On female sexual inversion and homosexuality in nineteenth- and early twentieth-century sexual science see Heike Bauer, "Theorizing Female Inversion: Sexology, Discipline, and Gender at the Fin de Siècle," *Journal of the History of Sexuality* 18, no. 1 (2009): 84–102; Chiara Beccalossi, "Female Same-Sex Desires: Conceptualizing a Disease in Competing Medical Fields in Nineteenth-Century Europe," *Journal of the History of Medicine and Allied Sciences* 67, no. 1 (2012): 7–35; Chauncey Jr., "Sexual Inversion"; Kirsten Leng, *Sexual Politics and Feminist Science: Women Sexologists in Germany, 1900–1933* (Ithaca, NY: Cornell University Press, 2017), 115–51; Matysik, "In the Name of the Law"; Katharina Rowold, "A Male Mind in a Female Body: Sexology, Homosexuality, and the Woman Question in Germany, 1869–1914," in *From Physico-Theology to Bio-Technology: Essays in the Social and Cultural History of Biosciences* (Amsterdam: Rodopi, 1998), 153–79.

19. Dickinson, *Sex, Freedom*, 210.

20. Sigmund Freud, "Über die Psychogenese eines Falls von weiblicher Homosexualität," *Internationale Zeitschrift für Psychoanalyse* 6, no. 1 (1920): 1-24.

21. These trials were sparked when journalist Max Harden gathered career-destroying evidence against prominent figures, including military commander Count Kuno von Moltke, and published it in the leftist journal *Die Zukunft* [The Future] in 1907. See Bauer, *Hirschfeld Archives*, 25–27; Norman Domeier, *Der Eulenburg-Skandal: Eine politische Kulturgeschichte des Kaiserreichs* (Frankfurt am Main: Campus, 2010); Spector, *Violent Sensations*, 139–58; Whisnant, *Queer Identities*, 48–59. On Hirschfeld's troubled involvement in these trials see Dose, *Magnus Hirschfeld*, 43–45.

22. For critical contextualization of these works see Oosterhuis, *Stepchildren*; Benjamin Kahan, ed., *Heinrich Kaan's "Psychopathia Sexualis" (1844)*, trans. Melissa Haynes (Ithaca, NY: Cornell University Press, 2016).

23. Oosterhuis, *Stepchildren*, 44–45; Volkmar Sigusch, *Geschichte der Sexualwissenschaft* (Frankfurt am Main: Campus Verlag, 2008).

24. On the "discursive explosion" see Foucault, *History of Sexuality*, vol. 1, 17. See also Spector, Puff, and Herzog, *After "The History of Sexuality."*

25. On this shift see for example Chauncey Jr., "Sexual Inversion"; Jay Prosser, "Transsexuals and the Transsexologists: Inversion and the Emergence of Transsexual Subjectivity," in *Sexology in Culture: Labelling Bodies and Desires*, eds. Lucy Bland and Laura Doan (Cambridge, UK: Polity, 1998), 116–31.

26. On Griesinger see Davidson, *Emergence*, 7–12; Oosterhuis, *Stepchildren*, 43, 77, 100ff.

27. Hirschfeld's *Jahrbuch* also published his important extended essay *Der urnische Mensch* [The Urning] in 1903: Magnus Hirschfeld, "*Der urnische Mensch*," *Jahrbuch für sexuelle Zwischenstufen* 5.1903: 1-193 (subsequently published as a monograph, Leipzig: Spohr, 1903). On literary and autobiographical depictions of homosexuality at this period see Claudia Breger, "Feminine Masculinities: Scientific and Literary Representations of 'Female Inversion' at the Turn of the Twentieth Century," *Journal of the History of Sexuality* 14, nos. 1/2 (January 2005): 76–106; Klaus Müller, *Aber in meinem Herzen sprach eine Stimme so laut: Homosexuelle Autobiographien und medizinische Pathographien im neunzehnten Jahrhundert* (Berlin: Rosa Winkel, 1991); Tobin, *Peripheral Desires*; Philippe Weber, *Der Trieb zum Erzählen: Sexualpathologie und Homosexualität, 1852–1914* (Bielefeld, Ger.: Transcript, 2008).

28. For overviews of this scholarship see Beachy, "The German Invention," 801–5; David F. Greenberg, *The Construction of Homosexuality* (Chicago: University of Chicago Press, 1988), 397–433.

29. See discussion in Introduction, and in particular, Anthony Giddens, *The Transformation of Intimacy: Sexuality, Love and Eroticism in Modern Societies* (Cambridge, UK: Polity Press, 1992), 2; Oosterhuis, "Sexual Modernity"; Rose, "Assembling the Modern Self," 225.

30. On these conceptual genealogies see Peter Cryle and Elizabeth Stephens, *Normality: A Critical Genealogy* (Chicago: University of Chicago Press, 2017), 262–79; Arnold I. Davidson, "Styles of Reasoning, Conceptual History, and the Emergence of Psychiatry," in *The Disunity of Science: Boundaries, Contexts, and Power* (Stanford: Stanford University Press, 1996), 75–100; Oosterhuis, *Stepchildren*, 64, 67, 114–15.

31. Richard Wetzell, *Inventing the Criminal: A History of German Criminology, 1880–1945* (Chapel Hill: University of North Carolina Press, 2000), 47.

32. R. von Krafft-Ebing, *Psychopathia sexualis: Mit besonderer Berücksichtigung der konträren Sexualempfindung: Eine medizinisch-gerichtliche Studie für Ärzte und Juristen*, 15th ed. (Stuttgart: F. Enke, 1918), 214; Oosterhuis, Stepchildren, 40, 51ff., 100–105.

33. See J. Edward Chamberlin and Sander L. Gilman, *Degeneration: The Dark Side of Progress* (New York: Columbia University Press, 1985); Spector, *Violent Sensations*, 46ff.

34. For an extensive analysis of Krafft-Ebing's shifting position on degeneration see Oosterhuis, *Stepchildren*, 42, 47, 100ff., 131–35, 172–73, 284.

35. Sigmund Freud, "Drei Abhandlungen zur Sexualtheorie (1905)," in *Sigmund Freud Studienausgabe Band V: Sexualleben*, vol. 5, 50–51.

36. Krafft-Ebing, *Psychopathia sexualis*, 281.

37. Krafft-Ebing, *Psychopathia sexualis*, 243, 246, 277. On Krafft-Ebing's earlier writings on this topic see Oosterhuis, *Stepchildren*, 140–48.

38. Ellis wrote the medical chapters in this co-authored volume: Havelock Ellis and John Addington Symonds, *Sexual Inversion: A Critical Edition*, ed. Ivan Crozier (Basingstoke, UK: Palgrave Macmillan, 2007), 166.

39. Albert Moll, *Die konträre Sexualempfindung* [1891], 3rd revised ed. (Berlin: Fischer's Medicin. Buchhandlung, 1899), 218–21.

40. Moll, 201, 203, 263.

41. Albert Moll, *Untersuchungen über die Libido sexualis* [1897] (Berlin: Fischer's Medicin. Buchhandlung, 1898), 213–16, 222, 224–33, 443–46.

42. Benjamin Tarnowsky, *Die krankhaften Erscheinungen des Geschlechtssinnes: eine forensisch-psychiatrische Studie*, 1886, as cited in Iwan Bloch, *Beiträge zur Aetiologie der Psychopathia sexualis. Mit einer Vorrede von Albert Eulenburg* (Dresden: Dohrn, 1902), 221.

43. Bloch, *Beiträge*, 222–26, 249.

44. Iwan Bloch, *Das Sexualleben unserer Zeit in seinen Beziehungen zur modernen Kultur* (Berlin: Marcus, 1907), 595–96.

45. Bloch, 551–52.

46. See, in particular, Kate Fisher and Jana Funke, "'Let Us Leave the Hospital; Let Us Go on a Journey around the World': British and German Sexual Science and the Global Search for Sexual Variation," in *A Global History of Sexual Science, 1880–1960*, eds. Veronika Fuechtner, Douglas E. Haynes, and Ryan M. Jones (Oakland: University of California Press, 2018), 51–69. On Bloch's cultural relativism and emphasis on literature and anthropology see also Leck, *Vita Sexualis*, 180–95; Vern L. Bullough, *Science in the Bedroom: A History of Sex Research* (New York: Basic Books, 1994), 56; Sigusch, *Geschichte der Sexualwissenschaft*, 285–307.

47. Bloch, *Sexualleben*, 595–97. On the complex relationships between Freud, Fliess, Weininger, and psychologist Hermann Swoboda, involving a testy plagiarism conflict surrounding the concept of bisexuality, see George Makari, *Revolution in Mind: The Creation of Psychoanalysis* (New York: Harper, 2008), 86ff., 151ff.; Michael Schröter, "Fliess versus Weininger, Swoboda and Freud: The Plagiarism Conflict of 1906 Assessed in the Light of the Documents," *Psychoanalysis and History* 5, no. 2 (2003): 147–73; Chandak Sengoopta, *Otto Weininger: Sex, Science, and Self in Imperial Vienna* (Chicago: University of Chicago Press, 2000).

48. Bloch, *Sexualleben*, 474–75, 517, 540, 560–61, 591–92; Schmidt, "Allies," 130. The "riddle" vocabulary can be traced back to Ulrichs's early pamphlets on male same-sex love: Spector, *Violent Sensations*, 93–94.

49. Gilman briefly considers Bloch's Jewishness in Sander L. Gilman, "Sigmund Freud and the Sexologists: A Second Reading," in *Sexual Knowledge, Sexual Science: The History of Attitudes to Sexuality*, eds. Roy Porter and Mikuláš Teich (Cambridge, UK: Cambridge University Press, 1994), 324. He also discusses the low status of dermatologists within the wider medical profession in Gilman, "Struggle of Psychiatry," 299. On the deep intersections between discourses of crime, Jewishness, and sexual otherness in prewar Central Europe, see Spector, *Violent Sensations*.

50. Magnus Hirschfeld, *Die Homosexualität des Mannes und des Weibes*, 2nd ed. (Berlin: Louis Marcus, 1920); Prof. Dr. P. Näcke, "Die Behandlung der Homosexualität," *Sexual-Probleme* 6, no. 8 (1910): 585–86. See also Paul Näcke, "Ein Besuch bei

den Homosexuellen in Berlin," *Archiv für Kriminalanthropologie und Kriminalistik* 15 (1904): 244-63; Paul Näcke, "Echte, angeborene Homosexualität und Pseudohomosexualität," *Deutsche medizinische Wochenschrift* 35, no. 34 (1909): 1477-79; Paul Näcke, "Die Diagnose der Homosexualität," *Neurologisches Zentralblatt* 27, no. 8 (1908): 337-51; Paul Näcke, "Einige psychiatrische Erfahrungen als Stütze für die Lehre von der bisexuellen Anlage des Menschen," *Jahrbuch für sexuelle Zwischenstufen* 8 (1906): 585–603; Paul Näcke, "Über tardive Homosexualität," *Sexual-Probleme* 7, no. 9 (1911): 612–34.

51. Krafft-Ebing, *Psychopathia sexualis*, 311–12, 317–18, 320, 324.

52. On the rise of hypnosis in central Europe after an initial period of resistance see Oosterhuis, *Stepchildren*, 121. On Schrenck-Notzing see Andreas Sommer, "Policing Epistemic Deviance: Albert von Schrenck-Notzing and Albert Moll," *Medical History* 56, no. 2 (2012): 270; Heather Wolffram, *The Stepchildren of Science: Psychical Research and Parapsychology in Germany, c. 1870–1939* (Amsterdam, Neth.: Rodopi, 2009).

53. August Forel, *Der Hypnotismus oder die Suggestion und die Psychotherapie: Ihre psychologische, psychophysiologische und medizinische Bedeutung*, 6th ed. (Stuttgart: Ferdinand Enke, 1911), 65, 435; Moll, *Die konträre Sexualempfindung*, 288–89; Bloch, *Beiträge*, 249–50.

54. Moll, *Die konträre Sexualempfindung*, 443. On Moll's work with hypnotism and medical psychology, a field he helped to pioneer in Germany, later founding the *Zeitschrift für Psychotherapie und medizinische Psychologie* [Journal of Psychotherapy and Medical Psychology, 1909–1924], see Andreas-Holge Maehle, "The Powers of Suggestion: Albert Moll and the Debate on Hypnosis," *History of Psychiatry* 25, no. 1 (2014): 3–19; Volkmar Sigusch, "The Sexologist Albert Moll—between Sigmund Freud and Magnus Hirschfeld," *Medical History* 56, no. 2 (2012): 185.

55. Magnus Hirschfeld, "Ursachen und Wesen des Uranismus," *Jahrbuch für sexuelle Zwischenstufen* 5, no. 1 (1903): 107. Näcke also points to Fuchs's treatment of "lighter" cases of homosexuality using this method; Fuchs was at this time an assistant in Krafft-Ebing's psychiatric clinic in Vienna. Näcke, "Behandlung," 603; Alfred Fuchs, "Therapeutische Bestrebungen auf dem Gebiete sexueller Perversionen," *Jahrbuch für sexuelle Zwischenstufen* 4 (1902): 177–86.

56. Hirschfeld, *Die Homosexualität*, 429 (emphasis in original).

57. Näcke, "Behandlung," 595–96 (emphasis in original).

58. See Moll, *Die konträre Sexualempfindung*, 276–89; Albert Moll, "Die Behandlung der Homosexualität," *Jahrbuch für sexuelle Zwischenstufen* 2 (1900): 13–19; Bloch, Beiträge, 250–51; August Forel, *Der Hypnotismus oder die Suggestion und die Psychotherapie. Ihre psychologische, psychophysiologische und medizinische Bedeutung mit Einschluss der Psychanalyse, sowie der Telepathiefrage. Ein Lehrbuch für Studierende sowie für weitere Kreise*, 12th ed. (Stuttgart: Ferdinand Enke, 1923), 237.

59. See August Forel, *Die sexuelle Frage: eine naturwissenschaftliche, psychologische, hygienische und soziologische Studie für Gebildete* (Munich: Reinhardt, 1905), 435; Hirschfeld, *Die Homosexualität*, 439ff.; Moll, "Behandlung," 6–7.

60. Moll, *Die konträre Sexualempfindung*, 275.

61. Moll, "Behandlung," 3, 10–11; Forel, *Die sexuelle Frage*, 435. On Hirschfeld's

position see Bauer, *Hirschfeld Archives*, 23. On Ulrichs' support of gay marriage see Leck, *Vita Sexualis*, 121; Tobin, *Peripheral Desires*, 43.

62. Hirschfeld, *Die Homosexualität*, 439ff. This translation is from "Adaptation Treatment": Magnus Hirschfeld, *The Homosexuality of Men and Women*, trans. Michael A. Lombardi-Nash (Amherst, NY: Prometheus Books, 2000), 504–25 at 506, 525. On this therapy, see also Elena Mancini, *Magnus Hirschfeld and the Quest for Sexual Freedom* (New York: Palgrave Macmillan, 2010), 86; Dose, *Magnus Hirschfeld*, 74–75.

63. Moll, "Behandlung," 22; Hirschfeld, *Die Homosexualität*, 414. Hirschfeld cites Moll, *Die konträre Sexualempfindung*, 453. On their professional relationship see Volkmar Sigusch, "Albert Moll und Magnus Hirschfeld. Über ein problematisches Verhältnis vor dem Hintergrund unveröffentlichter Briefe Molls aus dem Jahr 1934," *Zeitschrift für Sexualforschung* 8 (1995): 122–59.

64. Hirschfeld, *Homosexuality*, 438, 481–85. See also Moll, "Behandlung," 29.

65. Hirschfeld, *Homosexuality*, 488, 490.

66. Magnus Hirschfeld, "Kastratenstudien. Untersuchungen über sexuellen Chemismus," *Sexual-Probleme* 8, no. February (1912): 87; Näcke, "Behandlung," 601. On Hirschfeld's support for castration in certain circumstances see Bauer, *Hirschfeld Archives*, 71–72; Dose, *Magnus Hirschfeld*, 73–74, 77–78; Leng, "Magnus Hirschfeld's Meanings," 111–12.

67. Hirschfeld, "Kastratenstudien," 87; Hirschfeld, *Homosexuality*, 480. On Hirschfeld's relationship to Sadger and Steinach on the matter of a homosexual "cure" see also Manfred Herzer, *Magnus Hirschfeld und seine Zeit* (Berlin: de Gruyter, 2017), 144-47 (Sadger) and 244-51 (Steinach).

68. "Blutuntersuchungen bei Homosexuellen," *Jahrbuch für sexuelle Zwischenstufen* 14, no. 1 (1914): 72–73 (emphasis in original). See also Bloch, *Sexualleben*, 463, 588–91 at 590.

69. Hirschfeld, *Homosexuality*, 480–81.

70. On the life reform movement see Michael Hau, *The Cult of Health and Beauty in Germany: A Social History, 1890–1930* (Chicago: University of Chicago Press, 2003).

71. Tobin, *Peripheral Desires*, 83–84.

72. On this organization, its name, its key actors and its politics, see Bauer, *Hirschfeld Archives*, 43; Beachy, "The German Invention," 806–7, 831–32; Claudia Bruns, *Politik des Eros: Der Männerbund in Wissenschaft, Politik und Jugendkultur (1880—1934)* (Köln: Böhlau, 2008); Claudia Bruns, "The Politics of Masculinity in the (Homo-)Sexual Discourse (1880–1920)," *German History* 23, no. 2 (2005): 306–20; Marita Keilson-Lauritz, *Die Geschichte der eigenen Geschichte: Literatur und Literaturkritik in den Anfängen der Schwulenbewegung* (Berlin: Rosa Winkel, 1997); Marhoefer, *Sex and the Weimar Republic*, 24, 142–43, 151–54; Harry Oosterhuis, ed., *Homosexuality and Male Bonding in Pre-Nazi Germany: The Youth Movement, the Gay Movement, and Male Bonding before Hitler's Rise* (New York: Haworth, 1991); Schmidt, "Allies," 131–32; Tobin, *Peripheral Desires*, 53–82.

73. Bloch, *Sexualleben*, 823; Whisnant, *Queer Identities*, 36.

74. Dose, *Magnus Hirschfeld*, 35–36. On Röhm's involvement in masculinist homosexual circles, the scandals surrounding his sexuality within the Nazi movement, and the nationalist and anti-Semitic emphasis of Brand's society, "the most likely home for

fascists in the homosexual emancipation movement," see Marhoefer, *Sex and the Weimar Republic*, 146–73, cited at 152.

75. Bauer, *Hirschfeld Archives*, 43; Bruns, *Politik des Eros*; Bernd-Ulrich Hergemöller, "Hirschfeld und Blüher. Kontakte und Konflikte 1912–1922," in *Magnus Hirschfeld. Ein Leben im Spannungsfeld von Wissenschaft, Politik und Gesellschaft*, eds. Elke-Vera Kotowski and Julius H. Schoeps (Berlin: be.bra wissenschaft, 2004), 117–36; Marita Keilson-Lauritz, "Benedict Friedlaender und die Anfänge der Sexualwissenschaft," *Zeitschrift für Sexualforschung* 18, no. 4 (2005): 311–31; Keilson-Lauritz, *Geschichte*; Oosterhuis, *Homosexuality and Male Bonding*.

76. As Neubauer observes, he did so without first consulting with Blüher. In response, Blüher removed Hirschfeld's introduction from the second edition of his *Wandervogel* study. John Neubauer, "Sigmund Freud und Hans Blüher in bisher unveröffentlichten Briefen," *Psyche* 50, no. 2 (1996): 198–99; Hans Blüher, "Die drei Grundformen der Homosexualität," *Jahrbuch für sexuelle Zwischenstufen* 13 (1913): 139–65.

77. Letters, Freud to Blüher, 13 July 1912 and 31 July 1913: Sigmund Freud Archives, Library of Congress: Box 18, Folders 6 and 7 (General Correspondence 1871–1996: Blüher, Hans, 1912–1913, 1996). See also Hergemöller, "Hirschfeld und Blüher"; Jay Geller, "Freud, Blüher, and the Secessio Inversa: Männerbünde, Homosexuality, and Freud's Theory of Cultural Formation," in *Queer Theory and the Jewish Question*, eds. Daniel Boyarin, Daniel Itzkovitz, and Ann Pellegrini (New York: Columbia University Press, 2003), 90–120; Herzer, *Magnus Hirschfeld und seine Zeit*, 144-45 (on Freud's WhK involvement) and 227-33, where Herzer situates Blüher theoretically as "a kind of intermediary between Hirschfeld and Freud" (at 227).

78. Sigmund Freud, "Fragment of an Analysis of a Case of Hysteria (1905 [1901])," in *The Complete Psychological Works*, vol. 7, 1–122, at 50.

79. Sigmund Freud, *Three Essays on the Theory of Sexuality*, trans. James Strachey (London: Hogarth, 1962), 6, 38. Freud's commitment to biological approaches to psychiatry, particularly in the early stages of his career, is examined in detail in Frank Sulloway, *Freud, Biologist*.

80. Freud, "Drei Abhandlungen," 47–48, 60.

81. The terms "homosexuality" (*Homosexualität*) and "homoeroticism" (*Homoerotik*) appear primarily in revisions undertaken for subsequent editions in 1910, 1915, and 1920, where Freud offers a critical assessment of this terminology (e.g., Freud, "Drei Abhandlungen," 57n1).

82. Freud, "Drei Abhandlungen," 48–52.

83. Hirschfeld, *Homosexuality*, 397–98, 402.

84. Freud, *Three Essays*, 5; see also Freud, "Drei Abhandlungen," 49, 51, 132.

85. Freud, *Three Essays*, 102; see also Freud, "Drei Abhandlungen," 51–52.

86. Freud, "Drei Abhandlungen," 52, 56–57.

87. Freud, "Drei Abhandlungen," 132.

88. Freud, 56–57n1; Sigmund Freud, "Analyse der Phobie eines fünfjährigen Knaben ['Der kleine Hans'] (1909)," in *Sigmund Freud Studienausgabe Band VIII: Zwei Kinderneurosen*, vol. 8, 9–123; Sigmund Freud, "Eine Kindheitserinnerung des Leonardo da Vinci (1910)," in *Sigmund Freud Studienausgabe Band X: Bildende Kunst und*

Literatur, vol. 10, 120–24. On the development of Freud's theory of homosexuality see Richard C. Friedman and Jennifer I. Downey, "Psychoanalysis and the Model of Homosexuality as Psychopathology: A Historical Overview," *American Journal of Psychoanalysis* 58, no. 3 (1998): 250–51; Tim Dean and Christopher Lane, eds., *Homosexuality-Psychoanalysis* (Chicago: University of Chicago Press, 2001); Kenneth Lewes, *The Psychoanalytic Theory of Male Homosexuality* (New York: New American Library, 1988).

89. Freud, "Psychogenese."

90. "Historical Notes: A Letter from Freud," *American Journal of Psychiatry* 107 (1951): 786.

91. Friedman and Downey, "Psychoanalysis and the Model of Homosexuality," 249–50.

92. Freud, "Drei Abhandlungen," 69–70.

93. Freud, *Three Essays*, 11n.

94. Freud, *Three Essays*, 12n.

95. Freud, *Three Essays*, 11n.

96. C. G. Jung, *The Collected Works of C. G. Jung*, vol. 4, 182.

97. Sigmund Freud, "Über infantile Sexualtheorien (1908)," in *Sigmund Freud Studienausgabe Band V: Sexualleben*, vol. 5, 172.

98. August Forel, *Die sexuelle Frage. Eine naturwissenschaftliche, psychologische und hygienische Studie nebst Lösungsversuchen wichtiger sozialer Aufgaben der Zukunft*, 13th ed. (Munich: Ernst Reinhardt, 1920), 253.

99. Cryle and Stephens, *Normality*, 270, see also 267–79.

100. Oosterhuis, "Sexual Modernity"; Oosterhuis, *Stepchildren*, 43–50.

101. Moll, *Sexual Life*, 61–62.

102. Havelock Ellis, *Analysis of the Sexual Impulse, Love and Pain, The Sexual Impulse in Women*, vol. 3, *Studies in the Psychology of Sex* (Philadelphia: F. A. Davis, 1903), 223.

103. Westerink, for example, views Freud's *Three Essays* as both a break and continuation of aspects of Krafft-Ebing's thinking; in particular, he notes that there are no "perversions" in Freud's text in the way that Krafft-Ebing defined these as "neuropathic dispositions grounding a specific identity." See Herman Westerink, "Freud's Discussion with Psychiatry on Sexuality, Drives and Objects in 'Three Essays,'" in *Deconstructing Normativity?,* 28–34, cited at 34. In contrast, Sigusch attributes much more originality to Freud, arguing—rather too easily, as the studies by Oosterhuis, Cryle, and Stephens show—that one of Freud's greatest achievements lay in overturning what had once been considered oppositional concepts—biological versus psychological, mental function versus mental disturbance, and perversion versus normality. See Sigusch, *Geschichte der Sexualwissenschaft*, 277. Meanwhile, Dickinson finds that "what was most radical in Freud's theory was that he essentially denied the existence both of an authentic sexual self and of sexual normalcy." Dickinson, *Sex, Freedom*, 248. On psychiatry more broadly, see Elizabeth Lunbeck, "Psychiatry," in *From Natural Philosophy to the Sciences: Writing the History of Nineteenth-Century Science*, ed. David Cahan (Chicago: University of Chicago Press, 2003), 664.

104. Cryle and Stephens, *Normality*, 278.

105. Gilman, "Sigmund Freud," 341.

106. Freud, *Three Essays*, 108–9.

107. Freud, "Drei Abhandlungen," 44.

108. This section of this chapter represents a revised version of research previously published in an article coauthored with Birgit Lang: Lang and Sutton, "Queer Cases."

109. S. Ferenczi, "Zur Nosologie der männlichen Homosexualität (Homoërotik) [Vortrag, gehalten am III. Kongreß der 'Internationalen Psychoanalytischen Vereinigung' zu Weimar im Oktober 1911]," *Internationale Zeitschrift für Psychoanalyse* 2, no. 2 (1914): 132–36. Ferenczi notes that the term "Homoërotik" was developed by sexologist Ferdinand Karsch-Haack (*Das gleichgeschlechtliche Leben der Naturvölker*, Munich, 1911), cited at 133n1; it also featured in the legal writings of Ulrichs. Freud viewed Ferenczi's use of this term favorably in subsequent revisions to the *Three Essays*, describing it as superior to "homosexuality": Freud, "Drei Abhandlungen," 57n1; see also Tobin, *Peripheral Desires*, 137.

110. Wilhelm Stekel, "Masken der Homosexualität (Originalarbeit)," *Zentralblatt für Psychoanalyse* 2, no. 7 (1912): 368. Stekel had cofounded this periodical with Alfred Adler in 1911, with Freud holding veto power over submissions. See Makari, *Revolution in Mind*, 258. On Stekel's break with Freud see Peter Gay, *Freud: A Life for Our Time* (New York: Norton, 1988), 232.

111. Stekel, "Masken," 367–72.

112. See Ulrike May, "Ein Traum (1897) und ein Brief (1902): Zur frühen Beziehung zwischen Freud und Isidor Sadger," *Luzifer-Amor: Zeitschrift zur Geschichte der Psychoanalyse* 12, no. 24 (1999): 25–48; May-Tolzman, "Zu den Anfängen." See also Alan Dundes, "Introduction," in Isidor Sadger, *Recollecting Freud*, ed. Alan Dundes (Madison: University of Wisconsin Press, 2005); Nellie L. Thompson, Michael Schröter, and Ulrike May, "Gerettet aus der Verschollenheit: Zur englischen Ausgabe von Isidor Sadger's 'Erinnerungen an Freud,'" *Luzifer-Amor: Zeitschrift zur Geschichte der Psychoanalyse* 18, no. 36 (2005): 158–66.

113. J. [*sic*] Sadger, "Ein Fall von multipler Perversion mit hysterischen Absenzen," *Jahrbuch für psychoanalytische und psychopathologische Forschungen* 2 (1910): 78. See also Sadger, "Ist die konträre Sexualempfindung heilbar," 716. Freud revealed his opposition in a letter to Jung, as discussed in Angela Graf-Nold, *Der Fall Hermine von Hug-Hellmuth: Eine Geschichte der frühen Kinderanalyse* (München: Verl. Internat. Psychoanalyse, 1988), 37.

114. Sadger, "Ein Fall von multipler Perversion," 105, 111–12, 114. See also Isidor Sadger, "Sexuelle Perversionen," *Jahrbuch der Psychoanalyse* 6 (1914): 299–302; Isidor Sadger, "Zur Ätiologie der konträren Sexualempfindung," *Medizinische Klinik* 5, no. 2 (1909): 53–56.

115. Sadger, "Ein Fall von multipler Perversion," 90.

116. Isidor Sadger, "Welcher Wert kommt den Erzählungen und Autobiographien der Homosexuellen zu?," *Archiv für Kriminal-Anthopologie und Kriminalistik* 53, no. 1/2 (1913): 185; see also Wilhelm Stekel, "Ein Fall von multipler Perversion mit hysterischen Absenzen [Review]," *Jahrbuch für psychoanalytische Forschungen* 2 (1910): 74–77, 83. This view was echoed by M. Nachmansohn, "Die Psychoanalyse eines Falles von Homosexualität," *Internationale Zeitschrift für Psychoanalyse* 8, no. 1 (1922): 45–64.

117. Sadger, "Ist die konträre Sexualempfindung heilbar," 714.

118. See, for example, Sadger, "Ein Fall von multipler Perversion," 133.

119. Isidor Sadger, "Ketzergedanken über Homosexualität," *Archiv für Kriminal-Anthopologie und Kriminalistik* 59 (1914): 321–32; Sadger, "Welcher Wert," 182; Isidor Sadger, "'Wissenschaftlich-humanitäre' Propaganda der Homosexuellen," *Sexual-Probleme* 9, no. 11 (1913): 785–89.

120. Letter 119, Freud to Ferenczi, 3 March 1910, in *Correspondence of Sigmund Freud and Sándor Ferenczi*, vol. 1, 147–48. On Freud's stance on the WhK see also Freud, "Kindheitserinnerung," 124, 125n1.

121. Ferenczi, "Zur Nosologie," 139.

122. Isidor Sadger, "Magnus Hirschfeld, Die Homosexualität des Mannes und des Weibes [Review]," *Internationale Zeitschrift für Psychoanalyse* 2, no. 4 (1914): 392–96; Forel, *Der Hypnotismus (12th ed. 1923)*, 237.

123. Hirschfeld, *Homosexuality*, 436–37.

124. Sigmund Freud, "Stellungnahme zum Fall Prof. Dr. Beer," *Die Zeit*, October 27, 1905, sec. Morgenblatt. Cited in Hirschfeld, *Die Homosexualität*, 389. See also Herzer's discussion of the relationahip between Freud's *Three Essays* and Hirschfeld's theory of sexual intermediaries, which he examines via an extended review by Eugen Wilhelm in the *Jahrbuch für sexuelle Zwischenstufen*: Herzer, *Magnus Hirschfeld und seine Zeit*, 141-43.

125. See, for example, Sadger, "Welcher Wert"; Isidor Sadger, "Über den Wert der Autobiographien sexuell Perverser," *Fortschritte der Medizin* 31 (1913): 705–14, 736–49, 772–79.

126. Bloch, *Beiträge*, 251; Bloch, *Sexualleben*, 577, also 542–47.

127. Moll, *Sexual Life*, 313.

128. Moll, *Sexual Life*, 279.

129. This included the seduction hypothesis, which Moll criticized as "not suffic[ing] to account for the facts" (130), disregarding that Freud had long since retracted this aspect of his theory: Moll, *Sexual Life*, 130, 133, 137.

130. Moll, *Sexual Life*, 191.

131. Moll, *Sexual Life*, 100, 313, 316; A. A. Brill, "The Conception of Homosexuality," *Journal of the American Medical Association* 61, no. 5 (August 2, 1913): 336.

132. Moll, *Sexual Life*, 4–6, 103–4, 124–25, 190–91. For Moll's discussion of patient's dreams in his case studies see 81, 94–98, 178, 190.

133. P. Näcke, "Kleinere Mitteilungen. 7. Bemerkungen zu den Freudschen Symbolen," *Archiv für Kriminal-Anthopologie und Kriminalistik* 47, no. 3/4 (1912): 160; Havelock Ellis, *The Evolution of Modesty, the Phenomena of Sexual Periodicity, Auto-Erotism* (1910), 3rd edition, vol. 1, *Studies in the Psychology of Sex* (Philadelphia: F. A. Davis, 1925), 222.

134. Magnus Hirschfeld, *Geschlechtskunde (auf Grund dreißigjähriger Forschung und Erfahrung)*, vol. 1. Die körperseelischen Grundlagen (Stuttgart: Julius Püttmann, 1926), 221.

135. Moll, *Sexual Life*, 279.

136. Moll, *Sexual Life*, 279 (emphasis in original).

137. Hirschfeld, *Homosexuality*, 205. Näcke agreed that the Freudians "still owe us the scientific proof that homosexuality can really be cured, and for good." Näcke, "Behandlung," 597, 603.

138. August Forel, "Die Lehre Freuds und die Abstinenzbewegung," *Internationale Monatsschrift zur Erforschung des Alkoholismus und Bekämpfung der Trinksitten (Basel)* 23 (1913): 22. Forel advanced these arguments in an article advocating the benefits of abstaining from alcohol, one of his pet causes.

139. Forel, *Der Hypnotismus*, 12th ed. (1923), 205.

140. Prof. Dr. Friedländer, "Kritische Bemerkungen über neuere Arbeiten Freuds und seiner Anhänger," *Zeitschrift für angewandte Psychologie und psychologische Sammelforschung* 5 (1911): 595.

141. Moll, *Sexual Life*, 190, 103f.

142. Näcke, "Behandlung," 603 (emphasis in original).

143. Näcke, 604. Numa Praetorius was a pseudonym for Eugen Wilhelm.

144. Magnus Hirschfeld, "Das Ergebnis der statistischen Untersuchungen über den Prozentsatz der Homosexuellen," *Jahrbuch für sexuelle Zwischenstufen* 6 (1904): 109–78 at 178. See also Freud, "Drei Abhandlungen," 48n2.

145. M. Hirschfeld and E. Burchard, "Zu Dr. Stiers Artikel 'Ueber die Aetiologie des konträren Sexualgefühls,'" *Monatsschrift für Psychiatrie und Neurologie* 32 (1912): 550 (emphasis in original).

146. Sigmund Freud, "Meine Ansichten über die Rolle der Sexualität in der Ätiologie der Neurosen (1906)," in *Sigmund Freud Studienausgabe Band V: Sexualleben*, vol. 5, 155–56; Freud, "Über infantile Sexualtheorien (1908)," 172.

147. Havelock Ellis, "Sexual Problems: Their Nervous and Mental Relations," in *Modern Treatment of Nervous and Mental Diseases*, eds. William Anson White and Smith Ely Jelliffe (Philadelphia: Lea & Febiger, 1913), 102.

148. Magnus Hirschfeld, "Zur Methodik der Sexualwissenschaft," *Zeitschrift für Sexualwissenschaft* 1, no. 12 (1908): 684. Hirschfeld published a version of the questionnaire with 127 questions in this article, acknowledging the assistance of Abraham, Stein, Bloch, Juliusburger, van Roemer, and others. See also Mancini, *Magnus Hirschfeld*, 72; Sigusch, *Geschichte der Sexualwissenschaft*, 268–71.

149. Hirschfeld, *Homosexuality*, 399–402.

150. Stekel noted, however, that he was "of a different opinion" regarding Hirschfeld's distinction between "genuine" and "false" homosexuality: Wilhelm Stekel, "Magnus Horschfeld [*sic*]. Die Homosexualität des Mannes u. des Weibes [Review]," *Zentralblatt für Psychoanalyse* 4, no. 11/12 (1913): 614. Hirschfeld refers to a piece by Stekel in vol. 3:4/5 (1913) of the *Zentralblatt*: Hirschfeld, *Die Homosexualität*, 433.

151. Sadger, "Magnus Hirschfeld, Die Homosexualität [Review]," 393–94.

152. Sadger, 394–96.

153. Laura Doan, *Disturbing Practices: History, Sexuality, and Women's Experience of Modern War* (Chicago: University of Chicago Press, 2013), 21, chapter 4; Cryle and Stephens, *Normality*.

CHAPTER 3

1. Ernst Simmel, in *Psycho-Analysis and the War Neuroses*, International Psychoanalytic Library 2 (London: The International Psycho-Analytical Press, 1921), 30–43 at 36–37.

2. *Zur Psychoanalyse der Kriegsneurosen. Diskussion gehalten auf dem V. Inter-*

nationalen Psychoanalytischen Kongreß in Budapest, 28. und 29. September 1918 / 5th International Psychoanalytical Congress, Budapest (Leipzig and Vienna: Internationaler Psychoanalytischer Verlag, 1919); see also Paul Frederick Lerner, *Hysterical Men: War, Psychiatry, and the Politics of Trauma in Germany, 1890–1930* (Ithaca, NY: Cornell University Press, 2003), 171–74.

3. Sigmund Freud, "Einleitung," in *Zur Psychoanalyse der Kriegsneurosen*, 3. These sentiments were echoed by Sándor Ferenczi (10) and Eduard Hitschmann: E. Hitschmann, "Zur Psychoanalyse der Kriegsneurosen [Review]," *Internationale Zeitschrift für Psychoanalyse* 7, no. 4 (1921): 484. See also *Psycho-Analysis and the War Neuroses*.

4. For a historical overview of the diagnoses surrounding violent war trauma, see Marc-Antoine Crocq and Louis Crocq, "From Shell Shock and War Neuroses to Posttraumatic Stress Disorder: A History of Psychotraumatology," *Dialogues in Clinical Neuroscience* 2, no. 1 (2000): 47–55.

5. E. Burchard, "Sexuelle Fragen zur Kriegszeit," *Zeitschrift für Sexualwissenschaft* 1, no. 10 (1915): 373.

6. See Veronika Fuechtner, *Berlin Psychoanalytic: Psychoanalysis and Culture in Weimar Republic Germany and Beyond* (Berkeley: University of California Press, 2011), 19–20; Doris Kaufmann, "Science as Cultural Practice: Psychiatry in the First World War and Weimar Germany," *Journal of Contemporary History* 34, no. 1 (1999): 139–40; Lerner, *Hysterical Men*, 164.

7. Vern L. Bullough, *Science in the Bedroom: A History of Sex Research* (New York: Basic Books, 1994), 71. A recent exception is Leng's consideration of the writings of women sexologists during and about World War I: Kirsten Leng, *Sexual Politics and Feminist Science: Women Sexologists in Germany, 1900–1933* (Ithaca, NY: Cornell University Press, 2017), 221–63.

8. Ernest Jones, "Die Kriegsneurosen (war-shock) und die Freudsche Theorie," in *Zur Psychoanalyse der Kriegsneurosen*, 65. Jones attributes the term "war shock" to M. D. Eder, *War-Shock: The Psycho-Neuroses in War Psychology and Treatment* (London: Heinemann, 1917).

9. Erich Leed, *No Man's Land: Combat and Identity in World War I* (Cambridge, UK: Cambridge University Press, 1979), 164.

10. Lerner, *Hysterical Men*. The German Army Medical Service report for 1914–1918 listed 613,047 cases of "diseases of the nervous system": Kaufmann, "Science as Cultural Practice," 125.

11. These and other symptoms are discussed by Abraham, Ferenczi, and Simmel in *Zur Psychoanalyse der Kriegsneurosen*.

12. As Winter observes, "shell-shock" does not exist in the same form in French or German, with associations that can range from simple diagnosis to "a metaphor for the nature of industrialized warfare" itself: Jay Winter, "Shell-Shock and the Cultural History of the Great War," *Journal of Contemporary History* 35, no. 1 (2000): 8.

13. George Mosse, "Shell-Shock as a Social Disease," *Journal of Contemporary History* 35, no. 1 (2000): 101–8.

14. Elaine Showalter, "Rivers and Sassoon: The Inscription of Male Gender Anxi-

eties," in *Behind the Lines: Gender and the Two World Wars*, eds. Margaret Randolph Higonnet et al. (New Haven, CT: Yale University Press, 1987), 64.

15. Jason Crouthamel, "Male Sexuality and Psychological Trauma: Soldiers and Sexual Disorder in World War I and Weimar Germany," *Journal of the History of Sexuality* 17, no. 1 (2008): 60–84, esp. 62–63, 66–67; Jason Crouthamel, *An Intimate History of the Front: Masculinity, Sexuality, and German Soldiers in the First World War* (New York: Palgrave Macmillan, 2014), 46–55; Maria Tatar, *Lustmord: Sexual Murder in Weimar Germany* (Princeton, NJ: Princeton University Press, 1995).

16. Oswald Spengler, *Der Untergang des Abendlandes: Umrisse einer Morphologie der Weltgeschichte* (2 vols.) (Vienna [1918]; Munich [1919]: Braumüller; Beck, 1918). The term "soft aestheticism" is attributed to political economist Karl Rathgen, cited in Gunther Mai, *Das Ende des Kaiserreichs: Politik und Kriegführung im Ersten Weltkrieg* (Munich: dtv, 1993), 27; Kaufmann, "Science as Cultural Practice," 128. For analyses of such anxieties about moral disorder and national decline in the face of rapid industrialization and changing gender roles see Edward Ross Dickinson, "'A Dark, Impenetrable Wall of Complete Incomprehension': The Impossibility of Heterosexual Love in Imperial Germany," *Central European History* 40 (2007): 467–97.

17. Burchard, "Sexuelle Fragen," 375–76. On Eulenburg see Volkmar Sigusch, *Geschichte der Sexualwissenschaft* (Frankfurt am Main: Campus Verlag, 2008), 234–46.

18. Henriette Fürth, "Sexuelle Kriegsfragen," *Zeitschrift für Sexualwissenschaft* 2 (1915/1916): 133.

19. Ernst Jünger, *In Stahlgewittern: historisch-kritische Ausgabe*, ed. Helmuth Kiesel (Stuttgart: Klett-Cotta, 2013).

20. Andreas Killen, *Berlin Electropolis: Shock, Nerves, and German Modernity* (Berkeley: University of California Press, 2005), 129–30.

21. Kaufmann, "Science as Cultural Practice," 133, 139–40; Bernd Holdorff, "The Fight for 'Traumatic Neurosis,' 1889–1916: Hermann Oppenheim and His Opponents in Berlin," *History of Psychiatry* 22, no. 4 (2011): 465–76; Killen, *Berlin Electropolis*, 128, 131ff., 140ff.; Lerner, *Hysterical Men*, 61ff., 102ff. (on the Kaufmann method), 175.

22. See Killen, *Berlin Electropolis*, chapter 4; Jason Crouthamel, *The Great War and German Memory: Society, Politics and Psychological Trauma, 1914–1945* (Exeter, UK: University of Exeter Press, 2009), chapters 2–4.

23. See especially Lerner, *Hysterical Men*, 171–74, 181.

24. Joy Damousi, *Freud in the Antipodes: A Cultural History of Psychoanalysis in Australia* (Sydney: UNSW Press, 2005), 7.

25. Fuechtner, *Berlin Psychoanalytic*, 8–9, 18ff.

26. As Fuechtner explains, Simmel saw the repression of traumatic war events as causing a personality split, which resurfaces in debilitating physical symptoms that suggest their traumatic origin: Fuechtner, 29. See also Lerner, *Hysterical Men*, 171–74, 183ff.

27. Ernst Simmel, "Zweites Korreferat," in *Zur Psychoanalyse der Kriegsneurosen*, 42–60.

28. *Psycho-Analysis and the War Neuroses*, 31.

29. Lerner, *Hysterical Men*, 165–75.

30. Freud, "Einleitung," 5 in *Zur Psychoanalyse der Kriegsneurosen*, 5. For Lerner, the methods of doctors such as Simmel "parted from psychoanalytic tenets in important ways, and psychoanalysts alternately downplayed and emphasized these differences": Lerner, *Hysterical Men*, 164. See also Fuechtner, *Berlin Psychoanalytic*, 20, 39.

31. Lerner, *Hysterical Men*, 183–84.

32. Freud in *Psycho-Analysis and the War Neuroses*, 3.

33. Karl Abraham, "Erstes Korreferat," and Ferenczi, "Psychoanalyse der Kriegsneurosen," in *Zur Psychoanalyse der Kriegsneurosen*, 32–33; 25.

34. Abraham in *Zur Psychoanalyse der Kriegsneurosen*, 33–34.

35. J. [*sic*] Sadger, "Ein Fall von multipler Perversion mit hysterischen Absenzen," *Jahrbuch für psychoanalytische und psychopathologische Forschungen* 2 (1910): 111–12 (emphasis in original). See also Sigmund Freud, "Eine Kindheitserinnerung des Leonardo da Vinci (1910)," in *Sigmund Freud Studienausgabe Band X: Bildende Kunst und Literatur*, vol. 10, 87–159.

36. Abraham in *Zur Psychoanalyse der Kriegsneurosen*, 34; see also Lerner, *Hysterical Men*, 181–82.

37. Ferenczi in *Psycho-Analysis and the War Neuroses*, 18–20, at 19-20; see also Abraham, "Erstes Korreferat," in *Zur Psychoanalyse der Kriegsneurosen*, 35–36. The development of Ferenczi's ideas on this topic can be seen in Sándor Ferenczi, "Über zwei Typen der Kriegsneurose," *Internationale Zeitschrift für Psychoanalyse* 4, no. 3 (1916/1917): 131–45.

38. Ferenczi in *Psycho-Analysis and the War Neuroses*, 18–19.

39. Abraham in *Psycho-Analysis and the War Neuroses*, 29.

40. H. von Hug-Hellmuth, "Die Kriegsneurose der Frau," *Geschlecht und Gesellschaft* 9 (1914): 505–14, at 506.

41. Hug-Hellmuth.

42. Paul G. Dane, *Medical Journal of Australia*, April 25, 1925. See also Paul G. Dane, "Notes on Psycho-Analysis of War Neuroses," *International Journal of Psycho-Analysis* 8, no. 1 (1927): 72–73.

43. Lerner, *Hysterical Men*, 181–82.

44. Sigmund Freud, *The Ego and the Id*, ed. and translated by James Strachey (New York: Norton, 1961); Carl Müller-Braunschweig, "Das Problem der Angst in seinem Verhältnis zur psychoanalytischen Libidotheorie," *Zeitschrift für Sexualwissenschaft* 10, no. 9 (1924): 233–37.

45. Fuechtner, *Berlin Psychoanalytic*, 20.

46. Sigmund Freud, *Beyond the Pleasure Principle*, trans. James Strachey (New York: Norton, 1961). See Crouthamel, *Great War*, 66; Lerner, *Hysterical Men*, 189.

47. Ferenczi was the first analyst to engage explicitly with the question of impotence in 1908, while the ex-Freudian Stekel took up the question in the 1920s, arguing—albeit without pointing to any evidence—that hundreds of thousands of men had been made impotent by the war: Sándor Ferenczi, "Analytische Deutung und Behandlung der psychosexuellen Impotenz des Mannes," *Psychiatrisch-neurologische Wochenschrift* 10 (1908): 305–9; Wilhelm Stekel, "Krieg und Impotenz," *Medizinische Klinik* 30 (1920): 775ff.; Wilhelm Stekel, *Die Impotenz des Mannes (Die psychischen Störungen der*

männlichen Sexualfunktion, vol. 4., *Störungen des Trieb- und Affektlebens,* 2nd ed. (Berlin: Urban & Schwarzenberg, 1923). See also Christa Putz, *Verordnete Lust: Sexualmedizin, Psychoanalyse und die "Krise der Ehe," 1870–1930* (Bielefeld, Ger.: Transcript, 2011), 58–61, 176–77.

48. Crouthamel, *Great War,* 72–73; Angus McLaren, *The Trials of Masculinity: Policing Sexual Boundaries, 1870–1930s* (Chicago: University of Chicago Press, 1997), 150–64 (on psychoanalytic approaches to impotence after World War I); Putz, *Verordnete Lust,* 157–80.

49. Friedel Pick, "Über Sexualstörungen im Kriege," *Wiener klinische Wochenschrift* 45 (1917): 1418–19; Friedel Pick, "Über Sexualstörungen im Kriege," *Deutsche medizinische Wochenschrift,* no. 38 (1917). My discussion is based on Bloch's article on traumatic impotence and Pfeifer's review of Pick's work, cited below.

50. Dr. Pfeifer, "Dr. Fr. Pick, Über Sexualstörungen im Kriege. Vortrag, gehalten in der Vereinigung Prager Ärzte (D. M. W. 1917)," *Internationale Zeitschrift für Psychoanalyse* 6 (1920): 174–75.

51. Iwan Bloch, "Über traumatische Impotenz," *Zeitschrift für Sexualwissenschaft* 5 (1918/1919): 136. Further discussions of traumatic impotence in this journal include V. Desogus, "Störungen des Geschlechtstriebes bei den Kriegsverletzten," *Zeitschrift für Sexualwissenschaft* 8 (1921/1922): 177–80; H. Fehlinger, "Krieg und Geschlechtsleben," *Zeitschrift für Sexualwissenschaft* 3 (1916/1917): 124–26.

52. Bloch, "Über traumatische Impotenz," 139–41. Bloch cites the "epoch-making" works of Italian psychiatrist Ceni on the effects of concussion on the brain's "genital centers." See Carlo Ceni, "Die höheren Genitalzentren bei Gehirnerschütterung," *Zeitschrift für Sexualwissenschaft* 1 (1914 1915): 279ff. On Ceni see Angela Verlicchi, "Italian Pioneers of Neuroscience," *Progress in Neuroscience* 1 (2011): 11.

53. Bloch, "Über traumatische Impotenz," 135.

54. Sigmund Freud, "Hysterische Phantasie und ihre Beziehung zur Bisexualität," *Zeitschrift für Sexualwissenschaft* 1, no. 1 (1908): 27–34. In a letter to Jung, Freud explained that the article's redirection from the *Jahrbuch* had been due to "a bit of skullduggery on the part of the editors": Letter, Freud to Jung, 25 February 1908, in William McGuire, ed., *The Freud/Jung Letters,* 125–27. See also Andreas Pretzel, "Disziplinierungsbestrebungen. Magnus Hirschfeld und die Ärztliche Gesellschaft für Sexualwissenschaft," in *Magnus Hirschfeld: Ein Leben im Spannungsfeld von Wissenschaft, Politik und Gesellschaft,* 137–42.

55. Letter, Freud to Marcuse, 25 December 1908, in Box 37, Folder 13, Marcuse, Max, 1908–1910, Sigmund Freud Archives, Library of Congress: General Correspondence 1871–1996. Freud continued to work with Marcuse well into the 1920s, despite a few minor scuffles, contributing several pieces to the latter's 1923 *Handwörterbuch der Sexualwissenschaft* [Handbook of Sexual Science]. Bernd Nitzschke, Annelise Heigl-Evers, and Franz Heigl, "'Wo es in einer Sache nur Gegner oder Anhänger gibt': Ein bisher unbekannter Brief Sigmund Freuds an Max Marcuse," *Zeitschrift für Sexualforschung* 8, no. 3 (1995): 241–48. See also Max Marcuse, ed., *Handwörterbuch der Sexualwissenschaft. Enzyklopädie der natur- u. kulturwissenschaftlichen Sexualkunde des Menschen (1926),* 2nd ed. (reprint with new introduction by Robert Jütte) (Berlin: de Gruyter, 2001).

56. The Medical Society later became known as the Medical Society for Sexology and Eugenics; see Bullough, *Science*, 71; Sigusch, *Geschichte der Sexualwissenschaft*, 91–98; Andreas Pretzel, "Zur Geschichte der 'Ärztlichen Gesellschaft für Sexualwissenschaft' (1919–1933)," *Mitteilungen der Magnus-Hirschfeld-Gesellschaft*, no. 24/25 (1997): 35–122; Marcuse, *Handwörterbuch*, ix.

57. Jones, *Sigmund Freud, Life and Work vol. 2,* 117. See also postscript to letter 203F, Freud to Abraham, Vienna IX, Berggasse 19, 6 April 1914, *Correspondence of Sigmund Freud and Karl Abraham*, 228–30.

58. Bloch, "Über traumatische Impotenz," 137 (emphasis in original).

59. Bloch, "Über traumatische Impotenz," 139.

60. Felix A. Theilhaber, "Kleine Mitteilungen. Krieg und sexuelle Abstinenz," *Zeitschrift für Sexualwissenschaft* 2 (1915/1916): 464.

61. Iwan Bloch, "Aufgaben und Ziele der Sexualwissenschaft," *Zeitschrift für Sexualwissenschaft* 1, no. 1 (April 1914): 2, 6, 9.

62. Iwan Bloch, *Das Sexualleben unserer Zeit in seinen Beziehungen zur modernen Kultur* (Berlin: Marcus, 1907), 589; Albert Moll, *Sexual Life*, 26, 106–9. Moll explains that, whereas it was once believed that the sole function of the testicles and ovaries was sperm and ova production, it now appeared that the reproductive glands have a "duplex" function, also producing the "secondary sexual characters." As Sauerteig points out, however, he makes no explicit references to the emerging endocrinological literature: Lutz D. H. Sauerteig, "Loss of Innocence: Albert Moll, Sigmund Freud and the Invention of Childhood Sexuality Around 1900," *Medical History* 56, no. 2 (2012): 166.

63. Fürth, "Sexuelle Kriegsfragen," 134. On Fürth and other women sexologists during World War I see Leng, *Sexual Politics*, 221–63.

64. Helene Stöcker, "Kleine Mitteilungen: Krieg und sexuelle Abstinenz," *Zeitschrift für Sexualwissenschaft* 2 (*1915/1916*): 425ff.

65. See, for example, Fehlinger, "Krieg und Geschlechtsleben"; Burchard, "Sexuelle Fragen"; Otto Adler, "Perverses vom Kriegsschauplatz," *Zeitschrift für Sexualwissenschaft* 5 (1918/1919): 326ff.

66. Hirschfeld discusses his choice of terminology—both he and his critics noted that it remained imperfect, not least for its emphasis on clothing—in the section "Name, concept, prognosis and therapy of transvestitism," in Magnus Hirschfeld, *Die Transvestiten. Eine Untersuchung über den erotischen Verkleidungstrieb* (Berlin: Med. Verlag Alfred Pulvermacher, 1910), 299–304.

67. These concerns were expressed by psychiatrists Max Nonne and Robert Gaupp, respectively, in "Lecture at the 'War Conference,'" *Deutsche Zeitschrift für Nervenheilkunde* (1917): 39, 150, cited in Kaufmann, "Science as Cultural Practice," 137.

68. Paul Weindling, *Health, Race, and German Politics Between National Unification and Nazism, 1870–1945* (Cambridge, UK: Cambridge University Press, 1989), 291.

69. Kaufmann, "Science as Cultural Practice," 132. Cf. T. Bogacz, "War Neurosis and Cultural Change in England, 1914–22: The Work of the War Office Committee of Enquiry into 'Shell-Shock,'" *Journal of Contemporary History* 24, no. 2 (1989): 227–56.

70. See Robert Deam Tobin, *Peripheral Desires: The German Discovery of Sex*

(Philadelphia: University of Pennsylvania Press, 2015), 95; Derek J. Penslar, *Jews and the Military: A History* (Princeton, NJ: Princeton University Press, 2013), 103–20, 166ff.

71. For a detailed analysis of the experiences of homosexual male soldiers in World War I, and the ways in which many appropriated "militarized, nationalistic ideals of comradeship" to counter effeminate stereotypes, see Crouthamel, *Intimate History*, 123–45 at 123. On the legal situation of trans people during these decades see Katie Sutton, "'We Too Deserve a Place in the Sun': The Politics of Transvestite Identity in Weimar Germany," *German Studies Review* 35, no. 2 (2012): 335–54.

72. Otto Juliusburger, "Zur Kenntnis der Kriegsneurosen," *Monatsschrift für Psychiatrie und Neurologie* 38 (1915): 305–18.

73. On Juliusburger's psychoanalytic connections see also Fuechtner, *Berlin Psychoanalytic*, 8, 149.

74. "Sanitätsrat Dr. med. Otto Juliusburger," in *Institut für Sexualwissenschaft (1919–1913)*, online exhibition of the Magnus Hirschfeld Society, Berlin. URL: http://www.hirschfeld.in-berlin.de/institut/de/ifsframe.html?personen/pers 28.html; Ralf Dose, *Magnus Hirschfeld: The Origins of the Gay Liberation Movement*, trans. Edward H. Willis (New York: Monthly Review Press, 2014), 49.

75. K. Bonhoeffer, "Erfahrungen aus dem Kriege über die Ätiologie psychopathologischer Zustände mit besonderer Berücksichtigung der Erschöpfung und Emotion," *Allgemeine Zeitschrift für Psychiatrie und psychisch-gerichtliche Medizin*, 1917, 77. See also K. Bonhoeffer, "Psychiatrisches zum Krieg," *Monatsschrift für Psychiatrie und Neurologie* 36 (1914): 435–38; K. Bonhoeffer, "Erfahrungen über Epilsepsie und Verwandtes im Feldzuge," *Monatsschrift für Psychiatrie und Neurologie* 38 (1915): 61-71; G. Schwarz, "Zur Kenntnis der Gedächtnisstörung nach Granatenkontusion," *Monatsschrift für Psychiatrie und Neurologie* 40 (1916): 212ff.; A. Kutzinski, "Einige Bemerkungen zur Psychopathologie der sogenannten Intestinal-Neurosen im Anschluß an Erfahrungen bei Soldaten," *Monatsschrift für Psychiatrie und Neurologie* 40 (1916): 317ff. On Bonhoeffer see Andreas Ströhle et al., "Karl Bonhoeffer (1868–1948)," *American Journal of Psychiatry* 165, no. 5 (2008): 575–76; Kaufmann, "Science as Cultural Practice," 134.

76. Juliusburger, "Zur Kenntnis," 305–7.

77. Juliusburger, "Zur Kenntnis," 308.

78. Juliusburger, "Zur Kenntnis," 308–12, cited at 308 (emphasis in original).

79. Juliusburger, "Zur Kenntnis," 311.

80. Juliusburger, "Zur Kenntnis," 312.

81. See Laurie Marhoefer, *Sex and the Weimar Republic: German Homosexual Emancipation and the Rise of the Nazis* (Toronto: University of Toronto Press, 2015), 136–38, 143–45; Weindling, *Health, Race*.

82. Juliusburger, "Zur Kenntnis," 313.

83. Juliusburger, "Zur Kenntnis," 316.

84. Burchard, "Sexuelle Fragen," 376.

85. "Transvestitismus und Militärtauglichkeit," in Magnus Hirschfeld, *Sexuelle Zwischenstufen: Das männliche Weib und der weibliche Mann*, 2nd ed., vol. 2, *Sexualpathologie: Ein Lehrbuch für Ärzte und Studierende* (Bonn: A. Marcus & E. Webers,

1922), 145–66. On Hirschfeld's role as a medical expert for police-issued transvestite certificates see Hirschfeld, *Die Transvestiten*, 192ff., and Jane Caplan, "The Administration of Gender Identity in Nazi Germany," *History Workshop Journal* 72, no. 1 (2011): 173–75.

86. Hirschfeld, *Sexuelle Zwischenstufen*, vol. 2, 159. See also Rainer Herrn, *Schnittmuster des Geschlechts: Transvestitismus und Transsexualität in der frühen Sexualwissenschaft*, Beiträge zur Sexualforschung 85 (Gießen, Ger.: Psychosozial-Verlag, 2005), 76–77 (on Voo Doo), and 93–100 (on transvestites in World War I).

87. See Heike Bauer, *The Hirschfeld Archives: Violence, Death, and Modern Queer Culture* (Philadelphia: Temple University Press, 2017), 33–34.

88. On this discrepancy see also Lerner, *Hysterical Men*, 182.

89. Burchard, "Sexuelle Fragen," 377–78.

90. Kurt Mendel, "Kriegsbeobachtungen. XII. Transvestitismus und Homosexualität," *Neurologisches Zentralblatt* 38, no. 1 (1919): 13–20. For a contemporary discussion of legal questions associated with homosexual involvement in the military, including an assessment of legal culpability, see Joseph Wilmshöfer, "Beiträge zur forensischen Beurteilung der Homosexualität im Kriege," *Zeitschrift für Sexualwissenschaft* 6, nos. 10/11 (1920): 303–20 and 337–47. Herrn emphasizes the extent of the perceived threat among military doctors that effeminacy might infect other troops, and reads this as countering the sympathetic treatment by some army doctors. See Herrn, Schnittmuster, 97–99.

91. "Aus der Kriegszeit," *Vierteljahresberichte des Wissenschaftlich–humanitären Komitees während der Kriegszeit. Herausgegeben statt des Jahrbuch für sexuelle Zwischenstufen mit besonderer Berücksichtigung der Homosexualität* 17, no. 4 (1917): 155, 158. For examples of letters and poetry from the front see 158ff., and for an example of intimate friendship see 18, no. 1 (1918): 8–9.

92. "Frauen als Soldaten im Weltkriege (VI. Teil.)," *Vierteljahresberichte des Wissenschaftlich–humanitären Komitees während der Kriegszeit* 17, no. 1 (1917): 36. On male-to-female and female-to-male cross-dressing soldiers in the German military see Crouthamel, *Intimate History*, 110–18; Jason Crouthamel, "Cross-Dressing for the Fatherland: Sexual Humor, Masculinity and German Soldiers in the First World War," *First World War Studies* 2, no. 2 (2011): 195–215; Bauer, *Hirschfeld Archives*, 33, 148n126.

93. Aimed at a popular as well as professional audience, this volume brought together articles by prominent German and Austrian criminologists, sexologists, and other social commentators, including Erich Wulffen, Paul Englisch, and Curt Moreck, seeking to offer a "clear summary of existing literary and graphic materials on the relationships between the World War and the erotic." Magnus Hirschfeld, "Vorwort," in Magnus Hirschfeld, *Sittengeschichte des Weltkrieges*, 2nd ed. (Leipzig: Verlag für Sexualwissenschaft Schneider, 1930), v. See also Bauer, *Hirschfeld Archives*, 31–35; Crouthamel, *Great War*, 66–72.

94. See, for example "Die Frau als Soldat," *Die Freundin* 4, no. 12 (July 11, 1928): n.p.; P. W., "Frauen als Soldaten," *Die Freundin*, 9, no. 4 (January 25, 1933): n.p.; "Heldentaten einer Ungarin im Weltkrieg," *Frauenliebe* 5, no. 14 (1930): 1–2. I examine these publications in more detail in chapter 6.

95. Crouthamel, *Intimate History*, 111; Clare Sears, *Arresting Dress: Cross-Dressing, Law, and Fascination in Nineteenth-Century San Francisco* (Durham, NC: Duke University Press, 2015), 23–40.

96. Emi Wolters, "Transvestiten im Weltkriege [8-part series, 24 February to 13 April 1932, in 'Die Welt der Transvestiten' supplement]," *Die Freundin* 8, nos. 8 to 15 (1932). Article cited is from 23 March. Female imitators in the prisoner of war camps were also foregrounded in "Theater ohne Frau (Welt der Transvestiten) [Review]," *Die Freundin* 9, no. 2 (January 18, 1933): n.p. For an autobiographical response to Wolters's series see Hariet, "Als Fräulein in Belgien," *Die Freundin* 8, no. 26 (June 29, 1932): n.p.

97. Crouthamel emphasizes that most of the actual Weimar-era serial killers, such as Fritz Haarmann or Peter Kürten, were neither veterans nor "'war neurotics,' in the prevailing definition of the term": Crouthamel, *Great War*, 70, also 71–73. See also Crouthamel, "Male Sexuality," 67, 73–78; Fuechtner, *Berlin Psychoanalytic*, 39–46; Tatar, *Lustmord*.

98. Burchard, "Sexuelle Fragen," 379.

99. Hirschfeld, *Sittengeschichte*, 437 (emphasis in original).

100. See discussion in Crouthamel, *Great War*, 66ff. at 68; Crouthamel, "Male Sexuality," 70.

101. AP, "Trump Order Would Ban Most Transgender Troops from Serving," *NBC News*, March 24, 2018, https://www.nbcnews.com/news/us-news/trump-order-would-ban-most-transgender-troops-serving-n859686.

102. Lerner, *Hysterical Men*, 188.

CHAPTER 4

1. Magnus Hirschfeld, *Geschlechtskunde (auf Grund dreißigjähriger Forschung und Erfahrung)*, vol. 1. Die körperseelischen Grundlagen (Stuttgart: Julius Püttmann, 1926), 205. Hirschfeld does not give the year of his visit in *Geschlechtskunde*, but mentions it in a separate account in Magnus Hirschfeld, "Die Untersuchungen und Forschungen von Prof. E. Steinach über künstliche Vermännlichung, Verweiblichung und Hermaphrodisierung," *Jahrbuch für sexuelle Zwischenstufen* 17, no. 1 (1917): 3–20.

2. On the Viennese Institute see Deborah R. Coen, "Living Precisely in Fin-de-Siècle Vienna," *Journal of the History of Biology* 39 (2006): 493–523; Cheryl A. Logan, *Hormones, Heredity, and Race. Spectacular Failure in Interwar Vienna* (New Brunswick, NJ: Rutgers University Press, 2013); Gerd B. Müller, ed., *Vivarium: Experimental, Quantitative, and Theoretical Biology at Vienna's Biologische Versuchsanstalt* (Cambridge, MA: MIT Press, 2017).

3. Hirschfeld, *Geschlechtskunde*, vol. 1. Die körperseelischen Grundlagen, 206.

4. On this procedure see Eugen Steinach, "Verjüngung durch experimentelle Neubelebung der alternden Pubertätsdrüse," *Archiv für Entwicklungsmechanik* 46 (1920): 557-610; Harry Benjamin, "New Clinical Aspects of the Steinach Operation," *Medical Journal and Record*, no. 122 (1925): 452–57, 515–18, 592–594; Chandak Sengoopta, "Dr Steinach Coming to Make Old Young! Sex Glands, Vasectomy and the Quest for Rejuvenation in the Roaring Twenties," *Endeavour* 27, no. 3 (2003): 122–26.

5. Hirschfeld, *Geschlechtskunde*, vol. 1. Die körperseelischen Grundlagen, 206.

6. Sengoopta's pioneering history of hormone research places a strong emphasis on Hirschfeld, but very little on psychoanalysis; Schmidt also focuses particularly on Hirschfeld's uptake of this research. See Chandak Sengoopta, *The Most Secret Quintessence of Life: Sex, Glands, and Hormones, 1850–1950* (Chicago: University of Chicago Press, 2006), 76ff. (on Hirschfeld); 72, 80f., 87, 255n76, 260n123 (on Freud and psychoanalysis); other sexologists such as Krafft-Ebing and Bloch receive only brief mention; Chandak Sengoopta, "Glandular Politics: Experimental Biology, Clinical Medicine, and Homosexual Emancipation in Fin-de-Siècle Central Europe," *Isis* 89 (1998): 445–73; Günter Schmidt, "Allies and Persecutors: Science and Medicine in the Homosexuality Issue," *Journal of Homosexuality* 10, nos. 3–4 (1985): 127–40 at 128. Trask offers a rich new contextualization of the politicized uses of hormone research to "remake" German masculinity in the post–World War I era, focusing particularly on sexologists and constitutional biologists: April Trask, "Remaking Men: Masculinity, Homosexuality and Constitutional Medicine in Germany, 1914–1933," *German History* 36, no. 2 (2018): 181–206. Logan reads Steinach's research against that of Viennese contemporaries Julius Tandler and Paul Kammerer, situating these in relation to Austro-Hungarian anti-Semitism and heredity and race science. Logan, *Hormones*. In a similar vein, see Coen, "Living Precisely in Fin-de-Siècle Vienna." Walch uses Steinach's research to trace broader epistemological and technological developments in the human sciences, including a shift from "nerves" to "hormones" and the growing influence of the pharmaceutical industry: Sonja Walch, *Triebe, Reize und Signale: Eugen Steinachs Physiologie der Sexualhormone. Vom biologischen Konzept zum Pharmapräparat, 1894–1938* (Wien: Böhlau, 2016). In separate works, Stoff examines the science of "rejuvenation" between the nineteenth century and Nazi era, and traces these developments through to the 1970s, reading the twentieth-century history of hormone research against that of the vitamins and enzymes: Heiko Stoff, *Ewige Jugend. Konzepte der Verjüngung vom späten 19. Jahrhundert bis ins Dritte Reich* (Köln: Böhlau, 2004); Heiko Stoff, *Wirkstoffe: Eine Wissenschaftsgeschichte der Hormone, Vitamine und Enzyme, 1920–1970* (Stuttgart: Franz-Steiner-Verlag, 2012); see also Heiko Stoff, "Die hormonelle und die utopische Geschlechterordnung: Verjüngungsoperationen und der neue Mensch in den zwanziger Jahren," in *Verqueere Wissenschaft? Zum Verhältnis von Sexualwissenschaft und Sexualreformbewegung in Geschichte und Gegenwart*, eds. Andreas Pretzel, Ursula Ferdinand, and Andreas Seeck (Münster: Lit Verlag, 2005), 245–60.

7. E. H. Starling, "Hormones," *Nature*, December 1, 1923, 795–98. Discussed in Sengoopta, *Most Secret Quintessence*, 74.

8. Sigmund Freud, *Three Essays*.

9. For a long-view account of the changing evidentiary forms and conceptual frameworks of sexual science see Arnold I. Davidson, *The Emergence of Sexuality: Historical Epistemology and the Formation of Concepts* (Cambridge, MA: Harvard University Press, 2001).

10. See Robert Beachy, "The German Invention of Homosexuality," *Journal of Modern History* 82, no. 4 (2010): 801–38.

11. Wilhelm Reich, "Arthur Kronfeld: Sexualpathologie (Handbuch der Psychiat-

rie, Deuticke, Wien, 1923) [Review]," *Internationale Zeitschrift für Psychoanalyse* 10, no. 3 (1924): 312–13.

12. Anthony D. Kauders, *Der Freud-Komplex: Eine Geschichte der Psychoanalyse in Deutschland* (Berlin: Berlin Verlag, 2014), 108, see also 38–40, 109–11. See also Arthur Kronfeld, "Über die psychologischen Theorien Freuds und verwandte Anschauungen. Systematik und kritische Erörterung," *Archiv für die gesamte Psychologie* 22 (1911): 130–248; Ingo-Wolf Kittel, *Arthur Kronfeld: 1886–1941. Ein Pionier der Psychologie, Sexualwissenschaft und Psychotherapie* (Konstanz, Ger.: Bibliothek der Universität Konstanz, 1988).

13. Sigusch's history of sexual science may serve as exemplary here: while he describes Kronfeld as a key intellectual figure in Hirschfeld's Institute and notes his engagement with psychoanalysis, Kronfeld's actual research receives only fleeting mention: Volkmar Sigusch, *Geschichte der Sexualwissenschaft* (Frankfurt am Main: Campus Verlag, 2008), 268, 359–60. Herzer also briefly discusses Kronfeld's work at, and later break with, Hirschfeld's Institute due to scientific differences in Manfred Herzer, *Magnus Hirschfeld und seine Zeit* (Berlin: de Gruyter, 2017), 300-4.

14. Steinach was nominated for the physiology prize six times between 1921 and 1938, but never won. For later reflections on his life's work see Eugen Steinach and Josef Loebel, *Sex and Life: Forty Years of Biological and Medical Experiments* (London: Faber, 1940); Harry Benjamin, "Eugen Steinach, 1861–1944. A Life of Research," *Scientific Monthly*, December 1945, 427–42. On Steinach's popular reception, see Maria Makela, "Rejuvenation and Regen(d)eration: 'Der Steinachfilm,' Sex Glands, and Weimar-Era Visual and Literary Culture," *German Studies Review* 38, no. 1 (2015): 35–62; Florian Mildenberger, "'Verjüngung' und 'Heilung' der Homosexualität: Eugen Steinach in seiner Zeit," *Zeitschrift für Sexualforschung* 15, no. 4 (2002): 307–10; Sengoopta, "Dr Steinach."

15. Logan goes so far as to characterize the demise of Steinach's career and reputation as one of several examples of "spectacular failure" among fin de siècle Jewish Austrian scientists: Logan, *Hormones*, 189–90. See also Sengoopta, *Most Secret Quintessence*, 56–67; Walch, *Triebe, Reize und Signale*, 229–43.

16. Arthur Koestler makes this observation in *The Case of the Midwife Toad* (New York: Random House, 1971), 21–23, 122, cited in Sengoopta, *Most Secret Quintessence*, 58.

17. Steinach and Loebel, *Sex and Life*; Logan, *Hormones*, 7–8; Sengoopta, *Most Secret Quintessence*, 58, 64.

18. Steinach first introduced this term in Eugen Steinach, "Willkürliche Umwandlung von Säugetier-Männchen in Tiere [*sic*] mit ausgeprägt weiblichen Geschlechtscharakteren und weiblicher Psyche," *Pflüger's Archiv für gesamte Physiologie* 144 (1912): 74. See also Sengoopta, *Most Secret Quintessence*, 60–61, 64, and 240n150; Trask, "Remaking Men," 202–3.

19. Steinach and Loebel, *Sex and Life*, 47. The experiments that produced this finding are discussed at 29–39, 42, 89.

20. Steinach and Loebel, 108–19; see also Sengoopta, *Most Secret Quintessence*, 63.

21. Logan, *Hormones*, 25; Sengoopta, *Most Secret Quintessence*, 65–67.

22. See, in particular, Walch, *Triebe, Reize und Signale*, 72–73; Trask, "Remaking Men," 181–83.

23. Steinach and Loebel, *Sex and Life*, 115–19; Sengoopta, *Most Secret Quintessence*, 75–82 and 249n41; Walch, *Triebe, Reize und Signale*, 111–21.

24. Mildenberger, "'Verjüngung'"; Sengoopta, "Glandular Politics."

25. Sengoopta, *Most Secret Quintessence*, 36–38. See also Merriley Borrell, "Brown-Séquard's Organotherapy and Its Appearance in America at the End of the Nineteenth Century," *Bulletin of the History of Medicine*, no. 50 (1976), 309–20; Merriley Borrell, "Organotherapy and the Emergence of Reproductive Endocrinology," *Journal of the History of Biology* 18 (1985): 1–30; Laura Davidow Hirshbein, "The Glandular Solution: Sex, Masculinity, and Aging in the 1920s," *Journal of the History of Sexuality* 9, no. 3 (2000): 277-304.

26. On the prevalence of "quackery" arguments see Makela, "Rejuvenation."

27. Sengoopta, *Most Secret Quintessence*, 38, 70–72; Walch, *Triebe, Reize und Signale*.

28. Ralf Dose, *Magnus Hirschfeld: The Origins of the Gay Liberation Movement*, trans. Edward H. Willis (New York: Monthly Review Press, 2014), 31.

29. Michael Hagner, "Scientific Medicine," in *From Natural Philosophy to the Sciences: Writing the History of Nineteenth-Century Science*, ed. David Cahan (Chicago: University of Chicago Press, 2003), 66.

30. Steinach and Loebel, *Sex and Life*, 212–13, citing V. Blum, *Wiener medizinische Wochenschrift* 1936, Nos. 36–37.

31. Steinach and Loebel, *Sex and Life*, 209–10. Steinach first reported on his rejuvenation experiments in human subjects in Steinach, "Verjüngung durch experimentelle Neubelebung der alternden Pubertätsdrüse." See also Robert Lichtenstern, "Die Erfolge der Altersbekämpfung beim Manne nach Steinach," *Berliner klinische Wochenschrift* 57 (1920): 989–95; Harry Benjamin, "The Effects of Vasectomy (Steinach Operation)," *American Medicine* 28 (1922): 435–43. For analyses of these early rejuvenation experiments see Thomas Schlich, *Die Erfindung der Organtransplantation: Erfolg und Scheitern des chirurgischen Organersatzes (1880–1930)* (Frankfurt am Main: Campus, 1998), 159–61; Andreas Seeck, "'Verjüngungsoperationen' nach Steinach. Hinweise auf ein verändertes Verhältnis von Sexualität, Fortpflanzung und Leistungsfähigkeit," *Mitteilungen der Magnus-Hirschfeld-Gesellschaft*, no. 29/30 (July 1999): 45–48; Sengoopta, "Dr Steinach," 123–26; Sengoopta, *Most Secret Quintessence*, 81–89, 106–10; Trask, "Remaking Men," 184–85.

32. Fuchs in R. von Krafft-Ebing, *Psychopathia sexualis: Mit besonderer Berücksichtigung der konträren Sexualempfindung*, 15th ed. (Stuttgart: F. Enke, 1918), 327. Fuchs cites Steinach-Lichtenstern, "Umstimmung der Homosexualität durch Austausch der Pubertätsdrüsen," *Münchener Medizinische Wochenschrift* 65: 6 (5 February 1918).

33. On Viereck, who was later jailed for disseminating Nazi propaganda in America, see Sengoopta, *Most Secret Quintessence*, 272n258; Paul Weindling, *Health, Race, and German Politics Between National Unification and Nazism, 1870–1945* (Cambridge, UK: Cambridge University Press, 1989), 325. On Atherton see Trask, "Remaking Men," 181, and below.

34. On the use of "Steinach" as a verb see Logan, *Hormones*, 59; Sengoopta, "Dr Steinach," 123.

35. On Yeats' surgery, performed by Norman Haire, see Diana Wyndham, "Verse-making and Lovemaking—W. B. Yeats' 'Strange Second Puberty': Norman Haire and the Steinach Rejuvenation Operation," *Journal of the History of Behavioural Science* 39 (2002): 25–50.

36. Jones, *Sigmund Freud, Life and Work, vol. 3,* 104. Letter, Freud to Ferenczi, 22 January 1924, in Sigmund Freud, *Correspondence of Sigmund Freud and Sándor Ferenczi*, vol. 3, 119.

37. H. Benjamin, "Reminiscences," *Journal of Sex Research* 6, no. 1 (1970): 7. On Freud's operation, see also Patricia Gherovici, *Please Select Your Gender: From the Invention of Hysteria to the Democratizing of Transgenderism* (New York: Routledge, 2010), 79–83; Sengoopta, *Most Secret Quintessence*, 87.

38. Voronoff used ape rather than human testicles due to a prohibition in French law on removing human bodily parts. See David Hamilton, *The Monkey Gland Affair* (London: Chatto & Windus, 1986); Makela, "Rejuvenation," 47–55; Sengoopta, *Most Secret Quintessence*, 94–99.

39. Haire was a big fan of Steinach, Ellis, and Hirschfeld, in particular, although not of Moll, not least due to his adversity to Hirschfeld and to the birth control movement, which Haire himself was closely involved in. See Norman Haire, *Rejuvenation: The Work of Steinach, Voronoff, and Others* (London: Allen & Unwin, 1924). On Haire, see Ivan Crozier, "'All the World's a Stage': Dora Russell, Norman Haire, and the 1929 London World League for Sexual Reform Congress," *Journal of the History of Sexuality* 12, no. 1 (2003): 16–37; Ivan Crozier, "Becoming a Sexologist: Norman Haire, the 1929 London World League for Sexual Reform Congress, and Organizing Medical Knowledge about Sex in Interwar England," *History of Science* 39 (2001): 299–329; Diana Wyndham, *Norman Haire and the Study of Sex* (Sydney, Australia: Sydney University Press, 2012).

40. See Sengoopta, *Most Secret Quintessence*, 15–28 on oophorectomy, 39–45 on the move away from this surgery in the interwar period, 89–94 on female rejuvenation treatments more broadly, 42–45 and 89 on ovarian transplants, and 232n58 and 253n63 on graft rejections. On the last-mentioned see also Michael F. A. Woodruff, *The Transplantation of Tissues and Organs* (Springfield, IL: Charles Thomas, 1960), 67–69.

41. Letter, Haire to Ellis, 18 July 1927. Norman Haire Papers, University of Sydney: HAIRE No. 3.16.1 (1) Norman Haire/Havelock Ellis correspondence 1921–1933. See also Alfred Loeser's report on using these methods in older female patients at the 1926 International Congress for Sex Research: "Die Wirkung der Eierstocküberpflanzung auf die infantile, innersekretorisch kranke und alternde Frau," in Max Marcuse, ed., *Verhandlungen des I. Internationalen Kongresses für Sexualforschung. Berlin vom 10. bis 16. Oktober 1926. Veranstaltet von der Internationalen Gesellschaft für Sexualforschung* (Berlin, Köln: Marcus & Weber, 1928), 141–46.

42. Benjamin, "New Clinical Aspects of the Steinach Operation," 594. See also Logan, *Hormones*, 59–60; Sengoopta, *Most Secret Quintessence*, 88, 262n137.

43. Benjamin, "Reminiscences," 6. Benjamin's visits to Steinach's lab are detailed

in his diaries in the Kinsey Institute archive in Bloomington, Indiana, including in the journals "1923 Europe" (in May) and "1937 Europa" (again in May): Diaries 12 and 18 of 67, Harry Benjamin Collection: Series II: MS—Personal/Biographical/Historical, Box 2. B. Diaries and daily planners, 1913–1982. Benjamin also described these visits in Erwin Haeberle, "Der transatlantische Pendler. Ein Interview mit Harry Benjamin," *Sexualmedizin* 1 (1985): 44–47; Benjamin, "Eugen Steinach." Benjamin's correspondence with Steinach is held at the New York Academy of Medicine, however Steinach's personal papers do not appear to have survived confiscation by the Nazis in 1938; see Chandak Sengoopta, "Tales from the Vienna Labs: The Eugene Steinach–Harry Benjamin Correspondence," *New York Academy of Medicine*, no. 2 (2000): 2–7.

44. Sengoopta, *Most Secret Quintessence*, 40–45, 90–92; Makela, "Rejuvenation," 48–49, 60n39.

45. Makela, "Rejuvenation," 55–56; Joanne Meyerowitz, *How Sex Changed: A History of Transsexuality in the United States* (Cambridge, MA: Harvard University Press, 2002), 16–17 and 45–46 on the Steinach-Benjamin connection.

46. Curt Thomalla and Nicholas Kaufmann, *Der Steinach-Film (The Steinach Film)*, Documentary (Ufa Studios, 1922). On the film's popular reception see Rainer Herrn and Christine N. Brinckmann, "Of Rats and Men: Rejuvenation and the Steinach Film," in *Not Straight from Germany: Sexual Publics and Sexual Citizenship since Magnus Hirschfeld* (Ann Arbor: University of Michigan Press, 2017), 212–34; Makela, "Rejuvenation."

47. Katie Sutton, "Sexology's Photographic Turn: Visualizing Trans Identity in Interwar Germany," *Journal of the History of Sexuality* 27, no. 3 (2018): 442–79. On the use of photography in early twentieth-century German sexology see also Heike Bauer, *The Hirschfeld Archives: Violence, Death, and Modern Queer Culture* (Philadelphia: Temple University Press, 2017), 87–91; Kathrin Peters, *Rätselbilder des Geschlechts: Körperwissen und Medialität um 1900* (Zurich: Diaphanes, 2010); David James Prickett, "Magnus Hirschfeld and the Photographic (Re)Invention of the 'Third Sex,'" in *Visual Culture in Twentieth-Century Germany: Text as Spectacle* (Bloomington: Indiana University Press, 2006), 103–19; Katharina Sykora, "Umkleidekabinen des Geschlechts: Sexualmedizinische Fotographie im frühen 20. Jahrhundert," *Fotogeschichte: Beiträge zur Geschichte und Ästhetik der Fotografie* 24, no. 92 (2004): 15–30.

48. Letters from 20 March 1923, Haire to Ellis, and 14 and 19 July 1923, Ellis to Haire. Norman Haire Papers, University of Sydney: HAIRE No. 3.16.1 (1) Norman Haire/Havelock Ellis correspondence 1921–1933. See also Haire, *Rejuvenation*.

49. Samuel Wyllis Bandler, *The Endocrines* (Philadelphia: Saunders, 1921), iv; Louis Berman, *The Glands Regulating Personality: A Study of the Glands of Internal Secretion in Relation to the Types of Human Nature* (New York: Macmillan, 1922), 167; Sengoopta, *Most Secret Quintessence*, 72.

50. Arthur Kronfeld, *Über psychosexuellen Infantilismus, eine Konstitutionsanomalie*, ed. Magnus Hirschfeld, *Sexus: Monographien aus dem Institut für Sexualwissenschaft in Berlin* (Leipzig: Ernst Bircher, 1921). On this monograph series see Sigusch, *Geschichte der Sexualwissenschaft*, 262. On Kronfeld's life and career see Andreas Seeck, "Arthur Kronfeld (1886–1941)," in Volkmar Sigusch and Günter Grau, eds., *Personenlexikon der Sexualforschung* (Frankfurt am Main: Campus, 2009), 397–402;

Kittel, *Arthur Kronfeld*; Laurie Marhoefer, *Sex and the Weimar Republic: German Homosexual Emancipation and the Rise of the Nazis* (Toronto: University of Toronto Press, 2015), 134–35.

51. Kronfeld, *Über psychosexuellen Infantilismus*, 1–2, 24. See also Arthur Kronfeld, "Der konstitutionelle Faktor bei sexuellen Triebanomalien," *Zeitschrift für Sexualwissenschaft* 8 (1921): 2. See also Trask, "Remaking Men," 191–98 at 191.

52. Kronfeld, *Über psychosexuellen Infantilismus*, 61–65.

53. Magnus Hirschfeld and Ernst Burchard, *Der sexuelle Infantilismus*, Juristisch-psychiatrische Grenzfragen. Zwanglose Abhandlungen (Halle a.S.: Carl Marhold, 1913).

54. Kronfeld, *Über psychosexuellen Infantilismus*, 8–10.

55. Kronfeld, 3–5. See also Sigmund Freud, "Drei Abhandlungen zur Sexualtheorie (1905)," in *Sigmund Freud Studienausgabe Band V: Sexualleben, vol. 5*, 84–86.

56. Sigusch, *Geschichte der Sexualwissenschaft*, 268.

57. Kronfeld, *Über psychosexuellen Infantilismus*, 21–23.

58. Kronfeld, *Über psychosexuellen Infantilismus*, 23.

59. Letter, Freud to Ferenczi, 3 December 1919, Vienna. Sigmund Freud Archives, Library of Correspondence: General Correspondence 1871–1996, Box 25 Folder 16. Ferenczi, Sándor, 1903, 1915, 1919.

60. Editorial preface to Freud, "Drei Abhandlungen," 40.

61. Freud, 58. Citing A. Lipschuetz, *Die Pubertätsdrüse und ihre Wirkungen* (Bern: Bircher, 1919), 356–57. On Lipschütz see B. Günther, "Alexander Lipschütz (1883–1980). A Biographical Synopsis," *Biological Research* 27 (1994): 79–84.

62. Freud, "Drei Abhandlungen," 58n1.

63. Freud, *Three Essays*, 81.

64. Freud, 13n1. The editors of the Standard Edition cite two letters from Freud to Fliess from March/April 1896 (81–82). See also Sigmund Freud, "Meine Ansichten über die Rolle der Sexualität in der Ätiologie der Neurosen (1906)," in *Sigmund Freud Studienausgabe Band V: Sexualleben*, vol. 5, 147–57.

65. See Bauer, *Hirschfeld Archives*, 69–72; Schmidt, "Allies," 134; Andreas Seeck, ed., *Durch Wissenschaft zur Gerechtigkeit?: Textsammlung zur kritischen Rezeption des Schaffens von Magnus Hirschfeld* (Berlin: LIT Verlag, 2003), 45–48 ("Hirschfeld schweigt zu diesen Operationen—und kooperiert in Einzelfällen," 47); Sengoopta, Most Secret Quintessence, 81; Sigusch, *Geschichte der Sexualwissenschaft*, 216.

66. Here I am thinking particularly of Judith Butler's work on the conditions governing the recognition and livability of lives lived outside the terms of the heteronormative or ableist mainstream, and of Heike Bauer's recent application of such scholarship to Hirschfeld's oeuvre and subjects: Judith Butler, *Undoing Gender* (London: Routledge, 2004); Bauer, *Hirschfeld Archives*.

67. Elena Mancini, *Magnus Hirschfeld and the Quest for Sexual Freedom* (New York: Palgrave Macmillan, 2010), 58, see also 81–82; Dose, *Magnus Hirschfeld*, 73–74.

68. Dose, *Magnus Hirschfeld*, 74–75.

69. On these activities see, for example, Bauer, *Hirschfeld Archives*; Atina Grossmann, *Reforming Sex: The German Movement for Birth Control and Abortion Reform,*

1920–1950 (New York: Oxford University Press, 1995), 16–17. Dose notes that while Hirschfeld founded his Institute using his own money, his reasons were not entirely altruistic, but with a view to earning the prestigious imperial title of "Medical Councilor" (*Sanitätsrat*): Dose, *Magnus Hirschfeld*, 51–52.

70. Magnus Hirschfeld, *Naturgesetze der Liebe: eine gemeinverständliche Untersuchung über den Liebes-Eindruck, Liebes-Drang und Liebes-Ausdruck* (Berlin: Pulvermacher, 1912). This work is discussed in Magnus Hirschfeld, *Die Homosexualität des Mannes und des Weibes*, 2nd ed. (Berlin: Louis Marcus, 1920), 377, 416. See also Magnus Hirschfeld, "Operative Behandlung der Homosexualität," *Vierteljahresberichte des Wissenschaftlich–humanitären Komitees/Jahrbuch für sexuelle Zwischenstufen* 17 (1917): 189–90; Magnus Hirschfeld, "Hodenbefunde bei intersexuellen Varianten," *Archiv für Frauenkunde und Eugenetik* 7 (1921): 173–74; Magnus Hirschfeld, "Ist die Homosexualität körperlich oder seelisch bedingt?," *Münchener medizinische Wochenschrift* 65 (1918): 298–99. On Hirschfeld's theoretical articulation of the "sexual intermediaries" and homosexual rights activism see Sengoopta, "Glandular Politics."

71. Magnus Hirschfeld, "Kastratenstudien. Untersuchungen über sexuellen Chemismus," *Sexual-Probleme* 8, no. 2 (1912): 81–95; U. Duerst, "E. Steinach, Willkürliche Umwandlung von Säugetieremännchen in Tiere [*sic*] mit ausgeprägt weiblichen Geschlechtscharakteren und weiblicher Psyche. Arch. f. ges. Physiologie, Bd. 144, S. 71–108. V Tafeln. Bonn 1912 [Review]," *Sexual-Probleme* 8, no. 8 (1912): 590–92; Arno Ed. Lampé and Eduard Strauss, "Die Bedeutung der Organe mit innerer Sekretion für sexualpsychologische und -pathologische Fragestellungen," *Sexual-Probleme* 8, no. 8 (1912): 541–46; E. Stechow, "E. Steinach. Geschlechtstrieb und echt sekundäre Geschlechtsmerkmale als Folge der innersekretorischen Funktion der Keimdrüsen. Zentralbl. f. Physiologie. Bd. 24. Nr. 13. 1910. 18 S. [Review]," *Sexual-Probleme* 7, no. 9 (1911): 652–54.

72. Hirschfeld, *Die Homosexualität*, 416, see also 377.

73. Hirschfeld considers Freud's position on degeneration theory in detail, approvingly noting the psychoanalyst's acknowledgement of Bloch's rejection of the degeneration hypothesis. See Hirschfeld, 378, citing Freud, "Drei Abhandlungen" (2nd ed., 1910), 5. On Hirschfeld's stance on evolution and degeneration see Harry Oosterhuis, *Stepchildren of Nature: Krafft-Ebing, Psychiatry, and the Making of Sexual Identity* (Chicago: University of Chicago Press, 2000), 66–67; Mancini, *Magnus Hirschfeld*, 78–83; Marhoefer, *Sex and the Weimar Republic*, 136–38.

74. See Trask, "Remaking Men," 183. Trask also notes official recognition of this work, with both Hirschfeld's Institute and Moll awarded substantial sums from the Prussian government for their work on soldier populations, 189.

75. Hirschfeld, "Untersuchungen und Forschungen," 13 and 16. On Bloch's discussion of homosexuality as traceable to an embryonic stage see Iwan Bloch, *Das Sexualleben unserer Zeit in seinen Beziehungen zur modernen Kultur* (Berlin: Marcus, 1907), 589.

76. Hirschfeld, 12, 14–16. Hirschfeld engages in further self-promotion when he cites Steinach citing himself: "Permanent homosexuality, or that which occurs in the lives of individuals, can be traced back to the presence of a hermaphroditic puberty gland, as Hirschfeld correctly presumed when he speaks of the inborn homosexual disposition": Eugen Steinach, "Pubertätsdrüsen und Zwitterbildung," *Archiv für Entwick-*

lungsmechanik 42 (1916): 307, cited in Hirschfeld, 16–17. He also places Steinach's work within a longer genealogy of endocrinological research, including Moritz Nussbaum's fin de siècle frog testicle experiments. On the latter, see Sengoopta, *Most Secret Quintessence*, 231n52; M. Nussbaum, "Innere Sekretion und Nerveneinfluß," *Ergebnisse der Anatomie und Entwicklungsgeschichte* 15 (1905): 78–80.

77. Schmidt, "Allies," 133.

78. Magnus Hirschfeld, introduction to Kronfeld, *Über psychosexuellen Infantilismus*, vii–viii.

79. For further examination of Hirschfeld's shifting relationship to Freud and psychoanalysis see Manfred Herzer, *Magnus Hirschfeld: Leben und Werk eines jüdischen, schwulen und sozialistischen Sexologen*, 2., überarbeitete Aufl. (Hamburg: MännerschwarmSkript Verlag, 2001), 153–97; Mancini, *Magnus Hirschfeld*, 71–78.

80. Magnus Hirschfeld, *Geschlechtliche Entwicklungsstörungen mit besonderer Berücksichtigung der Onanie*, 1st ed., vol. 1, *Sexualpathologie. Ein Lehrbuch für Ärzte und Studierende* (Bonn: A. Marcus & E. Webers, 1917), 80.

81. Hirschfeld, *Geschlechtskunde*, vol. 1. Die körperseelischen Grundlagen, 225–26 (emphasis in original). In 1905 Freud had thrown a similar charge against Eugen Bleuler, successor to Forel as director of Burghölzli in 1898. As Makari observes, "Freud's stance made it impossible for Bleuler to have legitimate scientific questions that did not revert to his unconscious motives": George Makari, *Revolution in Mind: The Creation of Psychoanalysis* (New York: Harper, 2008), 257.

82. Hirschfeld, *Geschlechtskunde*, vol. 1. Die körperseelischen Grundlagen, 203, 208.

83. As noted in the Introduction, Foucault discusses the "rupture" caused by psychoanalysis to the "perversion-heredity-degenerescence system" in Foucault, *The History of Sexuality*, vol. 1, 119; see also 130, 150.

84. Isidor Sadger, "Fragment der Psychoanalyse eines Homosexuellen," *Jahrbuch für sexuelle Zwischenstufen* 9 (1908): 346. See also S. [*sic*] Sadger, "Ist die konträre Sexualempfindung heilbar," *Zeitschrift für Sexualwissenschaft* 1, no. 12 (1908): 712–20.

85. Sigmund Freud, "The Psychogenesis of a Case of Homosexuality in a Woman (1920)," vol. 18, *The Complete Psychological Works*, 151.

86. Freud, 171, 168.

87. E. Hitschmann, "Psychoanalyse trotz Hormonen," *Allgemeine Zeitschrift für Psychotherapie und psychische Hygiene* 1, no. 4 (1928): 478. For a similar view on the attractiveness of analysis in light of the unreliability of hormone treatments, see Max Hirsch, "Psychoanalyse oder Hormonbehandlung," *Archiv für Frauenkunde* 14, no. 5 (1928): 445.

88. Hermann Rohleder, *Moderne Behandlung der Homosexualität und Impotenz durch Hodeneinpflanzung* (Berlin: Fischer's medizinische Buchhandlung, 1917), 25. On Rohleder, see Andrea Hommel, "Hermann Rohleder (1866–1934) und die Anfänge der künstlichen Befruchtung in Deutschland," *Medizinhistorisches Journal* 29, no. 2 (1994): 121–48. Sengoopta emphasizes that research into glandular solutions for female homosexuality at this period remained at a very preliminary stage: Sengoopta, *Most Secret Quintessence*, 255n75. On contemporary sexological theories of female homosexuality see Katharina Rowold, "A Male Mind in a Female Body: Sexology,

Homosexuality, and the Woman Question in Germany, 1869–1914," in *From Physico-Theology to Bio-Technology: Essays in the Social and Cultural History of Biosciences* (Amsterdam: Rodopi, 1998), 153–79.

89. Freud, "Psychogenesis," 171–72.

90. Sigmund Freud, "Letter from Sigmund Freud to Anonymous, April 9, 1935," in *Letters from Sigmund Freud, 1873–1939*, ed. Ernst L. Freud (London: Hogarth, 1961), 423–24. The original letter is reproduced in Sigusch, *Geschichte der Sexualwissenschaft*, 272–73.

91. Ellis also notes Moll's skepticism concerning this method in his short book on homosexual therapy. Letter, Ellis to Haire, 17 September 1921. Norman Haire Papers, University of Sydney: HAIRE No. 3.16.1 (1) Norman Haire / Havelock Ellis correspondence 1921–1933. See also Albert Moll, *Behandlung der Homosexualität: biochemisch oder psychisch?* (Bonn: Marcus & Weber, 1921).

92. See Dose, *Magnus Hirschfeld*, 73–74; Rainer Herrn, "On the History of Biological Theories of Homosexuality," in *Sex, Cells, and Same-Sex Desire: The Biology of Sexual Preference*, eds. John P. de Cecero and David Allen Parker (Abingdon, UK: Routledge, 2013), 46; Logan, *Hormones*, 4; Sengoopta, *Most Secret Quintessence*, 81–82; Seeck, *Durch Wissenschaft*, 47–48.

93. George Sylvester Viereck, *Glimpses of the Great* (New York: Macauley, 1930), 266. Cited in Sengoopta, *Most Secret Quintessence*, 81.

94. Kronfeld, *Über psychosexuellen Infantilismus*, 67–68.

95. On Moll's rejection of the castration method see Sigusch, *Geschichte der Sexualwissenschaft*, 216.

96. Kronfeld, *Über psychosexuellen Infantilismus*, 66.

97. Logan, *Hormones*, 8; Trask, "Remaking Men," 206; Sengoopta, *Most Secret Quintessence*, 100–115.

98. Kronfeld, *Über psychosexuellen Infantilismus*, 67.

99. Sigmund Freud, "The Question of Lay Analysis (1926)," in *The Essentials of Psycho-Analysis*, trans. James Strachey (London: Vintage, 2005), 72.

100. Heinrich Meng, "Sexualpädagogik & Psychoanalyse," in *World League for Sexual Reform (Proceedings of the Second Congress): Sexual Reform Congress Copenhagen 1–5: VII; 1928*, eds. Hertha Riese and J. H. Leunbach (Copenhagen; Leipzig: Levin & Munksgaard; Georg Thieme, 1929), 133. On Meng, a member of the Association of Socialist Physicians and later cofounder of the Frankfurt Psychoanalytic Institute, see Veronika Fuechtner, *Berlin Psychoanalytic: Psychoanalysis and Culture in Weimar Republic Germany and Beyond* (Berkeley: University of California Press, 2011), 10–11, 75–78; Makari, *Revolution*, 398–99.

101. Sigmund Freud, "Lecture XXXIV: Explanations, Applications and Orientations," in *Sigmund Freud, New Introductory Lectures on Psycho-Analysis*, ed. and trans. James Strachey (London: Hogarth, 1974), 154.

CHAPTER 5

1. Helene Stöcker, "Die Ehe als psychologisches Problem," in *Sexualnot und Sexualreform. Verhandlungen der Weltliga für Sexualreform. IV. Kongress. Abgehalten zu*

Wien vom 16. bis 23. September 1930, ed. Herbert Steiner (Vienna: Elbemühl, 1931), 98. Emphases in original. On the influence of Romantic and Nietzschean philosophy on Stöcker's thought see Edward Ross Dickinson, *Sex, Freedom and Power in Imperial Germany, 1880–1914* (Cambridge, UK: Cambridge University Press, 2014), 190–91.

2. See Dickinson, *Sex, Freedom*, 190–214; Kirsten Leng, "Culture, Difference, and Sexual Progress in Turn-of-the-Century Europe: Cultural Othering and the German League for the Protection of Mothers and Sexual Reform, 1905–1914," *Journal of the History of Sexuality* 25, no. 1 (2016): 62–82; Kirsten Leng, *Sexual Politics and Feminist Science: Women Sexologists in Germany, 1900–1933* (Ithaca, NY: Cornell University Press, 2017); Kirsten Leng, "An 'Elusive' Phenomenon: Feminism, Sexual Science, and the Female Sex Drive, 1880–1914," *Centaurus, An International Journal of the History of Science and Its Cultural Aspects* 55, no. 2 (2013): 131–52; Kirsten Leng, "Permutations of the Third Sex: Sexology, Subjectivity, and Antimaternalist Feminism at the Turn of the Twentieth Century," *Signs: Journal of Women in Culture and Society* 40, no. 1 (2014): 227–54; Atina Grossmann, *Reforming Sex: The German Movement for Birth Control and Abortion Reform, 1920–1950* (New York: Oxford University Press, 1995); Atina Grossmann, "German Women Doctors from Berlin to New York: Maternity and Modernity in Weimar and Exile," *Feminist Studies* 19, no. 1 (1993): 65–88.

3. Dickinson, *Sex, Freedom*, 191–95; Leng, *Sexual Politics*, 74–75, 195–202; Edward Ross Dickinson, "Reflections on Feminism and Monism in the Kaiserreich, 1900–1913," *Central European History* 34, no. 2 (2001): 191; Tracie Matysik, *Reforming the Moral Subject: Ethics and Sexuality in Central Europe, 1890–1930* (Ithaca, NY: Cornell University Press, 2008), 70–81.

4. Magnus Hirschfeld, "Sexualreform im Sinne der Sexualwissenschaft," in *Sexual Reform Congress Copenhagen 1.-5.:VII:1928. W.L.S.R. World League for Sexual Reform/Weltliga für Sexualreform/Ligue mondiale pour la réforme sexuelle/ Tutmonda ligo por seksaj reformoj*, eds. Hertha Riese and J. H. Leunbach (Copenhagen: Levin & Munksgaard; Georg Thieme, 1929), 26, 29.

5. On Adler's break from Freudian psychoanalysis see George Makari, *Revolution in Mind: The Creation of Psychoanalysis* (New York: Harper, 2008), 257–67.

6. Stöcker, "Die Ehe als psychologisches Problem," 99.

7. Helene Deutsch, *Zur Psychoanalyse der weiblichen Sexualfunktionen* (Leipzig: Internationaler Psychoanalytischer Verlag, 1925).

8. See Lisa Appignanesi and John Forrester, *Freud's Women* (London: Basic Books, 1992); Mary Jo Buhle, *Feminism and Its Discontents: A Century of Struggle with Psychoanalysis* (Cambridge, MA: Harvard University Press, 1998); Christiane Ludwig-Körner, *Wiederentdeckt—Psychoanalytikerinnen in Berlin* (Gießen, Ger.: Psychosozial-Verlag, 1999); Joseph Schwartz, *Cassandra's Daughter: A History of Psychoanalysis* (London: Penguin, 1999); Nellie Thompson, "Early Women Psychoanalysts," *International Review of Psychoanalysis* 14 (1987): 391–408; Eli Zaretsky, *Secrets of the Soul: A Social and Cultural History of Psychoanalysis* (New York: Vintage, 2004), 193–216.

9. Paul Roazen, "Preface," in Helene Deutsch, *Psychoanalysis of the Sexual Functions of Women*, ed. Paul Roazen (London, New York: Karnac, 1991), xii–xiii. This was the first English translation of Deutsch's 1925 study; for more on her biography and intellectual contributions see Paul Roazen, *Helene Deutsch, a Psychoanalyst's Life*

(Garden City, NY: Anchor, 1985); Janet Sayers, *Mothers of Psychoanalysis: Helene Deutsch, Karen Horney, Anna Freud, Melanie Klein* (New York: Norton, 1921); Inge Stephan, *Die Gründerinnen der Psychoanalyse: Eine Entmythologisierung Sigmund Freuds in zwölf Frauenporträts* (Stuttgart: Kreuz, 1992).

10. Karen Horney, "Referat: Deutsch, Dr. Helene. Zur Psychologie der weiblichen Sexualfunktionen (Neue Arbeiten zur ärztlichen PsA. Nr. V.) Internat. PsA. Verlag, 1925," *Internationale Zeitschrift für Psychoanalyse* 11 (1925): 388.

11. Leng, *Sexual Politics*, 31. On the often intersectional exclusions at work in German sexual science in this period see also Heike Bauer, *The Hirschfeld Archives: Violence, Death, and Modern Queer Culture* (Philadelphia: Temple University Press, 2017).

12. In addition to the works by Leng, Dickinson, Matysik, and Grossmann cited above, historians of sexology have considered women's role in organizations such as the BfM and the WLSR (see below). Female analysts have been studied predominantly within a framework of psychoanalytic history or feminist theory, several key examples of which are cited in note 8 above.

13. Kathleen Canning, "Claiming Citizenship: Suffrage and Subjectivity in Germany after the First World War," in *Gender History in Practice: Historical Perspectives on Bodies, Class & Citizenship* (Ithaca, NY: Cornell University Press, 2006), 116–17. See also Renate Bridenthal, "Beyond Kinder, Küche, Kirche: Weimar Women at Work," *Central European History* 6, no. 2 (1973): 148–66; Susan Rouette, "Mothers and Citizens: Gender and Social Policy in Germany after the First World War," *Central European History* 30 (1997): 48–66; Michael Thomas Taylor, Annette F. Timm, and Rainer Herrn, eds., *Not Straight from Germany: Sexual Publics and Sexual Citizenship since Magnus Hirschfeld* (Ann Arbor: University of Michigan Press, 2017).

14. Edward Ross Dickinson, "'A Dark, Impenetrable Wall of Complete Incomprehension': The Impossibility of Heterosexual Love in Imperial Germany," *Central European History* 40 (2007): 467–97; George L. Mosse, *Nationalism and Sexuality: Respectability and Abnormal Sexuality in Modern Europe* (New York: H. Fertig, 1985).

15. See Katharina von Ankum, ed., *Women in the Metropolis: Gender and Modernity in Weimar Culture* (Berkeley: University of California Press, 1997); Claudia Breger, "Feminine Masculinities: Scientific and Literary Representations of 'Female Inversion' at the Turn of the Twentieth Century," *Journal of the History of Sexuality* 14, nos. 1/2 (January 2005): 76–106; Atina Grossmann, "Girlkultur or Thoroughly Rationalized Female: A New Woman in Weimar Germany?," in *Women in Culture and Politics: A Century of Change*, ed. Judith Friedlander et al. (Bloomington: Indiana University Press, 1986), 62–80; Marti M. Lybeck, *Desiring Emancipation: New Women and Homosexuality in Germany, 1890–1933* (Albany: State University of New York Press, 2014); Jill Suzanne Smith, *Berlin Coquette: Prostitution and the New German Woman, 1890–1933* (Ithaca, NY: Cornell University Press, 2013); Katie Sutton, *The Masculine Woman in Weimar Germany* (New York: Berghahn Books, 2011); Mara Taylor, "'We, Too, Belong to This Group of Krafft-Ebingers!' Women and Sexological Discourse in *Psychopathia Sexualis* and *Are They Women? Novel about the Third Sex*," in *Sexual-Textual Border-Crossings: Lesbian Identity in German-Language Literature, Film, and Culture. Yearbook of the Association of Third-Level Teachers of German in Ireland*, eds.

Rachel MagShamhráin, Hans-Walter Schmidt-Hannisa, and Sabine Strümper-Krobb (Konstanz, Ger.: Hartung-Gorre, 2010).

16. On the shifting possibilities of public discourse and political engagement in the Weimar era see Canning, "Claiming Citizenship"; Detlev Peukert, *The Weimar Republic: The Crisis of Classical Modernity*, trans. Richard Deveson (London: Penguin, 1991); Eric D. Weitz, *Weimar Germany: Promise and Tragedy* (Princeton, NJ: Princeton University Press, 2007). On the relaxation of censorship restrictions see Laurie Marhoefer, "'The Book Was a Revelation, I Recognized Myself in It': Lesbian Sexuality, Censorship, and the Queer Press in Weimar-Era Germany," *Journal of Women's History* 27, no. 2 (2015): 62–86.

17. On the German and Austrian sex reform movements see Dickinson, *Sex, Freedom*, 190–214; Grossmann, *Reforming Sex*; Leng, *Sexual Politics*; Elke-Vera Kotowski and Julius H. Schoeps, eds., *Magnus Hirschfeld. Ein Leben im Spannungsfeld von Wissenschaft, Politik und Gesellschaft* (Berlin: be.bra wissenschaft, 2004); Laurie Marhoefer, *Sex and the Weimar Republic: German Homosexual Emancipation and the Rise of the Nazis* (Toronto: Toronto UP, 2015); Britta McEwen, *Sexual Knowledge: Feeling, Fact and Social Reform in Vienna, 1900–1934* (New York: Berghahn Books, 2012); Andreas Pretzel, "Sexualreform im Spannungsfeld weltanschaulicher Voraussetzungen und sozialpolitischer Auseinandersetzungen," in *Verqueere Wissenschaft? Zum Verhältnis von Sexualwissenschaft und Sexualreformbewegung in Geschichte und Gegenwart*, eds. Ursula Ferdinand, Andreas Pretzel, and Andreas Seeck (Münster: LIT, 1998), 229–42; Kristine von Soden, *Die Sexualberatungsstellen der Weimarer Republik, 1919–1933* (Berlin: Hentrich, 1988). On feminist sex reformers and links to eugenics movements see Ann Taylor Allen, "Feminism and Eugenics in Germany and Britain, 1900–1940: A Comparative Perspective," *German Studies Review* 23, no. 3 (2000): 477–505; Ann Taylor Allen, "German Radical Feminism and Eugenics, 1900–1908," *German Studies Review* 11, no. 1 (1988): 31–56; Leng, "Permutations"; Cornelie Usborne, *The Politics of the Body in Weimar Germany: Women's Reproductive Rights and Duties* (Basingstoke, UK: Macmillan, 1992).

18. See Jill Suzanne Smith, "Richard Oswald and the Social Hygiene Film: Promoting Public Health or Promiscuity?," in *The Many Faces of Weimar Cinema: Rediscovering Germany's Filmic Legacy*, ed. Christian Rogowski (Rochester, NY: Camden House, 2010), 13–30; Ina Linge, "Sexology, Popular Science and Queer History in 'Anders als die Andern' ('Different from the Others')," *Gender & History* 30, no. 3 (2018): 1–16; Maria Makela, "Rejuvenation and Regen(d)eration: 'Der Steinachfilm,' Sex Glands, and Weimar-Era Visual and Literary Culture," *German Studies Review* 38, no. 1 (2015): 35–62; James Steakley, *"Anders als die Andern." Ein Film und seine Geschichte* (Hamburg: Männerschwarm, 2007).

19. Wilhelm Reich, "Die Sexualnot der werktätigen Massen und die Schwierigkeiten der Sexualreform," in *Sexualnot und Sexualreform. Verhandlungen der Weltliga für Sexualreform. IV. Kongress. Abgehalten zu Wien vom 16. bis 23. September 1930*, ed. Herbert Steiner (Vienna: Elbemühl, 1931), 72; Christine Diercks, "The Vienna Psychoanalytic Polyclinic ('Ambulatorium'): Wilhelm Reich and the Technical Seminar," *Psychoanalysis and History* 4, no. 1 (2008): 67–84; McEwen, *Sexual Knowledge*, 185–

87; Veronika Fuechtner, *Berlin Psychoanalytic: Psychoanalysis and Culture in Weimar Republic Germany and Beyond* (Berkeley: University of California Press, 2011).

20. Heike Bauer, *English Literary Sexology: Translations of Inversion, 1860–1930* (Basingstoke, UK: Palgrave Macmillan, 2009), 45, 49; Kate Fisher and Jana Funke, "'Let Us Leave the Hospital; Let Us Go on a Journey around the World': British and German Sexual Science and the Global Search for Sexual Variation," in *A Global History of Sexual Science, 1880–1960*, eds. Veronika Fuechtner, Douglas E. Haynes, and Ryan M. Jones (Oakland: University of California Press, 2018), 53.

21. The proceedings were published as A. Weil and Institut für Sexualwissenschaft, Berlin, eds., *Sexualreform und Sexualwissenschaft. Vorträge gehalten auf der I. Internationalen Tagung für Sexualreform auf sexualwissenschaftlicher Grundlage in Berlin* (Berlin: Julius Püttmann, 1922).

22. Hertha Riese and J. H. Leunbach, eds., *Sexual Reform Congress Copenhagen 1.-5.:VII:1928. W.L.S.R. World League for Sexual Reform/Weltliga für Sexualreform/ Ligue mondiale pour la réforme sexuelle/ Tutmonda ligo por seksaj reformoj* (Copenhagen: Levin & Munksgaard; Georg Thieme, 1929).

23. For an overview of the League's history see Ralf Dose, "The World League for Sexual Reform: Some Possible Approaches," *Journal of the History of Sexuality* 12, no. 1 (2003): 1–15; Manfred Herzer, *Magnus Hirschfeld und seine Zeit* (Berlin: de Gruyter, 2017), 310-25. On the British Society see Lesley A. Hall, "'Disinterested Enthusiasm for Sexual Misconduct': The British Society for the Study of Sex Psychology, 1913–1947," *Journal of Contemporary History* 30 (1995): 665–86.

24. Cited in Grossmann, *Reforming Sex*, 41.

25. Magnus Hirschfeld, "Presidential Address: The Development and Scope of Sexology," in *W.L.S.R. World League for Sexual Reform. Proceedings of the Third Congress (London)*, ed. Norman Haire (London: Kegan Paul, 1930), xi–xv.

26. Norman Haire, ed., *W.L.S.R. World League for Sexual Reform. Proceedings of the Third Congress (London)*. For a list of psychoanalytic speakers at the 1929 meeting see Ivan Crozier, "'All the World's a Stage': Dora Russell, Norman Haire, and the 1929 London World League for Sexual Reform Congress," *Journal of the History of Sexuality* 12, no. 1 (2003): 32–33.

27. Friedjung in P[aul] Krische, "Generalversammlung/Annual Convention," in *Sexualnot und Sexualreform. Verhandlungen der Weltliga für Sexualreform. IV. Kongress. Abgehalten zu Wien vom 16. bis 23. September 1930* (Vienna: Elbemühl, 1931), xxvii.

28. Magnus Hirschfeld, "Einführungswort des Vorsitzenden," in *Sexualnot und Sexualreform. Verhandlungen der Weltliga für Sexualreform. IV. Kongress. Abgehalten zu Wien vom 16. bis 23. September 1930*, ed. Herbert Steiner (Vienna: Elbemühl, 1931), xxxvii. On the Vienna meeting see McEwen, *Sexual Knowledge*, 175–95.

29. Herbert Steiner, ed., "Eröffnung des Kongresses (Begrüßungsansprachen)," in *Sexualnot und Sexualreform. Verhandlungen der Weltliga für Sexualreform. IV. Kongress. Abgehalten zu Wien vom 16. bis 23. September 1930* (Vienna: Elbemühl, 1931), xxxi, xxxiv.

30. McEwen, *Sexual Knowledge*, 175–195 on the Vienna meeting. See also Fisher and Funke, "'Let Us Leave'"; Leng, *Sexual Politics*, 265, 279n46.

31. This now-rare journal is held at the New York Academy of Medicine. On Stekel's positioning in relation to other psychoanalysts of this era see Jaap Bos and Leendert Groenendijk, *The Self-Marginalization of Wilhelm Stekel: Freudian Circles Inside and Out* (New York: Springer, 2007).

32. Charles E. McClelland, *State, Society and University in Germany* (Cambridge, UK: Cambridge University Press, 1980), 250; Patricia M. Mazón, *Gender and the Modern Research University: The Admission of Women to German Higher Education, 1865–1914* (Stanford: Stanford University Press, 2003), 10–11; Lybeck, *Desiring Emancipation*, 17–48.

33. Leng, *Sexual Politics*, 61.

34. See Ann Taylor Allen, "Mothers of the New Generation: Adele Schreiber, Helene Stöcker, and the Evolution of a German Idea of Motherhood, 1900–1914," *Signs: Journal of Women in Culture and Society* 10, no. 3 (1985): 418–38; Dickinson, *Sex, Freedom*, 44–45, 191–96; Volkmar Sigusch, *Geschichte der Sexualwissenschaft* (Frankfurt am Main: Campus Verlag, 2008), 82–91; Christl Wickert, Brigitte Hamburger, and Marie Lienau, "Helene Stöcker and the Bund für Mutterschutz (The Society for the Protection of Motherhood)," *Women's Studies International Forum* 5, no. 6 (1982): 611–18.

35. Peter Gay, *Freud: A Life for Our Time* (New York: Norton, 1988), 503.

36. Sigmund Freud, "Einige psychische Folgen des anatomischen Geschlechtsunterschieds (1925)," in *Sigmund Freud Studienausgabe Band V: Sexualleben*, vol. 5, 258.

37. See Jill Scott, *Electra after Freud: Myth and Culture* (Ithaca, NY: Cornell University Press, 2005).

38. Sigmund Freud, "Über die Psychogenese eines Falls von weiblicher Homosexualität," *Internationale Zeitschrift für Psychoanalyse* 6, no. 1 (1920): 1-24; Sigmund Freud, "Einige psychische Folgen des anatomischen Geschlechtsunterschieds," *Internationale Zeitschrift für Psychoanalyse* 11 (1925): 401–10; Sigmund Freud, "Über die weibliche Sexualität," *Internationale Zeitschrift für Psychoanalyse* 17 (1931): 317–32. The editors of Freud's collected works discuss his relative lack of female cases in the preface to the 1925 essay at 254–55. The "dark continent" quote—Freud included these two words in English in the original essay—is from Sigmund Freud, "Die Frage der Laienanalyse (1926)," in *Sigmund Freud Studienausgabe. Ergänzungsband* (10 vols.), vol., 271–349.

39. See, for example, Peter Cryle and Alison Moore, *Frigidity: An Intellectual History* (Basingstoke, UK: Palgrave Macmillan, 2011), 216–47; Leng, *Sexual Politics*, 264–306.

40. As Leng observes, such stigmatization sat in tension with the older sexological tendency to label sexually unrestrained women as "nymphomaniacs," a label underpinned by eugenic fears of unconstrained sexual freedom. Leng, *Sexual Politics*, 110–11.

41. Cryle and Moore, *Frigidity*, 4–5.

42. Cryle and Moore, *Frigidity*, 204.

43. On Krafft-Ebing and Schrenck-Notzing see Cryle and Moore, 194–203. Schrenck-Notzing is cited at p. 201.

44. On Ellis and Adler, see Cryle and Moore, 206–13. See also Otto Adler, *Die*

mangelhafte Geschlechtsempfindung des Weibes. Anaesthesia sexualis feminarum. Dyspareunia. Anaphrodisia [1904], 3rd ed. (Berlin: Kornfeld, 1919).

45. Adler, in Cryle and Moore, *Frigidity*, 212. For broader discussion of Adler's text see pp. 206–12.

46. Hitschmann, "Adler, San.-Rat Dr. Otto: Die mangelhafte Geschlechtsempfindung des Weibes. Fischers med. Buchhandlung H. Kornfeld, Berlin, 1924 [Review]," *Internationale Zeitschrift für Psychoanalyse* 11 (1925): 494.

47. Wilhelm Stekel, *Die Geschlechtskälte der Frau (Eine psychopathologie des weiblichen Liebeslebens)*, vol. 3., *Störungen des Trieb- und Affektlebens*, 2nd rev. ed. (Berlin: Urban & Schwarzenberg, 1921).

48. Wilhelm Stekel, *Frigidity in Woman in Relation to Her Love Life*, trans. James S. Van Teslaar, vol. 1, *Disorders of the Instincts and the Emotions. The Parapathia Disorders* (New York: Liveright, 1926), 101, 108.

49. Stekel, in Cryle and Moore, *Frigidity*, 218; see also discussion at 216–21.

50. Wilhelm Stekel, *Frigidity*, vol. 2, 276.

51. Stekel, *Frigidity*, vol. 2, 275.

52. Stekel in Cryle and Moore, *Frigidity*, 221.

53. Cryle and Moore, *Frigidity*, 222–47.

54. Cryle and Moore, *Frigidity*, 236–38.

55. See Leng's in-depth analysis of Vaerting's two-volume study *New Foundations of the Psychology of Man and Woman* (1921, 1923) and Lazarfeld's *Woman's Experience of the Male* (1931): Leng, *Sexual Politics*, 264–305.

56. Fuechtner, *Berlin Psychoanalytic*, 149.

57. See Karen Horney, "Zur Genese des weiblichen Kastrationskomplexes," *Internationale Zeitschrift für Psychoanalyse* 9 (1923): 12–26; Karen Horney, "The Flight from Womanhood: The Masculinity Complex in Women as Viewed by Men and Women," *International Journal of Psycho-Analysis* 7, no. 3/4 (1926): 314–39. On Horney's reputation and politics see Fuechtner, *Berlin Psychoanalytic*, 66, 148; Dagmar Herzog, *Cold War Freud: Psychoanalysis in an Age of Catastrophes* (Cambridge, UK: Cambridge University Press, 2017), 26–27; Makari, *Revolution*, 380–81; Susan Quinn, *A Mind of Her Own: The Life of Karen Horney* (Reading, MA: Addison-Wesley, 1988), 196–97.

58. Quinn, *A Mind of Her Own*, 63–66. For a summary of Stöcker's "New Ethic" see Dickinson, *Sex, Freedom*, 44–45, 193; Leng, *Sexual Politics*, 200–201, 328–29; Matysik, *Reforming*, 55–93.

59. Karen Horney, "Gehemmte Weiblichkeit. Psychoanalytischer Beitrag zum Problem der Frigidität," *Zeitschrift für Sexualwissenschaft* 13, no. 2 (1926): 67.

60. Horney, 68–73. On the "masculinity complex" see also Karen Horney, "Der Männlichkeitskomplex der Frau," *Archiv für Frauenkunde* 13, no. 1–2 (1927): 141–54.

61. Herzog, *Cold War Freud*, 26.

62. Horney, "Gehemmte Weiblichkeit," 72–73.

63. Horney, 76–77. In his essay on female sexuality, Freud had similarly drawn comparisons with "primitives" on matters such as breastfeeding practices. Sigmund Freud, "Über die weibliche Sexualität (1931)," in *Sigmund Freud Studienausgabe Band V*, vol. 5, 283.

64. See Leng, *Sexual Politics*, chapter 4.

65. Horney, "The Flight from Womanhood." This concept is examined in Herzog, *Cold War Freud*, 26; Quinn, *A Mind of Her Own*, 222–23.

66. Suzanne Gordon, "Helene Deutsch and the Legacy of Freud," *New York Times*, July 30, 1978, sec. SM, 6.

67. Pelin Gul, "Profile of Helene Deutsch," ed. A. Rutherford, *Psychology's Feminist Voices Multimedia Internet Archive*, 2010, http://www.feministvoices.com/helene-deutsch/; Roazen, *Helene Deutsch*; Brenda S. Webster, "Helene Deutsch: A New Look," *Signs: Journal of Women in Culture and Society* 10, no. 3 (1985): 553–71.

68. Deutsch, *Psychoanalyse*, 61.

69. See Sigmund Freud, "Drei Abhandlungen zur Sexualtheorie (1905)," in *Sigmund Freud Studienausgabe Band V: Sexualleben*, vol. 5, 124–25; Freud, "Über die weibliche Sexualität (1931)," 278.

70. Editorial preface, Freud, "Einige psychische Folgen," 2000, 256.

71. Vaerting, *The Dominant Sex* (1923), in Leng, *Sexual Politics*, 275, 281 (citing Vaerting, 51).

72. Freud, "Über die weibliche Sexualität (1931)," 290–91.

73. Freud, "Einige psychische Folgen," 2000, 259–64.

74. Freud, 266.

75. Deutsch, *Psychoanalyse*, 64, 44–45.

76. Joan Riviere, "Womanliness as a Masquerade," *International Journal of Psychoanalysis* 10 (1929): 303–13. In recent decades, these ideas have been taken up by feminist and queer theorists; see, for example, Judith Butler, *Gender Trouble: Feminism and the Subversion of Identity* (New York: Routledge, 1999), 61–73.

77. Deutsch, *Psychoanalyse*, 63–64. Deutsch also compares female and male sublimation in Helene Deutsch, "Psychologie des Weibes in den Funktionen der Fortpflanzung," *Internationale Zeitschrift für ärztliche Psychoanalyse* 11 (1925): 49.

78. Helene Deutsch, "Der feminine Masochismus und seine Beziehung zur Frigidität. Vortrag auf dem XI. Internationalen Psychoanalytischen Kongreß in Oxford im Juli 1929," *Internationale Zeitschrift für ärztliche Psychoanalyse* 16 (1930): 172–84.

79. Deutsch, 173. See also Horney, "Männlichkeitskomplex."

80. Deutsch, "Der feminine Masochismus," 176. Abraham and Horney had also published on the female castration complex in the years before Deutsch's piece, see Karl Abraham, "Äußerungsformen des weiblichen Kastrationskomplexes," *Internationale Zeitschrift für Psychoanalyse* 7, no. 4 (1921): 422–52; Horney, "Zur Genese."

81. See Kate Millett, *Sexual Politics* (New York: Avon Books, 1969), 176–203.

82. Irigaray in Cryle and Moore, *Frigidity*, 209. On Irigaray's criticism see also Elizabeth Grosz, *Sexual Subversions: Three French Feminists* (Sydney: Allen & Unwin, 1989), 133. The Freudian insistence on discussing female sexuality in relation to male norms has been the target of several decades of feminist criticism, with scholars frequently pointing to Freud's "phallocentric anti-female bias" (Richard C. Friedman and Jennifer I. Downey, "Psychoanalysis and the Model of Homosexuality as Psychopathology: A Historical Overview," *American Journal of Psychoanalysis* 58, no. 3 [1998]: 249–50.) For examples and discussions of this scholarship see Buhle, *Feminism and Its Discontents*; Richard Feldstein and Judith Roof, eds., *Feminism and Psychoanalysis*

(Ithaca, NY: Cornell University Press, 1989); Jane Gallop, *The Daughter's Seduction: Feminism and Psychoanalysis* (Ithaca, NY: Cornell University Press, 1982); Julie Mitchell, *Psychoanalysis and Feminism* (London: Allen Lane, 1974); Scott, *Electra*, 3, 8n9.

83. Deutsch, "Der feminine Masochismus," 177.

84. Deutsch, 179.

85. Deutsch, 182.

86. Deutsch, 184.

87. Hugo Sellheim, "Macht der Sport die Frau glücklich? Ein Epilog zu den Deutschen Frauen-Meisterschaften in Magdeburg 1931," *Uhu*, no. 1 (1931): 18–24. Sellheim also regularly wrote for sexological and gynecological journals during this period.

88. Prof. Dr. med. Ratner, "Über die Psyche des Weibes," *Zeitschrift für Sexualwissenschaft* 6 (1919): 350–51.

89. I explore such conservative critiques in more detail in Sutton, *The Masculine Woman*.

90. Deutsch, "Der feminine Masochismus," 184.

91. Webster, "Helene Deutsch," 554.

92. Stöcker in Dickinson, *Sex, Freedom*, 197. On maternal feminism see also Grossmann, "German Women Doctors"; Allen, "German Radical Feminism"; Leng, *Sexual Politics*, 184–220.

93. McEwen, *Sexual Knowledge*, 12; Leng, *Sexual Politics*, 293–94.

94. Leng, *Sexual Politics*, 290–306. See also Martina Siems, *Sofie Lazarsfeld. Die Wiederentdeckung einer individualpsychologischen Pionierin* (Göttingen: V&R Unipress, 2015).

95. Olga Knopf, "Über Frigidität," *Internationale Zeitschrift für Individualpsychologie. Arbeiten aus dem Gebiete der Psychotherapie, Psychologie und Pädagogik*, no. 1 (1930): 151–59.

96. Knopf, "Über Frigidität," 151.

97. Knopf, "Über Frigidität," 153 (emphasis in original). As Dickinson observes, the "affirmation of life" (*Lebensbejahung*) was a central concept in early-twentieth-century sex reform, seen as an essential creative force. It was first formulated by Wilhelm Bölsche, who had popularized Darwinian ideas in his study *Love-Life in Nature* (1898–1901): Dickinson, *Sex, Freedom*, 199.

98. Knopf, "Über Frigidität," 154.

99. Knopf, "Über Frigidität," 155, 158.

100. Here I follow Leng's application of Haraway's term to women sexologists of this era. See Kirsten Leng, "The Personal Is Scientific: Women, Gender, and the Production of Sexological Knowledge in Germany and Austria, 1900–1931," *History of Psychology* 18, no. 3 (2015): 239; Donna Haraway, "Situated Knowledges: The Science Question in Feminism and the Privilege of Partial Perspective," *Feminist Studies* 14, no. 3 (1988): 575–99.

101. Leng, *Sexual Politics*, 117; Heike Bauer, "Theorizing Female Inversion: Sexology, Discipline, and Gender at the Fin de Siècle," *Journal of the History of Sexuality* 18, no. 1 (2009): 84–102.

102. Birgit Lang and Katie Sutton, "The Queer Cases of Psychoanalysis: Rethinking the Scientific Study of Homosexuality, 1890s–1920s," *German History* 34, no. 3 (2016): 438.

103. Freud, " Psychogenese," 2.

104. Freud, 4–5.

105. Käthe Hoffmann, "Freud, Sigm.: 'Über die Psychogenese eines Falls von weiblicher Homosexualität' [Review]" *Zeitschrift für Sexualwissenschaft* 8, no. 2 (1921): 79–80. See also Freud, "Psychogenese," 1. Most of the in-depth psychoanalytic analyses of female homosexuality are relatively recent, as discussed in Maggie Magee and Diana C. Miller, *Lesbian Lives: Psychonanalytic Narratives Old and New* (London: Analytic Press, 1997); Judith M. Glasgold and Suzanne Iasenza, eds., *Lesbians and Psychoanalysis: Past to Present: Rethinking Theories* (New York: Free Press, 1995).

106. Erich Stern, "Zur Kennntnis der weiblichen Inversion," *Zeitschrift für Sexualwissenschaft* 7 (1920): 197–202 (emphasis in original).

107. Julie Bender, "Zur Frage der Homosexualität der Frau," *Zeitschrift für Sexualwissenschaft* 7 (1920): 324–26.

108. Dickinson, *Sex, Freedom*, 210.

109. See Helene Stöcker, "Homosexualität und Geschlechtsbewertung," *Geschlecht und Gesellschaft* 9, no. 7 (1914): 273-83, cited in Dickinson, *Sex, Freedom*, 210–11. On prewar debates about female homosexuality see also Lybeck, *Desiring Emancipation*, 83–116; Tracie Matysik, "In the Name of the Law: The 'Female Homosexual' and the Criminal Code in Fin de Siècle Germany," *Journal of the History of Sexuality* 13, no. 1 (2004): 26–48.

110. Leng, "The Personal," 241.

111. Johanna Elberskirchen, *Die Liebe des dritten Geschlechts. Homosexualität, eine bisexuelle Varietät keine Entartung-keine Schuld* (Leipzig: Max Spohr, 1904), 4. See discussion in Leng, "The Personal," 242, 244. See also Dickinson, *Sex, Freedom*, 211; Leng, *Sexual Politics*, 139–44. In an example of Elberskirchen's legacy for today's gay and queer rights movements, there are now plans in Berlin to establish an "Elberskirchen-Hirschfeld-Haus" as a museum and home for currently scattered LGBTIQ archival holdings: http://e2h.berlin.

112. Leng, *Sexual Politics*, 115–51 (Rüling is cited at 137).

113. Max Marcuse, "Über die Problematik der Sexualpsychologie des Weibes und der vergleichenden Sexualpsychologie der Geschlechter," *Zeitschrift für Sexualwissenschaft* 6, no. 9 (1919): 273–83; Julie Bender, "Sexualpsychologie des Weibes und Ärztin," *Zeitschrift für Sexualwissenschaft* 6 (1919): 351–52. Bender also authored a book during this period on sexual and social welfare: *Sexuelles Wohl und soziale Fürsorge* (Frankfurt am Main: Minjon-Verl. Pres. 1919).

114. Bender, "Sexualpsychologie," 352.

115. Freud, "Über die weibliche Sexualität (1931)," 276. Elsewhere in this essay Freud also acknowledges the work of Ruth Mack-Brunswick (287).

116. A. [Jeanne] Lampl-de Groot, "Zur Entwicklungsgeschichte des Ödipuskomplexes der Frau," *Internationale Zeitschrift für Psychoanalyse* 13, no. 3 (1927): 269–82. This reference is to the English version of the essay, published as A. Lampl-de Groot, "The Evolution of the Oedipus Complex in Women," *International Journal of Psychoanalysis* 9 (1928): 345.

117. Freud, "Psychogenese," 17.

118. Freud, "Über die weibliche Sexualität (1931)," 280n1. Cf. Horney, "The Flight from Womanhood"; Horney, "Zur Genese"; Karen Horney, "Die Verleugnung der Vagina," *Internationale Zeitschrift für Psychoanalyse* 19 (1933): 372–84. On Freud's positioning re women analysts see also Gay, *Freud: A Life*, 501–22.

119. Deutsch notes that she revised her already-drafted piece in response to Freud's. Helene Deutsch, "Über die weibliche Homosexualität," *Internationale Zeitschrift für Psychoanalyse* 18 (1932): 219n1.

120. Deutsch 1932, 221.

121. Deutsch, "Homosexualität," 231 (emphasis in original).

122. Leng, *Sexual Politics*, 11.

123. Freud, "Psychogenese," 22.

124. Freud, 22–23.

125. Deutsch, "Homosexualität," 234.

126. Freud, "Psychogenese," 21.

127. Freud, 8–13. This finding appears at p. 10; see also Lang and Sutton, "Queer Cases."

128. Deutsch, "Homosexualität," 237.

129. Deutsch, 239.

130. Roazen, "Preface," in Deutsch, *Psychoanalysis of the Sexual Function*, xv.

131. Freud, "Über die weibliche Sexualität (1931)," 275–76, 285.

132. Freud, 290.

133. See also Horney's discussion of Freud's focus on paternal overidentification in Horney, "Zur Genese," 22.

134. Deutsch, "Homosexualität," 225.

135. Herzog, *Cold War Freud*, 60.

136. Gay, *Freud: A Life*, 508. On Freud's reticence to engage directly with others' works see Roazen, Preface to Deutsch, *Psychoanalysis of the Sexual Function*, xii; and the editorial preface to Freud, "Über die weibliche Sexualität (1931)," 274.

137. Sara Ahmed, "'Making Feminist Points,'" *Feministkilljoys* (blog), September 11, 2013, http://feministkilljoys.com/2013/09/11/making-feminist-points. On the discursive power of citational practices see also Bauer, *Hirschfeld Archives*, 103, 109–17.

138. Herzog, *Cold War Freud*, 23, 26. On Horney's postwar impact on US psychoanalysis, and the schism in which she was later involved, see pp. 31–34.

CHAPTER 6

1. A note on gender and pronouns (I discuss my use of "transvestite" in the introduction to this book): where possible I follow the pronoun use that the sources indicate were preferred by historical subjects themselves, whether signaled directly or by an adopted name. Sometimes these pronouns comply with the sex assigned at birth, sometimes they do not. I also use the abbreviations, where relevant, AMAB for individuals assigned female but identifying as male or masculine, or AFAB for individuals assigned male but identifying as female or feminine (following the Oxford dictionary: https://

en.oxforddictionaries.com/definition/amab and https://en.oxforddictionaries.com/definition/afab. Where preferred pronouns are unclear, I use "they" and "their." In citing medical sources I reproduce the original texts, even though these often assigned pronouns by assigned birth sex rather than gender identity.

2. References to Hirschfeld's study in this chapter are to the second edition of 1925, which included a new preface by the author; the body of the text and page numbers are otherwise the same as the first edition, which appeared with the Med. Verlag Alfred Pulvermacher in Berlin in 1910. Magnus Hirschfeld, *Die Transvestiten: Eine Untersuchung über den erotischen Verkleidungstrieb*, 2nd ed. (Leipzig: Verlag "Wahrheit" Ferdinand Spohr, 1925), 6–14. Cited material at p. 9 (emphasis in original).

3. Wilhelm Stekel, "XV. Fragment der Analyse einer Transvestitin," in *Die Geschlechtskälte der Frau (Eine psychopathologie des weiblichen Liebeslebens)*, 2nd rev. ed. (Berlin: Urban & Schwarzenberg, 1921), 429–56. This volume appeared as part 3 of Stekel's series "Storüngen des Trieb -und Affektlebens (die parapathischen Erkrankungen)." In the following I cite the English translation, but note discrepancies with the German original as relevant: Wilhelm Stekel, "Fragmentary Analysis of a Transvestite," in *Frigidity in Woman, in Relation to Her Sex Life*, trans. James S. Van Teslaar, *Disorders of the Instincts and the Emotions: The Parapathiac Disorders* (New York: Liveright, 1943).

4. Toni Fricke, "Aus dem Empfindungsleben eines 'Transvestiten'! [Die Welt der Transvestiten]," *Die Freundin* 1, no. 2 (September 12, 1924): n.p.

5. Christa Putz, *Verordnete Lust: Sexualmedizin, Psychoanalyse und die "Krise der Ehe," 1870–1930* (Bielefeld, Ger.: Transcript, 2011), 178.

6. See, for example, Marhoefer's discussion of her adoption of a "microhistory" approach based on a single case, or Evans's close examination of the erotic photography of Herbert Tobias as offering insights into the "changing optics of queer desire in the second half of the twentieth century": Laurie Marhoefer, "Lesbianism, Transvestitism, and the Nazi State: A Microhistory of a Gestapo Investigation, 1939–1943," *American Historical Review* 121, no. 4 (2016): 1172; Jennifer Evans, "Seeing Subjectivity: Erotic Photography and the Optics of Desire," *American Historical Review* 118, no. 2 (2013): 433.

7. Scott Spector, *Violent Sensations: Sex, Crime & Utopia in Vienna and Berlin, 1860–1914* (Chicago: University of Chicago Press, 2016), 117; Michel Foucault, *The History of Sexuality*, vol. 1, 45 (emphasis in original).

8. The classification of human "kinds," according to Hacking, can change how people designated as "of that kind" see themselves: "that is, new knowledge about 'the criminal' or 'the homosexual' becomes known to the people classified, changes the way these individuals behave, and loops back to force changes in the classifications and knowledge about them." See Ian Hacking, *The Social Construction of What?* (Cambridge, MA: Harvard University Press, 1999), 105.

9. Sigmund Freud, "Psycho-Analytic Notes on an Autobiographical Account of a Case of Paranoia (Dementia Paranoides)," in *The Complete Psychological Works,* vol. 12. 1911–1913: The Case of Schreber, Papers on Technique and Other Works.

10. On these terminological parallels and shifts see Heike Bauer, "Theorizing Female Inversion: Sexology, Discipline, and Gender at the Fin de Siècle," *Journal of the*

History of Sexuality 18, no. 1 (2009): 84–102; Gert Hekma, "'A Female Soul in a Male Body': Sexual Inversion as Gender Inversion in Nineteenth-Century Sexology," in *Third Sex, Third Gender: Beyond Sexual Dimorphism in Culture and History*, ed. Gilbert Herdt (New York: Zone Books, 1994), 213–39; George Chauncey Jr., "From Sexual Inversion to Homosexuality: The Changing Medical Conceptualization of Female 'Deviance,'" in *Passion and Power: Sexuality in History*, eds. Kathy Peiss, Christina Simmons, and Robert A. Padgug (Philadelphia: Temple University Press, 1989), 87–117; Robert Deam Tobin, *Peripheral Desires: The German Discovery of Sex* (Philadelphia: University of Pennsylvania Press, 2015), 1–25.

11. On the masculinist homoeroticists see chapter 2. On the associations of the "masculine" woman with homosexuality see chapter 5. On how scholars have tended to overlook the transgender component of historical and medical accounts of inversion in favor of homosexuality, see Jay Prosser, "Transsexuals and the Transsexologists: Inversion and the Emergence of Transsexual Subjectivity," in *Sexology in Culture: Labelling Bodies and Desires*, eds. Lucy Bland and Laura Doan (Cambridge, UK: Polity, 1998), 116–31.

12. Hirschfeld, *Die Transvestiten*. On the gender imbalance and taxonomical problems plaguing Hirschfeld's discussion of transvestite cases, see Vern L. Bullough and Bonnie Bullough, *Cross Dressing, Sex, and Gender* (Philadelphia: University of Pennsylvania Press, 1993), 208; Darryl Hill, "Sexuality and Gender in Hirschfeld's *Die Transvestiten*: A Case of the 'Elusive Evidence of the Ordinary,'" *Journal of the History of Sexuality* 14, no. 3 (2005): 316–32; Geertje Mak, "'Passing Women' im Sprechzimmer von Magnus Hirschfeld. Warum der Begriff 'Transvestit' nicht für Frauen in Männerkleidern eingeführt wurde (transl. Mirjam Hausmann)," *Österreichische Zeitschrift für Geschichtswissenschaften* 9, no. 3 (1998): 384–99. As Mak notes, Hirschfeld did address female-to-male identifications in more detail in his extensive historical section.

13. Magnus Hirschfeld, "Die intersexuelle Konstitution," *Jahrbuch für sexuelle Zwischenstufen* 23 (1923): 3–27.

14. Havelock Ellis, "Sexo-Aesthetic Inversion," *Alienist and Neurologist* 34, nos. 2 (May) and 3 (August) (1913): 156–67 and 249-79; Havelock Ellis, *Eonism and Other Supplementary Studies* (7 vols.), vol. 7, *Studies in the Psychology of Sex* (Philadelphia: F. A. Davis, 1928). Ellis's article on sexo-aesthetic inversion also appeared one year later in German: Havelock Ellis, "Sexo-ästhetische Inversion," *Zeitschrift für Psychotherapie und medizinische Psychologie* 5 (1914): 134–62.

15. Letter, Ellis to Haire, 3 March 1925. Norman Haire Papers, University of Sydney: HAIRE No. 3.16.1 (1) Norman Haire/Havelock Ellis correspondence 1921–1933.

16. Ellis, *Eonism*, vol. 7, 27–28, 36, 101.

17. Ellis, *Eonism*, vol. 7, 32.

18. Karsch-Haack discussed his term "Transmutist" in a range of Weimar-era "third sex" publications; see for example Ferdinand Karsch-Haack, "Transvestismus und Aberglauben [Die Welt der Transvestiten]" 5, no. 14 (October 2, 1929); Ferdinand Karsch-Haack, "Junggesellin und Junggeselle (Die Transmutistin)," *Garçonne* 4 (1931): 1–4. See also Max Marcuse, "Ein Fall von Geschlechtsumwandlungstrieb," *Zeitschrift für Psychotherapie und medizinische Psychologie* 6 (1916): 176–93; P. Näcke, "Kriminologische und sexologische Studien. I. Zum Kapitel der Transvestiten nebst Bemerkungen

zur weiblicher [*sic*] Homosexualität," *Archiv für Kriminal-Anthropologie und Kriminalistik* 47, nos. 3/4 (1912): 237–52; Alfred Adler, "Psychischer Hermaphroditismus und männlicher Protest—ein Kernproblem der nervösen Erkrankungen," in *Praxis und Theorie der Individualpsychologie* (Munich: J. F. Bergmann, 1924), 11–15. On Adler's contributions to the field of trans psychology see also Christopher Shelley, *Transpeople: Repudiation, Trauma, Healing* (Toronto: University of Toronto Press, 2008), 168ff. Herrn discusses a number of further studies from this period, noting that these tended to either agree with Hirschfeld's position or ignored his work altogether except for its terminological innovation. See Rainer Herrn, *Schnittmuster des Geschlechts: Transvestitismus und Transsexualität in der frühen Sexualwissenschaft*, Beiträge zur Sexualforschung 85 (Gießen, Ger.: Psychosozial-Verlag, 2005), 74; Rainer Herrn, "Verkörperungen des anderen Geschlechts—Transvestitismus und Transsexualität historisch betrachtet," *Aus Politik und Zeitgeschichte*, Bundeszentrale für politische Bildung, 2012, no. 20/21 (Geschlechtsidentität) (2012): 41–48.

19. On the process of applying for a *Transvestitenschein* see Jane Caplan, "The Administration of Gender Identity in Nazi Germany," *History Workshop Journal* 72, no. 1 (2011): 171–80; Herrn, *Schnittmuster*, 134–42; Katie Sutton, "'We Too Deserve a Place in the Sun': The Politics of Transvestite Identity in Weimar Germany," *German Studies Review* 35, no. 2 (2012): 337–38.

20. On Institute activities relating to transvestite advocacy and research, and on Hirschfeld's own cross-dressing tendencies, see Heike Bauer, *The Hirschfeld Archives: Violence, Death, and Modern Queer Culture* (Philadelphia: Temple University Press, 2017), 48, 84–87; Herrn, *Schnittmuster*, 63ff. On Hirschfeld's study in the context of his clinical practice and theory of sexual intermediacy see Manfred Herzer, *Magnus Hirschfeld und seine Zeit* (Berlin: de Gruyter, 2017): 202-209.

21. Näcke, "Zum Kapitel der Transvestiten," 238.

22. My own research has focused on the emphasis on "respectability" in the Weimar transvestite media and political organizations, the significance of medical case histories for trans identity formation, and the role of photography in sexological and subcultural contexts. See Sutton, "Politics of Transvestite Identity"; Katie Sutton, "Sexological Cases and the Prehistory of Transgender Identity Politics in Interwar Germany," in *Cases and the Dissemination of Knowledge*, eds. Joy Damousi et al. (New York: Routledge, 2015), 85–103; Katie Sutton, "Sexology's Photographic Turn: Visualizing Trans Identity in Interwar Germany," *Journal of the History of Sexuality* 27, no. 3 (2018): 442–79; Katie Sutton, "From Sexual Inversion to Trans*: Transgender History and Historiography," in *Was ist Homosexualität? Forschungsgeschichte, gesellschaftliche Entwicklungen und Perspektiven*, eds. Florian Mildenberger et al. (Hamburg: Männerschwarm, 2014), 181–204. Herrn and Marhoefer have undertaken important research on Weimar as well as Nazi trans history, which has been particularly uncharted territory until recent years; see Herrn, *Schnittmuster*; Herrn, "Ver-körperungen"; Rainer Herrn, "Transvestitismus in der NS-Zeit: Ein Forschungsdesiderat," *Zeitschrift für Sexualforschung* 26, no. 4 (2013): 330–71; Marhoefer, "Lesbianism, Transvestitism"; Laurie Marhoefer, *Sex and the Weimar Republic: German Homosexual Emancipation and the Rise of the Nazis* (Toronto: University of Toronto Press, 2015), 55–65. Caplan provides a close analysis of the process of applying for a "transvestite certificate" and

Bauer focuses on the significance of Hirschfeld's Institute for German trans history (both cited above).

23. See, for example, discussion of Heinrich Hössli's writings of the 1830s in Tobin, *Peripheral Desires*, 42–43. On broader associations between LGBTIQ politics and human rights concepts see David S. Churchill, "Transnationalism and Homophile Political Culture in the Postwar Decades," *GLQ: A Journal of Lesbian and Gay Studies* 15, no. 1 (2009): 31–65; Leila J. Rupp, "The Persistence of Transnational Organizing: The Case of the Homophile Movement," *American Historical Review* 116, no. 4 (2011): 1014–39.

24. Werner Kn., "Der Kampf der Transvestiten," *Die Freundin* 4, no. 7 (April 2, 1928): 4. For a nuanced recent discussion of the imperialist and racialized implications of much early-twentieth-century German homosexual and trans politics see Laurie Marhoefer, "Was the Homosexual Made White? Race, Empire, and Analogy in Gay and Trans Thought in Twentieth-Century Germany," *Gender & History* 31, no. 1 (2019): 91–114.

25. Ellis, *Eonism*, vol. 7, 41.

26. Hirschfeld, *Die Transvestiten*, 31–54 at 31.

27. Hirschfeld, *Die Transvestiten*, 117.

28. Näcke, "Zum Kapitel der Transvestiten," 243.

29. See Geertje Mak, *Doubting Sex: Inscriptions, Bodies and Selves in Nineteenth-Century Hermaphrodite Case Histories* (Manchester: Manchester University Press, 2012); Geertje Mak, "'So We Must Go Behind Even What the Microscope Can Reveal': The Hermaphrodite's 'Self' in Medical Discourse at the Start of the Twentieth Century," *GLQ: A Journal of Lesbian and Gay Studies* 11, no. 1 (2005): 65–94.

30. Ellis, *Eonism*, vol. 7, 110.

31. Hirschfeld, *Die Transvestiten*, iii–iv.

32. "T.S." in Ellis, *Eonism*, vol. 7, 56.

33. Ivan Crozier, "Pillow Talk: Credibility, Trust and the Sexological Case History," *History of Science* 46 (2008): 382. See also Ivan Crozier, "Havelock Ellis, Eonism and the Patient's Discourse; Or, Writing a Book about Sex," *History of Psychiatry* 11 (2000): 138–46.

34. Hirschfeld, *Die Transvestiten*, 7–9 at 9.

35. "Mr. F." (Case 6), in Hirschfeld, 54–55. Emphases in original.

36. "Mr. F.," in Hirschfeld, 55.

37. "Mr. H.," in Hirschfeld, 69 (emphasis in original).

38. Ellis, *Eonism*, vol. 7:11–12.

39. "Mr. N.," in Hirschfeld, *Die Transvestiten*, 76 (emphasis in original).

40. Hirschfeld, 18, 76. Emphases in original.

41. "Mr. D." (Case 4), in Hirschfeld, *Die Transvestiten*, 30.

42. Hill, "Sexuality and Gender," 316.

43. Case 16, in Hirschfeld, *Die Transvestiten*, 136.

44. "Mr. C." (Case 3), in Hirschfeld, 20, 24.

45. Ellis, *Eonism*, vol. 7, 66. Several other of Ellis's cases similarly connect their gender identity to the desire for or perception of physical transformation; R. M., aged sixty-six, describes how, later in life, his transgendered "feelings seem to have stimulated the breasts, which had previously been almost as flat as a child's," 97.

46. Michael Hagner, "Scientific Medicine," in *From Natural Philosophy to the Sciences: Writing the History of Nineteenth-Century Science*, ed. David Cahan (Chicago: University of Chicago Press, 2003), 54. See also Thomas F. Tierney, "Foucault on the Case: The Pastoral and Juridical Foundation of Medical Power," *Journal of Medical Humanities* 25, no. 4 (2004): 271–90.

47. I examine this evidentiary shift in Sutton, "Sexology's Photographic Turn."

48. Sigmund Freud, *The Ego and the Id;* Sigmund Freud, *Civilization and Its Discontents.*

49. On the significance of the case-study genre for early psychoanalysis see John Forrester, "If *p*, Then What? Thinking in Cases," *History of the Human Sciences* 9 (1996): 1–25; Lang and Sutton, "The Queer Cases of Psychoanalysis": 419–44; Anne Sealey, "The Strange Case of the Freudian Case History: The Role of Long Case Histories in the Development of Psychoanalysis," *History of the Human Sciences* 24, no. 1 (2011): 36–50.

50. Bullough and Bullough, *Cross Dressing*, 212–13.

51. Stekel, "Fragment der Analyse." Translation: Stekel, "Fragmentary Analysis."

52. Ellis, *Eonism*, vol. 7, 17n2. See also Wilhelm Stekel, *Onanie und Homosexualität (Die homosexuelle Neurose)*, vol. 2, *Störungen des Trieb- und Affektlebens* (Berlin: Urban & Schwarzenberg, 1917); Wilhelm Stekel, *Der Fetischismus*, vol. 7, *Störungen des Trieb- und Affektlebens* (Berlin: Urban & Schwarzenberg, 1923).

53. On Stekel's status within early-twentieth-centuiry psychoanalysis see Jaap Bos and Leendert Groenendijk, *The Self-Marginalization of Wilhelm Stekel: Freudian Circles Inside and Out* (New York: Springer, 2007).

54. Stekel, "Fragmentary Analysis," 237 (emphasis in original; in the German text, the word "boy" is also in bold). Stekel, "Fragment der Analyse," 429.

55. Harry Oosterhuis, *Stepchildren of Nature: Krafft-Ebing, Psychiatry, and the Making of Sexual Identity* (Chicago: University of Chicago Press, 2000), 2; Spector, *Violent Sensations,* 116.

56. Thanks to Andrea Beckmann for assisting me to draw out these multiple interpretive possibilities.

57. Stekel, "Fragmentary Analysis," 237, 240.

58. Stekel, "Fragmentary Analysis," 248–49.

59. Stekel, 241. See also pp. 238, 243–44, 246–47 for further elements of the patient's self-diagnosis.

60. Stekel, "Fragment der Analyse," 437.

61. Stekel, "Fragmentary Analysis," 250–53, 254ff.

62. Stekel, 269. In the German text the "and" in "man *and* woman" is emphasized: Stekel, "Fragment der Analyse," 453.

63. Stekel, "Fragmentary Analysis," 259.

64. Stekel, 272. On the gendering of creative production versus biological reproduction see, for example, Maria Tatar, *Lustmord: Sexual Murder in Weimar Germany* (Princeton, NJ: Princeton University Press, 1995).

65. Karl Abraham, "Über hysterische Traumzustände," *Jahrbuch für psychoanalytische und psychopathologische Forschungen* 2 (1910): 22.

66. Ellis, *Eonism*, vol. 7, 16–17. Ellis provides an overview of pre-1928 psychoanalytic discussions of transvestism at pp. 16–27.

67. Bullough and Bullough, *Cross Dressing*, 213ff.; Herrn, *Schnittmuster*, 75–76.

68. Emil Gutheil and Wilhelm Stekel, "XVI. Analyse eines Falles von Transvestitismus," in *Der Fetischismus*, vol. 7, *Störungen des Trieb- und Affektlebens* (Berlin: Urban & Schwarzenberg, 1923), 534 (emphasis in original).

69. Letter from Elsa B., at Gutheil and Stekel, 537.

70. Gutheil and Stekel, "XVI. Analyse eines Falles von Transvestitismus," 538–39.

71. Gutheil and Stekel, "XVI. Analyse eines Falles von Transvestitismus," 540.

72. Gutheil and Stekel, "XVI. Analyse eines Falles von Transvestitismus," 558.

73. Gutheil and Stekel, "XVI. Analyse eines Falles von Transvestitismus," 569–70. Cf. Hirschfeld, *Die Transvestiten*, 203.

74. Arthur Kronfeld, "Ein Transvestit über seine Eigenart," *Sexualreform*, Mitteilungen aus dem Institut für Sexualwissenschaft, 11, no. 11 (1922): 167.

75. Arthur Kronfeld, "Sexualpsychopathologie," in *Handbuch der Psychiatrie*, ed. Gustav Aschaffenburg, Separate reprint (Leipzig: Franz Deuticke, 1923), 68–71 at 71. On Kronfeld's contributions see also Herrn, *Schnittmuster*, 77–78.

76. Kronfeld, "Sexualpsychopathologie," 70–71; Arthur Kronfeld, "Transvestitismus," in *Handwörterbuch der Sexualwissenschaft*, ed. Max Marcuse, 2nd enlarged ed. (Bonn: A. Marcus & E. Weber's Verlag [Reprint: Berlin: de Gruyter, 2001)], 1926), 776.

77. Ellis, *Eonism*, vol. 7, 16.

78. Ellis, *Eonism*, vol. 7, 17, 22–23. Later in this study, he clarifies that "Early environmental influences assist . . . but can scarcely originate Eonism" (109–10).

79. Gutheil and Stekel, "Analyse eines Falles," 563.

80. Gutheil and Stekel, "Analyse eines Falles," 564. Name emphasized in original.

81. Gutheil and Stekel, "Analyse eines Falles," 564–65.

82. Wilhelm Stekel, "Die Transvestiten [Review]" *Zentralblatt für Psychoanalyse* 1 (1910/1911): 55–58. On Stekel's ongoing attempts to prove that transvestites are latent homosexuals, a view shared by Sadger and psychiatrist Siegfried Placzek, see Herrn, *Schnittmuster*, 75–76. Others picked up on the question of masochism, with Näcke arguing that there was sometimes an overlap between masochistic desires and trans identifications, although he insisted that the latter were often quite distinct from sexual urges, which might be lacking altogether: Näcke, "Zum Kapitel der Transvestiten," 242, 245.

83. See, for example, Isidor Sadger, "Welcher Wert kommt den Erzählungen und Autobiographien der Homosexuellen zu?," *Archiv für Kriminal-Anthopologie und Kriminalistik* 53, no. 1/2 (1913): 179–87.

84. Kurt Hiller, "Sprechsaal: Die Transvestiten," *Monatsschrift für Kriminalpsychologie und Strafrechtsreform* 7 (November 1910): 613–15. See also Herrn, *Schnittmuster*, 75.

85. Marhoefer, *Sex and the Weimar Republic*, 6–7.

86. On Hiller and his role in the WhK, including an important revisionist account of the controversy leading to Hirschfeld's resignation, see Marhoefer, 112–44. See also Manfred Herzer, "Schwule Preussen, warme Berliner," *Capri: Zeitschrift für schwule Geschichte* 2 (1988): 16–18.

87. Magnus Hirschfeld, *Sexuelle Zwischenstufen: Das männliche Weib und der weibliche Mann*, 2nd ed., vol. 2, *Sexualpathologie: Ein Lehrbuch für Ärzte und Studierende* (Bonn: A. Marcus & E. Webers, 1922), 141–42 (emphasis in original).

88. Ellis, *Eonism*, vol. 7, 17–18. On further disagreements between Ellis and Stekel see Crozier, "Pillow Talk," 382. Stekel details his theory of the ways in which homosexuality is frequently "masked" in Wilhelm Stekel, "Masken der Homosexualität (Originalarbeit)," *Zentralblatt für Psychoanalyse* 2, no. 7 (1912): 367–72.

89. Ellis, *Eonism*, vol. 7, 22–23.

90. Ellis, 37.

91. Ellis's assessment of this case continues along Oedipal lines: "An infantile and always mainly unconscious absorption in the mother, on the part of a sensitive and sympathetic child, may well have furnished the point of departure for the attitude of Eonism which early began to develop in R. L." Ellis, vol. 7, 90–91.

92. Ellis, vol. 7, 26.

93. Ellis, vol. 7, 26.

94. Lothar Goldmann, "Über das Wesen des Umkleidungstriebes (Der Transvestitismus)," *Geschlecht und Gesellschaft* 12, no. 7–12 (1924): 285ff. at 285; Ellis, *Eonism*, 7:26.

95. See Herrn, *Schnittmuster*, 77–78.

96. Otto Fenichel, "The Psychology of Transvestism," *International Journal of Psycho-Analysis* 11 (1930): 211–14; Otto Fenichel, "Zur Psychologie des Transvestitismus [Vortrag auf dem XI. Internationalen Psychoanalytischen Kongreß, Juli 1929]," *Internationale Zeitschrift für Psychoanalyse* 17, no. 1 (1930): 21–25.

97. Herrn, *Schnittmuster*, 78.

98. See, for example, Heike Bauer, *English Literary Sexology: Translations of Inversion, 1860–1930* (Basingstoke, UK: Palgrave Macmillan, 2009); Heike Bauer, ed., *Sexology and Translation: Cultural and Scientific Encounters across the Modern World*, Sexuality Studies (Philadelphia: Temple University Press, 2015); Birgit Lang, Joy Damousi, and Alison Lewis, *A History of the Case Study: Sexology, Psychoanalysis, Literature* (Manchester: Manchester University Press, 2017); Klaus Müller, *Aber in meinem Herzen sprach eine Stimme so laut: Homosexuelle Autobiographien und medizinische Pathographien im neunzehnten Jahrhundert* (Berlin: Rosa Winkel, 1991); Tobin, *Peripheral Desires*; Philippe Weber, *Der Trieb zum Erzählen: Sexualpathologie und Homosexualität, 1852–1914* (Bielefeld, Ger.: Transcript, 2008).

99. On Kertbeny see Tobin, *Peripheral Desires*, 121–22. On Hirschfeld see Bauer, *Hirschfeld Archives*, 11, 37–56; Herrn, *Schnittmuster*, 76–77.

100. Magnus Hirschfeld and Max Tilke, *Der erotische Verkleidungstrieb (Die Transvestiten): Illustrierter Teil* (2 vols.), vol. 2 (Berlin: Alfred Pulvermacher, 1912).

101. Marie Weis, "Transvestitismus und Gesellschaft," *Frauen-Liebe* 5, no. 12 (1930): n.p.

102. Veronika Fuechtner, *Berlin Psychoanalytic: Psychoanalysis and Culture in Weimar Republic Germany and Beyond* (Berkeley: University of California Press, 2011), 21–22; Sarah Winter, *Freud and the Institution of Psychoanalytic Knowledge* (Stanford: Stanford University Press, 1999), 130–32.

103. See Marti M. Lybeck, *Desiring Emancipation: New Women and Homosexuality in Germany, 1890–1933* (Albany: State University of New York Press, 2014), 151–88; Laurie Marhoefer, "'The Book Was a Revelation, I Recognized Myself in It': Lesbian Sexuality, Censorship, and the Queer Press in Weimar-Era Germany," *Journal of Women's History* 27, no. 2 (2015): 67, 69; Marhoefer, *Sex and the Weimar Republic*, 54–79;

Clayton J. Whisnant, *Queer Identities and Politics in Germany: A History, 1880–1945* (New York: Harrington Park, 2016), 80–121.

104. "Die Transvestiten und die Polizei [Der Transvestit]," *Die Freundin* 1, no. 6 (November 1, 1924): n.p. I examine these developments in detail in Sutton, "Politics of Transvestite Identity." On the overlaps between masculine female homosexual and female-to-male transvestite subcultures and identifications see Heike Schader, *Virile, Vamps und wilde Veilchen. Sexualität, Begehren und Erotik in den Zeitschriften homosexueller Frauen im Berlin der 1920er Jahre* (Königstein/Taunus: Ulrike Helmer, 2004), 110; Katie Sutton, *The Masculine Woman in Weimar Germany* (New York: Berghahn Books, 2011), 116–20; Lybeck, *Desiring Emancipation*, 152, 196.

105. Friedel Werner, "Das transvestitische Empfinden [Die Welt der Transvestiten]," *Die Freundin* 5, no. 10 (September 4, 1929): n.p.; Fred Ursula, "Wär' ich doch eine Frau . . . ," *Die Freundin* 3, no. 3 (February 21, 1927): n.p.

106. Anne von den Eken, "Gibt es ein drittes Geschlecht?," *Das 3. Geschlecht*, no. 1 (1930): 2–7.

107. See, for example, E. E. Schweitzer, "Sadismus und Sadisten," *Das 3. Geschlecht*, no. 1 (1930): 32–38; Prof. Dr. K. F. F., "Sadistisches und Masochistisches im Sexualleben," *Das 3. Geschlecht*, no. 2 (1930): 27–37; Redaktion (editors), "Masochist und Transvestist," *Das 3. Geschlecht*, no. 3 (1931): 1; A. Hofstetter, "Transvestitismus und Metatropismus," *Das 3. Geschlecht*, no. 4 (1931): 14–15. On these connections see Rainer Herrn, *Das 3. Geschlecht. Reprint der 1930–1932 erschienenen Zeitschrift für Transvestiten* (Hamburg: Männerschwarm, 2016), 262–63.

108. See Roy Porter, "The Patient's View: Doing Medical History from Below," *Theory and Society* 14 (1985): 165–74.

109. Emi Wolters, "Die Welt der Transvestiten," *Die Freundin* 7, no. 11 (March 18, 1931): n.p.; Emi Wolters, "Welt der Transvestiten," *Die Freundin* 7, no. 26 (July 1, 1931): n.p. Wolters's name was sometimes written with a second "m," and sometimes with the aristocratic "von."

110. Toni Fricke, "Ein Transvestit ist vogelfrei," *Die Freundin* 3, no. 18 (September 19, 1927): n.p. Other contributors echoed this merging of the science on transvestite and intersex conditions, for example Hubert Rieck, "Paul und Pauline! Eine abstrakte Betrachtung der Wesensart mit wissenschaftlichem Hintergrund," *Das 3. Geschlecht*, no. 1 (1931): 7–8.

111. Goldmann, "Über das Wesen," 286.

112. Oosterhuis, *Stepchildren*, 10–12; Crozier, "Pillow Talk"; Scott Spector, "Introduction. After *The History of Sexuality*? Periodicities, Subjectivities, Ethics," in *After "The History of Sexuality"?*, 1–14; Weber, *Trieb*.

113. Eken, "Gibt es ein drittes Geschlecht?," 6–7.

114. On the Elbe case see Lili Elbe, *Ein Mensch wechselt sein Geschlecht. Eine Lebensbeichte; aus hinterlassenen Papieren*, ed. Niels Hoyer (Dresden: Reissner, 1932); Herrn, "Ver-körperungen," 48; Sabine Meyer, "*Wie Lili zu einem richtigen Mädchen wurde*": *Lili Elbe: Zur Konstruktion von Geschlecht und Identität zwischen Medialisierung, Regulierung und Subjektivierung* (Bielefeld, Ger.: Transcript, 2015). Elbe's story was the basis of *The Danish Girl* (dir. Tom Hooper, 2015).

115. These surgeries were conducted by Prof. Dr. Gohrbandt, director of surgery at

the Urbankrankenhaus in Berlin. Felix Abraham, "Genitalumwandlung an zwei männlichen Transvestiten," *Zeitschrift für Sexualwissenschaft* 18 (1931/1932): 223–26 at 223–24. For a detailed survey of German medical and surgical interventions sought or undergone by trans-identified individuals at this period, see Herrn, *Schnittmuster*, 167–218; Herrn, "Ver-körperungen." Dora/"Dorchen" was a domestic servant at Hirschfeld's Institute; for details see Bauer, *Hirschfeld Archives*, 86–87.

116. Abraham, "Genitalumwandlung," 226.

117. M. Ludwig, "Mädchenbub," *Das 3. Geschlecht*, no. 1 (1930): 10.

118. "Ein Transvestit über sich selbst. Lerne dich selbst erkennen!," *Das 3. Geschlecht*, no. 3 (1931): 22.

119. Foucault, *History of Sexuality*, vol. 1, *The Will to Knowledge*, 63. I explore this discursive genealogy further in Sutton, "Sexological Cases." On the discursive act of "coming out" see Judith Butler, *Excitable Speech: A Politics of the Performative* (New York: Routledge, 1997), 76ff., 107ff.

120. Ursula, "Wär' ich doch eine Frau. . . ."

121. Mimi, "Was wir Transvestiten leiden," *Die Freundin* 4, no. 10 (May 14, 1928): n.p.

122. Ursula, "Wär' ich doch eine Frau . . ."; E. K., [No title], *Die Freundin* 3, no. 13 (July 11, 1927): n.p.

123. Lauren Berlant, "On the Case," *Critical Inquiry* 33, no. 4 (2007): 670.

124. Lilly aus Hamburg, "Mein erster Ausgang als Dame," *Die Freundin* 6, no. 11 (March 12, 1930): n.p.

125. E. B., "Meinungsaustausch der 'Transvestiten,'" *Die Freundin* 3, no. 9 (May 16, 1927): n.p.

126. One posthumously published memoir told of a "pseudo-hermaphrodite" who had been assigned a female gender identity at birth but later chose to live as a man: N. O. Body (Karl M. [Martha] Baer), *Aus eines Mannes Mädchenjahren* (Berlin: Hesperus, 1907). English translation: N. O. Body, *Memoirs of a Man's Maiden Years*, trans. Deborah Simon (Philadelphia: University of Pennsylvania Press, 2005). On this text see Ina Linge, "Gender and Agency between 'Sexualwissenschaft' and Autobiography: The Case of N.O. Body's *Aus eines Mannes Mädchenjahren*," *German Life and Letters* 68 (2015): 387–405. A fictionalized "Diary of a Male Bride: Notes of a Homosexual" charted the experiences of a female imitator who lived as a woman both on and off stage; Mak examines this text as an example of "hermaphrodite" life writing: Walter Homann, ed., *Tagebuch einer männlichen Braut* (Berlin: Dreyer, 1907); Mak, *Doubting Sex*, 205–24.

127. Maria, "Brief eines Transvestiten [Die Welt der Transvestiten]," *Die Freundin* 7, no. 52 (December 28, 1932): n.p.

128. On queer "world-making" see Lauren Berlant and Michael Warner, "Sex in Public," *Critical Inquiry* 24, no. 2 (1998): 558. On the conditions required for queer lives to be "livable," see Judith Butler, *Undoing Gender* (London: Routledge, 2004). See also Nira Yuval-Davis, *The Politics of Belonging: Intersectional Contestations* (London: Sage, 2011).

129. Lina Es, "Transvestiten," *Die Freundin* 3, no. 4 (March 7, 1927): 3–4. Emphases in original. On historical conflations of cross-dressing with deception see Mar-

hoefer, "Lesbianism, Transvestitism," 1181–83. On Thomalla see Andreas Killen, *Homo Cinematicus: Science, Motion Pictures, and the Making of Modern Germany* (Philadelphia: University of Pennsylvania Press, 2017), 46.

130. Emi Wolters, "Welt der Transvestiten."

131. Friedrich Radszuweit, "Transvestitismus ist eine Krankheit," *Das 3. Geschlecht*, no. 4 (1931): 1. See also Friedrich Radszuweit, "Zum Kampf der Transvestiten," *Das 3. Geschlecht*, no. 4 (1931): 14. On Radszuweit's role in Weimar homosexual and transvestite politics see Herrn, *Das 3. Geschlecht*, 243, 260–61; Marhoefer, *Sex and the Weimar Republic*, 47–51, 57, 61–62, 78, 119, 130–31, 135–36, 170–71.

132. This was in contrast to *lesbian* narratives in Weimar-era magazines, where the possible biological basis of sexual identity was, as Marhoefer demonstrates, often not a great concern: Marhoefer, *Sex and the Weimar Republic*, 68.

133. Dolly S., "Transvestitenfragen," *Die Freundin* 4, no. 9 (April 30, 1928): n.p.

134. The Vereinigung D'Eon was named after the same French diplomat who had inspired Ellis's coinage of "Eonism." The subtlety of this name, observed leader Marie Weis, was intended to protect the privacy of members: Marie Weis, "Die Aufgaben der Vereinigung D'Eon [Der Transvestit]," *Garçonne*, no. 4 (December 1, 1930): 10.

135. Caplan, "Administration," 171–80; Herrn, *Schnittmuster*, 134–42.

136. St. A., "Verzweiflungskampf eines weiblichen Transvestiten," *Das 3. Geschlecht*, no. 2 (1930): 7.

137. Irene D., "Kann Transvestitismus anerzogen sein? [Welt der Transvestiten]," *Die Freundin* 7, no. 48 (December 2, 1931): n.p.; Irene D., "Kann Transvestitismus anerzogen sein? (Schluß) [Welt der Transvestiten]," *Die Freundin* 7, no. 49 (December 9, 1931): n.p.

138. Dr. Erich Maria Schwarz, "Die Welt der Transvestiten: Körpergerechte Männerkleidung," *Die Freundin* 7, no. 30 (July 29, 1931): n.p.

139. Editorial commentary (2 December 1931) on article: D., "Kann Transvestitismus anerzogen sein? [Welt der Transvestiten]."

140. Reply to Fräulein Gerda by Emma [Die Welt der Transvestiten], *Die Freundin* [cover missing, probably volume 6, no. 41, October 8, 1930].

141. F., "Sadistisches und Masochistisches im Sexualleben," 33.

142. Fricke, "Aus dem Empfindungsleben."

143. Anna Maria H., "Warum verzagen? [Die Welt der Transvestiten]," *Die Freundin* 7, no. 33 (August 19, 1931): n.p.; Fricke, "Aus dem Empfindungsleben."

144. R. C., "Meinungsaustausch der 'Transvestiten': Der alternde Transvestit," *Die Freundin* 3, no. 11 (June 13, 1927): n.p.

145. "Was wir Transvestiten leiden"; Loni Rex, "Die Welt der Transvestiten. Briefe die uns erreichen," *Die Freundin* 6, no. 43 (October 22, 1930): n.p.

146. Marie Weis, "Bericht über die . . . Zusammenkunft der transvestitischen Interessengemeinschaft 'D'Eon,'" *Garçonne*, 1930. n.p.

147. Sutton, "Politics of Transvestite Identity," 335–54 at 342.

148. Marhoefer, *Sex and the Weimar Republic*, 63–65, 202ff. Similarly, Lybeck discusses the exclusion of "undesirable" elements as a feature of female homosexual subcultures and politics of this era in Lybeck, *Desiring Emancipation*, 154–77.

149. This term is from Laura Doan, *Disturbing Practices: History, Sexuality, and*

Women's Experience of Modern War (Chicago: University of Chicago Press, 2013), 97ff. For recent discussions in the German context of both the relevance and limits of connecting contemporary LGBTIQ identity politics to historical sex-gender categories, and the necessity of recognizing the normative and restrictive as well as emancipatory elements of past movements, see Jennifer Evans, "Introduction: Why Queer German History?," *German History* 34, no. 3 (2016): 371–84; Kirsten Leng, "Magnus Hirschfeld's Meanings: Analysing Biography and the Politics of Representation," *German History* 35, no. 1 (2017): 96–116; Marhoefer, *Sex and the Weimar Republic*, 207–17; Marhoefer, "Was the Homosexual Made White?"; Tobin, *Peripheral Desires*, 230–49.

150. Forrester, "Thinking in Cases," 10.

151. Günter Grau and Claudia Schoppmann, eds., *Hidden Holocaust? Gay and Lesbian Persecution in Germany 1933–1945*, trans. Patrick Camiller (London: Cassell, 1995), 103ff.; Herrn, "Transvestitismus in der NS-Zeit"; Herrn, *Schnittmuster*, 157–65; Burkhard Jellonnek, *Homosexuelle unter dem Hakenkreuz: Die Verfolgung von Homosexuellen im Dritten Reich* (Paderborn, Ger.: Schöningh, 1990), 22ff.; Marhoefer, "Lesbianism, Transvestitism"; Bernhard Rosenkranz, Ulf Bollmann, and Gottfried Lorenz, *Homosexuellen-Verfolgung in Hamburg 1919–1969* (Hamburg: Lambda, 2009), 19ff.; Andreas Sternweiler, "'Er ging mit ihm alsbald ein sogenanntes "Festes Verhältnis" ein': Ganz normale Homosexuelle," in *Homosexuelle Männer im KZ Sachsenhausen*, eds. Joachim Knoll and Andreas Sternweiler (Berlin: Rosa Winkel, 2000), 57–78; Whisnant, *Queer Identities*, 221, 231.

152. See Joanne Meyerowitz, *How Sex Changed: A History of Transsexuality in the United States* (Cambridge, MA: Harvard University Press, 2002); Friedemann Pfäfflin, "Sex Reassignment, Harry Benjamin, and Some European Roots," *International Journal of Transgenderism* 1, no. 2 (1997), https://www.atria.nl/ezines/web/IJT/97–03/numbers/symposion/ijtc0202.htm.

153. Susan Stryker, *Transgender History* (Berkeley, CA: Seal Press, 2008), 150.

EPILOGUE

1. Letter, Hirschfeld to Haire, 15 March 1935. Norman Haire Papers, University of Sydney Library. HAIRE No. 3.20 (1) Correspondence. Magnus Hirschfeld.

2. Letter, Haire to Ellis, 29 August 1933, Norman Haire Papers, University of Sydney Library. HAIRE No. 3.16.1 (1) Norman Haire/Havelock Ellis correspondence 1921–1933.

3. Letter, Ellis to Haire, 14 January 1932. Norman Haire Papers, University of Sydney Library. HAIRE No. 3.16.1 (1) Norman Haire/Havelock Ellis correspondence 1921–1933.

4. In addition to Freud's former translator A. A. Brill, Simmel's application was backed by Erich Fromm, formerly of the Frankfurt Institute for Social Research before he escaped to Geneva and subsequently joined the New York Psychoanalytic Institute. Letter, David Brunswick to Monroe A. Meyer, 24 September 1933. The New York Psychoanalytic Society and Institute: Record Group 5 Box 1. Series 1, Folder 7. Pre-war

Rescue Efforts 1933–1938. On Fromm see Veronika Fuechtner, *Berlin Psychoanalytic: Psychoanalysis and Culture in Weimar Republic Germany and Beyond* (Berkeley: University of California Press, 2011), 135.

5. Letter, Nolan D. C. Lewis to George E. Daniels, 31 May 1938. The New York Psychoanalytic Society and Institute: Record Group 5 Box 1. Series 1, Folder 7. Prewar Rescue Efforts 1933–1938.

6. These events receive thoughtful consideration in Heike Bauer, *The Hirschfeld Archives: Violence, Death, and Modern Queer Culture* (Philadelphia: Temple University Press, 2017), 92–101; Ralf Dose, *Magnus Hirschfeld: The Origins of the Gay Liberation Movement*, trans. Edward H. Willis (New York: Monthly Review Press, 2014), 64–67; Günter Grau and Claudia Schoppmann, eds., *Hidden Holocaust? Gay and Lesbian Persecution in Germany 1933–1945*, trans. Patrick Camiller (London: Cassell, 1995), 31–33; Laurie Marhoefer, *Sex and the Weimar Republic: German Homosexual Emancipation and the Rise of the Nazis* (Toronto: University of Toronto Press, 2015), 174–75.

7. Biographical details drawn from Manfred Herzer, *Magnus Hirschfeld: Leben und Werk eines jüdischen, schwulen und sozialistischen Sexologen*, 2., überarbeitete Aufl. (Hamburg: MännerschwarmSkript Verlag, 2001); Volkmar Sigusch, "Albert Moll und Magnus Hirschfeld. Über ein problematisches Verhältnis vor dem Hintergrund unveröffentlichter Briefe Molls aus dem Jahr 1934," *Zeitschrift für Sexualforschung* 8 (1995): 122–59; Volkmar Sigusch, *Geschichte der Sexualwissenschaft* (Frankfurt am Main: Campus Verlag, 2008); Volkmar Sigusch and Günter Grau, eds., *Personenlexikon der Sexualforschung* (Frankfurt am Main: Campus, 2009).

8. Stephen Frosh, *Hate and the "Jewish Science": Anti-Semitism, Nazism and Psychoanalysis* (Houndmills, Basingstoke: Palgrave Macmillan, 2005); James E. Goggin and Eileen Brockmann Goggin, *Death of a "Jewish Science": Psychoanalysis in the Third Reich* (West Lafayette, IN: Purdue University Press, 2001).

9. August issue, 1931: *Süddeutsche Monatshefte*.

10. Fuechtner, *Berlin Psychoanalytic*, 12–13.

11. On these continuities and breaks between pre-Nazi and Nazi-era psychoanalysis, and the ongoing significance of psychoanalytic and psychotherapeutic research after 1933, see Geoffrey Cocks, *Psychotherapy in the Third Reich: The Göring Institute* (New York: Oxford University Press, 1985); Fuechtner, *Berlin Psychoanalytic*, 12–13, 114–15; Ulfried Geuter, *The Professionalization of Psychology in Nazi Germany* (Cambridge, UK: Cambridge University Press, 1992); Regine Lockot, *Erinnern und Durcharbeiten. Zur Geschichte der Psychoanalyse und Psychotherapie im Nationalsozialismus* (Frankfurt am Main: Fischer, 1985); George Makari, *Revolution in Mind: The Creation of Psychoanalysis* (New York: Harper, 2008), 462; Laurence Rickels, *Nazi Psychoanalysis* (Minneapolis: University of Minnesota Press, 2002); Eli Zaretsky, *Secrets of the Soul: A Social and Cultural History of Psychoanalysis* (New York: Vintage, 2004), 227–29.

12. On this period of exile and transition, and of the Nazi "cleansing" of Jewish analysts from the profession, see Karen Brecht et al., eds., *"Hier geht das Leben auf eine sehr merkwürdige Weise weiter . . .": Zur Geschichte der Psychoanalyse in Deutschland*, revised ed. (Giessen, Ger.: Psychosozial-Verlag, 2010); Nathan G. Hale

Jr., *The Rise and Crisis of Psychoanalysis in the United States: Freud and the Americans, 1917–1985* (New York: Oxford University Press, 1995); Anthony D. Kauders, *Der Freud-Komplex: Eine Geschichte der Psychoanalyse in Deutschland* (Berlin: Berlin Verlag, 2014), 117–59; Lockot, *Erinnern und Durcharbeiten*; H.-J. Wirth and T. Haland-Wirth, "Emigration, Biographie und Psychoanalyse. Emigrierte PsychoanalytikerInnen in Amerika," in *"Die biographische Wahrheit ist nicht zu haben." Psychoanalyse und Biographieforschung*, ed. K.-J. Bruder (Giessen, Ger.: Psychosozial-Verlag, 2003), 221–57; Zaretsky, *Secrets of the Soul*, 217–45.

13. RG8: Annual Meetings p. 7 Series 1. Agendas and Minutes· Folder APsaA Meeting of Members 1939. 19: Report of the Emergency Committee on Relief and Immigration. Presented to the Exec Council and the Exec Session of the AmPsaAss May 7 and 9, 1939; RG14 US Govt. S2. World War II Physician Immigration Activities. Reports of the Emergency Committee on Relief and Immigration of the APsaA 1938–1941. American Psychoanalytic Association Archives, Oskar Diethelm Library, Weill Medical College of Cornell University.

14. Dagmar Herzog, *Cold War Freud: Psychoanalysis in an Age of Catastrophes* (Cambridge, UK: Cambridge University Press, 2017), 3.

15. George Makari, "Mitteleuropa on the Hudson: On the Struggle for American Psychoanalysis after the Anschluß," in *After Freud Left: A Century of Psychoanalysis in America*, ed. John C. Burnham (Chicago: University of Chicago Press, 2012), 111. Assessing the extent of the émigré influence on the New York Society, Thompson notes that a full third of its members by 1948 were émigrés, more than half of whom were previously members of the Vienna Society: Nellie L. Thompson, "The Transformation of Psychoanalysis in America: Emigré Analysts and the New York Psychoanalytic Society and Institute, 1935–1961," *Journal of the American Psychoanalytic Association* 60, no. 1 (2012): 23. On the question of lay analysis as it was negotiated in the United States see Hale Jr., *Rise and Crisis*; R. Wallerstein, *Lay Analysis: Life inside the Controversy* (Mahway, NJ: Analytic Press, 1998).

16. Nellie L. Thompson and Helen Keable, "The Psychoanalytic Study of the Child: A Narrative of Postwar Psychoanalysis," *American Imago* 73, no. 3 (2016): 349, 361.

17. Makari, *Revolution*, 468–69.

18. On the impact of these events on Weimar-era sex reform see, in particular, Atina Grossmann, *Reforming Sex: The German Movement for Birth Control and Abortion Reform, 1920–1950* (New York: Oxford University Press, 1995), 136–88; Joachim Schlör, "'Wenn ich eines richtig gemacht habe . . .'. Berliner Sexualwissenschaftler in Palästina/Israel," in *Exilforschung. Ein internationales Jahrbuch*, eds. Claus-Dieter Krohn et al., vol. 16: *Exil und Avantgarden* (Mainz, Ger.: edition text + kritik, 1998), 229–52.

19. Letter, Stöcker to B.S.S., 6 Dec 1937, Zurich. B.S.S. collection Folder 9.4. B.S.S. Recip Stöcker, Helene.

20. Letter, Haire to Ellis, 20 June 1939. Norman Haire Papers, University of Sydney Library. HAIRE 3.16.2 Norman Haire/Havelock Ellis correspondence 1934–1939.

21. Letter, Brand to B.S.S., 29.11.33. B.S.S. collection Folder 4.2 BSS Recip Bf-Bre. Adolf Brand. Brand was another honorary overseas member of this society. On Röhm see chapter 2, and Marhoefer, *Sex and the Weimar Republic*, 146–73.

22. Cocks, *Psychotherapy*, 202–11; Harry Oosterhuis, "Medicine, Male Bonding and Homosexuality in Nazi Germany," *Journal of Contemporary History* 32, no. 2 (1997): 187–205.

23. On the "atom bomb" comparison and the wider impact of the Kinsey studies see Sarah E. Igo, *The Averaged American: Surveys, Citizens, and the Making of a Mass Public* (Cambridge, MA: Harvard University Press, 2007), 234, 260. See also Donna Drucker, *The Classification of Sex: Alfred Kinsey and the Organization of Knowledge* (Pittsburgh: University of Pittsburgh Press, 2014); Dagmar Herzog, "The Reception of the Kinsey Reports in Europe," *Sexuality & Culture* 10, no. 1 (2006): 39–48; Jennifer Terry, *An American Obsession: Science, Medicine, and Homosexuality in Modern Society* (Chicago: University of Chicago Press, 1999).

24. For an overview of developments in postwar Anglophone sexology see Vern L. Bullough, *Science in the Bedroom: A History of Sex Research* (New York: Basic Books, 1994); Paul Robinson, *The Modernization of Sex: Havelock Ellis, Alfred Kinsey, William Masters and Virginia Johnson* (New York: Harper & Row, 1976).

25. Louis Doyle, "A Scientific Sex Foundation," *Sexology*, 1938, 760.

26. Heike Bauer, "Sexology Backward: Hirschfeld, Kinsey and the Reshaping of Sex Research in the 1950s," in *Queer 1950s: Rethinking Sexuality in the Postwar Years*, ed. Heike Bauer and Matt Cook (Basingstoke, UK: Palgrave Macmillan, 2012), 133–49.

27. Howard Chiang, "Effecting Science, Affecting Medicine: Homosexuality, the Kinsey Reports, and the Contested Boundaries of Psychopathology in the United States, 1948–1965," *Journal of the History of the Behavioural Sciences* 44, no. 4 (2008): 307; Joanne Meyerowitz, *How Sex Changed: A History of Transsexuality in the United States* (Cambridge, MA: Harvard University Press, 2002), 214–26; Friedemann Pfäfflin, "Sex Reassignment, Harry Benjamin, and Some European Roots," *International Journal of Transgenderism* 1, no. 2 (1997), https://www.atria.nl/ezines/web/IJT/97–03/numbers/symposion/ijtc0202.htm.

28. Hale, Jr., *Rise and Crisis*, 276–99. See also Herzog, *Cold War Freud*.

29. Elizabeth Lunbeck, "Psychiatry," in *From Natural Philosophy to the Sciences: Writing the History of Nineteenth-Century Science*, ed. David Cahan (Chicago: University of Chicago Press, 2003), 665. See also Elizabeth Lunbeck, *The Americanization of Narcissism* (Cambridge, MA: Harvard University Press, 2014); Hale, Jr., *Rise and Crisis*, 245–56.

30. Herzog, *Cold War Freud*, 1.

31. Mary Jo Buhle, *Feminism and Its Discontents;* Diana Fuss, ed., "Pink Freud (Special Issue of *GLQ*)" 2, nos. 1–2 (1995).

32. Insert, *Zeitschrift für Sexualwissenschaft und Sexualpolitik*, Berlin, March 1932, A. Marcus & E. Weber's Verlag.

33. H. Vorwahl, "Zur Sexualsymbolik der Sprache," *Zeitschrift für Sexualwissenschaft und Sexualpolitik* 18, no. 5 (October 1931): 315.

34. Sigusch, *Geschichte der Sexualwissenschaft*, 276.

35. Sigusch, *Geschichte der Sexualwissenschaft*; Ulrich Clement, "Zum Verhältnis von Sexualwissenschaft und Psychoanalyse," *Zeitschrift für psychosomatische Medizin* 39 (1993): 63–74; Katerina Lišková, *Sexual Liberation, Socialist Style: Communist*

Czechoslovakia and the Science of Desire, 1945–1989 (Cambridge, UK: Cambridge University Press, 2018). A further strong source of postwar German sexological history is the journal *Zeitschrift für Sexualforschung* (1988–).

36. See Jane A. Russo, "Brazilian Psychiatrists and Psychoanalysis at the Beginning of the 20th Century: A Quest for National Identity," *Psychoanalysis and History* 14, no. 2 (2012): 297–312; Chiara Beccalossi, "Madness and Sexual Psychopathies as the Magnifying Glass of the Normal: Italian Psychiatry and Sexuality c. 1880–1910," *Social History of Medicine* 27, no. 2 (2014): 303–25; Jana Funke and Kate Fisher, "Sexual Science beyond the Medical," *Lancet* 387 (2016): 840–41.)

37. Herzog, *Cold War Freud*, 12, 22, 56–86; see also Dagmar Herzog, *Sex in Crisis: The New Sexual Revolution and the Future of American Politics* (New York: Basic, 2008), 77–79. On psychoanalytic homo- and transphobia see Tim Dean and Christopher Lane, eds., *Homosexuality-Psychoanalysis* (Chicago: University of Chicago Press, 2001); Meyerowitz, *How Sex Changed*. On the broader decline of psychoanalysis in mainstream US psychiatry see Hale Jr., *Rise and Crisis*, 300–344.

38. See, for example, Joy Damousi, *Freud in the Antipodes: A Cultural History of Psychoanalysis in Australia* (Sydney: UNSW Press, 2005); Mariano Ben Plotkin, *Freud in the Pampas: The Emergence and Development of a Psychoanalytic Culture in Argentina* (Stanford: Stanford University Press, 2001).

Bibliography

ARCHIVAL SOURCES

British Library Manuscripts and Archives, London
Havelock Ellis Papers
Harry Ransom Center, University of Texas, Austin
British Sexological Society Collection
Kinsey Institute Library and Archive
Harry Benjamin Collection
The Hirschfeld Scrapbook
Library of Congress
Sigmund Freud Collection
Oskar Diethelm Library, Weill Medical College of Cornell University
American Psychoanalytic Association Archives
University of Sydney Manuscripts Collection
Norman Haire Collection
Yale University Library
Ellis-Freud Correspondence MS195

PRIMARY SOURCES

A., St. "Verzweiflungskampf eines weiblichen Transvestiten." *Das 3. Geschlecht*, no. 2 (1930): 7–8.

Abraham, Felix. "Genitalumwandlung an zwei männlichen Transvestiten." *Zeitschrift für Sexualwissenschaft* 18 (1931/1932): 223–26.

Abraham, Karl. "Äußerungsformen des weiblichen Kastrationskomplexes." *Internationale Zeitschrift für Psychoanalyse* 7, no. 4 (1921): 422–52.

Abraham, Karl. "Über hysterische Traumzustände." *Jahrbuch für psychoanalytische und psychopathologische Forschungen* 2 (1910): 1–32.

Abraham, Karl. "Untersuchungen über die früheste prägenitale Entwicklungsstufe der Libido." *Internationale Zeitschrift für ärztliche Psychoanalyse* 4, no. 2 (1916): 71–97.

Adler, Alfred. "Psychischer Hermaphroditismus und männlicher Protest—ein Kernproblem der nervösen Erkrankungen." In *Praxis und Theorie der Individualpsychologie*, 11–15. Munich: J. F. Bergmann, 1924.

Adler, Otto. *Die mangelhafte Geschlechtsempfindung des Weibes. Anaesthesia sexualis feminarum. Dyspareunia. Anaphrodisia* [1904]. 3rd ed. Berlin: Kornfeld, 1919.

Adler, Otto. "Perverses vom Kriegsschauplatz." *Zeitschrift für Sexualwissenschaft* 5 (1918/1919): 326ff.

"Aus der Kriegszeit." *Vierteljahresberichte des Wissenschaftlich–humanitären Komitees während der Kriegszeit. Herausgegeben statt des Jahrbuch für sexuelle Zwischenstufen mit besonderer Berücksichtigung der Homosexualität* 17, no. 4 (1917): 155, 158.

B., E. "Meinungsaustausch der 'Transvestiten.'" *Die Freundin* 3, no. 9 (May 16, 1927): n.p.

Bandler, Samuel Wyllis. *The Endocrines*. Philadelphia: Saunders, 1921.

Bell, Sanford. "A Preliminary Study of the Emotion of Love Between the Sexes." *The American Journal of Psychology* 13, no. 3 (1902): 325–54.

Bender, Julie. "Sexualpsychologie des Weibes und Ärztin." *Zeitschrift für Sexualwissenschaft* 6 (1919): 351–52.

Bender, Julie. "Zur Frage der Homosexualität der Frau." *Zeitschrift für Sexualwissenschaft* 7 (1920): 324–26.

Benjamin, Harry. "New Clinical Aspects of the Steinach Operation." *Medical Journal and Record*, no. 122 (1925): 452-57, 515-18, 592-94.

Benjamin, Harry. "The Effects of Vasectomy (Steinach Operation)." *American Medicine* 28 (1922): 435–43.

Berman, Louis. *The Glands Regulating Personality: A Study of the Glands of Internal Secretion in Relation to the Types of Human Nature*. New York: Macmillan, 1922.

Bloch, Iwan. "Aufgaben und Ziele der Sexualwissenschaft." *Zeitschrift für Sexualwissenschaft* 1, no. 1 (April 1914): 2–11.

Bloch, Iwan. *Beiträge zur Aetiologie der Psychopathia sexualis. Mit einer Vorrede von Albert Eulenburg*. Dresden: Dohrn, 1902.

Bloch, Iwan. *Das Sexualleben unserer Zeit in seinen Beziehungen zur modernen Kultur*. Berlin: Marcus, 1907.

Bloch, Iwan. "Über traumatische Impotenz." *Zeitschrift für Sexualwissenschaft* 5 (1918/1919): 135–41.

Blüher, Hans. "Die drei Grundformen der Homosexualität." *Jahrbuch für sexuelle Zwischenstufen* 13 (1913): 139–65.

"Blutuntersuchungen bei Homosexuellen." *Jahrbuch für sexuelle Zwischenstufen* 14, no. 1 (1914): 72–73.

Body, N. O. *Aus eines Mannes Mädchenjahren*. Berlin: Hesperus, 1907.

Body, N. O. *Memoirs of a Man's Maiden Years*. Translated by Deborah Simon. Philadelphia: University of Pennsylvania Press, 2005.

Bonhoeffer, K. "Erfahrungen aus dem Kriege über die Ätiologie psychopathologischer Zustände mit besonderer Berücksichtigung der Erschöpfung und Emotion." *Allgemeine Zeitschrift für Psychiatrie und psychisch-gerichtliche Medizin* (1917), 77–95.

Bonhoeffer, K. "Erfahrungen über Epilsepsie und Verwandtes im Feldzuge." *Monatsschrift für Psychiatrie und Neurologie* 38 (1915): 61-71.
Bonhoeffer, K. "Psychiatrisches zum Krieg." *Monatsschrift für Psychiatrie und Neurologie* 36 (1914): 435–38.
Bühler, Charlotte. "Zum Problem der sexuellen Entwicklung." *Zeitschrift für Kinderheilkunde* 51, no. 4–5 (1931): 612–42.
Bullough, Vern L. *Science in the Bedroom: A History of Sex Research.* New York: Basic Books, 1994.
Burchard, E. "Sexuelle Fragen zur Kriegszeit." *Zeitschrift für Sexualwissenschaft* 1, no. 10 (1915): 373–80.
C., R. "Meinungsaustausch der 'Transvestiten': Der alternde Transvestit." *Die Freundin* 3, no. 11 (June 13, 1927): n.p.
Carpenter, Edward. *The Intermediate Sex: A Study of Some Transitional Types of Men and Women.* London: Allen & Unwin, 1908.
Ceni, Carlo. "Die höheren Genitalzentren bei Gehirnerschütterung." *Zeitschrift für Sexualwissenschaft* 1 (1914/1915): 279ff.
D., Irene. "Kann Transvestitismus anerzogen sein? (Schluß) [Welt der Transvestiten]." *Die Freundin* 7, no. 49 (December 9, 1931): n.p.
D., Irene. "Kann Transvestitismus anerzogen sein? [Welt der Transvestiten]." *Die Freundin* 7, no. 48 (December 2, 1931): n.p.
Dane, Paul G. "Notes on Psycho-Analysis of War Neuroses." *International Journal of Psycho-Analysis* 8, no. 1 (1927): 72–73.
Dane, Paul G. *Medical Journal of Australia*, April 25, 1925.
Darwin, Charles. "A Biographical Sketch of an Infant." *Mind*, June 1877, 285–94.
Desogus, V. "Störungen des Geschlechtstriebes bei den Kriegsverletzten." *Zeitschrift für Sexualwissenschaft* 8 (1921/1922): 177–80.
Dessoir, Max. "Zur Psychologie der Vita sexualis." *Zeitschrift für Psychiatrie* 50 (1895): 941–75.
Deutsch, Helene. "Der feminine Masochismus und seine Beziehung zur Frigidität. Vortrag auf dem XI. Internationalen Psychoanalytischen Kongreß in Oxford im Juli 1929." *Internationale Zeitschrift für ärztliche Psychoanalyse* 16 (1930): 172–84.
Deutsch, Helene. *Psychoanalysis of the Sexual Functions of Women.* Edited by Paul Roazen. London: Karnac, 1991.
Deutsch, Helene. "Psychologie des Weibes in den Funktionen der Fortpflanzung." *Internationale Zeitschrift für ärztliche Psychoanalyse* 11 (1925): 40–53.
Deutsch, Helene. "Über die weibliche Homosexualität." *Internationale Zeitschrift für Psychoanalyse* 18 (1932): 219–41.
Deutsch, Helene. *Zur Psychoanalyse der weiblichen Sexualfunktionen.* Leipzig, Ger.: Internationaler Psychoanalytischer Verlag, 1925.
"Die Frau als Soldat." *Die Freundin* 4, no. 12 (July 11, 1928): n.p.
"Die Transvestiten und die Polizei [Der Transvestit]." *Die Freundin* 1, no. 6 (November 1, 1924): n.p.
Doyle, Louis. "A Scientific Sex Foundation." *Sexology* (1938): 760-63.
Duerst, U. "E. Steinach, Willkürliche Umwandlung von Säugetieremännchen in Tiere

[*sic*] mit ausgeprägt weiblichen Geschlechtscharakteren und weiblicher Psyche. Arch. f. ges. Physiologie, Bd. 144, S. 71–108. V Tafeln. Bonn 1912 [Review]." *Sexual-Probleme* 8, no. 8 (1912): 590–92.

Eder, M. D. *War-Shock: The Psycho-Neuroses in War Psychology and Treatment*. London: Heinemann, 1917.

"Ein Transvestit über sich selbst. Lerne dich selbst erkennen!" *Das 3. Geschlecht*, no. 3 (1931): 19–25.

Eken, Anne von den. "Gibt es ein drittes Geschlecht?" *Das 3. Geschlecht*, no. 1 (1930): 2–7.

Elbe, Lili. *Ein Mensch wechselt sein Geschlecht. Eine Lebensbeichte; aus hinterlassenen Papieren*. Edited by Niels Hoyer. Dresden: Reissner, 1932.

Elberskirchen, Johanna. *Die Liebe des dritten Geschlechts. Homosexualität, eine bisexuelle Varietät keine Entartung-keine Schuld*. Leipzig: Max Spohr, 1904.

Ellis, H. Havelock. "Auto-Erotism: A Psychological Study." *Alienist and Neurologist* 19 (1898): 260–99.

Ellis, Havelock. "Analysis of the Sexual Impulse." *The Alienist and Neurologist* 21 (1900): 247–62.

Ellis, Havelock. *Analysis of the Sexual Impulse, Love and Pain, The Sexual Impulse in Women*. Vol. 3. 6 vols. Studies in the Psychology of Sex. Philadelphia: F. A. Davis, 1903.

Ellis, Havelock. *Eonism and Other Supplementary Studies*. 7 vols. Vol. 7. Studies in the Psychology of Sex. Philadelphia: F. A. Davis, 1928.

Ellis, Havelock. *My Life*. London: Spearman, 1967.

Ellis, Havelock. "Sexo-Aesthetic Inversion." *Alienist and Neurologist* 34, nos. 2 (May) and 3 (August) (1913): 156–67 and 249-79.

Ellis, Havelock. "Sexo-ästhetische Inversion." *Zeitschrift für Psychotherapie und medizinische Psychologie* 5 (1914): 134–62.

Ellis, Havelock. "Sexual Problems: Their Nervous and Mental Relations." In *Modern Treatment of Nervous and Mental Diseases*. Edited by William Anson White and Smith Ely Jelliffe, 100–142. Philadelphia: Lea & Febiger, 1913.

Ellis, Havelock. "The Bladder as a Dynamometer." *American Journal of Dermatology*, May 1902.

Ellis, Havelock. *The Evolution of Modesty, the Phenomena of Sexual Periodicity, Auto-Erotism* [1910]. 3rd edition. 7 vols. Vol. 1. Studies in the Psychology of Sex. Philadelphia: F. A. Davis, 1925.

Ellis, Havelock. "The Relation of Erotic Dreams to Vesical Dreams." *Journal of Abnormal Psychology*, September 1913, 137–67.

Ellis, Havelock, and John Addington Symonds. *Sexual Inversion: A Critical Edition*. Edited by Ivan Crozier. Basingstoke, UK: Palgrave Macmillan, 2007.

Ellis, Henry Havelock, and John Addington Symonds. *Das konträre Sexualgefühl*. Leipzig: Wigand, 1896.

Emi Wolters. "Welt der Transvestiten." *Die Freundin* 7, no. 26 (July 1, 1931): n.p.

Es, Lina. "Transvestiten." *Die Freundin* 3, no. 4 (March 7, 1927): 3–4.

F., Prof. Dr. K. F. "Sadistisches und Masochistisches im Sexualleben." *Das 3. Geschlecht*, no. 2 (1930): 27–37.

Fehlinger, H. "Krieg und Geschlechtsleben." *Zeitschrift für Sexualwissenschaft* 3 (1916/1917): 124–26.

Fenichel, Otto. "The Psychology of Transvestism." *International Journal of Psycho-Analysis* 11 (1930): 211–26.

Fenichel, Otto. "Zur Psychologie des Transvestitismus [Vortrag auf dem XI. Internationalen Psychoanalytischen Kongreß, Juli 1929]." *Internationale Zeitschrift für Psychoanalyse* 17, no. 1 (1930): 21–34.

Ferenczi, S. "Zur Nosologie der männlichen Homosexualität (Homoërotik) [Vortrag, gehalten am III. Kongreß der 'Internationalen Psychoanalytischen Vereinigung' zu Weimar im Oktober 1911]." *Internationale Zeitschrift für Psychoanalyse* 2, no. 2 (1914): 131–42.

Ferenczi, Sándor. "Analytische Deutung und Behandlung der psychosexuellen Impotenz des Mannes." *Psychiatrisch-neurologische Wochenschrift* 10 (1908): 305–9.

Ferenczi, Sándor. "Über zwei Typen der Kriegsneurose." *Internationale Zeitschrift für Psychoanalyse* 4, no. 3 (1916/1917): 131–45.

Forel, August. *Der Hypnotismus oder die Suggestion und die Psychotherapie: Ihre psychologische, psychophysiologische und medizinische Bedeutung*. 6th ed. Stuttgart: Ferdinand Enke, 1911.

Forel, August. *Der Hypnotismus oder die Suggestion und die Psychotherapie. Ihre psychologische, psychophysiologische und medizinische Bedeutung mit Einschluss der Psychanalyse, sowie der Telepathiefrage. Ein Lehrbuch für Studierende sowie für weitere Kreise*. 12th ed. Stuttgart: Ferdinand Enke, 1923.

Forel, August. "Die Lehre Freuds und die Abstinenzbewegung." *Internationale Monatsschrift zur Erforschung des Alkoholismus und Bekämpfung der Trinksitten (Basel)* 23 (1913): 21–22.

Forel, August. *Die sexuelle Frage: eine naturwissenschaftliche, psychologische, hygienische und soziologische Studie für Gebildete*. Munich: Reinhardt, 1905.

Forel, August. *Die sexuelle Frage. Eine naturwissenschaftliche, psychologische und hygienische Studie nebst Lösungsversuchen wichtiger sozialer Aufgaben der Zukunft*. 13th ed. Munich: Ernst Reinhardt, 1920.

"Frauen als Soldaten im Weltkriege (VI. Teil.)." *Vierteljahresberichte des Wissenschaftlich–humanitären Komitees während der Kriegszeit. Herausgegeben statt des Jahrbuch für sexuelle Zwischenstufen mit besonderer Berücksichtigung der Homosexualität* 17, no. 1 (1917): 36.

Freud, Anna. *Einführung in die Technik der Kinderanalyse: vier Vorträge am Lehrinstitut der Wiener Psychoanalytischen Vereinigung*. Vienna: Internationaler Psychoanalytischer Verlag, 1927.

Freud, Sigmund. "Analyse der Phobie eines fünfjährigen Knaben ['Der kleine Hans'] (1909)." In *Sigmund Freud Studienausgabe Band VIII: Zwei Kinderneurosen*. Edited by Alexander Mitscherlich, Angela Richards, and James Strachey, 8:9–123. Frankfurt am Main: Fischer, 2000.

Freud, Sigmund. *Beyond the Pleasure Principle*. Translated by James Strachey. New York: Norton, 1961.

Freud, Sigmund. *Civilization and Its Discontents*. Edited and translated by James Strachey. New York: Norton, 1962.

Freud, Sigmund. "Die Frage der Laienanalyse (1926)." In *Sigmund Freud Studienausgabe. Ergänzungsband*. Edited by Alexander Mitscherlich, Angela Richards, and James Strachey, Ergänzungsband: 271–349. Frankfurt am Main: Fischer, 2000.

Freud, Sigmund. "Die kulturelle Sexualmoral und die moderne Nervosität." *Sexual-Probleme* 1, no. 3 (March 1908): 107–29.

Freud, Sigmund. "Die Sexualität in der Ätiologie der Neurosen (1898)." In *Gesammelte Werke*, 1:489–516. London: Imago, 1952.

Freud, Sigmund. *Drei Abhandlungen zur Sexualtheorie*. Leipzig: F. Deuticke, 1905.

Freud, Sigmund. "Drei Abhandlungen zur Sexualtheorie (1905)." In *Sigmund Freud Studienausgabe Band V: Sexualleben*. Edited by Alexander Mitscherlich, Angela Richards, and James Strachey, 5:37–146. Frankfurt am Main: Fischer, 2000.

Freud, Sigmund. "Eine Kindheitserinnerung des Leonardo da Vinci (1910)." In *Sigmund Freud Studienausgabe Band X: Bildende Kunst und Literatur*. Edited by Alexander Mitscherlich, Angela Richards, and James Strachey, 10:87–159. Frankfurt am Main: Fischer, 2000.

Freud, Sigmund. "Einige psychische Folgen des anatomischen Geschlechtsunterschieds." *Internationale Zeitschrift für Psychoanalyse* 11 (1925): 401–10.

Freud, Sigmund. "Einige psychische Folgen des anatomischen Geschlechtsunterschieds (1925)." In *Sigmund Freud Studienausgabe Band V: Sexualleben*. Edited by Alexander Mitscherlich, Angela Richards, and James Strachey, 5:253–72. Frankfurt am Main: Fischer, 2000.

Freud, Sigmund. "Fragment of an Analysis of a Case of Hysteria (1905 [1901])." In *The Standard Edition of the Complete Psychological Works of Sigmund Freud*. Vol. 7: 1901–1905: A Case of Hysteria, Three Essays on Sexuality and Other Works:1–122. London, 1953.

Freud, Sigmund. "Hysterische Phantasie und ihre Beziehung zur Bisexualität." *Zeitschrift für Sexualwissenschaft* 1, no. 1 (1908): 27–34.

Freud, Sigmund. *Introductory Lectures on Psychoanalysis (Parts I and II)*. Edited by James Strachey. Vol. 15. *The Standard Edition of the Complete Psychological Works of Sigmund Freud*. London: Hogarth, 1963.

Freud, Sigmund. *Introductory Lectures on Psychoanalysis (Part III)*. Edited by James Strachey. Vol. 16: 1917–1917. *The Standard Edition of the Complete Psychological Works of Sigmund Freud*. London: Hogarth, 1963.

Freud, Sigmund. "Lecture XXXIV: Explanations, Applications and Orientations." In *Sigmund Freud, New Introductory Lectures on Psycho-Analysis*. Edited and translated by James Strachey. London: Hogarth, 1974.

Freud, Sigmund. "Letter from Sigmund Freud to Anonymous, April 9, 1935." In *Letters from Sigmund Freud, 1873–1939*. Edited by Ernst L. Freud, 423–24. London: Hogarth, 1961.

Freud, Sigmund. "Meine Ansichten über die Rolle der Sexualität in der Ätiologie der Neurosen (1906)." In *Sigmund Freud Studienausgabe Band V: Sexualleben*. Edited by Alexander Mitscherlich, Angela Richards, and James Strachey, 5:148–57. Frankfurt am Main: Fischer, 2000.

Freud, Sigmund. "Psycho-Analytic Notes on an Autobiographical Account of a Case of Paranoia (Dementia Paranoides)." In *The Standard Edition of the Complete Psycho-*

logical Works of Sigmund Freud. Translated by James Strachey. Vol. 12: 1911–1913: The Case of Schreber, Papers on Technique and Other Works. London: Hogarth, 1958.

Freud, Sigmund. "Stellungnahme zum Fall Prof. Dr. Beer." *Die Zeit*. October 27, 1905, sec. Morgenblatt.

Freud, Sigmund. *The Ego and the Id*. Edited and translated by James Strachey. New York: Norton, 1961.

Freud, Sigmund. *The Interpretation of Dreams*. London: G. Allen & Unwin, 1954.

Freud, Sigmund. "The Psychogenesis of a Case of Homosexuality in a Woman (1920)." Translated by James Strachey and Anna Freud. Vol. 18 (1920–1922): Beyond the Pleasure Principle, Group Psychology, and Other Works. *The Standard Edition of the Complete Psychological Works of Sigmund Freud*. London: Hogarth, 1955.

Freud, Sigmund. "The Question of Lay Analysis (1926)." In *The Essentials of Psycho-Analysis*. Translated by James Strachey. London: Vintage, 2005.

Freud, Sigmund. *Three Contributions to the Sexual Theory.* Authorized Translation by A. A. Brill, with Introduction by James J. Putnam. New York: The Journal of Nervous and Mental Disease Pub. Co., 1910.

Freud, Sigmund. *Three Essays on the Theory of Sexuality*. Translated by James Strachey. London: Hogarth, 1962.

Freud, Sigmund. *Three Essays on the Theory of Sexuality.* Authorized Translation by James Strachey. London: Imago, 1949.

Freud, Sigmund. *Totem and Taboo: Some Points of* Agreement between the Mental Lives of Savages and Neurotics. Translated by James Strachey. London: Routledge and Paul, 1950.

Freud, Sigmund. *Two Case Histories ("Little Hans" and the "Rat Man")*. Edited and translated by James Strachey. Vol. 10. *The Standard Edition of the Complete Psychological Works of Sigmund Freud.* London: Hogarth, 1955.

Freud, Sigmund. "Über die Psychogenese eines Falls von weiblicher Homosexualität." *Internationale Zeitschrift für Psychoanalyse* 6, no. 1 (1920): 1–24.

Freud, Sigmund. "Über die weibliche Sexualität." *Internationale Zeitschrift für Psychoanalyse* 17 (1931): 317–32.

Freud, Sigmund. "Über die weibliche Sexualität (1931)." In *Sigmund Freud Studienausgabe Band V: Sexualleben*. Edited by Alexander Mitscherlich, Angela Richards, and James Strachey, 5:273–92. Frankfurt am Main: Fischer, 2000.

Freud, Sigmund. "Über infantile Sexualtheorien." *Sexual-Probleme* 1, no. 12 (December 1908): 763–79.

Freud, Sigmund. "Über infantile Sexualtheorien (1908)." In *Sigmund Freud Studienausgabe Band V: Sexualleben*. Edited by Alexander Mitscherlich, Angela Richards, and James Strachey, 5:169ff. Frankfurt am Main: Fischer, 2000.

Freud, Sigmund. "Zur Ätiologie der Hysterie (1896)." In *Sigmund Freud Studienausgabe Band VI: Hysterie und Angst*. Edited by Alexander Mitscherlich, Angela Richards, and James Strachey. Vol. 6. Frankfurt am Main: Fischer, 2000.

Freud, Sigmund. "Zur sexuellen Aufklärung der Kinder (1907)." In *Sigmund Freud Studienausgabe Band V: Sexualleben*. Edited by Alexander Mitscherlich, Angela Richards, and James Strachey, 5:159ff. Frankfurt am Main: Fischer, 2000.

Fricke, Toni. "Aus dem Empfindungsleben eines 'Transvestiten'! [Die Welt der Transvestiten]." *Die Freundin* 1, no. 2 (September 12, 1924): n.p.
Fricke, Toni. "Ein Transvestit ist vogelfrei." *Die Freundin* 3, no. 18 (September 19, 1927): n.p.
Friedländer, Prof. Dr. "Kritische Bemerkungen über neuere Arbeiten Freuds und seiner Anhänger." *Zeitschrift für angewandte Psychologie und psychologische Sammelforschung* 5 (1911): 587–97.
Fuchs, Alfred. "Therapeutische Bestrebungen auf dem Gebiete sexueller Perversionen." *Jahrbuch für sexuelle Zwischenstufen* 4 (1902): 177–86.
Fürth, Henriette. "Sexuelle Kriegsfragen." *Zeitschrift für Sexualwissenschaft* 2 (1915/1916): 133–37.
Goldmann, Lothar. "Über das Wesen des Umkleidungstriebes (Der Transvestitismus)." *Geschlecht und Gesellschaft* 12, nos. 7–12 (1924): 281–88 (nos. 7/8); 289–96 (nos. 9/10); 334–78 (nos. 11/12).
Gutheil, Emil, and Wilhelm Stekel. "XVI. Analyse eines Falles von Transvestitismus." In *Der Fetischismus*, 7:534–70. Störungen des Trieb- und Affektlebens (die parapathischen Erkrankungen). Berlin: Urban & Schwarzenberg, 1923.
H., Anna Maria. "Warum verzagen? [Die Welt der Transvestiten]." *Die Freundin* 7, no. 33 (August 19, 1931): n.p.
Haire, Norman. *Rejuvenation: The Work of Steinach, Voronoff, and Others*. London: Allen & Unwin, 1924.
Haire, Norman, ed. *W.L.S.R. World League for Sexual Reform. Proceedings of the Third Congress (London)*. London: Kegan Paul, 1930.
Hall, G. Stanley. *Adolescence: Its Psychology and Its Relations to Physiology, Anthropology, Sociology, Sex, Crime, Religion and Education*. 2 vols. New York: Appleton, 1904.
Hariet. "Als Fräulein in Belgien." *Die Freundin* 8, no. 26 (June 29, 1932): n.p.
"Heldentaten einer Ungarin im Weltkrieg." *Frauenliebe* 5, no. 14 (1930): 1–2.
Hiller, Kurt. "Sprechsaal: Die Transvestiten." *Monatsschrift für Kriminalpsychologie und Strafrechtsreform* 7 (November 1910): 613–15.
Hirsch, Max. "Psychoanalyse oder Hormonbehandlung." *Archiv für Frauenkunde* 14, no. 5 (1928): 445.
Hirschfeld, M., and E. Burchard. "Zu Dr. Stiers Artikel 'Ueber die Aetiologie des konträren Sexualgefühls.'" *Monatsschrift für Psychiatrie und Neurologie* 32 (1912): 549–55.
Hirschfeld, Magnus. *Berlins Drittes Geschlecht* [1904]. Edited by Manfred Herzer. Berlin: Rosa Winkel, 1991.
Hirschfeld, Magnus. "Das Ergebnis der statistischen Untersuchungen über den Prozentsatz der Homosexuellen." *Jahrbuch für sexuelle Zwischenstufen* 6 (1904): 109–78.
Hirschfeld, Magnus. *Der urnische Mensch*. Aus: Jahrbuch für sexuelle Zwischenstufen 5.1903. Leipzig: Spohr, 1903.
Hirschfeld, Magnus. *Die Homosexualität des Mannes und des Weibes*. 2nd ed. Berlin: Louis Marcus, 1920.
Hirschfeld, Magnus. "Die intersexuelle Konstitution." *Jahrbuch für sexuelle Zwischenstufen* 23 (1923): 3–27.

Hirschfeld, Magnus. *Die Transvestiten. Eine Untersuchung über den erotischen Verkleidungstrieb*. Berlin: Med. Verlag Alfred Pulvermacher, 1910.

Hirschfeld, Magnus. *Die Transvestiten: Eine Untersuchung über den erotischen Verkleidungstrieb*. 2nd ed. Leipzig: Verlag "Wahrheit" Ferdinand Spohr, 1925.

Hirschfeld, Magnus. "Die Untersuchungen und Forschungen von Prof. E. Steinach über künstliche Vermännlichung, Verweiblichung und Hermaphrodisierung." *Jahrbuch für sexuelle Zwischenstufen* 17, no. 1 (1917): 3–20.

Hirschfeld, Magnus. *Die Weltreise eines Sexualforschers*. Brugg, Switz.: Bözberg, 1933.

Hirschfeld, Magnus. "Einführungswort des Vorsitzenden." In *Sexualnot und Sexualreform. Verhandlungen der Weltliga für Sexualreform. IV. Kongress. Abgehalten zu Wien vom 16. bis 23. September 1930*. Edited by Herbert Steiner, xxxvii–xliii. Vienna: Elbemühl, 1931.

Hirschfeld, Magnus. "Einteilung der Sexualwissenschaft." *Zeitschrift für Sexualwissenschaft* 1, no. 10 (1908): 569–88.

Hirschfeld, Magnus. *Geschlechtliche Entwicklungsstörungen mit besonderer Berücksichtigung der Onanie*. 3 vols. Vol. 1. Sexualpathologie. Ein Lehrbuch für Ärzte und Studierende. Bonn: A. Marcus & E. Webers, 1917.

Hirschfeld, Magnus. *Geschlechtskunde (auf Grund dreißigjähriger Forschung und Erfahrung)*. 5 vols. Vol. 1. Die körperseelischen Grundlagen. Stuttgart: Julius Püttmann, 1926.

Hirschfeld, Magnus. "Hodenbefunde bei intersexuellen Varianten." *Archiv für Frauenkunde und Eugenetik* 7 (1921).

Hirschfeld, Magnus. "Ist die Homosexualität körperlich oder seelisch bedingt?" *Münchener medizinische Wochenschrift* 65 (1918): 298–99.

Hirschfeld, Magnus. "Kastratenstudien. Untersuchungen über sexuellen Chemismus." *Sexual-Probleme* 8, no. 2 (1912): 81–95.

Hirschfeld, Magnus. *Naturgesetze der Liebe: eine gemeinverständliche Untersuchung über den Liebes-Eindruck, Liebes-Drang und Liebes-Ausdruck*. Berlin: Pulvermacher, 1912.

Hirschfeld, Magnus. "Operative Behandlung der Homosexualität." *Vierteljahresberichte des Wissenschaftlich–humanitären Komitees/Jahrbuch für sexuelle Zwischenstufen* 17 (1917): 189–90.

Hirschfeld, Magnus. "Presidential Address: The Development and Scope of Sexology." In *W.L.S.R. World League for Sexual Reform. Proceedings of the Third Congress [London]*. Edited by Norman Haire, xi–xv. London: Kegan Paul, 1930.

Hirschfeld, Magnus. "Sexualreform im Sinne der Sexualwissenschaft." In *Sexual Reform Congress Copenhagen 1.-5.:VII:1928. W.L.S.R. World League for Sexual Reform/Weltliga für Sexualreform/Ligue mondiale pour la réforme sexuelle/Tutmonda ligo por seksaj reformoj*. Edited by Hertha Riese and J. H. Leunbach, 26–29. Copenhagen: Levin & Munksgaard; Georg Thieme, 1929.

Hirschfeld, Magnus. *Sexuelle Zwischenstufen: Das männliche Weib und der weibliche Mann*. 2nd ed. 3 vols. Vol. 2. Sexualpathologie: Ein Lehrbuch für Ärzte und Studierende. Bonn: A. Marcus & E. Webers, 1922.

Hirschfeld, Magnus. *Sittengeschichte des Weltkrieges*. 2nd ed. Leipzig: Verlag für Sexualwissenschaft Schneider, 1930.

Hirschfeld, Magnus. *The Homosexuality of Men and Women*. Translated by Michael A. Lombardi-Nash. Amherst, NY: Prometheus Books, 2000.

Hirschfeld, Magnus. "Ursachen und Wesen des Uranismus." *Jahrbuch für sexuelle Zwischenstufen* 5, no. 1 (1903): 1–193.

Hirschfeld, Magnus. "Zur Methodik der Sexualwissenschaft." *Zeitschrift für Sexualwissenschaft* 1, no. 12 (1908): 681–712.

Hirschfeld, Magnus, and Ernst Burchard. *Der sexuelle Infantilismus*. Juristisch-psychiatrische Grenzfragen. Zwanglose Abhandlungen. Halle a.S.: Carl Marhold, 1913.

Hirschfeld, Magnus, and Max Tilke. *Der erotische Verkleidungstrieb (Die Transvestiten): Illustrierter Teil*. 2 vols. Vol. 2. Berlin: Alfred Pulvermacher, 1912.

Hitschmann, E. "Adler, San.-Rat Dr. Otto: Die mangelhafte Geschlechtsempfindung des Weibes. Fischers med. Buchhandlung H. Kornfeld, Berlin, 1924 [Review]." *Internationale Zeitschrift für Psychoanalyse* 11 (1925): 494.

Hitschmann, E. "Psychoanalyse trotz Hormonen." *Allgemeine Zeitschrift für Psychotherapie und psychische Hygiene* 1, no. 4 (1928): 477–80.

Hitschmann, E. "Zur Psychoanalyse der Kriegsneurosen [Review]." *Internationale Zeitschrift für Psychoanalyse* 7, no. 4 (1921): 484.

Hoffmann, Käthe. "Freud, Sigm.: 'Über die Psychogenese eines Falls von weiblicher Homosexualität' [Review]." *Zeitschrift für Sexualwissenschaft* 8, no. 2 (1921): 79–80.

Hofstetter, A. "Transvestitismus und Metatropismus." *Das 3. Geschlecht*, no. 4 (1931): 14–15.

Homann, Walter, ed. *Tagebuch einer männlichen Braut*. Berlin: Dreyer, 1907.

Horney, Karen. "Der Männlichkeitskomplex der Frau." *Archiv für Frauenkunde* 13, no. 1–2 (1927): 141–54.

Horney, Karen. "Die Verleugnung der Vagina." *Internationale Zeitschrift für Psychoanalyse* 19 (1933): 372–84.

Horney, Karen. "Gehemmte Weiblichkeit. Psychoanalytischer Beitrag zum Problem der Frigidität." *Zeitschrift für Sexualwissenschaft* 13, no. 2 (1926): 67–77.

Horney, Karen. "Referat: Deutsch, Dr. Helene. Zur Psychologie der weiblichen Sexualfunktionen (Neue Arbeiten zur ärztlichen PsA. Nr. V.) Internat. PsA. Verlag, 1925." *Internationale Zeitschrift für Psychoanalyse* 11 (1925): 388–94.

Horney, Karen. "The Flight from Womanhood: The Masculinity Complex in Women as Viewed by Men and Women." *International Journal of Psycho-Analysis* 7, nos. 3/4 (1926): 314–39.

Horney, Karen. "Zur Genese des weiblichen Kastrationskomplexes." *Internationale Zeitschrift für Psychoanalyse* 9 (1923): 12–26.

Hug-Hellmuth, H. von. "Die Kriegsneurose der Frau." *Geschlecht und Gesellschaft* 9 (1914): 505–14.

Hug-Hellmuth, Hermine. "Zur Technik der Kinderanalyse." *Internationale Zeitschrift für ärztliche Psychoanalyse* 4, no. 1 (1921): 179–97.

Jones, Ernest. *Sigmund Freud, Life and Work*. 3 vols. *Vol. 2 Years of Maturity 1901–1919*. London: Hogarth, 1955.

Jones, Ernest. *Sigmund Freud, Life and Work*. 3 vols. *Vol. 3: The Last Phase, 1919–1939*. London: Hogarth, 1957.

Juliusburger, Otto. "Zur Kenntnis der Kriegsneurosen." *Monatsschrift für Psychiatrie und Neurologie* 38 (1915): 305–18.

Jung, C. G. *The Collected Works of C. G. Jung: Freud and Psychoanalysis*. Edited by Herbert Read, Michael Fordham, and Gerard Adler. 20 vols. Vol. 4. Bollingen Series. New York: Pantheon Books, 1961.

Jung, C. G. "The Concept of Libido." In *The Collected Works of C. G. Jung*. Edited by Herbert Read, Michael Fordham, and Gerard Adler, 4:111–28. Bollingen Series. New York: Pantheon Books, 1961.

Jung, C. G. "The Theory of Psychoanalysis." In *The Collected Works of C. G. Jung*. Edited by Herbert Read, Michael Fordham, and Gerard Adler. Vol. 4. Bollingen Series. New York: Pantheon Books, 1961.

Jung, C. G. "Über Konflikte der kindlichen Seele." *Jahrbuch für psychoanalytische und psychopathologische Forschungen* 2 (1910): 33–58.

Jünger, Ernst. *In Stahlgewittern: historisch-kritische Ausgabe*. Edited by Helmuth Kiesel. Stuttgart: Klett-Cotta, 2013.

K., E. [No title.] *Die Freundin* 3, no. 13 (July 11, 1927): n.p.

Karsch-Haack, Ferdinand. "Junggesellin und Junggeselle (Die Transmutistin)." *Garçonne* 4 (1931): 1–4.

Karsch-Haack, Ferdinand. "Transvestismus und Aberglauben [Die Welt der Transvestiten]" 5, no. 14 (October 2, 1929).

Klein, Melanie. "Die Rolle der Schule in der libidinösen Entwicklung des Kindes." *Internationale Zeitschrift für ärztliche Psychoanalyse* 9 (1923): 323–44.

Klein, Melanie. "Frühstadien des Ödipuskonfliktes." *Internationale Zeitschrift für Psychoanalyse* 14 (1928): 65–77.

Kn., Werner. "Der Kampf der Transvestiten." *Die Freundin* 4, no. 7 (April 2, 1928): 4.

Knopf, Olga. "Über Frigidität." *Internationale Zeitschrift für Individualpsychologie. Arbeiten aus dem Gebiete der Psychotherapie, Psychologie und Pädagogik*, no. 1 (1930): 151–59.

Krafft-Ebing, R. von. *Psychopathia sexualis: Mit besonderer Berücksichtigung der konträren Sexualempfindung: Eine medizinisch-gerichtliche Studie für Ärzte und Juristen*. 15th ed. Stuttgart: F. Enke, 1918.

Krafft-Ebing, R. von. *Psychopathia Sexualis with Especial Reference to Antipathic Sexual Instinct: A Medico-Forensic Study*. English translation of 10th German ed. London: Rebman, 1899.

Krische, P[aul]. "Generalversammlung/Annual Convention." In *Sexualnot und Sexualreform. Verhandlungen der Weltliga für Sexualreform. IV. Kongress. Abgehalten zu Wien vom 16. bis 23. September 1930*, xxv–xxx. Vienna: Elbemühl, 1931.

Kronfeld, Arthur. "Der konstitutionelle Faktor bei sexuellen Triebanomalien." *Zeitschrift für Sexualwissenschaft* 8 (1921).

Kronfeld, Arthur. "Ein Transvestit über seine Eigenart." *Sexualreform*. Mitteilungen aus dem Institut für Sexualwissenschaft, 11, no. 11 (1922): 167–69.

Kronfeld, Arthur. "Sexualpsychopathologie." In *Handbuch der Psychiatrie*. Edited by Gustav Aschaffenburg, separate reprint. Leipzig, Ger.: Franz Deuticke, 1923.

Kronfeld, Arthur. "Transvestitismus." In *Handwörterbuch der Sexualwissenschaft*. Edited by Max Marcuse, 2nd enlarged ed., 776. Bonn: A. Marcus & E. Weber's Verlag (Reprint: Berlin: de Gruyter, 2001), 1926.

Kronfeld, Arthur. "Über die psychologischen Theorien Freuds und verwandte Anschauungen. Systematik und kritische Erörterung." *Archiv für die gesamte Psychologie* 22 (1911): 130–248.

Kronfeld, Arthur. *Über psychosexuellen Infantilismus, eine Konstitutionsanomalie*. Edited by Magnus Hirschfeld. Sexus: Monographien aus dem Institut für Sexualwissenschaft in Berlin. Leipzig: Ernst Bircher, 1921.

Kutzinski, A. "Einige Bemerkungen zur Psychopathologie der sogenannten Intestinal-Neurosen im Anschluß an Erfahrungen bei Soldaten." *Monatsschrift für Psychiatrie und Neurologie* 40 (1916): 317ff.

Lampé, Arno Ed., and Eduard Strauss. "Die Bedeutung der Organe mit innerer Sekretion für sexualpsychologische und -pathologische Fragestellungen." *Sexual-Probleme* 8, no. 8 (1912): 541–46.

Lampl-de Groot, A. "The Evolution of the Oedipus Complex in Women." *International Journal of Psychoanalysis* 9 (1928): 332–45.

Lampl-de Groot, A. [Jeanne]. "Zur Entwicklungsgeschichte des Ödipuskomplexes der Frau." *Internationale Zeitschrift für Psychoanalyse* 13, no. 3 (1927): 269–82.

Lichtenstern, Robert. "Die Erfolge der Altersbekämpfung beim Manne nach Steinach." *Berliner klinische Wochenschrift* 57 (1920): 989–95.

Lilly aus Hamburg. "Mein erster Ausgang als Dame." *Die Freundin* 6, no. 11 (March 12, 1930): n.p.

Lindner, Sámuel. "Das Saugen an den Fingern, Lippen, etc. bei den Kindern (Ludeln)." *Jahrbuch für Kinderheilkunde und physische Erziehung*, Neue Folge, 14 (1879): 68–89.

Lipschuetz, A. *Die Pubertätsdrüse und ihre Wirkungen*. Bern: Bircher, 1919.

Ludwig, M. "Mädchenbub." *Das 3. Geschlecht*, no. 1 (1930): 8–10.

Maeder, A. "A. Forel, Der Hypnotismus oder die Suggestion und die Psychotherapie [Review]." *Zentralblatt für Psychoanalyse* 1, no. 12 (1911): 598–99.

Marcuse, Max. "Ein Fall von Geschlechtsumwandlungstrieb." *Zeitschrift für Psychotherapie und medizinische Psychologie* 6 (1916): 176–93.

Marcuse, Max, ed. *Handwörterbuch der Sexualwissenschaft. Enzyklopädie der natur-u. kulturwissenschaftlichen Sexualkunde des Menschen* [1926]. 2nd ed. (reprint with new introduction by Robert Jütte). Berlin: Walter de Gruyter, 2001.

Marcuse, Max. "'Sexual-Probleme.' Ein Wort zur Einführung." *Sexual-Probleme* 1, no. 1 (1908): 1–5.

Marcuse, Max. "Über die Problematik der Sexualpsychologie des Weibes und der vergleichenden Sexualpsychologie der Geschlechter." *Zeitschrift für Sexualwissenschaft* 6, no. 9 (1919): 273–83.

Marcuse, Max, ed. *Verhandlungen des I. Internationalen Kongresses für Sexualforschung. Berlin vom 10. bis 16. Oktober 1926. Veranstaltet von der Internationalen Gesellschaft für Sexualforschung*. Berlin: Marcus & Weber, 1928.

Maria. "Brief eines Transvestiten [Die Welt der Transvestiten]." *Die Freundin* 7, no. 52 (December 28, 1932): n.p.

Mendel, Kurt. "Kriegsbeobachtungen. XII. Transvestitismus und Homosexualität." *Neurologisches Zentralblatt* 38, no. 1 (1919): 13–20.

Meng, Heinrich. "Sexualpädagogik & Psychoanalyse." In *World League for Sexual Reform (Proceedings of the Second Congress): Sexual Reform Congress Copenhagen 1–5: VII; 1928*. Edited by Hertha Riese and J. H. Leunbach, 133–38. Copenhagen; Leipzig: Levin & Munksgaard; Georg Thieme, 1929.

Mimi. "Was wir Transvestiten leiden." *Die Freundin* 4, no. 10 (May 14, 1928): n.p.

Moll, Albert. *Behandlung der Homosexualität: biochemisch oder psychisch?* Bonn: Marcus & Weber, 1921.

Moll, Albert. *Das Sexuelleben des Kindes*. Berlin: Walther, 1909.

Moll, Albert. "Die Behandlung der Homosexualität." *Jahrbuch für sexuelle Zwischenstufen* 2 (1900): 1–29.

Moll, Albert. *Die konträre Sexualempfindung* [1891]. 3rd revised ed. Berlin: Fischer's Medicin. Buchhandlung, 1899.

Moll, Albert. *Ein Leben als Arzt der Seele. Erinnerungen*. Dresden: Reissner, 1936.

Moll, Albert, ed. *Handbuch der Sexualwissenschaften: mit besonderer Berücksichtigung der kulturgeschichtlichen Beziehungen*. 2nd ed. (with G. Buschan). Leipzig: Vogel, 1921.

Moll, Albert. *The Sexual Life of the Child, with an Introduction by Edward L. Thorndike*. Translated by Eden Paul. New York: Macmillan, 1913.

Moll, Albert. *Untersuchungen über die Libido sexualis* [1897]. Berlin: Fischer's Medicin. Buchhandlung, 1898.

Müller-Braunschweig, Carl. "Das Problem der Angst in seinem Verhältnis zur psychoanalytischen Libidotheorie." *Zeitschrift für Sexualwissenschaft* 10, no. 9 (1924): 233–37.

Nachmansohn, M. "Die Psychoanalyse eines Falles von Homosexualität." *Internationale Zeitschrift für Psychoanalyse* 8, no. 1 (1922): 45–64.

Näcke, Paul. "Kleinere Mitteilungen. 7. Bemerkungen zu den Freudschen Symbolen." *Archiv für Kriminal-Anthopologie und Kriminalistik* 47, no. 3/4 (1912): 160–61.

Näcke, Paul. "Kriminologische und sexologische Studien. I. Zum Kapitel der Transvestiten nebst Bemerkungen zur weiblicher [*sic*] Homosexualität." *Archiv für Kriminal-Anthropologie und Kriminalistik* 47, no. 3/4 (1912): 237–52.

Näcke, Paul. "Die Diagnose der Homosexualität." *Neurologisches Zentralblatt* 27, no. 8 (1908): 337-51.

Näcke, Paul. "Echte, angeborene Homosexualität und Pseudohomosexualität." *Deutsche medizinische Wochenschrift*, 35, no. 34 (1909): 1477-79.

Näcke, Paul. "Ein Besuch bei den Homosexuellen in Berlin." *Archiv für Kriminal-Anthropologie und Kriminalistik* 15 (1904): 244-63.

Näcke, Paul. "Einige psychiatrische Erfahrungen als Stütze für die Lehre von der bisexuellen Anlage des Menschen." *Jahrbuch für sexuelle Zwischenstufen* 8 (1906): 585–603.

Näcke, Paul. "Über tardive Homosexualität." *Sexual-Probleme* 7, no. 9 (1911): 612–34.

Näcke, Prof. Dr. P. "Die Behandlung der Homosexualität." *Sexual-Probleme* 6, no. 8 (1910): 585–604.

Nordau, Max. *Degeneration* [Entartung, 1892]. New York: Howard Fertig, 1968.
Nunberg, Herman, and Ernst Federn, eds. "Diskussion über Molls Buch Das Sexualleben des Kindes, 58. Protokoll, Vortragsabend: am 11. November 1908, anwesend Prof. Freud, Bass, Federn, Graf, Hitschmann, Joachim, Rank, Rie, Reitler, Steiner, Sadger, Wittels." In *Protokolle der Wiener Psychoanalytischen Vereinigung*. Vol. 2. Giessen, Ger.: Psychosozial-Verlag, 2008.
Nussbaum, M. "Innere Sekretion und Nerveneinfluß." *Ergebnisse der Anatomie und Entwicklungsgeschichte* 15 (1905): 39–89.
Pfeifer, Dr. "Dr. Fr. Pick, Über Sexualstörungen im Kriege. Vortrag, gehalten in der Vereinigung Prager Ärzte (D. M. W. 1917)." *Internationale Zeitschrift für Psychoanalyse* 6 (1920): 174–75.
Pick, Friedel. "Über Sexualstörungen im Kriege." *Wiener klinische Wochenschrift* 45 (1917): 1418–19.
Pick, Friedel. "Über Sexualstörungen im Kriege." *Deutsche medizinische Wochenschrift*, no. 38 (1917).
Psycho-Analysis and the War Neuroses. International Psychoanalytic Library 2. London, Vienna, New York: International Psycho-Analytical Press, 1921.
Radszuweit, Friedrich. "Transvestitismus ist eine Krankheit." *Das 3. Geschlecht*, no. 4 (1931): 1.
Radszuweit, Friedrich. "Zum Kampf der Transvestiten." *Das 3. Geschlecht*, no. 4 (1931): 14–16.
Rank, Otto. "Die Symbolschichtung im Wecktraum und ihre Wiederkehr im mythischen Denken." *Jahrbuch für psychoanalytische und psychopathologische Forschungen* 4 (1912): 51–115.
Ratner, Prof. Dr. med. "Über die Psyche des Weibes." *Zeitschrift für Sexualwissenschaft* 6 (1919): 349–51.
Redaktion [Editors]. "Masochist und Transvestist." *Das 3. Geschlecht*, no. 3 (1931): 1.
Reich, Wilhelm. "Die Sexualnot der werktätigen Massen und die Schwierigkeiten der Sexualreform." In *Sexualnot und Sexualreform. Verhandlungen der Weltliga für Sexualreform. IV. Kongress. Abgehalten zu Wien vom 16. bis 23. September 1930*. Edited by Herbert Steiner, 72–87. Vienna: Elbemühl, 1931.
Reich, Wilhelm. "Arthur Kronfeld: Sexualpathologie (Handbuch der Psychiatrie, Deuticke, Wien, 1923) [Review]." *Internationale Zeitschrift für Psychoanalyse* 10, no. 3 (1924): 312–13.
"Theater ohne Frau (Welt der Transvestiten) [Review]." *Die Freundin* 9, no. 2 (January 18, 1933): n.p.
Rex, Loni. "Die Welt der Transvestiten. Briefe die uns erreichen." *Die Freundin* 6, no. 43 (October 22, 1930): n.p.
Rieck, Hubert. "Paul und Pauline! Eine abstrakte Betrachtung der Wesensart mit wissenschaftlichem Hintergrund." *Das 3. Geschlecht*, no. 1 (1931): 7–8.
Riese, Hertha, and J. H. Leunbach, eds. *Sexual Reform Congress Copenhagen 1.–5.:VII:1928. W.L.S.R. World League for Sexual Reform/Weltliga für Sexualreform/Ligue mondiale pour la réforme sexuelle/Tutmonda ligo por seksaj reformoj*. Copenhagen: Levin & Munksgaard; Georg Thieme, 1929.
Riviere, Joan. "Womanliness as a Masquerade." *International Journal of Psychoanalysis* 10 (1929): 303–13.

Rohleder, Hermann. *Moderne Behandlung der Homosexualität und Impotenz durch Hodeneinpflanzung*. Berlin: Fischer's medizinische Buchhandlung, 1917.

S., Dolly. "Transvestitenfragen." *Die Freundin* 4, no. 9 (April 30, 1928): n.p.

Sadger, Isidor. "Fragment der Psychoanalyse eines Homosexuellen." *Jahrbuch für sexuelle Zwischenstufen* 9 (1908): 339–424.

Sadger, Isidor. "Ketzergedanken über Homosexualität." *Archiv für Kriminal-Anthopologie und Kriminalistik* 59 (1914): 321–32.

Sadger, Isidor. *Recollecting Freud*. Edited by Alan Dundes. Madison: University of Wisconsin Press, 2005.

Sadger, Isidor. "Magnus Hirschfeld, Die Homosexualität des Mannes und des Weibes [Review]." *Internationale Zeitschrift für Psychoanalyse* 2, no. 4 (1914): 392–96.

Sadger, Isidor. "L. Loewenfeld, 'Über die Sexualität im Kindesalter,' Sexual-Probleme (Juli/August 1911) [Review]." *Zentralblatt für Psychoanalyse* 2, no. 3 (1912): 142–43.

Sadger, Isidor. "Sexuelle Perversionen." *Jahrbuch der Psychoanalyse* 6 (1914): 296–313.

Sadger, Isidor. "Über den Wert der Autobiographien sexuell Perverser." *Fortschritte der Medizin* 31 (1913): 705–14, 736–49, 772–79.

Sadger, Isidor. "Welcher Wert kommt den Erzählungen und Autobiographien der Homosexuellen zu?" *Archiv für Kriminal-Anthopologie und Kriminalistik* 53, no. 1/2 (1913): 179–87.

Sadger, Isidor. "'Wissenschaftlich-humanitäre' Propaganda der Homosexuellen." *Sexual-Probleme* 9, no. 11 (1913): 785–89.

Sadger, Isidor. "Zur Ätiologie der konträren Sexualempfindung." *Medizinische Klinik* 5, no. 2 (1909): 53–56.

Sadger, J. [*sic*]. "Über Urethralerotik." *Jahrbuch für psychoanalytische und psychopathologische Forschungen* 2 (1910): 409–50.

Sadger, J. [*sic*]. "Ein Fall von multipler Perversion mit hysterischen Absenzen." *Jahrbuch für psychoanalytische und psychopathologische Forschungen* 2 (1910): 59–133.

Sadger, S. [*sic*]. "Ist die konträre Sexualempfindung heilbar." *Zeitschrift für Sexualwissenschaft* 1, no. 12 (1908): 712–20.

Schwarz, Dr. Erich Maria. "Die Welt der Transvestiten: Körpergerechte Männerkleidung." *Die Freundin* 7, no. 30 (July 29, 1931): n.p.

Schwarz, G. "Zur Kenntnis der Gedächtnisstörung nach Granatenkontusion." *Monatsschrift für Psychiatrie und Neurologie* 40 (1916): 212ff.

Schweitzer, E. E. "Sadismus und Sadisten." *Das 3. Geschlecht*, no. 1 (1930): 32–38.

Sellheim, Hugo. "Macht der Sport die Frau glücklich? Ein Epilog zu den Deutschen Frauen-Meisterschaften in Magdeburg 1931." *Uhu*, no. 1 (1931): 18–24.

Spengler, Oswald. *Der Untergang des Abendlandes: Umrisse einer Morphologie der Weltgeschichte*. 2 vols. Vienna (1918); Munich (1919): Braumüller; Beck, 1918.

Spielrein, S. "Die Äußerungen des Ödipuskomplexes im Kindesalter." *Internationale Zeitschrift für ärztliche Psychoanalyse* 4, no. 1 (1916): 44–48.

Starling, E. H. "Hormones." *Nature*, December 1, 1923, 795–98.

Stechow, E. "E. Steinach. Geschlechtstrieb und echt sekundäre Geschlechtsmerkmale als Folge der innersekretorischen Funktion der Keimdrüsen. Zentralbl. f. Physiologie. Bd. 24. Nr. 13. 1910. 18 S. [Review]." *Sexual-Probleme* 7, no. 9 (1911): 652–54.

Steinach, Eugen. "Verjüngung durch experimentelle Neubelebung der alternden Pubertätsdrüse." *Archiv für Entwicklungsmechanik* 46 (1920): 557-610.

Steinach, Eugen. "Willkürliche Umwandlung von Säugetier-Männchen in Tiere [*sic*] mit ausgeprägt weiblichen Geschlechtscharakteren und weiblicher Psyche." *Pflüger's Archiv für gesamte Physiologie* 144 (1912): 71–108.

Steinach, Eugen, and Josef Loebel. *Sex and Life: Forty Years of Biological and Medical Experiments*. London: Faber, 1940.

Steiner, Herbert, ed. "Eröffnung des Kongresses (Begrüßungsansprachen)." In *Sexualnot und Sexualreform. Verhandlungen der Weltliga für Sexualreform. IV. Kongress. Abgehalten zu Wien vom 16. bis 23. September 1930*, xxxi–xxxvi. Vienna: Elbemühl, 1931.

Stekel, Wilhelm. *Der Fetischismus*. Vol. 7. Störungen Des Trieb- Und Affektlebens. Berlin: Urban & Schwarzenberg, 1923.

Stekel, Wilhelm. *Die Geschlechtskälte der Frau (Eine psychopathologie des weiblichen Liebeslebens)*. Vol. 3, *Störungen des Trieb- und Affektlebens*. 2nd revised ed. Berlin: Urban & Schwarzenberg, 1921.

Stekel, Wilhelm. *Die Impotenz des Mannes (Die psychischen Störungen der männlichen Sexualfunktion)*. Vol. 4. Störungen Des Trieb- Und Affektlebens. 2nd ed. Berlin: Urban & Schwarzenberg, 1923.

Stekel, Wilhelm. "Die sexuelle Wurzel der Kleptomanie." *Zeitschrift für Sexualwissenschaft* 1, no. 10 (1908): 588–600.

Stekel, Wilhelm. "Fragmentary Analysis of a Transvestite." In *Frigidity in Woman, in Relation to Her Sex Life*. Translated by James S. Van Teslaar. Disorders of the Instincts and the Emotions: The Parapathiac Disorders. New York: Liveright, 1943.

Stekel, Wilhelm. *Frigidity in Woman in Relation to Her Love Life*. Translated by James S. Van Teslaar. 2 vols. Vol. 1. Disorders of the Instincts and the Emotions. The Parapathia Disorders. New York: Liveright, 1926.

Stekel, Wilhelm. *Frigidity in Woman in Relation to Her Love Life*. Translated by James S. Van Teslaar. 2 vols. Vol. 2. Disorders of the Instincts and the Emotions. The Parapathia Disorders. New York: Liveright, 1926.

Stekel, Wilhelm. "Krieg und Impotenz." *Medizinische Klinik* 30 (1920): 775ff.

Stekel, Wilhelm. "Masken der Homosexualität (Originalarbeit)." *Zentralblatt für Psychoanalyse* 2, no. 7 (1912): 367–72.

Stekel, Wilhelm. *Onanie und Homosexualität (Die homosexuelle Neurose)*. Vol. 2. Störungen des Trieb- und Affektlebens. Berlin: Urban & Schwarzenberg, 1917.

Stekel, Wilhelm. "Die Transvestiten [Review]." *Zentralblatt für Psychoanalyse* 1 (1910/1911): 55–58.

Stekel, Wilhelm. "Ein Fall von multipler Perversion mit hysterischen Absenzen [Review]." *Jahrbuch für psychoanalytische Forschungen* 2 (1910): 116.

Stekel, Wilhelm. "Magnus Horschfeld [*sic*]. Die Homosexualität des Mannes u. des Weibes [Review]." *Zentralblatt für Psychoanalyse* 4, no. 11/12 (1913): 614.

Stekel, Wilhelm. "Ueber Coitus im Kindesalter." *Wiener medizinische Blätter* 16 (April 18, 1895): 247–49.

Stekel, Wilhelm. "XV. Fragment der Analyse einer Transvestitin." In *Die Geschlechtskälte der Frau (Eine psychopathologie des weiblichen Liebeslebens)*. 2nd revised ed., 429–56. Berlin: Urban & Schwarzenberg, 1921.

Stern, Erich. "Zur Kennntnis der weiblichen Inversion." *Zeitschrift für Sexualwissenschaft* 7 (1920): 197–202.

Stern, William. "Die Anwendung der Psychoanalyse auf Kindheit und Jugend. Ein Protest. Mit einem Anhang: Kritik einer Freudschen Kindes-Psychoanalyse, von Clara und William Stern." *Zeitschrift für angewandte Psychologie und psychologische Sammelforschung* 8 (1913/1914): 71–101.

Stöcker, Helene. "Die Ehe als psychologisches Problem." In *Sexualnot und Sexualreform. Verhandlungen der Weltliga für Sexualreform. IV. Kongress. Abgehalten zu Wien vom 16. bis 23. September 1930*. Edited by Herbert Steiner, 95–104. Vienna: Elbemühl, 1931.

Stöcker, Helene. "Homosexualität und Geschlechtsbewertung." *Geschlecht und Gesellschaft* 9, no. 7 (1914): 273-83.

Stöcker, Helene. "Kleine Mitteilungen: Krieg und sexuelle Abstinenz." *Zeitschrift für Sexualwissenschaft* 2 (1915/1916): 425ff.

Terman, Lewis M. "A Study in Precocity and Prematuration." *American Journal of Psychology* 16, no. 2 (April 1905): 145–83.

Theilhaber, Felix A. "Kleine Mitteilungen. Krieg und sexuelle Abstinenz." *Zeitschrift für Sexualwissenschaft* 2 (1915/1916): 464.

Thomalla, Curt, and Nicholas Kaufmann. *Der Steinach-Film (The Steinach Film)*. Documentary. Ufa Studios, 1922.

Ulrichs [pseud. Numa Numantius], Karl Heinrich. *Forschungen über das Räthsel der mann-männlichen Liebe (1864–1879)*. 12 vols. Reprint. Berlin: Rosa Winkel, 1994.

Ursula, Fred. "Wär' ich doch eine Frau. . . ." *Die Freundin* 3, no. 3 (February 21, 1927): n.p.

Viereck, George Sylvester. *Glimpses of the Great*. New York: Macauley, 1930.

Vorwahl, H. "Zur Sexualsymbolik der Sprache." *Zeitschrift für Sexualwissenschaft und Sexualpolitik* 18, no. 5 (October 1931): 315–18.

W., P. "Frauen als Soldaten." *Die Freundin* 9, no. 4 (January 25, 1933).

Weil, A., and Institut für Sexualwissenschaft, Berlin, eds. *Sexualreform und Sexualwissenschaft. Vorträge gehalten auf der I. Internationalen Tagung für Sexualreform auf sexualwissenschaftlicher Grundlage in Berlin*. Berlin: Julius Püttmann, 1922.

Weininger, Otto. *Geschlecht und Charakter. Eine prinzipielle Untersuchung*. München: Matthes & Seitz, 1997.

Weis, Marie. "Bericht über die . . . Zusammenkunft der transvestitischen Interessengemeinschaft 'D'Eon.'" *Garçonne*, 1930.

Weis, Marie. "Die Aufgaben der Vereinigung D'Eon [Der Transvestit]." *Garçonne*, no. 4 (December 1, 1930): 10.

Weis, Marie. "Transvestitismus und Gesellschaft." *Frauen-Liebe* 5, no. 12 (1930): n.p.

Werner, Friedel. "Das transvestitische Empfinden [Die Welt der Transvestiten]." *Die Freundin* 5, no. 10 (September 4, 1929): n.p.

White, W. "'Three Contributions to the Sexual Theory" by Prof. Sigm. Freud' [Review]." *Journal of Nervous and Mental Disease* 38 (1911): 126–28.

Wilmshöfer, Joseph. "Beiträge zur forensischen Beurteilung der Homosexualität im Kriege." *Zeitschrift für Sexualwissenschaft* 6, nos. 10/11 (1920): 303–20, 337–47.

Wolters, Emi. "Die Welt der Transvestiten." *Die Freundin* 7, no. 11 (March 18, 1931): n.p.

Wolters, Emi. "Transvestiten im Weltkriege [8-part series, 24 February to 13 April 1932, in 'Die Welt der Transvestiten' supplement]." *Die Freundin* 8, nos. 8 to 15 (1932).

Zur Psychoanalyse der Kriegsneurosen. Diskussion gehalten auf dem V. Internationalen Psychoanalytischen Kongreß in Budapest, 28. und 29. September 1918/5th International Psychoanalytical Congress, Budapest. Leipzig, Ger.: Internationaler Psychoanalytischer Verlag, 1919.

SECONDARY SOURCES

Ahmed, Sara. "'Making Feminist Points.'" *Feministkilljoys* (blog), September 11, 2013. http://feministkilljoys.com/2013/09/11/making-feminist-points.

Allen, Ann Taylor. "Feminism and Eugenics in Germany and Britain, 1900–1940: A Comparative Perspective." *German Studies Review* 23, no. 3 (2000): 477–505.

Allen, Ann Taylor. "German Radical Feminism and Eugenics, 1900–1908." *German Studies Review* 11, no. 1 (1988): 31–56.

Allen, Ann Taylor. "Mothers of the New Generation: Adele Schreiber, Helene Stöcker, and the Evolution of a German Idea of Motherhood, 1900–1914." *Signs: Journal of Women in Culture and Society* 10, no. 3 (1985): 418–38.

Amacher, Peter. *Freud's Neurological Education and Its Influence on Psychoanalytic Theory*. New York: International Universities Press, 1965.

Angelides, Steven. "Feminism, Child Sexual Abuse, and the Erasure of Child Sexuality." *GLQ: A Journal of Lesbian and Gay Studies* 10, no. 2 (2004): 141–77.

Ankum, Katharina von, ed. *Women in the Metropolis. Gender and Modernity in Weimar Culture*. Berkeley: University of California Press, 1997.

AP. "Trump Order Would Ban Most Transgender Troops from Serving." *NBC News*, March 24, 2018. https://www.nbcnews.com/news/us-news/trump-order-would-ban-most-transgender-troops-serving-n859686.

Appignanesi, Lisa, and John Forrester. *Freud's Women*. London: Basic Books, 1992.

Ariès, Philippe. *Centuries of Childhood; A Social History of Family Life*. Translated by Robert Baldick. New York: Knopf, 1962.

Bauer, Heike. *English Literary Sexology: Translations of Inversion, 1860–1930*. Basingstoke, UK: Palgrave Macmillan, 2009.

Bauer, Heike. "'Race,' Normativity and the History of Sexuality: The Case of Magnus Hirschfeld's Racism and Early Twentieth-Century Sexology." *Psychology and Sexuality* 1, no. 3 (2010): 239–49.

Bauer, Heike. ed. *Sexology and Translation: Cultural and Scientific Encounters across the Modern World*. Sexuality Studies. Philadelphia: Temple University Press, 2015.

Bauer, Heike. "Sexology Backward: Hirschfeld, Kinsey and the Reshaping of Sex Research in the 1950s." In *Queer 1950s: Rethinking Sexuality in the Postwar Years*. Edited by Heike Bauer and Matt Cook, 133–49. Basingstoke, UK: Palgrave Macmillan, 2012.

Bauer, Heike. *The Hirschfeld Archives: Violence, Death, and Modern Queer Culture*. Philadelphia: Temple University Press, 2017.

Bauer, Heike. "Theorizing Female Inversion: Sexology, Discipline, and Gender at the Fin de Siècle." *Journal of the History of Sexuality* 18, no. 1 (2009): 84–102.

Baumgardt, Manfred. "Die Homosexuellen-Bewegung bis zum Ende des Ersten Weltkrieges." In *Eldorado: Homosexuelle Frauen und Männer in Berlin 1850–1950. Geschichte, Alltag und Kultur*. Edited by Michael Bollé, 17–27. Berlin: Rosa Winkel, 1984.

Beachy, Robert. *Gay Berlin: Birthplace of a Modern Identity*. New York: Knopf, 2014.

Beachy, Robert. "The German Invention of Homosexuality." *Journal of Modern History* 82, no. 4 (2010): 801–38.

Beccalossi, Chiara. "Female Same-Sex Desires: Conceptualizing a Disease in Competing Medical Fields in Nineteenth-Century Europe." *Journal of the History of Medicine and Allied Sciences* 67, no. 1 (2012): 7–35.

Beccalossi, Chiara. "Madness and Sexual Psychopathies as the Magnifying Glass of the Normal: Italian Psychiatry and Sexuality c. 1880–1910." *Social History of Medicine* 27, no. 2 (2014): 303–25.

Behling, Katja. *Martha Freud: A Biography*. Cambridge, UK: Polity, 2005.

Benjamin, Harry. "Reminiscences." *Journal of Sex Research* 6, no. 1 (1970): 3–9.

Benjamin, Harry. "Eugen Steinach, 1861–1944. A Life of Research." *Scientific Monthly*, December 1945, 427–42.

Berlant, Lauren. "On the Case." *Critical Inquiry* 33, no. 4 (2007): 663–72.

Berlant, Lauren, and Michael Warner. "Sex in Public." *Critical Inquiry* 24, no. 2 (1998): 547–66.

Birken, Lawrence. *Consuming Desire: Sexual Science and the Emergence of a Culture of Abundance, 1871–1914*. Ithaca, NY: Cornell University Press, 1988.

Bland, Lucy, and Laura Doan. *Sexology in Culture: Labelling Bodies and Desires*. Cambridge, UK: Polity Press, 1998.

Blass, Rachael. "Understanding Freud's Conflicted View of the Object-Relatedness of Sexuality and Its Implications for Contemporary Psychoanalysis." In *Deconstructing Normativity: Re-Reading Freud's 1905 "Three Essays"* Edited by Philippe Van Haute and Herman Westerink, 6–27. London: Routledge, 2017.

Bogacz, T. "War Neurosis and Cultural Change in England, 1914–22: The Work of the War Office Committee of Enquiry into 'Shell-Shock.'" *Journal of Contemporary History* 24, no. 2 (1989): 227–56.

Borrell, Merriley. "Brown-Séquard's Organotherapy and Its Appearance in America at the End of the Nineteenth Century." *Bulletin of the History of Medicine*, no. 50 (1976): 309–20.

Borrell, Merriley. "Organotherapy and the Emergence of Reproductive Endocrinology." *Journal of the History of Biology* 18 (1985): 1–30.

Bos, Jaap, and Leendert Groenendijk. *The Self-Marginalization of Wilhelm Stekel: Freudian Circles Inside and Out*. New York: Springer, 2007.

Bourdieu, Pierre. "The Specificity of the Scientific Field and the Social Conditions of the Progress of Reason." *Social Science Information* 14 (December 1975): 19–47.

Boyarin, Daniel. *Unheroic Conduct: The Rise of Heterosexuality and the Invention of the Jewish Man*. Berkeley: University of California Press, 1997.

Braun, Christina von. "'Der Jude' und 'Das Weib.' Zwei Stereotypen des 'Anderen' in der Moderne." In *Deutsch-jüdische Geschichte im 19. und 20. Jahrhundert*. Edited by Ludger Heid and Joachim Knoll, 289–322. Stuttgart: Burg, 1992.

Braun, Christina von. "Die 'Blutschande.' Wandlungen eines Begriffs: Vom Inzesttabu zu den Rassegesetzen." In *Die schamlose Schönheit des Vergangenen. Zum Verhältnis von Geschlecht und Geschichte*. Edited by Christina von Braun, 81–111. Frankfurt/M, 1989.

Brecher, Edward M. *The Sex Researchers*. Boston: Little, Brown, 1969.

Brecht, Karen, et al., eds. *"Hier geht das Leben auf eine sehr merkwürdige Weise weiter . . .": Zur Geschichte der Psychoanalyse in Deutschland*. Revised ed. Giessen, Ger.: Psychosozial-Verlag, 2010.

Breger, Claudia. "Feminine Masculinities: Scientific and Literary Representations of 'Female Inversion' at the Turn of the Twentieth Century." *Journal of the History of Sexuality* 14, nos. 1/2 (January 2005): 76–106.

Bridenthal, Renate. "Beyond Kinder, Küche, Kirche: Weimar Women at Work." *Central European History* 6, no. 2 (1973): 148–66.

Bronfen, Elisabeth. "Geheimnisse einer Seele. Gedanken zu Pabsts psychoanalytischem Film." In *Psychoanalyse in der modernen Literatur: Kooperation und Konkurrenz*. Edited by Thomas Anz and Christine Kanz, 61–82. Würzburg: Königshausen & Neumann, 1999.

Bruns, Claudia. *Politik des Eros: Der Männerbund in Wissenschaft, Politik und Jugendkultur (1880—1934)*. Köln: Böhlau, 2008.

Bruns, Claudia. "The Politics of Masculinity in the (Homo-)Sexual Discourse (1880–1920)." *German History* 23, no. 2 (2005): 306–20.

Bugmann, Mirjam. *Hypnosepolitik. Der Psychiater August Forel, das Gehirn und die Gesellschaft*. Köln: Böhlau, 2015.

Buhle, Mary Jo. *Feminism and Its Discontents: A Century of Struggle with Psychoanalysis*. Cambridge, MA: Harvard University Press, 1998.

Brill, A. A. "The Conception of Homosexuality." *Journal of the American Medical Association* 61, no. 5 (August 2, 1913): 335–40.

Bullough, Vern L., and Bonnie Bullough. *Cross Dressing, Sex, and Gender*. Philadelphia: University of Pennsylvania Press, 1993.

Butler, Judith. *Excitable Speech: A Politics of the Performative*. New York: Routledge, 1997.

Butler, Judith. *Gender Trouble: Feminism and the Subversion of Identity*. New York: Routledge, 1999.

Butler, Judith. *Undoing Gender*. London: Routledge, 2004.

Cahan, David. "Institutions and Communities." In *From Natural Philosophy to the Sciences: Writing the History of Nineteenth-Century Science*. Edited by David Cahan, 291–328. Chicago: Chicago University Press, 2003.

Campt, Tina. *Other Germans: Black Germans and the Politics of Race, Gender, and Memory in the Third Reich*. Ann Arbor: University of Michigan Press, 2004.

Canguilhem, Georges. *On the Normal and the Pathological*. Edited by Robert Cohen, translated by Carolyn Fawcett. With an introduction by Michel Foucault. Dordrecht, Neth.: D. Reidel, 1978.

Canning, Kathleen. "Claiming Citizenship: Suffrage and Subjectivity in Germany after the First World War." In *Gender History in Practice: Historical Perspectives on Bodies, Class & Citizenship*, 212–37. Ithaca, NY: Cornell University Press, 2006.

Caplan, Jane. "The Administration of Gender Identity in Nazi Germany." *History Workshop Journal* 72, no. 1 (2011): 171–80.

Carter, Julian. *The Heart of Whiteness: Normal Sexuality and Race in America, 1880–1940*. Durham, NC: Duke University Press, 2007.

Carter, K. Codell. "Infantile Hysteria and Infantile Sexuality in Late Nineteenth-Century German-Language Medical Literature." *Medical History* 27, no. 2 (1983): 186–96.

Cetina, Karin Knorr. *Epistemic Cultures: How the Sciences Make Knowledge*. Cambridge, MA: Harvard University Press, 1999.

Chamberlin, J. Edward, and Sander L. Gilman. *Degeneration: The Dark Side of Progress*. New York: Columbia University Press, 1985.

Chauncey, George, Jr. "From Sexual Inversion to Homosexuality: The Changing Medical Conceptualization of Female 'Deviance.'" In *Passion and Power: Sexuality in History*. Edited by Kathy Peiss, Christina Simmons, and Robert A. Padgug, 87–117. Philadelphia: Temple University Press, 1989.

Chiang, Howard. "Effecting Science, Affecting Medicine: Homosexuality, the Kinsey Reports, and the Contested Boundaries of Psychopathology in the United States, 1948–1965." *Journal of the History of the Behavioural Sciences* 44, no. 4 (2008): 300–318.

Chiang, Howard. "Historicizing the Emergence of Sexual Freedom: The Medical Knowledge of Psychiatry and the Scientific Power of Sexology, 1880–1920." *Gender Forum: An Internet Journal for Gender Studies* 24 (2009): 1–6.

Churchill, David S. "Transnationalism and Homophile Political Culture in the Postwar Decades." *GLQ: A Journal of Lesbian and Gay Studies* 15, no. 1 (2009): 31–65.

Clark, Anna. *Desire: A History of European Sexuality*. New York: Routledge, 2008.

Clement, Ulrich. "Zum Verhältnis von Sexualwissenschaft und Psychoanalyse." *Zeitschrift für psychosomatische Medizin* 39 (1993): 63–74.

Cocks, Geoffrey. *Psychotherapy in the Third Reich: The Göring Institute*. New York: Oxford University Press, 1985.

Coen, Deborah R. "Living Precisely in Fin-de-Siècle Vienna." *Journal of the History of Biology* 39 (2006): 493–523.

Crocq, Marc-Antoine, and Louis Crocq. "From Shell Shock and War Neuroses to Posttraumatic Stress Disorder: A History of Psychotraumatology." *Dialogues in Clinical Neuroscience* 2, no. 1 (2000): 47–55.

Crouthamel, Jason. *An Intimate History of the Front: Masculinity, Sexuality, and German Soldiers in the First World War*. New York: Palgrave Macmillan, 2014.

Crouthamel, Jason. "Cross-Dressing for the Fatherland: Sexual Humor, Masculinity and German Soldiers in the First World War." *First World War Studies* 2, no. 2 (2011): 195–215.

Crouthamel, Jason. "Male Sexuality and Psychological Trauma: Soldiers and Sexual Disorder in World War I and Weimar Germany." *Journal of the History of Sexuality* 17, no. 1 (2008): 60–84.

Crouthamel, Jason. *The Great War and German Memory: Society, Politics and Psychological Trauma, 1914–1945*. Exeter, UK: University of Exeter Press, 2009.

Crozier, Ivan. "'All the World's a Stage': Dora Russell, Norman Haire, and the 1929

London World League for Sexual Reform Congress." *Journal of the History of Sexuality* 12, no. 1 (2003): 16–37.

Crozier, Ivan. "Becoming a Sexologist: Norman Haire, the 1929 London World League for Sexual Reform Congress, and Organizing Medical Knowledge about Sex in Interwar England." *History of Science* 39 (2001): 299–329.

Crozier, Ivan. "Havelock Ellis, Eonism and the Patient's Discourse; Or, Writing a Book about Sex." *History of Psychiatry* 11 (2000): 125–54.

Crozier, Ivan. "Pillow Talk: Credibility, Trust and the Sexological Case History." *History of Science* 46 (2008): 375–404.

Crozier, Ivan. "Taking Prisoners: Havelock Ellis, Sigmund Freud, and the Construction of Homosexuality, 1897–1951." *Society for the Social History of Medicine* 13, no. 3 (2000): 447–66.

Crozier, Ivan, and Heike Bauer. "Sexology, Historiography, Citation, Embodiment: A Review and (Frank) Exchange." *History of the Human Sciences* 30 (2017). http://www.histhum.com/?p=367.

Cryle, Peter, and Alison Moore. *Frigidity: An Intellectual History*. Basingstoke, UK: Palgrave Macmillan, 2011.

Cryle, Peter, and Elizabeth Stephens. *Normality: A Critical Genealogy*. Chicago: University of Chicago Press, 2017.

Cunningham, Hugh. "Histories of Childhood." *The American Historical Review* 103, no. 4 (1998): 1195–1208.

Cvetkovich, Ann. *An Archive of Feelings: Trauma, Sexuality, and Lesbian Public Cultures*. Series Q. Durham, NC: Duke University Press, 2003.

Dabhoiwala, Faramerz. *The Origins of Sex: A History of the First Sexual Revolution*. Oxford, UK: Oxford University Press, 2012.

Damousi, Joy. *Freud in the Antipodes: A Cultural History of Psychoanalysis in Australia*. Sydney: UNSW Press, 2005.

Danziger, Kurt. *Constructing the Subject: Historical Origins of Psychological Research*. Cambridge, UK: Cambridge University Press, 1990.

Davidson, Arnold I. "How to Do the History of Psychoanalysis: A Reading of Freud's 'Three Essays on the Theory of Sexuality.'" *Critical Inquiry* 13, no. 2 (1987): 252–77.

Davidson, Arnold I. "Styles of Reasoning, Conceptual History, and the Emergence of Psychiatry." In *The Disunity of Science: Boundaries, Contexts, and Power*, 75–100. Stanford: Stanford University Press, 1996.

Davidson, Arnold I. *The Emergence of Sexuality: Historical Epistemology and the Formation of Concepts*. Cambridge, MA: Harvard UP, 2001.

Dean, Carolyn J. *Sexuality and Modern Western Culture*. New York: Twayne, 1996.

Dean, Tim, and Christopher Lane, eds. *Homosexuality-Psychoanalysis*. Chicago: University of Chicago Press, 2001.

Dickinson, Edward R., and Richard F. Wetzell. "The Historiography of Sexuality in Modern Germany." *German History* 23, no. 3 (2005): 291–305.

Dickinson, Edward Ross. "'A Dark, Impenetrable Wall of Complete Incomprehension': The Impossibility of Heterosexual Love in Imperial Germany." *Central European History* 40 (2007): 467–97.

Dickinson, Edward Ross. "Reflections on Feminism and Monism in the Kaiserreich, 1900–1913." *Central European History* 34, no. 2 (2001): 191–230.
Dickinson, Edward Ross. *Sex, Freedom and Power in Imperial Germany, 1880–1914*. New York: Cambridge University Press, 2014.
Diercks, Christine. "The Vienna Psychoanalytic Polyclinic ('Ambulatorium'): Wilhelm Reich and the Technical Seminar." *Psychoanalysis and History* 4, no. 1 (2008): 67–84.
Doan, Laura. *Disturbing Practices: History, Sexuality, and Women's Experience of Modern War*. Chicago: Chicago University Press, 2013.
Doan, Laura. "Marie Stopes's Wonderful Rhythm Charts: Normalizing the Natural." *Journal of the History of Ideas* 78, no. 4 (2017): 595–620.
Doan, Laura. "Sexology's Afterlives: On the Queer Circuitries of Expert Knowledge in Modern Britain, 1913–1930." *Gender & History* 31, no. 2 (2019): 304–18.
Domeier, Norman. *Der Eulenburg-Skandal: Eine politische Kulturgeschichte des Kaiserreichs*. Frankfurt: Campus, 2010.
Dose, Ralf. *Magnus Hirschfeld: The Origins of the Gay Liberation Movement*. Translated by Edward H. Willis. New York: Monthly Review Press, 2014.
Dose, Ralf. "The World League for Sexual Reform: Some Possible Approaches." *Journal of the History of Sexuality* 12, no. 1 (2003): 1–15.
Eder, Franz X. *Kultur der Begierde: Eine Geschichte der Sexualität*. Munich: Beck, 2002.
Eder, Franz X. "National and Racial Images of the Sexual 'Other' in the German-Speaking Countries (1950s-1970s)." *Sexuality & Culture* 21, no. 2 (2017): 362–81.
Egan, R. Danielle, and Gail Hawkes. *Theorizing the Sexual Child in Modernity*. Basingstoke, UK: Palgrave Macmillan, 2010.
Ernst, Waltraud. "The Normal and the Abnormal: Reflections on Norms and Normativity." In *Histories of the Normal and the Abnormal: Social and Cultural Histories of Norms and Normativity*, 1–25. Abingdon, UK: Routledge, 2006.
Evans, Jennifer. "Introduction: Why Queer German History?" *German History* 34, no. 3 (2016): 371–84.
Evans, Jennifer. "Seeing Subjectivity: Erotic Photography and the Optics of Desire." *American Historical Review* 118, no. 2 (2013): 430–62.
Ewald, François. "Norms, Discipline, and the Law." *Representations* 30 (1990): 138–61.
Ewing, Christopher. "'Color Him Black': Erotic Representations and the Politics of Race in West German Homosexual Magazines, 1949–1974." *Sexuality & Culture* 21, no. 2 (2017): 382–403.
Falzeder, Ernst, ed. *The Complete Correspondence of Sigmund Freud and Karl Abraham, 1907–1925*. London: Karnac, 2002.
Falzeder, Ernst, Eva Brabant, and Patrizia Giampieri-Deutsch, eds. *The Correspondence of Sigmund Freud and Sándor Ferenczi*. Transcribed by Ingeborg Meyer-Palmedo, translated by Peter T. Hoffer. 3 vols. Vol. 1: 1908–1914. Cambridge, MA: Belknap, 1996.
Falzeder, Ernst, Eva Brabant, and Patrizia Giampieri-Deutsch, eds. The *Correspondence of Sigmund Freud and Sándor Ferenczi*. 3 vols. Vol. 3: 1920–1933. Cambridge, MA: Belknap, 2000.

Feldstein, Richard, and Judith Roof, eds. *Feminism and Psychoanalysis*. Ithaca, NY: Cornell University Press, 1989.

Fisher, Kate, and Jana Funke. "British Sexual Science beyond the Medical: Cross-Disciplinary, Cross-Historical, and Cross-Cultural Translations." In *Sexology and Translation: Cultural and Scientific Encounters Across the Modern World*, 95–114. Philadelphia: Temple University Press, 2015.

Fisher, Kate, and Jana Funke. "'Let Us Leave the Hospital; Let Us Go on a Journey around the World': British and German Sexual Science and the Global Search for Sexual Variation." In *A Global History of Sexual Science, 1880–1960*. Edited by Veronika Fuechtner, Douglas E. Haynes, and Ryan M. Jones, 51–69. Oakland: University of California Press, 2018.

Fisher, Kate, and Jana Funke. "The Age of Attraction: Age, Gender and the History of Modern Male Homosexuality," *Gender & History*, 31, no. 2 (2019): 266–83.

Fishman, Sterling. "The History of Childhood Sexuality." *Journal of Contemporary History* 17, no. 2 (1982): 269–83.

Forrester, John. "If *p*, Then What? Thinking in Cases." *History of the Human Sciences* 9 (1996): 1–25.

Foucault, Michel. *The History of Sexuality*. 3 vols. Vol. 1: The Will to Knowledge. London: Penguin, 1998.

Frevert, Ute. "Europeanizing Germany's Twentieth Century." *History and Memory* 17 (2005): 87–116.

Friedman, Richard C., and Jennifer I. Downey. "Psychoanalysis and the Model of Homosexuality as Psychopathology: A Historical Overview." *American Journal of Psychoanalysis* 58, no. 3 (1998): 249–70.

Frosh, Stephen. *Hate and the "Jewish Science": Anti-Semitism, Nazism and Psychoanalysis*. Houndmills, Basingstoke: Palgrave Macmillan, 2005.

Fuechtner, Veronika. *Berlin Psychoanalytic: Psychoanalysis and Culture in Weimar Republic Germany and Beyond*. Berkeley: University of California Press, 2011.

Fuechtner, Veronika. "Indians, Jews, and Sex: Magnus Hirschfeld and Indian Sexology." In *Imagining Germany, Imagining Asia*. Edited by Veronika Fuechtner and Mary Rhiel, 111–30. Rochester, NY: Camden House, 2013.

Fuechtner, Veronika, Douglas E. Haynes, and Ryan M. Jones, eds. *Towards a Global History of Sexual Science, 1880–1950*. Oakland: University of California Press, 2017.

Fuller, Steve. "Talking Metaphysical Turkey About Epistemological Chicken and the Poop on Pidgins." In *The Disunity of Science. Boundaries, Contexts, and Power*. Edited by Peter Galison and David J. Stump, 170–86. Stanford: Stanford University Press, 1996.

Funke, Jana. "'We Cannot Be Greek Now': Age Difference, Corruption of Youth and the Making of 'Sexual Inversion.'" *English Studies* 94, no. 2 (2013): 139–53.

Funke, Jana, and Kate Fisher. "Sexual Science beyond the Medical." *Lancet* 387 (2016): 840–41.

Fuss, Diana, ed. "Pink Freud (Special Issue of *GLQ*)" 2, nos. 1–2 (1995).

Galison, Peter. "Computer Simulations and the Trading Zone." In *The Disunity of Science: Boundaries, Contexts, and Power*. Edited by Peter Galison and David J. Stump, 118–57. Stanford: Stanford University Press, 1996.

Galison, Peter. "Introduction: The Context of Disunity." In *The Disunity of Science. Boundaries, Contexts, and Power*, 1–33. Stanford: Stanford University Press, 1996.

Gallop, Jane. *The Daughter's Seduction: Feminism and Psychoanalysis*. Ithaca, NY: Cornell University Press, 1982.

Gay, Peter. *Freud: A Life for Our Time*. New York: Norton, 1988.

Geissmann, Claudine, and Pierre Geissmann. *A History of Child Psychoanalysis*. London: Routledge, 1998.

Geller, Jay. "Freud, Blüher, and the Secessio Inversa: Männerbünde, Homosexuality, and Freud's Theory of Cultural Formation." In *Queer Theory and the Jewish Question*. Edited by Daniel Boyarin, Daniel Itzkovitz, and Ann Pellegrini, 90–120. New York: Columbia University Press, 2003.

Geuter, Ulfried. *The Professionalization of Psychology in Nazi Germany*. Cambridge, UK: Cambridge University Press, 1992.

Gherovici, Patricia. *Please Select Your Gender: From the Invention of Hysteria to the Democratizing of Transgenderism*. New York: Routledge, 2010.

Giddens, Anthony. *Modernity and Self-Identity: Self and Society in the Late Modern Age*. Cambridge, UK: Polity Press, 1991.

Giddens, Anthony. *The Transformation of Intimacy: Sexuality, Love and Eroticism in Modern Societies*. Cambridge, UK: Polity Press, 1992.

Gillis, Jonathan. "Bad Habits and Pernicious Results: Thumb Sucking and the Discipline of Late-Nineteenth-Century Paediatrics." *Medical History* 40 (1996): 55–73.

Gilman, Sander L. "Jews and Mental Illness: Medical Metaphors, Anti-Semitism, and the Jewish Response." *Journal of the History of the Behavioral Sciences* 20 (April 1984): 150–59.

Gilman, Sander L. "Sexology, Psychoanalysis, and Degeneration: From a Theory of Race to a Race of Theory." In *Degeneration: The Dark Side of Progress*. Edited by J. Edward Chamberlin and Sander L. Gilman, 72–96. New York: Columbia University Press, 1985.

Gilman, Sander L. "Sigmund Freud and the Sexologists: A Second Reading." In *Sexual Knowledge, Sexual Science: The History of Attitudes to Sexuality*. Edited by Roy Porter and Mikuláš Teich, 323–49. Cambridge, UK: Cambridge University Press, 1994.

Gilman, Sander L. "The Struggle of Psychiatry with Psychoanalysis: Who Won?" *Critical Inquiry* 13, no. 2 (1987): 293–313.

Glasgold, Judith M., and Suzanne Iasenza, eds. *Lesbians and Psychoanalysis: Past to Present: Rethinking Theories*. New York: Free Press, 1995.

Goggin, James E., and Eileen Brockmann Goggin. *Death of a "Jewish Science": Psychoanalysis in the Third Reich*. West Lafayette, IN: Purdue University Press, 2001.

Goldstein, Jan. "Foucault among the Sociologists: The 'Disciplines' and the History of the Professions." *History and Theory* 23 (1984): 170–92.

Golinski, Jan. *Making Natural Knowledge: Constructivism and the History of Science*. Cambridge, UK: Cambridge University Press, 1998.

Gordon, Suzanne. "Helene Deutsch and the Legacy of Freud." *New York Times*. July 30, 1978, sec. SM.

Graf-Nold, Angela. *Der Fall Hermine von Hug-Hellmuth: Eine Geschichte der frühen Kinderanalyse*. München: Verl. Internat. Psychoanalyse, 1988.

Graham, Loren R. "Science and Values: The Eugenics Movement in Germany and Russia in the 1920s." *American Historical Review* 82, no. 5 (1977): 1133–64.

Grau, Günter, and Claudia Schoppmann, eds. *Hidden Holocaust? Gay and Lesbian Persecution in Germany 1933–1945*. Translated by Patrick Camiller. London: Cassell, 1995.

Greenberg, David F. *The Construction of Homosexuality*. Chicago: University of Chicago Press, 1988.

Grosskurth, Phyllis. *Havelock Ellis: A Biography*. New York: Knopf, 1980.

Grossmann, Atina. "German Women Doctors from Berlin to New York: Maternity and Modernity in Weimar and Exile." *Feminist Studies* 19, no. 1 (1993): 65–88.

Grossmann, Atina. "Girlkultur or Thoroughly Rationalized Female: A New Woman in Weimar Germany?" In *Women in Culture and Politics: A Century of Change*. Edited by Judith Friedlander, Blanche Wiesen Cook, Alice Kessler-Harris, and Carroll Smith-Rosenberg, 62–80. Bloomington: Indiana University Press, 1986.

Grossmann, Atina. "Magnus Hirschfeld, Sexualreform und die Neue Frau: Das Institut für Sexualwissenschaft und das Weimarer Berlin." In *Magnus Hirschfeld: Ein Leben im Spannungsfeld von Wissenschaft, Politik und Gesellschaft*. Edited by Elke-Vera Kotowski and Julius H. Schoeps, 201–16. Berlin-Brandenburg: be.bra wissenschaft, 2004.

Grossmann, Atina. *Reforming Sex: The German Movement for Birth Control and Abortion Reform, 1920–1950*. New York: Oxford University Press, 1995.

Grosz, Elizabeth. *Sexual Subversions: Three French Feminists*. Sydney: Allen & Unwin, 1989.

Grünbaum, Adolf. *The Foundations of Psychoanalysis: A Philosophical Critique*. Berkeley: University of California Press, 1984.

Gul, Pelin. "Profile of Helene Deutsch." Edited by A. Rutherford. *Psychology's Feminist Voices Multimedia Internet Archive*, 2010. http://www.feministvoices.com/helene-deutsch/.

Günther, B. "Alexander Lipschütz (1883–1980). A Biographical Synopsis." *Biological Research* 27 (1994): 79–84.

Hacking, Ian. *Representing and Intervening: Introductory Topics in the Philosophy of Natural Science*. Cambridge, UK: Cambridge University Press, 1983.

Hacking, Ian. *The Social Construction of What?* Cambridge, MA: Harvard University Press, 1999.

Hacking, Ian. *The Taming of Chance*. Cambridge, UK: Cambridge University Press, 1990.

Haeberle, Erwin. "Der transatlantische Pendler. Ein Interview mit Harry Benjamin." *Sexualmedizin* 1 (1985): 44–47.

Hagner, Michael. "Scientific Medicine." In *From Natural Philosophy to the Sciences: Writing the History of Nineteenth-Century Science*. Edited by David Cahan, 49–87. Chicago: University of Chicago Press, 2003.

Hahn, Roger. *The Anatomy of a Scientific Institution. The Paris Academy of Sciences 1666–1803*. Berkeley: University of California Press, 1971.

Hale, Nathan G., Jr. *Freud and the Americans: The Beginnings of Psychoanalysis in the United States, 1876–1917*. New York: Oxford University Press, 1971.

Hale, Nathan G., Jr. *The Rise and Crisis of Psychoanalysis in the United States: Freud and the Americans, 1917–1985*. New York: Oxford University Press, 1995.

Hall, Lesley A. "'Disinterested Enthusiasm for Sexual Misconduct': The British Society for the Study of Sex Psychology, 1913–1947." *Journal of Contemporary History* 30 (1995): 665–86.

Halperin, David M. *One Hundred Years of Homosexuality: And Other Essays on Greek Love*. New York: Routledge, 1990.

Hamilton, David. *The Monkey Gland Affair*. London: Chatto & Windus, 1986.

Haraway, Donna. "Situated Knowledges: The Science Question in Feminism and the Privilege of Partial Perspective." *Feminist Studies* 14, no. 3 (1988): 575–99.

Harrowitz, Nancy A., and Barbara Hyams, eds. *Jews & Gender: Responses to Otto Weininger*. Philadelphia: Temple University Press, 1995.

Hau, Michael. *The Cult of Health and Beauty in Germany: A Social History, 1890–1930*. Chicago: University of Chicago Press, 2003.

Hegarty, Peter. *Gentlemen's Disagreement: Alfred Kinsey, Lewis Terman, and the Sexual Politics of Smart Men*. Chicago: University of Chicago Press, 2013.

Hekma, Gert. "'A Female Soul in a Male Body': Sexual Inversion as Gender Inversion in Nineteenth-Century Sexology." In *Third Sex, Third Gender: Beyond Sexual Dimorphism in Culture and History*. Edited by Gilbert Herdt, 213–39. New York: Zone Books, 1994.

Hergemöller, Bernd-Ulrich. "Hirschfeld und Blüher. Kontakte und Konflikte 1912–1922." In *Magnus Hirschfeld. Ein Leben im Spannungsfeld von Wissenschaft, Politik und Gesellschaft*. Edited by Elke-Vera Kotowski and Julius H. Schoeps, 117–36. Berlin: be.bra wissenschaft, 2004.

Herrn, Rainer. *Das 3. Geschlecht. Reprint der 1930–1932 erschienenen Zeitschrift für Transvestiten*. Hamburg: Männerschwarm, 2016.

Herrn, Rainer. "Der Anfang vom Ende—Die Don Juan-Figur in Sexualwissenschaft und Psychoanalyse." *Mitteilungen der Magnus-Hirschfeld-Gesellschaft*, no. 22 (1996): 27–37.

Herrn, Rainer. "On the History of Biological Theories of Homosexuality." In *Sex, Cells, and Same-Sex Desire: The Biology of Sexual Preference*. Edited by John P. de Cecero and David Allen Parker, 31–56. Abingdon, UK: Routledge, 2013.

Herrn, Rainer. *Schnittmuster des Geschlechts: Transvestitismus und Transsexualität in der frühen Sexualwissenschaft*. Beiträge zur Sexualforschung 85. Gießen, Ger.: Psychosozial-Verlag, 2005.

Herrn, Rainer. "Transvestitismus in der NS-Zeit: Ein Forschungsdesiderat." *Zeitschrift für Sexualforschung* 26, no. 4 (2013): 330–71.

Herrn, Rainer. "Ver-körperungen des anderen Geschlechts—Transvestitismus und Transsexualität historisch betrachtet." *Aus Politik und Zeitgeschichte*, Bundeszentrale für politische Bildung, 2012, nos. 20/21 (Geschlechtsidentität) (2012), 41–48.

Herrn, Rainer. "Vom Traum zum Trauma. Das Institut für Sexualwissenschaft." In *Magnus Hirschfeld: Ein Leben im Spannungsfeld von Wissenschaft, Politik und Gesellschaft*. Edited by Elke-Vera Kotowski and Julius H. Schoeps, 173–200. Berlin-Brandenburg: be.bra wissenschaft, 2004.

Herrn, Rainer, and Christine N. Brinckmann. "Of Rats and Men: Rejuvenation and the

Steinach Film." In *Not Straight from Germany: Sexual Publics and Sexual Citizenship since Magnus Hirschfeld*, 212–34. Ann Arbor: University of Michigan Press, 2017.

Herzer, Manfred. *Magnus Hirschfeld: Leben und Werk eines jüdischen, schwulen und sozialistischen Sexologen*. 2., überarbeitete Aufl. Hamburg: MännerschwarmSkript Verlag, 2001.

Herzer, Manfred. *Magnus Hirschfeld und seine Zeit*. Berlin: de Gruyter, 2017.

Herzer, Manfred. "Schwule Preussen, warme Berliner." *Capri: Zeitschrift für schwule Geschichte* 2 (1988): 3–25.

Herzog, Dagmar. *Cold War Freud: Psychoanalysis in an Age of Catastrophes*. Cambridge, UK: Cambridge University Press, 2017.

Herzog, Dagmar. *Sex in Crisis: The New Sexual Revolution and the Future of American Politics*. New York: Basic, 2008.

Herzog, Dagmar. *Sexuality in Europe: A Twentieth-Century History*. Cambridge, UK: Cambridge University Press, 2011.

Herzog, Dagmar. "The Reception of the Kinsey Reports in Europe." *Sexuality & Culture* 10, no. 1 (2006): 39–48.

Hill, Darryl. "Sexuality and Gender in Hirschfeld's *Die Transvestiten*: A Case of the 'Elusive Evidence of the Ordinary.'" *Journal of the History of Sexuality* 14, no. 3 (2005): 316–32.

Hirshbein, Laura Davidow. "The Glandular Solution: Sex, Masculinity, and Aging in the 1920s." *Journal of the History of Sexuality* 9, no. 3 (2000): 277-304.

"Historical Notes: A Letter from Freud." *American Journal of Psychiatry* 107 (1951): 786.

Hoffmann-Richter, Ulrike. "Die Wiener akademische Psychiatrie und die Geburt der Psychoanalyse." In *Gründe der Seele: Die Wiener Psychiatrie im 20. Jahrhundert*. Edited by Brigitta Keintzel and Eberhard Gabriel, 49–72. Vienna: Picus, 1999.

Holdorff, Bernd. "The Fight for 'Traumatic Neurosis,' 1889–1916: Hermann Oppenheim and His Opponents in Berlin." *History of Psychiatry* 22, no. 4 (2011): 465–76.

Hommel, Andrea. "Hermann Rohleder (1866–1934) und die Anfänge der künstlichen Befruchtung in Deutschland." *Medizinhistorisches Journal* 29, no. 2 (1994): 121–48.

Hothersall, David. *History of Psychology*. Philadelphia: Temple University Press, 1984.

Igo, Sarah E. *The Averaged American: Surveys, Citizens, and the Making of a Mass Public*. Cambridge, MA: Harvard University Press, 2007.

Jellonnek, Burkhard. *Homosexuelle unter dem Hakenkreuz: Die Verfolgung von Homosexuellen im Dritten Reich*. Paderborn, Ger.: Schöningh, 1990.

Kahan, Benjamin, ed. *Heinrich Kaan's "Psychopathia Sexualis" (1844)*. Translated by Melissa Haynes. Ithaca, NY: Cornell University Press, 2016.

Katz, Jonathan Ned. *The Invention of Heterosexuality*. New York: Dutton, 1995.

Kauders, Anthony D. *Der Freud-Komplex: Eine Geschichte der Psychoanalyse in Deutschland*. Berlin: Berlin Verlag, 2014.

Kaufmann, Doris. "Science as Cultural Practice: Psychiatry in the First World War and Weimar Germany." *Journal of Contemporary History* 34, no. 1 (1999): 125–44.

Keilson-Lauritz, Marita. "Benedict Friedlaender und die Anfänge der Sexualwissenschaft." *Zeitschrift für Sexualforschung* 18, no. 4 (2005): 311–31.

Keilson-Lauritz, Marita. *Die Geschichte der eigenen Geschichte: Literatur und Literaturkritik in den Anfängen der Schwulenbewegung*. Berlin: Rosa Winkel, 1997.

Kelley, Donald R., ed. *History and the Disciplines: The Reclassification of Knowledge in Early Modern Europe*. Rochester, NY: University of Rochester Press, 1997.

Kern, Stephen. "Freud and the Discovery of Child Sexuality." *History of Childhood Quarterly* 1 (1973): 117–41.

Killen, Andreas. *Berlin Electropolis. Shock, Nerves, and German Modernity*. Berkeley: University of California Press, 2005.

Killen, Andreas. *Homo Cinematicus: Science, Motion Pictures, and the Making of Modern Germany*. Philadelphia: University of Pennsylvania Press, 2017.

Kincaid, James. *Child-Loving: The Erotic Child and Victorian Culture*. New York: Routledge, 1992.

Kinsey, Alfred C., Wardell B. Pomeroy, Clyde E. Martin, and Paul H. Gebhard. *Sexual Behavior in the Human Female*. Philadelphia: W. B. Saunders, 1953.

Kittel, Ingo-Wolf. *Arthur Kronfeld: 1886–1941. Ein Pionier der Psychologie, Sexualwissenschaft und Psychotherapie*. Konstanz, Ger.: Bibliothek der Universität Konstanz, 1988.

Knorr-Cetina, Karin D., and Michael Mulkay, eds. *Science Observed: Perspectives on the Social Study of Science*. London: Sage, 1983.

Kotowski, Elke-Vera, and Julius H. Schoeps, eds. *Magnus Hirschfeld. Ein Leben im Spannungsfeld von Wissenschaft, Politik und Gesellschaft*. Berlin: be.bra wissenschaft, 2004.

Kuhn, Thomas S. *The Essential Tension: Selected Studies in Scientific Tradition and Change*. Chicago: University of Chicago Press, 1977.

Kuhn, Thomas S. *The Structure of Scientific Revolutions*. 3rd ed. Chicago: University of Chicago Press, 1996.

Lang, Birgit, Joy Damousi, and Alison Lewis. *A History of the Case Study: Sexology, Psychoanalysis, Literature*. Manchester, UK: Manchester University Press, 2017.

Lang, Birgit, and Katie Sutton. "The Queer Cases of Psychoanalysis: Rethinking the Scientific Study of Homosexuality, 1890s–1920s." *German History* 34, no. 3 (2016): 419–44.

Laqueur, Thomas. *Solitary Sex: A Cultural History of Masturbation*. New York: Zone, 2003.

Layne, Priscilla. "'Schwarz ist in': Racial Fetishism, Sexuality, and Black Masculinity in Lothar Lambert's *1 Berlin-Harlem*." *German Studies Review* 39, no. 2 (2016): 335–52.

Leck, Ralph M. *Vita Sexualis: Karl Ulrichs and the Origins of Sexual Science*. Urbana: University of Illinois Press, 2016.

Leed, Erich. *No Man's Land: Combat and Identity in World War I*. Cambridge, UK: Cambridge University Press, 1979.

Lemon, M. C. *The Discipline of History and the History of Thought*. London: Routledge, 1995.

Leng, Kirsten. "An 'Elusive' Phenomenon: Feminism, Sexual Science, and the Female Sex Drive, 1880–1914." *Centaurus, An International Journal of the History of Science and Its Cultural Aspects* 55, no. 2 (2013): 131–52.

Leng, Kirsten. "Culture, Difference, and Sexual Progress in Turn-of-the-Century Europe: Cultural Othering and the German League for the Protection of Mothers and Sexual Reform, 1905–1914." *Journal of the History of Sexuality* 25, no. 1 (2016): 62–82.

Leng, Kirsten. "Magnus Hirschfeld's Meanings: Analysing Biography and the Politics of Representation." *German History* 35, no. 1 (2017): 96–116.

Leng, Kirsten. "Permutations of the Third Sex: Sexology, Subjectivity, and Antimaternalist Feminism at the Turn of the Twentieth Century." *Signs: Journal of Women in Culture and Society* 40, no. 1 (2014): 227–54.

Leng, Kirsten. *Sexual Politics and Feminist Science: Women Sexologists in Germany, 1900–1933*. Ithaca, NY: Cornell University Press, 2017.

Leng, Kirsten. "The Limits of Transnationalism: The Case of Max Marcuse." In *A Global History of Sexual Science, 1880–1960*. Edited by Veronika Fuechtner, Douglas E. Haynes, and Ryan M. Jones, 422–43. Berkeley: University of California Press, 2018.

Leng, Kirsten. "The Personal Is Scientific: Women, Gender, and the Production of Sexological Knowledge in Germany and Austria, 1900–1931." *History of Psychology* 18, no. 3 (2015): 238–51.

Lennox, Sara. "Race, Gender, and Sexuality in German Southwest Africa: Hans Grimms 'Südafrikanische Novellen.'" In *Germany's Colonial Pasts*. Edited by Eric Ames, Marcia Klotz, and Lora Wildenthal, 63–75. Lincoln: University of Nebraska Press, 2005.

Lenoir, Timothy. *Instituting Science: The Cultural Production of Scientific Disciplines*. Stanford, UK: Stanford University Press, 1997.

Lerner, Paul Frederick. *Hysterical Men: War, Psychiatry, and the Politics of Trauma in Germany, 1890–1930*. Ithaca, NY: Cornell University Press, 2003.

LeVay, Simon. *Queer Science: The Use and Abuse of Research into Homosexuality*. Cambridge, MA: MIT Press, 1996.

Lewes, Kenneth. *The Psychoanalytic Theory of Male Homosexuality*. New York: New American Library, 1988.

Linge, Ina. "Gender and Agency between Sexualwissenschaft and Autobiography: The Case of N.O. Body's 'Aus eines Mannes Mädchenjahren.'" *German Life and Letters* 68 (2015): 387–405.

Linge, Ina. "Sexology, Popular Science and Queer History in 'Anders als die Andern' ('Different from the Others')." *Gender & History* 30, no. 3 (2018): 1–16.

Lišková, Katerina. *Sexual Liberation, Socialist Style: Communist Czechoslovakia and the Science of Desire, 1945–1989*. Cambridge, UK: Cambridge University Press, 2018.

List, Eveline. *Psychoanalyse. Geschichte, Theorien, Anwendungen*. Vienna: Facultas, 2009.

Lockot, Regine. *Erinnern und Durcharbeiten. Zur Geschichte der Psychoanalyse und Psychotherapie im Nationalsozialismus*. Frankfurt am Main: Fischer, 1985.

Logan, Cheryl A. *Hormones, Heredity, and Race. Spectacular Failure in Interwar Vienna*. New Brunswick, NJ: Rutgers University Press, 2013.

Ludwig-Körner, Christiane. *Wiederentdeckt—Psychoanalytikerinnen in Berlin*. Gießen, Ger.: Psychosozial-Verlag, 1999.

Lunbeck, Elizabeth. "Psychiatry." In *From Natural Philosophy to the Sciences: Writing the History of Nineteenth-Century Science*. Edited by David Cahan, 663–77. Chicago: University of Chicago Press, 2003.

Lunbeck, Elizabeth. *The Americanization of Narcissism*. Cambridge, MA: Harvard University Press, 2014.

Lybeck, Marti M. *Desiring Emancipation: New Women and Homosexuality in Germany, 1890–1933*. Albany: State University of New York Press, 2014.

Maehle, Andreas-Holge. "The Powers of Suggestion: Albert Moll and the Debate on Hypnosis." *History of Psychiatry* 25, no. 1 (2014): 3–19.

Magee, Maggie, and Diana C. Miller. *Lesbian Lives: Psychonanalytic Narratives Old and New*. London: Analytic Press, 1997.

Mai, Gunther. *Das Ende des Kaiserreichs: Politik und Kriegführung im Ersten Weltkrieg*. Munich: dtv, 1993.

Mak, Geertje. *Doubting Sex: Inscriptions, Bodies and Selves in Nineteenth-Century Hermaphrodite Case Histories*. Manchester, UK: Manchester UP, 2012.

Mak, Geertje. "'Passing Women' im Sprechzimmer von Magnus Hirschfeld. Warum der Begriff 'Transvestit' nicht für Frauen in Männerkleidern eingeführt wurde (transl. Mirjam Hausmann)." *Österreichische Zeitschrift für Geschichtswissenschaften* 9, no. 3 (1998): 384–99.

Mak, Geertje. "'So We Must Go Behind Even What the Microscope Can Reveal': The Hermaphrodite's 'Self' in Medical Discourse at the Start of the Twentieth Century." *GLQ: A Journal of Lesbian and Gay Studies* 11, no. 1 (2005): 65–94.

Makari, George. "Mitteleuropa on the Hudson: On the Struggle for American Psychoanalysis after the Anschluß." In *After Freud Left: A Century of Psychoanalysis in America*. Edited by Burnham, John C., 111–24. Chicago: University of Chicago Press, 2012.

Makari, George. *Revolution in Mind: The Creation of Psychoanalysis*. New York: Harper, 2008.

Makela, Maria. "Rejuvenation and Regen(d)eration: 'Der Steinachfilm,' Sex Glands, and Weimar-Era Visual and Literary Culture." *German Studies Review* 38, no. 1 (2015): 35–62.

Mancini, Elena. *Magnus Hirschfeld and the Quest for Sexual Freedom*. New York: Palgrave Macmillan, 2010.

Marhoefer, Laurie. "Lesbianism, Transvestitism, and the Nazi State: A Microhistory of a Gestapo Investigation, 1939–1943." *American Historical Review* 121, no. 4 (2016): 1167–95.

Marhoefer, Laurie. *Sex and the Weimar Republic: German Homosexual Emancipation and the Rise of the Nazis*. Toronto: University of Toronto Press, 2015.

Marhoefer, Laurie. "'The Book Was a Revelation, I Recognized Myself in It': Lesbian Sexuality, Censorship, and the Queer Press in Weimar-Era Germany." *Journal of Women's History* 27, no. 2 (2015): 62–86.

Marhoefer, Laurie. "Was the Homosexual Made White? Race, Empire, and Analogy in Gay and Trans Thought in Twentieth-Century Germany," *Gender & History* 31, no. 1 (2019): 91–114.

Markman Reubins, Beatriz. *Pioneers of Child Psychoanalysis: Influential Theories and Practices in Healthy Child Development*. London: Karnac, 2014.

Matysik, Tracie. "In the Name of the Law: The 'Female Homosexual' and the Criminal Code in Fin de Siècle Germany." *Journal of the History of Sexuality* 13, no. 1 (2004): 26–48.

Matysik, Tracie. *Reforming the Moral Subject: Ethics and Sexuality in Central Europe, 1890–1930*. Ithaca, NY: Cornell University Press, 2008.

May, Ulrike. "Ein Traum (1897) und ein Brief (1902): Zur frühen Beziehung zwischen Freud und Isidor Sadger." *Luzifer-Amor: Zeitschrift zur Geschichte der Psychoanalyse* 12, no. 24 (1999): 25–48.

May-Tolzman, Ulrike. "Zu den Anfängen des Narzißmus: Ellis-Näcke-Sadger-Freud." *Luzifer-Amor: Zeitschrift zur Geschichte der Psychoanalyse* 4, no. 8 (1991): 50–88.

Mazón, Patricia M. *Gender and the Modern Research University: The Admission of Women to German Higher Education, 1865–1914*. Stanford: Stanford University Press, 2003.

McClelland, Charles E. *State, Society and University in Germany*. Cambridge, UK: Cambridge University Press, 1980.

McEwen, Britta. *Sexual Knowledge: Feeling, Fact and Social Reform in Vienna, 1900–1934*. New York: Berghahn Books, 2012.

McGuire, William, ed. *The Freud/Jung Letters: The Correspondence between Sigmund Freud and C. G. Jung*. Translated by Ralph Mannheim and R. F. C. Hull. Bollingen Series. Princeton, NJ: Princeton University Press, 1974.

McLaren, Angus. *The Trials of Masculinity: Policing Sexual Boundaries, 1870–1930s*. Chicago: University of Chicago Press, 1997.

McRuer, Robert. "Compulsory Able-Bodiedness and Queer/Disabled Existence." In *The Disability Studies Reader*. Edited by Lennard J. Davis, 4th ed., 369–80. London: Taylor & Francis, 2013.

Meyer, Sabine. *"Wie Lili zu einem richtigen Mädchen wurde": Lili Elbe: Zur Konstruktion von Geschlecht und Identität zwischen Medialisierung, Regulierung und Subjektivierung*. Bielefeld, Ger.: Transcript, 2015.

Meyerowitz, Joanne. *How Sex Changed: A History of Transsexuality in the United States*. Cambridge, MA: Harvard University Press, 2002.

Micale, Mark S. "Preface." In *Beyond the Unconscious: Essays of Henri F. Ellenberger in the History of Psychiatry*. Edited by Mark S. Micale, translated by Francoise Dubois and Mark S. Micale. Princeton, NJ: Princeton University Press, 1993.

Mildenberger, Florian. "Kraepelin and the 'Urnings': Male Homosexuality in Psychiatric Discourse." *History of Psychiatry* 71, no. 3 (2007): 321–35.

Mildenberger, Florian. "'Verjüngung' und 'Heilung' der Homosexualität: Eugen Steinach in seiner Zeit." *Zeitschrift für Sexualforschung* 15, no. 4 (2002): 302–22.

Millett, Kate. *Sexual Politics*. New York: Avon Books, 1969.

Mitchell, Julie. *Psychoanalysis and Feminism*. London: Allen Lane, 1974.

Mort, Frank. *Dangerous Sexualities: Medico-Moral Politics in England since 1830*. 2nd ed. London: Routledge, 2000.

Mosse, George. "Shell-Shock as a Social Disease." *Journal of Contemporary History* 35, no. 1 (2000): 101–8.

Mosse, George L. *Nationalism and Sexuality: Respectability and Abnormal Sexuality in Modern Europe*. New York: H. Fertig, 1985.

Müller, Gerd B., ed. *Vivarium: Experimental, Quantitative, and Theoretical Biology at Vienna's Biologische Versuchsanstalt*. Cambridge, MA: MIT Press, 2017.

Müller, Klaus. *Aber in meinem Herzen sprach eine Stimme so laut: Homosexuelle Autobiographien und medizinische Pathographien im neunzehnten Jahrhundert*. Berlin: Rosa Winkel, 1991.

Neubauer, John. "Sigmund Freud und Hans Blüher in bisher unveröffentlichten Briefen." *Psyche* 50, no. 2 (1996): 123–48.

Nitzschke, Bernd, Annelise Heigl-Evers, and Franz Heigl. "'Wo es in einer Sache nur Gegner oder Anhänger gibt': Ein bisher unbekannter Brief Sigmund Freuds an Max Marcuse." *Zeitschrift für Sexualforschung* 8, no. 3 (1995): 241–48.

Oosterhuis, Harry, ed. *Homosexuality and Male Bonding in Pre-Nazi Germany: The Youth Movement, the Gay Movement, and Male Bonding before Hitler's Rise*. New York: Haworth, 1991.

Oosterhuis, Harry. "Medicine, Male Bonding and Homosexuality in Nazi Germany." *Journal of Contemporary History* 32, no. 2 (1997): 187–205.

Oosterhuis, Harry. "Sexual Modernity in the Works of Richard von Krafft-Ebing and Albert Moll." *Medical History* 56, no. 2 (2012): 133–55.

Oosterhuis, Harry. *Stepchildren of Nature: Krafft-Ebing, Psychiatry, and the Making of Sexual Identity*. Chicago: University of Chicago Press, 2000.

Oosterhuis, Harry. "The Pre-Freudian Modernization of Sexuality: Richard von Krafft-Ebing and Albert Moll." In *Deconstructing Normativity? Re-Reading Freud's 1905 "Three Essays."* Edited by Philippe Van Haute and Herman Westerink, 44–54. London: Routledge, 2017.

Parent, A. S., et al. "The Timing of Normal Puberty and the Age Limits of Sexual Precocity: Variations Around the World, Secular Trends, and Changes after Migration." *Endocrine Review* 24, no. 5 (2003): 668–93.

Penslar, Derek J. *Jews and the Military: A History*. Princeton, NJ: Princeton University Press, 2013.

Peters, Kathrin. *Rätselbilder des Geschlechts: Körperwissen und Medialität um 1900*. Zurich: Diaphanes, 2010.

Peukert, Detlev. *The Weimar Republic: The Crisis of Classical Modernity*. Translated by Richard Deveson. London: Penguin, 1991.

Pfäfflin, Friedemann. "Sex Reassignment, Harry Benjamin, and Some European Roots." *International Journal of Transgenderism* 1, no. 2 (1997). https://www.atria.nl/ezines/web/IJT/97–03/numbers/symposion/ijtc0202.htm.

Pick, Daniel. *Faces of Degeneration: A European Disorder, c. 1848–1918*. Cambridge, UK: Cambridge University Press, 1989.

Plastow, Michael. "Hermine Hug-Hellmuth, the First Child Psychoanalyst: Legacy and Dilemmas." *Australian Psychiatry* 19, no. 3 (2011): 206–10.

Plotkin, Mariano Ben. *Freud in the Pampas: The Emergence and Development of a Psychoanalytic Culture in Argentina*. Stanford: Stanford University Press, 2001.

Porter, Roy. "The Patient's View: Doing Medical History from Below." *Theory and Society* 14 (1985): 165–74.

Porter, Roy, and Mikuláš Teich. *Sexual Knowledge, Sexual Science: The History of Attitudes to Sexuality*. Cambridge, UK: Cambridge University Press, 1994.

Pretzel, Andreas. "Disziplinierungsbestrebungen. Magnus Hirschfeld und die Ärztliche Gesellschaft für Sexualwissenschaft." In *Magnus Hirschfeld: Ein Leben im Spannungsfeld von Wissenschaft, Politik und Gesellschaft*. Edited by Elke-Vera Kotowski and Julius H. Schoeps, 137–56. Berlin-Brandenburg: be.bra wissenschaft, 2004.

Pretzel, Andreas. "Sexualreform im Spannungsfeld weltanschaulicher Voraussetzungen und sozialpolitischer Auseinandersetzungen." In *Verqueere Wissenschaft? Zum Verhältnis von Sexualwissenschaft und Sexualreformbewegung in Geschichte und Gegenwart*. Edited by Ursula Ferdinand, Andreas Pretzel, and Andreas Seeck, 229–42. Münster: LIT, 1998.

Pretzel, Andreas. "Zur Geschichte der 'Ärztlichen Gesellschaft für Sexualwissenschaft' (1919–1933)." *Mitteilungen der Magnus-Hirschfeld-Gesellschaft*, no. 24/25 (1997): 35–122.

Prickett, David James. "Magnus Hirschfeld and the Photographic (Re)Invention of the 'Third Sex.'" In *Visual Culture in Twentieth-Century Germany: Text as Spectacle*, 103–19. Bloomington: Indiana University Press, 2006.

Prosser, Jay. "Transsexuals and the Transsexologists: Inversion and the Emergence of Transsexual Subjectivity." In *Sexology in Culture: Labelling Bodies and Desires*. Edited by Lucy Bland and Laura Doan, 116–31. Cambridge, UK: Polity, 1998.

Putz, Christa. *Verordnete Lust: Sexualmedizin, Psychoanalyse und die "Krise der Ehe," 1870–1930*. Bielefeld, Ger.: Transcript, 2011.

Quinn, Susan. *A Mind of Her Own: The Life of Karen Horney*. Reading, MA: Addison-Wesley, 1988.

Raphael, Lutz. "Die Verwissenschaftlichung des Sozialen als methodische und konzeptionelle Herausforderung für eine Sozialgeschichte des 20. Jahrhunderts." *Geschichte und Gesellschaft* 22, no. 2 (1996): 165–93.

Rich, Adrienne. "Compulsory Heterosexuality and Lesbian Existence." *Signs: Journal of Women in Culture and Society* 5 (1980): 631–60.

Rickels, Laurence. *Nazi Psychoanalysis*. Minneapolis: University of Minnesota Press, 2002.

Roazen, Paul. *Helene Deutsch, a Psychoanalyst's Life*. Garden City, NY: Anchor, 1985.

Roberts, Celia. *Puberty in Crisis: The Sociology of Early Sexual Development*. Cambridge, UK: Cambridge University Press, 2015.

Robinson, Paul. *The Modernization of Sex: Havelock Ellis, Alfred Kinsey, William Masters and Virginia Johnson*. New York: Harper & Row, 1976.

Roos, Julia. "Women's Rights, Nationalist Anxiety, and the 'Moral' Agenda in the Weimar Republic: Revisiting the 'Black Horror' Campaign against France's African Occupation Troops." *Central European History* 42, no. 3 (2009): 473–508.

Rosario, Vernon A. *Science and Homosexualities*. New York: Routledge, 1997.

Rose, Nikolas. "Assembling the Modern Self." In *Rewriting the Self: Histories from the Renaissance to the Present*. Edited by Roy Porter, 224–48. London: Routledge, 1996.

Rosenkranz, Bernhard, Ulf Bollmann, and Gottfried Lorenz. *Homosexuellen-Verfolgung in Hamburg 1919–1969*. Hamburg: Lambda, 2009.

Rouette, Susan. "Mothers and Citizens: Gender and Social Policy in Germany after the First World War." *Central European History* 30 (1997): 48–66.

Rowold, Katharina. "A Male Mind in a Female Body: Sexology, Homosexuality, and the Woman Question in Germany, 1869–1914." In *From Physico-Theology to Bio-Technology: Essays in the Social and Cultural History of Biosciences*, 153–79. Amsterdam: Rodopi, 1998.

Rupp, Leila J. "The Persistence of Transnational Organizing: The Case of the Homophile Movement." *American Historical Review* 116, no. 4 (2011): 1014–39.

Russo, Jane A. "Brazilian Psychiatrists and Psychoanalysis at the Beginning of the 20th Century: A Quest for National Identity." *Psychoanalysis and History* 14, no. 2 (2012): 297–312.

Sanfeliu, Isabel. *Karl Abraham: The Birth of Object Relations Theory*. Translated by Kate Walters. London: Karnac, 2014.

Sauerteig, Lutz. *Krankheit, Sexualität, Gesellschaft. Geschlechtskrankheiten und Gesundheitspolitik in Deutschland im 19. und frühen 20. Jahrhundert*. MedGG-Beihefte. Stuttgart: Franz Steiner Verlag, 1999.

Sauerteig, Lutz D. H. "Loss of Innocence: Albert Moll, Sigmund Freud and the Invention of Childhood Sexuality Around 1900." *Medical History* 56, no. 2 (2012): 156–83.

Sayers, Janet. *Mothers of Psychoanalysis: Helene Deutsch, Karen Horney, Anna Freud, Melanie Klein*. New York: Norton, 1921.

Schader, Heike. *Virile, Vamps und wilde Veilchen. Sexualität, Begehren und Erotik in den Zeitschriften homosexueller Frauen im Berlin der 1920er Jahre*. Königstein/Taunus: Ulrike Helmer, 2004.

Schaffner, Anna Katharina. *Modernism and Perversion: Sexual Deviance in Sexology and Literature, 1850–1930*. Houndmills, Basingstoke, UK: Palgrave Macmillan, 2011.

Schlich, Thomas. *Die Erfindung der Organtransplantation: Erfolg und Scheitern des chirurgischen Organersatzes (1880–1930)*. Frankfurt/Main: Campus, 1998.

Schlör, Joachim. "'Wenn ich eines richtig gemacht habe . . . .' Berliner Sexualwissenschaftler in Palästina/Israel." In *Exilforschung. Ein internationales Jahrbuch*. Edited by Claus-Dieter Krohn, Erwin Rotemund, Lutz Winckler, and Wulf Koepke, 16: Exil und Avantgarden: 229–52. Mainz: edition text + kritik, 1998.

Schmidt, Günter. "Allies and Persecutors: Science and Medicine in the Homosexuality Issue." *Journal of Homosexuality* 10, no. 3–4 (1985): 127–40.

Schoppmann, Claudia. *Nationalsozialistische Sexualpolitik und weibliche Homosexualität*. 2nd ed. Pfaffenweiler: Centaurus, 1997.

Schröter, Michael. "Fliess versus Weininger, Swoboda and Freud: The Plagiarism Conflict of 1906 Assessed in the Light of the Documents." *Psychoanalysis and History* 5, no. 2 (2003): 147–73.

Schultz, Duane P., and Sydney Ellen Schultz. *A History of Modern Psychology*. 9th ed. Belmont, CA: Thomson and Wadsworth, 2008.

Schwartz, Joseph. *Cassandra's Daughter: A History of Psychoanalysis*. London: Penguin, 1999.

Scott, Jill. *Electra after Freud: Myth and Culture*. Ithaca, NY: Cornell University Press, 2005.

Sealey, Anne. "The Strange Case of the Freudian Case History: The Role of Long Case

Histories in the Development of Psychoanalysis." *History of the Human Sciences* 24, no. 1 (2011): 36–50.

Sears, Clare. *Arresting Dress: Cross-Dressing, Law, and Fascination in Nineteenth-Century San Francisco*. Durham, NC: Duke University Press, 2015.

Sedgwick, Eve Kosofsky. "Jane Austen and the Masturbating Girl." In *Questions of Evidence: Proof, Practice, and Persuasion across the Disciplines*. Edited by James Chandler, Arnold I. Davidson, and Harry Harrotunian. Chicago: University of Chicago Press, 1994.

Seeck, Andreas, ed. *Durch Wissenschaft zur Gerechtigkeit?: Textsammlung zur kritischen Rezeption des Schaffens von Magnus Hirschfeld*. Berlin: LIT Verlag, 2003.

Seeck, Andreas. "'Verjüngungsoperationen' nach Steinach. Hinweise auf ein verändertes Verhältnis von Sexualität, Fortpflanzung und Leistungsfähigkeit." *Mitteilungen der Magnus-Hirschfeld-Gesellschaft*, nos. 29/30 (July 1999): 5–24.

Sengoopta, Chandak. "Dr Steinach Coming to Make Old Young! Sex Glands, Vasectomy and the Quest for Rejuvenation in the Roaring Twenties." *Endeavour* 27, no. 3 (2003): 122–26.

Sengoopta, Chandak. "Glandular Politics: Experimental Biology, Clinical Medicine, and Homosexual Emancipation in Fin-de-Siècle Central Europe." *Isis* 89 (1998): 445–73.

Sengoopta, Chandak. *Otto Weininger: Sex, Science, and Self in Imperial Vienna*. Chicago: University of Chicago Press, 2000.

Sengoopta, Chandak. "Tales from the Vienna Labs: The Eugene Steinach–Harry Benjamin Correspondence." *New York Academy of Medicine*, no. 2 (2000): 2–7.

Sengoopta, Chandak. *The Most Secret Quintessence of Life: Sex, Glands, and Hormones, 1850–1950*. Chicago: University of Chicago Press, 2006.

Shelley, Christopher. *Transpeople: Repudiation, Trauma, Healing*. Toronto: University of Toronto Press, 2008.

Shorter, Edward. *A History of Psychiatry: From the Era of the Asylum to the Age of Prozac*. New York: Wiley, 1997.

Showalter, Elaine. "Rivers and Sassoon: The Inscription of Male Gender Anxieties." In *Behind the Lines: Gender and the Two World Wars*. Edited by Margaret Randolph Higonnet, Jane Jenson, Sonja Michel, and Margaret Collins Weitz, 61–69. New Haven, CT: Yale University Press, 1987.

Shuttleworth, Sally. *The Mind of the Child: Child Development in Literature, Science, and Medicine, 1840–1900*. Oxford, UK: Oxford University Press, 2010.

Siems, Martina. *Sofie Lazarsfeld. Die Wiederentdeckung einer individualpsychologischen Pionierin*. Göttingen: V&R Unipress, 2015.

Sigusch, Volkmar. "Albert Moll und Magnus Hirschfeld. Über ein problematisches Verhältnis vor dem Hintergrund unveröffentlichter Briefe Molls aus dem Jahr 1934." *Zeitschrift für Sexualforschung* 8 (1995): 122–59.

Sigusch, Volkmar. "Fantasie oder Verhalten: Sigmund Freud und das Verhältnis von Psychoanalyse und Sexualwissenschaft." In *Geschichte der Sexualwissenschaft*, 261–84. Frankfurt am Main: Campus, 2008.

Sigusch, Volkmar. *Geschichte der Sexualwissenschaft*. Frankfurt: Campus Verlag, 2008.

Sigusch, Volkmar. "Heinrich Kaan: der Verfasser der ersten 'Psychopathia sexualis': Eine biographische Skizze." *Zeitschrift für Sexualforschung* 16 (2003): 116–42.

Sigusch, Volkmar. "The Sexologist Albert Moll—between Sigmund Freud and Magnus Hirschfeld." *Medical History* 56, no. 2 (2012): 184–200.

Sigusch, Volkmar, and Günter Grau, eds. *Personenlexikon der Sexualforschung*. Frankfurt am Main: Campus, 2009.

Singy, Patrick. "The History of Masturbation: An Essay Review." *Journal for the History of Medicine and Allied Sciences* 59, no. 1 (2004): 112–21.

Smith, Jill Suzanne. *Berlin Coquette: Prostitution and the New German Woman, 1890–1933*. Ithaca, NY: Cornell University Press, 2013.

Smith, Jill Suzanne. "Richard Oswald and the Social Hygiene Film: Promoting Public Health or Promiscuity?" In *The Many Faces of Weimar Cinema: Rediscovering Germany's Filmic Legacy*. Edited by Christian Rogowski, 13–30. Rochester, NY: Camden House, 2010.

Soden, Kristine von. *Die Sexualberatungsstellen der Weimarer Republik, 1919–1933*. Berlin: Hentrich, 1988.

Soffer, Reba N. *Discipline and Power: The University, History, and the Making of an English Elite, 1870–1930*. Stanford: Stanford University Press, 1994.

Sommer, Andreas. "Policing Epistemic Deviance: Albert von Schrenck-Notzing and Albert Moll." *Medical History* 56, no. 2 (2012): 255–76.

Spector, Scott. "Introduction. After *The History of Sexuality*? Periodicities, Subjectivities, Ethics." In *After "The History of Sexuality"? German Genealogies with and beyond Foucault*. Edited by Scott Spector, Helmut Puff, and Dagmar Herzog, 1–14. New York: Berghahn Books, 2012.

Spector, Scott. *Violent Sensations: Sex, Crime & Utopia in Vienna and Berlin, 1860–1914*. Chicago: University of Chicago Press, 2016.

Spector, Scott, Helmut Puff, and Dagmar Herzog, eds. *After "The History of Sexuality"? German Genealogies with and beyond Foucault*. New York: Berghahn Books, 2012.

Steakley, James. *"Anders als die Andern." Ein Film und seine Geschichte*. Hamburg: Männerschwarm, 2007.

Steakley, James. *The Homosexual Emancipation Movement in Germany*. New York: Arno Press, 1975.

Stephan, Inge. *Die Gründerinnen der Psychoanalyse: Eine Entmythologisierung Sigmund Freuds in zwölf Frauenporträts*. Stuttgart: Kreuz, 1992.

Sternweiler, Andreas. "'Er ging mit ihm alsbald ein sogenanntes "Festes Verhältnis" ein': Ganz normale Homosexuelle." In *Homosexuelle Männer im KZ Sachsenhausen*. Edited by Joachim Knoll and Andreas Sternweiler, 57–78. Berlin: Rosa Winkel, 2000.

Sternweiler, Andreas, and Hans Gerhard Hannesen, eds. *Goodbye to Berlin? 100 Jahre Schwulenbewegung*. Berlin: Rosa Winkel, 1997.

Stockton, Kathryn Bond. *The Queer Child, or Growing Sideways in the Twentieth Century*. Series Q. Durham, NC: Duke University Press, 2009.

Stoff, Heiko. "Die hormonelle und die utopische Geschlechterordnung: Verjüngungsoperationen und der neue Mensch in den zwanziger Jahren." In *Verqueere Wissenschaft? Zum Verhältnis von Sexualwissenschaft und Sexualreformbewegung in Geschichte und Gegenwart*. Edited by Andreas Pretzel, Ursula Ferdinand, and Andreas Seeck, 245–60. Münster: Lit Verlag, 2005.

Stoff, Heiko. *Ewige Jugend. Konzepte der Verjüngung vom späten 19. Jahrhundert bis ins Dritte Reich.* Köln: Böhlau, 2004.

Stoff, Heiko. *Wirkstoffe: Eine Wissenschaftsgeschichte der Hormone, Vitamine und Enzyme, 1920–1970.* Stuttgart: Franz-Steiner-Verlag, 2012.

Stolt, Carl-Magnus. "Why Did Freud Never Receive the Nobel Prize?" *International Forum of Psychoanalysis* 10, no. 3–4 (2001): 221–26.

Ströhle, Andreas, et al. (1868–1948)." *American Journal of Psychiatry* 165, no. 5 (2008): 575–76.

Stryker, Susan. *Transgender History.* Berkeley, CA: Seal Press, 2008.

Sulloway, Frank. *Freud, Biologist of the Mind: Beyond the Psychoanalytic Legend.* New York: Basic Books, 1979.

Sutton, Katie. "From Sexual Inversion to Trans*: Transgender History and Historiography." In *Was ist Homosexualität? Forschungsgeschichte, gesellschaftliche Entwicklungen und Perspektiven.* Edited by Florian Mildenberger, Jennifer Evans, Rüdiger Lautmann, and Jakob Pastötter, 181–204. Hamburg: Männerschwarm, 2014.

Sutton, Katie. "Sexological Cases and the Prehistory of Transgender Identity Politics in Interwar Germany." In *Cases and the Dissemination of Knowledge.* Edited by Joy Damousi, Birgit Lang, and Katie Sutton, 85–103. New York: Routledge, 2015.

Sutton, Katie. "Sexology's Photographic Turn: Visualizing Trans Identity in Interwar Germany." *Journal of the History of Sexuality* 27, no. 3 (2018): 442–79.

Sutton, Katie. *The Masculine Woman in Weimar Germany.* New York: Berghahn Books, 2011.

Sutton, Katie. "'We Too Deserve a Place in the Sun': The Politics of Transvestite Identity in Weimar Germany." *German Studies Review* 35, no. 2 (2012): 335–54.

Sykora, Katharina. "Umkleidekabinen des Geschlechts: Sexualmedizinische Fotographie im frühen 20. Jahrhundert." *Fotogeschichte: Beiträge zur Geschichte und Ästhetik der Fotografie* 24, no. 92 (2004): 15–30.

Tatar, Maria. *Lustmord: Sexual Murder in Weimar Germany.* Princeton, NJ: Princeton University Press, 1995.

Taylor, Charles. *Sources of the Self: The Making of the Modern Identity.* Cambridge, MA: Harvard University Press, 1989.

Taylor, Mara. "'We, Too, Belong to This Group of Krafft-Ebingers!' Women and Sexological Discourse in *Psychopathia Sexualis* and *Are They Women? Novel about the Third Sex.*" In *Sexual-Textual Border-Crossings: Lesbian Identity in German-Language Literature, Film, and Culture. Yearbook of the Association of Third-Level Teachers of German in Ireland.* Edited by Rachel MagShamhráin, Hans-Walter Schmidt-Hannisa, and Sabine Strümper-Krobb. Konstanz: Hartung-Gorre, 2010.

Taylor, Michael Thomas, Annette F. Timm, and Rainer Herrn, eds. *Not Straight from Germany: Sexual Publics and Sexual Citizenship since Magnus Hirschfeld.* Ann Arbor: University of Michigan Press, 2017.

Terry, Jennifer. *An American Obsession: Science, Medicine, and Homosexuality in Modern Society.* Chicago: Chicago University Press, 1999.

Thompson, Nellie. "Early Women Psychoanalysts." *International Review of Psychoanalysis* 14 (1987): 391–408.

Thompson, Nellie L. "The Transformation of Psychoanalysis in America: Emigré Analysts and the New York Psychoanalytic Society and Institute, 1935–1961." *Journal of the American Psychoanalytic Association* 60, no. 1 (2012): 9–44.

Thompson, Nellie L., and Helen Keable. "The Psychoanalytic Study of the Child: A Narrative of Postwar Psychoanalysis." *American Imago* 73, no. 3 (2016): 343–82.

Thompson, Nellie L., Michael Schröter, and Ulrike May. "Gerettet aus der Verschollenheit: Zur englischen Ausgabe von Isidor Sadger's 'Erinnerungen an Freud.'" *Luzifer-Amor: Zeitschrift zur Geschichte der Psychoanalyse* 18, no. 36 (2005): 158–66.

Tierney, Thomas F. "Foucault on the Case: The Pastoral and Juridical Foundation of Medical Power." *Journal of Medical Humanities* 25, no. 4 (2004): 271–90.

Tobin, Robert D. "Kertbeny's 'Homosexuality' and the Language of Nationalism." In *Genealogies of Identity: Interdisciplinary Readings on Sex and Sexuality*. Edited by Margaret Breen Sönser and Fiona Peters, 3–18. Amsterdam: Rodopi, 2005.

Tobin, Robert Deam. *Peripheral Desires: The German Discovery of Sex*. Philadelphia: University of Pennsylvania Press, 2015.

Trask, April. "Remaking Men: Masculinity, Homosexuality and Constitutional Medicine in Germany, 1914–1933." *German History* 36, no. 2 (2018): 181–206.

Turner, Frank M. "Public Science in Britain, 1880–1919." *Isis* 71, no. 4 (1980): 589–608.

Usborne, Cornelie. *The Politics of the Body in Weimar Germany: Women's Reproductive Rights and Duties*. Basingstoke, UK: Macmillan, 1992.

Van Haute, Philippe, and Herman Westerink, eds. *Deconstructing Normativity? Re-Reading Freud's 1905 "Three Essays."* London: Routledge, 2017.

Van Haute, Philippe, and Herman Westerink. "Introduction: Excavating a Theory of Sexuality." In *Deconstructing Normativity? Re-Reading Freud's 1905 "Three Essays."* Edited by Philippe Van Haute and Herman Westerink, 1–5. London: Routledge, 2017.

Verlicchi, Angela. "Italian Pioneers of Neuroscience." *Progress in Neuroscience* 1 (2011): 7–14.

Vidal, Fernando. *The Sciences of the Soul: The Early Modern Origins of Psychology*. Translated by Saskia Brown. Chicago: University of Chicago Press, 2011.

Walch, Sonja. *Triebe, Reize und Signale: Eugen Steinachs Physiologie der Sexualhormone. Vom biologischen Konzept zum Pharmapräparat, 1894–1938*. Wien: Böhlau, 2016.

Wallerstein, R. *Lay Analysis: Life inside the Controversy*. Mahway, NJ: Analytic Press, 1998.

Warner, Michael. "Introduction: Fear of a Queer Planet." *Social Text* 9, no. 4 (1991): 3–17.

Waters, Chris. "Sexology." In *Palgrave Advances in the Modern History of Sexuality*. Edited by H. G. Cocks and Matt Houlbrook, 41–63. Houndmills, Basingstoke, UK: Palgrave Macmillan, 2006.

Weber, Philippe. *Der Trieb zum Erzählen: Sexualpathologie und Homosexualität, 1852–1914*. Bielefeld, Ger.: Transcript, 2008.

Webster, Brenda S. "Helene Deutsch: A New Look." *Signs: Journal of Women in Culture and Society* 10, no. 3 (1985): 553–71.

Weikart, Richard. *From Darwin to Hitler: Evolutionary Ethics, Eugenics, and Racism in Germany*. New York: Palgrave Macmillan, 2004.

Weindling, Paul. "Bourgeois Values, Doctors and the State: The Professionalization of Medicine in Germany 1848–1933." In *The German Bourgeoisie*. Edited by David Blackbourn and Richard J. Evans, 198–223. London: Routledge, 1991.

Weindling, Paul. *Health, Race, and German Politics Between National Unification and Nazism, 1870–1945*. Cambridge, UK: Cambridge University Press, 1989.

Weitz, Eric D. *Weimar Germany: Promise and Tragedy*. Princeton, NJ: Princeton University Press, 2007.

Westerink, Herman. "Freud's Discussion with Psychiatry on Sexuality, Drives and Objects in 'Three Essays.'" In *Deconstructing Normativity? Re-Reading Freud's 1905 "Three Essays."* Edited by Philippe Van Haute and Herman Westerink, 28–43. London: Routledge, 2017.

Wetzell, Richard. *Inventing the Criminal: A History of German Criminology, 1880–1945*. Chapel Hill: University of North Carolina Press, 2000.

Whisnant, Clayton J. *Queer Identities and Politics in Germany: A History, 1880–1945*. New York: Harrington Park, 2016.

Wickert, Christl, Brigitte Hamburger, and Marie Lienau. "Helene Stöcker and the Bund für Mutterschutz (The Society for the Protection of Motherhood)." *Women's Studies International Forum* 5, no. 6 (1982): 611–18.

Wiegman, Robyn, and Elizabeth A. Wilson. "Introduction: Antinormativity's Queer Conventions." *Differences* 26, no. 1 (2015): 1–25.

Wigger, Iris. "'Black Shame'—the Campaign against 'Racial Degeneration' and Female Degradation in Interwar Europe." *Race & Class* 51, no. 3 (2010): 33–46.

Wildenthal, Lora. *German Women for Empire, 1884–1945*. Durham, NC: Duke University Press, 2001.

Williams, Meg Harris. "Psychoanalysis as an Art Form." *British Journal of Psychotherapy* 25, no. 3 (2009): 381–92.

Winter, Jay. "Shell-Shock and the Cultural History of the Great War." *Journal of Contemporary History* 35, no. 1 (2000): 7–11.

Winter, Sarah. *Freud and the Institution of Psychoanalytic Knowledge*. Stanford: Stanford University Press, 1999.

Wirth, H.-J., and T. Haland-Wirth. "Emigration, Biographie und Psychoanalyse. Emigrierte PsychoanalytikerInnen in Amerika." In *"Die biographische Wahrheit ist nicht zu haben." Psychoanalyse und Biographieforschung*. Edited by K.-J. Bruder, 221–57. Giessen, Ger.: Psychosozial-Verlag, 2003.

Wolffram, Heather. *The Stepchildren of Science: Psychical Research and Parapsychology in Germany, c. 1870–1939*. Amsterdam: Rodopi, 2009.

Woodruff, Michael F. A. *The Transplantation of Tissues and Organs*. Springfield, IL: Charles Thomas, 1960.

Wyndham, Diana. *Norman Haire and the Study of Sex*. Sydney: Sydney University Press, 2012.

Wyndham, Diana. "Versemaking and Lovemaking—W. B. Yeats' 'Strange Second Puberty': Norman Haire and the Steinach Rejuvenation Operation." *Journal of the History of Behavioural Science* 39 (2002): 25–50.

Yeo, Richard R. "Scientific Method and the Rhetoric of Science in Britain, 1830–1917." In *The Politics and Rhetoric of Scientific Method*, 259–97. Dordrecht, Neth.: D. Reidel, 1986.

Yuval-Davis, Nira. *The Politics of Belonging: Intersectional Contestations*. London: Sage, 2011.

Zaretsky, Eli. *Secrets of the Soul: A Social and Cultural History of Psychoanalysis*. New York: Vintage, 2004.

Index

Printed and bound by CPI Group (UK) Ltd, Croydon, CR0 4YY
16/09/2026
14963487-0008